P9-CES-018

The Mammoth Book of

# MURDER

# The Mammoth Book of

# MURDER

Edited by
Richard Glyn Jones

Carroll & Graf Publishers, Inc.
New York

First published in Great Britain 1989
First Carroll & Graf edition 1989

10 9 8 7 6 5 4

Carroll & Graf Publishers, Inc.
260 Fifth Avenue
New York
NY 10001

ISBN: 0–88184–529–9

Arrangement and introduction © 1989 Richard Glyn Jones

All rights reserved.

Printed by Collins Manufacturing, Glasgow

# Contents

Introduction ix
The Contributors xv

## 1. REGENCY RUFFIANS

JOHN WILLIAMS   *Nemesis in the Night (1811)*   2
SAMUEL GREEN   *America's First
Arch-Murderer? (1817–22)*   4
DOCTOR CASTAING   *The First Deadly Doctor (1823)*   8
WILLIAM CORDER   *The Red Barn Murder (1827–8)*   13
BURKE and HARE   *The Bodysnatchers (1828–9)*   18
LACENAIRE   *Poet and Murderer (1835)*   22
THOMAS WAINEWRIGHT   *Man of Letters –
and Poison (1837)*   29

## 2. VILLAINOUS VICTORIANS

JAMES RUSH   *The Killer in the Fog (1849)*   38
WILLIAM KIRWAN   *The Secret of Ireland's Eye (1852)*   47
FRANZ MULLER   *The First Railway Murderer (1864)*   52
PIERRE VOIRBO   *The Tell-Tale Tiles (1869)*   54
JEAN-BAPTISTE TROPPMANN   *Mass Murder
for Money (1870)*   60
JOHN BENDER   *Murder at a Wayside Tavern (1873)*   72
CHARLES PEACE   *Cat-Burglar and Murderer (1879)*   81
ARMAND PELTZER   *The Man Who Never Was (1882)*   91

## 3. DEADLY DOCTORS

DOCTOR WEBSTER   *Murder at Harvard*
*(1849)*                                                        104
WILLIAM PALMER   *The Amazing Autopsy (1855)*   108
DOCTOR SMETHURST   *Parsimony and the*
*Poisoner (1859)*                                              121
DOCTOR PRITCHARD   *Seducer and Slayer (1865)*   125
DOCTOR LAMSON   *'A Swell Pill-Taker' (1881)*     130
JACK THE RIPPER   *Eight Theories (1888)*         135
CARLYLE HARRIS   *The Fatal Capsule (1892)*       145
DOCTOR NEILL CREAM   *Poisoner of*
*Prostitutes (1892)*                                           151
DOCTOR BUCHANAN   *Belladonna (1895)*             160
H.H. HOLMES   *The Torture Doctor (1895)*         172

## 4. LATE-VICTORIAN VILLAINS

JOHN LEE   *The Man They Could Not Hang (1888)*   184
A.J. MONSON   *The Ardlamont Mystery (1893)*       185
TED DURRANT   *The Corpse in the Belfry (1895)*    191
ROLAND B. MOLINEUX   *The Killer at the*
*Knickerbocker (1895)*                                         196
WILLIAM GULDENSUPPE   *Willie's Legs (1898)*      202
JOSEPH VACHER   *The Jack the Ripper of*
*France (1898)*                                                206
SAMUEL DOUGAL   *So Much Slimy Clay (1899)*       223
GEORGE CHAPMAN   *The Lady Killer (1905)*         225

## 5. THE DAWN OF MODERN MURDER

JOHANN HOCH   *'I Have Done with Everybody'*
*(1905)*                                                        232
HARRY THAW   *Murder at Madison Square*
*Garden (1906)*                                                236
G.J. SMITH   *The Brides in the Bath (1915)*       238
DOCTOR WAITE   *The Deadly Dentist (1916)*        247
THOMAS ALLAWAY   *The Murder that*
*Misfired (1921)*                                              251

LANDRU   *The Bluebeard of Paris (1921)*                    257
HENRI GIRARD   *A Super-Poisoner (1921)*                    261
MAJOR ARMSTRONG   *The Nineteen*
*Dandelions (1922)*                                         267
PATRICK MAHON   *The Troublesome Typist (1924)*            278
FRITZ HAARMANN   *The Butcher of Hanover (1924)*           283

## 6.   EDWARDIAN ENIGMAS

THE GORSE HALL MYSTERY *(1909)*                            288
THE LUARD CASE *(1908)*                                    293
DOCTOR CRIPPEN   *Was He a Murderer? (1910)*               296
BELA KISS   *The Mystery Man of Europe (1915)*             303
THE AXEMAN OF NEW ORLEANS *(1911–19)*                      314
THE GREEN BICYCLE MYSTERY *(1920)*                         321
THE ELWELL CASE *(1920)*                                   331
HOLLYWOOD'S MOST BAFFLING MURDER *(1922)*                  334
THE DOT KING CASE *(1922)*                                 341
THE MINISTER AND THE CHOIR-SINGER *(1922–6)*               344

## 7.   CLASSIC CRIMES

LEOPOLD AND LOEB   *Murder by Genius (1924)*               350
DONALD MERRETT   *Motorcycles and*
*Matricide (1926)*                                         358
EARLE NELSON   *The Gorilla Murderer (1927)*               361
ALBERT SNYDER   *A 'perfect crime' (1927)*                 369
THE RIDDLE OF BIRDHURST RISE   *(1928)*                    375
CHUNG YI MAIO   *Death of the Jade Bride*
*(1928)*                                                   384
SIDNEY FOX   *Insurance and Arson (1930)*                  388
PETER KÜRTEN   *The Sadist (1930)*                         390
WILLIAM H. WALLACE   *Britain's Most Baffling*
*Crime (1931)*                                             398
A.A. ROUSE   *The Phoney Phoenix (1931)*                   403
BRUNO HAUPTMANN   *The Lindbergh Kidnapping*
*Case (1932)*                                              413
KENNETH NEU   *'Look at those nerves!' (1933)*             416
TONY MANCINI   *The Brighton Trunk Mystery (1934)*         418
BUCK RUXTON   *The Dismembering Doctor (1935)*             424
ROBERT JAMES   *The Reluctant Rattlesnakes (1935)*         429
ALBERT FISH   *The Cannibal Killer (1936)*                 433

## 8. MASS MURDERERS, AND MORE

DOCTOR PETTIOT   *Sixty-Three Victims (1944)*   436
NEVILLE HEATH   *The Cruel Bluff (1946)*   441
LEY AND SMITH   *The Chalk-Pit Murder (1946)*   452
DEATH OF THE BLACK DAHLIA   *(1947)*   456
JAMES CAMB   *Murder Overboard (1947)*   460
RAYMOND FERNANDEZ   *Slaying the Lonely Heart (1948)*   463
J.G. HAIGH   *The Acid-Bath Killer (1949)*   470
GASTON DOMINICI   *The Dirty Old Man Murders (1952)*   473
REG CHRISTIE   *The Monster of Rillington Place (1953)*   476
DOCTOR SAM SHEPPARD   *The 'Mysterious Stranger' (1954)*   478
ED GEIN   *Horror Heaped upon Horror (1957)*   483
CHARLES STARKWEATHER   *'A Little World All Our Own' (1958)*   490

## 9. THE SICK SIXTIES, AND BEYOND

JAMES HANRATTY   *The A6 Murder (1961)*   498
ALBERT DESALVO   *The Boston Strangler (1962–4)*   509
'JACK THE STRIPPER'   *The Thames Nude Murders (1964–5)*   511
IAN BRADY   *The Moors Murders (1965)*   515
RICHARD SPECK   *'Born to Raise Hell' (1966)*   519
ZODIAC   *The Sign of Death (1967)*   523
CHARLES MANSON   *Helter Skelter (1969)*   528
DALE NELSON   *A Regular Guy (1970)*   536
EDWARD PAISNEL   *The Beast of Jersey (1971)*   539
GRAHAM YOUNG   *A Psychopathic Murderer (1972)*   542
DEAN CORLL   *Loved Kids (1973)*   548
DAVID BERKOWITZ   *'Son of Sam' (1977)*   553
TED BUNDY   *'I Feel Like a Vampire' (1978)*   558
MARK CHAPMAN   *The Slaying of a Superstar (1980)*   565
PETER SUTCLIFFE   *The Yorkshire Ripper (1981)*   575
DENNIS NILSEN   *Killing for Company (1983)*   584

Sources and Acknowledgements   595

# Introduction

This is how I became addicted to murder.

I had an idea that I would write some mystery stories. I knew what kind of mysteries I enjoyed most, and they tended to be of the fantastic variety: the locked-room puzzles of John Dickson Carr, G.K. Chesterton's Father Brown tales and the witty novels of Edmund Crispin. But I also admired more serious crime novels by Patricia Highsmith, Julian Symons and Ruth Rendell, and I wanted to know what I should be aiming at in my own projected stories. So I started doing some background reading, ploughing my way through what I could find from the Haycraft/Queen list of the 'cornerstones' of crime fiction (an extremely tedious exercise) and acquainting myself with current critical opinion. This came out very strongly in favour of the realistic crime novel – the day of the ingenious puzzle and the eccentric detective was evidently long past – and it seemed to me that the next step was to look at some actual crimes, find out what happens in real life, and see if there were any possibilities there for fiction.

As chance would have it, a nearby second-hand bookshop had just acquired a large stock of paperback true-crime books, and I wandered in, picked one up, and began to read it. This happened to be Edmund Pearson's *Studies in Murder,* one of the best books of its kind ever written, and soon I was deeply immersed in the intricacies of the Lizzie Borden case. *Could* a stranger possibly have wandered into that house in Fall River and hacked Mr and Mrs Borden to death with an axe without being seen; *what* was the exact significance of Lizzie's laugh from the top of the stairs; *how on earth* could the entire family have dined on the same joint of boiled mutton at every meal for nearly a week, during one of the hottest spells on record?

I returned again and again to the bookshop, and soon had a small and bloody library, which I devoured during the weeks that followed, and I discovered that real murders are in many ways much more interesting than fictional ones. To begin with, they are much more extraordinary. Things that no novelist would dare to put into a story crop up all the time in reality: the most outrageous coincidences, completely irrational motives and actions, and details bizarre enough to intrigue the most committed fantasist. I found, too, that a well-written account of a murder can evoke a time, a place and a way of life with astonishing clarity, since it must examine people's everyday actions and focus on trivial details that the historian might easily miss. (Exactly how did public telephone boxes operate in 1931 Liverpool? – the Wallace case hinges upon it. How did women cope before sanitary towels were manufactured? – it is crucial to the Lizzie Borden case.)

There is also, of course, the fascination of the grisly elements in many of these cases. When I was spending a weekend with my sister and her family, I bought a book on Jack the Ripper containing some horrible photographs of his victims, and left it lying about. My sister asked if she could read it after me, and I left it with her. When it was eventually returned it was literally in tatters, having passed around the baby-sitting circle, with a request for more like that, please. This is not, I think, sheer morbidity. As Robert Meadley had pointed out, we do not seek out details of mutilated corpses from motor accident reports or casualty wards. What fascinates is the killer–victim relationship: the frisson of terror that we experience on behalf of the victim, perhaps, but even more powerfully the attempt to see inside the killer's mind. That, at any rate, is what I find endlessly interesting in these cases: the wondering whether, if I was in that situation or had undergone the same experiences as the murderer, I would have acted as he did. Could I, under the wildest extreme of provocation, poison my wife then saw her head off, as meek Dr Crippen evidently did? Can I, by any mad stretch of the imagination, put myself in the position of Dean Corll – another mild, quiet fellow – who killed some thirty boys for his own pleasure?

Murder is a mirror. A dark, distorting mirror in which we see unfamiliar faces. It shows us uncomfortable things, aspects of the human mind that we might not wish to see or acknowledge, but which are there nonetheless, and if we wish fully to understand ourselves we should look into it. Not too long or too hard, perhaps, but by glancing at murder from time to time we remind ourselves that this dark side does exist, and has to be reckoned with.

I never did get round to writing my novel. Detective fiction of the classic variety bears very little relation to real crime, I found. Real murder isn't a neat bullet-hole in the forehead of a well-dressed body in the library. On expiry, a body usually evacuates the bladder, and a corpse contains a surprisingly large amount of blood. But even the most hardboiled crime fiction tends to skip over this: the blunt fact that a dead body is a messy, smelly, indescribably banal thing. The crime novels that do try to get inside the murderer's mind – Ruth Rendell's *A Demon in my View* is stunning in its portrayal of a psychopathic killer – probably owe their psychological accuracy to looking inward rather than outward. For the rest, most crime fiction is indeed fantasy, despite the claims of the critics.

Which makes real murder all the more interesting. Once my own imagination was caught, I went on acquiring books about true murder cases until I had quite a sizeable library, and it is on this that I have drawn for this present collection. In it I have gathered short accounts of the 100 most notorious murderers of modern times. They make quite a collection. They range from John Williams, the subject of De Quincey's greatest and blackest essay (too long to include here), which brought into being the whole craft of writing about murder, through a whole gallery of those fascinating Victorian and Edwardian villains, right up to modern serial killers like Charles Manson, Ted Bundy and Dennis Nilsen, whose activities are so horrifically typical of our times. I have confined myself to *male* murderers, mainly for reasons of space and symmetry, and to 100 because there *are* about this number of murderers who stand out from the common herd. I hope that a companion volume of 100 great murderesses will follow.

It has been a pleasure to re-acquaint myself not so much with the murderers themselves but with the writers who describe their terrible exploits in the pages that follow. Some of them, such as the aforementioned Edmund Pearson, together with Colin Wilson, Damon Runyon, Julian Symons and Robert Bloch, are of course acknowledged masters of the genre, but there are many others whose writing deserves to be better known, and I am glad to be able to include some of it here.

Perhaps the most useful aspect of this collection is a very simple one: chronological order. Remarkably few true-crime books present their contents in the order in which they happened – if they have any order at all, it is usually alphabetical – and by disregarding chronology they throw away one of the most interesting possibilities, which is to show how the pattern of murder has changed over nearly two centuries. By presenting these cases in their proper order a pattern does emerge, and it is a fascinating one.

Colin Wilson has argued persuasively that murder is a product of the social stresses of the time, so that in more primitive periods, when the main concerns were simply a roof over one's head and enough food to ward off starvation, murder tended to be committed to gain precisely these things, and little else. As civilization advanced, and these basic necessities could be taken more for granted, people's needs extended to matters like happy and stable relationships, 'good' marriages, and of course money. Thus we find murders committed in order to dispose of unwanted spouses or purely for financial gain. This is where the modern age of murder really begins. Before that, we are in an age of ruffians and highwaymen where most murders are merely brutal. As we read further into the book, we enter an era of domestic murder, which had to be secretive because it took place in very tightly-knit communities. The case of Major Armstrong is perhaps the one *most* like a classic detective story and is probably the most extreme example of the 'closed' murder case.

As we progress to the murders of our own time, we find increasingly that killings are not committed for any obvious gain such as marriage or money, but for much more disturbing reasons. The final stage of Colin Wilson's argument is that our times are characterized not only by the complete fulfilment of our basic needs, but also by great personal freedom, and this combination leaves many people with little idea of their own place in the scheme of things. Perhaps because of the social pressures on us to acquire more and more goods and status – the carrots of a consumer society – a good many people at the bottom of the heap feel a burning resentment against this society and a sort of abstract desire for revenge upon it. In extreme cases this can only be expiated, it seems, in an orgy of killing, usually of victims weaker or in some sense 'inferior' to the murderer (usually women or children), all too often with a sickening sexual element. This is why Jack the Ripper's crimes were so exceptional and so hard to understand in 1888, and why characters like Dean Corll, Ted Bundy and the Yorkshire Ripper are all too typical now.

It is a valuable analysis, though one could add the more cynical view that there will always be a small minority of men who are driven to terrible violence. In a more restricted society they could not hope to remain undetected – in days of greater mobility, anonymous communities and wide freedom of choice it is all too easy for them to do so. To borrow William Goldman's brilliantly simple explanation of why some movie stars behave in so appallingly selfish a fashion: *they do it because they can*.

What *we* can do about it is a much more difficult matter. To call for some sort of 'return to Victorian values' is as impractical as it is meaningless. Society may have been more ordered then, but that order was built on grinding poverty and backbreaking work for the majority of people, with women and children forced to work in coal-mines and two million prostitutes in London alone. With affluence and leisure come dangers – freedom is always risky – and there will inevitably be some who abuse these privileges, who fail to take the responsibility that comes with freedom. It is not enough reason to take this freedom away, for it was hard-won, and any return to the sort of control that might curb the murder-rate implies a regime so staggeringly repressive that any advantage it brought in terms of law and order would be far outweighed by the huge personal price that we should all pay. A moral climate is largely beyond legislation and vague pleas for better standards will inevitably go unheeded. More and better policing would help, certainly, but purely on the grounds that the more likely it is that a criminal will be caught, the less likely he is to commit the crime. It is a practical matter.

The most encouraging development of recent years is the growing willingness of the police to work with psychologists to create 'profiles' of killers they are seeking. When victims are unknown to the murderer there are few clues. But as we learn more about these killers, it becomes possible to develop a kind of personality photo-fit. This has proved to be of great benefit – it *works*. There is every reason, then, for knowing and trying to understand the mind of the murderer.

This is the book that I wish had existed when I became interested in the subject – an Introduction to Murder.

Now it does. I trust that it will prove interesting.

RICHARD GLYN JONES

# The Contributors

| | |
|---|---|
| AA | Anthony Abbott |
| AK | Alistair Kershaw |
| AW | Alexander Woollcott |
| BM | Bill McGowran |
| CES | Charles E. Still |
| CJST | C.J.S. Thompson |
| CK | Charles Kingston |
| CR | Craig Rice |
| CW | Colin Wilson |
| DR | Damon Runyon |
| EA | Eric Ambler |
| EHS | Edward H. Smith |
| EL | Edgar Lustgarten |
| EP | Edmund Pearson |
| EQ | Ellery Queen |
| ESS | E. Spencer Shew |
| FB | Frederic Boutet |
| FDG | Francis D. Grierson |
| FES | F.E. Smith |
| FI | Francis Iles |
| FWC | Freeman Wills Crofts |
| GD | Grierson Dickson |
| GP | Giles Playfair |
| GS | (Judge) Gerald Sparrow |

| | |
|---|---|
| HGS | H. Greenhough Smith |
| HMH | H. Montgomery Hyde |
| HR | Helen Reilly |
| HRFK | H.R.F. Keating |
| HTFR | Henry T.F. Rhodes |
| | |
| JBr | Jimmy Breslin |
| JB | John Brophy |
| JCE | J.C. Ellis |
| JP | James Purvis |
| JRN | Jay Robert Nash |
| JS | Julian Symons |
| | |
| LC | Leslie Charteris |
| LG | Leonard Gribble |
| | |
| MP | Michael Prince |
| | |
| OS | Oscar Schisgall |
| | |
| RB | Robert Bloch |
| REM | R.E. Masters |
| RF | Rupert Furneaux |
| RGJ | Richard Glyn Jones |
| | |
| SHH | Stewart H. Holbrook |
| SJP | S.J. Peskett |
| SR | Sax Rohmer |
| | |
| WLQ | William le Queux |
| WM | Webb Miller |

# 1
# REGENCY RUFFIANS
## (1811–37)

# 1811

# JOHN WILLIAMS

## Nemesis in the Night

---

*Never, throughout the annals of universal Christendom,
has there indeed been any act of one solitary insulated
individual armed with power so appalling over the hearts
of men as that exterminating murder by which, during the
winter of 1811–12, John Williams, in one hour, smote two
houses with emptiness, exterminated all but two entire
households, and asserted his own supremacy above all the
children of Cain.*

*THOMAS DE QUINCEY*

The Ratcliffe Highway murders of 1811 are described in the
appendix to De Quincey's essay on 'Murder Considered as One
of the Fine Arts'. Towards midnight on 7th December, Timothy
Marr, who kept a hosier's shop in the East End of London, sent
out the servant girl to buy oysters; when she returned, it was to
find everyone in the house dead: Timothy Marr, his wife Celia,
their baby, and the apprentice boy, James Gowen. It looked as
if a giant with a sledge hammer had been at work. The force of
the blows had been so great that the apprentice's brains were
spattered over the ceiling. The hood of the baby's cradle had
been smashed, as if in a frenzy of violence; the child's head was
battered, and its throat cut. The murder weapon was found in
the bedroom: a type of sledge-hammer call a 'pen-maul' – which,
in a poster about the murders, can be seen to bear a striking
resemblance to the sacred pickaxe of the Thugs.

There was still no clue to the killer's identity – or motive –
when, two weeks later, a second family was slaughtered in the
same area. A publican named Williamson, his wife and their
maidservant, were slaughtered with an iron bar, and their
throats cut. A lodger named John Turner came downstairs
while the murders were taking place, and saw a man bending
over Mrs. Williamson's body, he tiptoed back upstairs, made a
rope of his bedsheets, and escaped from the bedroom window.

A crowd, attracted by his yells, broke into the house but the killer escaped through a rear window. (He seems to have been on the point of killing a fourteen-year-old girl in her bed when the noise disturbed him.) A certain amount of money had been taken.

The pen-maul was traced to a sailor's lodging house, and a young Irishman named John Williams arrested. He had access to the tool chest that contained the maul. On the morning of the murder, he had returned to a room he shared with other lodgers, and shouted at someone to put out a candle that was burning. The next morning, it was noticed that his shoes were muddy (the murderer had escaped by scrambling up a muddy bank); so were his socks, which he thereupon washed. A shirt was found to be bloodstained. Later on, bloodstained trousers were found in the bottom of the privy in the house. A coat belonging to William had heavy bloodstains in the pocket, as if it had held a knife; the bloodstained knife was later found in a mousehole. (De Quincey states, mistakenly, that it was found in the pocket.) Williams hanged himself before he could be brought to trial; his body was buried at the crossroads near the scene of the murders, with a stake driven through the heart.

In *The Maul and the Pear Tree* (1971), T. A. Critchley and P. D. James argue that Williams was probably 'framed'. The actual killer, they suggest, was a man named Ablass, a shipmate of Williams with a history of violence. The motive was robbery, and Ablass was probably aided by a man named Hart. The authors even suggest that Williams was actually murdered in Jail, with the connivance of the jailer. The theory is well-argued, but the basic objections remain. If the motive was burglary, why kill the baby? If two men were concerned, why did the lodger, Turner, see only one? But the basic objection is that the murders were committed with the ferocity of a maniac; talk about 'motive' is irrelevant. It is true that Williams had no history of violence, but on examination, it turns out that Ablass's 'violence' amounted to fomenting a mutiny on board ship. Ablass had reason to dislike Williams, who had escaped punishment after the mutiny; but again, what has this to do with the violence of the murders? The Ratcliffe Highway murders fascinated De Quincey's generation for the same reason that the Ripper murders fascinated the late Victorians: because of

their 'demonic' quality, because the killer was a man obsessed
by violence for it own sake.

C. W.

# 1817–22

# SAMUEL GREEN

## America's First Arch-Murderer?

'He was not the type of person a traveller would want to
meet in a lonely spot,' wrote one early-day crime historian
of Samuel Green, the terror of New England, and one of
America's first arch-murderers. Heavy-set, muscular, the five-
foot-eight-inch Green showed the world a savage-looking face
and burning dark eyes, but the strange fires raging inside him
were more fierce and threatening than his physical appearance.

Green was a product of the whip, that cherished item of
a young United States. To say that this inhuman killer was
created by the stern-minded adults who ruled his childhood is
an understatement in the annals of murder.

Born in the hamlet of Meredith, New Hampshire, Green's
poor, hard-working parents thought the child possessed at an
early age when he played the truant from school. As was the case
with most simple folk of that era, they resorted to thrashing their
child with switches. As a teenage apprentice to a blacksmith,
Green was caught stealing. He was horsewhipped. He was sent
home, where he was whipped again. He angrily sought revenge
by destroying a bed of onions. He was whipped for this offense
but refused to admit to the deed. Instead he grabbed the family
dog and threw it in the well. The drowned dog caused the water
to turn bad and the well had to be cleaned at great expense to the
Greens. For this transgression Green was, naturally, whipped.

In childish rage, Green stabbed the family pig. He was beaten
severely. His parents finally threw up their hands to Heaven
and sent their son off to Newhampton to live with man named
Dunne. For a short time Samuel settled down and attended

school without incident. He then grew bored with classes and began to play hookey. Apprehended, he was beaten. The boy stole a jew's harp from a local store and was flogged. Green fled back to his parents, who, upon hearing of his theft, beat him into unconsciousness, sending him back to Dunne, who, in turn, flayed Green's back until a layer of flesh was peeled back.

For this last beating, Samuel decide to kill Dunne. The boy cleverly arranged a large axe to fall upon his master when he entered his workshop. In case this failed, Green fixed a pitchfork, points aimed downward, at the top of the barn door. Dunne proved lucky. When he entered his workshop, the axe fell but only sliced away a part of his coatsleeve. As he raced into the barn in search of Green, the pitchfork shot downward, giving Dunne only a minor wound in the foot. For these clumsy attempts at homicide, Green was tied to the barn door and whipped until his back was a welted, bloody mass of flesh.

Again Green retaliated, destroying a hogshead of cider and stealing some bushels of Dunne's corn. He was whipped when caught. Green tried to burn down Dunne's barn. His master quickly put out the blaze. Green was beaten senseless with whips and fists.

This seesaw battle between guardian and boy continued for months until Dunne gave up the fight. By then the youth was old enough and strong so that no man could hold him. He then embarked on a career of passing counterfeit notes, along with another embittered youth named Ash, both of them supplied by a crafty old Fagin whose name they never uttered. They operated about Newhampton at the time. When both young men came under suspicion as having too much money for their station and age in life, they moved to other towns. As they passed a schoolhouse where children were playing, Green decided to wreak more vengeance upon those who represented his misspent youth. He threw a large timber beneath a speeding sleigh loaded with children, almost killing them.

The schoolmaster, a large man, collared both Green and Ash and beat them severely. That night the bruised youths waited for the man, waylaid him in a remote spot, and knocked him unconscious with rocks. They stripped him naked, tied him up, and left him to freeze to death. (The schoolmaster was found hours later and narrowly recovered.)

Green and Ash then moved through the town of Guilford, and then over to Burlington, Vermont, where Green enlisted with the army, being paid a bounty for his services. He immediately deserted but was caught and thrown into a guardhouse where, of course, he was flogged. He broke loose and fled back to his family in New Hampshire. Green was rich by then, having passed hundreds of dollars worth of counterfeit notes. With more than a thousand dollars to his name, the young man purchased a cow for his mother, the only sign of love he manifested in his life. The remainder of his loot he lavished upon himself in the purchase of fine clothes, jewelry, a fine horse and sumptuous meals.

When the money ran out, Green and Ash went back to passing counterfeit bills. Their elderly mentor and supplier taught the dedicated felon Green some backup trades in the lucrative fields of crime, showing him how to become an expert card cheat and how to pick locks and duplicate keys to enhance his methods of burglary.

Green went to Boston, where he hired out as a servant to wealthy men. Once inside their houses he played the dutiful servant, but late at night he robbed them of their valuables and fled.

Next, Green again teamed up with Ash and, outside of Bath, New Hampshire, they encountered a jewelry salesman in a tavern. The peddler imprudently allowed the two cutthroats to inspect his fine gems. Later that day, Green and Ash waited in ambush for the peddler. When he leisurely rode past them they sprang forth from bushes, knocked him off his mule with cudgels and took his money. Ash thought they should kill the man. Green hesitated. 'A dead cock never crows,' advised the wily Ash. Green winked at the reason and then brought his club downs upon the unconscious man, bashing in his head and killing him on the spot.

Green's wild exploits became less secretive as he ranged through New England, robbing and murdering at will. He was jailed several times on suspicion but evidence was lacking to indict him. On several occasions, Green did not wait for judgment. His friend Ash always managed to help him escape his cell. Once, when looting a jewelry store in Montreal, Green fought his way through an entire posse, shooting several men.

He was apprehended and thrown into jail. He was soon tried, convicted and sentenced to be hanged. Green, as his jailors half-expected, broke jail with his friend Ash's help and returned to the lonely mountains of New Hampshire. After hiding out for some months, Green again went on a crime spree, burglarizing stores in Albany, New York, and in New York City. He then went up to Middlebury, Vermont, where he robbed and shot to death a wealthy French traveler. Nothing was beyond the ambitions of Samuel Green. He left a trail of rape, horse-stealing, burglary, counterfeiting and murder from Montpelier, Vermont, to Schenectady, New York; from Saco, Maine, to Barre, Vermont. He became America's first Public Enemy Number One. In scenes reminiscent of the terrified villages with flickering torches and howling dogs searching for the Frankenstein monster, Green had aroused all of New England. Half the country was looking for him; the bounties to be paid for his capture were enormous.

The great fugitive's end began when he was arrested in Danvers, Massachusetts, for stealing thirty dollars' worth of goods from a store while blind drunk. He was convicted of this burglary. Green was sent to the State Prison at Boston to serve a four-year term. He attempted to escape many times, for which he was fitted for special shackles with weighted clogs to slow his movements; several more years were also added to his term.

Green learned that a Negro prisoner named Billy Williams had informed on him moments before his last escape attempt. Once released from solitary confinement, Green vowed revenge. He put poison into Williams' food but the wary convict did not eat it. Green finally cornered Williams alone in a shop on the morning of November 8, 1821. Wielding an iron bar, he pounced upon the informer. He brought the weapon down on Williams' head, giving him a fractured skull. While the man lay unconscious at this feet, Green kept hammering at him with the bar, breaking all of Williams' ribs and his arms and legs. Williams died a week later of these injuries.

It was the finish for Samuel Green, juvenile delinquent, whose final punishment, following a long trial, occurred on April 25, 1822. A rope was put about his neck instead of being applied to his back. Before Green was dropped to death, he told Father Taylor, who prayed at his side, that he had no words for those gathered to see him hang. 'They shall not know my fate,' he said cryptically. 'I have written out my confession in full.'

'Are you penitent, my son?' asked the priest.

'If you wish it,' droned Samuel Green.

J. R. N.

# 1823

# DOCTOR CASTAING

## The First Deadly Doctor

Dr. Castaing found himself some six months after he had qualified in the awkward position of having no money and no practice, and, to aggravate him still further, he was madly in love with the widow of a judge, whom he wished to marry at once.

To him Paris appeared to be overcrowded with doctors, and he knew that his only chance was to retire to the provinces, but he loved the gay life of the capital, and he was afraid that if he went away the lady might forget him.

It was a problem which could be solved only by hard work or crime, and, as Dr. Castaing was constituted, it is scarcely surprising he chose the latter alternative.

He had no elderly relatives likely to leave him any money, and so he searched amongst his acquaintances for someone whose death would benefit him financially. Finally his choice alighted on two brothers of the name of Ballet.

Hippolyte Ballet was a milksop; his brother, Auguste, was a fool who was spending his fortune rapidly by reckless dissipation. But the two brothers, who differed so completely, were deeply attached to one another, and, although Hippolyte considered Dr. Castaing his dearest and best friend, he made no secret of his intention to leave his fortune of one million francs to Auguste.

The young doctor hypocritically approved of his decision, and he urged him to mention only Auguste's name in his will. It was due entirely to Castaing's influence that until the last month of

Hippolyte's life Auguste was his sole heir.

Castaing and the elder Ballet were inseparables, who were seen together everywhere. Apparently the doctor had no intention of working at his profession, and the general opinion was that he was living on his private means. The truth was, however, that it was Hippolyte who was keeping him, although Castaing pretended to be only borrowing the money which paid their joint hotel bills monthly. But all this was part of the plan the doctor had conceived some months previously, for, unknown to his victims, each day's events were leading up to a double tragedy.

Castaing and his friend could never persuade Auguste to leave Paris and spend a quiet holiday with them in an obscure part of France, and it was after the two men had returned from a fortnight's residence in a farmhouse that Auguste, whose letters to Hippolyte asking for loans had been ignored, called on Castaing and informed him that he had come to the end of his resources.

'It's very bad news, my friend,' said the young doctor, sympathetically, 'and I regret I have worse news for you. Your brother has made a new will, and, with the exception of 5000 francs—bequeathed to you—the whole of his fortune goes to your sister, Madame Martignon.'

Auguste was astounded and dismayed. He was practically penniless, and he had contracted certain liabilities which if not met might involve him in a criminal prosecution. He now implored Castaing to try and persuade Hippolyte to alter his will.

'It would only be waste of time,' said Castaing, deliberately; 'Hippolyte had such confidence in you that when it was shattered by reports of your conduct he became embittered against you. No, the only way to save you would be to have the will destroyed, for if your brother died intestate under the law of France you would receive three-fourths of his estate and your sister one-fourth.'

There was something so suggestive in the doctor's tones that Auguste immediately took heart, and when he asked Castaing to explain how he could bring about the destruction of the will he protested that he had no intention of committing such a crime.

Auguste promptly apologised for even thinking of such a thing, and then Castaing proceeded to hint that the lawyer who was in possession of the will was a very great friend of his, and for a fee of 100,000 francs would put the important document in the fire.

'But I have not got 100,000 francs,' said Auguste, hopelessly.

'Give me your written promise to pay as soon as you inherit your brother's estate,' said Castaing, 'and I will guarantee to Lebret, the lawyer, payment in due course for his special services.'

Seven days later Hippolyte Ballet, Dr. Castaing's friend and benefactor, died after forty-eight hours of agony. The man who shared his apartments and his income very wisely did not attend to him during his last illness, but the doctor he sent for was old and incompetent, and was easily persuaded to certify that death was due to natural causes.

Search was made for a will, and when none was found Auguste inherited three-fourths of his late brother's million francs and Madame Martignon the remaining fourth. Auguste immediately handed to Dr. Castaing the sum 100,000 francs to pass on to Lebret, the lawyer, but as the story of Hippolyte's will had been a sheer invention the money remained in Castaing's pocket until it was utilised to settled his more pressing debts.

The first stage of this plan to obtain sufficient money to justify him marrying the widow was now completed. There remained, however, the most difficult part of the plan to be tackled. Hippolyte had been as clay in his hands, and had been willing to remain in his company day and night. With Auguste Ballet it was quite the other way. That young man had no liking for the simple life, and his idea of pleasure was spending money recklessly and enjoying himself without any thought of the morrow.

Castaing realised, therefore, that unless he murdered Auguste at once, the fortune for which he had already risked his neck by poisoning Hippolyte would be spent by Auguste, and there would be nothing for him.

But he had some hold on the young man, for Auguste believed the doctor had committed a very serious offence to obtain for him the greater part of his brother's estate, and as in the event of Castaing being accused of the crime of destroying the will he, Auguste, would be likely to be arrested too, he decided to come to some arrangement with his fellow-conspirator.

The two men had a conference on the subject, and Auguste,

under the impression that Castaing had not benefited a franc by the destruction of Hippolyte's will, agreed to make his own will immediately and bequeath everything to the doctor. So far as Auguste was concerned, it was a purely nominal act, because it must have been obvious to him that in a few years the will would be utterly valueless, on account of there being nothing to inherit under it.

Auguste, however, failed to see that he was dealing with a very thorough and crafty criminal. Had he suspected the character of his friend he would never have signed that will, because he would have known that it was as good as signing his own death-warrant.

Promptly taking advantage of Auguste's gratitude for services rendered, Castaing persuaded him to accompany him to an hotel at St. Cloud, ten miles from Paris. Ballet did not wish to leave his friends, but unwilling to offend the doctor, he accepted.

Soon after their arrival Auguste became ill, and Castaing was compelled by the agitated proprietor of the hotel to obtain the assistance of a specialist.

When the news reached Paris Auguste's sister, Mme. Martignon, and her lawyer promptly took up their residence at St. Cloud, but although they had started for the hotel the moment they heard of the young man's illness, they were not in time to see him alive.

'I wish this had not happened,' said Castaing to his victim's sister, 'because the only will Auguste made bequeaths everything to me.'

'That is, indeed, awkward,' commented the lawyer drily. Mme. Martignon instantly declared that Castaing should not receive a franc until it had been established beyond all doubt that there was no connection between Auguste's will and his sudden and mysterious death.

A post-mortem examination was ordered, and in preparation for it the police made inquiries about Dr. Castaing. But the most important piece of evidence they obtained was an admission from Castaing himself that the day previous to his friend's illness he had gone to Paris to buy some tartar emetic and acetate of morphia.

'Why did you want those poisons?' asked the detective.

'To kill rats in the hotel,' said the doctor, glibly.

'But why go ten miles when there is a chemist's shop less than a hundred yards from the hotel?' said the detective, and this time his question remained unanswered.

That evening Castaing was informed that he must consider himself under arrest, and that if he attempted to leave the hotel he would be conveyed to a cell and locked up.

Castaing, who knew that the tests for the poisons he had used were inadequate, and that they would fail to discover any trace of them in Auguste's body, accepted the decision of the police with a bow, and waited confidently for the report of the experts.

When the latter announced that they could not find the cause of the death, Castaing triumphantly demanded his release. Then he was told that, as the police had obtained a complete history of his relations with Hippolyte and Auguste Ballet, it had been decided that he was to be taken to prison to await his trial for the murder of the brothers and the destruction of Hippolyte's will.

Under English law the murderer would have escaped arrest, and there would have been no prosecution once the result of the post-mortem examination was signed by the doctors.

In France, however, the police are allowed greater latitude than here, and Castaing was kept a prisoner while the authorities built up a case against him, which at the assizes resulted in his conviction on 17th November 1823 for the murder of Hippolyte and Auguste Ballet.

Strenuous efforts were made to save him from the guillotine, but his crimes were so cold-blooded that his influential relatives found themselves powerless in face of public opposition to a reprieve, and Dr. Castaing, whining pitifully, was dragged to the guillotine to die the death of a coward.

C. K.

# WILLIAM CORDER
## The Red Barn Murder

Maria Marten, murdered in 1827, achieved a kind of immortality soon afterwards. She was the subject for pretty well the rest of the 19th century of numerous 'penny dreadfuls', the cheap story books of the Victorian era, and also of melodramas which were toured successfully through the larger and small towns, and some of the cities, by companies of actors and actresses who knew how to be heard at the back of the gallery and how to make it unmistakably clear which was the hero, which the villain, and which the innocent but betrayed heroine. In print and on the stage Maria Marten had only one serious rival – Sweeney Todd, the Demon Barber of Fleet Street, who cut his customers' throats while shaving them and tipped the corpses from the chair straight through the trap door into the cellar, where they were converted into meat pies.

Sweeney Todd never existed. He was drawn from the common stock of folk lore or invented by some author now anonymous. It is otherwise with Maria Marten, and the true story of her life and death needs no fictitious embellishments. Stangely enough, the crime done in the Red Barn at Polstead in Suffolk has some claim to be considered an intellectual murder. The killer was a man of some education and his plan for getting rid of Maria included one element which revealed an able and ingenious mind at work. William Corder, nearly twenty-four years old, as part of his plan, buried his victim, after shooting her, and later took himself off to the western outskirts of London, where he married and became a schoolmaster. In the eyes of some people schoolmastering is of itself a sign of an intellectual disposition for it involves the transmission of learning to others. What Corder's qualifications were for teaching remains vague. Physically he may be thought to fit the part of an intellectual for he is depicted as a short, plump man most attentively reading a book, and described as very near-sighted. When he was arrested his brother-in-law exclaimed: 'I should as soon have thought that tree growing yonder would walk as that he could have committed murder. . . . He is most kind, tender-hearted and indulgent husband.'

As a schoolmaster, at Ealing, Corder wore spectacles, possibly in order to disguise his appearance – but he did not change his name. He had sandy hair, a pale complexion and something of a squint. The spectacles re-appeared at his trial, for he put them on when, at the conclusion of the case for the prosecution, he was invited to defend himself. This he did, according to an old account, 'having drawn forth a quarto blue-covered copy book from his side pocket'. His speech, if indeed it was composed by himself, is literary in the newspaper style of the period and gave – if his own dying confession is to be believed – a false account of Maria Marten's death. The speech is nevertheless skilfully and, on the whole, economically composed, stating its arguments neatly and apparently with some detachment. Many an acknowledged intellectual has made a worse job of prose writing.

## 2

Maria Marten was nearly twenty-six when she died: her father – a mole catcher – seemed uncertain of the precise date of her birth. She worked as a domestic servant. When she was eighteen or so she had an illegitimate baby, which died. So did the alleged father. Soon afterwards she bore another child to a man named Matthews, a visitor from London, and then took up with William Corder, the younger brother of the father of her first child. By Corder she had yet another baby which did not long survive. Maria may be regarded as 'no better than she ought to be' and therefore not entitled to much sympathy, but there is hardly enough information to allow even a tentative judgement of her character. What is most likely is that she differed from other village girls chiefly in being rather prettier and less able to keep her head and resist the blandishments of some of the men that her prettiness attracted. At the trial there was a conflict of evidence about whether or not Maria had showed that she was anxious to marry Corder: this may indicate that for her he was less important as a lover than as a means of escape from her unfortunate situation, in a small village, as the mother of three bastards by different men. The father of the surviving child, Matthews, evidently would not or could not marry her. Corder also showed no eagerness, which may not have been entirely because of her promiscuous record and a baby that a new husband would have to accept as his own: Corder may have realised that for him to marry Maria would make neither of them happy for long.

Maria apparently went away to Sudbury for two months and bore Corder's baby there. After it died he promised (according to Maria's father, sister and step-mother) to take her to Ipswich and there marry her, but the reason Corder gave for the move to Ipswich was 'because John Baalham, the constable, came to me in the stable this morning and told me that he had got a letter from Mr. Whitmore' (the rector of Polstead) 'who was in London, to proceed against Maria about her bastard children.' At the trial Corder stated as an additional reason for moving Maria to Ipswich his desire to keep his mother ignorant of the contemplated marriage. Corder's father and three other children had all died recently of consumption, and his mother had apparently inherited the farm, of which he was manager or overseer. His livelihood, therefore, depended on his mother's good will, and he was most anxious that she should not hear that Maria had returned from Sudbury to Polstead. It was equally important to him that Maria should leave again without attracting attention.

### 3

He arranged that, after dark, he would call, with his gig, at the Red Barn (which stood in some isolation on his mother's farm land) and then drive Maria to Ipswich. However, it was soon after midday that he sent her to the Red Barn – a time when he had his labourers working elsewhere. He sent her in man's clothes: 'a brown coat, striped waistcoat and blue trousers.' She wore a man's hat but had 'one large and two small combs in her hair, and earrings in her ears.' Corder, with the complicity of Maria's step-mother, had concealed the birth, and the subsequent death, of his child – which was buried 'in the fields' – from his mother, his other relatives and from the parish officials who should have been notified. The ostensible reason for getting Maria away from her father's cottage dressed in a style which probably, at that time, offended against the Law was to ensure that, if anyone did chance to see her, from a distance, as she went through the fields to the Red Barn, she would be taken for a man working on the farm. By this device Corder broke, it was alleged, the link between himself and Maria Marten in the vicinity of Polstead. If and when she disappeared, her disappearance would seem to be from the town of Ipswich ten miles away, and in and beyond Ipswich no one would be able to trace her because, in fact, she would be dead and buried beneath the floor of the Red Barn, close to one of its wood slatted walls.

Deception is as essential to crime as to warfare and the provision of this false clue has a classic simplicity and directness. Unfortunately, for him, Corder's actions were inferior to his planning. He allowed Maria's father, sister and step-mother to know of the rendezvous at the Red Barn and even to watch Maria setting off on what was to be her last journey. Further, when it came – after a two hour interval – to burying the body he was forced to go to a neighbouring house to borrow a spade, and, this proving inadequate, go again to borrow a pick-axe. Such negligences and oversights may be regarded as characteristic of the intellectual or near-intellectual to whom theory always comes easier than practice. It is, however, just possible that Corder meant Maria no harm when he evolved the stratagem of smuggling her away from Polstead. If his intention was, as he said, to take her to Ipswich, the fact that he allowed her three closest relations to see her wearing man's clothes and to watch her depart for the Red Barn, makes better sense. Not only the brother of the young woman he married afterwards when he started a school at Ealing, but several people who had known him all or most of his life testified that Corder was a 'kind humane young man'. There was good evidence, too, that he spoke of, and to, Maria affectionately.

If such an interpretation of Corder's motives holds good then his defence at the trial, written and read out by himself, deserves fuller consideration. In it he said that, once inside the barn, Maria 'flew into a passion; told me that she did not care anything about me; that I was too proud to take her to my mother's and when married she did not think she should be happy, as my mother and family, she was sure, would never notice her. . . .

I felt myself so insulted and became so much irritated by her observations that I told her . . . I had then seen sufficient to convince me we should never live happily together, and I was, therefore, resolved, before it was too late, not to marry her, informing her that I should return home and that she might act as she thought proper respecting her future conduct.' This may be a transposed account of a quarrel which happened on another occasion but it is by no means impossible that Corder was telling the truth.

He went on to relate how he walked out of the barn and had got as far as the gate out of the barn-yard 'when I heard a loud report, like that a gun or pistol'. Running back, he found Maria lying on the ground. She was lifeless and only then did he realise that the pistol beside her was his. Some time passed before he made up his mind to conceal the body – it was found, a year later, only five inches below the surface of the barn floor – and to invent and tell lies to account for Maria's disappearance. Whether Maria killed herself, or was killed, Corder succeeded in diverting suspicion for a whole year. To that extent he succeeded in his subterfuge of disguising Maria as a man.

It is an ironic comment on the Marten family that what in the end stirred them to action was a clairvoyant dream experienced by the step-mother in which she saw Maria being murdered and buried in the Red Barn. Even so it was not until the dream recurred – some while later! – that anything was done. At Corder's trial the prosecution asserted, with expert medical evidence to support the assertion, that Maria had been stabbed while she was still alive. Corder most vehemently rejected this, suggesting that the body must have been injured when it was disinterred. He held firm on this point, both at the trial (when his defence was that she shot herself) and in his confession of guilt, taken down by the prison governer the night before he was executed, at Bury St Edmunds, on August 11th 1828. An old account says that, being questioned on the scaffold, he denied that he used any weapon but a pistol.

J. B.

# 1828–9

# BURKE and HARE

## The Bodysnatchers

In the early years of the last century a certain hideous criminal trade, but serving useful purposes, was carried on in England and Scotland by sinister individuals, 'Resurrectionists' as they were called.

At that period the laws of Great Britain, owing to the sentiment of respect for human remains which prevailed, absolutely prohibited dissection. The only exception was in respect to the corpses of criminals who had been executed. In some cases these might be placed at the disposal of surgeons, who had no other subjects for their anatomical investigations and who sought in vain to excite public opinion in the matter.

Being convinced of the immense importance of dissection to the pursuit of medical science, the surgeons availed themselves of the service of the resurrectionists to violate the cemeteries and bring them bodies from the graves.

It is easy to imagine the horrible circumstances attending these nocturnal expeditions—the seeking out of recent graves, the exhumation of the bodies, and the clandestine carrying of them to the hospitals. The resurrectionists took good care to rob the bodies on the spot of anything attached to them of any value. They delivered over the bodies quite naked. According to the law, the abstracting of the corpse was a matter of little importance, but the taking of the most minute article attached to it involved the severest penalty. The cleverest of the resurrectionists boasted that they could exhume a corpse sometimes in twenty minutes, counting from the moment when they climbed over the cemetery wall down to the moment when they got over it again carrying the body, having left the grave in such a condition that it looked untouched.

The resurrectionists had to be resourceful in their methods of conveying the body to the operation theatres of their medical clients. They would hide it between heaps of vegetables or bundles of wood piled up high on market carts or suchlike.

Once the body was safe in his laboratory, the doctor had nothing to fear, as the police were not allowed entrance to it. The prices paid for the bodies varied greatly. From four to eight pounds—sometimes much more—were given for 'good specimens.' The famous surgeon, Hunter, who initiated the anatomical museum at the College of Surgeons in London, paid more than £500 for the body of the famous Irish giant, Byrne.

Byrne was over eight feet high. He earned a good livelihood by exhibiting himself in London, but he had a bad constitution and was a loose liver, and it was manifest that he would not make old bones. In any case, Hunter yearned for those bones for his collection. He approached Byrne and offered him £800 down on the understanding that he should have Byrne's body on his decease. The giant was seized with a feeling of indescribable horror and refused. The surgeon persisted and tormented Byrne so much over the question that the latter made four trusty friends promise him on their oath that whenever he might die they would drop his body weighted with lead into the sea, well out from land, so afraid was he that if buried in the ordinary way his remains would be disinterred by body-snatchers in the pay of his fanatical persecutor.

But Hunter was not to be thus baffled. When the giant died he induced Byrne's friends to accept the above mentioned sum of £500 for the body. . . .

The evil fame of the resurrectionists spread all over the country and evoked a growing horror.

The inhabitants of London found it necessary to band themselves together in order to take steps to preserve their cemeteries from such profanation. Armed with loaded guns the citizens would mount guard during the night. Many accidents were incurred, shots being fired sometimes by mistake at inoffensive passers-by or at other men out on the same errand of defence. But while finding their work more difficult the resurrectionists continued to ply their trade.

The school of surgery at Edinburgh was in a particularly flourishing condition, and was held in very high repute.

It was being kept abundantly supplied with bodies for dissection, a certain Dr. Knox, in particular, never being at a loss in this respect. He was engaged at this time on a great anatomical work, the publication of which was presently to cause a sensation in the world of Science. This surgeon depended chiefly for his supply of bodies on a boot-maker named William Burke, who had a confederate named Hare.

Burke and Hare lived with their wives in Tanners' Close, one of the most miserable quarters of Edinburgh, a dark and filthy alley. Hare's dwelling, a single room, was in a basement, a wretched hovel reached by a long passage. Burke lived on the sixth floor of an old house tumbling into ruins.

At the beginning of 1828 mysterious disappearances began to occur in the city. At first these were confined to members of the poorer classes, especially drunkards and beggars.

Presently, however, a boy and a girl who were widely known vanished. The girl was famous for her great beauty; the boy, who was a beggar, was noted for his eccentricities, his bright disposition, and his simple goodness.

The girl vanished first, then the boy. The general public became excited, and strange rumours began to circulate about secret societies who lived on human flesh and who carried people off to devour them.

Months passed, other such disappearances took place, and the horror was becoming intensified when on November 1st a workman notified the police that he had discovered the body of an old woman who had evidently been murdered, hidden under a pile of straw in the room of one of his neighbours.

This neighbour was Burke. His room was searched, and certain clues found on the premises put the police on the track of a big box, addressed to Dr. Hare, in which the body was found.

Both Burke and Hare were arrested. The latter turned Queen's Evidence and confessed everything. They had begun their work, he stated, by selling the body of an old soldier who had died suddenly, owing them money. They had taken it to Dr. Knox, who had paid them something like £8 for it. Encouraged by this success, they had perfected and simplified the system which they had practised ever since. Instead of going to the cemeteries to disinter dead bodies with great difficulty, they had taken to 'manufacturing' the corpses in which they dealt.

Their method, invented by Burke, was always the same. On a foggy evening they would roam about the low quarters of the city and look out for some suitable victim, man or woman, by preference a drunkard. They would get into conversation wiith him and bring him home. On the table they would have whisky and some glasses. They would drink together. Burke, who had a fine voice, would begin to sing, and as soon as their guest was drunk enough, Hare would pass behind him and suffocate him by shutting his mouth and nostrils with his hands while Burke sat on his chest.

They had begun with an old woman, for whose body Dr. Knox had given them £10, without enquiry as to the cause of her death. They then had killed a mother and her daughter and another old woman and her grandson. Then a number of others. (Hare said he remembered sixteen in all but that there might have been more.) Among them was the beautiful young girl, whose body had been identified by a student who, however, had not allowed the fact of his recognition of her to become known, and the weak-minded young beggar, who had given the assassins a good deal of trouble as he was powerful and had struggled violently.

It was after their murder of this youth that Burke had invented the wax mask which from that time onwards they used to slap on the face of their victim to asphyxiate him.

Burke was hanged in 1829. Hare escaped hanging but only narrowly escaped lynching by Edinburgh crowds on more than one occasion. He is said to have lost his sight eventually, and to have become a beggar in the streets of London.

F. B.

# 1835

# LACENAIRE

## Poet and Murderer

---

The criminal world has its stars. Certain malefactors, by the enormity of their misdeeds, by the mysterious nature of their character, or just by chance—by the mere fact, perhaps, that they have had no great contemporary rivals—stand out conspicuously and become famous: leading actors in real life dramas, outstanding figures in a Chamber of Horrors.

Three names come to mind at once when we look back on the criminal annals of France during the last hundred years—three names of supermen in the field of robbery and murder, throwing all others into the shade: Lacenaire, Troppmann, and Landru—Landru, who never admitted his guilt. . . . Other names may be recalled, too: Dumollard, Jud, La Pommerais, Avinain, Faynayrou, Marchandon, Pel, Pranzini, Prado, Eyraud, Anastay, Carrara, Renard, Brière; but they are all of lesser rank.

Lacenaire, of the three, takes pride of place. He remains even now—nearly a century since his renown reached its height—the perfect exemplar of the accomplished criminal, cynical, capable, resolute.

He was, moreover, something of an innovator—as we shall see.

He was born in 1800, and was the son of a merchant of Lyons. He was educated first at Saint-Chamond; then at the seminary at Alix, and in Lyons.

He was a brilliant student—'a *rara avis*' some of the professors called him. One of them, however, shocked by his youthful wickedness, declared: 'This boy will end on the scaffold.' Lacenaire himself relates in his Memoirs, with that boastfulness in respect to his misdeeds which was one of his characteristics, that he was expelled from every school he went to, for unruliness, irreligion, and immorality.

When, towards the age of eighteen, he left college, he was unable to get to Paris to take his degree as had been intended, his father being ruined. Instead, he became a shop-messenger first, then a lawyer's clerk, then an employé in a bank. Finally, regarding these avocations as unworthy of him, he enlisted.

Did he enlist under an assumed name? Did he serve in the war in Morea? Did he desert in order to get to Paris and live there under an *alias?* Or did he make his way to Italy and commit his first murder in Verona? Investigations into his life at this early period yield no definite information.

He himself tells us that he deserted twice from the army, 'because he could not stay.'

His real career as a criminal begins in 1829.

He was then in Paris. His means were scanty, his tastes expensive. He was to declare in later years: 'I have never had any passion except a passion for gold.' And: 'I hate a vacuum—in my pockets.'

To fill the vacuum, he took to swindling.

Between whiles, he dabbled in literature, and composed songs of a kind no better and no worse than those of the pseudo-Bérangers of the period.

He was on friendly terms with some families of good repute, and exchanged visits with some young people in society.

It was at this time that took place the romantic and tragic incident of his duel in the *Fossés du Champs de Mars* with a nephew of Benjamin Constant.

Lacenaire, having stood up to the fire of his adversary, who missed, shot in his turn and killed him.

'The sight of his agony,' he records, 'caused me no emotion. My nature is marked by complete insensibility.'

This duel, although carried out in accordance with the rules, turned public opinion against Lacenaire, and closed all doors against him.

His first trial was for theft. He was sentenced to a year's imprisonment. While in prison he studied the characters of his fellow-criminals and learnt their methods of speech.

When set free he returned to literature, writing songs and

verses. But at the same time he perpetrated countless thefts, forgeries, etc. etc.

He now began to adopt all kinds of assumed names —Mahossier, Baton, Jacob Levy, Gaillard, Vialet. . . .

Under the name of Vialet he was again condemned to gaol, this time at Poissy, where with the help of the other prisoners he perfected himself in the theory and practice of crime.

But he dreamt of contriving new methods. He felt conscious of creative faculties. He was anxious to show his power and at the same time to effect a *coup* which would yield him wealth. He thought out a plan. Now he needed the right confederate. He studied his fellow-prisoners and ascertained the dates when they would be set free.

He himself was set free in August, 1834. He now bided his time. He had decided to make an accomplice of one of his Poissy fellow-prisoners, a young workman turned thief, named Avril, who seemed to him to possess all the necessary qualities and who would be given his freedom on November 25th that same year.

Accordingly he and Avril met on that day at Poissy. Avril had somehow contrived to amass a sum of 160 francs. The two drove together to Saint-Germain, where they breakfasted, and it was at this breakfast that Lacenaire divulged his plan. Avril agreed, but was intent first of all—having been shut up in prison for five whole years—to 'go a bust.'

Both men returned to Paris.

Avril, more than half drunk, left Lacenaire and went on his spree. His money all gone, he returned to Lacenaire, now ready to do his will.

Lacenaire's plan was marked by the simplicity of all great inventions. It consisted merely of luring a bank clerk into rooms rented specially taken for that purpose, and then killing him and getting the money which he had been misled into bringing with him.

This species of crime was in later years to become quite familiar. Carrara shone at it. So did some other miscreants recently brought to justice.

In Avril, Lacenaire found an accomplice worthy of him. The two men were equally resolute, equally formidable.

Lacenaire was a man of medium height, somewhat slight of build, athletic, and of a strong constitution. He had curly dark auburn hair, which had begun to grow thin over the temples by the time he was thirty-four. He wore a slight moustache and short whiskers. He had a broad forehead, grey eyes, a cleft chin. His features were delicate and regular. He liked generally to be well dressed.

Avril was small and lithe, but very robust and incredibly active and supple. His face would have been insignificant but for his extraordinary yellow eyes, which, like the eyes of a cat, lit up at moments of excitement and became ferocious. 'He has a taste for murder,' Lacenaire said of him admiringly.

The first effort proved a fiasco. A former friend of Lacenaire placed a room in the rue de Sartine at his disposal. The planned out communication was sent to the cashier of the Rothschild bank, and the two intending assassins lay in wait in the room with files sharpened for use as daggers.

But the bank messenger never came.

Lacenaire and Avril consoled themselves for the disappointment by making off with everything portable and saleable in the room which the friendly owner had lent them.

Lacenaire's next effort was of a quite different kind. Among his fellow-prisoners at Poissy, in addition to Avril, there had been an individual of evil character named Chardon, who made a show of piety, sold religious emblems, and lived with his old mother, on a first floor in the Passage du Cheval-Rouge. It was believed that the old woman had saved some money and that she owned some silver ornaments of value, while Chardon himself was said to have been given 10,000 francs by Queen Marie Amelie to found a place of refuge for reformed criminals.

Lacenaire and Avril, early one afternoon in December, knocked at the door of Chardon's dwelling. No answer. They went downstairs and met Chardon, who had just returned home, alone.

'We have just been to see you!'

'Good, come on up again!'

And they all went up together.

Of what happened when they entered Chardon's quarters, we know only the essential details. Avril seized Chardon by the throat while Lacenaire stabbed him in the back with a long sharp file. Chardon, falling to the ground, knocked open the door of a cabinet in which hung an axe. Avril seized hold of it and brought it down on Chardon's head.

Lacenaire now ran to the room in which old *mère* Chardon lay ill. He stabbed her repeatedly with his file, ransacked the room, and forced open a chest of drawers in which he found a sum of five hundred francs and some silver dishes. A fur coat also, a black cap, and an ivory statue of the Virgin.

Having taken possession of these things he went out of the place with Avril. Outside the door, they met two persons who had come to visit Chardon. 'He has gone out,' said Lacenaire, trying to pull the door shut, but Chardon's dead body was so lying that he could not do so.

Lacenaire and Avril now made for the estaminet de l'Episcié, a famous resort of criminals on the Boulevard du Temple. Lacenaire had put on the fur coat, Avril had donned the black cap. Discovering some bloodstains on their hands, they repaired to the Turkish bath establishment opposite for a wash, then dined and spent the evening at some place of entertainment.

The crime was not discovered until two days later. The police at first followed up clues which led them astray.

Meanwhile, Lacenaire, coming back to his idea of robbing a bank-messenger, took a new lodging for the purpose in the rue Montorgueil.

Again, a contretemps. Avril, having gone to the rescue of a young woman who had become his mistress, and who had just been arrested, was arrested himself. Lacenaire, attempting to save his friend, very nearly got arrested also.

Having lost Avril, Lacenaire now needed another accomplice. He choose a certain François, who had been in the army—a man who was remarkable for his bright red whiskers.

Lacenaire now contrived to arrange that a sum of money should be sent by messenger from a bank, in payment for an order to a Monsieur Marossier (himself).

The bank-messenger, a youth of eighteen, named Genevay, arrived in due course and was conducted by Lacenaire down into a basement room where François was sitting.

Genevay suddenly received a stab in the back, administered by Lacenaire, while François made to seize him by the throat.

Genevay struggled and yelled, and François, taking fright, made a bolt for it.

Lacenaire thereupon went after him, shouting: 'Stop, thief! Murder!'

Genevay's wound turned out not to be serious and he soon recovered from it.

Lacenaire and François came together again at a rendezvous to which they had arranged to make their way after accomplishing their crime. There was no immediate breach between them, but later François rounded on Lacenaire, told the police about his various *aliases,* and also gave them particulars regarding the murder of the Chardons.

Meanwhile, curious to relate, Avril also had gone back on his former chief and had offered to help to get him taken.

Lacenaire, when arrested, admitted everything, describing exactly the rôle he had played and the rôles played by his accomplices, now turned into his bitter foes.

He was imprisoned with them at la Force, but being a famous personage, and his revelations being of service to the police, he was never at a loss for money and was granted all sorts of favours.

François set the other prisoners against him, and one day Lacenaire was attacked in the prison and almost beaten to death. Balzac in *Splendeur et Misère des Courtisanes,* and Eugéne Sue in *Les Mystères de Paris* turned this scene to account.

Lacenaire's fame increased speedily. Men of fashion, men of letters, lawyers, doctors, elegant ladies came to la Force to see him.

The range of his knowledge, his philosophical bent of mind, the boldness of his theories, won the admiration of his visitors. He spoke of his forthcoming death sentence—as to which he felt no doubt—with the most perfect sang-froid. 'There was one day in my life,' he said with a smile, 'when I had to choose between suicide and crime. I preferred crime.'

This sang-froid did not leave him at the trial, when great crowds of people were present.

Complete master of himself, a trifle scornful, courteous and eloquent, Lacenaire showed clearly that he had only one aim—that of getting his accomplices condemned to death. Avril was duly sentenced. François was sent to a penal settlement.

While awaiting the scaffold, Lacenaire was sent to the conciergerie. There he excited the interest of the public even more than at la Force.

He contributed directly to this by writing to the papers to correct erroneous statements about himself and by announcing his Memoirs as forthcoming, and by composing verses in which he affirmed his principles, which amounted to an exposition of what we now call the Struggle for Life.

He hastened to disavow a poem which had been attributed to him and which represented him as a prey to remorse, and beseeching Divine pity. He replied to it by an invocation to the Divine Guillotine.

A great lady having asked him for his autograph, and having addressed him as *le sieur* Lacenaire, he replied coldly that *Monsieur* Lacenaire had very little time to give to such things. M. Gisquet, the Prefect of Police just then, who had in person brought him this request for his autograph (a circumstance illustrative of the times), tried in vain to obtain a few lines of a more amicable description from the Great Man.

Lacenaire took pleasure in disconcerting the Abbé Coeur, who tried to reconcile him with the Church, plying the good priest with philosophical jests and raillery. On the other hand he was quite willing that a cast should be made of his face.

He had forgiven Avril once he had secured that worthy's condemnation to death.

To cement their reconciliation he asked, and was given permission, to dine with his accomplice on the King's day. But he remained on his guard. 'Avril is as quick as a tiger,' he said to a police official. 'Keep your eyes on him and be ready to seize him.'

Six gendarmes stood on guard during the meal, which was an appetizing one and marked by gaiety and cordiality.

When coffee was served, however, Avril suddenly sat up in his chair, his eyes blazing, his whole face contracted, and said in low tones: 'All the same it is you, *Monsieur* Lacenaire, who are sending me to the scaffold.'

He had gripped his iron fork. . . .

He was seized and taken back to his cell.

Lacenaire did not weaken at the supreme moment. On his way to the guillotine, however, it was noticed that he experienced the aridity of lips and mouth which is to be observed almost always in the condemned prisoners walking to their doom.

He mounted the steps of the scaffold—the scaffold had seven steps at that period—and his neck went into the *lunette*, still wet with the blood of Avril, who had just been executed.

The knife, however, stuck in the groove and did not reach it. The knife had to be raised again.

Lacenaire with a convulsive movement managed to turn his head half round and saw the steel descending once more. This time he was decapitated.

F. B.

# 1837

# THOMAS WAINEWRIGHT
## Man of Letters—and Poison

Guardsman, artist, art critic, friend of Charles Lamb, dandy and *poseur*, forger and poisoner. There you have a breathless catalogue description of Thomas Griffiths Wainewright, whose prose style Lamb described as 'capital,' and whose appearance and manner amid the horrors of exposure and danger drew from that connoisseur of crime, De Quincey, a tribute of approval. Macready, the great actor, Forster, the biographer of Dickens, Talfourd, later a judge, and others of fame in their time, were delighted to admit him to intimacy and accept invitations to his house, where, dandified and affected, he gave them the choicest wines and foods amid an environment of almost perfect artistry. In the society of wit and knowledge he was not abashed, for if he was a skilful poisoner he was also a skilful conversationalist, and although invariably the youngest person present his intellectual attainments entitled him to the enviable position of an equal. But there were always two Wainewrights, and for years those who knew the kindly, good-natured side of an extremely clever man never suspected that there was another Wainewright who was capable of committing the most diabolical of murders.

One is tempted to credit Wainewright with a double dose of original sin at birth, but there is no proof whatever to support the theory that he inherited those criminal tendencies which were to render infamous even the fame of the man. The cynic might find adequate proof in the fact that his father was a lawyer and one of his grandfathers a publisher and editor, but all his immediate forbears were persons of exceptionally good character, and the mother who died at twenty-one in 1794 in giving birth to him deserved a better fate. The unfortunate baby grew into a pretty, intelligent and fascinating child; and when his father died, his grandfather, Dr. Griffiths, editor of the 'Monthly Review,' became his guardian and took him to live with him at Linden House, a spacious residence set in charming grounds and admired and envied by those who knew Turnham Green in the days when it was really green.

Amid such surroundings and under the benevolent supervision of such a man as his grandfather, the boy's artistic tastes developed. The editor of the 'Monthly Review' saw to it that he read only the best literature, and by the time Wainewright was eighteen he possessed a remarkable knowledge of English literature. Then, however, to the surprise of his relations he expressed a wish to enter the army, and as his trustees had sufficient money in hand to justify the adventure a commission was purchased for him in a Guards regiment, and for a brief while the lover of Shakespeare and Wordsworth and the amateur artist strutted about in uniform. Close acquaintance, however, with the army speedily disillusioned him and he was soon back again in civil life. Often afterwards when referring to his life as a soldier he would laughingly explain that it was the harshness of the colours that depressed him, adding, as he stretched out his long, white hands half covered with the jewellery which fashion dictated, that no artist should serve as a soldier unless permitted to design his own uniform.

Resignation from the army having left him without a profession, he turned to literature and painting, and at once met with success. He had an original style of his own and he could lighten the most learned art criticism by decorating it with fantasies and humour peculiarly his own. He was addicted to flippancy, but the discerning discovered the sound knowledge hidden from others and if his paintings did not conform to all the recognized rules they were too characteristic of the man to be worthless. No wonder, then, that when the 'London Magazine' was started in 1820 the editor invited Wainewright to join his band of contributors, and it is proof positive of his ability that he should have held his own in a company which included Charles Lamb, William Hazlitt, Allan Cunningham, De Quincey, Carlyle, and Hood.

But dilettante journalism combined with experiments in painting could not in the nature of things produce a satisfying addition to a private income of £200 a year, and when marriage with Miss Frances Ward failed to improve his financial position, something had to be done to meet his growing expenditure. The best was always good enough for Wainewright, whose naturally extravagant demands on life were now doubled and quadrupled by his anxiety to keep pace with the many famous persons with whom his membership of the 'London Magazine' circle brought him into contact. He felt it was worth while living at an uncomfortably extravagant rate when it gave him the honour of acting as host to Charles Lamb, John Forster, Macready, and other well-known men of the day. But even in the twenties of the last century £200 a year provided no more than bare necessities for a young married couple, and Wainewright, worried by the growlings of his Philistine creditors, decided that the future must be sacrificed for the present and the stock which provided his annuity sold.

Unfortunately for his plan the four trustees unanimously declined, and thereupon the genial art critic paused half-way in the writing of an article on the Italian Renaissance to practise imitations of signatures of four eminently respectable and stodgy old gentlemen, while the midnight oil burnt and not a sound was to be heard beyond the scratching of his pen.

It was said of Wainewright, the artist and critic, that he missed Parnassus because he was not thorough. That was probably true, but Wainewright, the criminal was thorough enough, and he laboured so strenuously as a student of forgery that his first completed effort achieved instant success. The young man who could talk so charmingly of the great poets and artists of all time, and one of whose pictures brought from William Blake an expression of emphatic praise, was cynical and affected, but only as an artist. Wainewright, the criminal, was thorough, efficient, and all the more daring because his daring was controlled by a cool and clever brain. It required coolness and courage as well as skill to present at the Bank of England a document demanding immediate payment of £2259 and bearing four very different and distinguishable signatures. It was, indeed, a remarkable instance of audacity triumphing, for the money was paid at once, and the forger became once more the dandified hoost whose house was a minor Mecca of the famous.

The proceeds of his first essay in forgery having been spent chiefly in riotous hospitality, Wainewright was soon grappling again with the problem of how to keep his creditors at bay. They had grown tired of being fed on mere scraps and now demanded payment in full, brushing aside the languid remonstrances of the artist, who, however, became desperate when he foresaw the possibility of an invasion of his house during one of his literary dinner parties. It was a crisis which had to be met squarely, and as Wainewright, the artist, was helpless he had to have recourse to the aid of Wainewright, the forger. Doubtless he would have preferred to devote exclusively his criminal self to the gentle art of forgery, but compelled to admit that a second attack on the Bank of England would meet with failure, his thoughts gravitated in the direction of the uncle who had inherited Linden House from his grandfather. Mr. Thomas Griffiths was of the race of kind and benevolent uncles, but he disturbed Wainewright's sense of proportion by displaying a youthfulness and vigour which were quite at variance with gradually approaching old age. And, as Wainnewright, the criminal, badly needed Linden House and the money it brought with it to enable Wainewright, the artist and connoisseur, to maintain his position in literary and artistic circles, he felt himself compelled to remove his uncle.

Previously to this stage in his career he had become acquainted with poisons, his interest in Italian literature having formed an introduction. An obscure pamphlet he came across by chance on the subject of poisons and poisoning fascinated him and he was already an amateur of poisons when he began to covet Linden House. To a criminal of his fastidious nature and to one who abhorred violence and the sight of blood, murder by any other means than a poison administered with finesse and subtlety was out of the question. The poisoning feats of the ancients had thrown a glamour over him, and he could see nothing vulgar in a form of crime which he considered worthy of an artist. He would have started back in horror at the thought of utilizing a knife or a bludgeon on the person of the elderly gentleman who, on hearing from his nephew that he and his young wife desired a stay in the country for the sake of their health, had warmly welcomed them and placed all the resources of his hospitality at their disposal. Murder of that sort would have been revolting, but there could be nothing crude or inartistic in an event brought about by a little strychnine cunningly administered.

It was easy to poison the wine of his uncle as they sat up late one night in the fine old library discussing literature and itts giants, and easier still to persuade him to empty his glass unsuspectingly. When shortly afterwards Mr. Griffiths died in a fit, there was no disturbing gossip to upset the handsome young nephew and heir whose pale, artistic features and general air of detachment from the sordid affairs of this world made him the most striking figure at the funeral.

Linden House and a fortune of some thousands of pounds now passed into the possession of Thomas Griffiths Wainewright, *littérateur* and artist, but unfortunately all the money with the exception of a few hundred pounds had to be paid out to insatiable creditors and, consequently, the maintenance of the house itself soon became a problem. Another was provided by the birth of a child, and yet another when his wife's mother, Mrs. Abercrombie, and her two daughters by her second husband, Helen and Madeleine, asked for a home. Wainewright had ever since his marriage lived so extravagantly and had talked so boastfully of his large income that his mother-in-law had no conception that they would be a heavy burden to him, and Wainewright himself would not confess the truth.

His position now was not only precarious but dangerous. His famous friends had begun to notice an unmistakable deterioration in his character, and there were ugly rumours to the effect that he had utilized his reputation as an art critic to sell as genuine spurious engravings. On the other hand, the position of the forger and poisoner was for the time being one of perfect safety. It was possible that some years later the forgery might be detected but he was not disturbed by this possibility, comforting himself with the undoubted fact that at the worst he had stolen only his own money. In the circumstances, therefore, the artist had to give way again to the stronger personality of the criminal, and Wainewright, who had obtained a small fortune by poisoning his uncle, now looked about him for a victim whose death would produce another.

His choice eventually alighted on Helen Abercrombie, who was pretty, twenty, and wholly under his influence. Helen had no money of her own, but her life was insurable, and the insurance companies had unlimited funds. He was certain that he had only to be his usually cautious self to eliminate risk, and he proceeded to show he had little to learn about the art of murder.

Had Wainewright, the *littérateur* and affected dealer in fine phrases, poisoned Helen Abercrombie, he would have done so hastily and clumsily, but Wainewright, the poisoner, was a totally different personality. Callous and unscrupulous in that character, he was the most practical of criminals, and he did not insure his sister-in-law's life until he had ascertained exactly the rules and regulations covering insurances. He was especially careful to ascertain his exact legal position, for Helen was under age, a fact which complicated the question of his insurable interest in her life.

Wainewright, the poisoner, therefore stayed his hand until the position and the way were both alike clear for him. As the poisoner he did not wish his name to be too clearly associated with the demand on the insurance company following her death, and although he had already invented a story of a suit in Chancery which could not come on for some years, and involved thousands of pounds rightfully belonging to Helen, to account for the necessity for insuring her, he induced her on the day she came of age to make a will in her sister's favour. For Wainewright, the poisoner, knew that Wainewright, the fascinating dilettante, would be able to extract the money from Madeleine with ease. All this duly accomplished, he began operations.

During the Christmas week of 1830 he took the Abercrombies to London for a few days and there acted as the most generous of hosts. There was a brief interval of sordid business, for which he laughingly apologized, when he got Madeleine to assign two of the policies on her sister's life to himself. They joked about an act which they agreed was superfluous, for Helen and death did not seem likely to meet for half a century yet, but all the same she was dead before the end of the year, and when her mother's hysterical innuendoes threatened to become permanent Wainewright poisoned her too. Then he ordered Madeleine to claim the £18,000 due from the insurance companies on her sister's death.

To his fury the companies declined to give the one touch needed to make his latest crime perfect by paying, and Wainewright, aware that his sister-in-law's action against the companies could not come on for some years, departed to Boulogne to avoid his creditors. Five years after his departure judgment in favour of the insurance companies was delivered in the courts, and a little later he heard that his forgery on the Bank of England had been discovered and that a warrant was out for his arrest.

For a time he wandered about the Continent haunted by fears and oppressed by penury, and at last he was driven to return to England in disguise, encouraged by the knowledge that his family and friends did not want the scandal of a public trial, and believing that his murders had not been suspected. In this he was wrong, for everywhere he was being spoken of as Wainewright, the poisoner; but when Forrester, the Bow Street runner, recognized him sitting at the window of an hotel in Covent Garden, it was only for forgery Wainewright was arrested and only for forgery was he tried.

Wainewright was now forty-three, and he bore only slight traces of the once pallid and interesting-looking dandy when he stood in the dock to hear his sentence of transportation for life. Queen Victoria had recently ascended the throne, and a new era had begun in which Thomas Griffiths Wainewright seemed out of place, even if many of his famous friends were living and linked his name to the new generation represented by Charles Dickens. It was Dickens, indeed, who in the company of Forster and Macready recognized Wainewright when the convict was waiting to be transferred to the ship which was to take him to Tasmania, and a great deal has been written of that encounter in Newgate which embarrassed all those who participated in it except the prisoner.

And to the end of his life—he died in 1852 at Hobart Town, at the age of fifty-eight—he remained unembarrassed. It was always the 'London Magazine' period with him and he refused to remember anything subsequent to it. He constantly boasted of his intimacy with the famous, and the convict who could paint portraits and landscapes was soon a prominent figure in the legion of the lost. But he was always mean and miserable in spite of his claims to ultra-gentility, and as each petition for a ticket of leave was rejected he shed tears and doubtless regretted he could not avenge himself by a little delicate poisoning. In the last few years of his life his temper and senile absurdities isolated him and he died lonely and derided.

Could he but know, however, of the considerable amount of literature his unparalleled career has inspired he would in his own peculiar fashion discover adequate consolation for the inconveniences his crimes entailed during the last twentyy years and more of his life. He might not care to see 'Janus Weathercock' transformed into 'Julius Slinkton' by Charles Dickens (in *Hunted Down*), and the character of 'Gabriel Varney' in Bulwer Lytton's *Lucretia* would not meet with his approval, but with William Hazlitt, Bryan Waller Procter (Barry Cornwall), De Quincey and Lamb recalling in print their acquaintance with him, and a younger and minor Hazlitt writing his life and editing his works, he would have reason for self-congratulation. Swinburne and Oscar Wilde have also helped to give him a permanent place in literary history, and Wainewright would be grateful to them too, especially to the Irishman, if only for the remark that 'the fact of a man being a poisoner is nothing against his prose'. The prose of Thomas Griffiths Wainewright is for all that no longer read, and the essayist and art critic is remembered now only because he was a criminal.

C. K.

# 2
# VILLAINOUS
# VICTORIANS
## (1849–82)

# 1849

# JAMES RUSH

## The Killer in the Fog

---

The Court House in Norwich was crowded as Mr. Baron Rolfe
entered through a side door and moved to take the Judge's seat.
Outside in the city streets there was the sunshine of early East
Anglian spring. The date on the calendar was March 29th, 1849.
Away in London a Swiss maid in the household of the Duchess
of Sutherland was attending to her duties and thinking of a
middle-aged Irishman. But several months were to pass before
everyone in that crowded court save one became familiar with
the name of Maria Manning. The exception was the portly man
with rounded cheeks and plump air of well-being who stared
around unconcernedly from the dock.

James Bloomfield Rush was his name. He was an auctioneer
and surveyor from Wymondham, in Norfolk, and that morning
he was on trial for his life. He had no one to defend him save
himself. As he had assured the court, he felt 'confident in his
own abilities and resources'. The trial was to last until April
5th, largely because the prisoner's abilities tended towards
lengthy and quite irrelevant cross-examinations of unimportant
witnesses. By that time he was to discover how misplaced was
his confidence. Had he glanced at the three men assembled to
question him he might have received his first doubt. Serjeant
Byles, aided by Mr. Prendergast and Mr. Evans, looked a
formidable team. They were.

In that protracted week they assured James Bloomfield Rush
of a permanent niche in the halls of ill-fame. They proved him
guilty of the murder of two men, a father and son, for little more
than an excess of savage spite against them.

Isaac Jermy had been Recorder of Norwich. He was the son of
a clergyman and a man of some substance locally. He lived with
his family at Stanfield Hall, near Wymondham, and Rush was
one of his tenants. The auctioneer had borrowed a considerable
sum of money from Jermy in 1844. The money was described
as a mortgage on Potash Farm, where Rush, a widower with

two daughters and a married son, sat down to meals each day opposite Emily Sandford, who after being his children's governess had been promoted to the dubious position of their father's mistress.

Jermy was frankly critical of the occupier of Potash Farm. Disputes arose between the two men, which found ventilation in October 1847 when Jermy brought an action against Rush for miscultivation of the farm. A solicitor named Clarke helped Jermy in his successful action and afterwards Rush, giving vent to the anger and frustration he felt, exclaimed in the hearing of a number of surprised persons: 'Damn them! I'll do for them at the first opportunity.'

It was considered the ranting of a bad loser. Proof that the feeling went deeper than supposed was provided some time later when Rush had privately printed a very scurrilous pamphlet, which purported to give an account of an action brought in March 1848 against him by Jermy and continued with an attack on Jermy's rights to Stanfield Hall and another estate. At this time Rush was indebted to Jermy for the sum of £5000, on which he was to pay interest at four per cent, until November 30th, 1848, when the money became due for repayment in full.

One passage of the vindictive diatribe against Jermy read:

> *I hope someone will come forward and oust this fellow, who has not half as much right to the property as I have. I hope this may be done by the steps I have taken, and am about to take. If there is truth in the Bible, such villainy is sure to be overtaken, and that when it is least expected.*

They read like idle words, not like a forewarning of doom. Most people who read them smiled, and did not bother to remember that in May 1848 Rush was declared bankrupt, and had loudly proclaimed his belief that Jermy had used secret influence to force Rush's creditors to foreclose.

So that between May and November of that year life at Potash Farm must have been lived in an atmosphere of strain and looming disaster. Hardly the atmosphere in which to win the affections of a young governess. But seemingly James Bloomfield Rush was more successful as a lover than auctioneer. Emily Sandford, who had been brought from London to teach the Rush children, found her employer's tumultuous vigour sufficiently attractive to succumb to his promise of eventual marriage.

A promise that weighed as lightly on Rush's mind as his debt to Jermy.

On the afternoon of November 28th, two days before he was due to repay the £5000 he owed, Rush thought a great deal about Robert the Bruce. He sat across the tea-table at Potash Farm and gloomed at Emily Sandford.

'Well,' he said, 'I've tried five or six times, too. I may succeed in my object this time.'

Emily Sandford filled his cup with tea and said nothing. She was accustomed to such outpourings, and took small notice of them. She did not take any notice when Rush donned his coat and hat at half past seven and went out. He did not say where he was going. But a thick fog was drifting across the fields, and after he had gone into the raw dampness she wondered what errand could have taken him out in such weather. But perhaps, very naturally, her mind turned more readily to the child she was carrying. If so, she was fortunate in not knowing that it would be born while its father occupied a cell in Norwich Gaol, waiting to be tried for murder.

Each step Rush took through the November fog brought stark tragedy closer to two families.

At eight o'clock that evening Isaac Jermy rose from his chair in the dining-room of Stanfield Hall and made his way to the front door. It was his custom each evening to stand in the porch smoking his after-dinner cigar. As he crossed the hall he heard the voices of his son and daughter-in-law. They were in the drawing-room playing picquet. He opened the front door, sniffed the swirling fog, carrying a dank tang from the moat, and stepped on to the porch. Almost at once a muffled figure sprang at him from out of the fog, and light from the hall behind him touched the pistol in a raised hand. The pistol exploded, and its load of slugs tore into Jermy's body, slashing his heart to shreds and breaking several ribs. He was dead before he collapsed on the floor of the porch.

The figure, muffled in a loose cloak, with flowing cape, turned and ran to a side-door, and entered the house. The butler appeared, and was roughly pushed aside just before the younger Jermy opened the door of the drawing-room and entered the hall.

Before he could ask what had caused the explosion the cloaked intruder levelled his weapon again and fired. The son of the house was killed instantly. Mrs. Jermy came running with her scared maid, Eliza Chestney. The maid called in terror to her mistress not to go forward. But Mrs. Jermy had seen the crumpled body of her husband, and was running to it. At that moment a figure moved away from the door of the dining-room. Both women saw the pistol. Before they could call out the intruder fired again—then once more. Mrs. Jermy's arm fell slack at her side. She turned and ran to the stairs. Eliza Chestney hurried after her, but went down in a moaning heap. She had been wounded in the hip.

The assassin turned and disappeared through the door by which he had entered. He was lost in the fog, which muffled his hurrying feet.

Shortly before half past nine Emily Sandford heard the porch door of Potash Farm rattling. She went to it, hesitated.

'Who is it?' she called.

'It's me—open the door!'

She recognized Rush's voice, but he sounded excited. She unbolted the door, and he almost ran into the farmhouse and upstairs without saying anything to her. When he came down she noted that he was unusually pale. He had taken off his jacket and shoes, and stood staring at her as though he didn't see her.

'Is anything the matter, James?' she asked.

He shook his head.

'No,' he said, as though the words were torn from him. 'Nothing. If any inquiries are made in the morning, you must say I was only out of the house ten minutes.'

His eyes ran over her, and he appeared to grow aloof as he told her she must sleep in her own room that night. It was three in the morning when he came to her room and woke her. He was trying to control an inner excitement, and not succeeding very well.

'You've got to be firm, Emily,' he insisted. 'If anyone asks you how long was out last night, you must say only ten minutes. Ten minutes, that's all.'

She sat up in bed, appalled by this agitated stranger who claimed her allegiance and demanded that she lie for him.

'What's happened, James?'

'Nothing,' he still insisted. But when he saw the denial did not satisfy her he added gruffly, 'At least, you may hear something in the morning.'

The he made her accompany him to the parlour, where he showed her a secret hiding-place in a cupboard. It was under a loose plank which could be raised with a chisel.

'I'm showing you in case of fire,' he said, and again she did not believe him.

Before dawn broke and the steamy fog lifted from the surrounding fields, no less than nine policemen had arrived at the scene of the crime. Constable George Pont, from Wymondham, was the first. He collected five irregular slugs of lead from the hall. They proved to be similar to those later removed from Isaac Jermy's body. Pont also found the ramrod of a large pistol.

By half past two the police had a reasonable notion that the killer was James Bloomfield Rush. James Watson, a footman, had caught sight of the fleeing figure, and was sure it was Rush. Eliza Chestney, questioned as she lay in bed, admitted she thought the assailant was the tenant of Potash Farm.

'He has a way of carrying his shoulders,' she told the attentive police, 'which can't be mistaken, and he keeps his head a little on one side.'

Pont and the other police started for Potash Farm. They arrived there shortly after Rush had shown Emily Sandford the hiding-place in the parlour cupboard. They surrounded the farmhouse as a dog began barking. A light appeared. Pont went forward and intercepted a lad named Savory who was employed about the house as handyman.

'Go and tell your master I want to speak to him,' he told the lad.

Savory was gone some minutes, then returned to say Rush was getting up. He let Pont into the house, and Rush entered the kitchen almost at once.

'What is this, Pont?' he asked.

Somewhat over-awed by the occasion, the policeman adopted a sententious manner.

'You must consider yourself my prisoner, Mr. Rush,' he said, 'on suspicion of having murdered the two Mr. Jermys last night.'

And according to Pont the prisoner acted as though overcome with surprise at the news. But perhaps he was merely thrown out of his stride at sight of the handcuffs manacling his heavy wrists.

He said: 'The two Mr. Jermys murdered! I don't like these handcuffs. God knows I'm clear of that!'

Before the police left they found a couple of double-barrelled guns in a locked cupboard in an upstairs room, with a wig and a supply of false hair. They did not find the intruder's cloak. It was never found.

While watching the search of his bedroom Rush tried to demonstrate his confidence by talking too much, and one of the things he said was a dangerous admission.

'It was about eight o'clock when the affair happened, some of you say?'

There was a sharp silence in the room, and Rush looked confused and disconcerted.

A constable from Norwich named Mortar said evenly, 'No one said that but yourself.'

The search revealed a deed cancelling the mortgage on Potash Farm. The scrawled signature read 'Isaac Jermy', but it was later proved to be a forgery. Jermy had to die so that he could not repudiate the bogus deed.

When the news of the shootings and the arrest spread through East Anglia the case created lively excitement and speculation. For at one time there was the possibility that the prisoner would be charged with four murders. Eliza Chestney was in a very critical condition, and her mistress had to have her shattered arm amputated. The story of Emily Sandford evoked pity for the deluded girl, but hardened the public's mind against the man who had duped her. The girl had to submit to being placed in an institution to await the birth of her child.

However, retribution overtook Rush through the very nature of his own conniving. He was certain he could browbeat Emily Sandford in court to make sure she gave him an alibi. In that he was exposing himself to well-directed legal shafts. Emily Sandford would not have crumpled before the questioning of

Serjeant Byles had Rush married her. She would not have been asked to testify against her husband.

Too late, the man conducting his own voluble and graceless defence realized how he had trapped himself. He did the only thing possible to a man of his smirched character. He smeared the reputation of the woman who had a short while before given birth to his child. It was a cheap, sordid device, doomed to return with boomerang certainty.

He also produced papers alleged to have been signed by Isaac Jermy and witnessed by Emily Sandford. It was established that the name of Isaac Jermy was already on the papers when Rush insisted upon the woman adding her own. Another bogus document was produced by the prosecution. It had been found in the hall of Stanfield Hall after the murderer had fled. It comprised the outside covers of a book, on which was written a melodramatic declaration:

> *There are seven of us—three outside and four inside the Hall, all armed. If any of you attempt to leave the premises you will be shot dead. Therefore all of you keep in the servants' hall, and you shall not be touched.*
>
> *J. Jermy, the owner.*

The writing was in an obviously disguised hand, and the signature was intended to suggest the note had been written by a Thomas J. Jermy, who had been involved in some previous claim to the property. Unfortunately for Rush, the Jermy in question was known to be in London on the night of the murders. Another piece of ill-conceived subterfuge had badly miscarried.

Although Eliza Chestney entered the court borne on a curtained stretcher, it was the entrance of Emily Sandford that riveted the concentrated gaze of the spectators, who included in their number the Bishop of Norwich. The emotional scene was reported in detail by an East Anglian newspaper.

> *On Emily Sandford being called by the usher, the most intense anxiety and excitement was manifested throughout the court. Every eye was turned on the door at which she was expected to appear, and as she came in with feeble and*

*tottering steps, draped in a black dress, whose ample folds
did not, however, conceal the outlines of her slender and
emaciated figure, a movement of some feeling closely allied
to regret ran through the audience.*

*The prisoner fixed his eyes on her with a severe and
watchful scrutiny, and his hands shook in every fibre.
When she got into the witness-box she raised a thick crêpe
veil which had previously concealed her face, and turned a
look full of anguish—almost of despair—upon the prisoner.
Her features were pale as death, the lips parched and white,
and her whole appearance that of one who was worn away
by grief.*

Rush at once attacked this picture of human dejection.
Addressing Baron Rolfe, he said: 'I must make an observation,
my lord. I have a higher power than yours to cite this witness.
She knows I am not guilty of the charge laid to me. But in every
respect I'm quite willing she should tell the truth.'

The Judge readily saw the implication, and promptly
reminded Rush that if the witness did not tell the truth she
would be liable to 'the pains and penalties of perjury in this
life, and punishment in the next'.

But Rush was like a dog worrying a bone.

'I wish her well to consider what evidence she is about to give,'
he said, red spots of anger in his fat cheeks as fear prompted the
words.

'You do yourself no good by that observation,' the Judge told
him.

'I cannot help it, my lord,' the humbug insisted. 'I must prove
my innocence,' quite ignoring the fact that the onus was on the
prosecution to prove his guilt.

Or was his avowed innocence so threadbare even to his self-
satisfied gaze?

As the sorry questioning continued the Judge felt forced to
interrupt harshly: 'I can't allow you, prisoner, to hurt the
feelings of the witness in this manner. All this has no bearing
on the case, and were you defended by counsel you would not
be permitted to put such questions at all.'

Justice leaned backwards to be fair to James Bloomfield
Rush. He in turn offered no mercy to Emily Sandford. He

questioned her about their closest intimacies in such a manner that cries of 'Shame!' rose from the court, which freely hissed the

prisoner as though he were a villain in a stage melodrama. The week-long trial finally drew to its close after the prisoner had harangued the jury interminably. They responded by bringing in their verdict of guilty within six minutes. The Judge, who had been patient and forbearing throughout a long and most difficult

trial, had some words of his own to say.

He said, addressing himself to Rush: 'To society it must be a matter of perfect indifference what your conduct may be during the few days of life that remain to you. No concealment of the truth in which you may continue to persevere will cast the slightest doubt upon the propriety of the verdict. No confession you can make can add a taper-light to the broad glare of daylight

guilt disclosed against you. I can only conjure you by every consideration of interest that you employ the short space of life that yet remains to you in endeavouring by penitence and prayer to reconcile yourself to that offended God before Whom you are so shortly to appear.'

A multitude of stories were told about Rush after he met his executioner on the terrace of the keep at Norwich Castle. He became a legendary fiend, responsible for untold atrocities and crimes. His father had died from gunshot wounds in strange circumstances. He had tried to poison Emily Sandford. His mother died strangely.

He had earned the public's spite, and the public was duly spiteful. But all accepted the truth of his going to the scaffold unfalteringly. His last words were to the hangman.

'This does not go easy,' he complained, twisting his neck in the noose. 'Put the thing a little higher. Take your time. Don't be in a hurry.'

He turned and died with his back to the gaping crowd.

L. G.

# 1852

# WILLIAM KIRWAN
## The Secret of Ireland's Eye

The picturesque spot called Ireland's Eye lies about a mile off Howth Harbour and is in the summer a favourite place for 'picnicking' and boating excursions. But none of the many thousands of visitors who have been there in the last hundred years or so has been able to discover the secret which it so jealously guards. This secret is exactly what happened on a certain September day in 1852, when a woman called Maria Kirwan met her death on the island. The evidence for and against foul play is so nicely balanced that, even if Sherlock Holmes himself had been called in, he would have been hard put to it to find the true solution.

On the morning of the day in question a man and a woman set out for Ireland's Eye from Howth Harbour. The man was an artist called William Kirwan, and the woman was his wife Maria. They had been married for about twelve years and were both in their thirties. Mrs. Kirwan, who was later described by witnesses as being extremely good-looking, was a good swimmer and very fond of bathing. On this occasion she brought a bathing dress with her, while, in addition to their 'picnic' lunch, her husband took his sketching materials. They reached the island in due course, and dismissed the boatman with instructions to return for them at eight o'clock in the evening. An hour or two later another party arrived, but they arranged to leave at four o'clock. As they were going, one of them offerd Mrs. Kirwan a seat in their boat if she wanted to return then, but she replied that she preferred to wait for her own boat.

During the next four hours the artist and his wife were alone together on the island. What passed between them will probably never be known beyond the fact that something occurred which caused the violent death of Mrs. Kirwan. Yet, curiously enough if the tragedy was unseen by human eyes, it was not unheard. During the afternoon and evening four people on the mainland, as well as a fisherman at sea, deposed on oath afterwards to hearing a series of strange cries coming from the island. Alicia Abernethy, who lived near the harbour at Howth, swore she heard, in her own words, 'a dreadful screech as of a person in agony and pain.' Some minutes later she heard another, not so loud, and then another, much fainter. Another woman, who lived near-by, described what she first heard as 'a very wild scream'. There were other screams, and the last was suddenly cut short. This was about seven o'clock. Three other people from the shore, and a fisherman who was cruising near Ireland's Eye, made similar statements, though none of them paid any particular attention to the cries at the time.

Shortly before eight o'clock the boat left Howth Harbour to pick up the Kirwans as arranged. There were four men on board, including the owner, whose name was Patrick Nangle. It was already dark when they arrived, and, seeing nothing of their party, they called out. The voice of Mr. Kirwan replied: 'Nangle, come up for the bag.' On going up Nangle found Kirwan alone on a high rock above the landing place. He asked where Mrs. Kirwan was, and the artist said she had left him to go and have a bathe about an hour and a half previously and he had not seen her since. 'Which way did she go? asked one of the boatmen. 'She went that way' said Kirwan, pointing in the direction of a rocky inlet, known as the Long Hole, on the seaward side of the island. The boatmen were, not unnaturally, rather annoyed at having to look for the woman at that hour, but nevertheless they set to work to comb the island. When they reached the Long Hole, Patrick Nangle cried out that he saw 'something white' lying on the rocks below. The object was the body of Mrs. Kirwan. She was lying, face upwards, on a wet bathing sheet, and she was wearing her bathing dress, which was also wet. There were scratches on the face and eyelids, and blood was issuing from the breast and ears. When he saw his wife's body, Kirwan was overwhelmed with grief, and threw himself upon it weeping and crying 'Maria! Maria!' Mrs. Kirwan's clothes were found on another rock near-by, where Kirwan said they might be, although—and here is a curious point—one the boatmen swore to having looked there previously and found nothing. The body was brought back to Howth, where it is was washed and laid out for burial. When it was pointed out to Kirwan that the police would not allow it to be touched until after the inquest, he exclaimed: 'I don't care a damn for the police; the body must be washed!' This was accordingly done. At the inquest a verdict of Found Drowned was returned, and the remains of Maria Kirwan were then interred in Glasnevin Cemetery.

Rumours of foul play now began to get about, and the suspicions directed towards Kirwan became much stronger when it became known that he had been leading what is sometimes described as 'a double life'. It appeared that he maintained another lady in Dublin, and that she posed as his wife. A neighbour of Kirwan's now stated openly that the artist had decided to do away with his wife on account of the other woman, and they were known to be on bad terms. The upshot of all this was that the late Mrs. Kirwan's body was exhumed, while the husband was arrested and charged with her murder.

William Kirwan was tried in Dublin in December, 1852. There were two judges, Mr. Justice Crampton and Baron Greene. The prisoner, who pleaded Not Guilty, had as his leading counsel Isaac Butt, founder of the Home Rule Party. Throughout the opening speech for the Crown there was no suggestion as to the method by which the accused had done the murder, but the prosecuting counsel laid great stress on two facts, one that the clothes were found in a place where Patrick Nagle had previously searched for them in vain, and second that a sheet was half under the body when it was first discovered. But it was not until towards the end of the trial, in answer to a challenge from the defending counsel, that the Crown prosecutor suggested to the jury the theory of the Crown as to how the murder had been committed. 'Let them suppose,' he said, 'that the prisoner induced the deceased to bathe in the Long Hole. He mediated her death. It must have been about seven o'clock when she bathed, and at that time the water was two feet nine inches deep. Let it be supposed that she was in this water, that the prisoner came into the hole with the sheet in his hand for the purpose of putting it over her head, that on seeing him approach in this manner his dreadful purpose at once flashed across the mind of his victim. Might she not then have uttered the dreadful agonising shriek that was first heard on the mainland? If he succeeded in forcing her under the water, notwithstanding her fruitless struggles with all her youthful energy against his superior strength, might they not in that respect expect the fainter agonising and dying shrieks, which both men and women swore they heard on the mainland, growing fainter and fainter?'

This was in answer to the defence's plea that the drowning was accidental. A Dublin surgeon, who was examined as an expert witness, gave it as his opinion that, from the appearance of the body at the post-mortem examination, death might have been produced by an epileptic fit without any additional cause. 'Epileptic patients often scream loudly,' said this witness, and he went on to say that in his opinion as a medical man sudden immersion in water with a full stomach might well bring on a fit of epilepsy. It later appeared that Mrs. Kirwan was subject to such fits, but, unfortunately for the prisoner, evidence to this effect was not put in at the trial.

After a long deliberation, which must have indicated how undecided they were, the jury brought in a verdict of guilty. 'Upon this verdict,' said Judge Crampton, 'it not my province to pronounce opinion, but after what has been said I cannot help adding this observation, that I see no reason or grounds to be dissatisfied with it, and, in saying this, I speak the sentiments of my learned brother, who sits beside me, as well as my own. You have raised your hand, not in daring vengeance against a man from whom you received—or thought you had received—provocation or insult; you raised your hand against a female, a helpless unprotected female, who by the laws of God and man was entitled to your protection, even at the hazard of your life, and to your affectionate guardianship. In the solitude of that rocky island, to which you brought her on the fatal 6th September, under the veil of approaching night, when there was no hand to stay and no human eye to see your guilt, you perpetrated this terrible—this unnatural—crime. . . . No human eye could see how the act was done, none but your own conscience and the all-seeing Providence could develop this mysterious transaction.'

The prisoner was then asked by the Bench whether he had anything to say before sentence was pronounced. He himself had not given evidence, since at that time prisoners on trial for murder were not allowed to do so, but he now declared in a clear steady voice: 'Convinced as I am that my hopes in this world are at an end, I do most solemnly declare in the presence of this Court, and before the God before whom I expect soon to stand, that I had neither act, nor part, nor knowledge of my late wife's death, and I state further that I never treated her unkindly, as her own mother can testify.'

Sentence of death was now pronounced, but, in view of representations being made to the Lord Lieutenant, this sentence was commuted to one of penal servitude for life. Islands were not of good omen for William Kirwan, for he was obliged to spend the next twenty-five years in the prison on Spike Island in Cork Harbour. He was in fact its last inmate. When he was at last released he went to America, where it is said he married the 'other woman' in the case—his former companion in Dublin. There is a tradition among the fishermen who sail near Ireland's Eye that, before he embarked, he revisited the scene of the tragedy at the Long Hole. He was then a decrepit old man with a flowing grey beard. If that be so, he guarded the secret of Ireland's Eye as well as the island itself has done ever since.

Whatever we may think of the innocence or guilt of William Kirwan, there is no doubt that his case illustrates the danger of convicting solely on circumstantial evidence. There is little doubt, too, that if the trial took place today and a similar verdict was returned, the proceedings would be quashed by the Court of Criminal Appeal. But that only means that there would not now be sufficient evidence to establish the prisoner's guilt beyond all reasonable doubt. Whether or not William Kirwan really did murder his wife is a mystery which still remains unsolved.

H. M. H.

# 1864

# FRANZ MULLER

## The First Railway Murderer

It shocked Great Britain in the year 1864. Sudden death while
ensconced in the safe protection of a railway train, 'Murder on
the Iron Way' as the press called it. Even the great and lofty
Matthew Arnold, poet and critic, wrote about it. Such things
had happened before – in America, and in France – but not
in the heart of England whose railways stood for all that was
regular, all that was Progress, all that was order. The very fact
of the trains running on fixed lines and according to laid down
timetables symbolised for the British public the unchangeability
of life within the railway system.

And now that had been brutally smashed, though for a good
many years yet, while the trains still ran scrupulously to time,
death on the lines was to be a staple for detective stories, sharp
in its contrast between murder and order, rich with possibilities
for devious alibi-faking. The murder on the iron way was to
affect real-life railways, too. Eventually it was responsible for
the introduction of the communication-cord and of carriages
with corridors linking their compartments, though at first the
authorities tried to increase public safety by putting portholes
between compartments – until there were complaints from ladies
about Peeping Toms.

But on the night of Saturday, 9 July 1864, each compartment
of the 9.50p.m. from London's Fenchurch Street terminus was
cut off from the others. When the train reached the suburb
of Hackney – it was for once four minutes late: the station
staff were much upset – two clerks entered a dimly-lit empty
compartment and found something sticky on the thick leather
seat cushions. No sooner had they decided this was blood than
they spotted a hat left behind as well. It was a 'black beaver' and
was to be the clue that led a murderer to the gallows.

The victim was a Mr. Thomas Briggs, aged seventy, chief clerk
at Robarts Bank in Lombard Street in the City, killed becaused
of the gold watch whose thick chain looped across his stomach, a

watch he often boasted was correct 'to every blessed fraction of a minute' so that he never missed those trains that departed on the dot. He was found beside the line later that night and died next day, having never recovered consciousness.

By then his murderer, a German called Franz Muller, was on the high seas, bound for America in the sailing-ship *Victoria*. But a jeweller in Cheapside by name John Death – preferring it pronounced Deeth – recognized Mr. Briggs' watch from the police description. Muller had exchanged it for some other jewellery, later pawned. Before long a cabman, James Matthews, recognized that 'Death' was the name on an empty jewel box Muller had given his little daughter, and he identified the black beaver which Muller had exchanged for his victim's respectable top hat.

Inspector Tanner of Scotland Yard set off across the Atlantic by fast steamer. He reached New York before Muller and successfully detained him. But his troubles had hardly begun. America was in the throes of the Civil War and at that stage Britain was favouring the South. So the extradition proceedings were turned into a major attack on a disliked nation, a full-scale pre-trial with much mention made of Muller's hat which he had cut down from Mr. Briggs's stately topper so as to destroy the telltale initials T.B. on the band. (Later there was a vogue for the shorter topper, known as the Muller cut-down.)

But Muller failed in his attempt to avoid extradition and was tried again at the Old Bailey in London where the Solicitor General, Sir Robert Porrett Collier, made great play, in attacking Muller's late-produced alibi, of the unreliability of 'the clock of a brothel', contrasted ironically with the unfailing regularity of railway clocks.

H. R. F. K

# 1869

# PIERRE VOIRBO
## The Tell-Tale Tiles

---

The famous Voirbo case, discussed fully by the well-known
French detective, Macé, in *Mon Premier Crime*, belongs to
1869. It opened with a complaint made by a restaurant keeper
regarding the smell and taste of the water in his well. He had
examined it and discovered that a human leg was floating on the
water. This man, named Lampon, at once informed the police.

The well was dragged, and the limb in an advanced state
of decomposition was recovered. Gustave Macé, then a
commissioner of police, was summoned and took charge of
the case. A further examination of the well was made under
his direction, and as a result another leg was recovered in a
parcel. The covering material was important. It was of black
calico, knotted at each end, and sewn with black thread. The
limb was further covered with a piece of trouser-leg of grey
cloth. All identifying marks had been removed, but on part
of a stocking to which a sock had been attached, which also
covered the leg, a mark was found. It consisted of a B with a
plus sign before and after it.

These clues were slight enough, but the establishing of
identification was complicated by a mistake made by the
medical experts who stated positively that they belonged to a
woman, and that they had been in the well for about a month.

The discoveries were connected with similar gruesome finds in
other parts of Paris—a thigh bone in the Rue Jacob and morsels
of flesh in one of the canals. Other suspicious circumstances
possibly relating to the crime were reports that a man had been
seen throwing what appeared to be small pieces of meat into
the river. When questioned he had replied that it was bait for
the fish so that they would rise well on the morrow. The date
of this incident was important. It was December 19th, two days
after the discovery of the thigh bone.

It was then recalled that on December 22nd in the early
morning a man had been interrogated by two sergeants since

he was carrying a parcel which they suspected contained stolen goods. He told a plausible story and was permitted to proceed. The man was not identified, but it was suspected that his parcel might have contained human remains.

The mistake regarding the sex of the remains caused delay. A careful analysis of the disappearances among women led to nothing.

The eminent Dr. Tardieu then re-examined the limbs. He pronounced them to be those of a man, and noted a scar on one leg which he considered recent. Identification was very difficult without the head, which was not recovered.

The laborious but brilliant reconstruction began.

Black calico and sewing suggested the work of a tailor, and a careful search for tailors in the neighbourhood of the Rue Princesse, where the body was found, was organized. No male tailor was traced, but after patient interrogation a seamstress named Mlle. Dard was reported as having lived in the neighbourhood. She had of late become a singer in the cafés. M. Macé discovered that she was supplied with work by a man who used to carry up water from the well for her.

Mlle. Dard was located and interrogated. She gave information quite willingly, and finally volunteered the information that a certain Pierre Voirbo was among her clients. It was he who carried the water upstairs for her.

Further questioning elicited the information that Voirbo was often in the company of a man named Désiré and his aunt, Madame Bodasse.

Madame Bodasse was interrogated and admitted that Désiré was her nephew. She had not seen him for some months, but this did not surprise her, since he was very eccentric and often disappeared for long periods. It was this witness who identified the wrapping on the remains. The grey tweed of the trousers was declared to correspond with that of her nephew's clothing. Madame Bodasse positively identified the initial B and the two plus signs as being the work of her own needle. Her nephew had suffered from the cold, and she was accustomed to sew the upper parts of stockings on to his socks to give increased warmth. The woman further gave evidence as to the existence of a scar on her nephew's leg.

There was now strong presumptive evidence as to the identity of the murdered man, and enquiries were therefore made at the house where he had his apartment. It was there suggested that he was still alive, since a light had been seen in his room not many days previously.

Whatever doubts this evidence may have raised, M. Macé kept the apartment under observation. Enquiries were made in the meantime regarding Voirbo, who, it was discovered, had a bad record. He had recently married, and had been heard to remark that his friend Désiré Bodasse had disappeared two days before the marriage, although he had promised to be present at the wedding. It was further ascertained that Voirbo had demanded a loan of 10,000 francs which had been refused.

Since nothing had been seen of Désiré despite the evidence of the light in his room, the detective decided to obtain a search-warrant and examine the apartment.

The room presented a most interesting appearance. It was in order, but obviously had not been occupied for some time, since there was a layer of dust on the furniture. The bed was undisturbed. Seventeen spent matches were found in the fireplace. On the mantelpiece were found two boxes of candles, one of which was empty while the other contained only one candle. It appeared, therefore, that fifteen had been burnt, the boxes having held eight eight each.

Experiments were carried out with this type of candle, and it was proved that it burnt on the average for three hours. The concierge confirmed the fact that the light had been observed to burn for about three hours and on some fifteen occasions. The inevitable conclusion was drawn that Désiré Bodasse had not burned these candles, but that someone who wished it to be thought that he was occupying his room had lighted them. As an additional precaution the trespasser had even wound up the clock, for it was going when the search was made.

It was now practically certain that there had been no mistake in identity, and that the remains were indeed those of Bodasse. The motive for the murder was also clear, since counterfoils relating to Italian Stock were found in the room, but the certificates themselves were missing. Bodasse was known to have kept such things in his own possession.

Further enquiry produced a description of the man last seen with Désiré Bodasse. He was independently identified as Voirbo, whom the police had already ascertained to be one of Bodasse's associates.

Voirbo was then identified by as money-changer as a man who, on or about a material date, December 16th, had cashed a share certificate of Italian Stock of 500 francs.

Police officers were sent to watch Bodasse's room in the hope that, suspecting nothing, Voirbo would return to repeat his deception of lighting the candles and winding the clock.

It is a curious fact that this man was himself a secret agent of the police, and it seems to have been for this reason that he did not fall into the trap. Either the police set to watch had not been informed as to the identity of the man who might visit the room or else they were taken in by his credentials as a secret agent and assumed that there was some mistake. They did not, at any rate, arrest him, but on the contrary, allowed him to enter the room.

The evidence against Voirbo was thus still incomplete, but he was summoned to the commissioner's office for interrogation. He endeavoured with great ingenuity to throw the blame upon three other men. They were shadowed, but no evidence against them could be found. Voirbo was again summoned for interrogation and finally arrested.

He was searched, and a steamship passage ticket was found upon him in the name of Saba. The *juge d'instruction* could extract nothing from him. The case did not look like being a simple matter, but Voirbo was held pending further investigations.

A thorough search was made of his rooms, but nothing incriminating was found. His wife, however, testified that he had possessed Italian securities to the value of 10,000 francs.

The only indication which was at all suggestive was a sewing machine which had been in his tailor's workshop. It had upon it one small spot of blood, a clue which might be without significance. In the workshop were found instruments which might have been used for dismemberment, cord similar to that used to tie up the parcels in which the remains had been enclosed, and labels said to be similar to those on the baskets carried by the man whom the police interrogated on December 22nd.

The cellar was searched and was found to contain two casks of wine. A short length of string was attached to the bung of one of these casks. At the other end was a metal container carefully closed and immersed in the wine. On opening it, the securities were found.

This was an important piece of evidence, but it remained to prove the vital point of the dismemberment. It was in this connexion that perhaps the most remarkable piece of reconstruction that has ever been carried out with regard to any crime was conceived.

There was in this case the formidable difficulty to which allusion has been made. A considerable time had elapsed since the crime had been committed. It was obvious from the evidence which the police had so laboriously collected that the murderer had covered his traces with cunning and ingenuity. It was suspected that the dismemberment had been carried out in the room which Voirbo had occupied. But to suspect this was one thing, to prove it was another.

Voirbo was photographed after resisting violently, and he was conducted on M. Macé's instructions to the supposed scene of the crime. The detective had noticed that the floor was tiled. A rearrangement of the furniture was made approximating to its position when Voirbo occupied the room. In the presence of the accused Macé stood in the middle of the room with a jug of water and poured it on the floor. Voirbo, who had remained calm up to this time, was noticed to show great agitation.

The water flowed over the tiles and settled in pools at certain points owing to the slope and inequalities in the tiling. These points were carefully marked and the water was mopped up. At the places noted the tiles were taken up. Beneath was found coagulated material of a dark colour which was subsequently shown to be blood.

Macé had proved his case by this discovery of direct evidence of a crime. He had assumed that if dismemberment had taken place in that room there must have been a considerable effusion of blood. This would naturally soak through he crevices between the tiles at those points where the blood had settled in pools.

It is stated that Voirbo's agitation was so great that he, who had never once betrayed himself, immediately made a full confession of his crime.

This affair is highly instructive from every point of view. It is typical of many others, but it does illustrate in a particularly striking way the value of being able to reconstruct from indications, more or less insignificant, a series of facts which, pieced together, produce a more or less clear picture of the events. In the first place the black calico seemed to associate a tailor with the crime. The marks on the clothing and the scar on the leg helped to establish identity. It is also worth noting how seriously a mistake in medical evidence may hinder an investigation. Had this not been rectified the mystery would never have been solved.

Most important of all is the reconstruction which related to the commission of the crime itself. The discovery of the candles and matches in Bodasse's room clarified the evidence as to the actual date of the victim's disappearance. The experiment with the water not only produced material evidence of the crime without digging up the entire floor, but revealed it in such a way as to demonstrate with absolute certainty the incidents which had taken place in the room. Part of the circumstances necessarily accompanying the crime was re-enacted, substituting water for blood. It is not difficult to see the significance of this. Had the floor been dug up, valuable evidence would have been destroyed for ever. It would not have been possible to demonstrate that the places where the blood had been found did in fact correspond with those points where pools would have formed. It is an example of scientific demonstration of proof; a production of and verification by experimental evidence.

H. T. F. R.

# 1870

# JEAN-BAPTISTE TROPPMANN

## Mass Murder for Money

On 25th November, 1869, near the ruins of the castle of Herrenfluch in Alsace, a group of men, which included two magistrates from Belfort, the Imperial Prosecutor Munschina, the examining magistrate Bardy, the Commissioner of Police from Cernay, Souvras, the secretary of Monsieur Claude (chief of the Paris *Sûreté*), aided by twenty local workers, had been looking for a body.

Towards evening, a cry from one of the searchers brought them all hurrying to a spot almost hidden by bushes and undergrowth. No doubt on the evidence of his secretary, Monsieur Claude dramatically describes a flight of crows which betrayed the grave of a murdered man. Does it not say in St. Luke that 'wheresoever the body is, thither will the eagles be gathered together'? These funereal creatures, as Monsieur Claude describes them, seemed reluctant to abandon their feast. The leader of the searchers leapt forward, as the last crow flew off, to discover some fragments of cloth, a brass button and the toes of a man's boots. It was by then too late to dig the body out, so guards were posted and the delicate task of exhumation was left to the following day.

On the morrow the party returned, accompanied by two doctors, and the gruesome work began. At first, all that could be distinguished was a mass of black clothing; then the man's livid face. He was lying on his back in sodden reddish earth which was infested with innumerable worms. The body was bent so that the legs almost touched the head. As the legs were moved there was seen to be crouched on the chest of the corpse an enormous toad, which one of the doctors seized and threw high into the air. What a loss to the Gothic novel when Monsieur Claude joined the police! The ruined castle, the sinister flight of crows in the evening light, the putrescent body, the worms and finally the toad; all this is pure Horace Walpole and Ann Radcliffe. Was the presence of this unclean beast, asks

Monsieur Claude, the symbolic revelation of the impurity which, before this horrible *dénouement,* was said to have cemented the spontaneous, intimate and mysterious association of these two men? He is speaking of the murderer, whom he has under lock and key in Paris, and the man now lying in the wet earth of Alsace. However, for all Monsieur Claude's rhetorical style, this was no laughing matter. The discovery of this man's body was the culminating piece of evidence in one of the most frightful crimes ever recorded.

The face of the dead man presented a terrifying picture of decomposition. One eye had disappeared and maggots crawled in the orbit. The other was still there under the eyelid. The nose was flattened and the moustache came away at a touch. The mouth was filled with earth. There were no wounds, no blood and no marks of violence.

These were the remains of one Jean Kinck, father of six children who, with their mother, had been found murdered not long before on the outskirts of Paris. This was thus the eighth body to be found, and the eighth victim of one of the most sensational murders in the history of crime.

For France the year 1869 was momentous. The grotesque Emperor Napoleon III had almost run his course and France stood before the defeat and humiliation of Sedan, from which she has not recovered to this day. A mounting series of crimes and scandals had undermined all confidence in the Emperor and his government. Of these the murder of the entire Kinck family, a tragedy of incomparable horror, was to be one more blow to a tottering administration. It appeared at that time as an omen of the wrath to come, which did indeed come in the general disintegration after 1870.

When the abolition of capital punishment is discussed, one is often moved by the moral and humanitarian arguments put forward, until mention is made of certain crimes which cry out to Heaven for vengeance. One may talk of degrees of murder and extenuating circumstances. One remembers that in these enlightened times the reform of the criminal comes before mass revenge, but there are some crimes for which there can never be forgiveness. Such a crime was that of Jean-Baptiste Troppmann.

If ever justice was done, it was done when the blade of the guillotine fell on the neck of that wild beast. There can be no question of his guilt, his sole guilt, yet such was the spirit of the time that the public were inclined to believe his wild stories of accomplices. Troppmann was from Alsace, which with Lorraine was to pass into German hands after the war of 1870. His was not the only crime associated with that unhappy territory and there is no doubt that, in the general spy fever of the time, several of these crimes were given a political flavour. It is clear that Troppmann was the last straw in the national disillusionment towards the end of the régime. His crime seemed to announce that this was the end of law and order. Thus the people blamed the régime more than the murderer, and destruction of the dossiers of the case under the Commune only added an air of mystery and uncertainty which persisted for many years afterwards.

The discovery of the body of Jean Kinck completed the case for the prosecution against Jean-Baptiste Troppmann, who stood accused of the murder of Madame Kinck and her six children. To the indictment could now be added the murder of the father.

On the morning of 20th September, 1869, a labourer discovered traces of fresh digging in a field about a mile from the Pantin Gate of Paris. He investigated with his pick and uncovered part of a face. He called the police, who in due course dug up the fresh bodies of a woman and five young children. There were four boys, aged five, eight, ten and thirteen, and a little girl of two. The final touch of horror was that the woman was sixth months advanced in pregnancy. All had been slaughtered with maniacal violence with a knife and pick-axe. The official account of the wounds inflicted, and the pitiful description of the clothing and possessions of the little victims, is a most distressing document to read. Suffice it to say that all the bodies had been terribly mutilated with the pick, as though the murderer had wanted to make certain of his work. Nevertheless, it is by no means certain that they were all dead when he buried them. The murder must have been very recent too, as the bodies were scarcely cold.

Identification was quickly established from indications on the clothing. In addition, the proprietor of the Railway Hotel at the Gare du Nord informed the police that a woman with five children had called at the hotel only the night before and had asked for Jean Kinck. They had then disappeared. The victims were identified as Madame Kinck and five of her children, who had lived up to the time of the murder at Roubaix, close to the Belgian frontier. Of the Kinck family two remained to be accounted for, the father and the eldest son, Gustave, a youth of sixteen. At the time of the discovery of the murders at Pantin, they were both missing, and it was thought that Jean Kinck was the murderer or at least one of the murderers, since it was difficult to believe that the night's killing could be the work of one man.

The night of 19th September was particularly dark, with a strong wind blowing heavy clouds across the feeble rays of the moon. Late that night, a cab drew up at the Porte de Pantin. The cabby seemed undecided about driving beyond the outskirts of Paris on such a night, but a man who was travelling inside put his head out and ordered him to drive on. In the cab, as the driver later reported, were a woman, her five children, and a young man who appeared to be a friend of the family. The young man was Jean-Baptiste Troppmann, a native of Alsace. They were all on their way to a property, which the father Jean Kinck, according to Troppmann, had purchased in the loneliest part of Pantin, and where they were to rejoin him. A strange story this, and a strange place to take a woman with five small children, tired from the recent long journey from Roubaix, so late at night.

Finally, the driver was ordered by the young man to stop at the edge of a field. Here Troppmann helped Madame Kinck to get down with the little girl and one of the small boys. He told the other three boys to stay in the cab while he went with the mother and the two children to find the father and bring him back to them. The three boys sat in the cab, and the driver got down and passed the time chatting with them. They said their friend Troppmann had brought them there to meet their father. Twenty-five minutes later Troppmann came back alone and told the three boys to get down. He informed the driver with ominous truth that it had been decided that they would all stay there, and that he could take his cab back to Paris. The driver, not a little surprised at this curious behaviour, drove off. The last he saw of the strange party was Troppmann taking the boys off into the darkness.

As we have seen, the bodies of all six were found next morning in their hurriedly dug grave. In the meantime the trusted friend of the family had left for Havre, where he told chance acquaintances that he was going to try his fortune in America. Unfortunately for him, he picked up one chance acquaintance who happened to be a police informer. He was unwise enough to ask this man to assist him in obtaining false papers. While they were seated in a café, a policeman walked in and, having nothing to do, asked the furtive-looking young man his name. Troppmann did not react very naturally, and the policeman's suspicions were roused. He told Troppmann to go to the police station with him, but on the way Troppmann bolted, ran along a jetty and threw himself into the harbour. He was eventually hauled out, and it was then found that his pockets were stuffed with papers and other personal property belonging to Jean Kinck. It was thus thought at first that it was the missing Jean Kinck who had been captured, but it was soon realised, however, that this could not be Jean Kinck, the father of a family. In any case, on the 24th, Troppmann admitted his identity. The hue and cry which had followed as soon as the murders were discovered and this rapid capture naturally caused a sensation throughout France.

Having identified himself, Troppmann was faced with the problem of talking himself out of what was, to say the least, an unenviable situation. Here began the first of a series of lying statements rich in ingenuity but rather lacking in coherence. His opening story was that Jean and Gustave Kinck together murdered the wife and children, Jean having suspected his wife of adultery. In this version of what happened, Troppmann admitted his presence on the fatal field but as a helpless onlooker, even grappling with the murderers in a vain attempt to save the victims. The bottom fell out of this story when the body of Gustave Kinck was found two days later, buried close to the grave of his mother and the rest of the family. Gustave had been stabbed seven times. The heart was pierced twice, the throat was torn open, and the knife was buried up to the hilt in the body.

Undeterred by the failure of this tale, Troppmann was reduced to blaming the murders on Jean Kinck alone. He adapted his story – in fact, all the stories in this strange affair – without turning a hair. It all fitted in, because in the second version of Troppmann's story Jean Kinck also murdered his son Gustave. Troppmann had not wished to accuse Jean of this further crime out of a sense of delicacy!

When the body of Jean Kinck, murdered with home-made prussic acid from Troppmann's do-it-yourself laboratory, was found in Alsace, the second story fell flat.

Throughout the whole trial there was only one thing which could be said in Troppmann's favour; it was incredible that this mass butchery could be the work of one man and a runt-like creature like Troppmann at that. Yet, despite his unathletic appearance, he was exceptionally strong and of an animal ferocity. It is difficult to believe that a whole family could have delivered themselves with complete confidence into the hands of this killer, young enough to be the son of Jean Kinck. How had this come about?

The story begins with Troppmann's arrival in Roubaix from Alsace. He had been sent by his father to set up a textile machine. The father's factory in Alsace produced these machines, and Troppmann had already carried out one mission to Paris to supervise the erection of one such machine at Pantin, where he was later to carry out seven of the murders.

At Roubaix he had fallen in with Jean Kinck, an Alsatian like himself, who had settled in Roubaix. Kinck was a plodder who had painstakingly built up a business worth a hundred thousand francs. Kinck took Troppmann home, and there he first met his victims, Hortense, the wife, an unlettered and timid woman, and her brood of six children. The future murderer became the young friend of the family. The knock on the door in *Macbeth* could not have been more dramatic than the appearance of Jean-Baptiste Troppmann at the Kincks' front door. he was then nineteen years old, a weak-faced, unhealthy-looking creature, secretive and boastful as the mood took him. Monsieur Claude has given us a detailed description of him. He had a broad forehead and abundant chestnut hair, of which he seemed vain. Below the noble brow the rest was the face of a fiend. Large ears, a straight, hooked nose, a large upper lip on which grew what Monsieur Claude calls a nascent moustache, and unsightly teeth, in all *une physiognomie sauvage*. With this went remarkable agility and strength, which were to test many of the guards whose duty it was to keep this wild beast caged. Madame Kinck, with that instinct one so often finds in otherwise unintelligent women, did not like him.

Jean Kinck suffered from chronic homesickness. Though he had been settled in Roubaix for thirty years, he longed for his native Alsace. This longing and the familiar sound of the dialect of his homeland must have played a big part in his attachment to Troppmann. Kinck, the self-made man, basked in the envy and admiration of his young countryman, and allowed himself to be amused and half-interested by Troppmann's romancing and ever-changing plans for making a fortune. The French do not care for Alsatians, and that doubtless threw the two of them together, the middle-aged man and the scheming boy of nineteen.

Among the hare-brained ideas which Troppmann discussed with Kinck was a scheme for making counterfeit money. Troppmann, so he said, had friends who would be ready to make over the plant to him for a consideration. Kinck surprisingly listened to the plan, which Troppmann said could best be realised in their own homeland in Alsace. Troppmann knew of a place beneath the ruins of the castle of Herrenfluch where everything could be organised and the plant set up in the greatest secrecy. Talk of travelling separately to the rendezvous made the whole business mysterious and alluring. Little did Jean Kinck realise that Troppmann had his own good reasons for not being seen with him. In the end Kinck took the bait, and he and Troppmann set off for Bollwiller in Alsace by different routes. In Troppmann's pocket was a bottle of prussic acid. From Bollwiller the two travelled to Sultz, where Kinck left his luggage. Troppmann had no luggage. All he needed was the bottle of prussic acid and a bottle of wine, which he bought on the way.

From Sultz the two travellers went on foot towards Cernay on a road which passes close to the ruined castle of Herrenfluch. This was the place which Troppmann had designated as the most suitable site for setting up the counterfeit plant. Kinck was never seen alive again.

The same night Troppmann returned to his home town of Cernay. He was seen to have a new watch, plenty of money and a satisfied but very mysterious air. In the afternoon of the following day he began to write letters. Among them was one to Madame Kinck. Will she please present a cheque for five thousand five hundred francs at Kinck's bank in Roubaix and send the money to Guebwiller post office? He explained that Jean Kinck had injured his hand and he, Troppmann, was therefore writing at Kinck's dictation. It is curious how often this thin story of the injured hand crops up in trial for murder and forgery. The signature on the cheque he enclosed was not Kinck's but a close enough imitation. Apart from the injury to Kinck's hand, wrote the friend of the family, all is going well.

In due course he went to Guebwiller. Madame Kinck had carried out his instructions, and the money was there at the post office awaiting him. But the package was addressed to Jean Kinck and the postmaster was maddeningly cautious. He refused to hand over the money until Troppmann could produce a satisfactory authority. So Troppmann went away, and came back two days later with an authority apparently signed by Jean Kinck, stating that the bearer, his son Jean, could collect. But French officialdom is a peculiarly immovable object. The signature of Jean Kinck had to be registered before a notary! Troppmann returned the next day with the same paper and renewed his efforts to get the package of notes over the counter. But this time another spanner was thrown into the carefully prepared works. A distant relative of Jean Kinck happened to come into the post office. She announced, in front of the postmaster, 'I am a relative of Jean Kinck by marriage, and he has no son named Jean!' The postmaster looked even more suspicious. Troppmann tried to put the woman off with a story that he was Jean Emile Kinck, and managed to make his escape while the woman was trying to puzzle it all out.

Troppmann drove back to Cernay in his cab. He had failed. Sterner measures were called for. He took leave of his family and left for Paris, where he put up at the Railway Hotel at the Gare du Nord. He wrote again to Madame Kinck in the name of her husband. In the letter he stated that 'Troppmann has put me in the way of half a million,' and gave instructions for Gustave, armed with the proper procuration, to go to Guebwiller and collect the package of money from the obstinate postmaster. He added that the whole family should then come to Paris.

So Gustave went off to Guebwiller and stayed with his aunt. Unfortunately he did not take with him the duly attested authority, which Troppmann had sent to be put in order at Roubaix at the town hall. Madame Kinck received it from the notary only after Gustave had left. She therefore sent it off to Guebwiler addressed to Gustave *poste restante*. But the poor muddle-headed Madame Kinck, worried by all the mystery and the long absence of her husband, somehow got the impression that she had addressed it to Gustave care of his aunt. This new setback in Troppmann's scheme could not be put right, as he could not guess what had happened. Gustave was afraid his father in Paris would be angry that he had left Roubaix without the document. He telegraphed to Paris after a few days, saying that he had not been able to obtain the money. Troppmann, always writing as Jean Kinck, countermanded the instruction for the whole family to come to Paris. Letters went to and fro between the harassed Madame Kinck and the impatient Troppmann. Finally, Gustave, tired of sitting at Guebwiller, wrote to his father that he was coming to Paris on 7th September. Troppmann received the news since he had registered at the hotel in the name of Jean Kinck. Troppmann met Gustave on arrival, and made him send a telegram to his mother, instructing her to come to Paris at once, bringing the children and all the family papers.

And that is all we know about Gustave until his body was dug up in the field at Pantin.

Meanwhile, Madame Kinck dressed the children in their best clothes, and on that fateful Sunday started the longest journey the poor woman had ever made in her life. This time it was a journey into death for herself and her children. Troppmann, ever busy, had been to an ironmonger's shop to buy a pick and spade. He insisted on stronger handles being fitted and called back later to collect the finished tools.

Exhausted by the long journey, Madame Kinck arrived at the hotel in Paris and inquired for Jean Kinck. She was not of course to know that the 'Jean Kinck' in the register represented the unholy person of Jean-Baptiste Troppmann. 'Jean Kinck' was out, buying certain tools as it happened, not entirely unconnected with the fate of Madame Kinck; so she went back to the station where she thought her husband might meet the next train.

At 10.45 p.m. she was met by Troppmann, a sinister figure in a long grey coat. When she asked for her husband, Troppmann said he was awaiting them at Pantin, and they would go out there in a cab at once.

It was then that the fateful *cortège* set off, Madame with the baby girl on her lap, and the two smallest boys, one on each side of her. Opposite sat Troppmann with the other two boys. We already know how Troppmann dismissed the cab, and we can only conjecture what horror was done that night as he took the two groups into the darkness to meet the father.

If there is any doubt as to whether this crime could be the work of one man, let us remember that mother and children trusted Troppmann implicitly, and were eagerly expecting the promised reunion with husband and father. All that was needed therefore was a surprise attack and savage, unrelenting ferocity. The only one who could hope to defend herself was the mother, and she was carrying the baby in her arms. From the autopsy it was revealed that she had been stabbed many times, and was probably unconscious before she could think of defending her little ones. These could be despatched quickly or rendered silent and helpless with one or two blows with the pick. Recovering his breath, Troppmann then went back for the other three boys. One of these, when found, had had his head smashed with one blow and was partly strangled. Another was choked with a cravat, and the third was struck through the centre of the forehead with the pick. The attack was clearly so sudden and unexpected that none had been able to make any defence, except the little Alfred, aged five, who was killed with his mother, and whose hands were cut with the knife as he tried to ward off the blows.

The good friend of the family then interred the six bodies – dead or dying, it mattered not to him – where they were discovered the next day. Taking the papers and the money, which Madame Kinck had brought with her, Troppmann left, and our next meeting with him is at Havre. Thus the picture is complete; the father poisoned and buried in his native earth of Alsace, the eldest son stabbed and buried in the same field where the rest of the family had been slaughtered.

Troppmann had been fished out of the water at Havre and taken to the local hospital. It is as well to mention that Troppmann did his best to drown the dock worker who had dived into the water to save him. The struggle in the water prevented him from disposing of the incriminating documents he was carrying and they were found on him when he was undressed at the hospital. As we may well imagine Monsieur Claude went up to Havre at once. He was having no nonsense from his half-drowned rat wrapped in a blanket in a hospital bed. He had him dressed at once for removal to Paris. Troppmann's arrival, carefully guarded, at the railway station, was met by a menacing crowd, who would most certainly have finished off the drowning job if they could have got their hands on him. He travelled in a first-class carriage to Paris, Monsieur Claude seated at his right hand. There were crowds at every stop, as at a Royal progress. At Rouen the crowd tried to storm the train and tear down the blinds on the carriage windows, and the train was delayed for twenty minutes before order was restored.

In Paris crowds had been gathering round the Gare Saint Lazare for two days. There is no doubt he would have been torn to pieces had he not been spirited away by cab from a private exit. More detectives followed in another cab. Not without difficulty the two cabs eventually arrived at the morgue. Monsieur Claude says that at the station in Paris Troppmann was on the point of collapse. His legs almost gave way under him and, as Monsieur Claude reports, his complexion was more than pale; it was green with fear. Having got nothing out of him during the journey from Havre, Claude decided to confront him with the bodies without delay, in the hope he would break down and confess.

In the mortuary the six unclothed bodies were laid out. The registrar of the morgue had signed a simple receipt for them:

*Received six bodies, sent by the Commissaire of Pantin.*
                                        *20th September, 1869*

What had been a happy young family, dressed in their best clothes and carrying the little toys and parcels of food found with their remains, only a day or two before, was now a row of horribly mutilated bodies on a mortuary slab. Knowing how they were killed, it is not necessary for us to examine each body in detail. Troppmann was unmoved when the *juge d'instruction* asked, 'Do you recognise these bodies?'

Troppmann stepped forward, scratching his ear like a cat, as Claude reports. He shrugged his shoulders and replied without emotion, 'Yes, that's Madame Kinck, that's Emile, that's Henri, that's Alfred, that's Achille and that's little Marie.' He pointed to each one as he spoke without deigning to take his hat off. This, for Monsieur Claude, was the last straw.

It was not until six days after the death of Madame Kinck and her five children that the body of Gustave, her eldest, was found in Pantin buried not far from the rest of the family. He had been stabbed in the throat with a kitchen knife which the murderer had left in the wound. In addition he had received blows with a pick in the chest and in the back of the neck. It was obvious that he had put up a good fight for his life. So the seventh corpse duly arrived at the morgue.

Troppmann, now in the Prison of Mazas, was at once pushed into a cab by Monsieur Claude to be driven to the morgue, though he was told he was being taken to the *Conciergerie*. The blinds of the cab were lowered so that Troppmann could not see where he was being taken. Claude again was trying sudden confrontation with the corpse to see if he could get an admission out of Troppmann. It was a surprise for him when he was suddenly shown the body of Gustave and for a moment he tried to cover his face with a handkerchief. 'Take that handkerchief away! shouted the *juge d'instruction*, 'Do you recognise this body?' 'Yes,' replied Troppmann, 'it's Gustave.' 'And it's you who murdered him!' said the *juge*. 'No! It was his father!' said Troppmann.

The *juge* then pointed out that Troppmann had stated that the father and son had committed the other murders. How then had one of the murderers suddenly become a victim? Then Troppmann produced his next card. 'It was probably because his father killed him to prevent him from ever revealing such an abominable crime!' Troppmann accompanied Claude back to the Mazas prison without saying another word. In the meantime the fatal field at Pantin had been trampled by a hundred thousand Parisians into a mire in which cartwheels stuck fast.

Monsieur Claude rightly guessed that the body of Jean Kinck – for it was highly doubtful if he was still alive – would be found in Alsace, but it was until November that his perseverance was rewarded.

By the time Troppmann had quite a problem on his hands to explain away the murder of the whole family. To the questions: Who was last seen with Jean Kinck? Who was last seen with Gustave? Who was last seen with Madame Kinck and the children? Who bought the tools? Who registered under the name of Jean Kinck at the hotel? Who tried to get the money at Guebwiller? Who had Jean Kinck's papers in his possession?, the answer is always 'Troppmann!'

Although valiantly defended by the famous advocate Lachaud, who based his arguments on the theory that this mass murder could not possibly be the work of one man and that there was substance in the story of the accomplices, Troppmann was found guilty.

S.J.P

# 1873

# JOHN BENDER
## Murder at a Wayside Tavern

Late in the year 1870, there appeared in Labette County, Kansas, a family of four persons: John Bender and his wife; their son, or reputed son, John, and his sister, Kate. Almost everything about them is in dispute, and it is often said that the younger man was really John Gebhardt, the son of Mrs. Bender by a former husband. It is also asserted that Kate Bender was not the sister, but the mistress of the younger man. Many imaginary but no authentic portraits of the quartette are in existence, and these differ as widely as do the written descriptions of them.

One portrait of old Bender shows him as a stolid peasant, not remarkable in any way; another makes him a shaggy-looking monster from a nightmare. The young John is depicted as a commonplace-looking man, under thirty; but, elsewhere, it is said that his face 'had the fierce malice of the hyena.' Concerning the appearance of Kate Bender, the writers have done their best, with the result that you may read that she was 'a large, masculine, red-faced woman'; that she was a rather good-looking red-haired girl; or that she was a siren of such extraordinary charms that one has to call on every famous beauty, from Cleopatra to Mrs. Langtry, for suitable comparisons. She was the most interesting of the family; her father was a poor second; while the elder Mrs. Bender and young John were tied for third place.

From some official descriptions of them, issued by Governor Osborn of Kansas at a time when he was dealing in facts, rather than impressionism, these details are selected: John Bender was about sixty years old, and of medium height. He was a German, and spoke little English. He was dark, spare, and wore no beard. His wife was ten years younger; heavy in frame; had blue eyes and brown hair. There was nothing distinctive about John Bender, Jr.; he was twenty-seven, of slight build, wore a light brown moustache, and spoke English with German pronunciation. Kate was 'about twenty-four years of age, dark hair and eyes, good-looking, well formed, rather bold in appearance, fluent talker, speaks English with very little German accent.'

Everybody agrees on two matters: old Bender was a disagreeable, surly fellow; and Kate was notably attractive to the men of that region, who found her pleasant, vivacious, and a desirable partner at the occasional country dance. She danced well, was a good horsewoman, and went to Sunday school and to 'meetin's' in the schoolhouse. For a few weeks, in 1871, she condescended to act as waitress in the hotel at Cherryvale. There was about her, however, a more marked peculiarity: she believed in spiritualism, lectured on the subject, and claimed to be a medium, with the power to call up spirits of the dead. Her lectures, in the various towns of the county, caused a mild sensation. This was the decade when lecturing women aroused great curiosity and antagonism; often they were accused, not only of the offence of seeking to vote, but also, like the Claflins, of advocating various degrees of laxity of morals. How much these lecturers actually risked by putting themselves too far in advance of their time, and how far the reports about them were the exaggerations of horrified men, determined to put down the pestiferous creatures, by foul means or fair, it is always hard to discover. The stories about Kate Bender's lectures soon pass over, I think, into legend as fantastic as the accompanying picture. The alleged fragment of one of her manuscripts, found in the house, in which she gravely advocates one or two crimes, including murder, may safely be attributed to some imaginative journalist.

Curious light is thrown upon Kate Bender's character by an advertisement which she seems to have had published in some of the newspapers in neighbouring towns, about a year before she became nationally famous. This was it:

> *Professor Miss Kate Bender can heal disease, cure blindness, fits and deafness. Residence, 14 miles east of Independence, on the road to Osage Mission. June 18, 1872.*

Nothing at all is really known about the antecedents of the Benders. The older man described himself to a neighbour, one of the township trustees, as 'a Hollander, who had lived in Germany, near the French line, where he had been a baker.' The younger man said that he had been born in the United States. A neighbour, by the way, at this date, and in this part of Kansas, might mean a man whose house was not more than ten miles distant.

As in the contemporary accounts of the murder of Captain White in Salem, the aspect of Essex County, Massachusetts, becomes wildly romantic, with caves, fastnesses, and gloomy forest glades, so the section of Kansas over which the Benders cast their spell has been described as one of dismal swamps, rugged cliffs, and other awe-inspiring bits of scenery. It was, in fact, cheerful and pleasant country: high, rolling prairie. For a short time, the Benders lived on the claim of a German named Rudolph Brockmann—a disastrous acquaintanceship for this harmless citizen. At last, however, after one move, they built a frame house on the main road from Parsons to Cherryvale, about seven miles northeast of the latter town. This road was used by travellers from Fort Scott and the Osage Mission to the town of Independence, and southwest to the Indian Territory, now Oklahoma.

Travellers were mounted as a rule, or driving a team—a pair of horses with a wagon or carriage. Men often went armed; the traditions of frontier days were not past, although there was seldom any use for weapons. The inhabitants were, ordinarily, peaceable, kindly folk; the horror which was aroused by subsequent events shows how shocking to them were lawlessness and bloodshed. Nevertheless, there were, still living, men of the pioneer times, and men who had been through both the wars—the lesser war and the great Civil War—which had racked Kansas. These men knew how to handle a horse and a rifle, and in the face of certain crimes did not always care to wait for the slow procedure of courts, nor for the aid of the public executioner.

The Bender family moved into their new house in the spring of 1871. It was built in a small hollow at the end of a long vale in the prairie. Near by was a stream, Drum Creek, bordered with thickets of wild plum and of cottonwood trees. The house seems to have had but two rooms, divided by a heavy curtain. The Benders professed to offer entertainment for man and beast: there was a small stock of tinned food and other supplies for sale in the front room; somewhere or other in the house sleeping space was found for travellers who cared to stay all night; while their horses could be sheltered in a stable in the rear. Back of the stable and house were a garden and orchard.

For a year and a half, the Benders seem to have lived the usual life of a family in that region, and to have attracted no especial notice, favourable or otherwise. Many of their neighbours, men and women who were living recently, remember meeting and talking with them. The two younger members of the family were often absent from their wayside tavern for days at a time; John Bender, Jr., on business unexplained, and Professor Miss Kate on her lecturing tours in Parsons, Oswego, Labette, or Chetopa, holding séances for the purpose of calling spirits from the grave; or perhaps exercising her remarkable curative powers upon persons afflicted with blindness, fits, or deafness. It is believed, however, that her most remarkable and permanent cures were effected, not during these visits, but upon patients who came for office consultation and treatment at her residence on the road to the Osage Mission.

It is impossible to determine exactly when it began to be rumoured in the country round about that there was something queer in the Bender ménage. Nearly everything about them and their performances depends upon statements never tested in a court of law; never sifted by cross-examination. Reputable persons can be found making assertions of an exactly opposite nature, and with perfect sincerity. With many people, no form of belief is held so tenaciously as that founded upon nothing more certain than local tradition and impressions acquired in childhood. They simply *know* that certain things are true because they have always been told that they were true. A number of the early adventures of travellers at the Bender house, and a number of fortunate escapes therefrom, sound much like things remembered—with additions—after the event. It is said, probably with truth, that the Benders did not begin their peculiar operations until the autumn of 1872, and that their entire career in the business which made them famous was during a period of about six months. Whatever they did during the autumn and winter of 1872 to 1873 caused no public outcry or investigation. It was not until the disappearance of Doctor York that any general suspicions were aroused.

Early in March, 1873, Dr. William H. York, who lived at Independence, was visiting his brother, Colonel A. M. York, at Fort Scott. On the ninth of the month, he left his brother, intending to ride to his own home. He was well mounted; had a good saddle; and carried a large sum of money and a fine watch. He spent the first night at Osage Mission, and left there on the morning of March 10th. Some of his friends met him, riding alone, on the road near the Bender house. He told them that he intended to stop for his midday dinner at the Benders'. And that was the last seen of Doctor York.

A considerable time, perhaps as much as two or three weeks, elapsed, and Colonel York was making a determined search for his brother. He traced him to a point on the road a few miles east of the Benders', but could get no farther in his investigations. At Independence he heard rumours of a strange adventure which two other travellers had experienced while dining with the Benders. These men had become convinced that they were about to be attacked; they left the house hurriedly; one of them went to the stable and brought out their carriage, while the other stood with a drawn revolver to cover the retreat. They believed that they were fired at, as they drove away toward the town of Parsons.

Colonel York prevailed upon twelve men from Cherryvale and elsewhere to visit the Bender house with him. They made the call on April 24th and had interviews with all that engaging group. Old Mrs. Bender, it was true, muttered something about a crowd of men disturbing a peaceable family, but the others were affable enough. Young John, who had been sitting by the side of the road with a Bible in his hand, searching the Scriptures, said that he had often been shot at by outlaws near Drum Creek. Doctor York had had dinner with them, Miss Kate had served it; on his departure, he had been foully slain, so the young Mr. Bender believed, by these same audacious bandits. One of the party, believing in spectral aid, asked Professor Miss Kate to consult the spirits, but she replied that there were too many unbelievers present; the spirits would be reluctant to assist. She made an appointment with him for a séance, alone, five days later. The men of the family helped Colonel York and his friends drag Drum Creek and search elsewhere. Altogether, they convinced Colonel York of their desire to aid him and of their ignorance of the fate of his brother. So the Colonel and his followers departed, and came not there again for eleven days.

On May 5th, with a larger number of men, who were still of the opinion that the Benders were somewhat maculate, he returned, to find the neighbours already on the premises. On the day before, May 4th, two brothers named Toles, who lived near by, were passing the Benders' house at eight in the morning. The agonized lowing of a calf attracted them; they found the animal nearly starved in its pen, while its mother was standing outside in as great distress to nourish her child as the calf was to be fed. They turned the two together, and then knocked on the door to see if the folk inside were ill and in need of help. There was no response; they looked in at the windows—the house was empty and in confusion, as if after a hurried departure of the family. This, in fact, had taken place. The Benders left, it is believed, on the night of April 29th, five days after Colonel

York's visit. The house had therefore been abandoned for four or five days.

On Monday, May 5th, when Colonel York and his men arrived, the door had already been broken open and the place was under examination. Aside from the clothing on the floor, household utensils, and 'manuscripts' of the lecturer, there was, at first, nothing remarkable to be seen. A trapdoor in the floor of the rear room was opened, and some of the men entered the cellar. This led by a tunnel toward the garden and orchard. On the floor of the cellar were damp spots which seemed to be human blood.

The search had been in progress for some length of time when Colonel York, standing in the rear of the house, and looking toward the orchard, suddenly remarked:

'Boys, I see graves yonder in the orchard!'

They laughed at him, and suggested that he had graves on the brain. Presently others were convinced that there were a number of long, narrow depressions, like graves, in the ground which old Bender had always kept freshly ploughed and harrowed. Soundings were made, with disquieting results, and presently spades were procured and one of the hollows was opened. At a depth of five feet, they discovered the naked body of a man, lying face downward. It was lifted out, and Colonel York's search for his brother was at an end.

Amid great excitement, everybody set to work, and other graves were opened, until the orchard was thoroughly excavated. They found eleven bodies: nine men, a young woman, a little girl. The skulls of all, except that of the child, had been crushed in one or more places from a blow with some blunt instrument like a sledge hammer. The girl was found lying under the body of her father, and from the absence of any wounds and from other indications, it appeared that she had died by suffocation; had, in fact, been buried alive.

Except for the young woman and one of the men, all the victims were identified, then or later. Three of the men, at least, had been known to be carrying large sums of money. These were a man named McKigzie, and two others, William F. McCrotty and Benjamin M. Brown. The two latter had three thousand dollars between them, so the Benders carried an unknown but considerable amount of loot when they fled.

The number of bodies varies in different accounts: to the eleven buried in the orchard are added, by one writer, two or three skeletons afterward discovered in or near Drum Creek and attributed to the work of the Benders. Other authorities set the figure at from seven to ten. The histories of Kansas set the number, conservatively, at seven. The names of the nine in the orchard who were identified are given, however, in more than one published account, so I think that, bearing in mind the counsel of the lady in the play to 'be just,' we can credit the Bender family with the murders of from ten to twelve persons.

The exact figures did not matter to the men who had carried on the search. When the body was exhumed of Doctor York—a man well liked and respected—and when the pitiful spectacle was revealed of the little girl, evidently put still living into the ground, and buried beneath the dead body of her father, there was an immediate desire for vengeance upon somebody, and the spirit of a lynching mob swept over the group.

Rudolph Brockmann, fellow countryman and neighbour of the Benders, had been helping in the search. He had worked as hard as any of the others; there was no reason to suppose that he did not share their horror at the murders. Nothing has been alleged against his character, but the mere fact told against him that he had talked with old Bender in a foreign language. He was questioned closely as to his knowledge of the crimes, and while the group of excited men stood around him, some one—the usual fool—shouted:

'Get a rope!'

This was done: a noose was put around Brockmann's neck, and he was pulled aloft from a tree branch or whatever was the nearest support. After a moment or two he was let down and given a chance to confess. He protested his innocence—and he probably spoke the truth. He was again hauled up and let down, until he was nearly choked to death. At last the mob were satisfied; the cooler and more reasonable men prevailed upon the others to cease; Brockmann was liberated and allowed to go home.

The process of the murders became apparent from an examination of the arrangement of the house, together with what could be learned from some of the surviving travellers who had taken a meal there. The diner sat on a bench or chair, with his back to the curtain which separated the two apartments. Sometimes he was entertained with pleasant conversation by whichever of the ladies was serving the meal. This was generally the younger one. One or two of the men of the family, attending behind the curtain with a sledge hammer, could await the moment when the guest, taking his ease, learned back and showed the outline of his head. Or the curtain was perhaps moved cautiously forward to meet him. The first blow, sufficient to stun him, if not to kill, was then delivered through the curtain. After that, the Benders worked rapidly. The body was dragged to the rear room, robbed and stripped. The trap-door being opened, one of the family cut the victim's throat and tumbled him into the cellar. If this happened by day, all was then secure, until night, when the dead man could be carried to the orchard and buried. Great precautions had been taken to keep the graves from becoming noticeable; these were successful at the time of Colonel York's first visit and nearly successful the second time.

Many stories are told of the part which Professor Miss Kate took, as the meal was served to a traveller. Sometimes she merely charmed him with her good looks, agreeable manners, and light table-talk. If he were docile, and took his chair as she set it, closely snuggled up against the curtain, she became an especially gracious hostess. But if he disliked the arrangement of things, became captious—as we all of us do at times—about the method of seating the guests, she would begin to sulk. Her conversation lost its sparkling qualities, and the dinner was practically a failure, from the point of view of both guest and hostess. One or two suspicious persons had moved to the other side of the table, so as to face the curtain; and two especially nervous gentlemen, who perhaps heard the sound of shuffling feet, and of heavy breathing behind the arras, insisted upon eating their meal standing up—which annoyed the Benders almost to the verge of incivility.

The romantic school, among the Benders' historians, have it that Kate dealt in mesmerism and other psychic methods of allaying suspicion and putting the traveller at his ease. There seems to be little doubt that she conversed with many of them upon spiritualism, and found willing listeners. The eagerness with which these hardy pioneers listened to her revelations upon the subject, suggests the facility with which all kinds of mediums, clairvoyants, crystal gazers, and soothsayers find their clients to-day, not among poets, artists, and the so-called impractical classes, but among 'hard-headed' business men.

E.P.

# 1879

# CHARLES PEACE
## Cat-Burglar and Murderer

Few names in the annals of crime are better known to the public than that of Charles Peace, whose effigy was for so long a principal attraction in the Chamber of Horrors at Mme Tussaud's exhibition of waxworks; though it is doubtful if many who familiarly refer to him as an arch-criminal could place the date of his trial within ten years. He was in fact tried for shooting at a Blackheath policeman with intent to murder in November 1878, under the name of John Ward; the discovery that he was the man for whom the police had been searching for two years for the murder of Arthur Dyson, at Banner Cross, near Sheffield, led to a further trial in February, 1879. He was found guilty, and was hanged on 25th February, 1879.

What has made the name of Charles Peace so notorious was not merely the crime for which he was executed, but other curious incidents of his career. Another man was sentenced to death for a murder of which Peace was guilty, the latter being present in Court during the trial. He was able on many occasions to escape detection by amazing powers of disguise and consummate daring. His nature was a curious mixture of sordid villainy and artistic tastes. He really loved music, and when he broke into a house—a very frequent habit with him—he could not resist taking violins and other instruments among his booty. Mr. Sherlock Holmes was accurate in saying, as we are assured he once did, that 'my old friend Charlie Peace was a violin virtuoso.'

It will be convenient to take the three principal trials in which

Peace was concerned—though in the first he was not in the dock—in chronological order. The first was that of John and William Habron (or Hebron), at Manchester, in November, 1876, before Mr. Justice Lindley. The two brothers, aged twenty-three and eighteen respectively, were charged with murdering Nicholas Cock, a policeman, at Whalley Range, near Manchester, on the night of 1st August. They were Irish labourers who were employed by a nurseryman in the neighbourhood and slept in an outhouse on his premises. In July Cock had summoned them for being drunk and disorderly; William was fined on 27th July and the charge against John was dismissed on 1st August. That night Cock was going his rounds with another policeman when they saw a man loitering suspiciously near the gate of a house. The two constables separated to investigate, Cock following the man into the grounds of the house. The man doubled back, scaled a wall, and was jumping down from it when he was confronted by Cock. Two shots were fire, the policeman fell, and the stranger ran away. Cock died half an hour later.

The Habrons were at once suspected, for they had been heard to utter threats against the man who had been responsible for summoning them. Police went at once to the outhouses where they lived and, finding them naked in bed, arrested them. A light had been shining through the window when the force arrived, but it was extinguished at the sound of their footsteps; this, for some reason, was supposed to point to the Habrons' guilt. Next day the police examined the scene of the crime and discovered a boot-mark in a patch of mud; they declared that it corresponded exactly with a boot worn by the elder brother, which was found to be covered with wet mud. Evidence was called also at the trial to prove that William had endeavoured on the afternoon of the murder to buy cartridges at an ironmonger's. Cock's companion at the scene of the crime deposed to seeing a man pass a few minutes before the shots were fired, whom he thought might be William Habron.

On the other hand, Cock said, before he died, that he did not know who had shot him. The defence was that the threats uttered by the prisoners—chiefly, it was pointed out, by the younger one—had been to 'shunt,' not to 'shoot,' the dead man. No weapon had been found either in their possession or in the neighbourhood of the crime. It was quite reasonable, in view of the weather, that William's boots should be muddy; it was unlikely that the boot-mark in the mud was clear enough for absolute identification. As for the cartridge incident, the witnesses were by no needs certain of Habron's identity, whereas there was other evidence that the men were working at the nursery at the time when one of them was alleged to be attempting to purchase the cartridges.

After two and a half hours' retirement the jury found William Habron guilty—with a recommendation to mercy on account of his youth—and his brother not guilty. William was sentenced to death. It was, however, generally felt that the evidence was insufficient for conviction; a petition, signed by many local residents, was forwarded to London, and the Home Secretary reduced the sentence to one of life imprisonment.

Just over two years later Charles Peace, lying in prison at Leeds under sentence of death, sent for a clergyman and confessed to him that he had shot Cock. He had intended, he said, to break into the house, was observed by two policemen, and, endeavouring to escape, ran into Cock's arms. Peace fired wide the first time to frighten him, and straight the second. 'I got away, which was all I wanted. Some time later I saw in the papers that certain men had been taken into custody for the murder of this policeman. That interested me. I thought I should like to attend the trial, and I determined to be present. I left Hull for Manchester, not telling my family where I had gone. I attended the Manchester Assizes for two days, and heard the youngest of the brothers, as I was told they were, sentenced to death. The sentence was afterwards reduced to penal servitude for life. Now, sir, some people will say I was a hardened wretch for allowing an innocent man to suffer for my crime. But what man would have done otherwise in my position? Could I have done otherwise, knowing, as I did, that I should certainly be hanged for the crime? But now that I am going to forfeit my own life, and feel that I have nothing to gain by further secrecy, I think it right, in the sight of God and man, to clear this young man, who is innocent of the crime.'

Peace drew a map of the spot and described his movements with sufficient accuracy to make it evident that he was indeed guilty; so the Home Office decided, after a certain natural hesitation. William Habron was given a free pardon and an indemnity of £800. He ought never to have been convicted.

It is somewhat significant that Peace committed the murder for which he was eventually hanged on the very day after he had watched this innocent man sentenced to death for his other crime. Habron was sentenced on 28th November, 1876; on 29th November, at Banner Cross, in Sheffield, Charles Peace shot and killed Arthur Dyson, an engineer employed by the North-Eastern Railway. Evidence at the inquest showed that Peace and the Dysons had previously been neighbours at Darnall, a suburb of Sheffield. Peace had for some time pestered the Dysons with his advances. When he was forbidden the house, he uttered threats against the Dysons, for which a summons was taken out against him. He did not appear in court to answer it; a warrant was issued, but he disappeared from the district. The Dysons moved from Darnall to Banner Cross, but Peace turned up there, shot Dyson dead and escaped. The jury at the inquest returned a verdict of wilful murder against Peace. Hue and cry were raised, and £100 reward was offered for his apprehension. No trace of him, however, could be found. Two years elapsed. Peace had disappeared, Mrs. Dyson went to America, and the Banner Cross murder seemed destined never to be avenged.

Nor, indeed, would it have been but for a curious succession of incidents.

In the years 1877 and 1878 a respectable old gentleman lived in a respectable little house in a respectable street of a respectable London suburb. His name was Thompson, and his address East Terrace, Evelina Road, Peckham, S.E. With him lived his wife, Mrs. Thompson, a young and handsome woman with a certain failing for drink. Their housekeeper, Mrs. Ward, and her son, Willie, occupied the basement. The house was well, almost richly, furnished. Thompson was a popular member of the congregation of the parish church. He had the endearing trait of loving animals, and kept many pets. Though he did not lack for money, he amused himself by assisting a neighbour in an invention designed to raise 'sunken vessels by the displacement of water within them by air and gases.' With this object they occasionally visited a pond in the neighbourhood to experiment on a toy yacht. They also wrote to the Admiralty offering to raise two vessels which had sunk; but their offer was rejected, as was a similar proposal to the German Government. Mr. Thompson, whose swarthy features suggested a tinge of negro blood, possessed a considerable collection of violins, guitars, concertinas and other musical instruments, and it was his pleasure to exhibit his skill on them to a few favoured acquaintances.

But the oddest thing about this household was that Thompson was Charles Peace. 'Mrs. Thompson' was a young woman with whom he had first become friendly in Nottingham; while 'Mrs. Ward,' the housekeeper, and her son were Peace's wife and stepson. And 'Thompson's' unlaborious employment with his neighbour did not prevent his spending a great part of the night in robbing suitable houses in the neighbourhood.

It was during such an escapade that he was arrested. One October evening in 1878, 'Mr. and Mrs. Thompson' and 'Mrs. Ward' spent a musical evening, he playing the violin, they singing and accompanying him on the harmonium. The women went to bed and Peace, as we may now call him, crept out and broke into a house at Blackheath. Two policemen happened to see a light moving in the house at two in the morning, called a sergeant, and kept the place under observation. Shortly afterwards a man came out and walked down the garden, where one of the policemen, named Robinson, was concealed. When he saw Robinson he fired two shots, both of which missed, shouting with an oath: 'Keep back, keep back, or I'll shoot you!' Robinson, however, closed with him; three more shots were fired, one of which entered the policeman's head and another his arm; fortunately they did not prove fatal. The other constable and the sergeant rushed up and overpowered the burglar, whose revolver was strapped to his wrist.

At the police station he gave his name as John Ward and his age as sixty. A set of housebreaking tools was found in his pocket, as well as a pocket-knife which had been stolen in another local burglary a few months before. He appeared on remand on 18th October, 1878. He engaged a solicitor to represent him and, after formal evidence had been given, he was remanded for a week, then for another week, and finally committed for trial at the Old Bailey. But while he was waiting for his trial, 'Ward' wrote to 'Thompson's' neighbour, the inventor, and begged him to visit an unfortunate man who, through the sin of drunkenness, found himself in a regrettable situation. The neighbour, mystified by this letter and not in the least connecting it with the disappearance of his friend, arrived, and discovered to his amazement that 'Ward' and 'Thompson' were identical. He communicated his discovery to the police, who hastened to communicate with the already alarmed Thompson menage. 'Mrs. Ward' and her son had run away with some of the plunder, but 'Mrs. Thompson' revealed the astounding fact that their prisoner was Charles Peace, who was wanted for the Banner Cross murder.

On 19th November, 'John Ward, alias Charles Peace, aged sixty,' appeared before Mr. Justice Hawkins for his Blackheath offence. Sir Harry Poland led for the prosecution; Peace was represented by two counsel.

During the hearing of the case Peace played the part of an unfortunate old man with whom fate had dealt hardly. He had given his age as sixty, and looked it; but he was actually fourteen year younger. When the jury found him guilty and he was asked by the Judge if he had anything to say, he made a long and miserable plea for mercy 'in a whining tone, with tears in his eyes, and almost grovelling on the floor.' He declared that he did not know the pistol was loaded, that he had only meant to frighten the policeman, not to hurt him, and that the shots which had wounded him had been accidentally discharged during the struggle. 'Oh, my lord, I know I am bad and base to the uttermost, but I know at the same time they have painted my case blacker than it really is. . . . So, oh, my lord, have mercy upon me, I pray and beseech you,' is a specimen of the appeal which, with many protestations of piety and repentance, he made to the utterly unresponsive Judge. Peace was sentenced to penal servitude for life, and removed to Pentonville Prison.

The discovery, now made, of the prisoner's true identity revived the Banner Cross case. Mrs. Dyson was sent for, and arrived at Queenstown from America early in January. Ten days later Peace was taken to Sheffield and charged before the magistrates with the murder of Arthur Dyson two years before. Mrs. Dyson gave the principal evidence, for she had been the only eye-witnesses of the crime. Peace frequently interrupted her and others witnesses, charging them with perjury. He complained also that the reporters in Court were sketching him. The trial was adjourned until the following Wednesday, the prisoner being taken back to London in the interval.

On the return to Sheffield on this Wednesday morning in the charge of two warders, Peace made a desperate attempt to escape from the train. It was moving at the rate of nearly fifty miles an hour, but Peace, an agile little man, flung himself through the window. One of the warders succeeded in grasping his boot; the other pulled the alarm signal. Peace hung out of the window for some moments, struggling; then he wriggled free of his boot and fell on his head in the snow by the side of the track. There he was found unconscious and bleeding when the train stopped.

As he was, or professed to be, too ill to go into Court, his examination was resumed in the passage outside his cell in the police station at Sheffield; he was carried in, bandaged and wrapped in rugs, and placed in an armchair. To what extent his pain was real cannot be known. Despite his apparent feebleness, he loudly declared that he had 'lots of witnesses who can prove that that base, bad woman has threatened my life, and has threatened her husband's life. But I can't talk to you, I am so bad. I feel very bad, but she has threatened to take my life often. . . . She has threatened her husband's, and hers as well.' He was also able at the end of the inquiry to instruct his solicitors in firm and decided tones, which suggests that he had again been exercising his undoubted skill as an actor.

He was lodged in Wakefield and Leeds jails pending the trial. From the former he wrote to 'Mrs. Thompson' to sell some of his goods and engage a barrister who would 'save me from the perjury of that villainous woman, Mrs. Dyson.' He did not know that 'Mrs. Thompson' had given him away to the police, for which she was afterwards to claim the £100 reward. His neighbour, the inventor, is also said to have claimed the reward. Peace wrote also to his real wife, as from her 'affectionate and unhappy husband'.

On 4th February, 1879, Peace was at last brought to trial for the murder of Arthur Dyson. The Judge was Mr. Justice Lopes, who afterwards became Lord Ludlow. Peace, who was represented by Mr. Frank Lockwood and Mr. Stuart Wortley, pleaded guilty. The prosecuting counsel described the crime. The Dysons and the Peaces lived next door but one to each other in a row of workmen's cottages at Darnall. Peace's apparent occupation was picture-framing, and the Dysons employed him to frame two or three small pictures for them. After a while Peace came to treat their house as his own, walking in at all times, whereupon Dyson wrote on a card: 'Charles Peace is requested not to interfere with my family,' and threw it into Peace's garden. Peace later in the same day tried to trip up Dyson in the street and, producing a revolver, threatened to kill both him and his wife. They took out a summons and he disappeared; to make themselves doubly safe from his attentions, they moved six miles away to Banner Cross. But when they arrived in sight of their new home, in front of which the furniture van was being unloaded, they saw Peace coming out of the house. He reiterated his intention to annoy them, but for a month they saw nothing more of him. In the evening of 29th November he reappeared, with a packet of letters and photographs which, he assured such of the Dysons' new neighbours as he could induce to listen, would show them the sort of people the Dysons were.

He loitered outside their house until Mrs. Dyson went down the yard, where he followed her. He pointed a revolver; she screamed, and her husband ran out of the house into the yard. Peace fired at him, and he fell. The prisoner then scaled a wall and escaped.

Mrs. Dyson was once again the principal witness. She repeated fairly exactly the evidence she had given at the inquest two years before and at the inquiry. The prisoner's counsel cross-examined her to suggest that her husband, who was an extremely tall and powerful man, attacked Peace in an access of jealousy, and that the revolver was accidentally discharged during the struggle. This she denied. Her acquaintance with Peace, however, proved to be rather more intimate than had hitherto been supposed. They had visited Sheffield Fair together, been photographed together, and visited a public-house together. He had given her a ring. A number of letters were produced which, Peace claimed, were written by her to him. If genuine, these suggested that they were accustomed to meet in the garret of an empty house between their dwellings at Darnall. One of the letters thanked him for a ring, and Mrs. Dyson had admitted receiving a ring from Peace. But she swore that the letters were not written by her.

Whether they were or not was, of course, not directly material in determining Peace's innocence or guilt of the murder of her husband. But her reliability as a witness was material, for she alone had seen what happened at the shooting. During Mr. Lockwood's speech to the jury the prisoner interjected occasional comments, such as: 'Hear, hear,' and 'I am not fit to die.' But there was no hope for him; the jury immediately brought in a verdict of guilty, and the Judge passed sentence of death.

While he was awaiting execution, Peace sent for a Darnall clergyman and confessed his share in the Whalley Range murder for which John Habron had been sentenced. At the same time he gave his account of the death of Dyson. Peace said he was standing on a wall at the back of the house, watching Mrs. Dyson, who had been his mistress, through a window; she was putting her little boy to bed. He whistled to her—a signal to which she was accustomed—and she came down. Peace wanted her to induce her husband to withdraw the warrant which had been issued against him, but she became abusive and an altercation followed. Dyson heard the noise, came out and seized Peace. The latter fired his revolver (which, as usual, was strapped to his wrist) in the air to frighten him; then, as this had no effect, he fired again, wishing to disable, not to kill him.

The chief interest of the career of Charles Peace does not lie in the sordid crimes for which he eventually paid the penalty. His complex personality and his remarkable powers of disguise single him out from the general run of murderers.

He was born about 1832 in Sheffield, his father being a wild-beast tamer employed by Wombwell's menagerie. The latter transmitted to his son an interest in animals and a love of music. But music did not exercise a restraining influence on the boy, who was always brutal and unruly. At an early age Charles, employed in a mill, injured his leg and his left hand in an accident. He never did any more honest work. Permanently lame, and with a maimed hand, he devoted himself to a life of crime.

Although his injuries should have made him conspicuous, he contrived to conceal his hand under his coat and to wear a false arm in his sleeve, terminating with a hook. He boasted, with reason, that he would walk past detectives who were searching for him without any danger of recognition. They only looked, he said, at one's face, and he had an abnormal power to protrude his lower jaw and to suffuse his face with blood, thus altering his whole appearance and taking on the likeness of a mulatto. So confident was he of his powers of disguise that, he claimed, he visited Scotland Yard to read the descriptive notices offering a reward for his apprehension. He later used walnut juice to effect a permanent change in his appearance.

He was one of the first 'cat burglars,' who were known in those days as 'portico thieves.' In the intervals of his burglaries and occasional minor terms of imprisonment, and also, no doubt, as a means of watching likely premises, Peace became an itinerant musician. He described himself modestly as 'The Modern Paganini' and 'The Great Ethiopian Musician,' and sang songs of his own composition to the accompaniment of a one-stringed fiddle of his own making. He also recited; Sir Archibald Bodkin, as a schoolboy at Highgate, was one of a juvenile audience who heard him declaim the grave scene from Hamlet.

Peace's professions of piety lasted to the end. He wrote to various members of his family assuring them of his repentance and enclosing specimens of prayers he had composed. And to his wife he sent a funeral card as follows:

*In*
*Memory*
*of*
*CHARLES PEACE*
*who was executed in*
*Armley Prison,*
*Tuesday, February 25th,*
*1879. Aged 47.*

*For that I don but never*
*intended.*

There must have been some slight particle of goodness in the man, for, as he was being taken to the scaffold and was permitted to address a group of reporters, his last words were a hope that no one would taunt or jeer at his wife and children on his account, 'but will have mercy upon them.'

A more curious and complicated personality than that of Charles Peace can rarely have existed.

F.E.S.

# 1882

# ARMAND PELTZER
## The Man Who Never Was

Paul Bourget, one of the finest of French novelists, wrote a celebrated murder-story, entitled 'André Cornélis.' The plot of this romance was not evolved from his imagination, but was based on the proceedings of an actual murderer named Peltzer—one of the most ingenious criminals on record. The facts of this strange story of real life, which Wilkie Collins might have envied, we are about to set before the reader.

Armand Peltzer, an engineer of Antwerp, had settled, in 1876, at Buenos Ayres, where he was building up a brilliant practice. But one morning, to his horror, he received a letter from his younger brothers, James and Léon, who were merchants in their native town of Antwerp, informing him that they had failed in business and, what was worse, that a charge was out against them of embezzlement. Armand, who had the brains of all the family, at once took ship for Europe, looked into their affairs, employed a clever counsel to defend them, saved them from shame and prison, and got them off scot-free. All this was excellent. But it so fell out that, during these events, he formed a friendship with his brothers' advocate, whose name was Bernays, and paid almost daily visits to his house. Now, Bernays had a young and charming wife. And that was fatal.

Julie Bernays was not exactly pretty; but the proud distinction of her features, crowned with a ruddy-golden cloud of hair, gave her a peculiar charm. Peltzer fell in love with her with passion—wildly, blindly. And he was one of those mad lovers who will stick at nothing. Cool and crafty, willing to wait, but inflexible of purpose, not to be turned aside by any peril, he resolved to have this woman, let the cost be what it might. In his favour, he had a certain fascination of his own. Slight of build, but of sinewy strength, with a dark-pale face, crisp beard and brilliant eyes, a winning manner and a flattering tongue, it was not long before he wound his way into her heart. His task was lightened by the fact that she was far from happy with her husband, a man not very easy for a girl to live with. Bernays, who was by race a Jew, was also, strange to say, a Roman Catholic. He was a man of a peculiar cast of character; cold, hard, and violent, and often acid with religious mania. Rather coarse in fibre, he failed to understand his wife, who was a girl of culture and refinement, sensitive, high-spirited, with nerves strung like wires. When they quarrelled, as they often did, he was wont to seek for consolation with the nursemaid of their only child—a little boy who was the only bond between them, for he was the idol of them both.

Such were the husband, wife, and lover—'the eternal triangle'—in this drama of real life.

If Armand looked upon his task as easy, he was soon to learn his error. Julie's ideal of love was very far from his. In spirit she was vestal, virginal. It was her wish to love as angels love, with a passion rather of the soul than of the flesh. Armand, who had no relish of the angel in him, sought in vain to wile her from her marriage vows. Yet, in her husband's absence, they went about together freely. In the month of August, 1881, they took a secret trip to Spa. This trip was their undoing. The child's nurse, Amelia Pfister, with whom Bernays had found solace, became aware of this adventure and conveyed the tidings to her master's ears.

Bernays was thunderstruck. His wife had ceased to love him, but he still loved his wife. In a fit of jealous rage he dashed into her presence and accused her of the guilt of infidelity. But he had caught a Tartar. With a white heat of passion that surpassed his own she told him that he ought to be ashamed to speak such wicked lies. When he called the nurse, she slapped that damsel's face with vigour, and sent her packing from the house. In the end the luckless Bernays was compelled to bribe the angry maiden with a sum of money and a dressing-case, to keep her tongue from wagging. His wife, when she came out of her hysterics, refused to speak another word.

Raging, he went off to Peltzer's lodging, where he burst in upon the villain like a tempest. But the storm was idle. The lover, in a tone of lofty scorn, informed him that he was a monster, who ill deserved to have an angel for a wife. He declared that he should come to Bernays's house that night as usual, and that he expected to be treated as, what he was, a friend. Bernays, overborne, and willing to believe that he had been mistaken, yielded, and in the evening Peltzer came to dine. But when the husband saw his wife and visitor smiling across the table in each other's faces, a new devil rose within him, and he kicked the lover out of doors.

Armand, always cool and calculating, saw, a chance of turning this event to his advantage. He sent his younger brothers, James and Robert, to challenge the obnoxious husband to a duel. Bernays, who perceived no reason why he should run the risk of being shot to throw his wife into the arms of her admirer, refused point-blank. And Armand, much incensed at being baffled by a coward, was forced to turn to another method which had long been ripening in his brain.

His brother Léon, after his acquittal, had gone to the United States, where he had wandered to and fro upon the earth, leading the life of an adventurer and often on the verge of prison. Armand, wrote to him to come to Paris. He sailed from New York on the *Arizona*, under the false name of Adolphe Prélat, and in due time the brothers met in secret, in a room in the Hôtel de Commerce. There they passed three days in consultation. Armand explained his scheme in detail. It was his design to call to being an assassin, as a wizard summons up an imp, who should commit the murder and then vanish like a dream. Léon was to put off his own identity, to disappear and cease to be, and in his place there was to come to life a new and wholly different being, by the name of Henry Vaughan. Recalling how he had secured his brother from dishonour, from infamy and prison, Armand won him over to his purpose. He further sealed the bond with a large sum of money. It was the price of blood.

Armand then caught the train to Antwerp. Léon, left in Paris, at once set to work. He went first to the shop of a costumier named Daumouche and explained that he required a fancy dress, as he was going to a masquerade. He proposed at first to represent an English dandy, with the style of whiskers known as Piccadilly weepers; but in the end he bought a dark brown wig and beard, a flask of kohl to tint the eyebrows black, and a box of amber-powder mixed with burnt sienna, to produce a swart complexion. Taking these with him to his rooms he set to work at making-up. Such was his skill that, when he finished, Léon Peltzer had ceased to be, and there had come to life a man of business, of Brazilian race—the gentleman whom his brother had already christened by the name of Henry Vaughan.

Next, he made up a roaring fire, and proceeded to burn every garment he possessed. This done, he dressed himself in clothes already purchased, every article completely new, even to shirt and under-linen, hat and boots. Then, wishing to put his work to the severest proof, he called again at the costumier's shop, and made some trifling purchase by the way of an excuse. Daumouche received him as perfect stranger, and had clearly no idea he had ever seen him in his life before. After such a test, he felt no fear of being recognized even by his oldest friends. And, indeed, he never was.

The next step was to obtain a weapon. At the shop of a gunsmith named Decante he demanded a revolver that would 'shoot hard with little noise.' He took away with him no less than seven, of various patterns, together with a stock of cartridges. Having tested these himself he sent the one he found the best to Armand, who made a trial of it at his own house in the Rue Jacobs, Antwerp, where, later on, a bullet of its calibre was found embedded in the woodwork of the overmantel, while other cartridges were fished up from a drain. For Armand was not satisfied with this revolver; and so keenly was he bent upon obtaining the right thing, that Léon was despatched to London; and there, at Baker's, the well-known gunmaker, he procured a weapon which they could hardly hope to better—a revolver 'that shot hard with little noise.'

And now came the most important step of all, the very essence of this most ingenious scheme. For this, it must be noted, was no mere case of a man assuming a disguise in order to commit a crime, but the creation of a living being who was yet a phantom. With this object, Léon now set forth upon a tour through Belgium, Holland, and North Germany, as the agent of the firm of Murray and Company of Australia, sent to Europe to organize a great new line of steamships between Amsterdam and Sydney. At Bremen, Hamburg, and Amsterdam he put up at the best hotels and called upon the heads of leading firms, explaining his gigantic scheme. In the course of a few weeks, his striking figure had become familiar in the world of shipping men—familiar, yet an apparition, which all the sleuth-hounds of the law might seek to track in vain.

When the time came for his return to Brussels, he took a flat at the address 159 Rue de la Loi. One room he furnished as a business office, with a roll desk and leather chair. But there were also features not so usual in an office—a thick carpet, heavy window-hangings, and a double curtain at the door. Their purpose was to deaden sound.

These preparations made, he wrote to Bernays in the name of Henry Vaughan:

> 'Sir,—*Friends of mine in London have favoured me with your address, informing me that you are one of the best advocates in Antwerp in affairs connected with the shipping business. The firm I represent are projecting an important line of inter-oceanic steamships, with one of its chief offices in Antwerp. The capital of this colossal scheme, which amounts to half a million sterling, has already been subscribed. There are certain legal points on which we now require the best advice, and we shall be happy if we can secure your services. I propose to call upon you to discuss details, but in the meantime I send a list of questions on which I should be glad of information on which I can rely. Will you be so good as to favour me with your opinions at your earliest convenience, as my course of action while in Brussels will be regulated by your answers? I have the honour to enclose a cheque for five hundred francs, in advance of fees.*
>
> '*I am, Sir, your obedient servant,*
>
> '*HENRY VAUGHAN.*'

Bernays was delighted. He drew up his replies and sent the document to Léon. Then an interview was fixed, at Bernays's office. But the night before the day appointed, Léon telegraphed that he was detained in Brussels by the illness of his son and that, as his time was taken up with daily consultations with the

Minister of Public Works, he was forced to ask the lawyer if he would be good enough to come to Brussels, and call upon him at his address in the Rue de la Loi. Bernays replied that he would come with pleasure. And so the trap was set and baited, and the prey was coming to the lure.

The next morning, which was Saturday, the seventh of January, 1882, Léon was waiting for him in his flat. And in the side pocket of his coat, all ready to his hand, was the revolver that shot hard with little noise.

At eleven o'clock the hall-bell rang. Léon, stepping to the door, opened it to Bernays. Greeting him in genial fashion, he helped him to take off his overcoat and to hang it on the rack which he had provided for the purpose—for the coat, with its thick winter collar, might deaden or deflect a bullet. Then, with a gesture, he motioned Bernays to precede him through the heavy double curtains which hung across the doorway of the office on the right. The lawyer was, of course, quite unsuspecting. What sign was there to warn him that he was going to his doom? Pushing apart the curtains, he stepped into the office. At the same moment, Léon, who was close behind him, drew the revolver from his pocket, raised it to the level of the other's neck, and pulled the trigger. The bullet whistled through the spine and came out below the chin. The end was instantaneous. Without a cry or struggle, the victim staggered a pace forward, and crashed down upon the floor beside the desk—stone-dead.

According to his brother's programme, for a reason we shall see, Léon should now have propped the body in the office chair. But, owing no doubt to the excitement of the moment, he forgot to carry out this part of his instructions. As soon as he had ascertained that all was over, leaving the dead man in a pool of blood, he went into the bedroom, where he burnt his wig and beard, and then washed all traces of the make-up from his face. In a few minutes Henry Vaughan, the assassin, had disappeared for ever, while Léon Peltzer, the stainless gentleman, had returned to life instead.

Then he walked out into the street—and disappeared.

When Bernays caught the early train to Brussels he left word that he expected to return that afternoon. His absence, therefore, caused surprise, and then alarm; and when the night, and then the next day, passed without a sign of his return, the members of his family put the matter into the hands of the police. The affair began to make a stir. The newspapers came out with scare-lines—'The Mysterious Disappearance of a Well-known Lawyer.' Various rumours ran from mouth to mouth. Some thought that, in an access of religious mania, he had sought seclusion in a monastery. Others, who were aware of his affairs of gallantry, believed that he had gone off with a mistress, and whispered that no doubt he would turn up again as soon as she began to prove a nuisance.

In the meantime the police were at a stand-still. If they guessed that Armand Peltzer had some inkling of the matter, there was nothing tangible to bring against him. He was to be seen daily in the company of Julie Bernays—whom, no doubt, he was consoling. But the one important point was certain—on the date that Bernays disappeared at Brussels, Armand had been conspicuous in Antwerp all day long. The alibi was perfect, unassailable.

And then a strange thing happened.

Ten days after Bernays vanished, the Coroner of Brussels received a letter that made him rub his eyes. It ran as follows:

'*BÂLE, 16 January*, 1882.
'*I am distressed to find from a newspaper this morning that M. G. Bernays is still missing. I infer from this that my previous letter has failed to reach the Coroner, and that, for this reason, the terrible accident that happened at my flat, 159 Rue de la Loi, on the seventh of the present month, is still undiscovered. The facts are these. M. Bernays called to see me by appointment, in connection with the Murray line of steamships. While we were talking, I happened to be handling a revolver, which I had taken from the table, and, at a moment when his back was turned, it accidentally exploded. M. Bernays fell. At first I thought that he was only*

*wounded, but the blood was flowing freely, and alas! I soon
discovered that he was dead—that I killed him!*

    *'I was paralysed with horror. At first I thought of rushing
out for the police, but then, in my despair, as I reflected on
my situation, without a friend in Brussels, with my wife and
child both suffering from illnesss, I yielded to the temptation
to fly with them to Switzerland. Ever since that fatal moment
I have been half crazy with despair.*

    *'I pray you to convey the terrible tidings to the family, and
to express my horror and despair at the calamity. I have no
wish to cast the responsibility upon any other person. I only
hope that God, in His mercy, will not demand the life of my
own child in return for the life that I have taken!*

    *'I am, Sir, your obedient servant,*

*'HENRY VAUGHAN.'*

Now, for what reason was this letter written? Who was this
Henry Vaughan, and why should he draw attention to his
'accident'? The police were as much puzzled as the public.
But to us, who hold the key, there is no mystery about the
matter. In the first place, it was meant to set the hunters on
the track of Henry Vaughan, whom they might seek for ever to
no purpose. Secondly, it was all-important that the body should
be discovered—for if left for weeks or months it might not be
recognizable; in which case Julie Bernays would not be a widow,
free to marry, but only the wife of a man who had disappeared
but who might still be living, so that Armand could not lead her
to the altar, which was the sole and single purpose of the crime.

The police went at once to Léon's flat. There they found, as
they expected, the dead body; but, what will surprise the reader,
it was no longer lying on the floor, as the murderer had left it,
but was sitting propped up in the office chair!

The party had two doctors with them. These experts arrived at
the conclusion that it had been placed there after death—some
two or three days after. A man had left his footprint in the pool
of blood congealed beside the chair. This man, it was assumed,
was Henry Vaughan—what else could be imagined? But—the
reader will again be startled—it was discovered later, by the size
and shape, that the print was never made by the assassin!

But by whom, then? We shall see.

And now began the hunt for Henry Vaughan. At Bâle, the town from which the letter had been written to the Coroner, there was no trace of such a person. But among the cities of the North, where he had made himself familiar, it was easy to discover scores of people who knew all about him. He had left his traces everywhere. But when it came to setting eyes upon him, it seemed as if the man had vanished from the earth. As, indeed, he had.

Week after week went by. The search relaxed—the police were foiled and beaten. Léon returned to Antwerp, where he took no pains to hide himself—as, indeed, why should he? As for Armand, whose plot had worked exactly as he had intended, he was courting Julie gaily, and with perfect ease of mind. He had sworn to her that he knew nothing of the disappearance of her husband, and she had believed him on his word. But this scheme, though clever to the last degree, was fated to be one of those that 'gang agley.' Like a Prince Rupert's drop, which, if the point is broken, flies to atoms, a touch was ready to explode it into dust.

The letter to the Coroner had been reproduced in all the newspapers. It happened that a merchant, who had done business with the Peltzers years before, detected a resemblance to the writing of his old acquaintance Léon, of which some specimens were still in his possession. These he took to the police. Experts were called in—among them M. Gobert, chief adviser to the Bank of France. In their opinion, the letter to the Coroner was in Léon's hand!

This was the single flaw in Armand's master-piece of murder. One may wonder how he came to let it pass. The risk was next to nothing, it is true; but if the letter had been typed it would have left no clue whatever. All would have gone as merry as a marriage bell. Armand would have wedded Julie and lived happy ever after. As it was, the game was up. From that moment all was over.

The police put two and two together. Léon Peltzer had no motive in the world for killing Bernays—but his brother Armand, whose affair with Julie was a scandal with the gossips, had the very best of reasons. On the fifth of March, at Antwerp, the police pounced upon the guilty pair.

They were first taken to the flat, in Brussels, where the

footprint in the blood had been carefully preserved. Léon's foot was quite dissimilar in size and shape; but Armand's fitted it exactly, even to the marks of wear upon the sole!

And now the mystery was clearing fast. It was Armand who, on learning of his brother's oversight, had gone in secret to the flat to prop the body in the chair. This was vital to his purpose—for if the revolver had gone off by accident, as the letter stated, while being handled carelessly, it could not possibly have sent a horizontal shot through the neck of a man standing.

The accused were lodged in prison to await their trial. There, Léon made two statements. In the first, while he confessed that he was Henry Vaughan, he stated that his letter gave a true account of what had happened. Then, when it was pointed out to him that the doctors' evidence had proved an accident to be impossible, he put forward an amended version. It is a strikingly dramatic story:

'When I opened the door of the flat to Bernays, it was evident that he did not recognize me. He took off his overcoat, and I showed him into the office. There, we discussed the schemes of the Murray line of steamships. But, all of a sudden, Bernays fixed his eyes upon me, and cried sharply, 'We have met before!' I was taken by surprise, but I answered calmly, 'I think you are mistaken.'

'But his suspicions were aroused. As I turned aside to conceal my discomposure he suddenly put out his hand and twitched my wig. 'What!' he cried out in an angry voice. 'It is you, Léon—*you*, the cheat and forger!' Then he darted to the door, exclaiming, 'I am going to summon the police!' I snatched up a revolver which was lying on the table, caught him by the coat and drew him backwards. As he struggled to escape the shot rang out. He turned a somersault, and as he fell his shoulder struck the desk. It all passed like lightning. I swear I fired the shot without intention, in a moment of intense and blind excitement.

'On seeing Bernays fall I almost lost my senses. It was some moments before I was able to approach the body. I thought he might be only wounded, and it was not until I came to lift him that I saw the blood was oozing from a wound behind the neck. I raised his head, and propped him up against the desk, while I went to fetch some water. I washed the wound—and it was then that I discovered that he was dead.

'I saw that I must fly. But, later on, the thought occured to me that I might represent the matter as an accident. And so I wrote the letter to the Coroner.'

To this romance he stuck through thick and thin—adding only, at the trial, that he himself had placed the body in the chair. It was known, of course, upon the clearest evidence, that the act was Armand's doing, two days later.

The trial took place at the Court of the Assizes, Brabant, in December. The police had taken several months in their inquiries, and these had been so thorough and complete that, when they finished, every detail of the plot had come to light. They discovered the costumier who had supplied the wig and beard, and the gunsmiths who had furnished the revolvers. They dug the bullet from the woodwork over Armand's mantelpiece, and fished up the cartridges which he had thrown down the drain. They discovered, also, in his house a new and striking piece of evidence—a batch of telegrams, in cipher, sent by Léon to his brother, which, when decoded, gave him news of how the plot was going, the last one telling him that Bernays, on the morrow, was to walk into the trap. The originals of these telegrams, when the forms were looked up at the post office, were shown to be in Léon's writing. Lastly, the police had gathered facts together, bit by bit, with such exactness that they were able to build up, to reconstruct in the minutest detail, the scene that actually occured in Léon's flat.

When, therefore, the trial opened there was practically no defence. The story of the crime was told at length as we already know it. Léon, who was calm, resigned, and even dignified, took all the blame upon himself. His brother Armand, he asserted, had no knowledge of the case whatever. He repeated the romance which we have given—how, on being recognized, he had shot the lawyer in a fit of blind excitement. Why he disguised himself at all—why he changed his name—why he invented Murray's firm, which had been proved to be a fiction—why he made his office sound-proof with a carpet and thick curtains—to these deadly questions there could be no real reply. His counsel pleaded that the other side had shown no motive for the crime. What fool would risk his neck to please his brother? But the speaker made no mention of the price of blood. Armand's bearing was completely different. He gave rather the impression of a dandy in a drawing-room than of a felon in the dock. He acted like a jackanapes, all bounce and chatter. But impudence was not the thing to save him. Nor could his counsel find a plea of any weight. He also claimed a lack of motive. Why should his client plot to murder Bernays? The lady was in love with him. Surely it must have been an easy matter to persuade her to elope? But Armand had not found it easy, as every gossip was aware.

Long before the end the auditors who crammed the Court to suffocation had no doubt about the verdict, and were ready to receive it with a cheer. It was delivered on the twenty-second of December. Both prisoners were found guilty of the crime of murder. As the penalty of death was not in force in Belgium, the only sentence possible was that of penal servitude for life.

The accused were asked if they had anything to say. Léon answered calmly, 'I accept the verdict. I shot Bernays. But my brother is innocent. The verdict against him is a legal crime.' Armand's exit was a piece of melodrama. All his flippancy had disappeared. Throwing one hand to heaven and pointing to the jury with the other, he cried in piercing tones, 'I call the wrath of God upon them all!'

And so with the curse upon his lips the master-murderer turned upon his heel and vanished for ever from the eyes of men.

H.G.S.

# 3
# DEADLY DOCTORS
## (1849–95)

# 1849

# DOCTOR WEBSTER

## Murder at Harvard

Until the gray and melancholy twenty-third of November, people of Boston, like most Americans, had been talking all through 1849 of nothing but the great California gold rush. But on that Friday, Boston had something nearer home to occupy its attention. Dr. George Parkman had disappeared in broad daylight. It was as incredible as if Bunker Hill Monument had sunk into the bowels of the earth. A Boston Parkman simply did not, could not, disappear and leave no trace. The police went to work, and so did hundreds of citizens, spurred by a reward of $3000 for the doctor, alive or dead.

That day the eminent doctor had left his Beacon Hill home about noon. He had gone to the Merchants' Bank. From there he had called at a greengrocer's to leave an order. Later he had been seen walking rapidly toward Harvard Medical College. At or near the college, it appeared, he had walked straight into Valhalla.

It was Dr. Parkman who had given the very land on which the then new Medical College stood. Moreover, he had endowed the Parkman Chair of Anatomy, occupied by Dr. Oliver Wendell Holmes. The Parkmans had been prominent from what, even by Boston standards, were ancient times. All the Parkmans were well-to-do; the doctor was so wealthy that his son, who never earned a penny in his life, was able to leave $5,000,000 for the improvement of Boston Common. The usually staid Boston press went into a dither and police arrested scores of persons.

Professor John White Webster made a call on the missing man's brother, and said that he had had an interview with the doctor in the Medical College on Friday afternoon, at which time he had paid Dr. Parkman $483. Dr. Parkman had then left the college, said the professor.

Webster, a graduate of Harvard Medical, had taught chemistry at Harvard for more than twenty years. With their four pretty daughters, the Websters were noted for the hospitality they lavished on the faculty. His professor's salary of $1200 annually was wholly inadequate. While it was known that Webster owed the doctor money and that the doctor had gone to collect it, the professor was not under suspicion. Who could suspect a faculty member of Harvard? It began to look as if some thug had waylaid the doctor, done away with him and made off with the $483 which Webster said he had paid Parkman.

Apparently nobody suspected Webster—except a morose and obscure man named Ephraim Littlefield, a janitor at Harvard Medical College. It appears to have been a generous act of Webster's that set Littlefield on his trail like a hound of hell. On the Tuesday following Parkman's disappearance, Webster presented a thumping big turkey to Littlefield—the first gift the janitor had received in seven years of work at the college. Littlefield not only brooded over the gift, but he was troubled because talk on the street had it that 'they'll sure find Dr. Parkman's body somewhere in the Medical College.' Medical colleges in those days were held to be notorious receivers of the products of professional body snatchers.

'I got tired,' said Littlefield in explaining his next move, 'of all that talk.' Accordingly, into his dismal basement apartment at the college he lugged drills, hammers, chisels, crowbars. He told his startled wife that he was going to dig through the brick vault under Professor Webster's laboratory room. Mrs. Littlefield was dreadfully frightened; suspicion of a Harvard professor was an act against nature, perhaps even against God.

A few days before Parkman's disappearance, the janitor explained to her, he was helping Webster in his laboratory. Suddenly Dr. Parkman appeared before them. 'Dr. Webster,' he cried, 'are you ready for me tonight?' Webster replied: 'No, I am not ready tonight.' Parkman shook his cane. 'Dr. Webster,' he said savagely, 'something must be accomplished tomorrow.' Then he left.

For the next several days, Littlefield had brooded and wondered whether on the next call Professor Webster *had* been ready. 'And *now*,' said the janitor to his wife, 'what do you think?'

So on Thanksgiving Day, while the turkey sputtered in the oven, he hammered and drilled his way into the solid brick wall. Progress was slow, but Littlefield was as determined as he was suspicious. At noon he refreshed himself with the great bird and cranberries, then returned to his labors. He continued his work on Friday, after his regular duties, and that night broke through. 'I held my light forward,' he related, 'and the first thing I saw was the pelvis of a man and two parts of a leg. I knew,' he added darkly, 'this was no place for such things.'

Littlefield called the police. Within a short time Webster was in a cell of the city jail. Next day the press and the town went delirious. 'Horrible Suspicions!!' screamed the normally sedate *Transcript*. 'Arrest of Professor J. W. Webster!' Harvard College and Beacon Hill seemed about to tumble into the Charles River.

Professor Webster was put on trial on the nineteenth of March, 1850. The state's star witness, janitor Littlefield, took the stand and his testimony was bad indeed for the professor. The defense presented a long and distinguished array of character and other witnesses. President Sparks of Harvard thought Webster 'kind and humane.' Nathaniel Bowditch, son of the celebrated mathematician, believed Webster to be 'irritable though kind-hearted.' Oliver Wendell Holmes testified both for the defense and the state. For the latter, he said that whoever had cut up the body alleged to be that of Dr. Parkman had certainly been handy with surgical knives.

The state was attempting to prove that the remnants of human mortality discovered in the vault—and in the laboratory stove—were those of Dr. Parkman; and the defense was doing its best to prove the fragments to have been almost anybody but Dr. Parkman. Day after day the trial continued and much of Boston sought to get into the courtroom. The marshal cleared the visitors' gallery every ten minutes, thus permitting thousands of persons to witness portions of the event of the century.

Slowly the coils closed around Professor Webster; and late on the eleventh day the jury was charged by Chief Justice Lemuel Shaw in an address which is still considered by lawyers to be one of the great expositions of all time on the subject of circumstantial evidence. Three hours later the jury returned a verdict of guilty.

Long before Professor Webster was hanged on August 30, 1850, he made a confession. On that fatal Friday, Parkman had called Webster a scoundrel and furiously shaken his cane in the professor's face. Then, said Webster, 'I felt nothing but the sting of his words, and in my fury I seized a stick of wood and dealt him a blow with all the force that passion could give it.' One blow was enough. Parkman fell, bleeding at the mouth. Webster bolted the doors, stripped the dead man, hoisted him into the sink and then dismembered him with the deft professional strokes that had been admired by Dr. Holmes.

The painful celebrity that came to Harvard has been dissipated in the century that has intervened, but more than one member of the faculty long felt the blight cast by Professor Webster. Bliss Perry once related how his mother, at Williamstown, Massachusetts, refused to entertain a Harvard professor who had come there, some twenty years after the crime, as a delegate to a convention of New England college officials. Mrs. Perry vowed firmly that she could not sleep 'if one of those Harvard professors was in the house.' The professor who had to find quarters elsewhere was James Russell Lowell.

Another incident concerns the lawyer (later the Union general) Ben Butler, to whom Harvard had somehow neglected to grant an LL.D. While he was cross-examining a witness in court, and treating him rather roughly, the judge intervened to remind Butler that the witness was no less than a Harvard professor. 'Yes, I know, Your Honor,' said Ben. 'We hanged one the other day.'

Professor Webster's fame is secure. He remains the only Harvard professor to have performed lethally while a member of the faculty, and the sole college professor to gain entrance to the chaste pages of the *Dictionary of American Biography* on the strength of his stout right arm.

S.H.H.

# 1855

## WILLIAM PALMER
### The Amazing Autopsy

More then 100 years ago there took place one of the most incredible farces in the history of medical jurisprudence. This was the first autopsy on the body of John Parsons Cook, performed before an audience of townspeople on November 26, 1855, in the assembly room of the Talbot Hotel at Rugeley, in Staffordshire.

Cook was a gambler and racehorse owner who had died at the age of twenty-seven, five days previously. He had been a heavy drinker, but free from any disease which could have caused his death. One of his close friends, who was also his suspected murderer, was another owner and gambler—thirty-one-year-old Dr. William Palmer of Rugeley.

It was high time, indeed, that Palmer was suspected of something. For some twelve years past this urbane little man, who had a certain superficial charm, had left behind him a trail of mysterious deaths. He solved even minor personal problems with a dose of poison.

Palmer is an interesting example of the effects of heredity and environment. His father was a swindler and his mother a woman of loose character. Many relatives on both sides of his family were drunkards and degenerates. But Palmer senior was at least a successful swindler, for when he died in 1836 he left his family £75,000. His son William was then twelve years old, and the boy's character must have been influenced not only by his awful ancestry, but by being brought up in an atmosphere of drink, immorality and easy money.

Apprenticed to a Liverpool chemist, William Palmer stole money and was dismissed after a few months. As pupil to a doctor he continued to steal. And before he was eighteen he had had illegitimate children by no fewer than fourteen different girls. He then went to continue his studies in medicine (and sex) at Stafford Infirmary.

Palmer went on to St. Bartholomew's Hospital, where he

found it much more interesting to study anatomy in Piccadilly than in lecture halls. He would never have qualified had not his mother promised £100 to a crammer if he would get Palmer through his final examinations. The crammer succeeded, and William Palmer became a M.R.C.S. in 1846 (as did Dr. Pritchard, another notorious wife-killer). But when the crammer had to fight for his fee in the courts, the resulting unpleasant publicity should have warned the good people of Rugeley that the young doctor putting up his brass plate in their High Street had not made a very encouraging start in his profession.

During the year after he qualified, Palmer married Annie Thornton, pretty, illegitimate daughter of a wealthy but unbalanced Army colonel, one of five brothers who all shot themselves. Annie and her bad-tempered, drunken mother inherited some £20,000, which is probably why Palmer married her. He must have been shocked to find that as a ward in Chancery she could draw little more than the interest on her capital. So it paid him in the meantime to keep her alive.

Within a year of his marriage he was borrowing money from his mother-in-law, who detested him but paid up for her daughter's sake. In January, 1849, Palmer invited the old lady to stay at Rugeley, and she went rather reluctantly, darkly prophesying to a neighbour that she did not expect to live a fortnight. This was an over-estimate, as she was dead within ten days, screaming, 'Take that awful devil away!' when her attentive son-in-law looked reproachfully into the sick-room not long before she died.

The death of Annie's mother from 'apoplexy' was certified by Dr. Bamford, a popular and kindly old man of over eighty with no qualifications but a high reputation. He completely trusted his young colleague, a fact which Palmer found very useful during the next few busy years. Unfortunately the mother-in-law's money seems also to have been tied up in Chancery, so her death may have served to improve Palmer's technique but not his financial position.

During the following year Palmer was at Chester races with a friend named Bladen to whom he lost £600. Bladen won another £500 which he collected in cash, and went off to stay at Rugeley, where Palmer said it would take him a few days to raise £600.

Within that time, however, Bladen was dead. Bamford signed the death certificate, and Palmer tried to convince Mrs. Bladen that her husband had actually died owing him money.

This profitable little exploit was so successful that Palmer almost duplicated it later in the case of a young man named Bly, who won £800 in bets from Palmer, was stricken with a strange illness and quickly died. Bamford signed the death certificate, and Palmer told Mrs. Bly that her husband had died owing £800.

In the meantime Palmer was keeping down the housekeeping expenses by effecting certain small economies fairly regularly. He permitted himself the luxury of keeping one son, but the other four children Annie bore him were slaughtered in infancy, in January, 1851, January and December, 1852, and January, 1854.

'What will people say!' murmured Annie to her sister-in-law. 'My mother died here, then Mr. Bladen, and now all these children!'

People were, in fact, saying plenty, but nobody did anything about it. It was assumed that when Palmer took the babies into his arms he gave them his finger to suck, having previously smeared it with honey and some deadly poison.

Apart from these small savings in the milk bill, the next really profitable proposition on Palmer's list was his Uncle Joseph, from whom he expected to inherit a useful sum. Joseph was, admittedly, no asset to the community as he was a worthless degenerate and, what was more helpful from his nephew's point of vview, a drunkard.

Palmer did not make the mistake of so many series-killers and keep strictly to a set routine, but he did sometimes feel that an artistic plan was too good to be abandoned after merely one success. So he suggested they should have a brandy-drinking competition. Joe eagerly accepted, drank whatever he was given, won, vomited, and died.

Reverting to a method more appropriate, Palmer next invited a wealthy old aunt to stay at Rugeley. To cure a slight indisposition her affectionate nephew gave her a box of pills before he went to bed. But she very ungratefully threw them out of the window, and by what may or may not have been a coincidence all Palmer's poultry were found dead next morning, after which Auntie went home, presumably missing breakfast.

By 1852 Palmer's income from his practice was negligible, which is hardly surprising. But his expenses had increased enormously as he had started his own racing stables at Hednesford where he employed a stableman named Bates, who will be heard of again.

Palmer was consistently unlucky on the turf, and by the end of 1853 he was in a desperate financial mess, blacklisted at Tattersall's for defaulting on bets and keeping other creditors at bay by borrowing from money-lenders at sixty per cent interest. He could offer no security, so he began to forge documents in the name of his mother, who was known to be worth some £30,000.

These loans eventually reached a total of about £16,000, with another £4,000 for interest and renewal charges.

He had by this time enlisted the help of two disreputable racing friends who should have been respected local characters. One was a rascally solicitor named Jeremiah Smith, one of the former lovers of Palmer's now sixty-year-old mother. Another was Cheshire, the Rugeley postmaster, who intercepted letters containing writs or demands for payment which might have made the old lady suspicious. Early in 1854 a substantial sum had to be raised somehow. So with Jerry Smith's professional assistance Palmer tried to insure his wife's life for £25,000.

He eventually succeeded in taking out a policy for £13,000 within a few days of killing the latest of his legitimate children. The annual premium was £760, and the insurance company apparently did not think it at all strange that a debt-ridden country doctor with a moribund practice should be so anxious to pay £15 per week for a life policy on a healthy twenty-seven-year-old wife.

From the moment the first premium was paid, with a handsome commission to Jerry Smith, Annie Palmer was doomed, and it is surprising that she survived so long. It was not until September of that year that she was taken ill. She was attended by Dr. Bamford, of course, also by a Dr. Knight, and was given pills by her attentive husband when his colleagues were out of the way.

Annie died nine days after taking to her bed, from what Dr. Knight certified as English cholera, but which was, in fact, antimony poisoning. That night the bereaved husband wrote in his diary: 'My darling Annie was called to-day by her God to the home of bliss so well deserved.'

A day or two later he demanded £13,000 from the insurance company, and finished a very satisfactory week by going with his seven-year-old son to take Communion on Sunday. He recorded the fact in his diary: 'Went with Willie to Church—Sacrament.'

Despite a warning that they should not pay without making investigation, the insurance company sent Palmer a cheque for £13,000 six weeks later, and the price of Annie's life was immediately grabbed by the moneylenders. So he was not much better off, and had to get busy with the next case on his death-list—his brother Walter.

It was a month or two before this could be put through, while he tried to insure Walter for a mere £82,000. The attitude of some companies was really hurtful.

At last, with the help of one of his moneylenders named Pratt, Palmer managed to insure Walter for £14,000. To such a lavish spender as Palmer it was a trifling sum, but it was much more than Walter was worth alive, anyway.

A busybody who might have wrecked the whole scheme was Walter's doctor, Wadell. He reported to the insurance company that his drink-sodden patient, who had tried to cut his own throat in a fit of *delirium tremens,* was 'healthy, robust and temperate.' But he added, rather unkindly, 'Most confidential. His life has been rejected in two offices. I am told he drinks. His brother insured his late wife's life for many thousands, and after first payment she died. Be cautious.' The fact that the company accepted the policy indicates either that the directors were half-witted, or that they never intended to pay out.

So debt-ridden brother William paid over a first premium of £780 (£120 being commission to Pratt the moneylender). And a slight snag, that when Walter died the money would be paid to his wife, was overcome by William's promising to lend Walter £400 in return for all rights under the policy being made over to himself. Which formalities cleared the air for Walter's now inevitable death.

Six months later Walter became ill, in spite of the restorative effects of drinking a quart of gin every day and three pints every night, as was sworn in evidence at the trial. Brother William generously paid for as much brandy as Walter could swallow, and gave him boxes of pills which he said, untruthfully, had been sent by Dr. Waddell—pills which the agonised Walter described as 'twisters.'

Duringg the last few days of his life he still drank three bottles of gin and brandy every day, and the only solids he consumed were in the form of prussic acid pills supplied by William. The end came on August 16, 1855, and within one hour of the death William had ordered a strong double coffin and had telegraphed to Shrewsbury racecourse for the winner of the Ludlow Stakes.

The results were not immediately satisfactory. The insurance company delayed making payment, and a demand to Walter's widow that she should forthwith settle a non-existent debt owing to brother William was rudely ignored.

But despite these little set-backs Palmer kept a stiff upper lip. He drank heavily but was never known to be intoxicated. His manner remained calm and composed, and his round, fresh-complexioned face usually bore the hint of a little smile. The sight of his victims lingering in dull pain or contorted with swift agony never affected the urbanity of his bedside manner.

Within a few weeks of Walter's unprofitable death the moneylenders were pressing Palmer for £4,000 interest and charges, which still left the original debt of £16,000 unpaid. So Palmer, feeling, perhaps, that there is no rest for the wicked, looked up his death-list, and sent a flattering dinner invitation to his stableman, Bates. And after a good meal Bates was persuaded to sign an application for a £10,000 life policy, one of several attempts totalling £25,000 on the life of a man who was little more than an illiterate labourer.

The £10,000 policy eventually went through, with the help of Jerry Smith, of whom the Attorney-General was to say at the trial, 'I blush for the legal profession to number such a man upon its roll.' And the insurance company were so delighted with this new business that they made Jerry their local agent and paid him five per cent on a first premium of £500.

But on second thoughts the company decided to send a couple of investigators to have a word with Mr. George Bates, who was described on the proposal form as a gentleman with a private income of £400 a year, 'living independent with good property and possessing a fine cellar of wine.'

The detectives found this fine old English gentleman spreading manure for a wage of twenty-four shillings a week.

They went round to see Palmer and said: 'The office has decided convictions that your brother was poisoned for the purpose of obtaining the £14,000 insurance money . . . and if a claim is preferred it will at once be met with a charge of murder.'

Wounded by these implications, and hounded to desperation by the moneylenders, Palmer had to start seeking not merely a new victim but also a new method of making murder pay.

On Tuesday, November 13, 1855, Palmer was at Shrewsbury races with a group of friends, and marked down as his next victim a man—it might have been anybody—who happened to have won a lot of money on Polestar in the Shrewsbury Handicap.

There cannot by any sentiment in business, but Palmer may even have felt a slight tinge of regret that he must kill his old friend John Parsons Cook. The decision must have been made very quickly, because Cook would not have been worth sixpennyworth of strychnine before the result of the race was known that afternoon.

But after the race Cook collected some £800 in cash and about £1,250 became payable to him at Tattersall's in London for credit bets. So leaving his friends to a drunken celebration at the Raven Hotel in Shrewsbury, which must have been a wrench, Palmer dashed home to Rugeley after the races, collected a supply of tartar emetic, in which the active poison is antimony, and was back in Shrewsbury early the following morning.

The first act of Operation Cook took place that evening, when a woman at the Raven Hotel saw Palmer in a pantry pouring a colourless liquid into a glass. He went into the lounge where the party was still going on, and shortly afterwards Cook took a swig of brandy and sprang to his feet crying out, 'Good God, how it burns my throat!' He became very ill, was put to bed, handed his £800 cash to a friend for safe custody and said, 'I believe that damned Palmer has been dosing me!'

From the fact that he did not die it may be assumed that Palmer did not know what was a fatal dose of tartar emetic, or else he did not allow for loss of poison by prolonged vomiting. He seems still to have had quite a lot to learn about poisoning.

Next morning Cook was well enough to walk to the racecourse, and he might never have been murdered if Palmer's horse, The Chicken, had won and broughtt its owner the £5000 for which it had been backed. But The Chicken was unplaced, and Cook was doomed.

Killer and victim went that night to Rugeley, where Cook booked a room at the Talbot Hotel, almost opposite to Palmer's house, and—still shaky after that ghastly cocktail of brandy and tartar emetic—went straight to bed.

Cook spent most of the next day in bed. The day after that, a Saturday, was busier. Palmer arrived at the hotel early and took some coffee up to Cook, who became very ill and vomited frequently, whilst Palmer bustled in and out of his room with food and medicines. On Sunday morning Palmer brought along his ancient stooge, Dr. Bamford, who was being groomed for signing another death certificate. It was to be the ninth he signed for known victims of Palmer's.

During the afternoon Jerry Smith sent Cook a bowl of soup from the Albion Hotel—not direct from one hotel to the other, which would have been unusual in itself, but via Palmer's house where it remained for an hour. It must have been very tasty soup because a Talbot Hotel chambermaid was tempted to sample a spoonful, after which she was very sick and spent the rest of the day in bed. Cook had taken only one or two spoonfuls when he also was sick, and was very ill all night.

At seven o'clock next morning Palmer looked in and must have been upset ot find that Cook was still alive. But he concealed his disappointment under a brave smile, quietly stole Cook's betting book, and said he must pop up to London on business. The business was to persuade a commission agent to collect winnings listed in the book as due to Cook, which Palmer could not do himself as Tattersall's had banned him. After collection the amounts were to be paid to the more threatening of Palmer's creditors.

The agent did his job conscientiously, assuming of course that the debts were owed not by Palmer but by Cook himself. He wrote to Cook to that effect, but the letter was tactfully intercepted by Cheshire, the Rugeley postmaster, and handed to Palmer, who had thus gained a little more time. But even after that highly successful trip to town Palmer's work for the day was not yet finished. He rushed back to Rugeley, collected three grains of strychnine, and looked in to see how his old friend Cook was progressing.

That strychnine was obtained gratis from a youngster named Newton, one of Palmer's drinking companions. He was assistant to a Dr. Salt, another Rugeley physician, and served in an 'open surgery' which was little more than a pharmacy where deadly poisons were sold across the counter.

There is conflict of evidence as to what happened at half-past ten that night in the sour atmosphere of Cook's sick-room, lit only by a single candle. Palmer may not have been really surprised to learn that during his absence in London, when other hands had given the invalid his meals and medicines, Cook had felt well enough to get up and talk to his trainer. But an hour after Palmer left him Cook was screaming and beating the bed in his agony, and when Palmer was sent for and gave him a drink, Cook's teeth snapped at the glass, which is a symptom of strychnine poisoning.

After a night of terrible torment, Cook was still obstinately alive next morning, however, and told a chambermaid, 'The pills Palmer gave me at half-past ten made me ill.'

Nettled by Cook's selfish refusal to die, Palmer was up early that morning and bought six more grains of strychnine from another pharmacy. To be on the safe side he also bought a supply of opium solution and some prussic acid. He tried to hide from Newton, who happened to come into the shop just then. But Newton was informed by the chemist that Palmer, who had had no practice for years, had just 'bought enough poison for the whole parish.'

That afternoon Palmer cunningly called in a third doctor, a Dr. Jones, who seems to have been just about as dotty as poor old Bamford. And that night, after Cook had had a disappointingly peaceful day, Palmer produced some pills from a box labelled in Bamford's handwriting and persuaded Cook to swallow two of them. Shortly after midnight Cook was shouting in agony again, his whole body contorted and jerking. When Palmer was sent for he arrived so quickly that he must obviously have been waiting up fully dressed to called.

By one o'clock, under the professionally calm gaze of Palmer, Cook died. 'The poor devil's gone,' Palmer remarked casually to the shocked chambermaids. He was caught by a maid, a little later, feeling under Cook's pillow. He handed Dr. Jones a watch and £5 which he said were in Cook's pockets. The balance of the £800 and the betting book had disappeared.

Cook's stepfather, an irritable but shrewd retired merchant named Stevens, who hated Palmer, arrived in Rugeley on the Thursday of that week. Palmer forced his company upon him, and mentioned that Cook owed him £4000, tactfully referring to Cook as 'the poor diseased beggar.' Stevens furiously replied that there would not be four thousand pence in Cook's estate, and asked nastily about that £800.

Insisting upon a post-mortem, Stevens saw the Strafford coroner on Sunday, and arranged for a Dr. Harland to carry it out on the following day. When Palmer heard about this interference in his affairs, he went round on Sunday night to see Newton, and asked whether strychnine could be found in a stomach after death.

'I think not,' said Newton.

'*That's* all right then!' exclaimed Palmer, and snapped his fingers in glee.

So at ten o'clock on the Monday morning, November 26, 1855, the first autopsy on the body of Cook began, a few doors from the room in which he had died. Dr. Harland, a feeble character without much experience, was nominally in charge, but the actual operation was left to two amateurs—Devonshire, who was a new and unqualified assistant to a Rugeley doctor, and Newton, the youngster who had given Palmer the strychnine, who knew absolutely nothing about pathology or anatomy and had never even seen a post-mortem.

Instead of the privacy desirable for such a delicate and vital operation, on which a man's life might depend, this affair attracted a large and excited audience. Those present in the assembly room of the Talbot Hotel, in addition to Harland and his enthusiastic amateurs, included Palmer, Bamford, Jones, two other Rugeley doctors, the crooked lawyer, Jerry Smith; the crooked postmaster, Cheshire; the hotel proprietor, the minister of the chapel and various morbid-minded townspeople.

The scientific equipment provided was, believe it or not, a single glass jar. There were no knives, scalpels or surgicals saws, no lenses, measuring glasses or scales—just one jar. Palmer,

who had arrived straight from a session of drinking brandy
with Newton, kindly offered to fetch his own instruments, but
Devonshire managed to borrow a set from his master.

The hit-or-miss butchery began at last, watched keenly by
Palmer, whose neck was at stake, and less keenly by decrepit
old Dr. Bamford, who stood unsteadily beside him.

Newton hacked out the stomach and handed it to Devonshire,
who tied the ends and proudly held it up for everyone to see.
A man's life would depend upon what a London analyst might
find among the fluids in the stomach. Then, for no reason it is
possible to conceive, Devonshire slit the stomach open from end
to end.

What followed was pure slapstick. Palmer was seen to
give Newton a deliberate shove—Newton, who had been
drinking brandy, cannoned against Devonshire—Devonshire
nearly dropped the stomach, and spilt practically all its contents.
When the lurching operators had regained their balance, the
empty and now useless organ was flung into the jar. Palmer
slapped his aged neighbour jovially on the back and said, 'They
won't hang us yet, Bamford!'

When order had been restored, Newton snipped off about a
yard of the intestines, which was thrown into the jar to become
well shaken up with the empty stomach. Harland tied and
sealed a double cover on the jar, and the audience resumed
watching the fumblings of Newton and Devonshire. Suddenly
a hue-and-cry was raised. Where was the jar? Actually Palmer
had grabbed it and scuttled out of the room with it. This irritated
even the long-suffering Harland, and during the ensuing fuss
Palmer reappeared, explaining that he thought the jar would
be 'more handy to take away' if he placed it near the door.
During the excitement the covers had been slit open and had
to be re-sealed. What medico-legal value the contents might by
then have retained seems problematical.

The jar was later to be taken by cab to the station, and Palmer
offered the driver ten pounds if he would overturn the cab and
smash the jar. 'A lot of fuss is being made about this affair
which is a humbugging concern;' he confided to the cabman,
who, however, churlishly refused to turn over his cab.

So the jar was eventually reached Professor Taylor, pathologist at Guy's Hospital, London, for analysis. It is hardly

surprising that in the stomach he found no strychnine, nor, indeed, anything else. 'The contents, if any,' he reported, 'had entirely drained away from it.' So Palmer still had a little more time.

A second autopsy had to be held, of course, and drugs now found in other organs examined were almost enough to hang Palmer.

Nine days after he died Cook was buried, and Palmer was weeping as he walked behind the coffin with Jerry Smith. The inquest had been fixed for December 5, after an adjournment, and on the day after the funeral Palmer dried his eyes and sent the coroner a gift of fish. He followed up this peace-offering a day or two later with a handsome hamper of game.

Then Cheshire dashed in excitedly one morning with Professor Taylor's report from London, which the postmaster had steamed open in transit and showed to Palmer before having it delivered. So, on December 13, the day after the inquest was reopened after a second adjournment, Palmer committed an act of almost incredible lunacy.

He wrote the coroner a long letter advising him to return a verdict of 'natural causes,' and clearly revealed that he had read Professor Taylor's report before it had reached its destination.

'Whatever Professor Taylor may say to-morrow,' said Palmer, 'he wrote from London . . . to say "We have finished our analysis, and find no trace of either strychnine, prussic acid or opium." . . . Mind you I know and saw it in black and white, what Taylor said.'

And as a parting insult to the outraged coroner Palmer enclosed a ten-pound note.

At eleven o'clock the next night, December 15, the inquest closed with a verdict of murder against Palmer. Police hurried across the road in the darkness to arrest him, and found that a sheriff's officer had just arrested him for forgery.

The bodies of Annie and Walter were exhumed a week later, and after the inquests a Grand Jury at Stafford returned a true bill against Palmer in March, 1956, in the cases of Annie and Cook. By this time public feeling could not have expected a fair trial in Staffordshire. During one of his journeys in custody, in fact, he had to be guarded by soldiers as well as police. So a special Act was rushed through Parliament—still known as Palmer's Act—enabling cases in which local juries might be influenced by prejudice to be tried at the Old Bailey in London.

And it was there, after a sensational fourteen-day trial in May, 1856, that William Palmer was at long last found guilty of murder and sentenced to death.

His behaviour at the end showed that he had either much courage or no imagination—if there is any difference. For in the very shadow of the scaffold he made grim little jokes and it is difficult not to feel a final fleeting spark of sympathy with a man who can do that.

True to what seems to be the unwritten code of the poisoners, Palmer refused to confess even on the morning of his execution, June 14, 1856.

With the hangman waiting to bind him, Palmer was offered a glass of wine. It had been poured out by someone with an understandably shaky hand, and there were bubbles on the surface. As Palmer blew off the bubbles he said, 'They always give me indigestion next morning if I drink in a hurry.'

The scaffold had been erected at midnight in the street outside the prison. Thirty thousand people had assembled, hundreds having waited all night. Prices for reserved seats in the twenty-three specially erected grandstands cost up to one guinea each. Palmer climbed the primitive ladder calmly—no easy feat with his arms strapped to his side—surveyed the vast hostile mob, and glanced up at the rope so that he should stand directly beneath it.

If he died without repentance, he did not die without dignity.

The story is told that a deputation of Rugeley residents later visited the Home Secretary, requesting permission to change the name of a town to which the murders had brought such unpleasant notoriety. He listened patiently whilst they put their case to him, and at last nodded. 'Yes,' he said, 'and why not name the place after me?'

The Home Secretary was Lord Palmerston.

G.D.

# 1859

# DOCTOR SMETHURST

## Parsimony and the Poisoner

---

That Dr. Smethurst murdered Isabella Bankes admits of no doubt, and it is difficult to approve of the action of the Home Secretary, who released him after he had been sentenced to death at the Old Bailey.

Smethurst owed his extraordinary escape to the way he tricked the expert Dr. Taylor into committing a blunder which enabled the defence to score its only point. It was a contest of wits between the quack and the expert, and for once the quack won.

Smethurst's disinclination for the hard work of his profession was the chief cause why he married a woman twenty years older than himself who had sufficient means to meet their weekly bill at the boarding-house in Bayswater, where they were residing when Isabella Bankes made their acquaintance.

Miss Bankes was one of those discontented women who in the late twenties look forty and are apt to pass their dull lives accumulating grievances. She was twenty-eight and decidedly commonplace, and the Smethursts took no notice of her until the doctor heard that the possessed between five and six thousand pounds.

Isabella Bankes had lived in the same house with Mrs. Smethurst, and yet for some strange reason she consented to marry the doctor.

It may be that Smethurst persuaded her that Mrs. Smethurst was not his legal wife. Whatever the reason the marriage of Thomas Smethurst and Isabella Bankes took place at Battersea Parish Church.

Smethurst's plan was to get her completely in his power, persuade her to make a will leaving her small fortune to him, and then dispose of her with the aid of arsenic, so that her money might come to him at once.

From the church they went to Richmond, and there they secured lodgings, and Isabella, pathetically proud of her new status, was so happy that she became really young for the first time in her life.

The few persons who met her were struck by her youth and her health, and it was therefore with a start of surprise that three days later they heard she was unable to leave her bed.

Her so-called husband went to a local doctor, and explained that his wife was suffering from an acute attack of biliousness, and when Dr. Julius called he prescribed a simple remedy and promised to come the next morning.

It was on the occasion of his second visit that he was alarmed by certain symptoms which at once suggested to him that the lady was being poisoned. His partner, Dr. Bird, confirmed his suspicions.

Meanwhile Smethurst, apparently unaware of what the doctors were saying about him, brought a solicitor to Isabella's bedside, and listened to her as she gave instructions for her will.

The two local doctors, after hesitating as to what they ought to do, informed the police of their suspicions, and the will was not twenty-four hours old when Dr. Smethurst was arrested on a charge of attempting to murder his wife by administering arsenic to her.

He protested his innocence, and as a result of appeals to the magistrate to release him so that he might attend the woman he professed to love he was discharged before a case against him could be made out.

It might have been supposed that he would have stayed his hand now, but the prospect of obtaining a few thousand pounds was sufficient to make him run the most terrible risk of all.

He might have been more careful had he not invented a plan which he was sure would put the authorities off the track and place him in a position to confound the experts to whom the task of analysing the content's of his wife's body might be entrusted.

His plan was the result of an article in the *Lancet* by a famous doctor explaining how the then recognised test for determining arsenic in the human body could be defeated.

The day after Smethurst's release by the order of the magistrates Isabella Bankes died, and the doctors who had attended her had no doubt whatever that she had been poisoned.

With this the police agreed, and for the second time Smethurst was taken into custody.

And now Dr. Taylor, the expert the Crown always retained in cases of murder by poisoning, appeared on the scene.

He believe that the arsenic must have been given to the woman in her medicine, and when he was shown the room where she had died he looked for a bottle which did not bear the labels of Dr. Bird and Dr. Julius, and containing some sort of liquid in which arsenic could have been mixed without betraying its presence.

Five minutes after he had entered the room he found a bottle nearly full of a colourless liquid, and this he guessed must be what he was in search of.

He took away the mysterious liquid, and apply to it what is known as Reinsch's test. This consists in mixing a small quantity of hydrochloric acid with the liquid to be tested, and then dropping the mixture into a copper gauze. If there is any arsenic present it will attach itself to the gauze.

Information having reached Smethurst of the proposed test, he offered no objection, merely asking that the remaining contents of the bottle should be preserved, and this was agreed to.

A little later he was informed that Dr. Taylor had reported that as a result of his experiment he had found arsenic in the gauze, and that therefore the case against the accused would be further strengthened by the renowned doctor's unfavourable opinion of his innocence. Smethurst heard this unmoved, because he knew better.

We know now that Smethurst purposely placed that bottle in such a position that Dr. Taylor could not fail to find it, and we also know that its contents included chlorate of potash, which the letter in the *Lancet* had stated would defeat Reinsch's test.

It was the intention of the poiisoner to instruct his counsel to dispute Dr. Taylor's evidence and thereby throw discredit on the prosecution and cause the jury to give him the benefit of the doubt.

But the Home Office expert discovered before the trial came on that he had made a mistake. He had the liquid examined again and discovered that there was no arsenic in it, and that the arsenic he had found in the gauze had emanated from the gauze itself.

The trick had succeeded, but the prosecution had plenty of evidence independent of Dr. Taylor's that Isabella Bankes had died of acute arsenical poisoning, and that the only person who could have administered it to her was the prisoner.

The defence laboured in vain so far as the jury was concerned, and rightly eliminating the evidence of Dr. Taylor, they judged the case on its own merits and found the prisoner guilty on 19th August 1859.

His condemnation to death was the signal for an outburst by those cranks who delight in pitying the living at the expense of the dead, and who clamour for mercy for the prisoner and forget his victim.

On this occasion it succeeded, and the public were astounded when they heard that Dr. Smethurst had been released.

It was thought that he would be discreet enough to leave the country immediately, but Thomas Smethurst had risked his neck for Isabella Bankes's money and he meant to get it; it mattered nothing to him that her friends and relations insisted on a charge of bigamy being brought against him. He waited to be arrested, and with amazing impudence he pleaded guilty, smiling with relief when the judge sentenced him to twelve months' imprisonment.

During his life in jail he was gradually forgotten by a public satiated by fresh sensations almost weekly, and it was therefore with more than ordinary surprise that they read in their newspapers one morning the statement that Dr. Smethurst, having served his year, was free again and had applied to the courts for probate of the will of Isabella Bankes.

As the will was in order, and as Smethurst's conviction for murder had been quashed by the Home Secretary, the judge acceded to his request.

For the next few years Smethurst led an irregullar life, and the money for which he had risked so much did not save him from dying in squalid misery and being buried in a pauper's grave.

C.K.

# 1865

# DOCTOR PRITCHARD

## Seducer and Slayer

---

Many murderers, long before their crime is revealed, disclose the trait of character which, when they are subjected to pressure,
leads them to kill. In a thousand little ways they expose their greed, their vanity, their viciousness, their cruelty, and their callousness.

Pritchard's weakness was vanity. He was a prodigious liar, for self-aggrandisement. He told fantastic stories about himself, stories from which he could get no material gain. He talked vividly of places he had never visited and posed as a friend of the Italian Liberator, Garibaldi, whom he had never met. He deceived himself more than others. He was quite convinced that he loved his wife whom he had slowly poisoned: he had the lid of the coffin lifted so that he could kiss her on the lips.

No adequate motive has been advanced why Pritchard murdered his wife. It is certain that he killed his mother-in-law because she suspected that her daughter was being poisoned. As regards the wife, it was suggested that Pritchard killed her to secure a life interest in two-thirds of the sum of £2,500, which seems inadequate, or to marry the young servant whom he had long before made his mistress, which seems unlikely.

Like many murderers, Pritchard was in financial difficulties and he was a seducer of woman. But the death of his wife was likely to add to rather than to reduce his difficulties. She did not interfere with his seductions and without her he would have had to provide someone to look after his children of whom he was very fond.

The most likely explanation is that Dr. Pritchard killed his wife chiefly to demonstrate to himself that he could do so without being detected. It would have pleased his vanity to be an unsuspected murderer. His frank confession to both murders on the night before his execution supports this view. He was an exhibitionist who was with difficulty restrained from addressing the crowd round the scaffold.

Born in 1825, the son of a Captain in the Royal Navy, Pritchard was apprenticed to a surgeon in Portsmouth. In 1846 he was commissioned as an assistant surgeon in the Navy in which he served until 1851. He married Mary Jane Taylor and he commenced practice at Hunmanby in Yorkshire.

Of his life at this period the *Sheffield Telegraph* wrote, after his conviction, fourteen years later: 'He was fluent, plausible, amorous, politely impudent and singularly untruthful. One who knew him well at Filey describes him as the 'prettiest liar' he ever met with. He pushed his way into publicity as a prominent member of the body of Freemasons, and made that body a means of advertising himself. His amativeness led him into some amours that did not increase the public confidence in him as a professional man: and his unveracity became so notorious that, in his attempt to deceive others, he succeeded only in deceiving himself. He was soon found out.'

In 1858 Pritchard, having been 'found out' sold his practice and, after travelling abroad for a year as medical adviser to a gentleman, he started a practice in Glasgow. But it was not long before his reputation there was similar to his reputation in Yorkshire. The other doctors of the city soon had Pritchard weighed up and he was unable to find anyone willing to propose him as a Fellow of the Faculty of Physicians and Surgeons. He had the effrontery to apply for the Andersonian Chair of Surgery, saying that he had had 'many opportunities, in almost every part of the world, of gaining practical experience and promulgating the principles of modern surgery'. The testimonials he submitted were in the names of famous English doctors, none of whom could possibly have heard of him. He was not given the post.

To build up a practice, and to satisfy his own vanity, it was necessary for Pritchard to become well known and popular and to this end he lectured on his travels and exploited his membership of the Freemasons. 'I have plucked the eaglets from their eyries in the deserts of Arabia, and hunted the Nubian lion in the prairies of North America,' he would say, or describe his sojourn in the South Seas, seldom telling the same version twice. But the most extraordinary display of vanity was his distribution of photographs of himself to all and sundry. He even gave one to a stranger encountered on a train.

Although nothing greater than suspicion was created at the time, Dr. Pritchard probably started his career as a murderer in 1863. A fire broke out at his house and a servant girl died. The fire started in her room but there was no indication that she had attempted to leave it, and the most likely inference is that she was already dead or unconscious when the fire started. How else could she have died of asphyxia and why else did her body exhibit no muscular contortion?

Moving elsewhere Pritchard engaged another servant, fifteen-year-old Mary M'Leod whom he soon seduced, and was later to accuse of the murders for which he was charged. Not long afterwards the Pritchards moved again to a house purchased for them by Mrs. Taylor, Mrs. Pritchard's mother. There in 1864 the doctor was discovered by his wife kissing Mary M'Leod, who was to swear at his trial that Pritchard had promised he would marry her after Mrs. Pritchard's death.

In November 1864, Mrs. Pritchard fell ill, taking to her bed, but getting better, she went to stay with her family in Edinburgh, and returned apparently in the best of health. She soon became ill again with vomiting and sickness, and she remained in her own room from then until her death in March 1865.

On the 8th December, Dr. Pritchard bought an ounce of Flemming's Tincture of Aconite, which is six times stronger than the ordinary tincture and he made three further similar purchases in the next three months.

On the 1st February Mrs. Pritchard became worse; she was in great pain and suffered from cramp. Her husband called in a relative, a Dr. Cowan from Edinburgh, to see her but he did not consider her to be seriously ill, and returned to Edinburgh. That night she became worse and Pritchard sent for a local doctor, Dr. Gairdner to whom he said his wife was suffering from catalepsy. Gairdner came a second time but was not asked to call again.

Dr. Gairdner however, was suspicious. He wrote to Mrs. Pritchard's brother, Dr. Michael Taylor, recommending Mrs. Pritchard's removal from her home, but when a visit to Dr. Taylor was suggested Dr. Pritchard declared that his wife was too ill to travel. When she heard of her daughter's illness, Mrs. Taylor set off for Glasgow.

Whether or not Mrs. Taylor suspected that something was wrong, Pritchard decided that she had to die, for while she remained at her daughter's bedside, his hands were tied. On the day of her arrival Mrs. Taylor, after eating some tapioca from a packet, which after Pritchard's arrest was found to contain antimony, became ill with symptoms exactly similar to her daughter's. Five days later Pritchard purchased another ounce of Fleming's Tincture of Aconite.

Mrs. Taylor recovered and until the 24th February lived in her daughter's room. That night at ten o'clock, screams were heard from the sickroom and the servants found Mrs. Taylor trying to be sick. When Pritchard came in he sent for yet another doctor, Dr. Patterson, to whom he said that Mrs. Taylor had been seized with apoplexy, adding, quite untruthfully, that 'she was in the habit of taking a drop'. He told Dr. Patterson also that his wife had been ill for some time with gastric fever.

Dr. Patterson found Mrs. Taylor lying fully dressed on her daughter's bed and it came to the conclusion that she was under the influence of some powerful narcotic. Mrs. Pritchard, Dr. Patterson thought, was under the influence of antimony. He said that Mrs. Taylor was dying and that nothing could be done. She died during the night.

Fortunately for Pritchard, a circumstance of Mrs. Taylor's life provided him with an opportunity to account for her death. She was in the habit of taking a patent medicine containing opium and Pritchard was able to suggest that she had taken too much. After his arrest the bottle she had in her pocket was found to contain both antimony and aconite. When Dr. Patterson was asked by Dr. Taylor for a certificate of his mother's death he refused to give it, and he wrote to the Registrar of Deaths, describing Mrs. Taylor's death as 'sudden, unexpected, and to him mysterious'.

Dr. Pritchard got out of the difficulty by certifying the death himself, attributing it to primary cause, paralysis, secondary, apoplexy. But as any doctor knows, paralysis is the result, not the cause of apoplexy.

Meanwhile Pritchard requested Dr. Patterson to visit his wife. Calling while Pritchard was in Edinburgh for his mother-in-law's funeral, Dr. Patterson came to the same conclusion as before—that Mrs. Pritchard was suffering from the effects of antimony.

Dr. Pritchard's final assault on his wife's life commenced with the week of the 13th March. That day he bought his final ounce of aconite.

The same night he sent his wife up a piece of cheese for her supper. Finding the taste nasty, Mrs. Pritchard gave it to the maid who remarked that it burned her throat. The cheese was taken back to the kitchen. Next morning, the cook, who also ate a piece, became violently ill.

His next attempt was on the 15th. The medium this time was a bowl of egg-flip to which he added two lumps of sugar, which he obtained himself, ostensibly from his consulting room which led from the dining-room. After drinking a full glass, Mrs. Pritchard was violently sick and suffered great pain. The cook, who also partook of the flip, had the same symptoms.

During the afternoon of the 17th, the cook entered the sickroom unexpectedly and found Pritchard giving his wife a drink. Shortly afterwards she had a severe attack of cramp and became delirious. When Dr. Patterson was called he wrote out a prescription for a sleeping draught and left, which, in light of his previous suspicious, was somewhat extraordinary.

That night Mrs. Pritchard died. Told that his wife was dead Pritchard exclaimed: Come back, come back, my dear Jane, don't leave your dear Edward'. He certified the cause of death as gastric fever and took the body to Edinburgh for burial. On his return to Glasgow he was arrested on suspicion of having caused his wife's death. The police had received an anonymous letter, which is believed to have been written by Dr. Patterson, although he denied being its author. Mrs. Pritchard's funeral was stopped and Mrs. Taylor was exhumed. Antimony was found in both bodies.

Proof of Dr. Pritchard's guilt was never in doubt. Both his mother-in-law and his wife had died of chronic antimony poisoning, Mrs. Pritchard's body being impregnated with that drug. While there was no direct evidence of administration, he alone had the opportunity and knowledge and he had purchased large quantities of that poison. On the night before his execution, the last public one in Glasgow, he confessed to both murders.

Dr. Pritchard's chief blunder lay in calling in other doctors when he could have certified the deaths himself, as in the end he had to do. It seems an extraordinary mental aberration for a medical plotter of murder to risk the presence of other doctors at the bedsides of his victims. Or did Pritchard think that his colleagues were such fools that they could be easily duped?

R.F.

# 1881

# DOCTOR LAMSON

## 'A Swell Pill-Taker'

It may be said of George Henry Lamson, doctor and poisoner, that his capacity for evil was almost equal to the ease with which he made friends.

The fact that from a very early age he exhibited unmistakable signs of degeneracy and criminality did not prevent him earning a reputation for bravery on the battlefield, or fascinating most people with whom he came in contact by a gentleness of demeanour which was irresistible.

And yet this was the man who carefully planned and carried out one of the most cold-blooded murders in the annals of crime.

In the late summer of 1881 the position of Dr. Lamson was a desperate one. He was not yet thirty, and he could point to a period of honourable service on the battlefields of the Balkans, but his natural inclination for evil, which he had for some time been feeding with morphine, had reduced him to a moral wreck.

He had swindled friends and strangers alike by means of worthless cheques, and there is every reason to believe that he had already attempted to poison the boy who was to be his victim a few months later.

No one ever succeeded in unravelling all the intricacies of Lamson's dark life, but there must have been some tremendous compelling force actuating him when, on his return from a fruitless trip to America, he made up his mind to murder his crippled brother-in-law, and so possess himself of the sum of £1500 to which his wife would be entitled should her brother die before reaching the age of twenty-one.

Lamson's professional attainments were meagre, but he had some knowledge of poisons, and when he selected aconitine as the medium by which Percy John was to be murdered, he believed that it would be very difficult to trace it. The fact that a dose of aconitine would entail an agonising death mattered little to the doctor who had once risked his life to tend the wounded.

Having chosen his poison, the doctor had to go through the formality of purchasing it, and, although the first chemist refused to supply it, he succeeded at the second attempt.

It was now necessary to prepare his brother-in-law for his visit, and, accordingly, he wrote him the following letter:—

'My Dear Percy,—

I had intended running down to Wimbledon to see you to-day, but I have been delayed by various matters until it is now nearly six o'clock, and by the time I could reach Blenheim House you would be preparing for bed.

I leave for Paris to-morrow, and so propose to run down for a few minutes before I go. Believe, my dear boy, your loving brother,

G.H.L.'

Now if there was one person who had every reason to trust implicitly Dr. Lamson, that person was Percy John.

He was nineteen years of age, and, unfortunately, crippled from the waist downwards, but ill-health had not robbed him of his sunny and optimistic disposition, while the inspiration of his young life was an almost idolatrous affection and admiration for his sister's husband. He counted the days between Lamson's visits, wrote constantly to him, and was ever pathetically anxious to spend his holidays with him.

The kindly disposition of the doctor, which had proved so alluring to experienced and cynical men of the world, seems to have hypnotised Percy John, the crippled schoolboy, and when, therefore, he received the doctor's letter he was overjoyed.

Blenheim House School was situated within a minute's walk of Wimbledon station, and at the time Percy John was there the proprietor and headmaster was a Mr. Bedbrook, the story of whose bad luck would fill a column.

But on that December evening when Dr. Lamson called, Mr. Bedbrook had no cause to anticipate any of the tricks fate intended to play on him. His school was prospering, and he was looking forward to enlarging it, unconscious of the pending tragedy in which he was to be involved.

The scene of the murder was the dining-room, and the crime is almost unique in that the poison was administered under the eyes of a witness.

The doctor had come with all his plans for the dreadful deed completed and matured. For days he had considered every possibility of failure and risk, and he was so confident of escaping the consequences that he deliberately invited the presence of the headmaster, so that if he were suspected of causing the death of the schoolboy he could retort by pointing out that he had never once been alone with his brother-in-law.

Immediately on his arrival Lamson had a few minutes' conversation with Mr. Bedbrook, and when a little later Percy John was carried into the room and deposited in an armchair the genial doctor exclaimed, as they shook hands:

'Why, how fat you are looking, Percy, old boy.'

'I wish I cold say the same of you, George,' remarked John, with a glance of of mingled affection and concern.

At this point the pupil who had brought Percy John into the room departed, and the two men and the boy were left alone.

Conversation now became general, and after Lamson had drunk a glass of sherry, in which he had mixed some sugar, brought into the room at his request, he took out of his black leather bag a Dundee cake and some sweets.

Now, there can be no doubt that one slice of the cake was already cut, but Mr. Bedbrook did not observe this, and when Lamson cut the cake and handed a slice to him and then to the boy, and started to eat a piece of it himself, he could be pardoned for having failed to notice the weakest spot in the murderer's plans.

Montagu Williams and Charles Mathews, later knight and Director of Public Prosecutions, both agreed that the dose of aconitine was place in a raisin in the slice of cake which Lamson had cut before he entered Blenheim House School, and as they defended the poisoner at his trial their statement cannot be parried.

Once he had got the poison in the youth's system by means of the Dundee cake, it became essential for the poisoner to strengthen his own position by putting Mr. Bedbrook and, through Mr. Bedbrook, the public and the medical experts on the wrong track.

'Oh, by the way,' he said to the headmaster, 'when I was in America I thought of you and your boys. I thought what excellent things these capsules would be for your boys to take nauseous medicines in. I should like to try one to see how easily they can be swallowed.'

The headmaster fell in with the suggestion, and then Lamson turned to his brother-in-law. 'Here, Percy, you are a swell pill-taker,' he remarked, with a laugh, 'take this and show how easily it may be swallowed.'

Percy John placed the capsule in his mouth and with one gulp it disappeared.

'That's soon gone, my boy,' exclaimed Mr. Bedbrook, and before young John could reply Dr. Lamson stood up and glanced towards the door.

'I must be going now,' he said, hurriedly.

There was some conversation about trains, but it was not of any importance. What was important was the fact that Lamson purposely left the two packets of capsules behind him. He clearly hoped that if ever he was arrested the prosecution would try to prove that he had administered the poison in the capsules, when, of course, he could easily disprove it.

With a hypocritical remark to the effect that his brother-in-law was obviously not long for this world, Dr. Lamson hurried away in the direction of the railway station. He was on his way to Paris when the doctors who had been summoned to Blenheim House School, and who had failed to relieve the agony of the boy who had been taken ill so soon after his relative's visit, announced that Percy John was dead.

Suspicion was, of course, directed at once against Dr. Lamson, and Chief Inspector Butcher, of Scotland Yard, was given charge of the case, and, with his assistants, set about discovering the hiding-place of the wanted man.

Great prominence was given to the tragedy in the London newspapers, and Dr. Lamson, purchasing one in Paris, read a statement which if couched in guarded language, plainly pointed to him as the criminal.

He was almost penniless, and he must have felt like a rat in a trap, for he knew the detectives were coming for him and he had not the means to place himself beyond their reach. But he had anticipated all this, and he now determined to try what a policy of bluff could accomplish.

Crossing over immediately he met his wife in London, and driving to Scotland Yard he asked to see Chief Inspector Butcher, to whom he introduced himself. There was a desultory conversation, and after the case had been considered it was decided to arrest the doctor and charge him with wilful murder of Percy John.

The trial before Mr. Justice Hawkins at the Old Bailey occupied six days and created an interest which was profound and world-wide.

The revolting nature of the very craftily-planned crime, the social position of the poisoner, the personality of his victim, and, above all, the possibility that the prosecution would be unable to prove the guilt of the accused, all tended to excite the public.

It is just possible that if Dr. Lamson's plans had not been quite so perfect his brilliant counsel would have extracted a verdict of 'not guilty,' or at the worst brought about a disagreement of the jury, but in spite of the many successes scored by Williams during his cross-examination of the witnesses, and a final speech which moved everybody who heard it, the jury returned a verdict which left the judge no option but to pass sentence of death.

The convict, looking much older than his years because of his beard and moustache, swept the court with one glance from his luminous black eyes, and, conventional to the end, protested his innocence.

He had, however, anticipated the result of his trial, for when the jury were determining his fate he returned to the dock to sign a document which his solicitor handed to him. That document was his will, and when it became known why he had reappeared the incident was to many the most thrilling of a sensational week.

The execution was fixed for 2nd April 1982, but it did not actually take place until 28th April, owing to an agitation which in view of the doctor's callous crime seems inexplicable.

Not only was there a concerted effort to gain a reprieve, but hysterical women sent him presents of flowers and fruit, and a meeting was actually held in Exeter Hall on his behalf. This was organised by Americans in London, Lamson being the son of an American clergyman.

The Home Secretary, however, was not to be stampeded.

C.K.

# 1888

# JACK THE RIPPER
## Eight Theories

For over one hundred years the world has sought the answer to the grimmest and ghastliest of all riddles. Detectives of all nations, scientists, criminologists, novelists and ordinary amateur students of crime like you and me have studied the clues and racked their brains to find the answer.

*Who was Jack the Ripper?*

Nobody knows. Nobody will ever know. But many people have claimed that they knew the identity of London's most mysterious and most ferocious mass-murderer. Many others have built up ingenious theories to suggest whom he *might* have been. But for purposes of practical record the identity of Jack the Ripper is a mystery as impenetrable as the song the Syrens sang or the name Achilles assumed when he did himself among the women.

But Sir Thomas Browne reminded us that even those classic puzzles are not beyond conjecture. Nor is the riddle of the Ripper.

Even after all these years it is hardly necessary to recapitulate the grisly story of the Ripper murders, those shuddering three months in 1888 when all London walked in terror after nightfall. Indeed, so revolting were the details of his slaying that few people could bring themselves to write, or read, of them in this more enlightened day.

Briefly, this is the story:

An unknown murderer butchered six women in the streets of the East End between August 7 and November 9, 1888. There were no murders during the month of October, and the slayings came to an end as suddenly as they had begun. Two of the women, Elizabeth Stride and Catherine Eddows, were killed on the same night, September 30, within half an hour of each other and within ten minutes' walk. The first of the two was killed in Berners Street, Whitechapel, and the second in Mitre Square, on the boundary of Whitechapel and the City of London.

All these crimes were committed in a very different East End from that which we know to-day—a sprawling, squalid area of slums and dismal alleys, dingy dead-ends and sinister courts all densely packed with beings who were never far removed from the starvation line.

The gin palaces and boozing dens were open all day and half the night. Drink was cheap, and many miserable wretches sought oblivion the easy way. Wife-beating was an accepted habit; criminals abounded, from the cheap sneak-thief to the most violent of murderers; sanitation was rudimentary. If ever there was a hell on earth, it was the East End of London in those dark years.

But it was in the night time that the East End wore its most sinister aspect. With the coming of darkness the stews and warrens of the Whitechapel Road became indeed appalling in their depravity.

All the murdered women were prostitutes, all the crimes were committed in the East End: three in Spitalfields, two in Whitechapel, and one in the City area. All the murders took place in the dead of night. All of them were characterised by the same maniacal ferocity, the bodies were hacked and gashed with a very sharp knife. In each case death apparently came with merciful swiftness, for the victim's throat was cut with one quick and powerful stroke. One of the women was actually beheaded.

But the most dreadful feature was the revolting treatment of the bodies after death, treatment which bore the unmistakable evidence of a hand and brain skilled in surgical knowledge.

Despite the fact that the strongest police cordons London had ever known up to that time were thrown round the districts in which he prowled, the Ripper was seen only three times—if, indeed, he was seen at all.

Witnesses, including one policeman, recalled after crimes had been committed having seen in the vicinity a tall, pale man with a black moustache. He wore a cap and a long coat, and walked with the vigorous stride of youngish man. That is all.

There was an appalling crop of imitative murders and outrages. For a time every crime of violence was automatically attributed to Jack the Ripper, but it was satisfactorily established that the Ripper was, in fact, responsible for six murders in about nine weeks excluding the month of October. The names of the victims and the dates were:

No.1. Aug. 7th, 1888—Martha Turner—George Yard Build-
ings, off Commercial Street, Spitalfields, in the
Borough of Stepney.
No.2. Aug.31, 1888—Ann Mary Nichols—Bucks Row, Spital-
fields.
No.3. Sept.9, 1888—Ann Chapman—in a courtyard off
Hanbury Street, Spitalfields.
Nos. 4 & 5. Sept. 30, 1888—Elizabeth Stride and Catherine
Eddows. Stride was murdered in an alleyway off
Berners Street, Whitechapel, and Eddows about ten
minutes' walk away in Mitre Square on the boundary
of Whitechapel and the City of London. The second
murder took place about half an hour after the first.
No.6. Nov. 9, 1888—Marie Kelly—the only victim to be killed
indoors, in a hovel in Millars Court on the dividing line
of the City and Metropolitan Police boundaries.

The ferocity of the outrages seemed to increase with each murder, until the final victim, Marie Kelly, was literally chopped into pieces by the murderer, who obviously took his time over the job.

I have seen in the Black Museum of Scotland Yard a faded photograph taken inside Marie Kelly's shabby room after the discovery of the crime. It is yellow with age and the details of the picture are not easily discernible, but even so it is a photograph so horrible that I still shudder at the bare recollection of it.

After his dreadful work of mutilation, the Ripper reconstructed poor Marie Kelly's face by laying out her features on the table in a sort of devil's jigsaw puzzle. Other mutilations requiring some degree of surgical skill had been performed and, incidentally, there is about them another minor mystery which has never been solved to this day. The room contained no illumination of any kind, the windows were completely stuffed up and there was no candle. The murderer must have performed his intricate task of dissection in complete darkness. Could it have been possible that the Ripper, who always struck in the dead of the night, possessed some cat-like power of seeing in the dark?

Such, then, in very brief outline, is the story of the murders. During the reign of terror which possessed the East End while the Ripper stalked the streets, and in the years since, many stories have been told and many theories advanced to 'prove' the Ripper's identity. In the main, they fall into these eight categories:

**1. THE FOREIGNER.** At the time it was commonly believed that Jack the Ripper must be a foreigner. The teeming slums of Spitalfields, Aldgate and Whitechapel were the melting-pot to which thousands of foreigners were flocking at that period from Germany, Poland, Russia and the Baltic countries. A foreigner 'on the run' could be sure of shelter there from his political adversaries.

Only a man who lived in the locality could be familiar with the bewildering maze of alleys and courts which made it possible to pass from Aldgate to Stepney right through Spitalfields and Whitechapel *by daylight* without touching a single main street.

But the foreigner theory was refuted by the Ripper himself—or so we may believe—in a postcard written in red ink and addressed to a newspaper. Its grimly jovial message caught the public imagination and gave the unknown murderer the name by which he was known for ever after:

> *'I'm not an alien maniac*
> *Nor yet a foreign tripper;*
> *I'm just your jolly, lively friend,*
> *Your's truly—Jack the Ripper.'*

Despite his denial, however, there was a strong popular belief that the murderer *was* an alien. Perhaps it soothed the jingoistic Victorians to think that no Englishman could be capable of this kind of killing.

In the tougher parts of Whitechapel and the Commercial Road the police patrolled always in couples. There was not unnaturally considerable public reaction to the Ripper crimes in this alien-infested locality. A Russian Jew, known as 'Leather Apron,' was almost lynched on suspicion of being the Ripper—merely because he was a foreigner. A Jewish butcher leaving the slaughter-house with blood on his clothes was another who had a narrow escape. So great was public alarm that all foreigners seemed to become automatic suspects.

After the third victim's death, a notice, written in a foreign language, was found nailed to an East End fence. The message sneered at the efforts of the police and spoke in high terms of the murderer. It was probably the work of a maniac, and had no real bearing on the Ripper.

But Sir Charles Warren, the police Commissioner for London, was so perturbed by the public fear, it was said, of an 'anti-foreign rising' in London. Coming immediately after the attacks on the police in the Press and Parliament for their lack of success, this incident led to Sir Charles Warren's resignation. He had to take the blame because the Ripper always got away.

**2. THE POLICEMAN.** In spite of the concentration of police in the district on the night of September 30, the Ripper got through the cordon and struck twice. 'Only a policeman or man in police uniform could have got through,' said the exponents of this theory. Some went further and suggested that the abrupt ending of the Ripper slayings was due to the discovery that they were committed by a high-ranking police official of such importance that the matter had to be hushed up.

This theme has been elaborated by Thomas Burke in one of his most compelling short stories, *The Hands of Mister Ottomole.*

After the death of the third victim, the police took the most extraordinary precautions. Many more officers were put on duty in the streets of the East End. Dozens of plain clothes officers supplemented the uniformed policemen. Beats were shortened; there was a general tightening-up to ensure that no officer had too much ground to cover.

Scotland Yard sent its best C.I.D. men to keep an eye on the East End, and dozens of civilians were enrolled in a Vigilance Committee to help the police. This peacetime 'Home Guard' armed themselves and patrolled the East End after dark with special powers of immediate arrest. So intense were the precautions that after Ann Chapman's murder the cordon was more than 5,000 strong round the area in which the Ripper roamed. Yet in spite of this the monster got through three weeks later to kill two men in one night. Could anybody but a police officer have done it?

**3.THE WOMAN.** Theorists who insisted that the Ripper must be a woman adopted a similar argument to that of the policeman school—'Only a woman could have got through the police without arousing suspicion.'

A New York paper, about forty years ago, published a story which was supposed to have been written by a Russian refugee who lived in Whitechapel at the time of the murders. He stated quite positively that the killings were the work of a woman named Olga Tchkersoff, and he told a circumstantial story of the domestic tragedy which unhinged her mind and led to the crimes. It was a romantic yarn of a wayward younger sister and an ancient father's discovery of a bloodstained sheath knife. It was, I fear, a little too highly coloured to ring true.

**4. THE MAD SURGEON.** Was Jack the Ripper a famous Harley Street surgeon—a dual personality on Jekyll-and-Hyde lines? One published version of this story alleged that the 'mad surgeon' was tracked down by a clairvoyant named Robert James Lees and committed to an asylum. To account for his disappearance his 'sudden death' was announced and funeral rites actually conducted.

A long and careful documented account of this medium's 'discovery' of the Ripper was recently republished in a leading spiritualistic organ. Robert James Lees is said to have enjoyed the patronage of Queen Victoria, and his daughter stated after his death that for his work in the Ripper case he received a pension from the Privy Purse.

According to those who support Lees' story the murderer was a vivisectionist who delighted in torturing animals. His wife and child had to intervene once when he was on the point of thrashing his own son to death, although normally he was quiet and gentle.

Lees, according to his published life story, had a vision of the first murder, a vision so complete that he was able to read the name George Yard Buildings on the wall. He was so impressed by this fact that he told the police about it before the murder was discovered.

After the sixth murder Lees, while riding on an omnibus, recognised the murderer whom he had seen in his vision. He told his wife that the passenger in the corner of the bus was Jack the Ripper—followed him off the bus and pointed him out to a policeman, who merely laughed at him.

Afterwards, as a result of further visions, the medium was reported to have taken the police along a 'psychic trail,' which led them to the West End house of a famous surgeon, the interior of which he described accurately to an inspector before they entered. The doctor was duly arrested and certified insane, but I fear this story takes a bit of swallowing, particularly as the details were revealed in a 'secret document' which was not published until after the medium's death.

A much more convincing version of the 'mad surgeon' theory was sent to me by an anonymous reader as a result of something I wrote about Jack the Ripper in the columns of the London *Evening News*. Though he refused to divulge his identity, my correspondent was obviously born and bred in the East End and very familiar with all the details of the Ripper murders.

His theory was that the Ripper was a surgeon, or possibly a student at the London Hospital which is in the Whitechapel Road and within easy walk of the scenes of all the murders.

The writer suggested that the 'mad surgeon' made nightly forays from the hospital in search of 'specimens.' It is reasonable theory, particularly as bloodstains in an operating theatre or surgical laboratory would be fairly easily explained in those days.

**5. A FATHER'S VENGEANCE.** Another published 'solution' is the story of another famous surgeon, demented by the death of his son, whose downfall was due to a woman of the streets. He sought news of her from other women, always killing his informants to cover his trail. The sixth victim, Marie Kelly, was the woman he sought, and after killing her he fled the country, finally revealing his identity on his deathbed in Buenos Aires.

**6. THE AMERICAN SAILOR.** One of the people who claims to have seen the Ripper was the policeman who discovered the third victim, Ann Chapman, in Bucks Row, a courtyard off Hanbury Street, Spitalfields. This policeman also referred to a witness, 'a seafaring man with an American accent,' who spoke to him the night after the murder on his beat and said that he, too, had seen the murdered on his beat and said that he, too, had seen the murdered woman in the company of a man just before the crime. He gave his name and address, but these proved to be false, and all attempts to trace him failed.

Four women witnesses said that they had also spoken to this 'seafaring man with an American drawl.'

Ann Chapman, like all the others, was killed instantly. But in some ways her murder was the most savage of all, for, in addition to inflicting the usual indescribable mutilations, the Ripper cut off her head and left it carefully placed upon her body.

The policeman who discovered her may well have been the only human being ever to see the Ripper, and to speak to him while he was on the prowl—apart, of course, from his victims. All the other descriptions of the mysterious 'sea-faring' man agreed with that of the constable. And it seems highly probable that the mysterious witness was none other than the Ripper himself.

He was described as being between forty-five and fifty years old, about five feet nine inches tall and with very dark hair, eyes and moustache. He wore a black trilby hat, black tie and appeared to have india-rubber soles on his boots. His silent approach, the deathly power of his face and the American drawl were stressed by all five people who saw him.

**7. GEORGE CHAPMAN.** A pole named Severino Klosowski, who took the name of George Chapman, owned a public-house in Southwark and was hanged in 1904 for poisoning three women. 'The Borough Poisoner' certainly had the pale face and dark moustache attributed to the Ripper. Having seen his photograph, I am convinced that this sinister-faced monster could have been capable of any crime.

The last Ripper murder took place on November 1, 1888, a week before Chapman left London. While he was living in New Jersey, an exactly similar chain of atrocities is said to have taken place in that State, and to have finished abruptly at the time when Chapman left the U.S. and returned to this country. Chapman was ambidextrous, so was the Ripper. Chapman had served in the Russian Army as a surgeon's assistant. During the period of the Ripper murders, Chapman worked in Whitechapel as a *barber*—an expert with the cut-throat razor.

Another link between Chapman and the mysterious 'man with the American accent' is to be found in the fact the Chapman had lived in America. At first sight it might seem that Chapman, of all the suspects, was the one with the greatest claim to be regarded as the Ripper; but murderers are invariably creatures of habit, and it hard to believe that a man with the Ripper's blood-lust should should suddenly change his methods to the more hum-drum killing by poisoning. In any case, Chapman richly deserved to die on the gallows, as he did; and if he was indeed the Ripper, then he took his secret with him to the grave.

**8. THE MAN WITH THE WHITE EYES.** To add to the general panic, East End hooligans developed the playful habit of springing out of alleys and courtyards to frighten women walking along the streets. One of these grim jokers was arrested. He was obviously insane. His face was blackened with burnt cork, upon which he had painted a pattern of white rings round his eyes and mouth to make his face look like a skull.

At this time, the height of the scare after the sixth and last murder, any arrest connected with the Ripper, however remotely, had to be communicated to police headquarters at Old Scotland Yard, then housed in Royal Palace Yard. The man was taken there for interrogation by two highly-placed officials. As soon as he was alone with them he grabbed an ebony ruler, laid them both out with this weapon, and dashed out of the building.

Three weeks later his body, with the face still painted, was found in the Thames near Hungerford Bridge. His identity was never established, and none of the witnesses who thought they had seen the Ripper could swear to identification of the decomposed body. But one policeman 'thought' it was the same man to whom he had spoken in the East End after the second murder.

One significant feature of this unknown body was that he had the remains of a moustache and wore rubber boots—again note the similarity with the man 'with the American accent,' who was seen after the Bucks Row killing.

Well, those are the principal theories. You can take your choice. From time to time there have been other fantastic 'solutions,' including one suggestion that the whole grisly cycle of killings was a Black Magic ritual tied up with human sacrifice and even Voodoo introduced by coloured seamen. But nobody took it very seriously. The secret is buried somewhere in an unsuspected grave and it will never be exhumed now. Your guess is as good as mine. . . .

One final word of warning. It is useless to go down to the East End in search of the spots where the poor butchered victims were found. Whitechapel and Spitalfields have changed out of recognition since the days and nights when the Ripper stalked their sinister alleys and lured his victims into their dingy courts.

The last of them to go was 'Murder Street,' which was the popular name given to a cul-de-sac off Duval Street in Spitalfields. Duval Street was formally known as Dorset Street and the cul-de-sac was none other than Millers Court where, in the house numbered 13, Jack the Ripper struck for the last time when he murdered Marie Kelly in September 1888.

'Murder Street' was swept away when the London Fruit Exchange was built in 1928, and now nothing remains of those days of fantastic terror and appalling discoveries but a grisly memory and a few faded photographs in the Black Museum of Scotland Yard.

B.M.

# 1892

# CARLYLE HARRIS
## The Fatal Capsule

The problem which Carlyle Harris, aged 22, medical student, set himself to solve was how to get rid of his schoolgirl wife, Helen Potts, without risking his own neck. Helen was still attending a high-class boarding-school and was only eighteen, but for a year she had been the secret wife of the young man who was regarded a one of the most brilliant pupils at New York's medical college, for only one other person knew of the marriage and that person was the bride's mother. Carlyle had met Helen in society and mutual infatuation had followed. In the circumstances a quick courtship and a secret marriage had seemed natural enough, for they could not afford to offend their relations, especially the bridegroom's and, although Mrs. Potts would have prevented the marriage had she been able to, the moment she heard of it—the contracting couple assumed false names for the ceremony—she did not insist on an immediate public repetition once her son-in-law had promised faithfully that as soon as he had qualified he would acknowledge Helen as his wife before the world.

Carlyle Harris, however, never intended to keep that promise, for he had never been really in love with Helen and he was too selfish and ambitious to link himself with a family which he considered not nearly as good as his own. Besides, he was certain that one day he would be one of New York's most famous physicians and surgeons and as such he deemed himself much too good for the pretty schoolgirl who was so much in love with him that the old saying, she worshipped the ground he walked on, best described their relations. It flattered his vanity that this should be so, but it did not soften his heart nor did it create any pity for the trusting, devoted and admiring young wife whose happiest moments, as she more than once said, were with 'dear Carl' or else dreaming of him when he was absent.

But she was in the way of Carlyle Harris, the ambitious medical student, the only son of a well-known American authoress and public lecturer who was accustomed in the course of her lectures to describe him as the perfectly brought up child. Mrs. Harris was a strong-minded woman, and it is likely that her son feared her, but what he feared more was the burden of having to support a wife whose presence would, as he put it, 'prevent him having a good time'. But how could get rid of his secret wife before her mother forced a public marriage? Helen lived with eight or nine other girls and was carefully guarded by suspicious and vigilant chaperones who never allowed her to go unaccompanied even to the most innocent of concerts. During vacation she went to her mother's house, and to that he had, of course, ready access, but the next vacation was some weeks off and he could not afford to wait so long because Mrs. Potts was threatening every day to force his hand by a public exposure in the newspapers.

He was still striving with the problem when by a subterfuge Helen eluded her guardians and met him in a café, and in the course of conversation complained that she was suffering from headaches. It was a casual remark, but in it Carlyle Harris discovered the solution of his problem and there and then he began to put it into motion.

'I know of a remedy,' he said, apparently distressed by her sufferings. 'A mixture of quinine and morphine which can't fail. I'll have some capsules made up and send them to you.'

The girl-wife thanked him with a look of love and devotion that only an inhuman monster could have ignored, and when at the end of the week a small box containing four capsules and marked 'C. W. H. student. One before retiring' arrived, Helen joyfully obeyed the instructions by taking the first of the four that night. But one of the four contained morphine of sufficient quantity to kill half a dozen persons, and it was, therefore, merely a toss-up as to whether the unsuspecting girl-wife died on the first, second, third, or fourth day of the 'treatment', for three of the capsules consisted of twenty-seven parts of quinine to one of morphine, and the fourth of morphine only.

For that was the plan Carlyle Harris had invented to get rid of his girl-wife, and he had no doubt whatever not only of its efficacy but of its perfect safety so far as he himself was concerned. From whatever point of view he looked at it he could find no flaw, no chance of the deadly morphine being traced to himself. He had gone to a well-known chemist shop and had ordered six capsules made up according to the harmless prescription which he had mentioned to Helen, but on receiving the six capsules he had put two of them in his pocket, and before sending the others to his wife had emptied one of the four of quinine and substituted morphine, thus converting that particular capsule into a terrible poison.

It was to be the perfect crime. As a medical student he knew that the doctors would have no difficulty in determining the exact cause of Helen's death, but he was certain that when they heard of the capsules they would immediately decide that the unfortunate girl had been poisoned as the result of a mistake by the chemist. No one could suspect the gallant, gay, and debonair Carlyle Harris, aged 22, of being a callous and cold-blooded murderer, but even if anyone did, there was always the evidence of the capsules which had been made up by the well-known chemist and not by Helen's husband.

Later, when New York Society was excited into a volcanic pity by the tragic death of the schoolgirl no one as yet suspected had been a married woman, Carlyle Harris remarked to a friend: 'I gave her only four of the six capsules the chemist compounded, and the two I kept out will show that they were perfectly harmless. No jury therefore could convict me with these specimen capsules in my possession, for analysis will prove them to be harmless.'

In that statement Carlyle Harris epitomized his perfect crime, but also in that statement was found the solution of the mystery because the two capsules he retained to save him actually convicted him. Had he not kept these capsules the State would never have been able to prove that the chemist who had made them up had not commited any blunder, but when Harris swore that they had formed part of the original six and the analysis duly proved them to be harmless it also proved that all six had been harmless when handed by the chemist to the young medical student. It was, therefore, obvious that some other person had substituted a large quantity of morphine for the quinine in one of the capsules, and it was equally obvious that this could have done only by someone who had had the box of capsules in his possession. Now it was admitted that only three persons had ever handled the box—the chemist, Carlyle Harris, and Helen Potts, and the two capsules kept back by Harris having established the fact that the chemist had not blundered the issue was narrowed down between Harris and Helen. As no one, not even her murderer, believed that she had committed suicide it was clear as sunlight that Carlyle Harris must be the murderer. No one else could have been, for no one else had had the chance of interfering with the capsules, and thus the author of the perfect crime proved at one and the same time the innocence of the chemist and his own guilt.

Before all this was to startled the country, however, there was to be a pathetic deathbed scene at the boarding-school where Helen Potts was finishing her studies. For three nights in succession she unknowingly took a chance in the lottery of death and each night unknowingly won the prize of a further extension of life. On the fourth day her mother came to see her, and Helen showing her the box with the last capsule in it good-humouredly complained that as Carl's remedy had been such a complete failure she had a good mind to throw the box out of the window.

'Don't, dear,' said the mother who adored her, 'just give the remedy another trial.'

No writer of fiction has ever conceived such a scene as this, no master of the tragic ever portrayed such a heartrending and yet starkly ironic situation. The young and beautiful girl holding in her hand the poisoned capsule and the mother who worshipped her and who was feeling happy because her son-in-law had just promised to re-marry her daughter on a certain date, urging her to swallow it! Surely, Helen's guardian angel might have intervened to save her! Surely something might have happened to prevent the tragedy! In fiction a dozen ways of escape would have been found, but this was real life, and life sometimes knows no pity. Helen, aware that her mother was anxious only for her happiness and health, obeyed her, and that night she swallowed the fourth capsule and was dead within a few hours.

While Helen lay dying and the doctors were struggling desperately to save her they sent for Carlyle Harris, the

C. W. H. of the capsule box, and he came, frightened and trembling, but only on his own account.

'They can't hold me responsible for this, doctor, can they?' he asked, almost sick with terror. The doctor answered roughly that they were trying to save a human life and had no time to bother about him, but all through the long battle Carlyle Harris whiningly asked questions concerning his own safety, and when the doctors lost the fight he vanished. No one suspected that it was his wife who had died in his presence. All that was known was that he and Helen had been very good friends, probably sweethearts, but of the secret marriage they had not an inkling. Before leaving, he announced that he had been to the chemist who had made up the capsules and had been assured by him that he had made no error. As a matter of fact, he had not been near the shop, a fact which was to tell heavily against him later. Criminals usually lie unnecessarily.

In due course Helen was buried, the general verdict being that she had died as the result of an error by someone unknown, and the perfect crime would have been consummated had it not been that a reporter on a New York newspaper decided to investigate the mystery on his own account. All he had to go on was the friendship between the medical student and the schoolgirl, but it was sufficient to lead him to the office where about a year before the tragedy two persons, calling themselves Charles Harris and Helen Neilson, had been married by an alderman. Now Neilson was Helen's second Christian name and Charles Harris was scarcely a disguise. This was sufficient to encourage the amateur detective, and very soon he was able to publish the news that the schoolgirl who had died mysteriously after swallowing capsules procured for her by Carlyle Harris had been actually the wife of Harris. This fact placed a different complexion on the whole case, and the body of Helen was exhumed. The autopsy revealed morphine poisoning, and immediately Carlyle Harris, who had recently graduated with honours and was now a fully qualified doctor, was arrested and charged with the wilful murder of his secret wife.

The trial ranks as one of America's greatest and most sensational, the social standing of the prisoner, his powerful and influential relations, the army of believers in his innocence, and, above all, the strong, masculine and fanatical figure of his devoted mother, combining to make it unique and memorable. The State brought all its resources into the conflict which was to determine whether a promising young doctor should live or die, and the country watched the contest with breathless interest.

Harris himself was the personification of coolness and confidence, and even when weeks of imprisonment had weakened him physically he was in every other respect stronger and more insistent that he must win. He still had a whole-hearted belief in the perfection of his plans and even now he could see no flaw in what he regarded as the perfect crime. Had he not the two capsules to prove that the box he had supplied to Helen contained no poison? And was it not admitted even by his enemies that he had not made up the capsules? The chemist confirmed that and also swore that the proportion of morphine had been only one twenty-seventh.

He, Carlyle, had given Helen nothing but the capsules—the prosecution did not contradict this—and, therefore, if the capsules were harmless he must be innocent. But as I have already pointed out it was his retention of the two harmless capsules that proved his guilt, because they proved that whoever had substituted the morphine the chemist had not. Little wonder then that the jury took only a short time to pronounce him guilty after they had heard the story of his secrets marriage, the efforts of Mrs. Potts to have it made public, and the young husband's mean tricks to postpone publicity. They also heard the real history of the 'perfectly brought up young man', and from that history emerged the figure of an utterly selfish and callous young scoundrel who had shown by his conduct, not only towards Helen but towards other women, that in pursuit of pleasure he was capable of committing any crime.

His appeals having been dismissed the murderer went to this death, and when seated in the electric chair protested his innocence. That lie was really a last moment effort to gain the sympathy of the governor and perhaps stay the hand which was ready to switch on the electric current, but Carlyle Harris, who, like all murderers, could deceive himself very easily, could not deceive anyone who had heard or read the evidence given at his trial, and the lie failed.

Three days before his execution his mother ordered that the inscription on his coffin should consist of the words: 'Carlyle W. Harris. Murdered, May 8, 1893'.

Murdered! Carlyle Harris was justly punished for a very cruel murder of which he could not have been convicted had he not retained the two capsules which he intended should round off and complete the perfect crime.

J.C.E.

# 1892

# DOCTOR NEILL CREAM
## Poisoner of Prostitutes

The coroner had just recorded the verdict of the jury that Ellen Donworth had been murdered by a person or persons unknown when one of the officials handed him a letter. Opening it hurriedly in the hope that it would afford a clue to the identity of the murderer, he was astonished to read a statement to the effect that the writer knew who was the guilty man, and that he was willing to impart the information for the sum of £300,000. The signature to this queer communication was 'O'Brien, detective,' but there was no address.

'H'm, evidently a lunatic,' remarked the coroner, giving the letter to the representative of the police who was present. The officer agreed with him, but, as in duty bound, he had it placed in a pigeon-hole at New Scotland Yard, for the mysterious death of Ellen Donworth was not the first of its kind, a few weeks earlier another young woman, Matilda Clover, having died in exactly similar circumstances.

But the work of destruction was not stopped by the publicity given to the death of Ellen Donworth, and although the police were striving their utmost to solve the problem the criminal, whoever he was, appeared to think that he could continue to murder with impunity. Two more girls residing in the neighbourhood of Waterloo Road, London, were poisoned, and the only clue that the authorities had was the description furnished by the policeman on duty near the house where the third victim lived of a man he had seen leave it in the early hours of the morning.

The position was a very serious one. Here was a man possessed of the deadliest poisons destroying human life, and there appeared to be no way of catching him. The mysterious assassin had a passion for writing anonymous letters, and once he actually wrote to Sir William Broadbent, the famous specialist, accusing him of one of the crimes, and demanding £1500 as hush money. Sir William merely sent the epistle on to Scotland Yard, and thought no more about it, for eminent men are accustomed to receiving unsigned letters, and he did not think it worth while to take any steps in the matter.

Such was the state of uncertainty when Neill Cream entered upon the scene.

The son of a Glasgow man, Cream had been taken as a small boy to Canada by his parents, who had been unfortunate in business. In the far west he had received a good education, and had qualified as a doctor, but there is every reason to believe that he was a born criminal. A good practice and plenty of friends could not keep him out of mischief, and one day he was arrested and charged with the murder of a patient. He ought to have been hanged, but for some reason his sentence was only twenty years' penal servitude, and he did not serve half his time, for on the death of his father he succeeded to a fortune, and his influential friends secured his release.

But while his acquaintances were anxious to get him outside the grim walls of the prison they had no desire to have him near them, and they persuaded him to go to England. He accepted their advice without any gratitude, and after paying a short visit to his native place, Glasgow, he came to London and took lodgings.

He gave his landlady to understand that he was a Canadian doctor anxious to study British medical methods at first hand, and she soon got accustomed to his coming and going at all hours. When the murders of the young women occurred she discussed them with her lodger, who was always, however, the first to mention the subject. Not once did the landlady suspect the smooth-tongued American. His manners were too plausible, and his desire to please too convincing, to give her opportunity to find fault with him.

Yet Neill Cream was the murderer of the four women, and in secret he gloated over what he called his triumphs until he reached such a pitch of mental exaltation that he was unable to keep his thoughts to himself. He wanted the world to know of his crimes, while anxious to avoid punishment for them, and after exhausting the subject as a topic of conversation he took to the dangerous game of trying to fool the police still further by making them arrest the wrong man.

It happened that lodging in the same house was a medical student, the son of a well-known Devonshire doctor. Neill Cream thought it would be a splendid joke if he had the student accused of murder, and, believing that he was doing a rather clever thing, he took into his confidence a gentleman of his acquaintance.

'What would you say if I told you that he murdered a girl?' asked Cream, after he had brought the conversation round to the personality of the medical student.

'I'd say you were mad,' answered his acquaintance, 'that chap wouldn't hurt a fly.'

'Well, I know for a fact that he poisoned a girl named Loo Harvey,' retorted the doctor, triumphantly; 'I shadowed them one night, and I saw him give her two pills. She collapsed immediately, and was found dead in the street. I imagine she was buried as an unknown.'

Now the gentleman whom Cream made his confidant was puzzled by this disclosure, and he frankly informed the doctor that he wished he had not mentioned the matter at all, for he did not want to be mixed up in a sordid drama. But after thinking the subject over he came to the conclusion that he ought to see one of the officials at Scotland Yard and ask his advice.

When he arrived at the headquarters of the police he was attended to by Inspector M'Intyre, who made a note of his story and filed it. But he first pointed out to him that no one of the name of Loo Harvey had been reported to the police as having been found dead.

'What is your friend's name?' asked M'Intyre, suddenly.

'Neill Cream,' answered the gentleman.

'I'll remember it,' said M'Intyre, quietly. 'Good afternoon.'

Strangely enough, up to this point no one thought of interviewing Neill Cream. Scotland Yard was not looking for a man of his class, and it seemed absurd to associate a well-to-do doctor with four very brutal and callous murders. Resting in various pigeon-holes were various anonymous letters dealing with the murders, and the fact that the handwriting was in all cases similar hardly afforded a clue. The police, however, could only wait and hope for the best.

And then they had a real 'lift-up' owing to one of those unexpected incidents which happen in real life but which would not be tolerated in a work of fiction.

Inspector M'Intyre was busy one afternoon writing out a report of another case when a superior officer entered his room.

'There's a chap waiting to see someone to make a complaint,' he remarked, with a smile, for they are accustomed to eccentric individuals calling at the Yard day and night. 'I don't know who he is or what he wants, but you might give him a few minutes.'

It was a command, of course, and M'Intyre obeyed at once. In the waiting room he found a rather lean person with small black eyes, wide forehead, thin lips, stooping shoulders and restless manner pacing up and down the room.

'It's a scandal that in a great city like this,' he began the moment he saw the officer, 'that I should be subjected to such an insult.'

The inspector looked sympathetic.

'Certainly,' he said, soothingly, 'but perhaps you'll kindly tell me your name. I can guess by your accent that you're an American.'

'My name, sir, is Neill Cream,' was the startling answer. 'I was born in Glasgow, but brought up in Canada. For the last few days my footsteps have been dogged by some villainous-looking persons. I believe they will try to murder me, and I want you to send a detective to protect me from them.'

Neill Cream. Instantly Inspector M'Intyre recalled the name of the man who had accused a young medical student of having murdered a young woman of the name of Loo Harvey, and he decided that the coincidence was not to be disregarded.

'I'm sorry you should be worried,' he said, gently, 'and I will do what I can to help you; in fact, I'll protect you myself.'

Cream impulsively shook him by the hand.

'I'll be delighted to have your company, sir,' he said, cordially.

The following afternoon M'Intyre, in his capacity of protector of Neill Cream, went for a walk with him down Waterloo Road. They passed one policeman only, and he apparently did not recognise the detective, but a few hours later that policeman was closeted with M'Intyre at the Yard.

'Well,' the latter asked, 'is that chap who was with me to-day anything like the man you saw come out of the house the night Ellen Donworth was poisoned?'

'He's very like him, sir,' answered the constable, 'but I wouldn't like to swear to it.'

'That's all right,' said M'Intyre, pleased with the information. 'My friend, Neill Cream, is evidently worth watching.'

So far there was nothing to found a charge on, and Neill Cream was permitted to go where he pleased. But somehow or other the detective was generally with him, and he soon managed to extract from him an account of his career.

Of course, Neill Cream told him only lies. He said that he was a traveller in drugs, and when reminded that he had styled himself a doctor he pointed out how easy it was to buy a medical degree in the States. However, M'Intyre did not expect to find anything to help him in Cream's own life-story. He had realised that he was dealing with a very sly scoundrel, but his wide experience of crime had taught him that sooner or later the cleverest of criminals will fashion the rope for his own neck.

The case was a ticklish one to handle, and a less efficient officer would have spoiled everything by acting hastily and arresting Cream. M'Intyre, however, was aware that he must first find convincing evidence, and so he continued to associate with Cream in the rôle of 'protector,' and never lost an opportunity for making progress.

One evening he obtained a specimen of Cream's handwriting, and when he compared it with the anonymous letters in the archives of the Yard he was hardly surprised at the resemblance. From that moment he was certain that Neill Cream was the slayer of the four unfortunate young women, but as yet he dare not take him into custody.

But when the Devonshire doctor, who was father of the medical student accused by Cream of the murder of Loo Harvey, forwarded to Scotland Yard a letter demanding £1500 hush money, Inspector M'Intyre felt that the end was near. To his surprise, however, the handwriting was entirely different to that of Neill Cream's and for the moment he was checkmated, for he refused to believe that Cream had a confederate.

M'Intyre did not acknowledge defeat for long, for it occured to him that the criminal might have had that letter written for him by someone who did not know his designs, but was wholly under his influence.

'I'll give Cream a call,' he said to a colleague, and at once proceeded to the doctor's lodgings.

Cream and M'Intyre were now on such friendly terms that the detective was able to walk upstairs and enter his room and greet him as he lay in bed reading the paper. After a few inquiries concerning his health, he casually asked Cream if he would write down the address of a certain shop he had recommended for a particular article. The doctor instantly complied with the request, and when he scribbled a line or two on his notepaper he handed it to M'Intyre, who carelessly thrust it into his pocket without glancing at it.

Once he was in the street, however, he took it out again and held it up to the light, and he thrilled with excitement when he read the water-mark, 'Fairfield—Superfine,' for it was exactly the same as the water-mark of the letter sent to the Devonshire doctor.

This was a clue that had to be developed at once. 'Fairfield—Superfine' might be the commonest of writing papers, and tens of thousands of persons might be in the habit of using it. M'Intyre took it to a paper manufacturer of his acquaintance and asked his opinion.

'It's not British made,' said the expert, decisively. 'I know all the British papers, and this isn't one of them.'

'Perhaps it's American?' suggested the detective.

'Yes, if I were you I'd inquire in Canada,' replied the manufacturer.

A long cable was despatched to a leading Canadian detective, and two days later he replied that 'Fairfield—Superfine' was a special paper manufactured in the town in Canada in which Neill Cream had lived for years, and which he had visited since the first murder in Waterloo Road. The report was what M'Intyre expected, and he kept a closer guard than ever on the doctor.

But meanwhile Cream had been growing more and more nervous. He was beginning to see a detective in every pedestrian, and a prison behind every door. Terror gripped him, and he spent sleepless nights, while he passed his days vainly trying to find the courage to flee. When M'Intyre was with him he suffered agonies, and so great did his distress become that he astonished the detective by blurting out a question that revealed his thoughts.

'I'm going away for a few days,' he said, suddenly. 'Do you think that I'll be arrested before I go?'

'Better come with me to Scotland Yard and see how you stand there,' answered M'Intyre, calmly.

'Very well,' said Cream, subsiding. 'Perhaps you're right.'

For some minutes they walked side by side, but the nearer they got to Scotland Yard the more nervous Cream became.

'I suspect a trap,' he said, coming to a standstill. 'I won't go any farther with you.'

'Please yourself,' remarked the detective, not to be ruffled.

From that moment, however, Neill Cream was shadowed day and night. Wherever he went there was always a lynx-eyed detective watching him, and in his lodgings there was another sleuth to see that the doctor did not give the authorities the slip.

Their precautions were necessary, for Neill Cream realised that he was in danger of arrest, and began hurried preparations for flight. Immediately this was communicated to Inspector M'Intyre he decided to run no more risks of losing his man, and, armed with a warrant, he called and notified the doctor that he was a prisoner, and that the charge was sending threatening letters. Later it was altered to murder.

Having seen him into a cell, the detective turned his attention to securing direct evidence of poisoning, and application was made to the Home Secretary for permission to exhume the body of Matilda Clover. The doctors discovered strychnine in the corpse, and M'Intyre next proceeded to find acquaintances of the murdered woman who had seen the prisoner in the company of his victims.

There was a most dramatic incident when Cream was brought before the magistrate at Bow Street for the first time. He was

charged with the murder of four women, and when counsel
for the prosecution informed the court that suspicion had been
directed against the accused because he had accused a medical
student of the murder of Loo Harvey he was interrupted by a
girl rising in the court and announcing that she was the young
woman who was supposed to have been killed.

'I am Loo Harvey,' she exclaimed, 'and I know the prisoner,
for he once gave me two long pills, thinking that I'd swallow
them, but I threw them away, and to that I owe the fact that I
am alive to-day.'

Cream started when he heard her voice, and those who
happened to be watching him saw a look of despair come into
his eyes. He must have known that Loo Harvey's evidence
would clinch the case for the Crown, and make his conviction
a certainty.

He was duly committed for trial, and, after a considerable
delay owning to the necessity for obtaining certain documents
from Canada, he was brought into the dock at the Old Bailey.
Mr. Justice Hawkins was the judge, and for the prosecution
there were Sir Charles Russell, Q.C., afterwards Lord Chief
Justice of England. He had with him three other counsel, while
the prisoner was defended by an equal number of barristers.

The chief witness was Loo Harvey, and her account of her
meeting with Neill Cream and of his attempt to poison her
clearly showed how it was that the poisoner found his victims.
The girl told how he had accosted her and induced her to
accompany him to a public-house, where he had treated her to
a glass of wine. Then he had made an appointment to meet her
again the next day, and when they met she had mentioned that
she was unwell. Thereupon Cream had revealed the fact that he
was a doctor, and, producing a pill-case, had given her two pills
which he described as a remedy.

But Loo Harvey did not like the appearance of the doctor, and
she thought that she saw danger in his demeanour. Despite his
anxiety to get on good terms with her she felt that he would be
a remorseless enemy if she offended him, and she had not the
courage to tell him that would not swallow the pills.

'You must take them at once,' he said to her.

'All right, I will,' she had answered. At that moment the
doctor had turned his head to glance after someone on the other

side of the bridge—the scene of the encounter was Waterloo Bridge—and instantly Loo Harvey had flung the pills into the Thames.

Cream went away, certain that inside an hour the young woman would be a corpse.

In addition to this witness Inspector M'Intyre had marshalled a solid phalanx of persons who had seen Cream in company with Ellen Donworth, Matilda Clover and the other two victims. The poisons were traced to him, the detective recovering the fiendish murderer's pill-case, which to-day is one of the most interesting relics in the Black Museum at Scotland Yard.

The authorship of all the letters was proved, and those not in Cream's handwriting were shown to have been written by the girl he was engaged to.

When counsel for the defence rose to deliver his final speech on behalf of the cowering culprit his task was a hopeless one. The very appearance of Cream was against him; his demeanour was that of a guilty man, and the barrister wisely relied upon his eloquence rather than upon any facts. Skilfully avoiding the unassailable points scored by the prosecution, he asked the jury to give Neill Cream the benefit of the doubt, because there was no reason why he should have taken the lives of four young women who had never offended him. But whatever the effect of his speech may have been on the jury, it was weakened considerably, if not obliterated, by the charge of the learned judge. Mr. Justice Hawkins had no doubt himself, and when he sent the jury out of court to decide the questions of life or death they quickly answered against the prisoner.

Neill Cream was sentenced to death, and when he was executed on 15th November 1892 there was no one who regretted his fate.

C.K

# 1895

# DOCTOR BUCHANAN

## Belladonna

---

In 1887, a young Nova Scotia physician, Robert W. Buchanan, arrived in New York from Halifax and hung out his shingle in West Eleventh Street. The placid old ninth Ward, now the colour patch called Greenwich Village, the home of romantics, radicals, artists, and pretenders, was at that time inhabited by quiet and unimaginative people, for whom the measure of any man's greatness was to be found on the books of the neighbourhood bank. This was quite as Doctor Buchanan desired, for he had brought with him a pretty young wife and a little daughter, whom he hoped to settle respectably while he established himself as a solid family practitioner.

For three years nothing happened. The doctor made a few friends, built up a modest clientele among the neighbours and kept himself obscure and busy. On November 12, 1890, however, Buchanan was granted a divorce on the ground of adultery. To the few men with whom the young doctor was acquainted there was nothing surprising in the announcement, for the doctor had previously said that his wife had gone away with someone else, leaving her little daughter behind. The divorce seemed therefore a natural consequence and, as there was no contest, the whole matter was settled by the courts without publicity, almost without notice.

On November 26, Thanksgiving Day, and only fifteen days after the granting of the divorce, Doctor Buchanan approached a friend, Richard W. Macomber, the keeper of a restaurant where the physician often took a meal and drank his ale, and asked the Boniface to go with him to Newark and act as witness to a will, which was to be drawn by a woman friend. Macomber accordingly accompanied his friend to New Jersey and was introduced to a most mature woman named Sutherland, who seemed extremely fond of the young doctor and who read her callers a will which she had just had drawn. The instrument provided that in case of her death all her property and money was to go to her husband. In case she proved to be unmarried at her demise, her estate was to be the property of her beloved friend and physician, Doctor Robert W. Buchanan. As there was some doubt as to the legality of making a will on Thanksgiving Day, the doctor and Macomber returned to Newark the following day and Macomber witnessed the signing of the will, seconded by a man named Doria, who presented himself as a former officer in the British army.

After the will had been endorsed and a few drinks had been absorbed in company with the sprightly widow, the three men left her house together and returned to New york, where some further libations were poured. Buchanan, being twitted about his incongruous charmer—a woman obviously fifty years old, while he was about thirty—replied that he had attended her as a physician and that she was grateful to him because he had served her well. He said, also, that he fully expected to be her heir, since there was no prospect of her marrying any one.

Two days later, on November 29, Doctor Buchanan went quietly to Newark and married Mrs. Annie B. Sutherland, who said in the application for a licence that she was a widow and gave her age as forty-one, a bit of fraudulent vanity, which deceived the lady's husband no more than others.

After the wedding Doctor Buchanan went back to his house in Eleventh Street and his wife remained at her home in Newark. The doctor did not tell his friends he had married. Instead, he repeatedly said he had had enough of women and marriage. After some months, however, Doctor Buchanan told his friend Macomber and some others that the lady in Newark had sold her house for nine thousand five hundred dollars and given him the money. He said he had added five hundred dollars of his own and bought the house in West Eleventh Street, where he had lived since coming to New York. Still later the Newark woman appeared at the doctor's home and was fully installed there, though Doctor Buchanan still pretended to some that she was not his wife but his housekeeper. Macomber and his intimates, however, knew the truth and there was evidently no further effort on the husband's part to conceal it, whatever may have been his earlier attitude.

It was not long before friction between the old wife and the young doctor began to manifest itself and to reach the attention of friends. Doctor Buchanan confided to Macomber and a few other cronies that his wife had an insufferable temper, that she used the vilest language before his little daughter, that she made constant scenes, and, finally, that he would have to get rid of her some way. Here his predicament presented itself, for when Buchanan spoke to Macomber about 'dumping the old woman,' the latter reminded him of the will and of the nine thousand five hundred dollars she had given toward the purchase of the Eleventh Street house. She would certainly revoke the will if Buchanan left her or treated her badly, and if it came to an open breach she would surely sue him for the money advanced and make a scandal for him. At such times Buchanan confessed his perplexity.

At this time, toward the end of 1891, the Carlyle Harris murder case was much in the newspapers, as recounted in a preceding chapter. At the time in question, the trial of Harris was approaching, and in January, 1892, he was heard and found guilty of murder. In the course of these weeks, according to Buchanan's friends, the doctor was several times asked his opinion of the Harris case and he answered that Harris was an amateur and a bungler. He had not been skilful in the use of poisons or he would have known how to hide the symptoms of morphine poisoning. Doctor Buchanan is said to have added that it was easy to poison a human being without being caught. All one needed was knowledge.

About the time these remarks were made, which must have been in January or February, 1892, Buchanan's trouble with his wife were growing more bitter. He confided to Macomber that it was more than he could bear and that he was actually growing afraid of the woman. Still later, Buchanan asked Macomber to take his little girl into the Macomber home, saying that his wife was using such vile language in the child's presence that his own house was unfit for his daughter to live in. So Buchanan moved the child away from its stepmother and her violence. The change had not been made long when Buchanan said his wife had a terrible scene and threatened to poison herself. He had laughed at her and said, 'Go ahead. You know where the poisons are kept.'

The following week Buchanan confided to Macomber that he stood in personal dread of his raging wife. She was in a desperate mood and he felt she was likely to put poison into his food. Could he not take his meals with the Macombers and his little daughter? Macomber consented, and so the Buchanans were practically divided, though the doctor still practised medicine from his home and kept office hours there. He also slept at home, but he hardly spoke to his wife and they certainly regarded each other with the blackest suspicion.

About nine o'clock on the morning of April 22, 1892. Doctor B. C. McIntyre was summoned to the home of Doctor Buchanan, who said his wife had been taken seriously and suddenly ill about an hour before. The summoned physician found Mrs. Buchanan suffering from hysterical symptoms and constriction of the throat, which latter he also attributed to hysteria. He prescribed sedatives and departed, saying he would return in the afternoon. When he did come back he found the woman worse off than before and, at Doctor Buchanan's suggestion, summoned another physician, Doctor H. P. Watson, from his office near by. These two men, without the interference of Doctor Buchanan, who said he knew better than to prescribe for his own family, examined the suffering woman carefully and could find anything wrong with her aside from a hysteria, which expressed itself in ravings and rigidity. They decided to increase the strength of the sedatives and went their way.

Early the next morning the two physicians returned found Mrs. Buchanan much worse, and were present when she died at about ten o'clock. She had been ill twenty-six hours. They promptly signed the certificate in keeping with the law and stated that death had been due to cerebral hemorrhage. Two days later, on the twenty-fifth, Mrs. Buchanan was buried in Greenwood Cemetery and a few day afterwards Doctor Buchanan closed his house and went to his old home in Nova Scotia, for a rest and change of scene, he told Macomber.

The young physician had wept no tears and suffered no pangs at the death of his wife. Neither had he made any pretence of sorrow or suffering. He had married his older woman to satisfy her whim. She had died, after two miserable years, and had left him possessed of her estate, which was estimated at from thirty to fifty thousand dollars. Why should he have wept? No one thought anything of the fact that he was dry-eyed and no one had the least suspicion that Mrs. Buchanan had not died naturally.

But Doctor Buchanan had not been more than two weeks on his vacation when a strange ghost began to walk. One night when there was the usual bustle and frenzy over the press hour of the first edition, an old man from Newark walked into the office of one of the big New York dailies and said he had some interesting information about the death of Mrs. Buchanan. He knew what the newspapers had done in the Carlyle Harris case and he felt what he could tell them would put them on the track of just as big a sensation. A reporter was assigned to listen to the man's story.

The caller, more than a little evasive and rambling, unfolded a strange tale. Mrs. Buchanan, formerly Mrs. Sutherland, had not been, as represented, the daughter of a Philadelphia banker and a respectable widow but the keeper of questionable houses in Newark. Doctor Buchanan had visited her house with some other men in the course of a slumming expedition to the New Jersey city. He had made love to the old woman and won her away from the informant, who by this confession revealed the springs of his spite and zeal.

The informant, who gave his name as James M. Smith, was a man of about sixty years. He was without an occupation. He had been the associate of Mrs. Sutherland for eleven years, until Doctor Buchanan had dislodged him. To the reporter, this part of the story was, however, of secondary interest. What excited him was the allegation that Doctor Buchanan had wooed the old woman long before his divorce from his first wife, that he had planned the will which made him the woman's heir months before it was executed, and that he would gain considerable money by her death. Smith gave various reasons for believing that Mrs. Buchanan had been poisoned and bade the reporter investigate.

For several weeks the newspaper detectives worked quietly and without much result. They discovered that the story of the woman's past had not been misrepresented, and found that Doctor Buchanan was under no illusions as to the identity of the woman to whom he gave his name. They found that he had long tried to conceal the facts of his marriage, that he had complained much about his wife, that he had made various suggestive remarks, that the illness had been sudden and mysterious, and that he had showed joy rather than grief at her demise.

But when the reporters went to see the physicians who had attended Mrs. Buchanan in her fatal illness they encountered a serious setback. Doctor McIntyre, a veteran practitioner of excellent repute, absolutely refused to entertain the idea of morphine poisoning, which was suggested. He said with the utmost positiveness that none of the conclusive symptoms of this poison had been present. The characteristic contraction of the eye pupil he had looked for and had not found. There could be no questions about the cause of death and all suggestions of murder were ridiculous. Doctor Waston enthusiastically supported him in this view. The reporters, after a brilliant start, were balked.

But it was not easy to discourage the newspaper men. They stuck to the case in spite of early reverses, and they were not long in being rewarded.

When nothing decisive could be discovered against Buchanan in New York, one of reporters set off for Halifax and there he quickly stumbled upon the fact that Buchanan had remarried his first wife when the second had been dead less than four weeks. Buchanan, alarmed and excited by the investigations of the reporters, made matters worse for himself by attempting to deny and conceal his remarriage. He declared that if the newspapers got after him it would be another Carlyle Harris case; that he would be railroaded by public opinion. To Macomber he confided that his wife had used morphine and that her exhumation would supply evidence that would be turned against him. He considered flight, and consulted his friend and also two attorneys on this question. They advised him to stay and defend himself, since an innocent man could not suffer.

Strangely enough, everything the man did and every chance remark he let drop that might be twisted into the semblance of a suspicion against him reached the assiduous reporters and was published by them or carried to District Attorney Nicoll, who, finally on June 5, just forty days after the burial of Mrs. Buchanan, ordered the body to be dug up.

Buchanan was immediately informed of this move, for he had anticipated that something of the sort would be done and had instructed his attorney to have a detective watch the grave. When the doctor heard of the disinterment he wanted to flee, but Detective Arthur Carey, later an inspector, was at his heels and he was arrested on the sixth and indicted on the ninth.

He pleaded not guilty the following day and was remanded on trial.

On the morning of March 20, 1893, the dread Recorder Smyth rapped for order at the opening of this famous trial, in many ways one of the most interesting and spectacular ever held in America. The prisoner was led in from the Tombs to face a crowded and partisan courtroom, a strange and impotent little figure to bear the weight of this heavy accusation.

Doctor Buchanan was seen to be a short, frail, little man of about thirty-five, pale, almost sickly looking, with sad, lustreless eyes, a drooping and sparse moustache of light hair, a thin, blond thatch and an unhealthy skin. Inside the rail of the courtroom he looked like a helpless white rat in a pit, beset by ravenous terriers. And this comparison is not altogether fanciful, for the little doctor saw ranged against him District Attorney Delancey Nicoll in person, Francis L. Wellman, fresh from the conviction of Carlyle Harris, and James W. Osborne, who began his notable career with this case. To defend him, Buchanan had Charles W. Brooke, one of the first criminal advocates of the day, and a newcomer, William J. O'Sullivan, who gained an immediate and unique repute through his conduct of this astonishing trial.

The circumstantial case which the State was able to set forth has already been fairly clearly indicated. Smith the discarded favourite of the former Mrs. Sutherland, told what he knew and what he suspected. Doria, the second witness to the will, testified to various suggestive remarks and bits of conduct on the part of Buchanan. Then Macomber, who was always thereafter suspected of some obscure motive of envy or pique, took the stand and recounted in great detail conversations and remarks of the accused doctor, all of which tended to become extremely suggestive when repeated in a courtroom against a man charged with a murder, though Macomber admitted he had thought nothing of them at the time they were uttered.

Finally Macomber told that he and Buchanan had several times discussed the Carlyle Harris case and that Buchanan had always scoffed at Harris as a bungling young fool. On one occasion Buchanan had told Macomber that if Harris had only known his poisons he could readily have concealed the symptoms of morphine poisoning, which were so obvious at the deathbed of Helen Potts and had helped to convict the medical student. If Harris had known his business, said Buchanan, he would have given the girl a little belladonna with her morphine. This would have prevented the telltale contraction of the pupils and otherwise confused the morphine symptoms.

The importance of this testimony struck the courtroom with its powerful point when Doctor McIntyre and Doctor Watson were called to the stand and questioned. After they had sworn that they noted none of the conclusive symptoms of morphine poisoning, they were asked whether they had taken into consideration the possibility that belladonna had been administered with the morphine and if they had made their deductions accordingly. Both admitted that they had not thought of this possibility and that such a double drugging might have escaped their suspicion and been the cause of Mrs. Buchanan's death.

The public interest and excitement were unbounded, but they were of a different quality from those exhibited the year before in the Harris case. Harris had been young and handsome. He had possessed a presence and a reputation for gallantry. Besides, his victim had been a beautiful young woman of good family, an attendant at a fashionable girls' school—a creature of the upper world. The man accused of this murder was romantic and attractive. He drew to himself a great following of the morbidly sentimental and the love-starved. Buchanan, on the other hand, was a curious-looking little fellow, almost a grotesque. The woman had been old, drab, and lewd. The whole affair was sordid. Furthermore, although the girl who had died at the hands of Harris was young and sweet, while Buchanan's alleged victim was a creature who probably deserved any fate, the unthinking public evinced nothing but loathing and contempt for this later defendant.

The struggle over the life of Robert Buchanan very soon resolved itself into a technical and scientific tournament, in which experts for one side vied with those of the other. The State showed that Mrs. Buchanan's body had been exhumed and examined both anatomically and chemically. Anatomists had made sections of the brain and discovered that there were no clots or lesions of any kind, so that the deathbed diagnosis of cerebral hemorrhage was mistaken. The chemists then took the stand and testified that they had found one-tenth of a grain of morphine in a small part of the dead woman's viscera—enough to indicate the presence of at least five grains in her body, more than sufficient to have caused death. They also stated that they had noted the presence of another drug, which, they were ready to testify, must have been belladonna or atropine or some other derivative of the deadly nightshade.

Other experts then testified that any of the nightshade poisons would have had the effect of confusing and changing the symptoms of the morphine poisoning. They stated that such drugs were commonly used in larger doses to counteract the effects of morphine and it was pointed out that at the deathbed of Helen Potts, atropine had actually been employed for this purpose, but to no avail. This drug, which is the active alkaloid of the plant Atropa belladonna, paralyses the accommodation of the eye and causes the pupil to distend.

Not much more than a century before the Buchanan and Harris trials, such a ruse as Doctor Buchanan is supposed to have employed would have been entirely successful, for chemical analysis was not used in post-mortem examinations and the detection of poisons by means of laboratory tests was so crude and uncertain that little dependence could be placed upon it. Courts and juries alike rejected it and prosecutors had to rely upon the symptomatic evidence. In this case, obviously, all testimony of the latter kind must have been in favour of the defendant and the culprit would almost certainly have gone free. With the more modern methods, however, there was another story to tell.

It was in this contest of test tubes, reagents, and colour reactions that Attorney O'Sullivan achieved a most striking personal triumph. This man, though new to the bar, had been a physician and had changed his profession later in life. He brought to the courtroom not only considerable legal resourcefulness and forensic power, but also a scientifically trained mind.

Again and again in the course of the trial O'Sullivan rose to attack the eminent and self-assured experts of the State and succeeded, time after time, in confusing and correcting them, forcing them into equivocations and expressions of doubt, where a less-well-equiped counsellor would have left them practically unimpeached. The reporters and onlookers were at first amazed and later thrilled by this exhibition of learning and resource. Before many days had passed it was freely whispered about that O'Sullivan had beaten the State at its own game and that Buchanan, for all the feeling against him, had an excellent chance of going free.

But O'Sullivan had not yet played his trump ace. In the course of cross-questioning the State's experts he asked each of them in turn with great particularly about colour reactions which were produced by treating human remains with acids. If there was a trace of morphine in the substance so treated, the test tube would show a brilliant red colour, would it not? The experts all answered that it would. This was because the acids, acting on the morphine produced a certain salt having a rose colour, was it not? Again the answer was yes. Now, the value of this test lay in the fact that these stated reagents would reproduce this colour by combination with no known substance except morphine. Was that not so? The experts again answered yes. In other words, O'Sullivan went on, the whole value of the test lay in the fact that morphine was the only chemical substance that would produce this red reaction. That was a well-known scientific fact, was it not? Once more came the affirmative answer.

When the time came Mr. O'Sullivan suavely trotted out Doctor Victor C. Vaughn, the celebrated toxicologist and chemist of the University of Michigan. Doctor Vaughn was asked about the Pellagri test for morphine. Yes, it was the one the State had laid such store by. Was it true, as the State contended, that these marked effects in the test tube could only be produced if the contents of the intestines held some morphine in solution or suspension?

For answer Doctor Vaughn had a table placed in front of the witness stand and went to work with his test tubes. He first took some of the ptomaine indol, produced in the decaying human intestine by bacterial action, added to it a tenth of a grain of morphine, as the State's experts had testified they had proceeded, and poured in his acids. Immediately there was the bright red colouration in the tube, the sure sign of morphine presence in connection with the indol.

But now came the shock and surprise. Doctor Vaughn took another test tube, some more of the ptomaine product but no morphine. He put in some other chemicals and then added his acids. A thrill of wonder and surprise ran through the courtroom, for there on the dark little table stood the tube, glowing red once more—a symbol of the State's defeat.

For upward of twenty days this brilliant struggle between the rival experts went forward session after session, while the insignificant little defendant was practically forgotten and Lawyer O'Sullivan stalked magnificiently through triumph after triumph, the hero of the case, a legal luminary arisen overnight. O'Sullivan revelled in it. He overlooked no opportunities for a display of brilliancy and he missed no chance to discredit the prosecution by a shaft of wit or barb of irony. If the onlookers had felt, in the early stages of his performance, that Buchanan had a good chance for his life, they were now ready to lay heavy odds in favour of acquittal. O'Sullivan had shot the State's case full of holes.

But the time came for the experts to cease, for O'Sullivan to retire from the centre of the stage, and for the miserable little man of medicine to come forward again into the limelight.

I mention the Carlyle Harris case again because it was constantly in the minds of the public, the jurors, the attorneys and the defendant in this trial. Harris had refused to take the witness stand and submit to cross-examination, and it was felt by many that it was this evasion of frankness which had caused his conviction. Buchanan evidently was obsessed by this idea and he took the stand over the protests of his attorneys, who knew they had won the case.

Here the black shadow of the executioner advanced across the courtroom. Doctor Buchanan, an excellent witness on the direct examination, was putty in the hands of Prosecutor Wellman, one of the most formidable cross-examiners who ever questioned an American witness. In an almost unbelievably short time he had the weak little physician reduced to a cringing, contradicting, contemptible poltroon, a man who had convicted himself out of his own mouth.

If more had been needed it was immediately forthcoming, for the State introduced a letter which Buchanan had written to Macomber from Nova Scotia, after the death of his wife. The treacherous former friend of the doctor had turned this up together with every other confidence the doctor had reposed in him. This letter has never been printed, for the most obvious reasons, and it was, if I remember correctly, not read in court, but passed from juror to juror and entered on the minutes of the trial without being testified to aloud. The contents of the thing were shocking, morally atrocious.

But, when all this is said and done, it must be admitted that the letter had absolutely nothing to do with the murder. It made no mention of anything at issue in the case and was, in fact, a mere vulgar recitation of things Buchanan was doing or, perhaps, imagining on his trip to his home country. The defence fought hard to have it excluded for these reasons, but the State pleaded that it showed the state of mind of the doctor within a couple of weeks of his wife's death and was thus part of the circumstantial chain. Recorder Smyth admitted it. Since the Court of Appeals refused to find any flaw in the trial, it must be concluded that this admission was legally correct, however erroneous it must seem in logic to try a man charged with murder on moral issues rather than upon the direct evidence of homicide.

Even after his miserable showing on the stand and the production of his befouling letter, Buchanan and his attorneys did not believe the jury would find against them. They had made an excellent defence and fairly riddled the crucial testimony of the State's witnesses. But they guessed without the scruples of an American jury. The panel retired late on the afternoon of the twenty-fifth of April, just a year after the burial of the victim. Twenty-eight hours later, on the evening of the twenty-sixty, the court received the verdict:

'Guilty of murder in the first degree.'

'Oh, that's impossible!' cried Attorney Brooke, rising in his chair, apparently astounded at the outcome.

When the verdict was repeated, Mr. Brooke, objected to the form in which the verdict was worded, saying that 'guilty' or 'guilty as charged' would have been sufficient. His point was, of course, that in this emphatic verdict the jury had exhibited its own passion and abhorrence, a charge which was more or less substantiated when the jurors said they had reached their verdict very early and that they had delayed so long in reporting because one of their number had taken ill and had slept and recovered before the final signing of the verdict was done.

But, be that as it may, the verdict had been delivered and it stood. The case went twice to the Court of Appeals and once to the United States Supreme Court on a writ of error. The Governor of the State granted two reprieves and reconsidered appeals for clemency. The British ambassador, Lord Pauncefote, was asked to intercede on behalf of a British subject, as Buchanan had never been naturalized. But all in vain. On the second of July, 1895, more than three years after his crime, Buchanan went to the chair and died the death of a rogue who is also a fool.

E.H.S.

# 1895

# H.H. HOLMES
## The Torture Doctor

I have often regretted that the science of criminal psychology had not developed sufficiently by the mid-1890s to justify a careful study of one of the most interesting mass murderers produced by America – Herman Webster Mudgett, alias H. H. Holmes, whose arrest in 1894 came about through the discovery of an insurance fraud. When the 'castle' – a huge house he had had built on 63rd Street, in Chicago's Englewood section – was examined, it was found to be a maze of trapdoors and secret rooms; and a large number of bones, skulls and teeth were found buried in the basement. It soon became clear that America had produced its most spectacular mass murderer. Newspapers spoke of two hundred victims, but the sum is probably about twenty – exceeded, so far as America is concerned, only by Pomeroy in those times.

Harry Howard Holmes – as he came to call himself – is a paradoxical character. Born in 1860 in Gilmanton, a small town in New Hampshire, he came of a secure middle-class background – his father was postmaster. He graduated at a school in Vermont, was a schoolteacher for a while, then went on to medical school at Ann Arbor, Michigan (a town that deserves a chapter to itself in the history of murder – it has had several remarkable cases). John Bartlow Martin believes that it was at medical school that Holmes practised his first swindle, an insurance fraud involving the theft of a body on its way to the dissecting room, and the faked death of a patient whom Holmes had insured. Presumably he and the patient split the proceeds. He had married at eighteen, but deserted his wife and child eight years later, after he had graduated from medical school. He combined the natural temperament of a swindler with a curious interest in hypnotism and the occult – Martin suggests that his later murders were an attempt to put into practice certain 'theories about human nature' that he does not specify. It is typical of him that, having deserted his wife, he arranged for her to hear indirectly that he had been in a train wreck and was probably suffering from amnesia.

Under his true name – of Mudgett – he practised medicine briefly in Mooers Forks, NY, but when he moved to Chicago in 1886, he had decided to call himself Holmes – presumably so as to be untraceable by his wife, Clara Lovering. In Wilmette, a northern suburb of Chicago, he met a pretty girl named Myrta Belknap, whose family was well-to-do, and married her bigamously in early 1887. The family broke with Holmes after he had forged the signature of her uncle John Belknap on a note, and it is recorded that he invited Uncle John up to the roof of his new house to discuss the matter. Some instinct told Uncle John not to go.

His only venture in legitimate business failing – it was a duplicating company – he discovered an interesting possibility on the south side: a Mrs. Holden, who ran a drugstore on 63rd Street, Englewood, needed an assistant. With his medical knowledge, Holmes was the ideal man. Three years later, in 1890, Holmes had become a partner in the store, and Mrs. Holden talked about rigged books and prosecution. Then Mrs. Holden vanished, and Holmes owned the store. No one knows what happened to her, and Holmes never told.

Soon he was doing so well in business that he built another house opposite the store – his 'murder castle'. His method here was to quarrel with the gangs of workmen every few weeks and pay them off – so that no one knew too much about the place. He apparently raised the money for the building by the sale of patent medicines for which he made spectacular claims. It was three storeys high; the ground floor contained shops, the next floor contained Holmes's 'chambers', the top floor consisted of apartments. The reason he gave for building the castle was that it was intended as a hotel for visitors to the Chicago World Fair of 1893. But he had gas pipes installed so that he could flood any room with gas – recalling Marcel Petiot – and secret peepholes into every room.

Now, with his second 'wife' safely at home in Wilmette, Holmes began to go in for seduction and murder. A jeweller named Conner moved into the drugstore – it was agreed that he should have a corner of the store for his watch-repairing business, while his wife Julia helped Holmes as a clerk. When Conner realised that Holmes and Julia were lovers, he moved out, leaving his wife and her sister Gertie – aged eighteen – behind. Both of them became his mistresses. Then Gertie became pregnant, and disappeared. Holmes took her in to a business acquaintance to say goodbye, and then told him some weeks later that Gertie had died. The business friend said, 'Holmes, you've killed her.' Holmes said: 'Pooh! what makes you think that?' and nothing more was said.

Holmes was attracted by a sixteen-year-old blonde named Emily van Tassel, who came to the ice-cream parlour, usually with her mother. When Emily disappeared one day, Holmes denied all knowledge of her whereabouts. She was never seen again.

In spite of now owning two drugstores and a 'hotel', Holmes preferred to live by various forms of confidence trickery. There was a machine which, he claimed, could make inflammable gas out of water by splitting up its hydrogen and oxygen. Actually, the machine was connected to the gas supply; but it was sold to a Canadian for two thousand dollars. Holmes discovered that the gaseous water was a mild stimulant (alcoholics still use gas bubbled into water when they can get nothing else), and sold it in the shop, claiming he had discovered a medicinal spring. The gas company found out and threatened to sue. He furnished the 'castle' on credit. When he failed to pay, the company tried to reclaim its property, but found the house empty. A porter who was bribed with twenty-five dollars told them that the furniture had all been put into a room whose door had been bricked up and then wallpapered; the company recovered its furniture. Huge quantities of crockery were found in a space in the roof, and repossessed. Holmes met a thief named Pitezel, who became a partner in his swindles. When Pitezel was arrested in Terre Haute for a dud cheque, Holmes posed as an Indiana congressman and bailed him out with another dud cheque.

Holmes' career as a seducer and murderer was also going forward swiftly. A new blonde secretary, Emily Cigrand, moved into the store. Julia showed signs of jealousy, and would tiptoe from her upstairs apartment to listen outside Holmes' door. Holmes had a buzzer installed under one of the steps to warn him. Finally he got tired of her jealousy; Julia and her eight-years-old daughter disappeared in early autumn, 1892. Miss Cigrand also vanished in December. The reason seems to have been that he had met a girl named Minnie Williams, who had inherited property to the value of twenty thousand dollars. Minnie, a pretty but brainless girl, lived with Holmes throughout the World Fair, which started on 1st May 1893. The upper apartments were kept permanently filled, and at least two of Holmes' female guests simply vanished; there may have been more. In June, Minnie's sister Annie came to stay with them. Like Minnie, she believed Holmes to be a wealthy businessman. In July, she wrote to the aunt who had brought them up: Brother Harry says you need never trouble any more about me, financially or otherwise.' She was going to Germany to study art. She vanished. Minnie continued to live with Holmes as his wife, and Pitezel often lived with them. (He also had a wife and five children.)

It should be clear by now that Holmes was not a successful confidence swindler; something always seemed to go wrong with his plans. But he had now got himself so far into debt that he could see no alternative. When the castle was empty again – the Fair being over – Holmes set fire to it, and tried to collect sixty thousand dollars from an insurance company for damage to its upper storeys. They were suspicious, and soon uncovered something of Holmes' past. Holmes was living in a small hotel with Minnie and Pitezel in November, when the insurance company lured him to their office to talk it over. Then a police inspector named Cowrie called on Minnie and sternly told her that the fraud had been discovered. She believed him, and confessed. Cowrie left with the policy, and the insurance

company decided not to sue for attempted fraud. But Holmes'
other creditors heard about it – no doubt Cowrie took care that
they should – and presented Holmes with bills totalling fifty
thousand dollars. On 22nd November, Holmes and Minnie fled
from Chicago. By this time, she had transferred all her property
to Holmes. It was time for her to disappear, and she did. Holmes
was later to accuse her of murdering Annie by hitting her with
a stool in a jealous rage.

Holmes had met a blonde girl with immense blue eyes
during the Exposition; her name was Georgiana Yoke, and
she demanded marriage if she was to surrender her virginity.
It made no difference to Holmes – he already had two wives;
so he married her in Denver in January 1894. Martin adds
the astonishing detail that Minnie was a witness, and that she
did not 'disappear' until some months later, which raises the
possibility that Minnie knew more of Holmes' affairs than his
previous mistresses had, and was an accomplice – perhaps even
in her sister's murder. With Minnie out of the way, Holmes and
Pitezel went to Fort Worth to realise her property. They used it
to raise a loan of sixteen thousand dollars, and also as collateral
for the purchase of a large number of horses. In June, Holmes
and Pitezel moved to Saint Louis, where Holmes bought another
drugstore, mortgaged the stock, then let Pitezel remove it all.
This fraud led to his only period in jail; he was arrested on 19th
July 1894, and bailed out by Georgiana on 31st.

It was in jail in St. Louis that Holmes met the celebrated train
robber, Marion Hedgepeth, of whom the detective Pinkerton
said, 'He was one of the worst characters I ever heard of. He
was bad all through.' Hedgepeth dressed like a banker, but was
reputed to have the fastest draw in the West; he once killed a
man whose gun was already out of its holster when Hedgepeth
started to draw. Women fought to get into the courtroom when
the good-looking Hedgepeth was tried.

Holmes told Hedgepeth that he had worked out a perfect
insurance swindle. It involved insuring a man's life, getting him
killed in an apparently accidental explosion, and substituting
another body for the 'victim'. (It will be recalled that Holmes
started his career with a similar swindle). He asked Hedgepeth if
he knew of a suitable crooked lawyer to deal with the insurance
company. Hedgepeth put him on to one Jephta D Howe. Pitezel

was to be the 'victim', who could be insured for ten thousand dollars. In the event of a successful swindle, Hedgepeth would get five hundred dollars, Howe two thousand five hundred dollars, and Pitezel and Holmes would share the rest.

What Pitezel did not know was that Holmes had no intention of finding a corpse to substitute for his own. Holmes had a much simpler method. Kill Pitezel, and take his share of the money.

For the purpose of the fraud, Holmes and Pitezel moved to Philadelphia, and rented a house at 1316 Callowhill Street, which backed on the morgue. No doubt Holmes told Pitezel he intended to get the body from the morgue. Under the name of B F Perry, Pitezel moved into the house and erected a sign that claimed he was a dealer in patents. He moved in on 17th August. A carpenter named Eugene Smith brought him a device for setting saws. Pitezel told him to leave it. On 3rd September, Smith called in to find how the sale of his patent was going, and found the place empty, with the door open. After waiting for a while, he looked upstairs – and found Pitezel's swollen and decomposing corpse. The police were called in, and soon decided that Pitezel had been conducting some experiment using chloroform, and had made the mistake of trying to light his pipe too close to it. The inquest found that his death was accidental. Five days later, the Fidelity Mutual Life Insurance Company on Walnut Street received a telegram from their St. Louis branch declaring that B F Perry was actually Benjamin Fuller Pitezel, and that he was insured by them. A few days later, the company received a letter from the lawyer Jephta D Howe saying that he represented Pitezel's widow Carrie and would be calling on them. The insurance company tried to trace Pitezel's former address in Chicago, and found their way to Myrta Belknap, the second Mrs. Holmes. Holmes apparently kept in touch with her, for she agreed to send him a message – he was on 'business trip' – and in due course, Holmes contacted the insurance company. By this time, Pitezel was burried. Eventually, Holmes arrived in Philadelphia, and offered to identify the body. Jephta D Howe also arrived with Pitezel's second eldest daughter, Alice, and the body was exhumed and quickly identified. The insurance company paid up without hesitation. But Holmes was less willing to part with the five hundred dollars he had promised Hedgepeth, not to mention the two thousand five hundred dollars for Howe. Howe told his elder brother about his grievance, and since the elder brother was Hedgepeth's lawyer, he advised the train robber to make some capital out of it by denoucing 'Howard' (Holmes' alias) and trying to get his sentence reduced for his public spiritedness. This did not work – he was still sentenced to twelve years – but the insurance company suddenly realised they had been defrauded. The alarm went out for Holmes. But he had returned to St. Louis, and taken away two to the remaining four children – Nellie, aged eleven, and Howard, nine – claiming that they were on their way to rejoin Pitezel. Alice had been left in Indianapolis – no doubt Holmes was afraid that she would reveal the body *was* that of her father after all – and Holmes then rejoined her.

For the next week or so, Holmes was nowhere to be found. It was later established that he visited his family in New Hampshire, and even his first wife. He defrauded his brother of three hundred dollars, then went back to Burlington, Vermont, where Pinkerton detectives finally traced him. He was living with Georgiana, and Mrs. Pitezel, with two remaining children – a girl of sixteen and a baby – were living nearby. The detectives traced Holmes by following the trail of Mrs. Pitezel from St. Louis to Detroit and Toronto. When the fugitives moved to Boston, and Holmes began making the round of steamship offices, the police decided it was time to pounce, and Holmes was finally arrested on 17th November 1894. His career of murder had been brief – from 1890 to 1894 – but eventful.

On the way back to Philadelphia (with Mrs. Pitezel), Holmes lied fluently and involvedly, an offered the guard five hundred dollars if he would allow him to hypnotise him. (This raises an interesting possibility about why Minnie Williams and so many other women were so completely in his power.) When he arrived in Philadelphia, it was to find that Pitezel's body had been exhumed again, and that it had now been discovered that he died of chloroform poisoning, not of the explosion. It must have begun to dawn slowly on Mrs. Pitezel about now that her husband was dead and the three children had vanished. Holmes had told her he had no idea what Pitezel had done with them, and suggested that the eldest girl Dessie should be sent to join him.

A detective named Geyer did a remarkable piece of work in tracing what had become of the children. Geyer plodded from hotel to hotel in Cincinnati – where Mrs. Pitezel thought Holmes had taken the children – until he found one where a man had stayed with three children. Holmes had used an alias, of course. After weeks of checking hotels and houses, he had the photographs of Holmes and the children published in the press, and this led him to a house in Toronto where a man and two girls had arrived in late October. Holmes had borrowed a spade from the old gentleman next door. The bodies of the girls were found in the cellar, buried under a few feet of earth. The boy Howard was more difficult to trace. Evidence showed that he had never even reached Toronto. Accordingly, Geyer returned to Indianapolis, and began patiently checking hotels in every outlying town. At last there was only one left – Irvington; and it was in Irvington that Geyer at last discovered that Holmes had arrived at a rented house with a nine-year-old boy and a large stove. The boy had watched two workmen erect the stove; later in the day, he ended up in it. Geyer found a few charred bones and teeth in the kitchen chimney.

In his *Book of Remarkable Criminals* (1918), H B Irving has quoted from the letters the children wrote to their mother on that last trip from town to town, bringing home their misery and home-sickness so sharply that they are almost unbearable to read. And suddenly, it becomes very hard to understand how Holmes can have gone through with it, or why he did it. He was covering up his trail; he had killed Pitezel, now he had to kill the rest of the family to escape detection. All for a few thousand dollars. Mrs. Pitezel, Dessie and the baby Wharton were next on the list.

Police now opened Holmes' 'castle' and examined it from cellar to roof. There was a large stove in the cellar with charred human bones in it. More bones were buried under the floor. A dissecting table in the corner was heavily stained with blood. Greased chutes ran from the second and third floor down to the cellar. A handyman who had worked for Holmes now gave the information that Holmes had once given him a male skeleton to mount, and on another occasion, asked him to finish removing the flesh from another skeleton. He said he assumed Holmes was engaged in surgical work. The skeletons were then sold to medical schools. Holmes did not believe in wasting anything.

Holmes lied on to the end. He kept a diary in which he recorded his sense of shock at the discovery of the children's bodies, and how he recalls the 'innocent child's kiss so timidly given' before they waved him goodbye. He accused Minnie Williams of hiring someone to do the murder to spite him. When condemned to death – as he inevitably was – he wrote a long confession for the newspapers in which he admitted to twenty-seven murders, then, after selling it for seven thousand five hundred dollars, he repudiated the whole thing and again declared himself innocent. He conducted his own defence and did it well; but it made no difference. He was hanged on 7th May 1895, at Moyamensing Prison.

It is true that, to a very large degree, Holmes was merely a confidence swindler. It is surprising how many mass murderers began as confidence swindlers – Landru, Joseph Smith, Petiot, Fernandez and Beck. But there is reason to think that he was a man who was fascinated by crime, as Lacenaire was. Martin talks about his 'lifelong preoccupation with cadavers', and one can sense this in reading the full account of the case. One might add: his lifelong preoccupation with sex. The wife of Arthur Rouse referred to him in a letter as a 'sex maniac' – meaning by that a man who needed all the sex he could get, rather than a rapist. Holmes was a sex maniac in this sense. A short, well-dressed, dapper man – he was five feet seven inches tall – with a large droopy moustache and a pink complexion, he had exactly the same kind of sexual vanity as Rouse. Writers on the case who talk about his baleful power over women are talking romantic nonsense – as are the writers who talk in the same way about Landru and Joseph Smith. Any fairly presentable man with a glib tongue can spend his life in seduction if he wants to. Most men over twenty-five are married; most unmarried girls are anxious to marry, and prefer the security of a father-figure, particularly a property owner who claims to be wealthy. But it must also be remembered that Holmes was not living in the mid-twentieth century when very few girls are virgins when they marry. He was living in America – basically a Puritan country anyway – at the end of the nineteenth century, when fiction was full of the awful fate of girls who rashly surrendered their virginity. A girl who did so felt like a criminal.

The business partner Frederick Nind, to whom Gertie Conner came to say goodbye – and who later accused Holmes of killing her – described how Holmes had come into the office one day, and described how he had been out with Gertie the night before and 'committed an indiscretion'. It may be that Holmes was preparing his partner for his later admission that Gertie was pregnant; but the fact that he thought it worthy of remark demonstrates that he was not seducing women every other day. And why did the sixteen-year-old Emily van Tassel vanish? She had no money, she was not living in the castle. It is fairly obvious that Holmes managed to get her into the castle one night, chloroformed and raped her, then put her body into the chute to the basement. The larger number of his victims were women; from what we know of his sexual appetite, it is probable that he violated most of them either before or after death; if Martin is correct about his 'lifelong preoccupation with cadavers', the probability is that it was after death. What was his aim in building a house with peepholes into every room and secret passageways? That he intended to use it, to some extent, for confidence trickery cannot be doubted; but not *every* room. He was a voyeur; and unlike most voyeurs, he wanted to do more than look. A solitary girl could be rendered unconscious by gas piped into the room after she was asleep, then chloroformed to keep her unconscious, and later disposed of in the stove. What of the two male skeletons the caretaker mentioned? Were they the husbands of women Holmes particularly wanted? It is true that they might just as well have been men he had killed for their money. But in that case, why this odd touch of selling the skeletons instead of disposing of them in the normal way? They could not have brought in all that much money – a medical student can buy his own skeleton for a few dollars – and they were a considerable risk. But Holmes was a strange kind of power maniac, a man who enjoyed the feeling of being a wolf preying on society. It would have increased his pleasure in possessing the wife to think that her husband had not been able to protect her – that, in fact, he would soon be an exhibit in a medical school, murdered by Holmes, the super-criminal and super-ravisher.

It is true that, as a super-criminal, Holmes is disappointingly unlike Conan Doyle's Professor Moriarty; no 'Napoleon of crime', but a bungling confidence man. But real super-criminals are like that; if they had the brains and imagination to turn them into Moriartys they wouldn't be criminals. At worst, they might write obscene books, like Sade.

It is a disquieting thought that Holmes could have killed off the Pitezel family and continued his career of murder for years if it had not been for the denunciation by Hedgepeth. Martin professes himself baffled by Holmes's motive in telling Hedgepeth about his scheme of collecting insurance – for obviously, he could have asked Hedgepeth about a crooked lawyer without telling him everything. But there is really no problem about the motive. Hedgepeth was the 'handsomest outlaw in the West', one of the most famous criminals of his day. Holmes no doubt looked at him with involuntary respect, and then told himself that *he* was a far more successful criminal and lady's man than Hedgepeth. He wanted to boast to Hedgepeth about the superiority of is own methods. I am not now drawing the usual moral that all criminals are trapped by their vanity; Holmes was no more vain than the rest of us. The desire to boast to 'the handsomest outlaw in the West' was natural, if incautious.

C.W.

# 4
# LATE-VICTORIAN
# VILLAINS
## (1888–1905)

# 1888

# JOHN LEE
## The Man They Could Not Hang

John Lee is remembered not for the murder he did, or for any dramatic occurrences at his trial, but for 'cheating the gallows'.

Lee, middle-aged and balding in 1884, was employed as the footman to Miss Emma Keyse, who had once been a maid to Queen Victoria. One November night the staff found the dining room ablaze and, in it, Miss Keyse with a battered head and a cut throat. There had been some awkwardness: she had reduced Lee's wages for some trivial offence, and it was thought that he had been angry about this. So, although the evidence was purely circumstantial, Lee was tried for her murder, found guilty and sentenced to hang.

Hangman Berry placed the hood over Lee's head, attached the noose, pulled the lever – and nothing happened. The lever was tested, and Berry jumped up and down on the trapdoors, but still nothing happened. Lee was taken away so that the apparatus could be tested with a weighted dummy, and with the dummy it worked perfectly, but when Lee took its place the drop once again refused to function. Hangmen take a pride in their work, and this was getting too much for Berry, who now ordered Lee to be removed once more so that completely thorough checks could be made. Again, the test drop worked without a hitch.

Lee was brought back and once more the lever was pulled – and *still* the trap would not open, leaving Lee standing quivering with 8 feet of rope draped loosely about his shoulders. It was thought that heavy rains might have swollen the wood, so Lee was removed yet again and an army of prison staff set to work to make sure that nothing would go wrong – but there were no further tries, for the Sheriff ordered a stay of execution pending instructions from the Home Secretary, and when these came they said that Lee should be jailed, not hanged.

He served 22 years, and after release disappeared from view. An early movie was made about him as *The Man They Could*

*Not Hang*, and somewhere along the way he became a sort of West Country folk hero. It has even been argued that he was innocent and was spared by divine intervention. A rock group has named itself after him.

R.G.J.

# 1893

# A.J. MONSON

# The Ardlamont Mystery

It is a raw December day in Edinburgh. Prosperous folk hurrying in the streets shiver involuntarily as the coin of their charity is seized by the blue fingers of the ragged beggar. . . .

But inside the gloomy building they are passing more than one brow is damp with the sweat of a suspense so painful that the atmosphere seems almost suffocating.

It is the High Court of Justiciary.

The Lord Justice-clerk, impassive on the Bench, glances from the pale, cultured-looking man in the dock to the foreman of the jury, which for ten days has listened to the evidence of nearly one hundred witnesses and the arguments of brilliant counsel, and has now to utter a verdict on which hangs a human life.

A wigged figure breaks the tense silence with a fateful question, and the foreman bends forward a little to reply:

'*Not proven!*'

A pause. Then a murmur runs round the court—of relief, of surprise, of dissent, according to the views of those who have heard the tangled story that has been told and debated inside and outside those walls.

A few formalities, and then Alfred John Monson, whose life has hung in the balance for three months, leaves the dock, a free man—free, but with neither the vindication of innocence nor the stigma of guilt.

Such was the closing scene of a case which in its day aroused as great public interest and as keen controversy as any of the notorious trials of history.

In its main outlines the case of the Ardlamont Mystery—as it had been called, because its scene was laid near Ardlamont House, a property in Argyllshire—was neither more nor less sordid or unusual than many others in which, according to the allegation of the prosecution, a desperate need for money was the motive, rather than those of love or revenge.

It was, however, especially noteworthy for its contribution to the age-old controversy regarding the value of circumstantial evidence.

'A witness may lie,' a famous judge has declared, 'but if you see smoke coming out of a chimney you may reasonably conclude that there is a fire in the house.'

But, as Professor Hans Gross, the 'Father of Criminology,' insisted, it is comparatively easy to accumulate a mass of such evidence, but quite another to decide what deductions may be justly drawn from it.

It was exactly on this No Man's Land that the battle was fought between the eminent experts called by the prosecution and the defence respectively in the Ardlamont Mystery.

The two chief figures in the case were: Alfred John Monson, a well-educated man of early middle-age, who was accused on two counts of murdering and of attempting to murder Windsor Duley Cecil Hambrough, who at the time of his death on August 10, 1893, was a twenty-year-old lieutenant in the 3rd (Militia) Battalion of the West Yorkshire Regiment.

Cecil Hambrough was the son of Major Dudley Hambrough. The major held a life interest (in Scotland he would be called the heir of entail) in the Hambrough family estates, which were producing between £4000 and £5000 a year, and he also had a prospective interest in other property.

He was not, however, very wise in money matters, and was admittedly in serious financial difficulties when his son reached the age of seventeen, and it became necessary to think of preparing the lad for the Army career for which Major Hambrough destined him.

The major had had financial dealings with a certain Mr. Tottenham, a London financier, and Tottenham introduced Alfred Monson to him in 1890, with the suggestion that Monson should undertake Cecil's tuition and guidance at a fee of £300 a year.

This was arranged, and Cecil went to Yorkshire, where Monson and his family were living near Ripley.

For some time Major Hambrough and Monson continued to be on good terms, and Monson figured in some rather complicated negotiations aimed at extricating the major from his difficulties. They were not successful, however, and a coolness ensued which ended in Major Hambrough trying to induce his son to return home.

Cecil, however, preferred life with the Monsons to the ups and downs of his father's existence, and refused to return. He had already entered the Militia (in those days a stepping-stone to the Regular Army), and he and Monson were excellent friends.

For some time, it was admitted, both Monson and Cecil had been receiving financial aid from Mr. Tottenham—aid which in Monson's case was necessary, for in August, 1892, he was adjudged a bankrupt.

In the following January he and Cecil tried to raise money on the young man's expectancy in the Hambrough estates, but the effort was not successful.

In May (1893), Monson secured a lease of Ardlamont House, an Argyllshire property in the Kilfinan district to which one could travel by streamer from Glasgow, disembarking preferably at the Kames pier, about five miles from the house. As Monson could not himself contract the lease, it was done in the names of Cecil Hambrough and a Mr. Jerningham, the latter being put forward by Monson as Cecil's guardian, and as sound security for the rent, which was to be £450 for the season, payable in portions.

Monson, his wife and children, and a governess, went to Ardlamont, and Cecil joined them there after finishing his period of training with the Militia.

In July there began attempts to effect an insurance on Cecil's life, and although at first unsuccessful, the Mutual Life Assurance Company of New York and Glasgow finally accepted the young man's proposal for a £20,000 insurance, divided into two policies of £10,000 each. The first premium (£194) was paid by Monson.

Now comes a point which was subsequently to become an important issue in Monson's trial.

The policies were dated August 4, and on August 7 Cecil wrote to an official of the insurance company asking him to deliver them to Monson's wife, to whom he wished to assign them.

Cecil also executed a letter to Mrs. Monson assigning the policies to her.

*. . . as security against all liabilities incurred by you on my behalf, and in the event of my death occurring before the repayment of these moneys you will be the sole beneficiary of these policies.*

Here, it may be pointed out—as Monson's counsel did at the trial—that if Cecil died (as he did) before reaching the age of twenty-one, the policy money could not be recovered. As Monson declared that he was unaware of this fact, the suggestion was that the whole transaction was due merely to Cecil's desire to reward those for whose kindness to him he was grateful.

And now there comes into the picture a character whose proceedings formed one of the greatest mysteries in the whole affair.

On Tuesday, August 8, the day after Cecil had written the two letters mentioned, there arrived at Ardlamont a man introduced by Monson as one Scott, who was described as an engineer, who had come to inspect the boilers of a yacht which Monson had brought on Cecil's behalf.

Cecil, enjoying to the full the opportunities for outdoor sport afforded by the estate, made Scott a welcome guest, and the three men got on excellently.

On the Wednesday (August 9) after dinner, Monson, Cecil and Scott went to Ardlamont Bay to fish. Scott remained on shore, but Monson and Cecil put out in a boat. When they all returned to the house about midnight, Monson and Cecil were wet through, but they laughingly explained that they had had a mishap.

On this incident, however, the Crown later based its charge against Monson of attempting to murder Cecil. It was found that a hole had been cut in the boat. Monson's account of the affair was that in the darkness the boat had struck a rock and capsized. Cecil, who could not swim, clung to the rock, while Monson swam to the shore, obtained another boat and picked Cecil up.

'In fact,' said Monson, 'so far from trying to murder him I saved his life.'

Early next morning (Wednesday, August 10), Mrs. Monson, the children and the governess left to go by boat to Glasgow, where they were to spend the day, and soon afterwards Monson, Scott and Cecil set out on what was to be the latter's last adventure.

They were going shooting, and Monson carried a 12-bore shot-gun. Cecil's gun was a 20-bore.

A witness named James Dunn saw them enter a field, and presently they entered a wood and were lost to his sight.

Soon afterwards Monson and Scott returned to the house and informed the butler that Cecil had shot himself accidentally. The butler and other servants hurried with Monson to the north end of the wood, where Cecil's dead body was found, with a gunshot wound in the head. He was lying on his back, with his head to the north, between the edge of the wood and a plantation of trees.

A doctor was called. He saw no cause for suspicion. Scott then left Ardlamont, and was not heard of again until nearly a year later, long after Monson's trial had ended.

Cecil's body was taken to Ventnor (Isle of Wight) for burial, and no more was heard of the matter until officials of the insurance company, who had been approached by Mr. Tottenham on Mrs. Monson's behalf, began investigations. These inquiries led to the exhumation of Cecil's body, and the arrest of Monson on August 29.

After three months' preparation the case came into court, Mr. Asher, Q.C., the Solicitor-General, leading for the Crown, and Mr. J. Comrie Thomson for the defence.

It was an extraordinary legal battle conducted on both sides with admirable forensic ability that never passed the bounds of the strictest equity. Of the ninety-four witnesses, many were experts. They included Sir Henry Littlejohn, the famous medical authority, Dr. Matthew Hay, Dr. P. H. Watson, Dr. Joseph Bell, Mr. Speedy, a naturalist, and others.

The contention of the defence was that Cecil had been carrying his gun at the 'trail,' when he stumbled in getting over a fence, and the weapon exploded and shot him. When it was proved (a point which had escaped the doctor who first saw the body) that he had been killed by shot from a 12-bore gun, Monson explained that he and Cecil had exchange guns shortly after leaving the house.

Monson declared that he and Scott (who could not be called, having disappeared) had not seen the accident happen. They had heard a shot, called out to Cecil, and, on receiving no reply, had walked in the direction of the sound and found the young man lying dead.

'The case is purely one of circumstantial evidence,' said the Lord Justice-clerk in charging the jury. 'Everything in it depends on inferences to be drawn, and it is quite certain that, in a case where the evidence is purely circumstantial, if every link in it is a sound link and is well welded into the next, there cannot be a stronger case than that.'

The defence argued, with reason, that Monson had no motive for taking the life of a young man on whom his financial future appeared to depend.

There can, one thinks, be no doubt that the Crown failed to prove that Monson killed Cecil Hambrough.

In an English court Monson would have been either acquitted or convicted; as it was, the law of Scotland allowed him to be sent forth under a cloud.

A point made, for example, by the Crown was the position of the dead youth's body. It was argued that this showed that he had been struck by shot from a gun held horizontally. The point was met by the contention that Monson and Scott had moved the body from the spot where they found it.

Another question raised was the distance at which a charge of shot fired from a gun will begin to spread, but competent witnesses were oddly at variance on the point.

When Mr. Scott failed to appear at the trial the Court pronounced sentence of 'outlawry' against him. In May of the following year, however, he turned up, figuring in a conjurer's entertainment in an Edinburgh music-hall. While there he appealed to the Court of Justiciary to withdraw the sentence of outlawry pronounced against him, and this the Court did.

So closed the last chapter of the story—leaving the Ardlamont Mystery still as much as ever.

F.D.G.

## 1895

# TED DURRANT

## The Corpse in the Belfry

Among the silly ideas which no fiction writer in his senses would try to sell an editor, I think you could safely count a story about a church with a curse on it. It is therefore with particular pleasure that I bring to your notice the Emmanuel Baptist Church of Bartlett Street, San Francisco—a church which I deeply regret having failed to create myself, in one of my Saint stories.

This church was a well-found establishment with an unusually active congregation, ambitious enough to possess a library of improving literature, and topped by a genuine belfry complete with bell. Nevertheless, from the day it was consecrated this church seems to have been saddled with a hoodoo. One of its first pastors committed suicide in his study. The next incumbent went out and bumped off a leading citizen. He was acquitted by a sympathetic jury, but naturally became somewhat *persona non grata* with the board of trustees, who promptly advertised for a replacement. The one they got turned out to be a clerical Casanova who stirred up such a commotion among the flock that his resignation had to be asked for. The elders must have inspected the next applicant with an exceptionally leery eye.

The Reverend J. George Gibson, however, who took over, successfully survived their scrutiny. Although he was only thirty-five and still a bachelor, his references from his former parishioners seemed to guarantee his reliability. As to any latent tendencies he may have had towards indulgence in -cide, whether sui- or homi-, the trustees presumably could only keep their fingers crossed.

Among the most enthusiastic of the younger helpers whom

he inherited was one William Henry Theodore Durrant. Ted Durrant, as he was generally called, was a stocky young man of twenty-three, not unlike Gibson in appearance, even to sporting a similar scrubby moustache. Durrant voluntarily served as church librarian, secretary of a the Christian Endeavour Society, and assistant superintendent of the Sunday school. He was a medical student at Cooper College. He neither drank nor smoked and was regarded by most members of the Emmanuel Church as quite a paragon of youthful virtue.

However, to forestall the sceptics who will already be suspecting such a model of purity, let us immediately reveal that Ted Durrant does appear to have had quite a jolly girl friend.

Her name was Blanche Lamont. She had arrived in San Francisco only two months before the Reverend Mr. Gibson, and was living with her uncle and aunt, Mr. and Mrs. George A. Noble. She was studying to be a teacher at the Powell Street Normal School.

She was a pretty girl of twenty-one years, sixty-seven inches, and 122 nicely distributed pounds, with big brown eyes and beautiful auburn hair. She had joined the Emmanuel congregation, and was known as an industrious church worker. And yet, paradoxically, it was rumoured that she was no better than she should be, if as good.

These rumours were sufficiently widespread to give considerable concern to her aunt, Mrs. Noble, and to her best friend—a slim, shy, perhaps even prettier girl of nineteen, named Marian Elora Williams, whom they called Minnie.

On Wednesday, April 3, 1895, Blanche Lamont went to school as usual. After classes, at three o'clock three other girls saw her meet a young man, whom they later identified as Ted Durrant, and get on a street-car with him. Later in the afternoon other witnesses saw them together near the Emmanuel Church; and a Mrs. Caroline Leak, who lived opposite the church and knew them both, saw them go in.

What happened after that no living person will ever know, for Blanche Lamont was never seen alive again.

Durrant himself went to Mrs. Noble and said he would help try to find her niece.

'But I think you ought to be careful about making a public fuss about it,' he advised. 'You know, those rumours . . . If it turned out she'd left town to avoid a scandal, the publicity would only make matters worse.'

Minnie Williams had other ideas.

'That Ted Durrant knows a lot more about Blanche's disappearance than he's talking about,' she told several acquaintances.

Minnie Williams, poor girl, was perhaps too young to grasp fully all the occupational hazards of shooting off the mouth.

April 12 was Good Friday, but not for her. That afternoon she visited a family named Voy in the Mission district, and, at about the time she would have crossed the Bay to San Francisco, Ted Durrant was seen at the ferry building by several of his fellow medical students. Minnie left the Voys at eight o'clock in the evening to go to a Christian Endeavour meeting. And once again the story lapses into one of those exasperating silences; for she never got there.

The following morning Mrs. George Noble received a peculiar package in the mail. It contained three of Blanche's rings, wrapped in a piece of newspaper, on the margin of which were hand-printed the names of three pillars of the Emmanuel Baptist Church: George King, the organist; George Schoenstein, a music teacher; and Ted Durrant.

It was highly mystifying, but all Mrs. Noble could think of was Ted Durrant's warning and her fear that the rumours about her niece might be disastrously vindicated. She hastily re-wrappped the package and put it away, saying nothing to anyone.

At 8 a.m. that same Saturday morning, the Reverend J. George Gibson arrived at the church and found the lock on the vestibule door leading to the library broken. But he had his Easter sermon to work on, and nothing seemed to have been stolen, so for the time being he put the broken lock out of his mind and went to his study.

He had not been working long when the janitor, Frank Sademan, came in and told him about the lock.

'I know,' said Gibson. 'I'll have it investigated. But leave it to me—don't say anything about it.' He wrote steadily for an hour and then went home to the near-by boarding-house where he lived.

A little later, a gaggle of female volunteers swarmed into the church and began to decorate it for the Easter Sunday service.

It was about ten-thirty when one of them, a Mrs. Herman Nolt, went into the library to look for a vase. Peering into a small adjoining room used for the storage of extra books, she saw, on the table inside, the dead and mutilated body of a girl.

Mrs. Nolt let out a banshee squawk which brought the rest of the decorating detail running, while she herself hustled down the street to tell the pastor.

Mr. Gibson, while properly shocked, waited to collect one of his trustees to go with him to view the body.

The victim had obviously fought desperately for her life, but she could not have called much for help, for a cloth gag had been stuffed into her mouth and rammed home with a stick. Her dress was in shreds. A piece of a broken dinner knife was stuck in her chest, and she was slashed so viciously that neither Gibson nor the trustee could positively identify her, although Blanche Lamont's library card lay close beside her.

'You'll have to excuse me,' said the Reverend Mr. Gibson, in great distress. He headed straight for the nearest undertaker's.

'There's a dead body in the church—murdered,' he told the undertaker. 'I want it removed at once. There must be no publicity.'

The undertaker stared at him. 'I can't do that,' he protested. 'It's against the law.'

It was probably one of the most stupid things George Gibson ever did in his life, and, combined with his earlier unconcern about the broken lock on the library door, was to earn him a great deal of embarrassing attention from the Detective Bureau. The only explanation he could give, later, of his conduct was that he was temporarily so overwhelmed by the realisation that his ill-starred church was about to burst into another riot of unsavoury headlines that he lost his head.

The police, however, in the shape of Patrolman Barney Riehl, had already been summoned. A few hours later the victim was identified as Minnie Williams.

Blanche Lamont was still inexplicably missing. But not for long.

On Easter Sunday, April 14, 1895, Officer Barney Riehl, all on his own, went back to the church for another look. He didn't just look in the library and the store-room where Minnie's body had been found. He had a hunch. He climbed a winding stairway to the belfry, observing footprints in the thick dust, and other marks that looked as if something heavy had been dragged up the stairs. And there, in a little tower-room under the big bronze bell, he found Blanche Lamont.

There was no trouble this time about identifying her. She had not been mutilated or disfigured, only strangled. She was naked. Her clothing was stuffed between the bare studs and laths of the tower. She lay on her back, hands folded on her breast, her head pillowed on a block of wood.

Of course, the detectives came back and took over again, elbowing Barney Riehl back into obscurity. They determined, with their high-falutin craft, that Blanche had been strangled by a left-handed man with square-cut finger-nails; they had already found horse hairs on the torn clothing of Minnie Williams. On the strength of this, and because he was the last person known to have been with Blanche before she vanished, and also because he had been lurking around Minnie the day she disappeared, they arrested Theodore Durrant, who was ambidexterous, had square-cut finger-nails, and like riding horses.

He went on trial before Judge D. J. Murphy and a jury on July 22, 1895. It was a long trial, which dragged on until November 1, when the jury took only twenty minutes to find him guilty of murder in the first degree.

He succeeded four times in obtaining a stay of execution. But finally, on January 7, 1898, William Henry Theodore Durrant climbed to the scaffold in San Quentin prison and felt the noose around his neck. To the hundred witnesses who were gathered to see him go, he said: 'I forgive everybody who has persecuted me, an innocent man whose hands have never been stained with blood; and I go to my God with forgiveness for all men.'

It has not been my intention to submit this case as a classic of crime, detection, and punishment. Durrant was convicted purely on circumstantial evidence. After he died there were several 'confessions' by other people, but police never gave any credence to them. Durrant himself never confessed, even to the last, which always leaves a doubt.

But one thing we can be sure of, which I started out with, was the hoodoo on the Emmanuel Baptist Church. In 1909 the Reverend Mr. Gibson resigned as pastor because there was lack of income. Later the church was demolished to make way for newer buildings. It is to be hoped that, when it disappeared, the strange hoodoo that dogged its historical footsteps vanished with it.

L.C.

# 1895

# ROLAND B. MOLINEUX
## The Killer at the Knickerbocker

A slip of paper hanging on a hook in the Coroner's office in the Criminal Courts Building introduced the Molineux case to crime's Hall of Fame. Katherine B. Adams had died suddenly in her home at 61 West Eighty-sixth Street. A routine report filled out on a regular form appeared as just another item in the grist of a coroner's day. But newspaper men sensed significance in it and before long Roland B. Molineux was in the Tombs under indictment for the murder.

Molineux was one of the most active members of the Knickerbocker Athletic Club, organized in 1895. It was at Forty-fifth Street and Madison Avenue. The chief athletic instructor in the club was Harry Cornish. He and Molineux chose not to be friends. Their interests clashed constantly. They appeared to be in competition in a race to win the good will of the club members. Cornish was a man who never pulled his punches and was not above taking any sort of an advantage. Molineux was a chemist and the son of Gen. Edward L. Molineux, one of Brooklyn's most respected citizens.

Soon after the club was opened Molineux and Henry Crossman Barnet became bachelor members and lived there. Barnet was forty and wore a brown beard that was barbered down to a point. He was a broker, and his outdoor pastime was yachting, and he had a way among the women. Molineux was superintenddent of a chemical factory in Newark. He went back and forth daily from the club where he became a member of the house committee. Cornish spent most of his time there. Barnet had little to do with Cornish. Molineux and Cornish first clashed in the spring of 1896 when the club prepared to stage an amateur circus. Cornish saw an opportunity to show off his athletic skill to good advantage, while Molineux had worked on the stage long enough to learn some tricks of showmanship.

The break came when Molineux complained to fellow committeemen that Cornish was not keeping to his place as a paid employee. Cornish retaliated with reflections on Molineux's character. Cornish then was critical of Bartow S. Weeks, the president of the New York Athletic Club, and the Knickerbocker Club was asked to dismiss Cornish. An apology to Mr. Weeks closed the incident but didn't heal the breach between Cornish and Molineux.

Cornish called Molineux a vile name and Molineux retorted that the club was not big enough to hold both of them; that either he or Cornish must go. Molineux resigned. Cornish refused to quit. In the meantime Molineux had been elected to the Board of Governors of the New York Athletic Club. Things then ran more smoothly at the Knickerbocker and in 1898 Cornish moved to the home of Mrs. Adams. In her household was Mrs. Adam's daughter, Laura Rogers, who had been separated from her husband. An elderly woman to whom Cornish was distantly related and who was called 'Aunt' also lived there.

In the same spring Blanche Cheseborough appeared on the scene as a lover of both Barnet and Molineux. She was then 22 years old. She had sex appeal and vivaciousness so that she never lacked for male admirers.

A native of Westerly, R. I., she came to New York in 1894 and within two years she found herself alone, her father and mother both having died. She sang in a church in Brooklyn and a sister helped to maintain her. She met Molineux while cruising in Maine. The following spring Molineux introduced Barnet to her at the opera. From then on life was a merry round for her. She was almost constantly out with Barnet or Molineux.

On Thanksgiving Day, 1897, Molineux proposed marriage to Blanche. She wasn't impressed. Barnet took her to the amateur circus at the Knickerbocker. There were some misgivings, but they soon passed. Blanche did not see Barnet after June, 1898. On October 30 of that year he was taken ill at the club and sent for Dr. Henry Beaman Douglass who found his patient in the barroom weak but able to walk. He had all the symptoms of diphtheria and a culture was taken. The doctor gave Barnet 2,000 units of anti-toxin and Barnet said he had taken a dose of Kutnow's powder from a box that had been sent him by mail.

The diphtheria test failed, but in a day or two traces of mercurial poisoning showed up. The effervescent laxative powder that had been sent Barnet was examined. It contained cyanide of mercury. Barnet was critically ill but he refused to tell who sent him the powders saying he would attend to that when he got well. But he never got well. Three days later he died. Dr. Douglass's certificate said his patient had died of heart failure.

Molineux did not attend the funeral, explaining that he had not been invited. He had known of Barnet's illness but he was fearful of diphtheria. Miss Cheseborough did not call but she did send flowers. Molineux and Blanche were married on November 29, 1898, less than three weeks after Barnet's death, at the Waldorf-Astoria. They remained at the hotel for a few days and then went to live in a boarding house operated by a mutual friend, a Mrs. Bellinger, at 257 West End Avenue. Molineux continued to commute to Newark daily. He also maintained three rooms at the factory, Mamie Melando acting as caretaker.

On the day before Christmas Cornish found on his desk a small square package addressed to 'Mr. Harry Cornish, Knickerbocker Athletic Club, Madison Avenue and 45th Street, City.' Inside was a Tiffany pasteboard box containing a silver bottle holder and a blue bottle bearing the label of a brand of bromo-seltzer. Henry A. King, a club member, noticed the powders and remarked that he would take a dose. He went over to the water cooler but there was no water, so the bottle was put back unopened. Two days after Christmas Cornish took it home and showed it to Mrs. Adams. The holder fitted some silver ornaments in the room and Cornish took only the bottle into his room and placed it on a desk. Meanwhile Cornish was wondering who sent him headache powders, something he had never taken in his life.

The next morning Cornish went to his kitchen to get his newspaper. He met Laura Rogers wearing a bandage around her head. A few minutes later she told Cornish her mother had a headache and wanted some of his powder. He gave the bottle to Mrs. Rogers. It was sealed with paraffin, and she was having difficulty in opening it until Cornish took it over. Mrs. Adams poured a glass of water and Cornish put it in a liberal dose of powder. Mrs. Adams drank it. She said it tasted sour and 'queer.' Cornish assured her it was all right and took a small dose of it himself. Three minutes later Mrs. Adams called for help and when Cornish started to get up his knees felt weak. He managed to reach Mrs. Adams but, athlete that he was, he did not have the strength to help her. Her face was drawn and ashen. Doctors were called but when the first one arrived Mrs. Adams was dead.

There was a hallmark on the holder which showed it had been sold by F. A. Lebkeucher & Co., manufacturing jewelers of Newark. It was retailed by Hartdegen & Co., also of Newark. It was sold three days before Cornish received it. The police did not link Cornish or Mrs. Rogers to the case, although Cornish had been married and divorced. His wife lived in Buffalo.

But while preliminary investigations were under way members of the Knickerbocker Club were asking each other such questions as 'Who had a motive to kill Harry Cornish? What was behind the death of Henry Barnet?'

On January 2, 1899, a New York newspaper linked Roland B. Molineux with the many rumors then afloat. A friend of General Molineux read that paper and at 7 o'clock that same morning went to the General's house. Together they went to the home of George W. McClusky, the chief of detectives. They were assured that Roland was under suspicion.

The following day the public was let in on the circumstances surrounding the death of Barnet. McClusky at the same time summed up the situation saying, 'The same mind sent both poisons.' Then followed a number of breaks that helped the police materially. One was the discovery that a letter box had been rented at 1629 Broadway in the name of Harry Cornish. The man did not in the least resemble Cornish. Another man at 247 West Forty-seventh Street rented a box in the name of H. C. Barnet. He likewise bore no resemblance to Barnet. The police were getting nowhere, but finally Col. Asa Bird Gardiner, the District Attorney, decided to take over the case which he turned over to James W. Osborne, his assistant. Osborne began hammering away at everything in sight. Coroner Hart held an inquest and all of the available witness were heard. Mrs. Molineux was a witness and she denied any improper friendship with Barnet. Cornish stated: 'You will have to look into some New York club for the poisoner. Molineux has lied about me on the stand and under oath. He has shown enmity to me from first to last. On one occasion Barnet left the clubhouse to go on a yachting trip. He came back unexpectedly, and when I asked him why he did not go he said it was because Molineux was on board. Does that indicate that Molineux and Barnet were friendly?'

Molineux had testified that he was Barnet's friend up to the very end. Osborne then called the Forty-second Street letter box man who positively identified Molineux as the man who called for mail under the name of H. C. Barnet. Molineux then seemed momentarily to lose his reason. Seven handwriting experts swore that Molineux penned the address on the poison package. Colonel Gardiner had edged himself back into the case and, as the head prosecutor, he summed up the evidence before the coroner's jury. The verdict was that Molineux sent the powder to Cornish that subsequently killed Mrs. Adams. That night Molineux spent in the Tombs.

Nearly a year passed before Molineux was put on trial, but interest in the case never waned. The first indictment against Molineux was thrown out becasue it linked the Barnet case with the Adams case. Another grand jury refused to indict. Molineux was promptly released on bail but was rearrested when a subsequent grand jury returned a true bill. He pleaded not guilty on August 2, 1899, to the charge he had killed Mrs. Adams in an effort to kill Cornish.

The proof in the Adams case was quite satisfactory from a legal point of view and a dozen handwriting experts pinned the evidence on Molineux. But Osborne wanted to get before the jury the circumstances surrounding the death of Barnet. He wanted the jurors to couple this case with the death of Mrs. Adams. He finally got it before the jury over the objection of Bartow S. Weeks, Molineux's trial counsel. There was much testimony that Molineux picked up his mail at the two rented mail boxes, and that much of it contained patent medicines and drug samples.

Osborne proved by a servant that Molineux had lived under the name of Cheseborough in a house in West Seventy-fifth Street. This was in 1897, before he went through the marriage ceremony. This was a severe blow to General Molineux who was seated with his son while the testimony was being given. When the prosecution ended the defense sprang a surprise. It announced that there would be no further defense than that developed through the people's witnesses. In his summing up Weeks attacked Cornish's testimony and dramatically announced, 'We stand here on our sworn statement that we are innocent of anything connected with these cases. The prosecution failed to prove that the defendant was the writer of the address on the wrapper that covered the bottle of poison. It has failed to demonstrate the connection between the hired boxes and the sending of the poison package.'

Osborne, summing up for the state, pointed dramatically to Blanche Cheseborough Molineux who sat beside her husband and shouted, 'There sits the motive.'

Late on a Saturday night the jury, after eight hours' deliberation, found Molineux guilty of murder in the first degree. The verdict was reversed on the error of permitting the Barnet death to be brought into the trial.

Molineux's second trial was held before Justice Lambert of Buffalo. The handwriting received less latitude in their testimony and Molineux put in a defense—an alibi—that he was at Columbia University when the poison package was left at the postoffice on the afternoon of December 23. Cornish was a witness, but at times it seemed that he was the defendant, so bitterly did Molineux's counsel deal with him. On November 12, 1902, almost four years from the day Mrs. Adams died, the jury acquitted Molineux. He fell into his aged father's arms and went back to Brooklyn where his wife awaited him. She divorced him a year later. Molineux wrote a play called 'The Man Inside,' which was produced by David Belasco. On November 7, 1913, Molineux married a second time. In the autumn of 1914 Molineux went insane, and on November 2, 1917, he died in the State Hospital at King's Park, Long Island.

Blanche Cheseborough married the lawyer who obtained her divorced.

C.E.S.

# 1898

# WILLIAM GULDENSUPPE
## Willie's Legs

---

A pekin duck was responsible for uncovering one of the most extraordinary murders in the annals of crime in New York. A woman and two men were involved in the grisly business of murder and scattering fragments of his body about the city.

Mrs. Augusta Nack, Martin Thorn, a barber, and William Guldensuppe, rubber in the Murray Hill Baths, were the principal actors in this tragedy. Mrs. Nack was a buxom German woman. Her husband, Herman, for several years after they came to this country, operated a bologna and delicatessen store on Tenth Avenue, near Twenty-eighth Street. Nack and his wife got along well until he took to drink. He neglected his business and when his wife chided him on his habits he beat her. Once he threw her down a flight of stairs to prove, he said, that he was the boss of the household. One day, Mrs. Nack learned that her husband's business had been taken over by a stranger. Nack had sold out and gone on a protracted spree. When it was all over Mrs. Nack took her husband back and set him up in business again in West Sixty-second Street, out of her own funds. But the sheriff soon moved in and Nack went to work on a bakery wagon.

Mrs. Nack rented a room to a good-looking German who said his name was William Guldensuppe, a bath rubber.

Mrs. Nack was much in demand as an experienced midwife. She was thrifty. Nack's increasing demands for beer money made him unpopular at home, and when Guldensuppe moved in, Nack moved out. The arrangement worked out well. Guldensuppe came and went as he pleased. The upkeep of the establishment was low and his contributions were in proportion. One day Mrs. Nack answered an advertisement by a man who wanted a room on the West Side, and Martin Thorn entered the picture. He, also, was a German, thirty-three years old and weighed about thirty pounds less than the bath rubber.

Like Guldensuppe, he wore a mustache. Both men regarded Mrs. Nack quite highly. Thorn worked as a barber at 836 Sixth Avenue and his boss was Conrad Vogel. While the other barbers talked about William Jennings Bryan, Tod Sloan and Bob Fitzsimmons, Thorn talked about women. He spoke of progress he was making with Mrs. Nack, whom he described as a handsome woman who was in love with him. Guldensuppe also had progressed to the point where he was able to borrow money from Mrs. Nack instead of paying his share of the expenses. Thorn also worked his way into Mrs. Nack's good graces, by taking her to the theater.

The showdown between the barber and the rubber could not be definitely far off. There was a fight and Thorn got the worst of it. It was humiliating enough to be beaten up in the presence of Mrs. Nack but to meet the taunts of his fellow barbers was more than Thorn's pride could withstand. He boasted he would have killed Guldensuppe except that his rival and adversary had taken his gun from him. He had lost the respect of Mrs. Nack and tried to poison her mind against Guldensuppe.

In June Mrs. Nack and Thorn, now back in her good graces, went to Woodside and rented a seven-room house. She paid the rent of $15 in the names of Mr. and Mrs. F. Braun, and went back to Manhattan. In the meantime, Mrs. Nack and Thorn had done some shopping, purchasing among other things, six yards of red oilcloth and two pounds of plaster of Paris.

Then she invited Guldensuppe out ostensibly to look over the new home which she said was to be a baby farm. Thorn went in by the back door, for which he had a key, and Mrs. Nack remained at the front door. Thorn secreted himself in a closet upstairs. Guldensuppe viewed the place and said it met with his approval. Mrs. Nack then invited him to see the interior. Upstairs he opened a closet door and as he did so Thorn shot him. Mrs. Nack was in yard and heard the shot. Immediately Thorn came down and announced the job had been done. Mrs. Nack said she had heard the shot and understood. At

Thorn's direction, Mrs. Nack went to New York and returned at 5 o'clock. She busied herself at home by changing the flowers on her hat and replacing the yellow roses with bright red ones.

When she returned, all signs of the murder had been removed. All she saw were a number of packages, well wrapped. 'You take this one,' Thorn ordered. 'It is nothing but clothes. I will take this one.' He held up a heavy package and with a flourish announced, 'It is his head.' He was as cool as that.

A trolley car took them to the ferry from Astoria to the foot of East Ninety-second Street, Manhattan. It was the least patronized of the East River ferries. Mrs. Nack rode in the bow while Thorn wandered about aft. When no one was looking he dropped his package over the rail and walked away. Guldensuppe's head, encased in plaster of Paris, dropped out of sight and Thorn breathed a sigh of relief.

Mrs. Nack's bundle was consumed in the kitchen stove at the town apartment. Night was upon them and they could do no more that day, but the following morning they returned to the Woodside cottage. Thorn bundle up Guldensuppe's legs and went by trolley to the Thirty-fourth Street ferry. On the way over he flung the bundle into the river and after buying a drink in a waterfront saloon, he went back to Woodside. In his absence Mrs. Nack had been busy with scrubbing brush and soap. There was no evidence of murder, to the casual observer.

Then they left together, Thorn bearing a package containing Guldensuppe's trunk and arms. Crossing the Greenpoint ferry to Tenth Street he threw his bundle overboard. They had lunch at the Nack flat in Ninth Avenue and in the afternoon hired a surrey from an Eighth Avenue undertaker and drove to Woodside, where they picked up the last bundle. It held the lower part of the trunk. By way of the Astoria ferry they came to New York and then drove uptown to what was then known as Ogden's Woods, where this package was dropped in the underbrush. It was on Underhill Avenue, south of Fordham.

On the day after the murder, Thorn sent a note to Guldensuppe's employer and signed Guldensuppe's name, saying he had been detained on business. He also wrote a letter signed 'F. Braun,' advising the agents for the Woodside house that because of his wife's illness they could not move in for two weeks. He then sent a messenger to Mrs. Nack's house with a note signed with Guldensuppe's name asking that Guldensuppe's clothes be delivered to the bearer. The note, of course, was a blind to throw any chance inquirer off the scent.

Guldensuppe was out of the way and Thorn was congratulating himself on his success when fate intervened. Two boys made a grisly discovery in the river at the foot of East Twelfth Street. Guldensuppe's chest had floated ashore. Almost simultaneously, two other boys found the package that had been dropped in Ogden's Woods.

The newspaper reported at length the story of the finding of the dismembered body of an unidentified man and the police got to work. The police held to the theory the victim had been stabbed to death. The fact was that Thorn's shot did not kill him and he completed the job with a razor. The oilcloth was difficult to trace. A dozen men were identified as the victim but not Guldensuppe. One night a reporter went to the Murray Hill Baths and while there heard some of the rubbers speak of their missing associate. The reporter asked some questions and by daybreak he had piloted three of them at the morgue. In the meantime a pair of human legs had come ashore near the Navy Yard in Brooklyn. One foot was identified by a rubber as that of his fellow worker, Guldensuppe. Another rubber also remembered that Mrs. Nack had called on Guldensuppe and the boss recalled that Guldensuppe had told about going over to Long Island with an old woman. Mrs. Nack was arrested within an hour. She was identified by a shopkeeper as the buyer of the oilcloth in which portions of the body were wrapped. She was taken to the morgue to see what the police had recovered. She looked on the gruesome objects without flinching. Her only remark was, 'I don't believe those are Willie's legs.'

Nack was then run down. He said if his wife had been living with Guldensuppe it was no concern of his. He had known it for eighteen months. His story satisfied police who looked elsewhere for the accomplice. But Thorn was not clever. One day when his tongue was loose with liquor, he told the whole story of the murder to John Garta, a fellow barber. Garta told his wife and she told the police. Thorn was arrested at Eighth Avenue and One Hundred and Twenty-fifth Street. The rest was easy. Thorn and the woman were indicted in Long Island City, where the actual murder took place. Thorn ably defended by William F. Howe, one of the leaders of the bar, went on the stand and told stories that he afterward admitted were lies. The jury found him guilty of murder in the first degree and he paid the penalty in the electric chair on August 1, 1898. Thorn's conviction was assured when Mrs. Nack turned State's evidence and was sent to prison. She was released in 1908, after serving nine years. She returned to the Ninth Avenue section and for many years ran a fancy goods store and later a delicatessen business.

Had it not been for the duck perhaps the case would have been unsolved. The water had been left running in the tub by Thorn who thought it entered a sewer. Instead it ran on the surface, thus making a pool in which the duck wallowed. One day the duck came home with his breast feathers all red. His owner trailed him and in this manner the spot where Guldensuppe was lured and murdered was found.

C.E.S.

# 1898

# JOSEPH VACHER
## The Jack the Ripper of France

'About thirty years old, medium height, black hair, black beard, sparse and unkempt on the cheeks, brown moustache, rather heavy black eyebrows, bony face.

'His upper lip is raised; it is twisted to the right and his mouth contorts when he sppeaks. A scar runs vertically from his lower lip to the right side of his upper lip. All the white of his right eye is bloodshot and the lower lid has no lashes and is slightly raw. The man's appearance makes a disagreeable impression . . .

'The wanted man is thin; his cheeks are lined; his face is pale with yellowish patches; his features are drawn and he looks sickly. He has a reasonably masculine voice which he seldom raise in speaking but, if he is excited, it becomes sharp and he talks with difficulty on account of the deformity of his mouth.'

This portrait, tilted, if either way, on the side of flattery, is extracted from a notice circulated in July of 1897 by M. Emile Fourquet, *juge d'instruction* of Belley. Two years before, a youth named Victor Portalier had been murdered in the district with an obscene ferocity never matched unless by London's Jack the Ripper a decade earlier. M. Fourquet had not taken up his judicial post when Portalier was hacked to death but, from the time of his appointment to the district in April, 1897, he became unremittingly interested in the crime, and it was his opinion that the murderer was an unknown vagabond seen by a number of local residents on the day of the killing. From these witness—and from other witnesses in other localities on later occasions—he assembled the foregoing description and despatched it to police stations throughout France. It was a sufficiently good likeness to result, by the end of the following year, in the execution of Joseph Vacher—'*Jack l'éventreur du sud-est*'—without question the most detestable, the most monstrous, the most pitiful murderer in French criminal records.

The killing of Portalier was not the first of Vacher's hideous butcheries, nor was it was last, but it was the one which attracted M. Fourquet's ardent interest and the one for which the '*éventreur*' was ultimately arraigned and executed. All in all, he confessed to eleven murders, uniform in their frenzy and in the nature of the acts which followed on the actual killing. The 'dark odyssey' (as the presiding judge termed Vacher's career during the trial) began, as far as can be proved, on 20th May, 1894.

A twenty-one-year-old factory girl, Eugénie Delhomme, living at Beaurepaire near Vienne, was that night waiting on a quiet country road to meet her lover. In his place came Joseph Vacher, soft-footed and, as always when about his murderous business, horrifying voiceless. 'It seems to me,' he stated after his arrest, 'that my lust to kill was less in the case of my first victim than with the others.' Sinister relativity! And hardly supported by the facts, for Eugénie Delhomme's body had been spared few of the mutilations which were Vacher's trade-marks. She had been seized with such violence that her throat still bore the marks of devilish fingers, while a hand had been clasped so cruelly over her mouth that her own teeth had pierced though her lower lip.

The sweetheart for whom she had been waiting was, needless to say, the first suspect; and, when he clearly demonstrated his innocence, a former admirer was questioned. But no passion as commonplace as jealousy had operated in this slaughter: 'a sort of frenzy drove me blindly forward to commit my crimes. Never did I look for victims: chance meetings decided their fates. The poor creatures need not be pitied. None of them suffered longer than ten minutes . . .' The man who uttered these words was not among the friends or lovers of Eugénie Delhomme; each of these in turn established his alibi and the murder became a mere entry in the local files, to remain unconsulted until ten more lives had been ended by the same hand and knife.

Six months later to the day, in a stable near Blais (Var) was found the atrociously savaged corpse of thirteen-year-old Louise Marcel. She had evidently sought to hold off the blade which slashed her throat, for the fingers of her left hand were deeply cut. For suspected complicity in the crime, a M. Roux was taken into custody—and released.

Adèle Mortureux, seventeen, died in the Bois de Chêne (Côte d'Or) on 12th May, 1895. For the strangling, disembowelling and mutilation of the girl, a M. Grenier was arrested, and his case even proceeded as far as the *Chambre des Mise en Accusation* which very properly declined to send him up for trial.

On 24th August of the same year, Mme Morand was attacked in her lonely house at Saint-Ours (Savoie). It was early morning and the sixty-year-old widow's only son, Jean-Marie, was working in the fields. The Ripper found her preparing breakfast and plucked up a knife from the kitchen table—a curious economy since his own knife was certainly in his pocket. He raped the disembowelled corpse and left it to be found by Jean-Marie on his return.

The rhythm quickened: a week after the murder of Mme Morand, Vacher was again at work, and on 31st August committed the crime which was to bring him, exactly three years and four months later, to his own execution. A younger shepherd, Victor Portalier, set off from the hamlet of Onglas, in the Belley district, to graze his flock. The time was a little after noon but he was to see no nightfall. Vacher's own laconic story supplies the only facts which seemed to him essential:

'I went up to the shepherd—I said nothing to him—I seized him suddenly by the throat and I killed him with a knife—I don't know which one. The child put up a fight—he yelled a lot . . .'

Impressively detached, the men of science instructed to examine the body add one or two details:

'. . . Another wound exists in the stomach . . . another wound in the thoracic region . . . another in the breast . . . three in the neck . . .'

In the absence of Alfred Davaine, *juge d'instruction* of the district, his temporary replacement, Léon-Anthelme du Vachat, occupied himself with the affair, arriving on the scene of Vachat's fearful surgery at dawn next morning. Neither he nor his assistants, for all their efforts, were able to collect any data apart from the testimonies of a number of local folk that a suspicious vagabond had been encountered thereabouts: he had visited several farms demanding food and had impressed everyone by his surly manner and his repulsive appearance. The unpromising onset of this stock figure, the sinister tramp, marks the first step towards the guillotine for Vacher. A description was circulated, less detailed than that already quoted, and leading only to the stern interrogation of the innocent; but the dossier which was to challenge M. Fourquet's interest had been opened.

Various suggestions were put forward as to the identity of the individual responsible for Portalier's death. The Brigadier Sornay submitted that Portalier's mother, angered that her estranged husband had bequeathed all 10,000 francs of his estate to Victor, had hired a killer to assassinate the boy. Among much else which militated against acceptance of this pretty theory was the circumstance that no 10,000 francs had been left by Portalier *père* to anyone. Then, on 30th September, the director of the asylum of Saint-Robert reported the escape a month previously of a lunatic names Jean-François Bravais and resembling the man described by the police. Within a few days Bravais, protesting his innocence, was arrested—and, on 12th November, exculpated and returned to Saint-Robert. No one at the asylum gave a thought to Vacher who had been discharged from the place as cured barely eighteen months before.

Something over three weeks passed after Portalier's death before Vacher next wielded on human flesh one of the knives from the little set which he invariably carried; it may have been during that time that his restless hads carved—perhaps with the very implement which he had used on Portalier—the words discovered later on his cudgel: 'Mary of Lourdes: Who does good, finds good,' On 22nd September, 1895, he found worthier employment for his knife, cutting down an adolescent girl near Truinas. His victim's throat had been gashed open and the killer was starting on his supplementary task when he was startled by the arrival of a cart. He had only time to drag the girl's body some way to the side of the road when the driver of the vehicle hailed him, alarmed by the spectacle of the crouching figure with its blood-bespattered face. To the solicitous inquiry yelled at him, Vacher had sufficient presence of mind to respond: 'It's all right. I suffer from epilepsy and I just hurt myself falling down during an attack.' The driver was content to leave the epileptic to recover unaided, and drove on. Vacher continued his work without further interruption.

The assaults which follow need not be described in elaborate detail: all of them are obviously the work of one man and marked by the same abominable technique. They can be summarised as follows:

Pierre Massot-Pelet, fourteen-year-old shepherd, was killed near Saint-Etienne-de-Boulogne (Ardèche) and mutilated and sexually assaulted on 29th September, 1895. The solitary suspect was acquitted. Marie Moussier, nineteen, died on 10th September, 1896, after the same manner as the others. One point only distinguished her death: her face bore the marks of human teeth. In the Haute-Loire, on 1st October of the same year, a shepherdess of fourteen was killed, mutilated, and raped. A vagabond of the same age was killed, mutilated and sexually assaulted towards the end of May of in the following year. His body was hidden near the scene of the murder at Tassin-la-Demi-Lune and only discovered on information supplied by Vacher himself. A thirteen-year-old shepherd, Pierre Laurent, was murdered in the Monts du Lyonnais on 18th June, 1897.

In some, but not all, of these cases, witnesses came forward to report having seen a peculiarly repellent beggar in the neighbourhood. Slowly, the too-easily memorised traits of Vacher's torn and malformed countenance were added together.

During the period 1894–97 Vacher met with but one check—apart from that which led to his capture and trial. On 1st March, 1896, Alphonsine-Marie-Joséphine Derouet, aged eleven, was attacked near Noyen while on her way to early morning Mass. A game-keeper running in the direction of the child's screams found Vacher crouching in a ditch. There was a brief struggle, Vacher struck out with his foot, achieved a momentarily crippling blow on the game-keeper's leg, and ran for it. His assailant was at least able to provide the police with a description and, later in the day, Vacher was actually detained by one of the rural constabulary, solemnly cycling along the road in search of the would-be rapist. Smart work, a little diminished by the policeman's failure to detect any resemblance between his captive and the man described by the game-keeper. Eight days later, no one suspecting that the demoniac of the region had been trapped, Vacher was again arrested—for vagrancy and assault—and sentenced to one month's imprisonment.

Additional to the eleven killings which he acknowledged, mention must be made of three other crimes of which in all likelihood Vacher was the author. The first of these took place on 29th September, 1890, in the village of Varacieux (Isère). Nine-year-old Olympe Buisson was stabbed to death, disembowelled, and subjected to a sexual assault—and Vacher was in the neighbourhood.

Francine Rouvray, thirty, on 6th September, 1895, was almost decapitated with a knife and then eviscerated. There is reason to believe that Vacher was then near Autun where the murder occurred.

On 23rd February, 1897, at Lacaune (Tarn), Célestin Gautrais was similarly butchered. Vacher, without confessing to the crime, revealed during his interrogation that he had been in the area at approximately that time.

## 2

Joseph Vacher was born on 16th November, 1869 (Fourquet's guess as to his age was a fairly good one), at Beaufort (Isère), the fifteenth of his parents' children. His family, as far as is known, were respectable and healthy people, nor does his ancestry reveal any trace of insanity. Physically, the auguries were that he should grow into a sturdy French peasant; spiritually, his development was entrusted to the Marist Brotherhood, of whose instruction he recalled nothing but a talk given by an informative missionary on ritual mutilations among savage tribes. On the whole, no conditions could have been more favourable for the emergence of yet another useless, valued social unit.

Vacher himself blamed his deviation from so estimable a prototype on the fact that, when about eight years old, he was bitten by a mad dog, arguing that the resultant illness had permanently affected his brain. Some mysterious potion was obtained from the local magician and Vacher consumed the entire bottle at one gulp—an impulsive performance which (village magicians being what they are) might well have contributed more to a mental collapse than the original bite. His family substantiated the story, but the *Acte d'Accusation* included the statement: 'It has been established that Vacher was never bitten by a mad dog; it would seem that he was merely licked by a dog suspected of hydrophobia. . . .Expert medical opinion is that this fact could not in any way have influenced his mental condition.'

Just how it was established that he had never been bitten as he claimed is not revealed, nor is any denial made that he consumed some unknown, and possibly toxic, remedy; moreover, no attention is paid to the possibility that the incident, however trivial in its physical effects, may yet have had some powerful and abiding effect on Vacher's mind. To the expert advice of contemporary alienists, we may oppose the fact that in at least two cases, and possibly more than two, there was the gruesome circumstance of the murderer himself acting like a mad dog and worrying the body with his teeth. Finally, there is the unalterable evidence that his violence, his surliness, his melancholia dated from the time when he was in contact witth the dog.

Vacher's first employment after quitting the Marist brothers was a brief one as farmhand. Never attached to the practice of hard work, he evinced an incongruous enthusiasm for the contemplative life and returned to the Marist establishment as a postulant. He was to remain with the Brotherhood for a short time only, as, in their own words, 'We found him insufficiently serious and altogether too eccentric for the religious life.' In 1888 he was back at Beaufort, manifesting his breach with the traditions of monkish segregation by attempting to rape a young male servant.

At this time, from causes unrevealed but not altogether beyond guessing at, he contracted orchitis, an inflammatory condition of the scrotum, for which he was treated at Grenoble. A recrudescence in the following year obliged him to submit to an operation at Antiquaille by which a portion of one testicle was removed. It is not difficult to relate this, in conjunction with other events in his life, to the manner in which he mutilated the male victims who later lay at the mercy of his knife.

On his discharge from the hospital he obtained employment at a warehouse in Lyons, there, as everywhere else, making himself notorious for his violent and unpredictable rages alternating with a morose taciturnity almost as alarming. On at least one occasion, in the course of a dispute with a fellow-employee, he drew the knife which lay always in his pocket, and no suggestion has been made that any popular dismay was expressed at the warehouse when, in November of 1890, he was called up for service with the army and attached to the 60th Infantry Regiment at Besançon.

According to Lieutenant Greilsemmer, 'Vacher's conduct during his service in the company was always very good; not even the slightest irregularity was recorded against him, he was of a high moral stature, his honesty and correctness were unquestioned; he was noted for his sobriety,' but one or two witnesses, Lieutenant Greilsemmer among them, have furnished other details which tend to lessen the effect of this testimony.

Some amusement can be derived from the fact that his promotions seemed to follow almost as a direct consequence of his more maniacal performances, and Lieutenant Grünfelder has left a naïve account of Vacher's elevation to the rank of corporal: 'He had not been able to get his promotion from acting lance-corporal to full corporal and, in a state of despair, he cut his throat with a razor; he was taken to the hospital, from where he complained in writing to the Colonel who, after interviewing him, admitted that he knew his drill very well [*sic*] and promoted him to full corporal.'

Lieutenant Greilsemmer noted that, 'Pursued by his persecution mania, Vacher believed himself to be surrounded by spies and enemies. His nervous state caused attacks of insomnia during which he would talk ramblingly and make threatening gestures, and the slightest irritation caused by his comrades only increased his over-excited condition. Vacher would then threaten to cut their throats with a razor. His room-mates went to bed in fear of their lives and always kept their bayonets handy. I might add that when Vacher was in this state he seemed like a sleep-walker and was obsessed with only one idea—his need to see blood flowing.'

Shortly after the period to which this lively description relates, he was promoted to sergeant.

Grünfelder, not without some perturbation it may be thought, was granted the privilege of sharing quarters with Sergeant Vacher, and at the latter's trial gave evidence as to the charms of the arrangement:

'During ten or fifteen consecutive nights he would wake, get up or stay in bed leaning on his elbow, uttering incoherent words accompanied by threatening gestures. I regularly distinguished the words: blood . . . they don't know what I'm capable of . . . I'll kill him. Fearing that he planned to attack me, I made up my mind to have my bayonet with me when I went to bed, hiding it under the sheets; then I informed Lieutenant Greilsemmer of what was going on, and he instructed me to embody all the facts in a report for submission to the Colonel. A few days later . . .'

A few days later, it being apparently decided that Vacher did not know his drill well enough to be promoted still higher, he was, by way of alternative, sent to hospital for observation. He entered the infirmary in May of 1893, and the *expertise* of the establishment had him roaming about on sick leave within a matter of days. On 25th June he was in Baume-les-Dames, where a Mlle Louise B. lived with her family.

Vacher had always been as little popular with women as with men: there was nothing attractive about his appearance and it would have needed a singularly jaded and perverse temperament to find any charm in his vicious nature. But along with his strong homosexual tendency went a more than ordinary preoccupation with women, and his lack of sexual triumphs with them was a continual exasperation and hurt. Louise, however, had been less severe than most in her rejection of his approaches (although it is unlikely that she was his mistress) and Vacher's chagrin when she showed an unmistakable preference for someone else was correspondingly intense. There were repeated disputes, threats were made by Vacher, and, on the day mentioned, he came to the girl and fired three bullets at her—an uncharacteristic choice of method and one which was less efficacious than the technique for which he became renowned. One bullet struck the girl in the jaw, two others wounding her in the neck, but she was so slightly harmed as to be back at work a fortnight later; Vacher himself was less fortunate. He turned the revolver on himself, and though the bullet which entered his head failed to deprive the public executioner of his fee, it had the effect of rendering complete Vacher's unprepossessing mask. His right eye was damaged and remained ever afterwards in a condition of suppuration; a facial nerve was severed and caused a partial paralysis of the right side; his features were scarred.

The court at Baume-les-Dames discovered in this contretemps and Vacher's past history some reason to doubt his mental stability, and on 7th July, 1893, he was committed to the asylum of Saint-Ylie where his behaviour—even by the not over-exacting standards of his fellow lunatics—was remarkable for its unwavering ferocity. He had requested the removal of the bullet which had lodged behind his eye, but at the last moment he changed his mind, and the spectacle of this maniac with his ravaged face and dribbling, half-blind eye must have been among the most gratifying available to interested visitors to the place.

Nothing gives more conclusive proof of the existence of natural protective devices than the facility with which habitual criminals are able to effect escapes. Vacher was a splendid example of this aspect of natural history. True, he was usually recaptured within a short space of time, but the primitive alertness never atrophied; he was always on the lookout for a fresh chance, and when it appeared was endowed with an extraordinary agility for seizing it. Thus, on 25th August, he broke out from Saint-Ylie and, although recaptured soon afterwards, made another break while being returned to the asylum by train and remained at liberty for several more days. It would be interesting to know how he employed his freedom but, if he wielded his knife at all, it was on some friendless and insignificant creature like Beaupied whose disappearance caused as little concern as would Vacher's own.

In view of Professor Lacassagne's subsequent assurances that Vacher was as sane as the rest of us, it would be as well at this point to note the opinions of him formed by the doctors at Saint-Ylie. Dr. Guillemin considered that he was 'suffering from mental derangement characterised by delusions of persecution (and) not responsible for his actions'. Dr. Bécoulet, still more precise, noted that Vacher, 'victimised by depression, gloomy and taciturn, believes himself to be the butt of everyone's persecution and jealousy. He last attempted to commit suicide by dashing his head against the wall . . .' while Dr. Chaussinand discreetly hinted that he required 'constant and rigorous supervision'.

In December, 1893, Vacher was transferred to the asylum of Saint-Robert, where for a time he enacted the rôle of the resigned and reformed character. His guardians were soothed by his behaviour to such an extent that any vigilance they may have originally exercised was eventually discarded. At the appropriate moment Vacher made another escape. Recaptured, he abandoned his wily affectation of normality and, at each station on the journey back, screamed wildly at the people on the platform. All of which was profoundly significant to the trained observer: on 1st April, 1894, Dr. Dufour, director of Saint-Robert, discharged his patient as cured—one of the happiest April Fools' Day jests recorded.

Even assuming that all the facts are available, it is apparent that Vacher delayed but briefly before entering on the work for which he was so uniquely fitted. The murder of Eugénie Delhomme was on 20th May, 1894, roughly six weeks after his release. Thereafter, he wandered about the country, surviving by begging from each farm he came upon. No one, he stated during his interrogation, wanted to employ a man so distressingly ugly, but it is conceivable that the reluctant potential employers detected in him an intangible quality more threatening than the scar or the slowly-weeping eye. Or, again, it is possible that Vacher's disinclination for work ('I wasn't born to work') impelled him to adopt a less irksome, if less reliable, method of keeping alive; but he sentenced himself to death when he elected to follow a career which brought him before so many eyes.

For three years he moved about a random, mostly in the south-east. There exists a photograph of the baggage which he carried throughout this period: strangely grotesque and displeasing, that jumble of antique garments and objects—a sack, maps, a change of clothing, an umbrella, an accordion, a cudgel, a pair of scissors, a cleaver, and a set of knives in assorted sizes.

3

Once installed at Belley, M. Emile Fourquet inevitably heard more talk about the murder which had aroused the district two years before his appointment as *juge d'instruction* than about any other topic; and he was struck—as others had been—by the similarity between the local calamity and certain murders which, from time to time, had appalled various adjoining areas. It was his perception of the pattern in these massacres which decided him to despatch his circular, of which some passages were quoted at the beginning of this study and which might now be given in full:

'I, Emile Fourquet, *juge d'instruction* of the district of Belley:

'In reference to the case against the missing man X, wanted for murder;

'Hereby give a rogatory commission to my colleague at . . . to inquire in his district for the wanted man, a description of whom follows:

'About thirty years old, medium height, black hair, black beard, sparse and unkempt on the cheeks, brown moustache, rather heavy black eyebrows, bony face.

'His upper lip is raised; it is twisted to the right and his mouth contorts when he speaks. A scar runs vertically from his lower lip to the right side of his upper lip. All the white of his right eye is bloodshot and the lower lid has no lashes and is slightly raw. The man's appearance makes a disagreeable impression. Sometimes he wears a beret and sometimes a wide-brimmed straw hat, his headgear being pushed up at the back and pulled low over his eyes.

'These are the most important points to bear in mind.

'The wanted man is thin; his cheeks are lined; his face is pale with yellowish patches; his features are drawn and he looks sickly. He has a reasonably masculine voice which he seldom raises in speaking, but if he is excited it becomes sharp, and he talks with difficulty on account of the deformity of his mouth.

'At the time of the crime, this man was wearing wooden-soled shoes, carrying a cloth bag which looked as if it contained linen or clothes, and he was carrying a stick.

'He generally asks for soup or bread and buys wine or milk alternately; he frequents farms where he often tries to get work as a shepherd, and claims variously to be from Bresse, the Department of the Seine, or Dauphiné.

'He pretends to be lame and older than he looks, and talks of having left his family after a quarrel. Finally, he sometimes speaks the dialect of Dauphiné, or even of Bugey, and wanders about begging, particularly in villages, at church doors, convents or monasteries.

'This is the man referred to in the press as "Jack the Ripper of the South-East".

'If located, telegraph this office.

'There is a warrant for his arrest.

'Please circulate this notice throughout your district.'

The uneasy farmers and farmers' wives of the south-east had observed to some purpose.

By the time M. Fourquet's document was issued there was a nightmarish terror throughout the countryside; that obscene and malevolent figure walked beside every solitary person on lonely roads and was responsible for every knock on the doors of isolated farms. Great as was the dread created in London by the Ripper there were still the gas-lit stalls and packed streets to provide some vague reassurance; in the territory which Vacher made his own, loneliness and silence intensified the fear.

Fourquet succeeded in stimulating yet further the already considerable police activity and a number of arrests were made from among the 250,000 vagabonds estimated to be in France at that time. All those seized were later released.

4

The day began early for Joseph Vacher on 4th August, 1897. At 6 a.m. he came to the door of Jean-Pierre Badel's house at Gravil near Tournon, playing an accordion as he approached—an accompaniment as incongruous and grotesque as the organ requiems which J. G. Smith played for his murdered wives. Mme Badel, alone in the house, peremptorily ordered him to stop, and gave him a sou and a piece of bread in the hope of getting rid of him. Vacher was disposed to chat; he stood outside the door muttering incoherent comments, his eyes straying from side to side as he talked. Did Mme Badel suspect that the mumbling beggar was the '*éventreur*'—or did her mind shy fearfully away from so ghastly a notion? She has left no answer to the speculation but at some point, in an abrupt spasm of disquiet, she slammed the door in his face and watched him from the window as he slouched off along the road.

Three hours later he was in the Bois de Pelleries, and it was there that he encountered Mme Marie-Eugénie Plantier, the Amazonian female who was to bring him face-to-face with furious and uncomprehending society.

Mme Plantier had gone to the wood with her husband and children to gather pine-cones, but she had become separated from the others and was seemingly alone when Vacher saw her. His stealthy approach gave no warning and she was taken completely by surprise. He grabbed her from behind, clasping his hand across her mouth. Mme Plantier struggled more vigorously than any of her predecessors had been able to do; she freed herself from Vacher's grasp just long enough to call out.

Her husband heard her screams and ran to her. He stooped, picked up a stone and hurled it at the assailant. It smashed heavily into the contorted mouth. Then he flung himself upon Vacher, while his wife (who could clearly have handled the whole thing on her own if necessary) and the children contributed haphazard kicks and blows to the contest. Vacher's quickness of wit emerged once again. In the hope of persuading his opponent to withdraw from the battle, he gasped out, 'I didn't attack your wife—it was my mate,' and, as additional proof that he had an ally, he managed to release himself for moment and blow shrilly on a whistle as though summoning aid. Husbandly ire was such, however, that M. Plantier was indifferent to the size of the opposing forces, and he sprang once again on the Ripper. The latter had by now plucked out his great scissors with which he met Plantier's charge, stabbing and slightly wounding him.

Henri Nodin, a peasant working nearby, had heard the sounds of the struggle and now appeared on the scene. Together, he and Plantier overcame Vacher and dragged him towards the road, the wretched creature bleeding from the mouth and clinging anguishedly to branches and tree trunks as he was hauled along. On the road they encountered two more men and the four of them marched Vacher to the nearest building, a wayside inn.

'I'm an unhappy man, a cripple, a good-for-nothing,' Vacher is said to have remarked on the way. 'I should be in hospital. I desire women and they spurn me. If I go into a brothel they take my money, are disgusted with me, throw me out without giving anything in exchange. I'm accused of assaulting people. But if I *do* do wrong, it's God who makes me and he will protect me.' A little while after, he called to a passer-by, 'Why am I being dragged off? Do you know why, you? It's because I wanted a woman. Yes, and if I could have I'd have raped her. And if she'd been twelve or thirteen, it would have been ever better. I like young shepherdesses best.'

If Vacher did, in fact, make these statements, it is remarkable that none of his captors suspected that they had trapped '*l'éventreur du sud-est*' whose monstrous exploits were the prime subject of local discussion. It seems they did not guess at his identity; and Vacher, recovering his spirits, struck up an inappropriately jolly tune on his accordion as he was led into the inn to await the arrival of the gendarmerie from Saint-Peray.

More peculiar even than the failure of M. Plantier and his friends to see any significance in Vacher's helpful self-revelations was the blankness of the *Procureur de la République* at Tournon, whither Vacher was transferred the day after his capture. This official saw in the case no more than a—one hesitates to say 'everyday'—commonplace lech somewhat out of control, an unpremeditated succumbing to Mme Plantier's vigorous charms. It was on a charge of having offended against public decency that Vacher was remanded for trail before the *Tribunal Correctionel* of Tournon.

The local *juge d'instruction* was more observant. He remarked Vacher's scarred, grim face—that unmistakable face—and brightly hit on the similarity of the man standing before him to the man described in M. Fourquet's circular. He thereupon addressed a letter to his colleague at Belley and would have included a photograph but for the quaint reluctance of Tournon's solitary photographer to confront so ill-favoured a subject. This artistic sensibility resulted in the question of whether Vacher was or was not the '*éventreur*' being left unresolved until after his trial for offending against public decency. On that ironic count Vacher was sentenced to three months' imprisonment and, on the day after, 9th September, was taken to Belley. An attempted escape *en route* was foiled.

His first appearance before M. Fourquet on 10th September was undramatic and followed the customary pattern of such confrontations. To the charge that he had killed Victor Portalier, Vacher maintained a calm denial; and the witnesses from around Onglas who had given the *juge d'instruction* material for his circular were no great help. After a lapse of two years they were unable to be definite as to the identification needed, in surprising contrast to the blithe manner in which witnesses usually identify the first man brought before them. Subsequent interrogations, and accusations respecting other murders, brought no more satisfactory results, and among twelve witnesses of the sinister tramp only one, Joséphine Vettard, was able to assert that the man she had previously seen now stood in her presence. It was a temporary hitch merely. One by one, the others began to recognise the accused man, and by 7th October he knew that he had lost the first trick.

Suddenly he changed his line. That same day he sent a letter to M. Fourquet, its pietistic babble utterly unlike letters which he had addressed not so long before to the director of Saint-Robert. Typical of the latter was a note written on 30th March, 1894:

'Since I am shortly to leave you, I feel it my duty . . . to thank you as well as M. Boinet for the aid which you have given me since I have been in the asylum, and to testify to the gratitude which I owe you for the kindness which your goodwill and sense of justice have caused you to show me . . .

'As I have told you, *Monsieur le Directeur*, I intend on leaving here to go to the Marist brothers to seek a position as domestic servant there . . . I would be very happy if you would feel able to provide me with the reference which would certainly greatly assist me to obtain this. . . .'

A prettier example of below-stairs humility could not be wished for; but, under an ornately-lettered heading of

'God—Right—Duty', he wrote in a notably different style to M. Fourquet:

'So much the worse for you if you hold me responsible.

'Even your method of working makes me pity you.

'If I have kept the secret of my miseries it is because I believed it to be in the general interest, but since I am perhaps mistaken I will tell you the whole truth. Yes, it is I who committed all the crimes with which I am charged—and I committed them in moments of frenzy.

'As I have already told the doctor in charge of the medical service at the Belley prison, I was bitten by a mad dog when I was seven or eight years old—I'm not quite sure myself—but I do remember very well that I took some remedy for it. Only my relations can assure you that I was bitten; I myself have always believed, even since I thought about the incident, that it was the medicine which infected my blood . . .'

'Yes, it is I who committed all the crimes . . .' M. Fourquet must have been astonished at his luck. Further interviews followed swiftly on his receipt of the letter and Vacher was now a garrulous as he had previously been taciturn. He detailed the killing of Portalier, commenting that 'I killed him—but I didn't rape him—I bit into his testicles.' He was equally informative in respect of the other assassinations which he had performed, and even volunteered the news that M. Fourquet had left a gap in the ghastly list: this was the killing of Beaupied, and the police located the body from Vacher's directions on 25th October, at Tassin-la-Demi-Lune.

The essential points in Vacher's statements were an insistence that he was mad as a result of being bitten by the dog, and a reproachful preoccupation with the revulsion felt for him by all those with whom he came into contact. There is no reason to question that his agonised hunger for love was indeed the source of his corruption, but precisely what solution could be proposed it is difficult to see. A Sister Seraphina might have considered an intimate relationship with him as a simultaneous device for solacing and constraining the man and chastening her own flesh and spirit; but Seraphinas are hard to come by . . .

Vacher, for whatever reason or complex of reasons, was a wanderer outside life, withheld from communication with his fellows by the accident of malformation. Rejected by men and women, there was only one relationship he could establish—the intimate relationship of death. Few murders are public; but none were committed in a more desolate solitude than his.

Mad or sane, the jury found him guilty on the night of 28th October, 1898, and he was sentenced to die. Even humanitarians would find it hard to suggest any other solution to the despair of this outcast.

He was carried insensible to the guillotine on the last day of the year, and a large and eager horde, seeing the motionless figure, thought he had cheated them and screamed their disappointment. But he was not dead, only afraid of quitting a life which had been an incessant anguish. Before he lost consciousness, desperately contemplating an imaginary future as a free man, what could he have hoped for that would not have been more hideous than death?

The public executioner, Louis Deibler, ended whatever hopes Vacher may have had—the last guillotining he performed before delegating his duties to his son. Vacher's head was handed over to the experts in order that they might conduct an autopsy. They were unable, even so, to settle the academic wrangle between themselves.

A.K.

# 1899

# SAMUEL DOUGAL
## So Much Slimy Clay

---

Had Samuel Dougal, practised forger, ceaseless lecher, really murdered the fifty-five-year-old lady he had lived with as 'husband' during the year 1899 at the isolated Essex house, Moat Farm, or not? Unless the body could be found the police did not dare prosecute.

Dougal's 'wife', Miss Camille Cecile Holland, whom he had met a year earlier when she was a wealthy paying guest in the fashionable Bayswater district of London, had gone off with him one morning in the trap saying to the maid 'Goodbye, Florrie, I shan't be long.' It was the last time anyone saw her. Dougal first told Florrie she had gone up to London, and to later inquirers he said she was on 'a yachting expedition'.

It was an expedition that apparently lasted all of four years. At the end of that time the police suspicions of the cheques signed by Miss Holland, which Dougal continued to cash, mounted up and they began investigations. Dougal tried to run off, was arrested in London and charged with forgery.

But where was the woman known locally as 'Mrs. Dougal'?

The police began to search. They poked into every corner of the old farmhouse. Then they began on the areas round it. They drained the moat which surrounded the house, after which Dougal had re-named the farm when he had bought it with Miss Holland's money. For hours they waded waist-deep in the thick black slime that lay at the moat's bottom, still without success.

They dug away at the heavy clay of the garden. They probed with long iron rods. From his cell Dougal threatened to sue the chief constable for £1,000 for the damage done. After weeks of work they were on the point of giving up when one of the rods pushed through the thick clay struck something hard. They dug again and at last came upon the tiny, size 2 shoes Miss Holland had worn and in her skull found a bullet, identified as being made by the Union Metallic Ammunition Company of America, fired by a revolver Dougal owned.

In the meanwhile they had been digging, too, into Samuel Dougal's past. He had had two wives before, both of whom had died from eating poisoned oysters. He had a third wife, still living, whom he had brought to the farm as soon as Miss Holland had disappeared. The night before his departure with Miss Holland she had found him trying to get into the maid's room and had scorned his explanation that 'I only wanted to wind up the clock.'

More, much more, was found out, too, about his life at the farm since Miss Holland's going. A Mrs. Wisken, a widow with whom the couple had lodged while Moat Farm was being repaired and who afterwards adopted Miss Holland's little spaniel Jacko and had him stuffed when he died, told a journalist, 'All the time he was going about drinking and amusing himself at hotels and inns, and in other ways acting like the thorough villain he was.' Those 'other ways' included having relations with a mother and her three daughters and the arrival at the farm of servant girls by the dozen, rapidly made pregnant and then leaving usually without bitterness. Indeed, Dougal wrote to one suggesting that since many of them would be witnesses at his trial they should club together and hire transport. 'It is a delightful drive through undulating country, and at this time of year it would be a veritable treat for them all.'

Another of his activities had been teaching girls to ride the new bicycles, which he thought best done without clothes on. 'What a picture,' commented Miss F. Tennyson Jesse, who edited the book on Dougal's trail, 'in the clayey, lumpy field, the clayey, lumpy girls, naked, astride that unromantic object, a bicycle.'

At the end of the trial the chief constable read a statement praising 'the dogged persistence' of his men among all that slimy clay. Dougal was hanged on 14 July 1903

H.R.F.K.

# 1905

# GEORGE CHAPMAN
## The Lady Killer

Jack the Ripper, still unidentified and still the most famous of all serial murderers was not altogether true to type. The typical serial murderer kills once too often and gets caught. Almost half a century after Palmer, 'the Rugeley poisoner' came to a bad end, another serial murderer (who had similarly been trained in medicine) went a little too obviously to work and on April 7th 1903 paid the penalty at Wandsworth Prison. He was executed as George Chapman, but his real name was Severin Klosovski. Born in Poland in 1865 he was apprenticed, in his teens, for a five year term, to a surgeon in the town of Zvolen. About the beginning of 1888 he arrived in London and soon got a job as a barber in Whitechapel High Street, then more or less a 'colony' of immigrants from Eastern Europe. These presumably supplied most of the customers at the barber's shop, and it is not certain whether Klosovski combined a little elementary medical practice with his barbering, as he had done in Poland and, indeed, as had been quite customary in England up to the eighteenth century. He had left a wife behind him in Poland. She came to London, found him living with another Polish woman, and presently returned to Poland, leaving the 'other woman', Lucy Baderski, in possession of Klosovski's bed and name. In the autumn of 1889 he migrated with this pseudo-wife to the United States, but she returned, without him, in February 1981. Soon afterwards Klosovski followed – the date of his return, as of his first arrival in England, cannot be fixed. He joined his pseudo-wife, who had by then borne him two children, but soon afterwards either he deserted her or she turned him out of the house. He seems to have been an habitual philanderer, whose purpose was always physical seduction, and he was not so much promiscuous as fickle by temperament. He might be described as a serial seducer, dropping one woman as soon as another engaged his attention. So far as is known he had not yet taken to murder.

About 1893 or 1894 he was living with a young woman known as Annie Chapman. After this episode he gave himself the very English name of George Chapman, and it was as George Chapman that he was charged, tried and convicted. He would never admit that he was the same person as Severin Klosovski, which may or may not signify that he felt guilt and apprehension because in early years in London (and perhaps in New Jersey) he had committed offences more terrible than the seduction and desertion of women. In his later career as George Chapman he murdered, by poison, three women in succession each of whom was living with him as his wife. The first, Mary Isabella Spink, kept her blonde hair as short as a man's, lathered the faces of customers in the barber's shop Chapman took over at Hastings, and then, while they were being shaved, entertained them at the piano. The business, however, proved not so profitable as Chapman had hoped and he returned to London, where he became a publican in the City Road. There his wife fell ill and Chapman himself prepared the medicines prescribed by the local doctor. She died on Christmas Day 1897, the doctor certifying the cause of death as consumption.

Chapman kept the City Road pub and advertised for a resident barmaid, selecting from several applicants one Bessie Taylor. He 'married' her in the way usual with him, driving away from the pub one Sunday and returning before evening with a claim that the wedding had been at St. George's Cathedral, Southwark. Not long afterwards, Chapman gave up the London pub and took a lease of another in the country town of Bishop's Stortford. There his pseudo-wife had an operation, performed in hospital. Chapman, as fickle with 'licensed premises' as with women, soon returned to London, where he obtained a lease of the Monument Tavern in the Borough. On those premises, after a long illness, Bessie Taylor died, on February 13th 1901, the doctor in attendance attributing her death to 'exhaustion from vomiting and diarrhoea'; to a layman this would seem to be confusing the malady with its symptoms. The body was conveyed about two hundred miles away, to Lynn in Cheshire, near where Bessie had been born thirty-six years earlier. The valedictory verses on the tombstone are said to have been composed by Chapman, but are probably standard doggerel, available to the bereaved at any 'monumental mason's' workshop. Even so, in view of what had happened and was later to be disclosed, there is a grim, hypocritic undertone in the clumsy rhythms.

> *Farewell, my friends, fond and dear,*
> *Weep not for me one single tear;*
> *For all that was and could be done,*
> *you plainly see my time has come.*

Chapman's third victim, Maud Marsh, was also engaged by him as a barmaid. This was six months after the death of Bessie Taylor. It was not long before Chapman 'married' his new barmaid, driving away from the Monument Tavern and returning a little later with a 'bride' wearing a wedding ring.

Her parents lived only ten miles away at Croydon. When they visited the Monument Tavern they began to dislike and distrust Chapman. The new wife fell ill with what must have been to Chapman very familiar symptoms, including vomiting and diarrhoea. She went into Guy's Hospital, where her malady was diagnosed as peritonitis. She soon recovered and went back to domestic and bar room duties at the Monument Tavern. When the symptoms recurred, she was put under the care of the doctor, named Stoker, who had attended Chapman's previous wife, Bessie Taylor, in her last illness in the upper room of the same pub. The coincidence of the circumstances, including the patient's symptoms, appears to have made no impression on the doctor. Indeed, when Chapman removed his home to yet another pub, the Crown, Dr. Stoker was so satisfactory to the husband that he continued his attendance on the sick wife.

Her mother came to nurse her: her father and her sister were often at her bedside. At length her father went to consult his own doctor at Croydon about the mysterious, debilitating illness, and to tell him also that the patient's husband insisted on preparing with his own hands all the food – by this time it was always liquid food – offered the sick woman. The Croydon doctor visited the new pub, the Crown, and on his way back decided that the woman was being poisoned. He made up his mind to go and see Dr. Stoker again, but was too late: next day the patient died, and at the post-mortem examination it became clear that Chapman had finished her off with a still stronger dose of antimony probably in the form of tartar emetic.

## 2

It was his persistence in carrying through this plan for poisoning to its fatal end – although he must have known that he was suspected by Maud Marsh's father and mother – which exposed Chapman first as a murderer, then as a serial murderer. The two earlier deaths of pseudo-wives were quickly brought to the notice of the law. Tartar emetic, although so conveniently soluble in water, has the effect of preserving the tissues of the body for unusually long periods, and when the corpses of Mary Isabella Spink and Bessie Taylor were exhumed, there was no difficulty in proving that they also had died by poisoning. Chapman was a systematic murderer, making and carrying out his plans with great deliberation, yet he had little to gain and can hardly be classed either with Smith, Burke and Hare, Landru, Haigh, and others who made a business of murder, or with Palmer, Madeleine Smith, Crippen and those who may seem to have been driven to murder by pressure of outward circumstance. The compulsion on Chapman seems to have come from within, and presumably he developed such a liking for poisoning his pseudo-wives that he evolved a pattern of behaviour to which he felt obliged to conform.

Habitual seducers are not often handsome or even prepossessing, and Chapman, to judge from surviving photographs, had commonplace features, a skin rough in texture and dull colour, hair coarse and a moustache grown so long that it drooped some four or five inches below his mouth. He nevertheless seems to have found dozens of women, perhaps more than a hundred in all, willing to sleep with him 'for love'. He may have poisoned more than the three taken into account at his trial. It would be a possible explanation of his behaviour that he seduced women in order to suppress and contradict his awareness of his own physical handicaps. If this is a correct interpretation, his pattern of seduction, varied with occasional murder, arose from the fact that, having demonstrated his virile attractions by the 'conquest' of one woman, he quickly lost interest in her. As soon as that happened – and because in fact he remained, and knew it, an ugly man of meagre physique, with something ignoble and baboon-like about him – he again felt the need to demonstrate his sexual attractiveness and so needed another woman to seduce. It is also possible that some part of the compulsion upon him came from circumstance, and that he began to poison his pseudo-wives because he wanted to retain his social status as the licensee of a pub: a 'wife' who died an apparently natural death would not damage that status, whereas to dismiss her and replace her with another would hardly be respectable.

### 3

It has often been suggested that George Chapman was the same person as 'Jack the Ripper', whose first murder was on August 6th 1888, about the time Chapman reached London, and in Whitechapel, where Chapman then lived. The Ripper was thought to have been trained in surgery: Chapman certainly was. The description of a man seen in the company of one of the Ripper's victims shortly before she was killed, so far as it goes, would fit Chapman: 'Height 5ft 6in; age 34 or 35; dark complexion, with moustache curled at ends.' The last known Ripper murder in London occurred on November 9th 1888. In May 1890 Chapman went to America and ran a barber's shop in Jersey City: there were 'slashing' murders in that vicinity but they had ceased by 1892, when Chapman returned to London. There is a possibility that the two murderers were one and the same man, but it is very doubtful if any precedent or parallel could be found for such an abrupt switch from stabbing and mutilation murders, all but one done out of doors and all with prostitutes as victims, to slow secret, domestic poisoning, from an exhibitionist and demented technique to the most secretive of all methods of murder. Moreover, if Chapman committed the Ripper murders in Whitechapel, it was while he was still using his real name, Severin Klosovski, and while his command of the English language, never very precise or reliable, must have been still elementary. The two handwritten communications, one on a postcard, both signed 'Jack-the-Ripper', which the police received in 1888 appear, from intrinsic evidence, authentic and they are the work of someone reasonably well educated and completely at home with English idioms and slang.

J.B

# 5
# THE DAWN OF
# MODERN MURDER
## (1905–24)

# JOHANN HOCH

## 'I Have Done with Everybody'

Inspector George Shippy of the Chicago police knew he had a mass-murderer on his hands, a man he knew had slain perhaps a dozen women, and yet Shippy was compelled to set him free. The detective's tedious investigation into the murky career of Johann Hoch—one of the scores of aliases used by this unique killer—had produced a sinister portrait of an American Bluebeard that, at least in the sense of longevity, was unequaled in the annals of homicide.

Johann Otto Hoch, who married and murdered for nineteen years until his own lethal bigamy overcame him, was born John Schmidt in 1862 in Horweiler, Germany. He married Christine Ramb, and deserted her and three children in 1887. While investigating a charge of bigamy and another charge of swindling a used-furniture dealer, Inspector Shippy first came in contact with Johann Hoch in 1898, when he was using the alias 'Martin Dotz.'

Shippy had no way of knowing that Hoch-Dotz had murdered a dozen women from coast to coast but his suspicions were aroused when he received a letter from a Rev. Hermann C.A. Haas of Wheeling, West Virginia. Rev. Haas, who had good reason to look for Hoch, had recognized the bigamist's picture in a Chicago newspaper. He sent along another picture of Hoch, stating it was this man who was suspected of killing a Mrs. Caroline Hoch in the summer of 1895.

Hoch, a middle-aged, balding, burly man of medium height with piercing, light blue eyes and a thick handlebar mustache, stood behind the bars of his cell and looked at the picture Shippy held in his hand.

'Is this you, Dotz?'

'It is me,' Hoch replied.

'That's curious,' Shippy mused. 'According to my information, the man in this picture committed suicide in the Ohio River three years ago.'

Hoch glared at the detective for a moment and then turned to his cot, remaining silent. Shippy managed to collect enough evidence to convict Hoch-Dotz of swindling. While Hoch was serving a year in the Cook County Jail, Shippy, acting on a tip, began to search for a dozen missing wives. The detective began with Hoch's murderous exploit in Wheeling, West Virginia.

Hoch first appeared in Wheeling in February 1895, using the name Jacob Huff. He opened a saloon in a German neighborhood. He played the zither and led boisterous customers in drinking songs. Upon arrival, Hoch also began to seek out marriageable widows or divorced women with money. He found Mrs. Caroline Hoch, a middle-aged widow.

The couple married in April. Three months later, Rev. Haas, who had performed the wedding ceremony even though he suspected Hoch of foul play, found his once healthy parishioner, Mrs. Caroline Hoch-Huff, dying in agony. The parson saw Huff administer a white powder to his wife and concluded it was poison. He did not act, however, and the woman died some days later in great pain. Huff insisted she be buried immediately. After withdrawing all of the nine hundred dollars from his wife's bank account, selling her house, and collecting twenty-five hundred dollars on her life insurance, Jacob Huff disappeared.

Rev. Haas, in a series of letters sent three years later to Inspector Shippy, described what he thought happened. Huff walked to the nearby Ohio River on the night of his disappearance. He stripped naked and waded into the waters. Hoch placed his good watch, with his picture inside the locket, and a suicide note on his pile of clothes and then, holding a heavy sack aloft, walked up the river in neck-high water for a hundred yards until he reached a rowboat. He climbed into the boat, which he had earlier anchored, and then quickly dressed in another set of clothes. Next he calmly rowed up river, pausing only once in deep water to drop the large weighted sack he had so carefully carried. He continued on until he reached the Ohio side of the river, where he set the boat adrift and continued on his strange journey. But he was no longer Jacob Huff; now he was Johann Otto Hoch. It was peculiar to Hoch that he often took the last name of the woman he had either deserted or murdered. 'A warped keepsake stored in that evil mind,' Inspector Shippy concluded years later.

For almost a year Shippy tried to follow Hoch's strange, fading trail. He found a score of dead and deserted women, from San Francisco to New York, most of the victims being in the Midwest.

He would unearth more years later, as many as fifty and perhaps more than that—women in St. Louis, Minneapolis, Philadelphia. Incredibly, Inspector Shippy could not produce enough evidence to convict Hoch. Desperately, he wrote to the authorities in Wheeling, West Virginia, and begged them to exhume the body of Mrs. Carolina Hoch, telling them to look for arsenic poisoning.

In Wheeling, the body of Mrs. Hoch was dug up, and officials gasped as the coffin lid was opened. There was no middle to the body; all of the widow's vital organ had been surgically removed. (That, authorities later decided, was what Hoch had carried in the weighted sack and dropped into the middle of the Ohio River when feigning his suicide.) There was no case against Johann Otto Hoch. At the end of his term for swindling, he was let loose, 'to murder again,' moaned Shippy, 'God knows how many women, God knows where.'

From 1900 to 1905, Hoch, under various aliases, married at least another fifteen women, murdering most of them. His *modus operandi* was to marry and then slowly poison his wives to death, calling in doctors he knew would innocently diagnose the wife's disease as nephritis, a disease of the kidneys, for which there was then no treatment. Hoch, at the beginning, took his time, spending patient months to murder his wives systematically.

Hoch's careful method, however, fell to pieces after his release in Chicago. He knew he was a suspected killer and prolonged stays in any city would invite further suspicion. He began killing in record time—marrying rich widows he met within hours and heavily dosing them with arsenic within days, his gruesome job sometimes completed within a week. Such lethal frenzy ended his career. He married his last victim, Mrs. Marie Walcker, in Chicago on December 5, 1904, and quickly poisoned her.

On the night of Marie Walcker's death, the victim's estranged sister, Amelia, appeared. Hoch embraced the sister and kissed her. 'Upstairs my poor wife is dying,' he said. 'I cannot be alone in this world. Marry me when she goes.'

Amelia Walcker was stunned. 'What? How can you say such a thing?'

Hoch drew back into the shadows, his massive chest heaving. 'The dead are for the dead,' he intoned. 'The living are for the living.'

Marie Walcker-Hoch was buried the nest day without being embalmed. Amelia Walcker married Hoch within six days. The killer had received $500 from Marie's insurance policy and Amelia gave him another $750. Then he disappeared and Amelia went to the Chicago police. Inspector Shippy immediately had Marie Walcker's body exhumed and Hoch's poison was found. Shippy sent photos of Hoch to every major newspaper in the country.

In New York, a landlady and widow, Mrs. Katherine Kimmerle, spotted Hoch's picture and realized that it was a photograph of her new boarder, Henry Bartels, a strange lodger indeed since Bartels had proposed marriage to the widow only twenty minutes after he took a room. Mrs. Kimmerle rushed to the police. Hoch-Bartels was soon in custody.

'I'm Hoch, all right!' he admitted to the police. 'But I am a very much abused and misrepresented man.' Found in Hoch's room were $625, several wedding rings with the inscriptions filed off, a dozen suits with labels ripped out, a loaded revolver and a fountain pen that contained fifty-eight grams of arsenic. ('The poison is for me,' Hoch insisted. 'I was planning suicide.') While being extradited to Chicago to stand trial for the murder of Marie Walcker-Hoch, the killer told his train guards: 'There are lots of Hochs but I'm not the one they want.'

'You're the one,' Inspector Shippy shouted when he picked up the killer at Union Station.

During his long trial, the mass-murderer hummed, whistled and twirled his thumbs in court. He was innocent, he insisted to the end. When convicted of murdering Marie Walcker-Hoch and sentenced to be hanged, Hoch only whispered: 'It's all over with Johann.' Then he murmured as he was led away, 'It serves me right!'

Yet Hoch clung to hope to the hour of his death. He remained awake all night before the day of his execution, eating huge meals and demanding more and more food. Every now and then he would smile at his astonished guards and say: 'Now look at me, boys. Look at poor old Johann. I don't look like a monster now, do I?' No one replied.

On the scaffold on February 23, 1906, Hoch piously proclaimed his innocence, and then nodded for the sheriff to place the rope around his neck. 'I have done with everybody.' He shot through the trap moments later and died of a broken neck.

A reporter standing next to the galllows spoke to the still-swinging corpse: 'Yes, Mr. Hoch . . . but the question remains . . . *what* have you done with everybody?'

J.R.N.

# 1906

# HARRY THAW

## Murder at Madison Square Garden

The ambush, retaining its primitive simplicity but adapted to modern conditions, was the method chosen by Harry Thaw, the young American millionaire who in 1906 shot and killed Stanford White, an older man almost as rich as his murderer. Thaw arranged to be at the theatre known as the Madison Square Roof Garden for the first night of a play called *Mam'selle Champagne*. For the same opening performance a table, where food and drink could be served, was engaged for Stanford White – who had, following his profession of architecture, designed the theatre. White was thus shot dead in the most public circumstances and on premises which could be, and were, described as his 'artistic creation'.

Harry Thaw's behaviour that evening was more dramatic than anything enacted on the stage. White attended the theatre alone but Thaw took his young wife with him and two men guests, after giving them all dinner at another restaurant. The presence of the two guests showed forethought on Thaw's part: they were to escort his wife to her home after he had done the deed and surrendered himself to the police. About halfway through the second act of *Mam'selle Champagne* the Thaw party left, apparently at the suggestion of Mrs. Thaw, who said in evidence afterwards, that 'the play did not interest' her. She thus started Thaw's timetable for murder working. Thaw brought up the rear of the party and, unseen by the other three, turned back, walked to the table where Stanford White was sitting and shot him three times. According to the Assistant District Attorney, prosecuting, Thaw then 'turned the pistol upside down in his hand, holding it by the muzzle, and faced the audience in that way. The audience understood that his act was complete, what he intended to do had been done, and the audience understood him and there was no panic.' The simplicity and directness of this murder contrasts so strongly with the secrecy, the precautions taken against identification, the creation of false alibis, the readiness to throw the blame on some other person, the elaborately prepared escape from the scene of the crime which is associated in the public mind with most real life murders and still more with murders in novels, short stories and plays that it was not surprising many people took the view that a man with so little care for his own life must be mad.

The first lawyer engaged to defend Thaw advised that he should plead insanity. Thaw objected, perhaps because he realised that with such a plea there might be no full process of trial and therefore the dead man's 'sex life' could not be 'exposed' in court. Thaw's mother objected because the plea would require to be supported by evidence of insanity in other members of the family. At the trial Temporary Insanity was pleaded and at a second trial Thaw was acquitted on those grounds and consigned to an asylum but released in 1915.

The Thaw trial was reported at length in newspapers all over the world because of its background of wealth and debauchery: in that respect it is comparable with the 1963 scandals in London associated with the resignation of the Under Secretary for War in the Macmillan government, Mr. Profumo. Mrs. Thaw alleged that, when she was a photographer's model and showgirl aged 16, she had been given drugged champagne and, while unconscious, raped by Stanford White, waking afterwards in 'a room whose walls and ceiling were covered with many mirrors'. It may have been the effect of these details in his wife's story which prompted Thaw to choose the Madison Square Roof Garden and the 'first night' of a play called *Mam'selle Champagne* for the public punishment of Stanford White. The case survives in American social history because the defence and ultimate liberation of Harry Thaw is often regarded as an example of the power of the 'Almighty Dollar' within what appears to be a democracy.

J.B.

# 1915

# G.J. SMITH

## The Brides in the Bath

The Englishman's pet word, 'extraordinary,' is but a mild one to describe the career of George Joseph Smith. If it were not for a distrust of superlatives I would say that his case is the most astonishing ever heard in a court. It is no narrow spirit of patriotism which makes me think that the murders in this country, in Fall River, in 1892, are more interesting than the performances of Mr. Smith in three towns of England. For their amazing novelty, however, the achievements of this humorless Londoner should have entitled him—had there been any such decoration—to the De Quincey Medal, with the statement that, in his honor, the award would not be made again for fifty years. Brutal as were his crimes, they also had a grotesque quality, a dreadful approach to comedy, which often causes a description of them to be received with smiles. A bathtub, useful and desirable piece of furniture though it may be, is not exactly dignified. Like the folding bed, it has figured in too many jests to fit into a tragedy. And when the name of Mr. Smith became associated with three bathtubs, and three tragedies, it is apparent why some folk look upon his misdeeds as perilously close in resemblance to a French farce.

Mr. Eric Watson, the learned and very readable biographer of G.J. Smith, calls him 'the most atrocious English criminal since Palmer.' Well, the question of 'atrocity' is one of opinion, and hard to decide. Palmer, the sporting doctor of Rugeley, was a convivial soul, who died game: at first thought he hardly seems in Smith's class. Then one remembers the pious entries in his diary, and the string of poisonings which he probably committed. Yes, he belongs with Smith, wherever the latter may be, and so perhaps does Doctor Cream. But these men were crude and conventional by comparison with Mr. Smith.

For Smith invented a new way to commit murder, and one which enabled him to face coroners' juries and come forth triumphant, 'without a stain on his character.' I have heard a writer of detective novels, one with a lively fancy, begging for 'a new kind of murder,' yet this stodgy Mr. Smith, without the imagination of a greengrocer (and they are notoriously duller than grocers of any other color), thought out, in minute detail, a most successful plan for homicide, and only went to ruin because, like so many great artists, he could not resist one more farewell appearance. He had taken to heart, too literally, the advice of Mr. Tilden to the aspiring tennis player: *Never change a winning game.*

Smith's performances answer all but one of the requirements for a good murder. The lack was in the personality of Smith himself. His was not a hitherto blameless character; he was not an educated man; and he had lived in anything but the odor of sanctity. He was a habitual, although petty, criminal, whose early associations were those of a reformatory, where he lived from the age of nine to sixteen. As he always was 'bad,' it would be argued, by some humanitarians, that he had never had a 'chance,' and so should not have been punished. The same folk, by the way, would also excuse from punishment anybody who had, prior to his offense, always been 'good,' so the advantages of a criminal career, under these rulings, seem to be undeniable. Smith had done time in prison more than once between his release from the reformatory and the age of twenty-seven,, when he entered upon his career of wholesale matrimony and murder.

One other feature of Smith's crimes does much to enhance their interest: a considerable mystery still surrounds them. We do not know exactly his methods, either physical or (if there were any) psychical. He never confessed. To the end, the view of himself which he wished the world to adopt was that of an afflicted man who had suffered from what he called 'a phenomenal coincidence'—that three of his wives had died in their bath. In court, he interrupted the judge to protest at the charge to the jury as 'a disgrace to a Christian country.' He added that he was not a murderer, although he might be 'a bit peculiar.' As this seems to have been his method of admitting the fact that he had seven times committed bigamy, it is apparent that he had so mastered the art of modest understatement that he might have been envied even by an Oxford man. He never murdered a woman if he could, just as easily, rob her of every penny without taking her life. This fact throws doubt upon the theory that he enjoyed murder for its own sake.

Mr. Smith's matrimonial campaigns began in 1898; they were ended by his arrest early in 1915. His one lawful wife, Miss Thornhill, after difficulties with the police which both of them shared, retired to Canada, perhaps about 1902. She returned to England to testify at the trial in 1915. Some of his other courtships need not be described in detail: they merely involved a bigamous marriage, innocently if incautiously entered into on the part of the lady; and her subsequent grief when her husband decamped with all her cash and as much of her clothing as she did not happen to be wearing. It is not recorded that he left any of his living brides without at least the conventional 'stitch' to cover her. The marriage with a lady known to the public only as Miss—, in the respectable neighborhood of the Registry at St. George's, Hanover Square; the robbery of 'Mrs. F.W.' after a proposal of marriage; the marriage with 'Miss F.' at Southampton; and the marriage with Miss Alice Reavil at Woolwich in 1914 are all items in a rather monotonous program. Mr. Watson tabulates one of them—it is typical—in this way:

> *29 October. Marries Miss F. at Southampton.*
> *5 November. Absconds with all Miss F.'s property.*

It is queer that he took so long about it; either Miss F. was of unusual attractiveness, or else something delayed the bridegroom in his business arrangements, which customarily were prompt. Miss Reavil was humble in social station; she is described as a 'domestic servant.' Most of the other brides were, as he said, 'a notch above' him.

Leaving these minor incidents in Smith's career, let us consider his most remarkable marriages—four in number. In 1908, and for the first time under his own name, he was married at Bristol to Miss Edith Pegler. To her he was what might almost be called a good husband. That is, he never murdered her and he never robbed her. Indeed, she profited, in a small way, and quite innocently, by his robbery of another. From one of his mysterious absences, he returned bringing her an outfit of clothing. He 'had been doing a deal in ladies' secondhand clothing'—in other words, he had robbed poor Alice Reavil of her small outfit. Edith Pegler was the Catherine Parr to this Henry VIII; she survived him, and she had, comparatively speaking, small cause for complaint against him. She was forced to appear and give testimony, and when the tale of her husband's escapades was told, her sensations must have been far beyond description.

It was Smith's custom, when hard up—and that was his chronic state, for he never worked—to wander from this town to that, ostensibly as 'a dealer in antiques.' One of the worst deeds of this wicked man was to bring a reproach upon a business hitherto associated with nothing impure, by representing himself as a buyer and seller of antiquities and objects of art. In his wanderings, having left Miss Pegler somewhere or other, he met, and quickly wooed and won, Miss Beatrice Mundy. This was a respectable lady, thirty-three years of age, and the heiress to twenty-five hundred pounds by the will of her late father, a bank manager. Smith, as 'Henry Williams,' married her, inquired about her money, and found to his distress that it was so tied up that he could not lay his hands upon it. The sum of one hundred and thirty-eight pounds was available, however. He seized that and departed, leaving behind, as a gratuitous insult, a letter in which he charged the innocent woman with being diseased—the result of profligacy!

By a strange but real coincidence, some months later he met Miss Mundy at Weston-super-Mare. Despite everything, she instantly agreed to rejoin him. This time he resolved to get all of her money. It could be done only if she died, having willed her fortune to him. The deluded woman readily consented to a will; Smith, at the same time, making his own will in her favor. His was quite worthless, as he hadn't a penny. The wills were signed July 8, 1912. On July 9, Smith went to a shop in Herne Bay, where he and Miss Mundy were living, and bargained for a bathtub. He beat the dealer down from two pounds to one pound, seventeen shillings and sixpence. On July tenth, he took his 'wife' to a doctor, saying that she had had a fit. Miss Mundy remembered nothing of any fit, she had merely complained of a headache. The doctor was called twice on July twelfth, although there seemed to be nothing much the matter with the lady. On Saturday, July thirteenth, the doctor was sent for again: Smith (Mr. Williams, as he called himself) had found his wife dead in her bath. A policeman and a woman neighbor were also called; Smith led them upstairs and exhibited, to their astonishment and horror, the naked body of the dead woman, lying on the bathroom floor. Owing to the shrewdness exercised in the preliminary visits to the doctor, the coroner's jury found that the death was accidental: an epileptic fit followed by drowning. Smith buried his wife in a cheap grave, and commenced proceedings to obtain probate of the will. After some difficulties, he secured more than two thousand pounds. Later in the summer, he rejoined Miss Pegler, telling her that he had made one thousand pounds on the sale of a Chinese image.

During his next expedition, in the latter part of 1913, he met, at Southsea, Miss Alice Burnham, a nurse. She was a plump young woman of twenty-five, with a father who had sufficient perspicacity to distrust Smith at sight. It should be said, by the way, that Smith's easy conquests over women were equaled by the dislike he seems to have aroused in most men. Miss Burnham and Smith visited her home at Aston Clinton, and her father afterward described his prospective son-in-law as a man of very evil appearance; in fact, Mr. Burnham 'could not sleep while Smith was in the house.' Mr. Burnham's insomnia did not interfere with his daughter's romantic intentions, and she was married to 'George Joseph Smith, 40, bachelor, of independent means' at Portsmouth on November fourth. The name and age of the groom were correctly given. Miss Burnham's funds, from all sources, were about one hundred and thirty-two pounds and sixpence, and Smith soon had these in his care. On December fourth, he insured her life for five hundred pounds. Four days later she made her will—in favor of the man whom she honestly supposed to be her husband.

In two days they were at Blackpool, seeking lodgings—lodgings with a bath. They rejected rooms in one house, because a tub was lacking. After they had found quarters, they called upon a doctor; Miss Burnham said she had a headache. The next day she called for a bath, which was prepared for her. While she was upstairs, the landlady, like the one in *Tess*, looked at the ceiling and saw a stain, not of blood, but of water. The tub, for some reason, had overflowed. Smith went out on an errand: to buy two eggs for breakfast. When he returned he talked with the landlady for a few minutes, and then went upstairs. He was soon calling for a doctor, for the same one who had seen his wife yesterday. Mrs. Smith was dead—most unaccountably drowned in her bath. Soon after the inquest, Smith departed from Blackpool, leaving his address on a postcard with the landlady. That person had formed an unfavorable opinion of the sorrowing husband, and the gift of prophecy seems to have been vouchsafed to her. On the reverse of the postcard she wrote:

*Wife died in bath, I shall see him again some day.*

Smith returned to Miss Pegler at Bristol; he had been, he told her, trading in Spain, where he had done fairly well. So he had: in a few weeks the insurance was paid, and it amounted to five hundred and six pounds.

In September of the next year, 1914, occurred the marriage with Alice Reavil, who escaped without any bathing incident. Three months later, Smith married, at Bath—with rare irony—Margaret Elizabeth Lofty, whose occupation was that of companion to elderly ladies. She was a clergyman's daughter, and a spinster of thirty-eight. The bridegroom appeared as 'John Lloyd, land agent.' Miss Lofty had but nineteen pounds in cash; but her thoughtful fiancé had her insured for seven hundred pounds, *before* the wedding. They repaired immediately to Highgate, and Smith engaged rooms—after a quarrel at one house where they did not like his manner as he asked about the bath. Then followed the usual procedure: the visit to a doctor, a will made in the husband's favor, a hot bath, requested by the wife at 7:30 P.M., and at 8:15 a police constable called in to view the naked body of a drowned woman.

Another 'phenomenal coincidence'—but it was one too many. Mr.Burnham, and another man, who had met Smith at the time of an earlier bereavement, saw a newspaper account of this distressing death of a bride in her bath. They each communicated with Scotland Yard, and an investigation began which carried the detectives into more than forty towns of England, and led to the interviewing of 50 witnesses, of whom 112 were called at the trial. Smith was identified with 'Williams' and 'Lloyd.' He soon ceased to deny the many marriages and the deaths; he always insisted that the deaths were accidental. He was tried, in June, 1915, at the Old Bailey, for the murder of Miss Mundy. It was remarked that all the solicitous care of an English court of justice was exercised to determine whether one worthless man should live or die—and this at a time when hundreds of the best and bravest men of Great Britain were daily giving up their lives in battle for their country.

The trial of Professor Webster indicated how accurately circumstantial evidence may lead to the discovery of truth, and the trial of Smith illustrated its value, and showed how absurd is the position of those who, ignorant of the meaning of the words, talk as if 'circumstantial evidence' means incomplete or unsatisfactory evidence. Nobody had seen Smith kill any of the three women; nobody could even testify that he was in the room when they died. He took care to seem to absent himself. But the long string of coincidences fell upon him with crushing force. There were no less than thirteen points of similarity in the three deaths; of these, the wills, the insurance policies, the inquiries about the baths, the visits to a doctor, the ostentatious absence just after the time of death, and the fact that the brides were more profitable to Smith if they died than if they lived, were some of the most remarkable. Evidence as to 'system' was admitted; that is, evidence of the two later deaths was allowed, to prove the earliest one. It would be interesting to know whether this would have been permitted in an American court, or whether the frequent rule against such evidence—a rule so fair in the abstract, and so apt, in the particular case, to restore a murderer to his loving friends—would have prevailed instead.

One of the mysteries of the case—to men, at least—was Smith's extraordinary powers of fascinating women; of prevailing upon them to marry him after the shortest courtships; of making them accept insult and sometimes abuse, and causing them to entrust to him their lives and fortunes. A few elderly women disliked him; upon men he either made no impression at all or else an unpleasant one. Perhaps the explanation of his marriages is that he selected the victims with care, from among that class which Sherlock Holmes described as one of the most dangerous in the world—

> . . . *the drifting and friendless woman. She is the most harmless . . . of mortals, but she is the inevitable inciter of crime in others. She is helpless. She is migratory. . . . She is lost, as often as not in a maze of obscure pensions and boardinghouses. She is a stray chicken in a world of foxes. When she is gobbled up she is hardly missed.*

If Smith had one good quality, one amiable trait, or even one agreeable human failing, it does not appear. He was abominably closefisted; his idea of a wedding journey was to take his bride to a free picture gallery, or to some shilling treat. He could cheat his victims, and anybody else, out of pounds or out of pence, with equal deliberation. And when he had killed Miss Mundy, and thereby come into two thousand pounds, he returned the tub, over which he had haggled with the dealer, and refused to pay for it at all.

It is still unknown how the murders were accomplished. The simplest explanation is that he suddenly seized his victim by the feet and lowered her head beneath the water. One of the detectives in the case prevailed upon a young lady whom he knew, an experienced swimmer, to get into a tub of water—discreetly clad in a swimming suit—and let him make the experiment. They were both convinced that it might be done; the girl quickly had to give the signal that she had enough, and wished to be pulled up again. Perhaps some folk were disposed to remark that these crimes could never have taken place except in modern American tubs; with the gill of water in the old tin-hat tubs of Queen Victoria's glorious days, Smith would have been baffled.

Sir Edward Marshall Hall, the famous barrister, who defended Smith, thinks that the murderer hypnotized his wives in advance. This, he believes, explains the curious fact that the bathroom doors were invariably left unlocked—and in strange houses. It has been suggested that, as a result of hypnotic suggestion, Smith did not even have to enter the bathrooms; that the brides drowned themselves! Drugs have also been offered as an explanation, and 'poisonous vapour' in the water. There is certainly something odd in the dazed condition noted in the brides by one or two of the doctors who interviewed them. Smith was heard to prompt them in their replies, and in their inquiries of their prospective landladies whether there was a bath in the lodgings. One of the most bizarre theories is that Smith had a mania, an irresistible impulse, which could not be denied, once he saw a woman in a tub. He simply must drown her. This notion is based on the fact that he warned Miss Pegler, just before the murder of Miss Lofty, against bathtubs!

'I should advise you to be careful of those things,' he said, 'as it is known that women often lose their lives through weak hearts and fainting in a bath.'

Assuredly it is impossible to say what are all the fantastic impulses of sexual psychopathy, but there was too much careful planning, too much calculation of pounds, shillings, and pence, to let an English jury be hoodwinked into thinking that Smith was not responsible for his acts.

In Great Britain, murderers could not insure the safety of their own necks by taking care to commit their murders in an especially atrocious fashion. Nor did the law, in that kingdom, summon swarms of alienists to entertain the court for days with descriptions of the prisoner's 'phantasies' at the age of five and a half. One of the consequences is that, with a population of forty millions, there were less than half as many murders in a year as in the city of Chicago, with three millions.

Smith had lived by his victories over women, and to the end women were attracted by him. At the police court, they thronged around him in the dock; coming early in the morning and staying all day. They hemmed him in, pressing so closely that they actually touched him. At his trial, in the Old Bailey, the pretty ladies of London were there to watch, and to comment upon his fascination. Men found him insignificant and common: 'Just like any butcher!'

When his last morning came—a day in August—he was in complete collapse. The executioners led him from his cell across the prison yard. Outside the wall, a crowd had collected—many of them women—and the loud chatter of women's voices reached the inside of the prison, drowning the tones of the chaplain as he recited the service for the Burial of the Dead.

E.P.

# 1916

# DOCTOR WAITE
## The Deadly Dentist

As sordid a murder by poison as ever came to light occurred in 1916 when Dr. Arthur W. Waite confessed that he had killed his father-in-law and his mother-in-law, Mr. and Mrs. John E. Peck, who were living with him and his wife at 435 Riverside Drive. It was the last important homicide in New York in which poison was the agency and it was important too because Waite was known as a formidable tennis player. He had come with his wife's parents from Michigan and money was the murder motive. He never collected anything, for the moment the hand of the law dropped on his shoulder he confessed and then attempted to kill himself. But he lived to expiate his crime in the electric chair at Sing Sing prison.

The circumstances surrounding the case were unusual. The family minister who was suspicious of the cause of the Pecks' deaths turned detective and came to New York in disguise, set out to obtain evidence. He was the Rev. Alfred Wishart of Grand Rapids. As pastor of a local church there he had known the Peck and Waite families for years. Out in his own bailiwick he was called a crusader but he turned determined sleuth when he learned of the death of his old friend John Peck. Peck and his wife were here on a visit. Mrs. Peck was the first to die. There was nothing outwardly suspicious about her death, but when shortly afterwards the elderly Mr. Peck died, some whose suspicions were aroused sent Mr. Wishart a telegram suggesting an autopsy.

An examination proved that Peck had died of arsenical poisoning. An examination showed traces of arsenic in Mrs. Peck's vital organs. Obviously an interview with Dr. Waite was in order. His actions had caused comment at about the time the aged pair began to show signs of illness. Detectives took him in custody and much to their surprise he confessed not only the murder of the Pecks but that it had been his intention to kill his own wife and a maiden aunt who lived in the Riverside Drive home. It was a most astounding story that the doctor told. Then excusing himself for a moment, he went into another room and took a draught of poison. He was taken to Bellevue Hospital, and his plan to cheat the electric chair was thwarted.

Waite's volubleness at his trial was a torment to his lawyers. He insisted on repeating his confession and went into details in describing his motive. His brain conceived the plot when he was a young man in Michigan. He had decided he would never work for a living even after his parents financed him through a dental college. There he was more interested in tennis than in his studies and was known far and wide as a crackerjack on the courts.

In the course of his athletic career he met Miss Peck, who admired him because he was in the public eye. They were married and almost immediately he managed to get hold of a considerable sum of money which he spent lavishly. When this money had been dissipated, Waite began looking around for more, more determined than ever to live without working. An aunt, who had taken a fancy to the young dentist, was the donor of the $50,000 wedding gift, and when she refused more he included her in the list of those he proposed to get rid of by poison.

Waite was 28 years old when he committed the crimes for which he paid with his life. He was tried for the murder of Mr. Peck. On the day Waite took the witness stand the courtroom was filled to standing room only. Waite appeared eager to reach the witness chair. He had groomed himself with unusual care. His lawyer was helpless. Waite's babble put him nearer the electric chair with every word. Brazenly he told the jury about the death of Mr. Peck. 'I gave him large doses of about everything I had, diphtheria, pneumonia, typhoid, influenza germs but they did not seem to affect him. Then I tried tubercular sputum and procured a nasal spray into which I put it. I induced Peck to use that but it did not work. I then got a lot of calomel and fed him that in order to weaken his system so that he could not resist the germs, but that failed. I tried many other things in the hope that he would succumb. I would open the windows and dampen his bedsheets with water. That made no difference. I tried hydrochloric acid but that didn't do him any harm. Then I tried to get him out in an automobile with me. My idea was to stall at the top of a hill with him in the back seat. I planned to jump and let him go over a cliff in the car. I couldn't do that either. One night I turned on the gas in his room, but the superintendent came up and told me about the leak. I had to shut it off.

'Then I gave him arsenic. I don't remember what day it was. I gave him a lot of it in his food. One night I was left to watch by his bedside while my wife got some rest. The old man was groaning with pain. I looked over the medicine bottles beside his bed and found a small vial of chloroform. I saturated a rag with some of it and went over to him and said: "Father, here is some ether and ammonia which will relieve your pain." I gave him a smell and then I gave him another dose. At last he fell asleep. I continued to put on more until he became unconscious. Then I got a pillow and placed it over his face and held it there until he died.'

All through this gruesome recital Waite sat with his head erect and at no time showed any emotion. He rattled off the story as well he might for he had confessed it to practically everybody with whom he had come in contact. He had told me the details in private previously. He became most friendly with me for I had seen him the day he was brought from Bellevue and he had left standing orders in the Tombs prison that he would see me whenever I called. This was quite often because the newspapers gave much space to the case.

It took the jury twenty minutes to take one ballot and return with a verdict that sent Waite to his death. He was completely unmoved. He said he deserved whatever fate was meted out to him; that he had no regrets and that he would go to the electric chair with a firm step and a smile on his face.

Dr. Wishart did not appear publicly in the prosecution of Waite but he was the man who started the ball rolling. He had come to New York in what he called a disguise consisting of a black suit, but wearing at a jaunty angle a light fedora hat. He worked fast and soon learned from interviews in the home just what happened the night Waite was left alone to care for Peck. Later the minister told of his part in the investigation saying: 'And may God forgive me for the lies and deceit that I practiced then. I have done more lying since I have been here than in all the rest of my life. I have lied and deceived, and I expect I have broken your laws. The Lord forgive me. I did it for what I believed to be the right. I have gone down on my knees and prayed for forgiveness for those sins.'

The authorities admit that had it not been for Dr. Wishart the murder of the Pecks would probably have been unsolved.

Dr. Wishart preached the funeral service over Mr. Peck while Waite sat nearby. Waite stared into the face of the dead man. All during this time the minister watched Waite's reactions. At the close of the service he was convinced that Waite was responsible for the death of the aged man.

After Waite's conviction he was quickly taken to Sing Sing by train. I was in the party. At the railroad station both in New York and in Sing Sing he was almost playful, saying that he was going to a nice quiet place where later he would have a nice long rest. As the doors closed behind him he waved a cheery good-by to me, and I did not see him again until he walked into the death chamber for execution. I was there and saw him step into the room. I saw him advance the few steps to the chair. Waite blinked at the glare of the lights; he might have seen me but I doubt it. He did wave his hand but there were twenty people in that room and probably they all looked alike to him. He was strapped in the chair, the current was turned on, and in five minutes he was pronounced dead.

Under the law an autopsy must be made at once and that is done in a small chamber directly behind the room in which the execution takes place. It was suspected that Waite was not sane; that he had a brain affection and an enlarged heart due to his athletic activities. I was one of a half dozen reporters who awaited the result of the post mortem only to learn that Waite was normal, exceptionally well developed physically, and that he had not suffered in the slightest through any indulgences.

Several years ago a reporter on the New York *World* wrote a series of articles under the caption 'Murderers I Have Known.' I have never known many murderers, although I have seen no less than one hundred condemned to die.

E.H.S.

# 1921

# THOMAS ALLAWAY
## The Murder that Misfired

The crime of Thomas Henry Allaway is one of the extremely rare instances in which a man has with the utmost deliberation, coolness and cunning, planned the murder of a person entirely unknown to him. That alone would make it memorable, but from first to last the story of the crime teems with the sensational and the unusual, and not the least the fact that had it not been for a blunder on the part of the murderer the brilliant work of the detectives would have been wasted.

On the 22nd of December, 1921, an advertisement appeared in the *Morning Post* in which Miss Irene Wilkins, of Streatham, offered her services as a lady cook. Miss Wilkins knew that an application for such work in Christmas week would bring a quick response and, therefore, she could not have been surprised when a few hours later a telegram arrived from Bournemouth asking her to travel there by the 4.30 train and promising to send a car to meet her. In due course she caught the train and on arrival at Bournemouth Central Station soon after seven was accosted by a chauffeur in uniform who conducted her to a car. Now it happened that a gentleman travelling by the same train had his attention drawn by some trivial incident to the meeting between the lady and the chauffeur, but he thought no more of it until he read in the papers that the body of a woman, who had obviously been murdered, had been found in a lane some three miles from Bournemouth Central Station. He then communicated with the police who promptly filed his statement.

The discovery created a profound sensation which was intensified by the pathos of Miss Wilkins's last day on earth. She had had no enemies, and it was plain there could be no pecuniary gain to her murderer. Who, then, had lured her to Bournemouth—the telegram had been bogus, of course—what fiend had planned an elaborate hoax so that he might get her at his mercy in a lonely lane? These questions were asked by millions, but they were not to be answered for six months.

Superintendent Garrett, of Bournemouth, took the investigation in hand conscious that as murderer and victim had been complete strangers to one another his task was an extremely difficult one. But with the aid of the traveller who had noticed the meeting between the lady and the chauffeur and with information from other sources he decided that whether the murderer was a chauffeur or not he had worn the uniform of one when he went to meet Miss Wilkins. But who was the chauffeur? Bournemouth is a town with a large proportion of prosperous persons who employ chauffeurs, and it was, of course, always possible that the cunning murderer might have assumed the uniform as a disguise. However, when he had got into the thick of the case Superintendent Garrett came to the conclusion that the uniform had not been a disguise, and on this assumption he started to 'comb out' Bournemouth, relieved by the knowledge that his labours were lightened by this narrowing of the area of investigation.

Meanwhile, facsimile copies of the decoy telegram to Miss Wilkins were circulated throughout the world. They were published in remote American newspapers, all over the continent of Europe and even in Africa and Asia. As a result letters began to pour in upon the Bournemouth police, and retired detectives and policemen had to be recalled from their leisure to help in the sorting and the reading of them. Superintendent Garrett and the detectives were working eighteen hours a day now and before the crime was a month old they had interviewed every chauffeur in Bournemouth and neighbourhood. Each man was called upon to account for his movements on the night of the 22nd December, and we may be sure that each man, except the actual murderer, willingly submitted to the ordeal, for the chauffeurs of Bournemouth were as eager as any class in the community to bring the cowardly criminal to justice.

Amongst those examined was a chauffeur in private employment named Thomas Henry Allaway, a young married man with a seven-year-old daughter, who was noted for his fondness for female society and who appeared to be better off than the majority of his fellows. Allaway cheerfully answered every question, readily described his movements on the all-important night, and eagerly wrote down the half-dozen sentences which were dictated to him. Then when his handwriting had been compared with that of the decoy telegram and found to bear no resemblance to it he was permitted to leave the station, and he must have been a very happy man when with his usual swagger he turned into the street.

Another chauffeur took his place on the other side of the desk and so the inquiry proceeded, an inquiry which seemed to an excited and indignant public to be wasting too many days, for there were no arrests and, apparently, no one was suspected. Meanwhile, the well-meaning but stupid continued to hamper the detectives with useless information. They sent more than 20,000 letters to Superintendent Garrett, all of which were read carefully and, where there was a gleam of promise, tested. But not one of them was of any use, and thus week after week went by and the murderer was still at large.

Crowds daily visited the scene of the murder and the lane had become a place of pilgrimage when one afternoon a young man holding by the hand a little girl of seven walked up to the policeman on duty and courteously inquired the way to the scene of Miss Wilkins's death. The officer, accustomed to the question, answered briefly and turned away, unaware, of course, that the inquirer was Thomas Henry Allaway, the Bournemouth chauffeur who was some months later to die at the hands of the hangman for the murder that was then puzzling the whole country.

But from the moment news of the crime had been published no one distinguished himself more by talking about it than did Thomas Henry Allaway. He was a very sociable person, a member of at least two clubs, and a familiar figure in certain hospitable public-houses and inns. He spent his money freely, and had a good eye for feminine beauty, but once the Bournemouth mystery had taken hold of the imagination of the man in the street Allaway made it his own special subject. Night after night he would discuss and argue about it, criticizing the police for their failure and hazarding explanations of the immunity of the murderer. He was so cool and confident that he could speak freely without the least of betraying himself. He had no cause to be nervous now, he felt, for had he not endured the ordeal of facing one of the cleverest detectives in Bournemouth and had he not emerged triumphant from that ordeal?

No doubt he believed that he had committed the perfect crime, arguing that although cleverer men than himself had tried it before and failed he had succeeded because he had carefully thought out every act step by step. The telegram in a disguised handwriting had been dispatched from a post-office where he was unknown and he had requested Miss Wilkins to travel by a train which was always met by dozens of motor-cars. In the hustle, bustle, and confusion of a dark December night with everybody intent on getting away as quickly as possible there would be no one to observe him, at any rate, not closely, and once his purpose had been accomplished it would be impossible to link his life with that of the lady from London. He had thought all that in advance, and the result was the perfect crime.

So he became the most prominent debater on the topic of the Bournemouth mystery in his own circle, went about his affairs with the peace of mind of the innocent, and chaffed those of his comrades who were so sensitive as to be upset by the suspicion attached to members of their calling in Bournemouth. Not that he was not sensitive either; indeed, explaining that as a chauffeur's uniform was regarded with suspicion he would no longer wear his except when actually on duty, ever afterwards he was never seen in uniform except when driving his employer.

Then, some months after the murder, Superintendent Garrett, still firmly of opinion that the murderer was a chauffeur, although every chauffeur had been closely questioned and his movements on the 22nd of December accounted for, decided to have a list compiled of those chauffeurs who might be considered by a stretch of the imagination to be still under suspicion. On that list was the name of Thomas Henry Allaway, but there was nothing definite against him, and there were others who appeared to be just as likely as he to be the guilty one. But when that list was about to be acted on the man who thought he had committed the perfect crime suddenly provided the police with the all-important clue they lacked, and he did so by ignoring the fact that the collar he wore rubbed the back of his neck.

It happened one morning that the detective told off to shadow Allaway—all the men on the second list were being shadowed simultaneously—noticed as he was following him that his collar bore traces of a heavy grease which on closer investigation proved to have come from his neck, leaving a patch of natural tinted skin. The obvious inference was that the complexion of the chauffeur's neck and face was not natural and it only required a brief glance to see that Allaway for some reason had disguised his complexion by using a grease favoured by actors and actresses when 'making up'. In other words, he had altered his appearance by giving his skin a touch of bronze, and it seemed that there could be only one reason why he should do this. And that reason was a desire to make it impossible to identify him should he ever be paraded before anyone who had seen the lady and the chauffeur meet on the night of the 22nd of December at Bournemouth Central Station.

This was the murderer's trivial and yet fatal mistake. He had laid all his plans with amazing cunning and the luck had favoured him, but he blundered to his shameful death when he failed to realize that the collar which rubbed the back of his neck was also rubbing away the grease he had obtained from one of his many female friends, a chorus girl in a touring company.

Once the police discovered that Allaway had altered his complexion they forgot every other name on the second list and concentrated on him. In the guise of tradesmen they wrote him apparently harmless and unimportant letters to which he replied, unaware that their letters were so worded that his replies had to contain words which had formed part of the decoy telegram. They dare not, of course, try to lure him in to writing the word 'Wilkins', for that would have put him on his guard, and so far they had no evidence to bring before a jury, but they circumvented this difficulty by a ruse which brought from him a letter containing the words 'will' and 'kinsman'. A combination of these produced 'Wilkins', in handwriting which persuaded Superintendent Garrett that he was on the right track.

The net now began to close around him and the perfect murderer proved himself a perfect fool by forging cheques in his employer's name and providing the police with what they wanted, an excuse to put him under lock and key for a comparatively trivial charge while they investigated his past with a view to arraigning him for the capital offence. He lied, of course, and lied stupidly and inartistically. He protested that he did not write the decoy telegram, and when specimens of the letters he had written when a soldier at the Front were shown to him he declared that they had been written for him by certain of his fellow soldiers whom he named. It was a desperate lie because he had been identified by the clerk to whom he had handed the telegram to Miss Wilkins on the 22nd of December, but this would not have been sufficient for a jury which would have wanted something more than an alleged recognition after six months. The chief object of the police was, therefore, to prove beyond a shadow of doubt that the decoy telegram had been written by Thomas Henry Allaway. On that fact the question of his guilt or innocence turned, and Allaway knowing this lied for all he was worth, hoping that the two fellow soldiers he had named could never be brought to confront him. It was a chance shot which seemed likely to score, for they might easily have been killed in action or since the Armistice might have gone abroad. But with the assistance of the War Office the men were traced and when in the month of July, 1922, Allaway was tried at the Winchester Assizes for the murder of Miss Wilkins in the previous December, the two men he had hoped were dead or lost proved that his letters to his wife were not in their handwriting. There was other evidence against him, but it was the decoy telegram that convicted him, and he might never have been connected with the telegram had it not been for the collar that rubbed the back of his neck.

Allaway was a brute beast with the brain of a degenerate and he committed murder like a brute beast. And when Mr. Justice Avory passed him on to the hangman that official performed a public service in ridding society of one of the most callous and cruel of murderers.

J.C.E

# 1921

# LANDRU

## The Bluebeard of Paris

The most monstrous criminal character in modern annals was probably Henri Désiré Landru, whose head I saw chopped off at dawn on February 25, 1922. He was convicted of the cold-blooded murder of ten women and one boy, whom he had hacked to pieces and burned in his cookstove at Villa Ermitage in Gambais, near Versailles; he had been the lover of 283 women.

Over a period of five years Landru had pursued the grim business of systematic lovemaking and slaughter. Relations duly reported the mysterious disappearances of his 'fiancées' to the police, but each time the circumstances and the name of 'the man in the case' were different; the police found no clue and did not connect the disappearances as the crimes of one man. The disorganization of civilian life during the war favored Landru's schemes. The husbands of many of the women were at the front; others, whose husbands had been killed, were only too anxious to listen to offers of marriage. Then, by pure chance in April 1919, the sister of one of the missing 'finacées' caught a glimpse of Landru in Paris, followed him to his apartment and informed the police. Without realizing they had made one of the greatest catches in Parisian criminal history, the police took him into custody.

The whole fantastic story began to come out when, on the way to the station, detectives caught Landru attempting to throw away a little notebook. It was the famous *carnet* containing the key to the entire series of astounding crimes. The entries look like notations of business transactions and remained a mystery until police compared the names of the women in the *carnet* with the names of scores of women missing since 1915 and found that ten tallied.

Then the police pieced together a bizarre drama. They learned that Landru had lived in eleven different places in Paris, under at least fifteen names (he sometimes adopted the name of his previous victim). He was the son of a respectable Parisian businessman who had become insane in later life and committed suicide. In youth Landru was studious, bright and normal; but as he attained manhood criminal tendencies asserted themselves. He served two brief prison terms for petty fraud and about 1914 hit upon the unique idea of wholesale lovemaking as a business. By matrimonial advertisements and offers to purchase furniture, he came in contact with hundreds of women and made violent love to every one of them. At first he seems to have confined his operations to swindling his enamored victims.

Henri Désiré's courtships were so skillfully ardent that he was able to propose matrimony at the second or third meeting. His diary revealed him at times courting seven women simultaneously, maintaining a passionate correspondence and turning out love letters by the score. A bundle of such letters was found in his villa, ready for use.

During this time Landru maintained a separate home for his wife and son and was a good husband and family man. He explained his frequent excursions to the villa as 'business trips.' Neither wife nor son knew the nature of his business and often unknowingly helped dispose of the property of his victims.

Landru's unforgettable trial, in the fall of 1921, was better than anything the *Folies-Bergères* ever put on. All Paris stormed the doors, Landru maintained an imperturbable dignity; under questioning he would smile deprecatingly and say, 'It's an affair of honor. I do not kiss and tell.' One day he sent for the judge, saying he was remorseful and wanted to talk. At last, buzzed the prosecution, Landru is going to confess. But to the judge Landru sighed and said: 'I must tell you. I am remorseful about all the 283 infidelities to my wife.' The prisoner's story ricocheted around the courtroom to roars of laughter.

But day by day the prosecution unraveled the cryptic entries in the 'death *carnet*.' The first was the name of the widow Cuchet, whom Landru met through a matrimonial advertisement. After a whirlwind courtship she went to live with him at the fateful Villa Ermitage (railroad station, Vernouillet), under promise of marriage. Then came the stark inscription: 'One round-trip, two single tickets to Vernouillet,' with the cost. Mme. Cuchet and her seventeen-year-old son disappeared from the face of the earth from that day forth. Some of her furniture later turned up in the apartment of Landru's wife. Landru's wife and her son's sweetheart were found to be wearing some of Mme. Cuchet's jewelry when Landru was arrested.

Entries in the *carnet* marked with monotonous regularity a fatal jaunt to Vernouillet and the disappearance of one more victim. The majority were widows, but one was a nineteen-year-old girl; and at the time of Landru's arrest Fernande Segret, an attractive girl of twenty-nine, was wearing the 'death ring'—the engagement ring Landru had used for ten other 'fiancées.' At the same time he was engaged to Jeanne Falque, from whom he had borrowed 2000 francs. Despite Mlle. Segret's knowledge that she had narrowly escaped the fate of ten predecessors, she refused to testify directly against him. 'He was always affectionate and respectful to me,' she said. 'I loved him and would have married him.' At the trial she avoided his gaze. When she finally looked at him she swooned in the witness box.

As climax to a crushing array of circumstantial evidence, a celebrated criminologist produced 256 fragments of human bones from the ashes of the cookstove at Villa Ermitage and testified that they came from at least three bodies. Another expert testified that the soot in the chimney contained a high content of fat. An ashcan yielded bits of half-melted corset ribs and buttons from women's clothing. One closet contained scores of bottles that had contained tissue-destroying fluids. Neighbors testified they had often seen dense clouds of nauseating smoke coming from the mysterious villa.

Alienists and scientists who examined Landru confessed they could not understand his uncanny attraction for women. Except for his extraordinary eyes, which were large and serpentlike in their fixity and brilliance, he had no outward feature to account for it. He was fifty-five years old, of medium build and sallow complexion. At first glance his only unusual features were his remarkably shaped bald head and his Assyrian beard, of which he was inordinately proud. Parisian men about town tried to elicit Landru's system of winning women. But he smiled mysteriously and said: 'Our relations were mostly of a business nature, and those of a private nature are a matter between them and me.'

Henri Désiré Landru was sentenced to have his head cut off in front of the Versailles jail at dawn on February 25, 1922.

About 4 a.m that morning, word came that Anatole Deibler, the famous executioner, had arrived with his guillotine, and we hurried to the prison. Four hundred troops had drawn cordons at each end of the street and permitted only possessors of little mimeographed tickets to pass. The only light came from the few electric street lights and the flickering candles in the workmen's old-fashioned lanterns as they bolted the grisly machine together.

Nearly a hundred officials and newspapermen gathered in a circle around the guillotine; I stood fifteen feet away. News arrived from the prison that Landru, whose long black beard had been cut off previously, had asked that he be shaved. 'It will please the ladies,' he said. He wore a shirt from which the neck had been cut away, and cheap dark trousers – no shoes or socks.

Just as the first streaks of chilly dawn appeared, a large horse-drawn van arrived and backed up within a few feet of the guillotine. Deibler's assistants pulled two wicker baskets from it, placed the small round one in front of the machine where the head would fall and the large coffin-shaped one close beside the guillotine.

Suddenly the great wooden gates of the prison swung open. Three figures appeared, walking rapidly. On each side a jailer held Landru by his arms, which were strapped behind him, supporting him and pulling him forward as fast as they could walk. His bare feet pattered on the cold cobblestones and his knees seemed not to be functioning. His face was waxen and, as he caught sight of the ghastly machine, he went livid.

The jailers hastily pushed Landru face downward under the lunette, a half-moon-shaped wooden block, which clamped his neck beneath the suspended knife. In a split second the knife flicked down, and the head fell with a thud into the basket. As an assistant lifted the hinged board and rolled the headless body into the big wicker basket, a hideous spurt of blood gushed out.

An attendant standing in front of the machine seized the basket containing the head, rolled it like a cabbage into the larger basket and helped shove it hastily into the waiting van. The van doors slammed, and the horses were whipped into a gallop. Since Landru had first appeared in the prison courtyard, only twenty-six seconds had elapsed.

W.M.

# 1921

# HENRI GIRARD

## A Super-Poisoner

In the little township of Montreuil-sous-bois near Paris, in the year 1909, there was probably no resident more popular and better known than Henri Girard.

He was a man close on forty years of age, of goood appearance, tall, slim and debonair. Always immaculately dressed in pressed trousers and patent-leather boots, he was regarded as the local leader of fashion and elegance, in so much that he was usually known as 'Gentleman Girard.'

He was an Alsatian by birth, his father being a well-to-do chemist. About 1888 the family left Alsace in order to allow the father to take up an appointment in the Excise stationed in the Department of the Seine. Henri was sent to a boarding-school in Paris and then to the Lycée St. Louis. He was expelled from both of these establishments for thefts from his fellow-pupils and finished his education in an institution at Vincennes. At the age of eighteen he enlisted for four years in a cavalry regiment and became a non-commissioned officer, but during the last year of his service he lost his rank.

His father did his best to settle him in life, but he was always extravagant, spending his money freely and often on the turf. After stealing from his father a sum of between seven and eight thousand francs, he bought a business for warehousing beer in Paris. Although this was a failure, he continued his fast living and kept several mistresses at once. He at length married one of them while still keeping the others.

Always pressed for money, he next tried to start business as a wine-broker; then in turn became a book-maker and an insurance agent. Together with a partner he found with some money, they established the Crédit Général de France, which had for its object the buying-up of lottery tickets and parcels of securities. These were supposed to be the property of the shareholders and were to be sold on the Bourse, the proceeds being afterwards divided. Subsequent operations showed that Girard was dealing fraudulently with them and he was charged in Court and received twelve months' imprisonment.

He afterwards carried on as an agent to various insurance companies, trusting to his powers of persuasion and plausibility to attract clients.

He settled for a time at Montreuil and while there made the acquaintance of a wealthy man named Pernotte, and eventually succeeded in insuring his life in two different companies for a total sum equivalent to about £8400, which was to be payable to him in case of the insured man's death. M. Pernotte's wife and his two sons were apparently ignorant of the transaction. A short time afterwards the Pernotte family were taken ill with typhoid fever. It was attributed to water they had all drank from an earthenware vessel in which was kept a house supply. On their recovery they went away for a holiday, but after their return M. Pernotte still complained of feeling unwell.

He was constantly visited by his friend Girard, who professed to have some knowledge of medicine and told him one day he could give him a hypodermic injection which would soon put him on his feet again. It, however, had the reverse effect, for M. Pernotte got rapidly worse and died soon afterwards.

Although his doctors were suspicious and doubtful as to the cause of his death, an examination of the body showed nothing to inculpate Girard. It was not long before he claimed the money from the insurance companies and received it without trouble. This coup having been brought off successfully, after a little time had elapsed Girard decided to carry out another. Among his neighbours at Montreuil was a man called Godet with whom Girard had established friendly relations. Godet later agreed, at the suggestion of his friend, to take out a joint life insurance for £8000 on the terms that in case of the death of one, the money was to go to the survivor.

The two friends were frequently together and paid visits to Paris. One day after lunching, Godet was seized with an illness and had to be taken home. He proved to be suffering from typhoid fever, but after a long time gradually recovered. Something now made him suspicious of Girard and he resolved to avoid him in future and refused to see him again.

When war broke out in 1914 Girard was called up and drafted into the heavy artillery, but was eventually transferred to the motor transport. He soon became popular owing to his generosity to his comrades, giving and lending money with a lavish hand. When his supply became exhausted in 1917 he turned to thieving again and was arrested red-handed for shop-lifting in one of the large stores.

While in the army he had become on very friendly terms with a comrade called Delmas, and having by a ruse obtained possession of his papers, succeeded in insuring his life for £1600, payable to himself. A few weeks later, after lunching with Girard, Delmas too was taken ill and developed typhoid fever. Fortunately for him he was sent to a military hospital and eventually recovered his health.

Girard, however, was not disheartened by this failure to achieve his purpose and next cast his eye on a Post Office employé named Duroux, whom he thought might prove an easy victim. Duroux, who was known to his associates as 'Mimiche,' seemed to have become fascinated with his clever friend Girard, and they frequently met.

In May, 1917, Girard invited him to dine with him at his flat in the Avenue de Neuilly to which he had recently removed. He accepted the invitation and was received in the apartment by one of Girard's lady friends. An excellent dinner was served and 'Mimiche' spent a very pleasant time and suffered no ill effects from the repast. He little knew, however, that the servant had been instructed not to wash up the dishes but after the meal when he had left, Girard and the lady washed the plates, knives and forks in a bath of antiseptics.

In December of that year 'Mimiche' twice visited a café with Girard and each time was taken violently ill afterwards. He told some of his friends of this strange coincidence and on their advice he declined to accept further invitations from his plausible acquaintance.

Meanwhile, Girard was on the lookout for another victim.

His wife, who was known as 'Mademoiselle Drouhin,' used to lunch at a cheap restaurant in Paris, and there made the acquaintance of a Madame Monin, who at the time was a temporary clerk in the War Ministry. This lady had been a milliner, and became on such friendly terms with Madame Girard that she offered to make hats for her in her spare time.

On April 30th, 1918, Madame Monin went to the Girard's flat, which was then in the Faubourg St. Denis, to take a hat she had been making. It was about seven o'clock in the evening when she arrived and found Girard and his wife taking an apéritif in the dining-room. The table was set out with glasses and bottles of wine and bitters. She was invited to join them. Meanwhile, Madame Girard drew her into another room to inspect and try on the new hat. When the ladies returned they found Girard had poured out a glass of quin-quina for Madame Monin, which she drank. As the Girards were going out, she left the flat with them and they parted company at the corner of the Boulevard Magenta.

She took the Metro at the Gare de l'Est, but had scarcely reached the platform when she was seized with violent pain and dizziness. Two policemen who saw her plight went to her assistance, put her in a taxi and took her home to her flat, into which she had to be carried. Her neighbours came to her help, but it was soon evident that she was in a serious condition. A doctor was sent for, but before he arrived she was dead.

The Girard's were informed of her death but they took no notice. The week following, Girard presented himself at the office of the Insurance Nationale and asked for payment as a beneficiary. A sum of 20,000 francs was paid over to him without question. In the other three insurance companies in which Girard had taken out policies on Madame Monin's life, another woman had presented herself and had undergone all the necessary medical examinations and signed herself

'Veuve Monin Jeanne Drouhin.' This was the name under which Girard's wife passed, and later she confessed it was she who had undergone the examinations and falsified the signatures. Two of the companies concerned paid, but the 'Phoenix,' the third, raised difficulties, and refused to pay without further inquiries while they lodged a complaint with the Public Prosecutor's Department. Meanwhile, a post-mortem examination was made on the body of Madame Monin which, however, revealed nothing to account for her death, but the medical experts stated their belief from her symptoms that she had been poisoned by mushrooms.

This led to the arrest of Henri Girard for further investigations and for some time the matter was wrapped in mystery.

The police in the course of their inquiries found that the deceased woman had been insured four times within the year. Girard was the agent who had secured the business in each case, and according to custom, had been paid the first premium as his commission. Madame Monin's death took place before the second premium became due.

The police investigations, which lasted over three years, revealed that Girard had for a long time been carrying on a series of scientific murders of an astonishing character.

He was a man who possessed an extraordinary power of personal attraction and was an adept in gaining the confidence of elderly people inexperienced in matters of business and ready to entertain any proposal which might conceivably return them money.

After cultivating their acquaintance and gaining their trust, his favourite plan was to take out a joint insurance policy with the victim, under which, when one died the other was to receive a considerable sum of money. This done, he set about with great cunning to get rid of the person insured. The method he first used and which he thought was the least likely to arouse suspicion, was not that of the crude poisoner who seizes on arsenic or other mineral poison which was so easy of detection, but to subtly infect the body of his victim with some deadly germs. He began to devote himself seriously to the study of bacteriology and bought the necessary apparatus and latest books on the subject. Further, he succeeded in obtaining quantities of typhoid cultures from wholesale chemists in Paris.

When the police searched his apartments at Neuilly they discovered a regular laboratory fully equipped for bacteriological research. In it was found a box containing bacteriological cultures, including tetanus, anthrax and Eberth's bacillus. There were also capsules of strychnine and potassium cyanide, a microscope and a pair of rubber gloves, together with many books on pharmacy and toxicology.

Apparently, when he found that the pathogenic germs could not always be relied upon to achieve the end he sought, he turned his attention to poisonous mushrooms, the deadly principles in which were little known and difficult to determine.

Like Landru and other criminals, he kept a note-book or diary, some of the mysterious entries in which threw a light on his activities. In it were found notes concerning poisons, 'to prepare bottles and tubes' and 'to buy rubber gloves and microbe books.' Appointments with 'Mimiche' at six o'clock at Gare l'Est, and a significant note that he had swollen legs. Opposite the dates May 10th and 11th, 1917, was the word 'Mushrooms,' and on May 14th, 'an invitation for "Mimiche" to dinner,' which leaves no doubt as to the poison he intended to use on his victim.

The two methods he employed in his crimes were first by infecting his victims by hypodermic injections or in food, with such deadly diseases as typhoid fever, and second, by the extracts he made from certain poisonous fungi for which he gave orders to be supplied with those of a particularly dangerous kind.

As far as could be ascertained, two of his victims died and three recovered from the effects of his attempts to murder.

Before the date of his trial was fixed he was subjected to a medical examination as to his mental condition, as it was contended that he had no other ulterior motive in making the poisons beyond morbid curiosity. He tried with considerable cunning to make out that he was not responsible for his actions, but in this he failed to convince the experts who examined him.

He was sent to the Chamber of Criminal Indictment, and when the case was brought up before the Seine Assize Court in October, 1921, it was stated that Henri Girard had died some months previously in prison. His two women accomplices, however, were tried, one receiving penal servitude for life and the other twenty years' imprisonment. Henri Girard, by his most fiendish cunning and ingenuity, succeeded in concealing his crimes for years. Eventually they were unmasked, but not before death had seized him and put an end to a career which is perhaps unequalled in the annals of crime.

C.J.S.T.

## 1922

# MAJOR ARMSTRONG
## The Nineteen Dandelions

There was a tennis party, and Major Armstrong was skipping about the court, playing in a set of doubles. He was correctly and spotlessly dressed in flannels, and was as fussy and polite as usual.

Suddenly a figure of gloom appeared at the sidelines, and Mrs. Armstrong's voice boomed out:

'Come, Herbert! It's six o'clock—how can you expect the servants to be punctual, if the master is late for dinner?'

Now, the little Major, in obeying his wife, was a perfect lamb. So he tucked his racquet under his arm, apologized to his astonished partner and opponents, and trotted away behind Mrs. Armstrong—who was a good six inches taller than himself.

Of course, the match was ruined for the three remaining players. They stood staring for a moment, until they were reminded that others were waiting for the court. Then they moved resentfully off, and sat down with the spectators—who were smiling and whispering. The only ones who were much astonished were those who did not know the Armstrongs very well.

Almost everybody in the town of Hay did know the Armstrongs. The Major was pretty well liked, and he was even courted by some who thought it wise to keep on good terms with him. Mrs. Armstrong was respected, and, moreover, was probably admired by ladies who approved of her system of keeping a husband under strict discipline.

She gazed forbiddingly from behind steel-rimmed spectacles. She was a martyr to frail health—nothing much the matter with her. Her ideas of etiquette were firm; she even let young Mr. Martin, the lawyer, feel her disapproval for coming to one of her tea parties in flannel trousers and a sports coat. Martin was Major Armstrong's brother lawyer, and for that reason, if for no other, had been treated by the older man with courtesy.

But to Mrs. Armstrong, her husband's military rank, his university education, and his position as Clerk of Courts were matters of importance. You did not attend Mrs. Armstrong's tea parties in tennis clothes any more than you would try to get into Buckingham Palace in shirt sleeves.

Tennis seemed to get small consideration from Mrs. Armstrong. It had no claims on her good manners. On another occasion she broke up the Major's game by reminding him that this was his 'bath night.'

You could not fail to notice Major Armstrong. When you talked with him, you were constantly aware of his blue eyes. Very blue they were—light blue—someone said they were the color of forget-me-nots. And they shone, as with a light, while he looked straight at you, and talked—at great length—about himself and his affairs. It is not true that all murderers have blue eyes, but it is true that they have been a noticeable feature in a number of men whose careers were full of danger to people about them.

The Major was small and very dapper. He weighed ninety-eight pounds. He was neatly made, and carried himself so well—perhaps as a result of military training—that he did not seem little until he stood near someone of ordinary height.

His dress and adornment expressed his personality, for it was of a kind only to be described as 'natty.' He wore a boutonnière; his straw-colored mustache was waxed at the ends; his collars and cravats were a joy to the haberdasher. His glasses—behind which glittered those eyes of heaven's blue—were of the *pince-nez* variety, and I think they were secured by a slender gold chain and a gold hook which encircled his right ear.

He was concerned with tiny details and fond of dickering over trifling matters of business, and playing with mechanical gadgets. Yet this little henpecked man, with his gold eyeglasses and his nice manners, became a terror in the community. People were afraid to eat or drink in his presence, and two of his neighbors—a man and wife—lay awake at night fairly trembling at the thought of the blue-eyed Major.

Most of us think of murder as something far distant. It happens among gunmen or gangsters, generally among people a long way off. Certainly, not among our neighbors; not on our own street. If we know anything about life in a small town, it is hard to imagine that someone whom the neighbors respect is, as a matter of fact, as dangerous as a rattlesnake. That while he is talking to you, he may be deciding that you will be the next on his list. That if he offers you a cup of tea or if he invites you to dinner you will accept at your peril.

'No,' we say, 'that does not happen in our town.'

And that is what the people of the town of Hay would have said until they found out about Major Armstrong. Hay is a little place, on the border of England and Wales, and it had no more respectable citizen than the Major.

He was Master of Arts of Cambridge University, and held the King's commission in the Great War. He had not dropped his military title, but insisted on being addressed as Major. His law firm had borne the quaint name of Cheese and Armstrong, but now Mr. Cheese was dead. The Major had only one rival for the legal business of the whole region. This was Mr. Martin.

Armstrong may have looked back upon the years of the war with longing. Living with Mrs. Armstrong was a little like being married to the president of the W.C.T.U., the general director of the Anti-Tobacco Society, and the author of an encyclopedia of etiquette, all at once.

She was a rigid teetotaler; therefore her husband must not drink wine or spirits. When they dined out, and the servant prepared to fill Armstrong's glass, the Major would be given no chance to decline for himself. From the other end of the table, Mrs. Armstrong's stentorian voice would be heard:

'No wine for the Major!'

Mrs. Armstrong played the piano with acid correctness, and she disapproved of tobacco. The Major actually smuggled his pipe into his pocket, or tossed his cigar over a hedge—like a schoolboy caught by the master—if he met his wife coming along the street. In his own home, there was one room only in which she permitted him to indulge in the foul practice of smoking.

The Major must have been one of those men who read with amusement the resolutely gloomy novels which so many literary men have written about the horrors of war, the dreadful life of camp and trench. A career under military regulations must have seemed lightsome and free as compared with the way he was kept goose-stepping at home.

His house was a pleasant villa called 'Mayfield,' and here he had a number of enemies. They were dandelions. He had a fine lawn—what Mr. Kipling called a mint-sauce lawn—and he had also a garden. The lawn was infested with dandelions, and the Major hated them. He used to come out and glare at the weeds, marring his closely mown turf. Then he would sigh heavily, go downtown, and order five more gallons of weed-killer. Sometimes, for variety, he would buy half a pound of arsenic. He even bought arsenic in the winter, which was a curious time to prepare for dandelions. Still, it is always well to be ready for the changing seasons. Probably he murmured, 'If Winter comes, can Spring be far behind?'

He had a little squirt-gun, a delightfully delicate thing, with a tiny nozzle. This was for punishing dandelions. You see, if your lawn is like a putting green, to dig up a dandelion makes a nasty hole. But if you fill a squirt-gun with powdered arsenic, and then tiptoe gently up to the dandelion when it is off its guard, insert the nozzle near the root, and then—quick—press the plunger, why the dandelion begins to peak and pine, and pretty soon it passes away altogether. Without harming the grass.

The Major had great fun with his dandelion destroyer.

About this time—it was in July, 1920—Mrs. Armstrong made a new will. She had some property, which had been willed in part to her children, and in part to her husband. Now, another will was made—all in the Major's handwriting, and rather irregularly witnessed. The whole property now was to go her husband.

In August, the dandelions began to get bold and mischievous once more, and the Major resolutely went out and got three cans of poisoned weed-killer. He would show 'em!

In the same month, Mrs. Armstrong's health declined. She had obscure complaints, and it was said she was not altogether right in her mind. Rheumatism, it is true, she had had for years.

But these new troubles were serious, and, from now on, the poor lady is entitled to sympathy. Even the hardest-hearted tennis player or wine drinker must admit that. She was frightfully sick, and in the midst of it all was certified as insane, and carried off to a private asylum. Her doctors and her sister agreed that this was wise. Nobody could be more attentive—no one could, to all appearances, be a more dutiful husband than the little Major.

At the asylum, she seemed slowly to get better, mentally and physically. By January she had made such a recovery as to be able to come home. It was just before her return that the Major bought, in midwinter, the half-pound of arsenic. Still thinking of his lawn, and the accursed dandelions!

Mrs. Armstrong's improvement, so marked while she was away, did not continue when she was back at 'Mayfield.' Soon she was ill again, and a nurse was called in. The delusions returned; she heard people walking about the house. She could take or retain no food, and spent most of the time in bed, slowly getting feebler.

The Major was solicitous, often coming home from his office in the middle of the day, and sometimes relieving the nurse on watch. This was not the dandelion season; he had no present foes in the garden or on the lawn, and the squirt-gun, presumably, was put away.

At last, late in February, after weeks of distressing sickness, Mrs. Armstrong died. Dr. Hinckes, the local physician, and a good one, certified that she had a complication of diseases. She was buried in the churchyard. Only a few friends came to the funeral; they noticed that the widower seemed calm. In fact, while the coffin was being brought down, he was chatting with one of the other mourners about fishing rights.

Next Sunday his grief was more apparent. At the church they held a kind of memorial service for the late parishioner, and Major Armstrong, himself, read the lesson, 'with great eloquence and feeling.'

Winter vanished, and the warmer days arrived. Dandelions began to threaten the lawn at 'Mayfield' and the Major planned his spring offensive. He had been away for a few weeks, for rest and change of scene, and during these holidays renewed his wartime acquaintance with the mysterious lady known only as 'Mrs.—.' After he got back to Hay, he gave little dinner parties, mostly for gentlemen. Wine was no longer forbidden. From one of these dinners, a guest—the local inspector of taxes—went home rather ill, and had a bad night.

It is a curious thing about the poisoner: one success almost always makes him try again. The crime for which a poisoner is arrested is usually not his first, nor even his second. The employment of poison gives a sense of power; a feeling which seems to make the poisoner say to himself:

'Nobody knows what a weapon I have. People, if they recognized my power, would respect me more—and fear me more.'

Poison is, therefore, frequently the weapon of quiet, furtive people; of small, inoffensive-appearing persons; of meek-looking women; of men who are a little effeminate, a bit sly in manner.

The Major's next experiment may have been upon Mr. Davies, from the neighboring city of Hereford. He had a small business controversy with Major Armstrong, and came to Hay to discuss it. The Major invited him to his house to tea. How the business was settled I do not know, but Mr. Davies no sooner got home than he had a very bad pain. He called the doctor, and they operated for appendicitis. When the certificate came to be signed, it appeared that Mr. Davies had had acute appendicitis, resulting in peritonitis, which, in turn, resulted in death.

Summer was a-coming in. 'Mrs.—' appeared on the scene again. She made a brief visit to 'Mayfield,' and seems to have been considering a proposal of marriage. The Major showed her his garden and lawn, and perhaps told her of his triumphs over the dandelions. It was her great good luck that she took some time to consider whether she wished to become the bride of this man.

The legal business meanwhile was improving, with nobody but the friendly Mr. Martin to dispute it, or to appear on the opposite side in litigation. Mr. Martin, who was a wounded veteran of the war, had persuaded a young lady to marry him. He brought his bride to the town of Hay, where they set up housekeeping. In the late summer, they received a package by mail; a present of some chocolates. There was no name enclosed, and they mildly wondered who sent them.

There are still people who receive these strange gifts, from nobody in particular, and who go right ahead and eat them. Others let them stay around till someone else tastes them. The Martins did not care for chocolates, but put them in a dish and brought them out at a dinner party. Someone took a bite, and this someone was beastly sick. Afterwards—when many other things had happened—the remaining chocolates were found and examined. On the under side of a number of them there was a small hole, as though a tiny nozzle had been inserted. And in these chocolates there was a little bit of arsenic.

Mr. Martin and the Major were representing the parties to a business deal—a sale of land. The Major's client did not complete the contract and Martin had to press him, and, after a year's delay, to threaten to declare the contract broken and demand return of the deposits. The Major was agitated and kept pleading for more time. In October, after postponement, Martin's client finally refused to go on with the sale, and insisted that the deposits be returned.

Major Armstrong's remedy for this was tea. There is something about tea conducive to friendliness, and it seemed to him that these troubles would clear up, if he could only get the other lawyer looking at him across a tea table. You must remember that at this time nobody had examined the chocolates, and that the deaths and illnesses which had occurred were attributed to various diseases.

After repeated invitations, Mr. Martin did go, late one afternoon, to 'Mayfield,' where his soft-spoken little host received him with smiling courtesy. The two lawyers' offices were directly opposite each other, on the business street of the town, but the Major had gone home first—to see that everything was prepared and pleasant.

There was tea, and there was bread and butter, and there was bread with currants in it, and there were buttered scones. The two men did not discuss legal business at all, except in a general way, and the question of the land contract did not come up. But very soon after the tea was poured, the Major—for a man so fussy and so well-mannered—did a strange thing. He reached across and picked up a buttered scone, which he put on Mr. Martin's plate with the remark:

'Please excuse fingers.'

Mr. Martin ate the scone; then he had some currant bread,

smoked a cigarette, talked a while and went home. He found himself with poor appetite for dinner, although he ate a little. In the evening he tried to do some work, dictating to a secretary, but had to give it up. He became, first, very uncomfortable, and then, for twenty-four hours, violently sick. The same doctor who had attended Mrs. Armstrong was his physician.

Martin remembered the urgent invitations to tea; he recalled the scene; and, during the week that followed, as he slowly returned to health, he resolved to deny himself the pleasure of any further teas with the Major. He had a father-in-law who was a chemist, and this gentleman thought that he recognized something about the symptoms of his son-in-law's illness. He insisted upon an analysis. When this revealed the presence of arsenic, both of them, as well as the doctor, thought it time to communicate with the government.

The officials did not hurry; they agreed that things were suspicious, but nothing more than suspicious. The doctor began to remember peculiar circumstances of Mrs. Armstrong's last illness. And all of them warned Mr. Martin not to accept any more treats at 'Mayfield.'

It was good advice, even if not needed. But it was hard advice to follow. Major Armstrong began to talk about tea once more. He called on his brother lawyer, as soon as he returned to work; commiserated him upon his illness, and playfully recalled that he had warned him against lack of exercise. In the Major's opinion, Mr. Martin was taking too little exercise. He ought to walk more, and use his motor car less.

'And it may seem a curious thing to say,' added Major Armstrong, 'but I fear you will have another attack just like that one!'

Mr. Martin looked at him, and almost turned green. He hoped not.

'And now, old man,' pursued the affable Major, 'we must have another talk about that sale. My clients have a proposal to make. Come to tea to-morrow.'

Mr. Martin was sorry. He had an engagement. No, positively. He could not come.

'Oh, very well,' returned Armstrong.

But next day he was back again—this time by telephone.

'Come in to tea, won't you?'

'Sorry,' said the terrified Martin, 'not taking any tea today.'

Next day the business really did require a settlement, and Martin realized that he must talk with his neighbor.

'Will you come over to tea, this afternoon?' telephoned the Major.

'No,' was the reply. 'I can't come to tea. But I will look in afterwards—around six o'clock.'

But this wouldn't do. There was something about this contract that could be settled only over the teacups.

'Well, never mind,' the Major replied, 'come to tea tomorrow.'

Then it occurred to Armstrong that taking your tea in your office is a good English custom. Perhaps Martin didn't like to go so far as 'Mayfield.' The Major set up a tea caddy, cups and spoons in his office, had his housekeeper send down some scones, and instructed one of his clerks to order some bread and cake from the restaurant nearby.

'I tell you what,' said he, 'we'll have tea in my office. Come over about half-past four.'

Mr. Martin could only stammer. He had run out of excuses. He and his wife were thoroughly agitated now; they saw the Major's gleaming blue eyes everywhere. They actually took turns in keeping awake all night; one of them on guard while the other slept. Evidently they expected the Major to come climbing up the wistaria vine, armed with an arsenic bottle.

That afternoon the telephone rang again.

'Where are you?' came the Major's voice. 'The tea is spoiling; been waiting half an hour.'

'Oh, I've had my tea,' said the wretched man. 'Had it here in my office.'

After this, Martin—while the police investigated—was reduced to bringing tea into his own office and hastily gulping it.

I have wondered why he didn't accept someday; go over, and give Major Armstrong every opportunity to prepare the dishes; take them from his hands, then turn on him, and say:

'Oh, Major, I couldn't think of taking these. Look, this cup of tea, so nice and hot! And this lovely buttered bun! I want *you* to have these!'

And back the little viper right into a corner with the stuff.

But this might have given the show away, and ruined Scotland Yard's investigations. The Major, so far, had the whip hand, and he knew it. Martin was frightened. When the tea invitations ceased at last, and Armstrong began to ask Mr. and Mrs. Martin to dinner, the younger lawyer was desperate.

All this time Scotland Yard was working on the case, and telling Martin to hold out a little longer. It was a serious thing to arrest such an important and respectable person as the Major, and to accuse him of the extraordinary offense of trying to murder a fellow lawyer with a poisoned scone. It would not do to make a mistake.

Finally, a detective inspector came down from London, and, to the utter amazement of everyone—except the Martins, and one or two others—arrested the Major for attempted murder.

At the same time—a dark winter night—strange men appeared in the town and strange lights were seen in the churchyard. England's famous pathologist, Sir Bernard Spilsbury, and his aides were exhuming the body of Mrs. Armstrong.

As soon as the coffin was opened, all the doctors knew, by the extraordinary manner in which the body was preserved, that this was probably a death by arsenic. And the autopsy revealed the largest amount of that poison ever found in such circumstances.

It was for murder, the murder of his wife, that the Major was tried. He was defended by one of the great criminal lawyers of the day, Sir Henry Curtis Bennett, who did his best to show that Mrs. Armstrong—utterly helpless at the time—might have arisen from bed, and taken the poison herself.

Mr. Martin's story of the tea party was admitted as evidence, and the judge (Lord Darling) took a vigorous part in cross-examining the prisoner. In the United States, it is probable that the Major's lawyers would have succeeded in excluding Martin's evidence, and the prisoner would have escaped. The theory of Mrs. Armstrong's suicide might have seemed stronger if her husband had not been revealed as a systematic poisoner.

Major Armstrong sat bolt upright in court, calm and attentive—staring, with his pale blue eyes, straight ahead. While he was on the witness stand, he and the judge had a long verbal duel, conducted with icy politeness. The Major described how he had made up twenty little packets of arsenic, each containing a deadly dose for a dandelion.

It was also, the judge pointed out, a deadly dose for a human being, was it not?

And he had used nineteen of these packets on nineteen dandelions. As the Major describeed the process, in his precise voice, you could almost see the graves of the nineteen dandelions.

And there was one little packet left over (as the judge observed) and it was found in his pocket, when he was arrested, in December.

The jury—most of them farmers—were capable of noting that in December the dandelion season is practically over.

A year or two later, that graceful writer, Mr. Filson Young, visited the town of Hay, and sat on the lawn at 'Mayfield.' The dandelions, he says, were thicker than ever.

They had triumphed. The Major was far away. He was not even lying in that churchyard whither he had sent one, or two, or how many others? For the concluding words of the dread sentence of the law in England are:

'. . . and that you be there hanged by the neck until you be dead; that your body be buried within the precincts of the prison in which you shall last be confined; and may the Lord have mercy on your soul.'

And the chaplain, standing behind the judge, replies:

'Amen!'

E.P.

# 1924
# PATRICK MAHON
## The Troublesome Typist

Patrick Herbert Mahon, was extremely attractive to women, a fact of which he took zestful advantage. But probably none of his many amorous adventures, wearily forgiven by his long-suffering wife, lasted so long, or gave him so much pleasure as his love affair with himself, which was as richly satisfying as it was permanent. Criminologists used to talk of the 'born murderer'. The phrase has since gone out of fashion, but if it *were* possible to isolate the 'born murderer' as a separate and recognizable type one might expect to find in him, as an unvarying characteristic, the exaggerated self-love, the unrestrained egotism of a Patrick Mahon. The most noticeable symptom of his condition was Mahon's colossal personal vanity. In his prison cell, even with death standing at his elbow, he spent much time worrying about what he should wear at his trial and how to give his handsome features an illusion of sunburn. (In the end he ordered a new and expensive suit, and actually distilled an artificial sun-tan out of tobacco juice). Deeper-seated, but stemming from that same self-love, was his obsessive desire to be liked and admired. To achieve all that was necessary to him in the way of admiration and respect he plainly required not only a comfortable income but also a settled domestic and social background.

By the spring of 1922 it looked as if Patrick Mahon had achieved both. Behind him was an unsavoury police record, including prison sentences for forgery, embezzlement, bank robbery and assault, but nothing was known of this amongst the numerous and rapidly expanding circle of friends and acquaintances who surrendered so easily to his infectious charm. They accepted him at his face value—as a hard-working and enterprising young chap, who had a responsible job as a sales manager and was making money fast. He had a charming and capable wife, a comfortable flat at Kew, and, as the popular secretary of the local bowling club, the sort of social success which, although limited and suburban, was necessary to support his ego.

All this was suddenly put in peril by the importunate demands of a girl who had not the sense to know when enough was enough. Emily Kaye, a typist in Mahon's office, had cheerfully embarked upon a flirtation with the handsome sales manager. Before she knew what was happening to her she had fallen violently in love. Mahon had taken what was so readily offered, and then, having appropriated Miss Kaye's savings, which amounted to the tidy sum of four hundred pounds, had sought to disengage himself. This was not easy, for Miss Kaye, who was about to bear his child, was not disposed to let him go. She plagued him to throw up everything, his job, his prospects, his wife, his friends, his easy and comfortable life, and to go away with her. Mahon had no intention of doing anything of the kind, but hesitated to break the unpleasant truth to Miss Kaye, who was plainly in a position to do him a great deal of harm if sufficiently provoked. To gain time Mahon fell in with her naïve proposal for a 'love experiment', by which Miss Kaye hoped to convince him, upon the basis of a few agreeable weekends, that they were 'meant for each other' and, as such, destined to live happily ever after—together. For the purposes of the 'experiment'—which happened to fit in neatly enough with some plans of his own—Mahon, using the name Walling, rented a bungalow on the Crumbles, that stretch of lonely beach between Eastbourne and Pevensey, which had been the scene of a particularly repulsive murder only a few years before. It was now to be the setting of another.

On 12th April 1924, having first purchased a chef's knife and a saw at a shop in Victoria Street, London, Mahon travelled down to Eastbourne by train, and was met at the station by Miss Kaye. They went together by cab to the bungalow, which had once been the home of the officer in command of the coast-guard station, and was variously known as Officer's House or Langney Bungalow; there the 'love experiment' began. The pair returned to London on the following Tuesday. Mahon—still temporizing—had agreed to apply for a passport so that they could go abroad together, but when he met Miss Kaye at Victoria Station in the evening he admitted that he had not been to the Passport Office and had no intention of going there.

This led to a violent quarrel in the train. That night, in the lonely bungalow, Miss Kaye presented her final ultimatum. 'Pat' must make up his mind to leave his wife and his job and make a new life for himself and Emily in South Africa. The two were alone. Only Patrick Mahon survived to tell the tale of what happened next. His account is given below—there is no other:

> *She suddenly picked up a weapon—an axe—a coal axe—and threw it at me; it struck me on the shoulder and glanced off and hit the door of the bedroom, breaking the shaft. . . . I felt appalled at the fury she showed and realized suddenly how strong the girl was. She followed up the throw by dashing at me and clutching at my face and neck. In sheer desperation and fright I closed with her, doing my best to fight back and loosen her hold. We struggled and eventually, in the course of the struggle, we fell over an easy chair and Miss Kaye's head came in violent contact with the round coal cauldron. . . . My body, of course, being on top when she fell, her hold relaxed a bit, and she lay apparently stunned or dead. The events of the next few seconds I cannot remember except as a nightmare of horror, for I saw blood beginning to ooze from Miss Kaye's head where she had struck the cauldron. I did my utmost to revive her, and I simply could not at the time say whether I strangled her or whether she died of the fall, but from the moment she fell and struck her head she did not move. By this time, the excitement of the struggle and the fright and the blows I had received had reduced me to a condition of nervous exhaustion, and as the realization of the terrible position flooded my brain I think my mind was at the breaking strain. . . . I think I wandered or sat down in the garden for some time in a state bordering on madness.*

Mahon carried the body into the spare bedroom. He had now to face the problem of how to dispose of it. He had laid his plans well enough, as was shown by his purchase of a chef's knife and a saw, but he lacked the nerve to carry them out right away. Mahon locked up the bungalow and went into Eastbourne, where he spent the night. He did not begin the work of dismemberment until the following Friday—it happened to be Good Friday—when he cut off the legs and head, then stuffed the mutilated body into a trunk. That week-end he spent at the bungalow with a girl whom he had met casually in the street at Richmond, Surrey, a week before, and who had joined him at his urgent invitation—he had sent her the money for her fare. They were together at the bungalow on the Friday night and the whole of Saturday and Sunday—during all that time the partially dismembered body of Emily Kaye was lying in the trunk in the spare bedroom. The girl returned to London on the Easter Monday, suspecting nothing.

At his trial Mahon explained why he had taken such a desperate risk; contrasted with his various posturings in the witness-box it has the appearance of truth. 'The damn place was haunted,' he said, 'I wanted human companionship.' And again: 'I should have gone stark staring mad if I had not had her with me.' The day after the girl's departure—that is, on the Tuesday—he built a fire in the sitting-room grate, and at midnight he placed upon it the head of Emily Kaye. At that moment a thunderstorm broke with semi-tropical violence almost directly overhead. As the head lay upon the coals the eyes opened, and Mahon fled in terror from the bungalow and out on to the rain-swept and deserted shore. When he had calmed his nerves sufficiently to return the head had already been partly consumed; the poker went through it. Mahon found the disposal of the various parts of the body a long and laborious business. After burning the head and legs on the Tuesday he went back to his wife, and for the rest of the week he was working at his office. On the following Saturday and Sunday he resumed his grisly task at the bungalow. Some of the flesh he boiled in a cauldron, and this, together with the leg bones, he put into a Gladstone bag. On the Sunday evening he threw these remains out of the window of a train between Waterloo and Richmond. Mahon spent that night at Reading, returning to London on the Monday, and leaving the bag in the cloakroom at Waterloo Station.

This proved to be his undoing. Mahon's wife found the cloakroom ticket and was puzzled by it. She showed it to a friend, who had formerly been a police officer. Together they went to Waterloo and presented the ticket. Mahon's bag was handed to them. It was locked, but the ex-detective was able to ease it open sufficiently to see that it contained a large knife and some pieces of bloodstained silk. He did not tell Mrs. Mahon about this, but, having re-deposited the bag, simply asked her to return home and replace the ticket where she had found it; he then informed Scotland Yard.

On the following Friday, 2nd May, Mahon went to Waterloo for the bag. As he was leaving the cloakroom with it, he was stopped by a C.I.D. officer and taken to Kennington Road Police Station, and afterwards to Scotland Yard. There the bag was opened, and was found to contain two pieces of silk, a pair of women's torn knickers, a towel and a silk scarf (all bloodstained), a brown canvas racquet case and a cook's knife. 'I am fond of dogs,' Mahon explained. 'I must have carried meat for the dogs in it.' After sitting silent for a quarter of an hour, he added, 'I wonder if you can realize how terrible a thing it is for one's body to be active and one's mind to fail to act.' Half an hour later Mahon spoke again. 'I am considering my position,' he said, and then, after a further period of silence, 'I suppose you know everything. I will tell you the truth.' He then made a very long and detailed statement to show how Miss Kaye had died and the means he had used to dispose of her body.

Mahon was tried at Lewes Assizes in the following July. The case for the Crown was presented by Sir Henry Curtis BBennett K.C., and Mahon was defended by Mr. J. D. (afterwards Mr. Justice) Cassels K.C. Rarely has a murder trial produced a more strikingly dramatic scene than that which occurred whilst Mahon was giving his evidence. It was almost at the end of his examination-in-chief. Mr. Cassels asked him: 'Did you desire the death of Miss Kaye?' Mahon answered, calmly, 'Never at any time.' And at that precise moment the courtroom was illumined by a flash of lightning, followed by a violent clap of thunder. Mahon shrunk into a corner of the witness-box, his artificial sun-tan serving only to emphasize the ghastly pallor of his face; he was trembling with fear, a pitiable figure. No one who was there will ever forget the moment when the heavens opened to remind Patrick Mahon of the midnight scene in the bungalow on the Crumbles, with the dead eyes of Emily Kaye opening in the fire, while the thunder pealed overhead. He was a broken man when he came to face the deadly cross-examination of Sir Henry Curtis Bennett, who ever afterwards spoke of him with loathing as the most callous and brutal murderer he had ever known. Being found guilty and sentenced to death,

Mahon was executed at Wandsworth Prison on 9th September 1924.

E.S.S

# 1924

# FRITZ HAARMANN
## The Butcher of Hanover

Modern Germany has been the world's shop window for perversion. Post-war periods are notorious for degeneracy. Haarmann was a German of the lower middle class who reached forty in the first year after the First World War (which he spent in a civil jail for a string of thefts). Economic and social institutions were dissolving – to produce the collapse of the Mark and the emergence of the Nazis; to foster and facilitate the vile career of Haarmann. 'His,' said William Bolitho, 'is the sum of all their guilt [referring to mass murderers]. . . . This man was the *chief* murderer, the *worst* man, the *last of the human race*.' The italics are mine, but not the unique condemnation; in thus singling out Haarmann among devils, it goes too far. Only just too far, however. Judge from the facts.

At that time Hanover roughly compared in size with Bristol, Stockholm, Edinburgh, Toronto. A population of somewhere about four hundred thousand. An historic name and a geographical position which made it a naturally centripetal metropolis, a Mecca of the discontented for miles around. And especially the discontented young. Boys whose fathers had perished at Vilna or Verdun; boys who sought escape from hungry villages; hobos in the making, delinquents on the make – they poured by the thousand, by the day, into Hanover. Only to find it as stricken as elsewhere. Queues – queues for everything. Cigarettes, chocolate, clothing, milk, fish, bread. No jobs which they could do, no lodgings which they could afford. Most did not want to leave again; the big city at least promised opportunities – and besides, where could they go? So they tended to congregate, a constantly increasing, floating multitude, at their point of arrival. Hanover's head railway station. There they could find shelter, company, and warmth. There they created for themselves a substitute home.

In this transformed Hanover, Haarmann fell on his feet. He made a basic living in the black market as a meat hawker; his effeminate mannerisms and falsetto voice gained him contemptuous popularity – like that of a female impersonator or an epicene droll. He augmented his income – and dressed in a little brief authority – as a paid police spy (*Anglice*, copper's nark), appointed despite, or because of, his police record (which included indecent assaults as well as burglary and fraud). He obtained relaxing entertainment at the railway station; drawn thither like the pimps to King's Cross and St. Lazare. At night, he would move among the swarm of rootless boys, noting and cannily appraising each newcomer; readily invoking his official contacts if anyone challenged his role of benefactor; joyfully escorting acquiescent choices to the perilous intimacy of his basement room. Only the lucky ones escaped as walking casualties.

Haarmann might have gone on undisturbed, indefinitely, had he confined his transgressions to sex. Once, when a missing boy was tracked right to his door, parental insistence compelled the police to search their colleague's hideout – and, catching him *in flagrante delicto,* reluctantly to arrest him (he was sentenced to nine months). But the German police, in general, did not harry sexual perverts, even when they were debauching juveniles. Nor did the German courts, in general, itch to punish them. The situation may have been like that held to exist at one time on the Oxford circuit, where, it was said, no jury would ever convict of buggery, 'because eleven of them don't know what it is and the twelfth does it himself'.

Haarmann could never have been dismissed as an innocuous deviant. Sex criminal of course he was – but was he a sex murderer? Were his killings part and parcel of his sexual impulses? Or were they incidental and distinct – and secondary?

In trying to answer that one must remember there were two Haarmanns. Two characters within that thick, fat frame, behind that coarse moon face. The pedlar, out for profit. The pederast, out for pleasure. That he defiled his pick-ups cannot be doubted.

That he killed many, took their belongings, cannot be doubted either. But which project was uppermost in his mind as he prowled the railway station? Which was the primary driving force – material greed or sex?

According to Haarmann, he killed in paroxysms of erotic frenzy. Criminals are not the most trustworthy guide to their own motives, but psychological probabilities support him. One cannot imagine a shrewd, experienced rogue embarking on such a systematic course of murder merely to get hold of such pitifully small possessions. Cheap cuff links. A few loose coins. A pocket comb. All such things were to be found only on the better off. Most of these boys had nothing more than the garments they stood up in. But Haarmann, particularly at a time of shortages, could not bring himself to forego such tiny trifles which chance, or his own wickedness, delivered to his hand. Besides, there was someone else who had a say. His regular partner – sexual, domestic, and professional. An elegant young man less than half his age.

Hans Grans was a homosexual queen who, in most respects, ruled his older consort. He did not object to – often encouraged – Haarmann's infidelities; he liked the implicit licence to pursue his own. He demanded a cut, though, of any residual booty, and – if his eye was taken by a suit or by a trinket – he might suggest and urge that booty should be snatched. He did not drive Haarmann to murder; Haarmann did not need driving – he murdered in hot blood. But Grans sometimes gave a prod or incentive to cold robbery, as an influential and like-minded spouse. Partners to a marriage, they shared and shared alike, for better or for worse – with one solitary exception. There is much to indicate that Grans was an accomplice, even a principal, in sodomy and murder. There is nothing to indicate that he was a principal, even an accomplice, in consuming or marketing human flesh.

Haarmann was a rarity among mass murderers, best remembered and most detessted for actions other than those of which he was accused. Anthropophagy may not be among penal offences, but it offends – both morally and aesthetically – more than the gravest crime expressly recognized by law. The idea of murder does not excite such abhorrence, such revulsion, as the idea of man feeding upon man. This feeling is so universal that in civilized communities cannibalism, unlike murder, is virtually unknown. Except in mortal extremities of hunger – and very seldom even then. One human being would generally rather die than devour another. Haarmann, though, seems to have been free from this inhibition, which operates as strongly on sinners as on saints, on murderers as on missionaries. The first hint transpired in his capacity as a purveyor; supplies of smuggled meat were continually dwindling, and, as easily as he took clothes for Hans, he took the disposable parts of the carcasses for his stall. His customers, long subsisting on tainted beef or pork, accepted the peculiar flavour – and survived. It was a small step then to sampling his own wares. Impelled first, perhaps, by curiosity. Tempted to continue, one would guess, by the free meal. In the end, addicted – who knows? – to the taste.

When youths and boys from many districts were reported missing, the Hanover police displayed no excess of zeal; flotsam and jetsam, drifters, might turn up anywhere. When the remains of their remains did turn up – in the river, the police did not exhaust themselves by close investigations; fleshless skulls, whitened bones, might be anybody's. And anyway, why should they suspect 'Detective' Haarmann? But under pressure of suspicion, they carefully searched his room. Under pressure of discoveries they made there – items of property, extensive stains of blood – Haarmann admitted committing twenty-four separate murders. (As he didn't plead insanity like Christie or Haigh, that may be considered a moderate computation.) He implicated Grans – a bitchy pay-off to a lover's quarrel.

Properly, the trial should have taken place in solemn silence, interrupted only by *frissons* of sheer horror. Instead, it descended into *opéra bouffe*. Haarmann chatted to the judges, rebuked or commended witnesses, exhorted Grans – glacial beside him – to follow his honourable example and confess. He incessantly cracked 'in' jokes for the delectation of brethren and partisans in the public gallery. The music of their laughter – gratifying to his queer ego – must have been one compensation for his expected sentence.

Another – gratifying his spitefulness – must have been the long jail term imposed on his beloved Hans.

E.L.

# 6
# EDWARDIAN ENIGMAS
## (1909–26)

# 1909

# The Gorse Hall Mystery

At the beginning of November, 1909, Mr. George Henry Storrs was murdered at his home, near Stalybridge, under circumstances which have never been cleared up.

Mr. Storrs was a wealthy builder and mill-owner, and lived with his wife and his wife's niece, Miss Lindley, in a large house named Gorse Hall. There were three servants—a cook and housemaid resident in the building, and a coachman living with his wife over the stables.

Mr. Storrs was a kindly and popular man, a good employer, and had no known enemies. He and his wife were a devoted couple, and both were on affectionate terms with Miss Lindley. The household may, indeed, be called a happy one.

Its peace, however, was destined to be rudely broken. About 9.30 on the night of September 10, 1909, when the family were sitting in the dining-room, a shot was suddenly fired through the window.

Seeing that no one had been hit Mr. Storrs rushed to the window and pulled aside the blind. He could just see a dark figure disappearing into the shrubbery. When the ladies asked if he knew the man he replied, after a slight hesitation, that he did not.

Mrs. Storrs was more alarmed than her husband, and next day she insisted on the police being informed and asked to keep a special watch on the house. She also had a large alarm bell put on the roof, and it was agreed that if this were sounded the police should instantly hurry over. It was suggested that the man was a homicidal maniac, and she was afraid that he might return.

Nothing unusual happened, however, for some seven weeks, and then, on the last Saturday of October, Mr. Storrs called on the police and asked them to be particularly vigilant in their watch. He said he had no special reason for making the request, but that he 'wanted to be sure.'

That night about midnight the alarm bell sounded and the police hurried tot he house. But nothing was wrong. Mr. Storrs said apologetically that he had wished to be sure that the alarm was really efficient, and had rung it as a test.

Sunday and Monday passed uneventfully, but on Monday evening tragedy really did visit the house. Some time after dinner the housemaid had to pass the scullery door, when she saw that the gas was alight. She looked in and found that the window had been broken open, but before she could investigate further a man jumped out from behind the door and seized her wrist. He had a revolver in his hand and he swore that if she made a sound he would shoot her.

Instinctively she twisted away from him, running screaming through the house. He did not fire, but followed her till they reached the hall. There Mr. Storrs, attracted by the noise, rushed out of the dining-room. As soon as the man saw him he cried: 'I've got you at last!' Again he did not fire, but as Mr. Storrs ran forward he closed with him and a terrible fight began.

In the meantime Mrs. Storrs and Miss Lindley had also rushed out. For a moment they tried to join in the struggle. Mrs. Storrs actually succeeding in tearing away the man's revolver. Then they saw him draw a knife. But Mr. Storrs gasped out: 'The bell! Give the alarm!' and Mrs. Storrs rushed off to ring it, while Miss Lindley fled down the drive to summon help from the Stalybridge Central Club, which was close by.

When assistance came the murderer had disappeared and Mr. Storrs was at the point of death. He had received fifteen terrible knife wounds, and died without making a statement.

While neither the ladies nor the servants were able to give a detailed description of the murderer, declaring that there was nothing distinctive about him, they agreed that he was youngish and poorly dressed, with a slight moustache and long fair hair. The revolver was of a cheap type, and yielded no clue.

A young man called Howard was arrested and charged with the murder. He was a cousin of Mr. Storrs, though he was personally unknown to the ladies. The evidence against him seemed purely circumstantial, but the police had a stronger case than was anticipated. When at the trial Mrs. Storrs and Miss Lindley were asked if they could identify the murderer, they pointed dramatically to the prisoner, and swore he was the man.

No possible question of their bona fides arises; at the same time it became evident during the course of the trial that 'they were mistaken. Howard's innocence being proved beyond question. The verdict of Not Guilty was received with applause, and Howard left the court a popular hero.

Months afterwards a second man named Wilde was charged with the crime, stood his trial at Chester Assizes, and was also acquitted.

Since then the Gorse Hall Tragedy has remained a complete mystery, and no trace of the real murderer has ever been found.

In attempting to reconstruct what may have taken place in this strange tragedy, certain facts at once stand out as significant.

First, the murderer, whom for want of a better name I shall call John, had a definite grievance, real or imaginary, against Mr. Storrs. This is proved by the facts that he said: 'I've got you at last,' and that he did not gain materially through his crime.

Second, Mr. Storrs knew of this grievance and of his own danger. From his manner on the occasion of the attempt on September 9, it is almost certain that he recognised the man, and when he went to the police on the last Saturday in October, he evidently expected a further attack. Moreover, when he saw his assailant in the hall on the night of his death, he gave no exclamation of surprise, but grappled at once as with a known foe.

Third, Mr. Storrs obviously wished to keep the affair secret. If he knew his own danger, as I have suggested he did, the fact that he made no statement on the subject proves this. But it is supported by his other action. He did not inform the police of the first attack until assailant had had time to get away. I will suggest presently that a second attack was made on the Saturday night on which the alarm was sounded, and that on his occasion Mr. Storrs suppressed any mention of John's presence for the same reason: to give him time to escape.

Fourth, owing to Mr. Storrs's upright character and kindly disposition, the secret was nothing with which he could reproach himself.

Fifthly, certain of John's actions seem to indicate an unbalanced mind. He entered the house on the night of the murder by smashing a window, and then committed the folly of turning on the gas. When he was discovered by the housemaid he followed her through the house, though he must have known her screams would attract attention. Again, to strike as many as fifteen times with his knife shows a fury quite abnormal.

With these salient points in mind, can we suggest any circumstances which might meet the facts?

I think we can.

At first sight it might seem as if the crime were committed by some epileptic or homicidal maniac, subject to recurrent fits of illness. But this theory would not account for the facts that Mr. Storrs undoubtedly recognised his assailant and yet kept his identity secret. If he had not had some definite and personal reason for silence, he would surely have told the police who the man was.

Let us then try to fit a theory on to the facts we know. Let us begin by assuming that John is like Howard in personal appearance, and of an extremely unbalanced and excitable temperament. Let us further assume that he nurses a bitter hatred against Mr. Storrs.

The cause of this hatred—that is, the motive for the crime—we do not know. There is not the slightest indication as to its nature in the evidence. All that we really know is that John had some overwhelming but mistaken sense of grievance against Mr. Storrs.

We are probably on firmer ground when we picture John brooding over his fancied wrongs until his desire for revenge grows first into an obsession and then into actual mania.

On going to see Mr .Storrs John blurts out his grievance and threatens vengeance. Mr. Storrs, however, has no ill-feeling towards his visitor; in fact, he is sorry for him.

His kindly disposition makes him regret the young man's sense of injury, and he is willing to discuss the affair. But John, half insane, will not listen to reason, and Mr. Storrs in self-defence is obliged to summon help.

John, seeing his chance gone, hurries away, determined to succeed at the next opportunity. The person who was called does not realise what he has prevented, and Mr. Storrs, finding the whole matter painful, does not discuss it.

This reconstruction is still speculative and unsupported by direct evidence. But it is clear that John and Mr. Storrs must have had some interview of the kind, in order to account for what follows. This interview, further, was probably not at Gorse Hall, as John was not seen by the inmates.

On September 10, John, who has bought a revolver, goes to Gorse Hall to make his attempt. He reaches the house, creeps up to the only lighted window, find the blind does not exactly fit and that he can see Mr. Storrs, and fires at him through the window. He sees that he has missed, and noticing that there are other people in the room, realises that if he remains for a further attempt he may be identified. So he hurries off.

Mr. Storrs realises he is in danger, and asks the police to be specially vigilant. That night John makes his third attempt, but Mr. Storrs sees him and rings the alarm. John again finds that if he remains, he will be caught. Mr. Storrs, full of pity for the misguided youth, and hoping eventually to bring him to reason, tells the police he was only making a test, in order to give the young fellow time to escape.

It is obvious that there must have been some special circumstances about this attempt which enabled Mr. Storrs to ring the alarm before being attacked. Perhaps, for example, he may have discovered John in the act of swarming up a balcony pillar or a waterpipe, or in such other position that the young man could not use his weapon.

On Monday, John again goes to Gorse Hall. Determined this time to make an end of the matter, he breaks in and commits the murder. He escapes from the country and is therefore not found by the police.

The above reconstruction, indicates the lines along which I believe the explanation of this mysterious crime must lie.

F.W.C.

# 1908
# The Luard Case

Caroline Mary Luard, aged fifty-eight, wife of Major-General Charles Edward Luard, of Ightham Knoll, Ightham, near Sevenoaks, Kent, was on 24th August 1908, found lying dead on the veranda of a summer house in Fish Pond Woods on the neighbouring estate. She had been shot twice through the head with a small-calibre revolver. Prolonged investigation by the police yielded no clue to the identity of the murderer, but it was not long before the voices of calumny and malice began to suggest whom it might be. General Luard, the distracted widower, received through the post dozens of anonymous letters, some of which, not content with heaping abuse upon him, accused him of having killed his wife.

Now, if there were one thing which the abortive police inquiries had established beyond of doubt it was that General Luard *could not have been the murderer*. Motive there was none. The Luards were an exceptionally devoted couple who were never seen to treat each other with anything but the most touching affection. General Luard, living in retirement after thirty years' service in the Royal Engineers, a man of means and position, stood to gain nothing, financially, from the death of his wife; he was a man healthy in body and mind and of most equable temper. However, many murders have been committed by persons who appeared to have no motive. Far more important was the fact that ten minutes after Mrs. Luard had been murdered—the time was fixed by two independent witnesses who had heard the shots. Luard was seen on the golf course of Godden Green, at so great a distance from the summer house that even if he had run the whole way he could not possibly have got there in the time.

Hoping that in fresh surroundings he might be able to find some relief from his distress, a friend of his, Colonel Warde, persuaded General Luard to come to stay with him at his home near Maidstone. There the General seemed to be easier in his mind. But early in the morning of 18th September, before most of the household was astir, he walked out of the house, and

concealing himself behind a clump of bushes at the side of the
railway line, waited until he heard a train approaching, when
he threw himself in front of it and was cut to pieces. He had
left behind him this pathetic letter, addressed to his host:

> *My dear Warde,*
> *I am sorry to have to return your kindness and long
> friendship in this way, but I am satisfied it is best to join
> her in the second life at once as I can be of no further use
> to anyone in future in this world, of which I am tired and
> in which I do not wish to live any longer. I thought that
> my strength was sufficient to bear up against the horrible
> imputations and terrible letters which I have received since
> that awful crime was committed and which robbed me of
> my happiness. And so it was for long and the goodness,
> kindness and sympathy of so many friends kept me going.
> But somehow in the last day or two something seems to have
> snapped. The strength has left me and I care for nothing
> except to join her again. So good-bye my dear friends to
> both of us.*
> > *Yours very affectionately,*
> > > *C. E. Luard.*
> *P.S.—I shall be somewhere on the line of the railway.*

Rarely can 'poison pen' letters have led to a more hideous result.
On the surface, robbery appeared to have been the motive for
the murder of Mrs. Luard. Rings had been stripped from her
fingers with such violence as to tear the skin; the pocket of
her dress had been cut out and her purse stolen. Yet it seems
that the officers who conducted the investigation did not share
that popular theory that Mrs. Luard had been killed by some
tramp who had surprised her, alone and defenceless, as she
was walking through the wood; they were clearly inclined to
doubt whether robbery was the motive at all. Let us consult
the facts. At about 2.30 on the fatal afternoon, General and
Mrs. Luard, accompanied by their Irish terrier, set out together
to walk in the woods. Because she was expecting a friend to tea
and wanted to be back at the manor house in time to entertain
her, Mrs. Luard did not intend to go much further than the
summer house. The General, on the other hand, proposed to
walk as far as the Godden Green golf course. Therefore, at

a point some little way beyond the summer house—La Casa, as it was called—General Luard and his wife parted company. Mrs. Luard started to walk back along the bridle path in the direction of the summer house, and the General continued on his way with the dog. The time was about 3 p.m. General Luard was seen to arrive at the golf course at about 3.25. He got back to Ightham Knoll just over an hour later, having accepted a lift in a friend's car. Mrs. Luard's guest had arrived, but of the hostess there was no sign. General Luard apologized for her as best he could. Tea was served, and immediately afterwards the General said he was feeling so uneasy about his wife's absence that he thought he ought to go to look for her.

As he came within sight of the summer house, which was deep in the heart of the wood, he saw his wife stretched face downwards on the veranda. His first thought was that she had fainted, but when he came closer, a pool of blood on the floor and extensive bloodstains on her face and head revealed to him the horrible truth. Two witnesses, each independently of the other, were able to fix the precise hour at which Mrs. Luard had been killed. Both of them had heard the shots fired; both were certain of time—3.15p.m. What puzzled Scotland Yard at the time, and what has puzzled most people who have studied the case since, is why, a quarter of an hour after leaving her husband, Mrs. Luard should have got no further on her way home than the summer house. She was hurrying back, it should be remembered, because she was expecting a guest for tea. By 3.15 she ought at least to have reached the edge of the wood; indeed, she should already have been in the meadows leading to the house. Why had she lingered at La Casa?

To the officers engaged on the case the delay carried the strong suggestion that Mrs. Luard may have had an appointment to meet someone at the summer house, and that it was this 'someone' who had killed her. It further appeared to the police that the evidence which suggested robbery as the motive for the crime had a curiously contrived air about it. Why, they asked, should a man who was in so much of a hurry to rob Mrs. Luard of her rings that he had torn the skin of her fingers in wrenching them off bother to cut out her pocket to steal her purse? Why should he not simply have taken the purse out of the pocket? Did not the evidence appear to be a trifle over-done? Nothing

of all this ever got beyond the realm of speculation, and in that
condition it remains to this day.

E.S.S.

# 1910

# DOCTOR CRIPPEN
## Was He a Murderer?

It is ironical that the name of the man who, of all the classical
murderers, was the least certainly guilty, should have become
almost a synonym for the word 'murderer.' It is no less ironical
that a man whose chief characteristics were his kindness and
gentle charm, should be remembered only as an inhuman
monster.

Few murder cases have remained as famous as that of
unfortunate little Hawley Harvey Crippen. Many people to-day
have never heard of Seddon, whose case, within a year or two
of Crippen's, aroused almost as much interest at the time; yet
who is there even now who does not think he knows all about
Crippen?

In point of fact he knows very little about Crippen: not
even that most important thing of all, namely the very great
possibility, amounting almost to probability, that Crippen never
committed murder at all.

At the time of his tragedy Hawley Crippen was nearly fifty
years old. Here is an interesting point for a beginning. I have
never seen any statistics regarding the age of murderers, but
one would be inclined to say off-hand that few are as old as
this.

If murder is in the blood, it will come out before half a
century. Moreover Crippen's alleged crime was one of passion.
Is not fifty a little late in life to begin committing murder for
love? We may bear the point in mind later.

Crippen is usually referred to as 'Dr. ' Actually, he was not a
qualified medical man. He underwent a sketchy kind of training

in his own country (he was a native of Michigan, U.S.A.) and in 1883, when he was twenty-one years old, paid a visit to London where he attended several London hospitals in a haphazard way.

The only degree he ever achieved was a diploma in 1883 as an ear and eye specialist at the Ophthalmic Hospital in New York, which may or may not have given him the right to call himself a 'doctor,' but certainly did not make him one. In view of the profession he was practising in London at the time of his wife's death, this point will also become important.

After obtaining his diploma, Crippen practised during the next fifteen years at a variety of places, including Detroit, Santiago, Salt Lake City, New York, Philadelphia, and Toronto, never staying more than two years in any of them; though whether this was due to restlessness of disposition or inability to make a living, we do not know.

In 1887 he married for the first time; his wife died three or four years later leaving a son who, at the time of his father's trial was living in California. In 1893 he fell in love with a young girl who was not too young to have acquired a bad reputation even at the age of seventeen. This girl passed under the name of Cora Turner. Her mother was a German and her father a Russian Pole, and her real name was Kunigunde Mackamotzki; so that Cora Turner was certainly a change towards simplicity.

Crippen married her and, in 1900, brought her to London, when he obtained the post of manager of the English branch of a patent medicine firm.

If Crippen really did murder his wife, it cannot be denied that Mrs. Crippen almost brought the deed upon herself. She was not a pleasant women. Possessed of an almost pathologically swollen vanity, she fancied herself for honours on the music-hall stage; at one time indeed, she expected to bring the world to her feet in grand opera, though her voice was no better than that of any of the young women who, at that time, used to sing ballads in the drawing-room after supper.

In any case, arrived in London, Cora Crippen made all preparations to take it by storm. She chose the stage name of 'Belle Elmore,' she laid in a huge stock of expensive gowns, she joined the Music-hall Ladies' Guild, she did in fact everything except make a success on the stage; for she only appeared on it once, and was then promptly hissed off it by the audience.

Soured by this reception, and the impossibility of obtaining another engagement, Mrs. Crippen proceeded to take it out of the indulgent little husband who had paid for all the gowns, the singing-lessons, the agents' fees, and everything else: for at this time Crippen adored his shrewish wife, believing in her talents when no one else did.

She hen-pecked him unmercifully, quarrelled with him, insulted him before his friends, and did not draw the line at assuaging her wounded vanity with the attentions, and more than the attentions, of other men.

In short, Cora Crippen did what so many stupid, shrewish wives have done before her and literally drove her amiable little husband out of love with her.

And to drive out of love with his wife a man who has been accustomed to love is tantamount to driving him into the arms of another woman. Mrs. Crippen drove her husband into the arms of a typist at his office, Ethel Le Neve.

All this, of course, took time. It was 1900 when the Crippens came to London; it was 1910 when Cora Crippen died; and during those ten years there is no doubt that Crippen's home life was becoming more and more intolerable. Between him and Miss Le Neve there sprang up a love which, on Crippen's side at any rate, was to prove stronger than the fear of death.

And then Mrs. Crippen died.

There is no need to give the events which followed in any close detail, for they are still well known. Crippen made blunder after blunder—so incredibly foolish that there is surely some inference to be drawn from that very foolishness. He pawned his wife's jewellery qquite openly; some of it he gave to Miss Le Neve, and let her wear it openly; he had even bought the hyoscin from which his wife was to die quite openly from a chemist who knew him well and had signed the book in his own name.

If these were indeed the acts of a deliberate murderer then surely a more stupid murderer never existed. I suggest that they were not the acts of a deliberate murderer.

Then, by this small detail and that, an inaccuracy here and there, suspicion was aroused among Mrs. Crippen's friends;

information was lodged at Scotland Yard, and a Detective-Inspector went to Hilldrop Crescent to interview Crippen.

The Inspector viewed the visit as a formality; Crippen's demeanour confirmed his expectation that it was all nothing but a mare's nest. But three days later a small point took the Inspector up to Hilldrop Crescent again—and Crippen had fled. If Crippen had stood his ground then, neither you nor I would ever have heard of him.

The events that followed roused the excitement of two continents.It was not merely a case of an insignificant little man being wanted for wife murder; every romantic ingredient was present to turn the affair into the greatest of all classical murder hunts.

There was the identification of the pair on the liner *Montrose* by means of the new-fangled wireless telegraphy; there was the fact that Ethel Le Neve was disguised as a boy; there was the fact that the dead wife's body had been not merely buried under the cellar floor, but dismembered first—and dismemberment invariably rouses public's horror; there was the dramatic chase of the *Montrose* across the Atlantic by Inspector Dew in a faster boat, with the eyes of the whole world on the race except only those of the *Montrose's* own passengers; there was the love affair which had caused the whole tragedy; and there was finally, the character of Crippen himself as it began to leak out—a gentle, affectionate, mild, precise little man in late middle age, the last little man in the whole world, one would have said, to commit a callous and inhuman murder.

Inspector Dew did reach America first. Crippen was arrested on the *Montrose* when she docked, brought back to England, tried, condemned and hanged. On the evidence before them the jury could have returned no other verdict. Miss Le Neve, tried separately as an accessory after the fact, was acquitted. The letters Crippen wrote to her from prison as he awaited execution are among the most touching documents ever penned.

What, then, is the truth? How can it be asserted, in face of these facts, that Crippen never did commit murder? What considerations, pointing to this conclusion, never came before the jury at all?

It is always easy to argue, on one side or the other. Facts alone can determine truth; and there is one fact in Crippen's case which appears to me insurmountable, in the absence of any greater facts to confute it.

Unfortunately, however, it is a fact of psychology; and psychology, even psychological fact, carries little or no weight in a court of law. Evidence may be given as to character, but it influences little but the sentence. And yet it is character that determines action.

The insurmountable fact is this: there is overwhelming evidence that Crippen was mild, gentle and kindly—and mild, gently, kindly men simply do not commit murder. That is surely incontrovertible. One does not remain gentle and throwing off the mask, reveal oneself kindly for forty-eight years and then, suddenly as a fiend.

That elementary fact of psychology has been recognised for at last two thousand years. It is, after all, a long time since the rule was laid down that *nemo fuit repente turpissimus* (no one ever became vile all of a sudden). And there is no evidence that Crippen ever slid at all down the path of vileness; it is just assumed that he took it in one single bound.

Admit that one psychological fact, if to prove no more than that there is something queer behind the scenes here, and instantly the whole case becomes full of difficulties.

Take, for instance, the choice of poison. Very little was known in 1910 about hyoscin, or henbane. It had never been used in a case of murder. It was, I fancy, not even in the British Pharmacopoeia. Why did Crippen choose it?

Consider Crippen's profession. He was not a bona fide doctor, nor did he practice as such. He filled a succession of posts in firms concerned with patent medicines. Almost up to his last moments he was engaged in compiling a formula for a patent medicine of his own, be called *Sans Peine*.

He was, in fact, used to dealing with drugs, but not in the way of the recognised prescriptions: he was used to experimenting with them.

Now put these two considerations together, and look at them in the light of a very curious piece of evidence which was certainly never put forward at the trial, for it was not known then. This evidence takes us from an insignificant villa in London to no less a place than the Royal Palace in St. Petersburg, Russia.

It has been reliably established that, at just about the same time as Crippen was dabbling with hyoscin here, the court Magician, or Conjurer, at St. Petersburg, a man named Papus, was dosing the Tsar and Tsarina with a mixture of hyoscin and hashish, which was said to produce singularly pleasing effects, the admixture of hashish having been found to neutralise much of the toxic properties of hyoscin. What does this give us? It shows us that at this time, the quacks of Europe were experimenting with hyoscin, of which all they knew for certain was that it had properties as a narcotic. And Crippen was a quack.

This seems not only to offer a possible explanation of Crippen's very puzzling choice of a drug; but it goes some way, too, to suggest that his intention was not murderous. That suggestion is more than strengthened by the absence of any concealment of the purchase—the last thing, surely, that one would expect with a guilty intention.

Now, it is a theory of my own that dismemberment seldom enters into any plan of calculated murder. That is to say, when dismemberment occurs it almost amounts to proof that murder had not been planned ahead, and shows that the killing was, if not accidental, at any rate decided only on the spur of the moment.

But a poisoning is never decided on the spur of the moment. Therefore a poisoning, followed by dismemberment, which in turn is followed only by ordinary burial, and not by some such method as a piecemeal burning of the body, carries all the appearances of unexpected instead of expected death.

If, further, we admit dismemberment as indicative of an absence of plan, we see more and more evidence to the same effect. When obvious blunder after obvious blunder is made the conclusion is difficult to resist that nothing was thought out in advance.

Yet the use of poison for purposes of murder is equally strong evidence of premeditated planning. The only way of reconciling these opposing factors in the case of Crippen is that he did not intend to kill with his poison.

What, then, did he intend to do?

The late Sir Edward Marshall Hall, who believed strongly in Crippen's innocence, propounded a theory to answer this question which seems to me from every point of view convincing. It was his belief that Crippen, knowing of hyoscin only as a narcotic, used it upon his wife, not with any intention of killing her, but in order to put her into a drugged sleep so that he could spend the evening with Miss Le Neve.

This, I think, is what must have happened. But Crippen, in his ignorance, either administered an overdose or perhaps mixed his hyoscin with some agent which did not neutralise it sufficiently. In any case he discovered that he had killed instead of drugged, and lost his head. For plainly he did lose his head. Crippen was not of the stuff of which murderers are made.

There is, actually, a piece of evidence supporting this theory which came out at the trial, though its significance was missed then. On the night before her death Mrs. Crippen had some friends in, who left at about midnight. At Miss Le Neve's trial her landlady gave evidence that one night at the end of January Miss Le Neve came home very late in a state of considerable distress, quite horror-stricken, in fact, as if she had suffered a great shock, and the time mentioned was *two o'clock in the morning*. Mrs. Crippen died on January 31. If Crippen had intended to murder his wife he would not have had Miss Le Neve in the house at the time. If Miss Le Neve was in the house, it may be almost certainly said thhat murder was not intended.

All these considerations convince me that Crippen was innocent of premeditated murder. That he was responsible for his wife's death is, of course, indubitable, and the defence he adopted, of a blank denial of everything, was the worst possible one. At worst he was guilty only of manslaughter.

Why, then, did he not make a clean breast of the facts and plead manslaughter, or even accident?

The answer to that question is one of the most striking features of the whole case. He was in fact pressed to do this, but he refused. His reason was that to substantiate his plea he would have to admit that Miss Le Neve was in the house that night; and, if anything went wrong with the case and the jury did bring in a verdict of murder, this might have been prejudicial to Miss Le Neve.

He was almost assured of an acquittal from the murder charge if he permitted this defence, but on the quite slender danger of entangling Miss Le Neve he decided upon almost certain death for himself.

I always feel very sorry for Crippen. He has been dreadfully maligned. I cannot believe that he was a monster. Certainly he was, as the late Lord Birkenhead said of him, 'a brave man and a true lover.'

F.I

# 1915

# BELA KISS

## The Mystery Man of Europe

In the early spring of 1912 a tall rather elegant man of exquisite manner, thin-faced, blacked-haired, with high cheek-bones and a countenance of almost Tartar type, arrived with his young and pretty wife from Budapest at the charming little summer resort of Czinkota, a few miles from the Hungarian capital. The place is much frequented by holiday folk on Sundays, it being a centre for excursions to Visegrad, Nagy-Moros and Budafok. The stranger, who was about forty years of age, was named Bela Kiss, his wife being about fifteen years younger. After searching the district for a house he eventually took a rather spacious one standing back in a large garden on the Matyasfold road, in a somewhat isolated position, and for a few months lived happily there, going into Budapest alone about once or twice a week. It afterwards transpired that he had been a tinsmith in a large way of business, but had retired.

The pair formed few friendships, for Kiss seemed a somewhat mystical person, and had often been heard to discuss psychic subjects with his wife. He was also something of an amateur astrologer and possessed many books upon the subject, while his wife had a small crystal globe into which she was fond of gazing. The pair seemed a most devoted couple, and went about together in the small and rather dilapidated car which the husband possessed, and in which he often went into Budapest.

The wife was extremely good-looking, and Kiss was apparently extremely jealous of her. Indeed, he forbade her to make any male acquaintances. She was a native of Zimony, on the Danube, in the extreme South of Hungary, a place long noted for its handsome female inhabitants. According to village gossip, however, little Madame Kiss had a friend in a certain Paul Bihari, an artist of Budapest, who sometimes spent the day with her wandering in the acacia woods and picnicking together during her husband's absence. The handsome young fellow was well known in the capital and especially at the Otthon Club, where Hungarian authors, artists and journalists assembled nightly.

## 2

Matters proceeded in this manner for nearly six months, Paul being a frequent visitor to the house, and the pair making many excursions to the beauty spots in the vicinity. One evening, however Bela Kiss on his return from Budapest found the house locked up. After waiting till near nightfall he broke open the door, and found lying upon the dining-table, a note from his wife saying that she had fled with her lover, and asking forgiveness. In a frenzy of anger he burnt the note, and then rushing to a neighbour named Littman, who lived in the vicinity and who was one of the few persons with whom he had formed a friendship, told him of the staggering blow he had received.

Next day all Czinkota was agog, knowing what had occurred. But it was only what they had long expected.

Crushed by his disillusionment, the heart-broken husband shut himself up and became almost a recluse. He drove sometimes to Budapest, but he had no servant and did his own cooking and looked after his few daily wants himself. In fact, he became a woman-hater and devoted his time to the study of psychometry and mysticism. His eccentricity now became the more marked, but as months wore on his health appeared to be failing until it was noticed that he had not been seen out for over a week, while the house appeared to be closed. Yet each night there appeared a light in his bedroom.

The neighbour in whom he had confided how his wife had deserted him began to wonder, so one day he called. The knock on the door's brought Bela, pale, half-clad and very feeble. He told his friend that he had been ill in bed for some days. The friend at once suggested that he should have somebody to nurse him, and that the village doctor should be called. At first Kiss demurred, saying: 'After all, if I die what matters? I have nothing to live for, now that my dear one has left me!'

The neighbour uttered comforting words, and eventually the doctor visited him—much against his will—and an old woman from the village, named Kalman, was left in charge.

His eccentricity had, it seems increased to a marked degree. In one room there were laid out carefully upon the table the clothes and shoes that his wife had left behind, and into that room the invalid forbade the old woman to enter. For nearly three weeks the village woman was most assiduous, and carefully nursed him back to health, until at last he became quite well again. So he paid her and she left, leaving him to the dull, isolated life which he had lived ever since his young wife had gone.

### 3

Soon he resumed his business visits to Budapest, usually leaving the house in the afternoon and often not returning until midnight and after. Very naturally the woman Kalman was questioned by her friends as to the condition of the house of the poor grief-stricken man. It was also but natural that she should describe to her neighbours what she had seen—how, though forbidden to enter the room where the erring wife's clothes were displayed, she had entered it in secret while her patient was asleep, and passing through it had peered through the keyhole of the room beyond, where she saw five large tin drums ranged along by the wall.

The old woman's curiosity had been aroused by sight of these, and soon her friends, to whom she described what she had seen, suspected the eccentric, grief-stricken man to be in league with some illicit distillers who had their secret factory somewhere in the neighbourhood. The gossips were naturally sorely puzzled to account for those big receptacles for fluid. Some laughed and said that he had a big store of wine bought at the previous year's vintage. Littman, his neighbour and confidant, hearing about it, one day mentioned to him what the old woman Kalman had seen, whereupon Kiss laughed heartily and replied:

'Well, that is really amusing! They think I am one of those who distil alcohol against the law and sell it in secret to the night cafés in Budapest—eh? Well, let them think so! I would be afraid to engage in such a dangerous trade, lucrative as it is. No. The fact is that I have my store of petrol here. I bought it cheaply from a man who was about to be made bankrupt.'

Quickly the truth went round the village, and suspicion was at once allayed. Indeed, a man of such exemplary conduct as Bela Kiss surely could never be engaged in any illicit transactions.

Once Littman expressed surprise that he had not followed the runaway pair and divorced his wife. To this, Kiss replied: 'If they are happy in Vienna, as I hear they are, why should I wreck her life? I loved her more than anything on earth. So that is enough. I was a fool! That's all!' And refused to discuss the matter further.

From that moment, however, suspicions regarding Kiss became increased. His many journeys to Budapest were regarded as mysterious, and an evil-tongued woman who distrusted him declared that he practised black magic. He had drawn the horoscope of a woman of her acquaintance who believed in astrology, and thus a fresh theory was set up to account for his aloofness and eccentricity.

Whenever he motored to Budapest, as he did twice a week, it was noted that he never returned until early hours of the morning, when the whole village was asleep. The villagers heard his noisy, ramshackle car speeding through the streets homeward bound. Of money this retired tinsmith had plenty. The village policeman, who, by the way, had also had his curiosity aroused by the malicious gossip, struck up an acquaintance with, and soon discovered him to be real good fellow, kind, generous and hospitable. They often spent evenings together, for the representative of the law was, in addition to Littman, the only person he ever invited to cross his threshold since his wife's flight. The constable naturally reported the result of his inquiries to his chief, and all suspicions were set at rest.

## 4

One wintry morning in January 1914, the exquisitely dressed Bela Kiss was seen walking with a pretty young woman, also handsomely attired in furs, about half a mile from the village and this fact, which soon got about, gave rise to the theory that the disillusioned husband had fallen in love again. The gossips kept watch, but only on that one occasion was the lady seen. It was, no doubt, an illicit meeting, for the well-dressed lady had, it was known, come from Budapest and had spent the day with her admirer.

About a month later a farmer driving from Czinkota to Rakosfalva noticed a man and a woman walking in the afternoon along a secluded footpath on the edge of a wood, and on approaching recognised Kiss arm in arm with well-dressed young girl, to whom he was earnestly talking. The spot was nearly four miles from the village, and near by stood Kiss's old motor-car, muddy and unwashed.

Just about that time a strange story was told to the police of the Josefvaros quarter in Budapest by a young girl named Luisa Ruszt, daughter of a well-know draper in the Karoly Korut, one of the principal shopping thoroughfares.

She said that one evening she had met a man in the Somossy variety theatre, and he had taken her next day for a long motor drive. On their way back to Budapest, they had stopped at his country house and there had some refreshment. Afterwards they returned to the city, when he invited her to his flat somewhere near the Margaret Bridge. They had dinner at a restaurant, when he told her that if she cared to go back to his flat he would tell her fortune. Like most girls she was eager to know her future, therefore she consented and went.

On arrival he offered her some pale yellow liqueur which seemed very strong, and then setting her at a table he told her to gaze intently into a small crystal globe. In fun he promised that she would see her future husband.

She did as he instructed, and had been gazing intently for some time when she began to experience a strange dizziness, probably due to the liqueur. Suddenly, on looking up from the crystal she saw in a mirror at her side the man standing behind her with a piece of green silk cord in his hand. It had a noose and a slop-knot, and he was about to place it over her head!

Sight of the changed face of her friend—a pale, evil countenance, with glaring dark eyes which had in them the spirit of murder—held her breathless. She fainted, and knew no more until she found herself lying beneath the trees in the Erszebet Park at dawn with all her jewellery and money gone.

She described to the police, as well as she could, the man with his house in the country and his flat in the town, but, though some inquiries were made, neither flat nor house could be identified, and they apparently dismissed the story as the imaginings of a romantic girl.

Curiously enough, however, about three weeks later a very similar story was told by a young married woman of good family, and whose husband was a wealthy merchant, to the police of the Belvaros quarter of Budapest. The lady, who lived on the handsome Franz Josef's Quai, facing the Danube, had met a smartly dressed man one Sunday morning as she came out alone after service in the Terezvaros Church, which was highly fashionable during the Budapest season. She was nearly run down by a passing taxi when he had grabbed her arm and pulled her back. Thus they became acquainted. They walked together for some distance, when he told her that his name was Franz Hofmann, a jeweller's traveller, and that he was greatly interested in spiritualism. She happened to be also interested in spiritualism, hence a friendship was formed. Her husband was away in Paris, therefore she invited him to dine at her house a few days later, and at the dinner she appeared wearing some valuable jewellery, while he, as a jeweller, admired it greatly.

Later that evening Hofmann invited her to go to one of the most select night cafés for which Budapest is famous, and she accepted. Afterwards, at two o'clock in the morning, he persuaded her to accompany him to his flat, where he would tell her fortune by the crystal. She went, and almost the same thing happened. She drank the liqueur, and he tried to strangle her. She fought with him, was overpowered, and when she came to her senses found herself in the hands of the police devoid of her jewellery. She had been found lying in a doorway unconscious.

This second story aroused the interest of the Budapest police, and inquiries were made, but neither woman could say where the flat in question was situated. They had been taken there, they said, by a roundabout route. The taxi had been dismissed in what seemed to be a cul-de-sac, and they had walked the remainder of the distance. They both described the inteerior in identical terms and their description of the man left no doubt that it was the same individual in each case.

Then, when a third girl told a similar story a fortnight later, and when a dealer in second-hand jewellery had shown the police a ring the description of which had been circulated, a real hue and cry was raised. But just at that moment war broke out and the country was thrown into disorder. The police system quickly broke down, and every available man was called up to fight against the Allies on the side of the Germans.

Bela Kiss was among those called up. He had been living a quiet, lonely, uneventful life, and as soon as the call to arms came he ordered from a blacksmith a number of iron bars, which he fixed inside the windows of his house to keep óut thieves during his absence. Then, a week later, he left Czinkota and joined the colours.

## 5

Eighteen months passed. He fought in Serbia, and once wrote to his friend Littman from Semendria, on the Serbian shore of the Danube, after a great battle had been fought. Littman, who was over military age, replied but the letter was returned some four months later with an official intimation that Kiss had died of wounds in a military hospital near Belgrade. Then the village gossips of Czinkota knew that the poor deserted husband, who had led such a lonely life, had given his life for his country, and his name was later on engraved upon the local war memorial.

In the meantime, however, a sensational discovery had been made, quite by accident, of the body of a young woman in an advanced state of decomposition buried under about six inches of earth in the same wood of acacias wherein the farmer had seen Bela Kiss walking with a young woman. Upon the finger of the corpse was a wedding-ring engraved on the inside by which she was identified with the young wife of a furrier in a large way of business in Vienna, who had before the war run away with a middle-aged man, taking with her a quantity of jewellery and the equivalent of two thousand pounds in money. She had left her husband and entirely disappeared, after sending a letter to a friend from Budapest.

Inquiries were at once instituted, of course, and it was found that her husband had been killed within the first week of the war. Therefore, as far as the police—unfortunately a very inefficient service in those days—were concerned, they could do no more. But within three months yet another body was turned up by the plough in the vicinity. The records of missing persons were inspected, and they found that the unfortunate woman was named Isabelle Koblitz, a niece of the Minister of Commerce, who was known to have studied spiritualism, and who had disappeared from Vienna in July 1913.

The chief of the detective police of Budapest then began further inquiries. From Berne a report came that a wealthy Swiss lady named Riniker, living at Lausanne, had been staying at a well-known hotel in Budapest, from which she had written to her sister in Geneva, but had, in October 1913, mysteriously disappeared. A description was given of her, together with the fact that she had a red scar upon her cheek and that she had a slight deformation of the left leg. Within three days the Hungarian police established the fact that the body of the lady was that which had, six months before, been found in a disused well at Solymar, a little place about twenty miles away, at which the festival of the Queen of the Roses is celebrated each year.

The police now became much puzzled. Yet they did not connect the stories of the women who had gazed into the crystal with the discovery of the bodies of others.

Suddenly an order to commandeer all petrol went forth, and all garages and private persons were compelled to deliver it over for military purposes and receive receipts for it, which the Government eventually paid. At first the commandeering took place only in the big towns, but after three months a further thorough 'comb-out' of petrol was ordered, and commissioners visited every village, including Czinkota. There they searched for petrol, whereupon the old woman Kalman recalled the fact that poor Kiss who had died possessed quite a stock of petrol. This quickly reached the ears of the commissioner, who went at once to the dead man's house, broke down the iron bars, and found the big drums of spirit. From their appearance both the commissioner and a constable suspected them to be full of smuggled brandy. Indeed, the constable obtained a tin mug from the kitchen in order to sample the spirit when they bored a hole. They did so—and found it to be crude alcohol.

Further investigation, however, led to a most ghastly discovery. On cutting open the top of the big drum a quantity of female clothing was seen. This was removed, and beneath was the nude body of a woman bound with cord and so well preserved in the spirit that her features were easily recognisable. Indeed, around her neck was a thin red line, showing plainly the manner in which she had been murdered—namely, by strangulation with a cord and slip-knot!

And each of the other drums contained the body of a woman, each showing traces of strangulation. Upon these gruesome facts—perhaps the most horrible discovery ever made in the annals of the police of Europe—we need not dwell.

Search of Bela Kiss's belongings brought to light a number of receipts for advertisements inserted in several of the most important newspapers in Vienna and Budapest, and upon examination of the files of those papers the advertisements in question were easily identified.

One, which was repeated in ten different issues of the paper, read:

> *Bachelor: aged 40: lonely; good income from commercial enterprises averaging £3000 per annum, is desirous of corresponding with educated lady with a view to matrimony. Address: De Koller, Poste Restante, Granatos, Budapest.*

A number of other similar advertisements were traced by the receipts, all of which were either alluding to matrimony or trying to induce girls to learn their future. Indeed, when the police came to inquire at the Post Office in Budapest they found no fewer than fifty-three letters awaiting the mysterious De Koller undelivered!

In a Vienna daily newspaper the following advertisement was found: 'Know Yourself!—Those who wish to know their future and thus frame their lives should consult Professor Hofmann of Budapest. Write: Poste Restante, Vienna.' To this one advertisement there were twenty-three replies awaiting him, all from women eager to have their fortunes told. It then became plain that the fellow's habit was to lure women possessing even paltry sums of money or modest jewellery, either to his flat in Budapest, or to take them out by night to his house at Czinkota, and there strangle them. The tin drums of spirit he evidently used in order to preserve the bodies of his victims until he could bury them in secret or otherwise dispose of them.

A number of prisoners of war were at once set to work digging in Kiss's garden and in the acacia woods, the result being that no fewer than twenty-six other bodies of women and girls were found at various spots. Over one hundred and sixty pawn-tickets relating to women's clothing were found concealed under the carpet of the dining-room, and by the recovery of the clothing and some jewellery, fourteen of his victims were eventually identified. They were mostly of women of the better class, and in every case had worn jewellery, and had money in their possession when they had gone to consult him.

The method he adopted never varied. His first crime was committed by means of a cord slipped over the head and drawn tight ere his victims could utter a cry—thus adopting the method of the notorious Frenchwoman Gabrielle Bompard—and so successful was he that he always pursued the same course. Among the bodies recovered in the garden was one which was identified as the young wife who was supposed to have fled with the artist, Paul Bihari. The latter was found in Agram, and when questioned by the police stated that one day, while at the house in Czinkota, Kiss came home unexpectedly, and after a fracas he left and had not seen the lady or heard of her since.

The monster Bela Kiss had, however, died of wounds received while fighting in Serbia, therefore the police hushed up the terrible affair, and soon the gruesome discovery was forgotten by all except the villagers of Czinkota.

About a year later, however, Inspector Resch, of the detective force of Budapest, learned that a man closely resembling Franz Hofmann had been seen a week before by the girl Luisa Ruszt—who had had such a narrow escape while gazing into the crystal globe. At first he was not inclined to believe her, but so positive was she that she had actually seen him in the flesh, that the police officer decided to go the hospital at Belgrade and learn details at first hand of the assassin's death.

On arrival he found that Bela Kiss had died from wounds, and he was given the dead man's papers, which proved his identity beyond question. By mere chance the nurse who had tended him in his dying moments was still there, and naturally the inspector questioned her as to the end of such a callous and elusive criminal.

'But surely,' she remarked, 'Such a very frank and pious-minded boy could not have committed such awful crimes!'

'Boy!' echoed the inspector. 'What do you mean? Bela Kiss was over forty years old.'

'Well, the Bela Kiss who died here was about twenty!' was her reply.

Again the surprised detective examined the identification papers, and saw that without doubt they were the genuine ones belonging to Bela Kiss of Czinkota. Hence the assassin had, no doubt, exchanged papers with the poor young fellow who had died and been buried under his name.

With this astounding knowledge Inspector Resch sped back to Budapest, and a thorough search was at once made for the assassin. The police of Europe were warned, and as it was believed that the assassin had fled to London, Scotland Yard became active, as well as the Paris Sûreté. But the fellow managed to slip through their finger.

W.L.Q.

*Five years later, a man who has just emerged from the French Foreign Legion informed the Sûreté that a fellow-soldier called Hofmann was in the habit of amusing his friends with lurid stories of garrottings; moreover, he answered the description of the wanted man. But by the time the authorities acted, Hofmann too has deserted.*

*There were rumours that he had fled to the United States, and in 1932 a detective in New York's Homicide Squad claimed to have spotted Kiss in Times Square, but again he proved too elusive to be apprehended.*

*He was never caught.*

R.G.J.

# 1911–19

# The Axeman of New Orleans

Jake Maggio lay silently on his bed and tried to gather his thoughts. A faint light was beginning to show through the window and Jake guessed it to be nearly five A.M. For a second the young man blinked rapidly, trying to understand why he had awakened so early.

Then the groans came again. They were accompanied by a rasping, gurgling sound that made Jake's hair stand on end. There was a moment of silence and then the sounds were heard once more. Suddenly realizing that they were coming from his brother and sister-in-law's room on the other side of the wall. Jake jumped up and roused his older brother. Andrew. Together they rushed out into the hall and flung open the adjacent bedroom door. What they saw stopped them in their tracks.

Their sister-in-law lay sprawled on the floor in a mass of blood. Her head had been badly bludgeoned and her throat was split from side to side, almost completely decapitating her.

Their brother, Joseph, lay back on the bed. His head, too, was badly beaten and his throat was slit, but by some miracle he was still alive. It was from him and his bloody throat that the horrible moans and gurgling sounds had come.

When Joseph saw his brothers he tried to get up and half fell out of the bed. Jake and Andrew called the police at once and set about doing what they could.

The Maggios both owned and lived over a small grocery store and when the police arrived they found a panel of the door had been chiseled out. A blood-soaked axe was discovered outside on the back steps. The razor that had been used to slash the throats was found near the bodies.

The year was 1918 and the place was New Orleans. The infamous Axeman had struck. In the months to follow his terrible exploits would turn the Mardi Gras city upside down, terrorize the Italian community, baffle police, and create a mystery that lingers to this day.

The police investigating the attack that early summer day seemed hopelessly confused from the start. The major portion of their initial efforts was spent questioning the neighbors. Acting on a spurious tip that Andrew had come home late that night, the police on the scene promptly arrested the two brothers and charged them with murder.

A short time later a message was found chalked on the sidewalk near the house of death. It said, 'Mrs. Maggio is going to sit up tonight just like Mrs. Tony.' Detectives in homicide quickly recalled that in 1911 there had been three axe murder cases, all strikingly similar to the Maggio crime. In all three, the victims had been Italian grocers and their wives. In the last case the victims's name had been Tony.

The next day an embarrassed police department released Jake and Andrew. They had been revealed to be hard-working, honest men. And it had also been shown that on that fateful night Andrew had been returning from a party to celebrate his draft call. Several people were available to testify that he was too drunk to attack anyone, much less his beloved brother.

The newspaper gave a lot of play to the crime, but as weeks passed and no new developments occurred, interest in it waned. The Great War was reaching its bloody climax and the terrible stories coming from the Continent quickly eclipsed the murder in the public mind.

Then, in the early morning of June 28, a local baker making his deliveries arrived at the grocery store of Louis Besumer. Finding the store still closed, the baker went around to the back to leave the fresh bread. To his horror he found a panel of the back door chiseled out. Remembering the Maggio crime and terrified that the killer might be there he knocked timidly. The baker jumped a mile when the door opened almost immediately.

Instead of the killer, however, the baker was confronted by

Louis Besumer, his face pale and shocked, blood streaming from a deep wound on his head.

The baker rushed into the house and found Mrs. Besumer lying unconscious on the bed. She, too, was covered in blood and had a terrible gash in her skull. An axe was found in the bathroom still glistening red.

Both attack victims survived and Louis was released from the hospital the next day. He was no sooner back on his feet, though, when he became engulfed in some rather strange developments. The local newspapers had discovered that he was Polish and had only recently come to New Orleans from South America. It was also learned that he spoke several languages fluently and that he regularly received letters from abroad. With that the local papers began a campaign of innuendo, implying that Besumer might be a spy for the Kaiser. When approached by the papers Louis quickly denied being a spy or a killer. He said he was innocent, a victim himself, and that he was Polish and not German, for God's sake!

Further difficulties were created by Besumer's statement that he was not married to the woman he had been living with. She did not recover consciousness until July 5. By that time she had been identified as Mrs. Harriet Lowe. Almost as soon as she was able to talk and hear what was going on, Mrs. Lowe gave a statement. 'I've long suspected that Mr. Besumer was a German spy,' she said. Louis was quickly arrested.

The next day Harriet gave another statement. 'I did not say Mr. Besumer was a German spy. That is perfectly ridiculous.' Louis was released.

A few days later Harriet started talking about the attack. She described the assailant as a stranger, yet the specific information she gave out started everyone thinking of Louis as a spy again. A war fever gripped the city and Mr. Besumer became a very unpopular man.

A month later Harriet passed away after surgery. She died mumbling that Louis had hit her with the axe. Louis went back to jail.

The harassed police were very happy to finally have a murder suspect firmly under lock and key (Harriet now being unable to change her story). The same night that Louis was arrested, however, the Axeman struck again.

The new victim was the young pregnant wife of Edward Schneider. Schneider returned home late that night and was horrified to find his bride lying on their bed, unconscious, in a pool of blood.

The Schneiders were lucky. Mrs. Schneider recovered completely and was able to give birth to a healthy child.

Police questioned her closely but all she could remember was opening her eyes, seeing a dark form standing over her with an axe, and seeing the weapon come down at her. Combining her descriptions with those of Louis and Harriet, police came up with a description of a rather tall, heavyset white man. There was nothing else to go on.

The latest attack set the local papers off on a new track. The day after the Schneider assault the *Times-Picayune* carried a large type headline: 'IS AN AXEMAN AT LARGE IN NEW ORLEANS?' The city didn't have to wait long to find out.

On August 10, four days after the headline, Joseph Romano was attacked in his bedroom. The attack was interrupted by a young niece, who got a brief glimpse of the Axeman as he fled. Romano staggered out to the living room and managed to walk to the ambulance, but two days later he died from the massive wound he had received.

Once again a door panel was found chiseled out. Once again the bloody axe was found in the backyard. Once again nothing was stolen. A pattern had been established. The only difference in this case was Romano's profession. He was a barber.

A wave of hysteria began to sweep the Italian community, especially among the grocers. Dark rumors of Mafia activities began to circulate. Families began to set up night watches, making sure that someone in the household was awake all night. Other families left the city.

As the newspaper picked up the cry, the hysteria swept to other parts of the metropolis. The police began receiving all sorts of reports about the Axeman. Several Italian grocers claimed to have had their doors panels chiseled out, or to have seen a man with an axe in or near their home. Others claimed to have seen a man with an axe fleeing through their backyards.

As the police began to feel pressure, they turned back to the only suspect they had, poor Louis Besumer. The general attitude seemed to be that no matter what else had happened, or whether he was guilty of any of it, Louis killed Harriet and we're going to make him pay.

In March of 1919 the Axeman struck again. The latest victims were a family of Italian grocers named Cortimiglia. On the evening of March 10, Iorlando Jordano, another Italian grocer living across the street, heard screams coming from the Cortimiglia house. He rushed over, followed by his younger brother, Frank. Inside they found Charles Cortimiglia lying on the floor, his body covered with gaping wounds. Mrs. Rosie Cortimiglia sat in the middle of the floor clutching the bloody body of her two-year-old daughter. Mrs. Cortimiglia was hysterical and refused to let anyone take her dead daughter from her. When the police arrived, they found all the now too-familiar signs: the chiseled door panel, the bloody axe, and the absence of theft. Both Charles and Rosie survived.

When Rosie was able to talk she described the attack in detail. She said she awakened to see her husband struggling with a large white man, armed with an axe. After a long struggle the intruder broke free and delivered a brutal blow with the axe that dropped her husband to the floor. With that the Axeman swung around towards Rosie.

Rosie said she promptly grabbed her daughter, who was asleep in a nearby crib, and hugged her to her breast, screaming, 'Not my baby! Not my baby!' The Axeman swung twice, finally hitting the baby and wounding Mrs. Cortimiglia.

A few days later Charles recovered enough to leave the hospital. No sooner was he out than Rosie changed her story. To everybody's amazement she began to accuse the Jordanos (who owned a competing grocery store in the same block) of committing the murder.

The police immediately questioned her husband. He was incredulous. No, the Jordanos didn't do it. Yes, they came in to rescue us. Despite this very strange testimony the police proceeded to arrest the Jordanos.

The elder Jordano, who was sixty-nine and in poor health, protested his innocence, citing the unlikelihood of his being able to commit the crime. It was quickly shown that the younger Jordano, who was a big man, could hardly have squeezed through the door panel. Shortly after the arrest Rosie was released from the hospital. She proceeded to the jail where, in front of the press, she screamed at the Jordanos and fainted.

The Jordanos were scheduled for trial in May. Before the authorities could attempt to convict them, however, they had to try Louis Besumer, who was still waiting in another jail cell. Louis went on trial on April 30. The trial was very short and the prosecution looked rather foolish. Federal agents admitted they had no evidence whatsoever of espionage. Police accusations and testimony became very shaky on the stand. Flat statements given out to the press earlier turned out to be hearsay and rumor. Louis was acquitted.

By now all of New Orleans had been caught up in an 'Axeman Craze.' The papers played up every sensational angle and every man in the street had a theory. 'Axeman' parties were held and a local songwriter turned out a tune entitled 'The Mysterious Axeman's Jazz.'

On March 14, a letter signed 'The Axeman' was received by the *Times-Picayune*. In the letter he said he planned to visit New Orleans on the night of March 19 and added that he loved jazz and would pass by any house playing it. When the nineteenth came the noise was incredible. Bars and nightclubs were packed and residential streets echoed with the sounds of thousands upon thousands of record players blaring out jazz at full volume.

In May the Jordanos went on trial. The courtroom was packed and the whole thing got intensive play in the media. Witness after witness took the stand, but only Rosie's testimony suggested the Jordanos were guilty. Charles (now separated from his wife) got on the stand and vehemently denied that the Jordanos were involved. Despite this the jury somehow found the Jordanos guilty and sentenced Frank to hang.

A few months later the Axeman went back to work. On the evening of August 10 an Italian grocer named Frank Genusa answered a knock at his door. He opened it to have his friend and fellow grocer Steve Boca fall into his arms. Boca's skull was cleaved open and he was covered with blood.

Boca recovered enough to talk the next day. Police searched his home and found all the usual signs. Following what was now appearing to be normal police procedure in New Orleans, they arrested Genusa for the murder. Boca himself cleared his friend and the cops turned back to their fruitless investigation.

Three weeks later the Axeman struck at the home of a druggist but was scared away when the man fired a revolver through the door.

The next day a nineteen-year-old-girl was found badly beaten and unconscious in her bed. No door panel was missing (the intruder came in through a window) but an axe was found outside.

On October 27 of that year the Axeman made a deadly appearance at the home of Mike Pepitone, still another Italian grocer. Mrs. Pepitone surprised the attacker in the bedroom with her husband just after the attack had occurred. Mike was dead and his blood covered the wall and ceiling. The Axeman fled as Mrs. Pepitone began screaming. Once again the police were left with only a very general description of the killer.

It was at this point that Rosie Cortimigilia rushed into the city room of the *Times-Picayune* and demanded to see a reporter. She was highly emotional. Thin and gaunt she hardly seemed the same person who had appeared in court. Throwing herself on her knees in front of the reporter who listened to her, Rosie screamed, 'I lied! I lied! God forgive me, I lied!' A few days later the Jordanos were freed.

By now the citizens of New Orleans, especially the Italian citizens, had given themselves up to fear. The police had proven worse than useless in catching the killer and the Axeman seemed insatiable.

But just at that moment, when everything seemed hopeless, the attacks stopped. Mike Pepitone was the last person to fall under the killer's axe. There was no sign, no word to indicate why the attacks stopped. The police doggedly continued their investigation but virtually nothing was turned up. Only one incident provides any possible solution to the mystery.

About the time of Rosie Cortimiglia's confession, a New Orleanian named Joseph Mumfre was shot dead in Los Angeles. He had been walking down the street when a veiled woman dressed in black stepped out and emptied a revolver into his body. The woman made no attempt to flee and was promptly arrested. She turned out to be Mrs. Mike Pepitone. She told police she had seen Mumfre in her husband's bedroom and traced him to Los Angeles. She said he was the Axeman.

Mrs. Pepitone pleaded guilty in court. There was a lot of public support for her and she was sentenced to ten years in jail. She was freed after three.

The New Orleans police had Mumfre on file. He had a long jail record and the dates when he had been locked up dovetailed perfectly with the gaps in the Axeman's activity. Despite this the police refused to accept Mumfre as the killer and left the case open. The consensus of public opinion also held that the mass murderer's identity had not been discovered. The newspapers held the same view.

Many people feel that there was more than one Axeman. Some still insist the Mafia was responsible. Others speak of a vendetta against Italian grocers. The answered now are jumbled and worn with time. Whoever the Axeman really was will remain a secret forever.

J.P.

# 1920
# The Green Bicycle Mystery

There was a murder case in England which not only needed a Sherlock Holmes but seemed as if it had been devised in solemn conclave by Conan Doyle, Holmes, and Watson themselves. It could be entitled The Mystery of the Green Bicycle; or, The Curious Incident of the Dead Raven.

Unfortunately, there was no great hawk-faced detective from Baker Street in it. Only, at the beginning, a local constable named Hall. Perhaps that is why one of the men best informed on this case says that it has 'considerable claims to be regarded as the most fascinating murder mystery of the century.'

Bella Wright was twenty-one and lived with her father and mother in a tiny placed called Stoughton. This is within a mile or two of the city of Leicester, and in that city she was employed in a rubber factory.

She was a girl with good looks and good character, and was engaged to be married to a stoker in the navy.

The country round about Leicester is full of little villages connected by old Roman roads or by lanes with high hedges. To the north is the famous hunting center of Melton Mowbray.

The lanes are charmingly picturesque and lonely, but were made for a less motorized age. They are sometimes full of surprises and excitement for the pedestrian or the cyclist. At a curve he may suddenly be confronted by a flock of sheep just as an enormous motor bus, brushing the hedge on either side, comes up behind him.

Miss Wright was accustomed to go to and from her work on a bicycle, and sometimes, in the long daylight hours of the English summer evenings, to cycle from one hamlet to another to do errands or to call on her friends. Her uncle, a man named Measures, lived in the village of Gaulby, three miles from her home.

She was on the late shift at the factory, and one Friday evening in July rode home from her work at eleven o'clock, going to bed soon after. Next day seems to have been a holiday, so she thoroughly made up her sleep, not getting up again till four o'clock Saturday afternoon. Then, after writing a few letters, she rode with them to the post office at Evington. Again she came home, but finally, at 6:30 P.M., set out on her cycle in the opposite direction, away from Leicester. Her mother had seen her start for Evington, and never after that saw her alive.

At nine twenty that evening (still daylight) a farmer named Cowell was driving cattle along the old Roman road called the Gartree Road or *Via Devana*. At a point about two miles from Gaulby, where the way is very lonely and the hedges, at that season, more than eight feet high, Cowell found Bella Wright lying dead in the road. Her head was covered with blood, and her cycle lay askew, with its front wheel pointed toward Stoughton—that is, toward home.

The farmer supposed that she had been killed by a fall or similar mischance. He placed her on the grass at the side of the road. Her body was still warm. Close to the spot where it was found—and this may be important—there was an opening in the hedge: a field gate which led into the grassy meadow beyond.

Constable Hall and a doctor came later, after it was dark. The doctor's hasty examination led to nothing more than a general impression that Miss Wright, being thrown from her bicycle, had fractured her skull on a stone. Cowell's statement as to his discovery of the body seems to have been accepted as quite satisfactory. This was due, I suppose, to his good reputation, since the only witnesses he could call to prove his story were his cows.

Miss Wright's body rested that night in a cottage nearby. Early next morning Constable Hall decided to make further investigation. He carefully examined the road; and seventeen feet from the bloodstain which marked the spot where the girl's head had lain in the dust he found a bullet, caliber .45, partly embedded in the road as if it had been stepped on or run over.

He made another exceedingly curious discovery: the gate which led into the field was painted white, and on the top bar were marks of claws—marks in blood—twelve such sets of tracks, six going and six returning—leading from the body to the gate. In the field the constable came across a large bird with black plumage—dead. The bird was found to be gorged with blood. Indeed, that surfeit of blood was supposed to have killed it.

In England everybody is keen about birds and their habits. As soon as the Leicestershire police said that this bird was a raven, other folk flew to the defense of ravens. They said that (a) there were no ravens around Leicester; and (b) if there were, they had never been known to drink blood.

(The bird of which the Book of Job says 'Her young ones also suck up blood' is not the raven but the eagle.)

This creature, said the bird experts, must be a rook or a carrion crow.

Whatever bird it was, there are two schools of thought about it, and all the authorities, Messrs. H. R. Wakefield, Edward Marjoribanks, and others, have discussed it. There are the severely practical ones, who thinks that the raven (or rook) had no connection with the death of Bella Wright; and there are the romantics, who believed there was a very close connection.

At all events, how did the bird obtain so much blood from the poor dead or dying girl as to cause its own death? Was that really the cause of its death? How did it chance to be in that vicinity at the moment? Since the body is supposed to have been found within a few minutes of death, how was there time for all this gruesome feasting and tracking back and forth from road to gate?

Let's return now to Constable Hall and the bullet. He and the doctor made another examination of the girl body. After the blood had been washed from the girl's face, they found a small bullet wound one inch below the left eye, and another slightly larger, the mark of the exit of the bullet, in her hair. Thus it seemed that this heavy bullet had passed through the girl's head, yet had gone no farther than seventeen feet from her!

At all events, this was murder; and it was the duty of the police to inquire where she had been, and with whom, between six thirty and nine twenty of that summer evening—daylight all the time.

At seven thirty she had ridden up to the cottage of her uncle, Mr. Measures, in Gaulby. Calling on Measures at the time was his son-in-law, a man named Evans. So both of them were important witnesses to her arrival and departure. With her, when she came, was another cyclist, a young man. Bella Wright went in, leaving the young man outside. She remarked that he was 'a perfect stranger,'and added:

'Perhaps if I wait a while he will be gone.'

Yet she did not ask her uncle to drive him away, as if he were objectionable. And when, an hour or more later, they came out again, the young man was still there—having either returned or waited. This time, he greeted her, so said Measures and Evans, with the remark:

'Bella, you *have* been a long time. I thought you had gone the other way.'

Evans had some friendly conversation with the stranger about his bicycle. And finally, the girl and the young man pedaled away together—at, say, eight forty. Forty minutes later, or thereabouts, Cowell, the farmer, was finding Bella's dead body in the Gartree Road.

Now, as the reader has noticed, there are some contradictions in this. If the man was 'a perfect stranger,' how had he progressed so far as to call her Bella? This has been answered by the statement that what he really said was 'Hello!' And that certainly goes more reasonably with the rest of his remark.

How is this for an explanation of the incident? That he was a stranger, as she said, who had joined her as she rode along; and that, while his company was perfectly tolerable to her, she had offered a little tribute to strict propriety when she said to her uncle that if she waited around a bit he would go away. Girls do not, today—if they ever did—scream and say, 'Sir, I have never met you!' when a presentable stranger starts conversation, while riding along a country road. They may welcome it, or they may simply bear it, not wishing to make a fuss, and knowing that, in most cases, the man will soon go away without becoming an annoyance.

Measures and Evans had had a good look at this man and his cycle, and so in a few days the police were offering a reward for a man of thirty-five, about five feet seven to nine inches in height, hair turning gray, and with rather a high–pitched voice. They gave a description of his clothes and various other particulars.

The notable thing was that he rode *a green bicycle*.

And for the next few months each man in Leicestershire unfortunate enough to own a green bicycle wished to heaven that he had never bought it. After he had satisfied the police as to where he had been on that July evening, he had to encounter the jeering remarks of his friends as to his diversions and his murderous disposition.

But the man really sought—the last man alive with Miss Wright—was not so easily discovered. Scotland Yard had a try at it, but could do nothing with the murder, the missing green bicycle, or the dead raven.

Half a year went by, and Bella Wright had long been lying in the churchyard, past which she rode that evening. Then, one day in February, something happened: a most peculiar chance, which, for a time, probably revived faith in the ancient falsehood, 'Murder will out.'

A canal boat was passing through Leicester, carrying a load of coal to the rubber works where the dead girl had been employed. A boatman named Whitehouse was idly watching his towrope when he saw it slacken down into the water and then tighten. As it became taut it brought up part of a bicycle, which hung in plain sight for a moment—long enough to change the whole current of a man's life—then slipped back into the water. Whitehouse had not forgotten all those police advertisements and the reward: he came back next day and dragged the canal. He hauled up the bicycle frame again, and, as he hoped, it was green.

The police were soon busy—dragging the canal for other interesting objects and examining the one the boatman had found. From the canal they fished other parts of the machine; also a revolver holster with twelve ball and seven blank cartridges in it.

The green bicycle was of a special model, made in Birmingham, and from it the name and number plate and other identifying marks had carefully been removed. But, in an obscure place, was found the number 103,648—and this was the number of a bicycle sold years before to a Mr. Ronald Vivian Light.

This gentleman was found teaching mathematics at a school in Cheltenham. He was a good-looking, rather earnest man; a little prematurely old in appearance, possibly as a result of his experiences in the war. He was a Rugby School boy; a civil engineer, who had served four years in France, part of the time with an officer's commission. Shell-shocked and slightly deaf since the great German attack in 1918, he had been discharged in 1919. For about a year thereafter (the year 1919, in the summer of which Miss Wright was killed) he had been out of work and living in Leicester with his mother. His present position dated only from January, 1920, the month before the discovery of the green bicycle.

Invited by a police inspector to explain how the fragments of his bicycle happened to be at the bottom of a canal, Mr. Light proceeded to tell a pack of lies. He said he had never owned a green bicycle; he had never seen Bella Wright; he had never been in the village of Gaulby—certainly not on that crucial evening last July.

Naturally, there was nothing to do but arrest him—especially as Bella's uncle, Mr. Measures, and Evans also, positively identified him as the mysterious man who rode away with her so shortly before the murder. And two little girls, Muriel Nunney, aged fourteen, and Valeria Caven, twelve, believed they recognized him as a man who had followed and frightened them about five thirty on the day of the murder, and in the same vicinity. They remembered this many months after the event. Some of the cartridges, by the way, found in the holster suspiciously near the sunken bicycle, had bullets like the one found in the road. But of course Mr. Light denied the holster as firmly as he did all the other relics.

Now, here was a beautiful case of circumstantial evidence. The net was drawn tight round the poor young man, who would, of course, be convicted—as in the detective novels.

About three months after his arrest, Ronald Light was placed on trial. The Attorney General stated the case against the prisoner in all its deadly detail. He began to prove by his witnesses that the bicycle belonged to Light; that he was with the girl shortly before her death; that he had concealed evidence, and lied about it, over and over again.

In the middle of this testimony, the prisoner's counsel quietly interrupted. This war Sir Edward Marshall Hall—the famous defender of accused persons, for whom everybody sent in time of great trouble. Sir Edward courteously intimated that the learned Attorney General was going to unnecessary pains. He need not prove that the bicycle belonged to the prisoner; they admitted it. He need not prove that his client rode up to Mr. Measures's house that evening, with Bella Wright; they admitted that. Most of the Crown witnesses would not be cross-examined by the defense; only one or two points did they deny.

The Attorney General and the police were probably somewhat disgusted. Here was the defense conceding three quarters of the case at the outset. What about the other quarter?

Sir Edward denied, and his client would deny, that his client had used the name 'Bella.' He had said 'Hello.' And Sir Edward took in hand, very kindly and gently, the two little girls, who said they had met Ronald Light near the scene of the murder, and who described him going about the lanes seeking to molest unprotected damsels.

When he got through with Miss Muriel and Miss Valeria, they no longer looked like two little angels of justice, but rather more like two busy little brats who, feeding for months on sensational newspaper and pictures, had suddenly begun to remember something which *might* have happened to them on some day or other—but which they obligingly fixed for a *certain* day, after the police had suggested the date.

At the end of the trial the judge advised the jury not to trouble themselves at all with the testimony of Miss Muriel and Miss Valeria.

When he began to present his case, Sir Edward played his ace. He called the prisoner to the witness stand. Ronald Light was serious, calm, and dignified. He was what we call 'a shell-shocked veteran,' who had, moreover, become partially deaf as the result of an exploding shell. There was no attempt to emphasize Light's wartime services, except in so far as his shattered nerves might explain some of his conduct.

Light now testified that he had never had a revolver or pistol since he had been sent home from France on a stretcher. On the evening of the murder he left home at about five forty-five for a bicycle ride, expecting to return at eight o'clock. He rode through Gaulby, a district he did not know very well, and at six forty-five he was near a place called Little Stretton. He did not see the two small girls anywhere. As it was still early, he turned about to go home by the long route, and this led him again toward Gaulby.

He met a girl, who was a stranger to him, standing at the roadside examining her bicycle. She asked if he had a wrench. He had not, but he looked at the front wheel, which seemed merely to wobble a little. There was nothing he could do for it. They rode on together, chattering as they went. She said that she was going to see some friends in Gaulby, and added:

'I shall only be ten minutes or a quarter of an hour.'

Light then testified:

'I took that as a sort of suggestion that I should wait and we should ride back together. I waited for ten minutes or more, then walked my machine up the hill to the church. Here I got on the bicycle to ride back to Leicester, when I found the rear tire flat. I pumped it up, and sat down on a gate; but the tire went down again and I had to mend the puncture. By this time it was eight fifteen, and I knew I was late anyhow. I thought I would ride back and see if this girl had come out. She came out the gate as I rode along, and I said, "Hello, you've been a long time. I thought you'd gone the other way." I talked with Evans, and all that he says is correct, except that I did not say "Bella."'

He further testified that they rode together for only about ten minutes; that he had still more trouble with his tire; and that the girl left him at a crossroads. He kept on the upper or more direct road; she took the lower, the Gartree Road. He had to walk nearly all the way home and did not arrive till nearly ten. On the following Tuesday he heard of the death. He read the description of Bella Wright and of his own bicycle and came to the conclusion that he was the man wanted.

He was utterly terrified. Both for his own sake and for his mother's, who was an invalid, he wanted to escape the horror of an investigation, perhaps a trial. Foolishly, as he now admitted, he refrained from going to the police at once, and drifted into a policy of silence, then of concealment, and finally of falsehood. He never went out on the green bicycle again, but hid it and at last broke it up and threw it (together with the holster) into the canal. He now frankly admitted all the lies told when the police came to him.

'I see now, of course,' he said to the judge, 'that I did the wrong thing.'

He must have been astounded again when the evidence rose against him from the canal. It is recorded that he had looked at this water from his cell, while he was awaiting trial, and exclaimed:

'Damn and blast that canal!'

Ronald Light's story, as he now told it, could not be contradicted or disproved in any detail. Five hours of cross-examination failed to trip him once.

His lawyer, who was himself an expert on firearms, sharply questioned the Crown witnesses who testified on technical points: about the wound, and about the bullet. Sir Edward maintained that such a heavy bullet, fired as they thought, from a distance of seven feet, would have blown out the back of the skull. It was absurd that it should not have traveled farther. The only explanation would be that she was shot as she lay on the ground, and even this was not wholly satisfactory.

That it was the same caliber as bullets found in Light's holster meant nothing: bullets like this one had recently been made in England by the thousand million. Sir Edward suggested that the bullet found in the road might not be the fatal one at all, and that she might have been killed by an accidental shot fired from the neighboring field. It could be a rifle bullet.

No one had appeared who could testify that Light and the girl were together on the Gartree Road; he was never placed at or even very near the scene of the crime.

The Crown had shown no motive. It was not a lovers' quarrel; the two were strangers. There had been no sexual assault. Why should Light have shot her?

The defense, of course, slid over the fact that certain kinds of murders, particularly of women and children, are committed for no apparent motive whatever.

The judge, in his charge, seemed rather to lean to the side of the defense. The jury argued the case for three hours, standing nine to three in favour of the prisoner. Then the three were won over, and they reported Ronald Light 'not guilty.' The verdict was cheered.

But who did kill Bella Wright? Probably we shall never know. Probably, also we shall never know whether we ourselves, if innocent, but in a predicament like that of the rider of the green bicycle, would behave any better.

Now to come back to our raven. A gentleman named Trueman Humphries went down to the Gartree Road, took pictures, and looked about. At the end he wrote, for the *Strand*, an entertaining bit of fiction. He imagines a scientific detective challenged to solve the mystery of the green bicycle. This detective organizes, in the neighborhood of Gaulby and Little Stretton, a shooting match. A prize is offered and all the boys and men in the region are drawn in.

There are various targets: disappearing images of deer, running rabbits, or the like. All of them are sprung upon the contestants suddenly and as a complete surprise. Before one of these sportsmen—a young lad—as he lies on the ground, firing, there rises what seems to be a dark hedge cut in the middle by a white gate. And on this gate sits a raven!

The boy tumbles over in a faint. When he comes to, he is ready to make his confession. He was in the field near the Gartree Road that July evening. He hd sighted a bird of some kind on the white gate. He lay behind a sheep trough two or three hundred yards away (there is really such a trough) and fired. He killed the raven—but the bullet also killed the girl who rode by the gate at that moment.

Far-fetched? Very likely. But it's not unworthy of the great Sherlock!

E.P.

# 1920
# The Elwell Case

In a sense which would have delighted Sherlocks Holmes, the Elwell murder was marked by a set of extremely prominent teeth. You may remember the mystery in which Holmes called the attention of the Scotland Yard inspector to the curious incident of the dog in the nighttime.

'But,' said the obliging inspector, 'the dog did nothing in the nighttime.'

'That,' said Holmes, 'was the curious incident.'

In the murder of Joseph B. Elwell, his false teeth provided a similarly curious incident. In fact they were so conspicuous by their absence that they became important evidence in the case.

When Elwell's housekeeper, arriving for work as usual on the morning of June 11, 1920, found her kind employer dying in the reception room with a bullet wound in his forehead, the gleaming teeth which had illumined many a seductive smile in his career as a philanderer, were not where she had always seen them. They were upstairs in the glass of water beside his bed.

Upstairs also was the entire collection of toupees which had long helped to maintain the illusion that he was still a dashing young blade. Forty wigs there were in that hidden collection, yet not one of them was on his head when his fate came roaring at him out of the muzzle of a .45 automatic on that June morning seventy years ago.

Before that day's sun was high in the heavens, detectives and reporters were delightedly swarming over the Elwell house, which, since his housekeeper, valet and chauffeur all slept out, was exceptionally convenient for hanky-panky.

In particular the reporters relished the boudoir delicately furnished for a guest, the monogrammed pajamas left behind there by one greatly embarrassed visitor, and the long telephone directory—obviously complied with loving care—of fair ladies, each of whom was promptly called upon for an alibi.

But if one thing is certain about Joseph Elwell's death, it is that he would have shot himself rather than let one of these ladies see him as the bald and toothless old sport he really was.

The press yearned to assume that that bullet was fired by a woman scorned, but although there is no doubt that Elwell was a ladies' man, the one who killed him was certainly no lady.

This case caused the greater stir at the time because not since a Pittsburgh defective named Harry Thaw shot and killed the great Stanford White had the victim of a murder been a man already so widely known. For this Joseph B. Elwell was the Ely Culbertson of the bridge world shortly after the turn of the century.

In the days when contract was undreamed of and the courtesy of the time said that one might not even lead at all until one's partner had replied, 'Pray do,' to the question, 'Partner, may I play?' all earnest addicts studied *Elwell on Bridge*.

Elwell left the writing of these textbooks to his wife, and he also left his wife.

After their separation, he moved on up in the sporting world, with houses of his own at Palm Beach, Saratoga Springs, and Long Beach and for a final touch of magnificence, a racing stable in Kentucky.

It was, however, in his New York house at 244 West 70th Street that he was killed, and only the night before he had been dining at the Ritz and attending the Midnight Frolic on the Ziegfeld Roof in company with men and women whose names and faces were already familiar in what later was to be known as Café Society.

All the evidence tends to suggest that he went home alone and remained alone at least until after the first visit of the postman next morning, for he had come downstairs barefoot and in his wrinkled pajamas, and was reading a letter out of the morning mail when he was shot.

Now the postman dropped that mail at 7:10 and the murderer had departed before the arrival of the housekeeper one hour later. It is difficult to escape the conclusion that the murderer was someone Elwell himself admitted, maybe someone he had sent for and was expecting, perhaps someone bringing a report from the early morning workout at a racing stable, certainly someone in whose presence he would not mind sitting with his wig off and his teeth out, reading a letter.

But why not a burglar trapped in the house and shooting his way out? Or why not an enemy—Elwell had more than one man's share of enemies—who, having gained access the day before, had been biding his time ever since? To each of these questions there are many answers, but one conclusive answer fits them both. It is difficult to imagine why any unexpected person would (or how any unexpected person could) have come around the calmly seated Elwell (whose chair, with its back to the wall, faced the fireplace), stood squarely in front of him and shot him between the eyes.

No, Elwell must have known Mr. X was there. He merely did not know that Mr. X was going to kill him.

One other point. The upward course of the bullet led the police to suspect that Mr. X shot from the pocket or from the hip. Of course there is always the possibility that he may have been a midget, a belated suggestion which will either amuse or annoy him if he happens to read this memoir of his successful but anonymous achievement. Whoever he was, or wherever he is, he also has it on his conscience that he brought into this world one of the most irritating detectives in the whole library of criminous fiction.

It was the nice people problem presented by the Elwell murder which prompted a previously obscure pundit named Willard Huntington Wright to try his hand at his first of many detective stories. Under the pen name of S.S. Van Dine he turned Elwell's obituary into *The Benson Murder Case*, introducing for the first time that laboriously nonchalant, cultured, and tedious detective, Philo Vance.

A.W.

# 1922
# Hollywood's most Baffling Murder

Although Hollywood has filmed many a four-star mystery in its time, its greatest opus in this category never went before the cameras. It was too fantastic to meet even the minimal requirements of credibility.

Only real life, which regularly gets away with murder, could have produced it.

The scene was a white stucco cottage overlooking Westlake Park in Los Angeles, the cast included some of the most publicised personalities of the film world, and the victim was the top director of one of the most important motion-picture companies of the day.

The was only one shot—from a .38-calibre revolver—but it was heard around the world. That shot not only took the life of forty-five-year-old William Desmond Taylor, but also wrecked the careers of two famous women stars and laid bare the details of a biography few screen writers would have had the temerity to palm off as fiction.

It happened in Hollywood's lush and lusty silent days, upon which the sedate film capital of today looks back with no nostalgia whatever. Every great American industry has had its rip-snorting, wild-oats-sowing youth, and the motion-picture industry is no exception. By an irony of timing, only a few days before Taylor's murder leaders of the film companies had hired Will H. Hays, Postmaster-General in President Harding's cabinet, to act as morals and policy czar of the industry.

That was the year Aimee Semple McPherson threw open her gigantic Angelus Temple to five thousand worshippers per service, who ecstatically obeyed her cries of: 'Don't let me hear any silver!'

The Rudolph Valentino madness of female America was in full cry. Mary Pickford and Doug Fairbanks reigned over the celluloid empire, more regal and less approachable than the Bourbons. And William S. Hart was inspiring small boys from Maine to California to plague their fathers for cowboys suits and six-shooters.

Just a few months before that shot, Mr. George Arliss had made *Disraeli*, Miss Pauline Frederick *Madame X*. That year was to see the world's first documentary, Robert J. Flaherty's *Nanook of the North. The Sheik, Tol'able David, The Covered Wagon* had not yet been filmed. Norma Shearer was still three long years from discovery, a thin Swedish actress named Garbo a still longer four.

It was the heyday of Richard Barthelmess, the young Gish girls, Harold Lloyd, Milton Sills, Pola Negri, Charles Ray, Wallace Reid (who was soon to die a victim of the dope traffic which was to haunt the Taylor case so persistently).

And two of the twinkliest stars in the Hollywood firmament were comédienne Mabel Normand and ingenue Mary Miles Minter—the one reputedly whom Taylor loved, and the other reputedly who loved him.

The key figure of the case was born William Cunningham Deane-Tanner in County Cork, Ireland, in 1877. His father, a British Army officer, wanted him to follow a military career. William's eyes, however, were fixed on the stage. Luckily for him they were defective eyes, and they kept him out of the British Army. At eighteen he became secretary of a theatrical company.

This unaccountable preference his military father squelched by buying him an American ranch and shipping him off to the New World.

Two years of ranching in Harper, Kansas, merely confirmed young William's conviction that he was an actor born. He gave up the ranch. But dramatic fame played coy, for in 1901 we find him selling British antiques in a shop in New York.

That year he married the daughter of a broker. Two years later Mrs. Deane-Tanner presented him with a daughter, Ethel.

Here the incredibilities begin.

By the time Deane-Tanner was thirty-one he was vice-president and manager of the swank antique shop, and he and his family were popular residents of Larchmont, a fashionable suburb of New York.

About noon on October 23, 1908, Deane-Tanner left the shop to go to lunch.

He never came back, either to his shop or to his home. The next morning he telephoned from a hotel, requesting his cashier to send a messenger to him with six hundred dollars. The cashier complied—and that was the end of William Cunningham Deane-Tanner. No one of *that* name was ever heard again!

Second incredibility: William Cunningham Deane-Tanner had a younger brothed named Dennis. Dennis also married an American girl, who bore him two children. Dennis was employed in a shop on lower Fifth Avenue. In 1912, without warning or explanation, the vanished William Cunningham Deane-Tanner's brother Dennis also vanished. And no one of *that* name was ever heard of again!

Third incredibility: William's deserted wife obtained a divorce in 1912. She remarried in 1914. Several years later she took her daughter to the movies. A tall, handsome actor with penetrating eyes appeared on the screen.

It was her daughter's father—her first husband!

The stage-struck boy from Ireland had found his heart's desire at last.

Under the name of William Desmond Taylor our hero—as in Larchmont, New York—became one of Hollywood's most popular and respected citizens.

From acting he leaped to directing, becoming the white-haired boy of the powerful Famous Players-Lasky lot and president of the Motion Picture Directors' Association. His career was crowded with beautiful women, a number of whom Taylor's influence helped to fame and fortune. He acted as literary adviser to many Hollywood stars who were his friends, notably the screen's number one comédienne, Mabel Normand.

Taylor was also up to his neck in a struggle with one cadre of the underworld. For, attracted by the wealth and luxury of the boom-town film capital, narcotics racketeers had descended on Hollywood. They found their prey only too easily. Dope threatened the health and careers of many film people, among them some of Taylor's close friends. Taylor began a grim one-man crusade against the vicious trade. He campaigned ruthlessly against the peddlers, vowing that he would drive them from the film colony.

According to a reputable source, Taylor spent more than fifty thousand dollars of his own money in the fight. Information he furnished Federal narcotics agents caused drug-criminal arrests from coast to coast.

Never a well man—Taylor suffered from a stomach ailment—he nevertheless enlisted in July, 1918, in the Canadian Army. He was discharged with the rank of captain late in 1919.

Taylor's two-storey stucco cottage was one of a group of eight such cottages forming a U and fronting on South Alvarado Street. One of his close neighbours was Charlie Chaplin's leading lady in many films, Edna Purviance. Across the spectacular courtyard gardens lived film star Douglas MacLean and Mrs. MacLean.

Now in 1921 a man calling himself Edward F. Sands lived with Taylor in that cottage. Nothing was known of Sands's background except that he had used other names in the past and had seen military service. Sands was presumably Taylor's valet and chauffeur. Actually, there is reason to believe he was considerably more than that. He seemed to have a hold of some sort on Taylor. He may have learned certain secrets involving Taylor and Taylor's friends of the film colony which they preferred not to become public knowledge.

That year Taylor went to Europe, leaving Sands in charge of the cottage. On his return he found Sands gone. Taylor reported that the man had forged his name to many cheques, had pawned a great many of Taylor's valuables, stolen some of Taylor's clothing and wrecked two of his cars.

That winter Taylor's cottage was broken into twice. In due course the burglary victim received in the mail an envelope containing some pawn tickets. They turned out to be redemption certificates for the articles stolen from the cottage—articles which had been pawned in the name of William *Deane-Tanner*!

Incredibility number four: As a result, one of the most curious theories of the Taylor murder case was to arise—that Edward F. Sand was *Taylor's long-vanished brother, Dennis*.

The truth or falsity of this theory might go a long way towards solving the unsolved Taylor case. But from that day to this "Sands" has neither been found nor identified.

The crucial events of the case took place during approximately one hour and a half on the evening of Wednesday, February I, 1922.

Some time after 6 p.m. Taylor telephoned Mabel Normand's apartment on West Seventh Street. Miss Normand's maid, Mamie Owens, answered. Miss Normand, she told Taylor, was out shopping. Taylor left a message: he had two books for Miss Normand, which either she could pick up at his cottage or he would deliver.

A few minutes later, Miss Normand phoned her maid to say that she was going to stay down-town to see the new Harold Lloyd picture. Mamie Owens told her that her studio had called—she was to be on location, dressed and made up, early the next morning. The maid also gave her mistress Taylor's message. Miss Normand replied that in that case she would pick up the books at Taylor's cottage and then come home.

Taylor usually left his front door open, even at night. When the film star reached the cottage, she heard him talking on the telephone. She waited outside for a few minutes, then rang the bell.

Taylor answered in person. He took her in cordially and mentioned the books he had for her.

She agreed to stay for cocktails. While Henry Peavey, Taylor's recently hired house-man, prepared them, Taylor indicated a number of cancelled cheques on his littered desk. Most of them, he said bitterly, were forgeries by 'that fellow Sands', but Sands's work had been so expert that Taylor himself was unable to separate the forgeries from the genuine ones.

'I'd like to lay my hands on Sands,' he told the film star grimly, 'but he seems to have vanished completely.'

House-man Peavey served the cocktails. Peavey then finished a few chores and left for the night (he did not sleep in).

Shortly afterwards Miss Normand also left. Taylor was seen walking her to the kerb, where her car waited.

At a little before 8 p.m.—only a few minutes after Taylor re-entered his cottage—Mr. and Mrs. Douglas MacLean and Mrs. MacLean's maid across the courtyard all heard a sudden sharp, loud report. Mrs. Maclean was curious enough to step out on her upstairs veranda for a look.

She saw a man, she testified later, leave the Taylor cottage. He was below average height and stockily built. He wore a mackinaw, a muffler, and a cap pulled down over his eyes. This man shut the Taylor door, looked casually around, then went down the cottage steps, turned left, and strolled out of Mrs. MacLean's view.

Neither the MacLeans nor the maid followed the incident

up. Presumably they dismissed the report they had heard as the backfire of some car.

About seven-thirty the following morning, house-man Peavey appeared at the Taylor cottage for the day. His cries aroused the neighbours.

The famous director and crusader against dope lay on his living-room floor by his desk, near an overturned chair. The .38-calibre bullet had entered his back near the left shoulder-blade.

Incredibility number five: Taylor was found lying with his legs and feet neatly together and his arms straight along his sides in a perfectly composed attitude. His clothing was not mussed. His coat was buttoned.

The position of the corpse, while "composed", was, of course, completely unnatural. After Taylor fell dead, *someone had arranged the body and limbs in that position!*

Taylor, then, had been murdered the night before, at a few minutes before 8 p.m., shortly after he had seen Miss Normand to her car and returned to his living-room.

Who was the short stocky man in the mackinaw and cap?

How had he gained entry to the Taylor cottage?

Who had arranged the body afterwards? Why?

These crucial questions have never been answered.

One of the first results of the house-man Peavey's cries was that neighbour Edna Purviance rushed to her telephone.

Her first call was to Mabel Normand. The famous comédienne, close friend of the murdered man—presumably the last person to see him alive except his killer—said later that when Miss Purviance gave her the tragic news she was first 'incredulous, then stunned'.

Edna Purviance immediately made a second call. This call was to Mary Miles Minter. Miss Minter was then at the peak of her fame. Small, pretty, with blonde curls, she was barely past mid-teens, but already a star.

Mary Miles Minter reacted with extraordinary violence to Miss Purviance's news. Her mother, Charlotte Shelby, tried to restrain her film-star daughter, but was unsuccessful. The little ingenue, favourite of millions, rushed to South Alvarado Street and ran into a courtyard milling wildly with police, reporters, camera-men, neighbours, and passers-by.

She was hysterical. She fought to get through the police
cordon guarding the Taylor cottage. She clawed at her famous
blonde curls. She screamed senselessly and hammered with
her small fists on the chests of watchful detectives . . . for
the detectives could not fail to be interested in Mary Miles
Minter's behaviour. They had found in the Taylor cottage two
pink silk night-gowns initialled M.M.M. The foot of one of
the dead man's riding-boots was to yield letters indicating that
Miss Minter had been madly infatuated with the sophisticated
forty-five-year-old director.

Only later was Miss Minter to state that she and Taylor had
been secretly engaged and had planned to marry when she
became eighteen years old. Her mother, it came out, had been
strongly against her relationship with Taylor.

The immediate consequences to Mabel Normand were
nightmarish. Her apartment was brutally invaded by detectives,
reporters, photographers, rubber-necks. A thousand questions
were fired at her from every side, reducing her to exhausted
tears. She was to say later that she never got over the shock
of realising that she was suspected by some of having murdered
her friend Bill Taylor.

It was a suspicion which in some quarters—against all the
evidence—was to follow her to her grave.

The inquest brought out nothing new, except when Mrs.
Douglas MacLean testified about the man she saw leaving the
Taylor premises shortly after the shot.

She was sure the man she had seen leave the cottage could *not*
have been Edward F. Sands. And, asked the direct question,
Mrs. MacLean replied that, yes, the stranger *could* have been
a disguised woman!

For a long time afterwards Los Angeles police insisted that
Taylor's murder resulted from his fight against the drug
racketeers. His crusade against dope had earned him the
enmity of powerful underworld forces. But this remained an
unsubstantiated theory, as did another widely held—that Taylor
had been murdered by a professional killer hired by someone
who feared and hated his influence on a person prominently
involved in the case.

And there the mystery of the death of William Desmond
Taylor stands. After thirty years nothing more is known. No

solution has ever been formally offered.

The consequences of Mary Miles Minter's involvement in Taylor's life were, to her, crushing and catastrophic. Her glamorous, profitable film career ended abruptly. She was to become embroiled with her own mother over the disposition of the more than one million dollars she had earned portraying pure young American girlhood on the screen. As *Juliet Reilly*, she disappeared from public life. She never married.

By its necessarily exposed position, Hollywood has always had to maintain far higher standards of behaviour than other groups. This at times has caused the innocent to suffer along with the guilty for the crime of mere association. Mabel Normand's career, too, was ended by that single crashing shot in Bill Taylor's cottage. The end in her case came more slowly, but it was even more crushing and final than Mary Miles Minter's.

A broken, defeated woman, Mabel Normand died of tuberculosis in a California sanatorium eight years almost to the day from that fateful evening when her friend Bill Taylor bade her good-night in the courtyard and retraced his steps to keep his rendezvous with death.

E.Q.

# 1922
# The Dot King Case

This much you will have to admit: the fact that a man lies about his whereabouts at the time of a murder doesn't necessarily prove he committed the murder.

Or does it?

Before you decide, there are certain events to consider. The other day Alberto Guimares, age fifty-six, died in his bed at the Hotel Madison in New York; but the country was too busy with a Korean war and an election campaign to pay any attention to his passing. And yet, hardly thirty years ago, his name flared across the nation. Guimares—who has been cremated at the request of his estranged wife—was

one of the key figures in the fabulous murder of Dot
King.

Dot King, who had been born Anna Marie Keenan and whose
extraordinary beauty had earned her the nickname Broadway
Butterfly, was a girl who could—and did—win the favours of
a millionaire. When it came to bestowing her own affection on
someone, however, she chose a penniless dancer—this same
Alberto Guimares, fugitive from the Boston police on a charge
of fraud.

On the morning of Thursday, March 15, 1923, Guimares
was mixing himself a drink in his room at the Hotel Embassy
when Detectives William Jackson and Francis Traynor came to
question him.

Guimares looked surprised but not frightened. He was a
Puerto Rican, slim and handsome in the prevailing Valentino
fashion, and he spoke with a Spanish accent. He demanded:
'What are you talking about?'

The detectives told him. Earlier that morning Dot King's
coloured maid, Billy Bradford, had found her mistress dead—
with chloroform stains around her lips. A broken chloroform
phial lay near-by, beside a man's pocket comb; and the condition
of the bed indicated a frantic struggle. The maid had gone
screaming for a policeman.

'But why come to me?' Guimares challenged.

'The maid said you were Dot King's lover.'

'She was my woman, yes,' Guimares readily admitted. 'But I
did not kill her. Why should I? She gave me much money.'

'How much?'

That was when Guimares made his amazing disclosures.
Within a short period of time, Dot King had given him
$10,000 to pay night-club tabs and other incidental expenses
when they went out together; $2,500 to clear himself of the
Boston fraud charge; a large but indeterminate sum to buy a
share in a stockbrokerage house; a $1,500 platinum watch; a
$750 fur-lined coat; and thousands more in minor gifts including
a $500 course in English.

'Where did she get it all?' a detective asked.

'From her Philadelphia millionaire!'

In Dot King's room detectives had found part of a love
letter—an impassioned note in which a man had written:

'I want to see you, oh, so much, and kiss your pretty pink toes.' According to the maid, the elderly admirer's name was Marshall. Guimares scornfully corrected the misconception. He identified the millionaire as J. Kearsley Mitchell, one of the famed Stotesbury clan.

Detective Jackson noticed that Guimares's right hand was swollen and scarred. 'How did you get that?' he demanded.

Guimares shrugged. 'Last night. Don't ask me where— I was too drunk to remember. I hit somebody. Can't tell you why or who.'

'And where were you between seven and nine this morning?' That, according to the medical examiner, was when Dot King had been murdered.

'Right here', Guimares said. 'Haven't been out. Had breakfast in bed.'

If you remember the case even vaguely, you must recall the sensationalism that reached its climax when the respectable Mr. Mitchell humbly admitted his infatuation for Dot King—an infatuation he had expressed in many letters and in gifts of tens of thousands of dollars.

The affair became increasingly ugly when Guimares confessed he had repaid Dot King's generosity to himself by beating her, usually when they were both drunk. Why had he beaten her? Because he had wanted to blackmail Mitchell with the letters, and Dot had refused to give them up; had refused to kill the golden goose. (The police, by the way, later found the letters.)

But all these sordid circumstances did not prove that Guimares had killed Dot King.

Even among detectives, the Puerto Rican had many defenders. Some insisted a burglar must have murdered Dot King; many of her gems were missing. Others said it might have been Mitchell, attempting to retrieve the letters. Theories popped up by the hundreds.

But there was never any conclusive proof against anyone. Though almost sixty years have passed, police never have convicted the slayer of Dot King.

Guimares had to be released from custody—though he later served a jail term for using the mails to defraud. Then he vanished from public notice and became an 'investment adviser' to Puerto Ricans. He married three times.

Now he is dead. No one will ever know whether he told the truth or lied on the morning Dot King was murdered. But I ask you to ponder on one curious fact: Guimares, living in a hotel, said he'd had breakfast in his room—and signed a chit for it—at the time Dot King was killed. *But the records of the Hotel Embassy showed no breakfast charges for his room that morning, nor did any waiter say he had served Guimares.*

Guimares changed his story. Perhaps, he said, he'd paid cash. He didn't remember.

The hotel checked its records again. No cash payments on the day in question were for the dishes Guimares said he'd ordered.

Strange? Suspicious? Of course. It seemed to prove Guimares had lied. But what stymied the police was what I pointed out at the outset: the fact that a man lies doesn't necessarily prove he committed a murder.

Or does it?

O.S.

# 1922–6

# The Minister and the Choir-Singer

On a Saturday morning in September 1922, the Rev. Edward W. Hall, a lusty and handsome bucko who, for two anxious nights, had been missing from the comfortable rectory of the Protestant Episcopal Church of St. John the Evangelist in New Brunswick, was found dead under a crabapple tree on an unusually abandoned farm which lies on the outskirts of that Jersey town. A clear case of murder most foul, it will always command a place in the archives of those of us who, as spectators, sit forward in our seats whenever such an irruption of violence turns into melodrama the comedy of a seemingly humdrum life.

By the clergyman's side, bedded with him in death, was the once troubling body of Eleanor R. Mills who, in life, had been a choir-singer in his church and the wife of his sexton. She too, had been shot, probably at the same time and presumably by the same hand, and for good measure her throat had been cut. Scattered on the ground around the bodies—strewn by that hand or, perhaps, merely by the wind—was a handful of tell-tale letters from her to him, an unwisely hoarded correspondence which, unless they were artful forgeries, made clear that the rector and the choir-singer had for some years past been enjoying, or at least experiencing, a love affair.

That element lent the case its peculiar savor and assembled its enormous audience. At that very time, over in a shrouded theater on Broadway, a magnificent actress named Jeanne Eagels was rehearsing for her long and punishing engagement in *Rain*, at which, through five seasons, the American playgoers watched a hot-eyed missionary overwhelmed by his passion for a rowdy harlot he had thought he was trying to redeem. Such little slips by the clergy always fascinate the urchin hearts of the laity, and the Hall-Mills case enjoyed its long run for the selfsame reason.

If we assume—as every hypothetical solution of the mystery always *has* assumed—that the double murder was somehow a sequel to the amorous skulduggery, then there was one moment of fatal weakness when Edward Hall had turned into the path which led to his grisly tryst under the crabapple tree. That moment came along before his unquiet eye first rested on his sexton's wife. It came when, out of a ruinous sense of filial duty, and against his own feeling that he had no call to the pulpit, he allowed his widowed mother to persuade him to study for holy orders.

The Hall-Mills murderer was never brought to book, and may even now be reading, with mild interest, this résumé of his bloody handiwork. If he is at liberty to do so, it is because, while the trail was not yet cold, there was no competent police work applied to it. You may labor under the naïve delusion that if you, yourself, are ever discovered some morning with a knife in your back, a vast, inexorable machinery will automatically start tracking your murderer down. But that machinery will prove more dependable if you can manage to be killed in a metropolitan area, and preferably at a good address. Out on the outskirts of New Brunswick, the limited resources of the local constabulary were further strained by the capricious circumstance that the bodies were found on the border-line between two counties, and in each the prosecuting authority was guided at first by a thrifty hope that the costly job would be handled by the other. The Hall-Mills murderer (or murderers) would probably have long since paid the penalty if the bodies had been found under a bush in Central Park instead of under a tree in De Russey's Lane—that crabapple tree which, while the impress of those bodies was still visible on the turf, was hacked to bits, root and branch, and carried off by souvenir-hunters.

Thanks to the newspapers, there were plenty of amateur sleuths on the job. Inevitably the reporters assumed (perhaps too hastily) that the blow was struck either from the Mills household or from the Hall household, and since the press is incurably snobbish, they all kept a rather more hopeful eye on the latter because locally the Halls were people of some social consequence, and suspicion directed their way made the better story. However, it is improbable that there would ever have been action by the grand jury if, long afterwards, the late Philip Payne, then managing editor of the *Daily News*, had not, like so many before him, become enamored of a well-advertised attraction known as Peggy Hopkins Joyce. Promptly the *News* broke out in a rash of her photographs, and Payne became so inattentive to his less interesting duties that he was fired. Stepping at once into the same post on the *Mirror*, it became with him a matter of professional pride that now this less successful rival of the *News* should pass it in circulation. Casting about him for a good opening gun, Payne, who was to be lost the next year in a disastrous attempt to fly the Atlantic, stirred up the dust which, for four years, had been gathering on the exhibits of the Hall-Mills case.

With the quite baseless allegation that the 'wealthy and fashionable' connections of the murdered clergyman had hamstrung the earlier investigations, he actually dragooned the New Jersey authorities into indicting Mrs. Hall and arresting her privily at midnight so that the *Mirror* would have a head start on the story. She had been Frances Stevens, a spinster of some means in Mr. Hall's congregation and considerably older than himself. Indicted with her were two brothers and a cousin, and the preposterous case against them relied almost entirely on the testimony of a raffish and cock-eyed old girl named Jane Gibson who, at the time of the murder, was precariously housed near De Russey's Lane. Such nuts volunteer as witnesses in all sensational cases and, if necessary, will even confess to the crimes. The reporters, who had happily named her the Pig Woman, were catnip to Mrs. Gibson and, in no time, she was not only insisting that she had heard the fatal shots, but that, oddly riding by on her mule in the midnight darkness, she had seen all these defendants on the spot since they either held up flashlights for the purpose or obligingly crouched in the headlights of a car as she passed by. At the trial, this farrago of transparent nonsense, when contrasted with the engaging candor and obvious honesty of Willie Stevens on the stand, made the acquittal a foregone conclusion.

As a gesture, the defendants then sued the over-zealous *Mirror* for libel, and when this suit was discreetly settled out of court by a payment of fifty thousand dollars, even so comparatively scrupulous a newspaper as the *New York Times* which, while the case was news, had wallowed in it for countless columns, made only a microscopic report of that settlement and printed that report as inconspicuously as possible. And the *Mirror* has not yet caught up with the *News*.

A.W.

# 7
# CLASSIC CRIMES
## (1924–36)

# 1924

# LEOPOLD AND LOEB
## Murder by Genius

Exceptional ability is by no means to be equated with an admirable character and some highly gifted people are so impressed by their own gifts that they consider themselves, on that account, exempted from moral responsibilities and social obligations. Very often, however, a man or woman endowed with an exceptional talent quickly gets used to it and learns to take it for granted. By contrast, some of those with an insignificant talent, or a bogus talent, seem to be driven into pretentiousness, perhaps in a pitiable attempt to compensate for what they regard, secretly, as an inferiority. An intellectual is pretty well bound to be a theorist, and is subject to a continual temptation to adapt his mental picture of the external world, including other people, so that it yields him the illusion that all his theories work perfectly. If and when he begins to confuse such a subjective picture with objective reality he is defeated, and under the smart of defeat his manner may become arrogant, and he may take up the attitude that he need not bother about the feelings and interest of other people because they are his inferiors. Such an attitude is at least potentially criminal. It may also be humourless, for humour above a certain low level tends to be adult, that is to say ironic, and irony is a great destroyer of arrogance.

The arrogance of the petty or pseudo-intellectual can be observed in the adolescent minds of the two Chicago law students, Nathan Leopold and Richard Loeb, who in 1924 essayed a 'perfect' murder with an intellectual motive, an intellectual purpose and a plan which, although they bungled it, might also be considered intellectual. Leopold and Loeb were the sons of rich Jewish business men: so was their victim, a fourteen-year-old named Robert Franks. At the time of the murder Leopold was nineteen, Loeb eighteen. Presumably a certain amount of discipline was accepted by them at the University of Michigan, where they had both studied, but perhaps rather less at the University of Chicago to which they had transferred when they took up the study of law.

Whatever the reason for Leopold and Loeb studying law, they studied other subjects also, including science and philosophy. Leopold, who was regarded as good at languages, made a serious hobby of 'bird watching', specialising in the habits of the 'Kirtland Warbler', till then neglected by other bird watchers. The philosophy which most appealed to him was that of Nietzsche. A strong emotional attachment existed between the two youths. Both were certainly intelligent, although Loeb, spoken of as 'charming', was content, it seems, to follow where Leopold led. Paradoxically it was Leopold who formulated the theory that Loeb was or could be a Nietzschean 'Superman' to whom he himself would act as a kind of adjutant and chief disciple.

How far their attempts to practise a Nietzschean philosophy burlesqued that philosophy those who are able to read such elaborate systematisations may be able to judge. To a non-philosopher it appears that whenever Nietzsche's writings are linked with the political and military aggressions of Germany in the first half of the twentieth century, authors and journalists spring up by the dozen to portray Nietzsche as misunderstood and even to represent him as a crusading pacifist. The notion of superiority by birth is ancient and almost universal: it is at the root of every form of hereditary aristocracy. In a collective form it is cherished by almost every state or nation and by those groups of nations or tribes who feel themselves to be united into a 'race' by a common language or by similarities of physical appearance. It springs from or releases powerful emotions and is most dangerous, as an excuse for oppression, when it is highly theoretic. The belief in hereditary superiority can be seen in the Jewish conception of a race descended from a common ancestor and chosen for special privileges by God, and seen again in the modern history of Germany and of Dutch colonial settlements in South Africa. In Leopold and Loeb the heady words of Nietzsche apparently brought ancient Jewish and modern German ideas – both families were of German-Jewish origin – explosively together. Now, looking back across the interval of four decades, the youths can be regarded, at the very moment they were claiming to exercise unrestricted power over other people as being themselves moved like puppets, by historic forces.

Leopold and Loeb were, or affected to be, bored by life. They were able to buy almost anything they wanted and they believed they understood those things which are not purchaseable with money because they had read about them and discussed them. Boredom is an impasse into which the children of the very rich are always liable to find themselves heading: it also afflicts many *soi-disant* intellectuals and may descend on criminals between bouts of law-breaking. Leopold and Loeb qualified for boredom on two of these three counts, and in escaping from what might have been a temporary malaise they turned themselves into criminals. As punishment for their crimes they were made to endure, in prison, the boredom of long periods of enforced inaction.

Most people, during adolescence, undergo manic-depressive instabilities of mood, losses of confidence and a certain amount of genuine unhappiness. Those who do not have such experiences either are remarkably well adapted to the needs of the society they are growing up into or for some reason their adolescence is belated and will overtake them later, when they are nominally mature. Leopold and Loeb seem to have escaped most of the instabilities and humiliations of normal adolescence. No unhappiness greater than boredom or pique distressed them and, although their moods might be described as variable and, sometimes, quarrelsome, they showed all the calm confidence appropriate to a Superman and his deputy-cum-creator. This they reinforced with intellectual arrogance obtained from reading and from philosophic discussions. They made a kind of mental cocoon for themselves inside which they organised a coterie for the benefit of the only two members. The coterie excluded not only other people but the ideas of right and wrong acknowledged in the outside world.

The two youths had in effect insulated themselves against society. Such an insulation can be observed, in an extreme form, in the minds of desperate criminals and in the hopelessly insane. To various extents, however, and in varying intensities, it characterises many sub-divisions of society, including religious bodies, military formations, trades unions and professions. Members of such specialised communities keep sane, and avoid trouble with the law, because they are not soldiers, sailors, airmen, believers, trades unionists, lawyers or doctors all day and everyday : they have private lives which involve them with people of widely different interests. Another safeguard is that any organisation to which they belong will almost certainly have a large membership. When members are few, as in societies for proclaiming that Shakespeare was someone else or in literary scratch-my-back cliques, the ready reckoners of sanity – a sense of proportion, a sense of humour and common sense – may not be able to operate. This is what happened to the two Chicago youths when they insulated themselves within an intellectual coterie of two.

## 2

To demonstrate their emancipation from standards of right and wrong, Leopold and Loeb became thieves, on a small scale. They obtained pistols and masks and stole, from the University of Michigan where not long before they had been students, a portable typewriter. They had not then entirely lost a sense of proportion, however, and realising that this was an unworthy activity for Supermen, they enlarged their ambitions suddenly and resolved to add swindling to theft and murder to swindling. They made up their minds to kill a victim selected almost, but not quite, at random. The victim was to be anyone, if the circumstances were favourable, whom they knew to be the son of a rich man. They made this qualification so that, after the father of the dead boy had been swindled into believing him to be alive and in the hands of kidnappers, he could be swindled again into paying a ransom. The murderers would take the ransom not because they needed the money but to demonstrate – to themselves and each to the other – their superior status. As an intellectual exercise they would plan and carry out the crime so that it would remain concealed long enough for the ransom to be paid. They themselves – who would leave no clues and whose motive only the two members of the cocoon-coterie could possibly guess – would never be suspected, much less brought to trial and convicted. It was to be a 'perfect' murder.

They first prepared a false trail by a method probably learned from books, rather than at the cinema. For the crime they needed a car other than those they owned and those which belonged to their families. A stolen car might, because in 1924 cars were rarer objects than today, expose them to the possibility of interference from the police or even from the owner. They needed a hired car but one not easily traced back to them. Leopold therefore hired such a car, using a false name – Ballard – for the transaction and also to register at three different hotels and open a bank account. Loeb sent letters addressed to Ballard to the hotels. The purpose of these preliminary operations was to create a substantial illusion of a young man named Ballard, so that if the hired car should later be connected with the murder they planned, police investigations would begin a search all over the United States, with all the complex interactions of Federal and State law to hamper them, for a young man named Ballard whose description might well apply to hundreds of thousands of other young men.

The plan was to kill the victim in the car, first knocking him unconscious with a heavy chisel they had bought for the purpose, then strangling him with a length of rope. The plan provided that each should hold one end of the rope and tug, thus sharing equally in the act of murder. This part of the plan was not carried out but it may be taken as a by-product of some non-Superman conception of responsibility and guilt; if so, it acknowledges by implication the validity of the external, 'normal' world and its morality. It also implies, perhaps, that neither Leopold nor Loeb trusted each other or expected to be trusted by the other.

### 3

The murder was committed on the afternoon of May 21st 1924. Using the hired car, the two youths drove to a stretch of open country, stopped to observe a number of boys at play and selected as their victim one they knew, named Levinson. It was obviously essential that they should not come close enough to be recognised by any of the boys but their foresight had not run to the provision of long distance glasses. They therefore drove back to the Leopold house, whence Leopold fetched a pair of field glasses which he used when he went bird watching. They returned but Levinson had departed. Another boy, however, also Jewish, a fourteen-year-old named Robert Franks, whom they knew as a school friend of Loeb's younger brother, quitted the game a little later and began to walk home. He accepted a lift in the hired car. Almost at once a gag was put into his mouth, the chisel was used to knock him unconscious, and he was laid flat on the floor of the car and covered with a rug so that he could not be seen whether the car was moving or at a standstill. In fact the blows with the chisel had already killed the boy, the rope was not needed.

With the dead body in the back, Leopold and Loeb drove around the Chicago streets until dusk. Then they drove to a marsh well known to Leopold because he had done some of his bird watching there. They took the clothes off the dead boy and threw hydrochloric acid over his face to make it unrecognisable. After that they put the corpse into what is described as 'a drain'; it may have been a short culvert or a ditch. They presumed – rashly – that the body would soon be 'washed away'. Some of the victim's clothes they buried and they destroyed other things in a cellar furnace at the Loeb house. The chisel with which the murder had been done they threw away in the marsh. They then posted a letter – written before the murder took place and typed on the typewriter stolen from the University of Michigan – to the dead boy's father, stating that 'he is at present well and safe' but making threats about what might happen if a ten thousand dollar ransom were not paid at once. The letter gave most precise and lucid instructions for the payment in 'old bills of the following denominations – any attempt to include new or marked bills will render the whole venture futile'.

This letter would not reach the dead boy's father until the following morning but the murderers impatiently, or sadistically, telephoned his house and, learning that he was not there, told his mother, using the name 'Mr. Johnson', that the boy had been kidnapped for ransom and it would be better for him if she did not inform the police. They left the hired car overnight on the drive of the Leopold's house, after washing the interior. This in itself was more than enough to connect Leopold with the fictitious hirer of the car, Ballard. The forethought and imagination of the two youths had not anticipated bloodstains, and their plan for a demonstration of a 'perfect' murder had included no provision for taking the hired car to the house. They dared not leave it anywhere else. Next morning bloodstains were still visible inside the car and needed further washing. When the family chauffeur offered to help they refused (which probably surprised him) and explained the stains as due to spilt wine. With undiminished confidence they went on with the plan. They commanded the father of their victim, by telephone, to drive with the ransom money, carried in a cigar box, to a drug-store where he would find a further letter of instruction awaiting him. The father had no sooner replaced the receiver than he learned from the police that his son's dead body, not washed away and not unidentifiable, had been discovered in the marsh.

The Chicago police examined the ransom letter and declared it to be typed, with little skill, on a portable machine. The text, they decided, was the work of an 'educated' person, except that the word 'kidnapped' had been spelt with only one 'p'. They therefore arrested three of the teaching staff at the dead boy's school, apparently in the belief that one of them would confess to the crime. There is, no doubt, an implied criticism in this not only of the Chicago police but of the schoolteachers of that vast city.

Within a week, however, a newspaper reporter came to the rescue of the police and led them to the true culprits. The reporter had possession of a pair of spectacles with horn rims, which had been picked up near the dead boy: he discovered an optician who had sold the glasses, or a very similar pair, to Nathan Leopold. The youth was taken by the police (whose minds, or collective mind, seem to have worked somewhat eccentrically) to a hotel and there questioned. He was unable to produce another pair of such glasses, but was able to name a number of people who would testify to his respectability. He had an alibi for the time of the murder – Richard Loeb had been with him, and the two respectable youths had thrust out of the car, in one of the Chicago city parks, a pair of pick-up girls, leaving them to walk home. The typewriter was not to be found – it had been thrown into a lake by that time – but a typescript of essays, done for the University of Chicago at the Leopold house, had demonstrably been typed on the same machine as the swindling ransom letter. This evidence also was discovered not by the police but by the same newspaper man who had carried a pair of spectacles from one optician's shop to another until he got the answer he sought.

The chauffeur told about the hired car with the red stains inside, and first Loeb, then Leopold confessed. At their joint trial they pleaded Guilty. Nevertheless the law of the State of Illinois compelled the prosecution to prove its case but before a Judge without a jury. An immense expenditure of words by defence counsel, Clarence Darrow and his assistants, presumably ensured that sentence of death was not passed. Instead, both Leopold and Loeb were sentenced to life imprisonment with the Judge's recommendation that they should never be released on parole. That was for murder. For the kidnapping they were each sentenced to 'ninety-nine years' imprisonment'.

Loeb died in prison in 1936, killed during a riot or brawl. Leopold, despite the Judge's double sentence and recommendation, was released on parole in 1958, when he was fifty-three and had spent thirty-four years in prison. He has been described as an almost unrecognisably changed character. A murder with points of comparison occurred in Holland in August 1960. A fourteen-year-old boy, Theo Mastwijk, was killed by three friends little older than himself – two brothers, Boudewyn and Eward Henny, sons of a well-to-do insurance broker, and Henny Werkhoven, son of a carpenter. All were alleged to have been concerned in shop breaking and thefts of cycles. Theo Mastwijk, having run away from home, is believed to have been secretly sheltered in an upper room of the large house, at Baarn near Utrecht, belonging to the parents of the Henny boys. When they had the place to themselves, the boys are said to have killed Theo Mastwijk and concealed his body in a disused well in the garden, where it was discovered a year later.

J.B.

# 1926

# DONALD MERRETT

## Motorcycles and Matricide

Another monster who, perhaps more dimly, must have been intermittently aware of his own dual nature is recorded in the annals of crime under two names. As an undergraduate at Edinburgh, known by his right name, John Donald Merrett, he murdered his mother in 1926 and successfully passed off the crime as suicide. After an interval of twenty-eight years, during which he had become known as Ronald Chesney, he murdered his wife and his mother-in-law. Merrett was only seventeen when he killed his mother, eighteen when he stood trial at Edinburgh in February 1927. He was sent to prison for twelve months on the subsidiary charge of presenting forged cheques. The foreman of the jury reported: 'The verdict under the first charge' [murder] 'is Not Proven, by a majority, and under the second charge [uttering] 'Guilty, unanimously.' This was a very odd decision indeed, so much so that Mr. William Roughhead published a full account of the case as a volume in the *Notable British Trials* series. That is to say, the case became a standard reference book for lawyers and criminologists, and a book to be found on the shelves of most public libraries, from 1929 onwards. Among the illustrations were photographs of Merrett as a small boy, quite good looking, mild and normal as could be, and two others of Merrett at the time of the trial: these are hardly to be identified as pictures of the same person, for the whole face has coarsened, the nose becoming longer and broader and the ears thicker, while the wide mouth is pushed outwards in an ugly pout.

 Donald Merrett would doubtless have liked to change his face as well as his name, when he married the daughter of his mother's friend, Mrs Bonar, who preferred, for no sinister reasons, to be known as Lady Menzies. The best he could do was to grow a beard, wear a gold ear ring and a yachting cap and move to the south coast of England. He had money, almost £50,000, inherited from a grandfather, and under advice he settled £8,400 on his young wife on the terms that she would draw the interest while she lived, but that, if and when she died, the capital sum would revert to him. He took the name of Chesney and bought himself an aircraft, a high powered car and a small sailing vessel. With these he set up as a free lance smuggler between France and England, under cover of being a gentleman of independent means with a taste for the sea.

He stood six foot high and was stoutly built, a hearty, jovial man: the touch of the buccaneer about him (which nobody except the few aware of his smuggling activities took seriously) was considered attractive. Like Neville Heath, Ronald Chesney was popular with both men and women, and he had established a second personality so pleasing to his vanity that, unlike Heath, he could keep the monster under control after its first murderous outbreak. He kept it under control, in fact, for nearly thirty years. Two reasons can be suggested for this: his monster was brutal but not sadistic, and his alternative personality, the Jolly Buccaneer, was a more picturesque and altogether grander rôle to play than Heath's ne'er-do-well. The alternative personality gave Chesney physical outlets too. It led him into gun-running from Tripolitania to Spain and in 1939 into a wartime career as a Lieutenant-Commander in the Royal Naval Volunteer Reserve.

After the end of the war he went back to smuggling, making his headquarters in Occupied Germany. In 1954, finding himself in need of money, he decided to kill his wife so that the capital sum he had settled on her in more prosperous days might revert to him. His wife was then living with her mother in a London suburb, Ealing. Chesney, who had shaved off his beard but had left the moustache, visited her there openly and made sure that he was seen and identified by various people, all the way back, by Liverpool Street station, Harwich and the Hook, as Ronald Chesney. When he returned a week later he was clean shaven, wore spectacles and had removed the ear ring. He had brushed his hair in a different style and he carried a passport fraudulently obtained in the name of another man to whom he bore some resemblance. On this journey he was not the Jolly Buccaneer but the Monster, skilfully disguised and drawing no attention to himself.

He flew from Amsterdam to London Airport, arrived undetected at his wife's house and entered in undetected by anyone but his wife. What happened will never be known in detail. All that is reasonably certain is that, perhaps using the technique of George Joseph Smith, he drowned her in the bath. It was presumably after this that he encountered his aged mother-in-law inside the house. He killed her by blows with a pewter vase and by strangulation. This was no part of his 'perfect murder' plan: he killed the old woman because she recognised him but, although he thus eliminated an essential witness, at the same time he disclosed his motive and virtually disclosed his identity. The second nocturnal murder in the red brick house at Ealing gave away the fact that the first was not what he had made it look like – death by accident while intoxicated. The plan, which involved an ingenious timetable, had collapsed. Nevertheless Chesney tried to complete it. He was to fly back to Amsterdam by early morning, so that he might appear never to have left his hotel room there. Because of fog, however – it was February – the aircraft was diverted to Dusseldorf. It was late in the morning when he reached Amsterdam, with his alibi in ruins.

Unlike Heath, Chesney (or Merrett) did not wait to be caught but committed suicide, shooting himself in a wood near Cologne. In the letters he left behind there were incidental protestations of innocence which must seem hypocritic unless they are read as coming from the Jolly Buccaneer who, although a law breaker, could claim that he had suppressed and supplanted the murderous Monster for twenty-eight years. Possibly he held that the deed spoke louder than the written word and regarded his suicide as sufficient acknowledgement from him that the Monster was not fit to go on living.

J.B.

# 1927

# EARLE NELSON

## The Gorilla Murderer

---

America has never seen anything like him before or since. There have been killers who were just as methodical and who carried out their brutal murders with just as much religious fervor—but none had the transcontinental intensity that overflowed from the poisonous wells inside Earle Leonard Nelson.

He was a killer apart, a killer's killer, a mass murderer who worked from coast to coast with a Bible in his hand.

Earle Nelson loved God. He said he did. His words oozed with sanctimonious tones, and his Bible was thumb-worn and ink-stained at his favorite passages.

Nelson carried his Bible everywhere, especially when trying to rent a room from a landlady. It was a disarming device which worked effectively—so effectively that it cost eighteen landladies their lives.

Earle Nelson was a common-looking little boy when his mother died. The orphan was taken in by a kindly aunt, Mrs. Lillian Fabian, whose religious beliefs bordered on fanaticism and who constantly chanted that 'Earle will be a minister someday.'

Mrs. Fabian encouraged her young charge to read his Bible and say grace at every meal. His whole appearance exuded purity, from his sensitive, slightly quivering mouth to his unblinking blue eyes.

If it hadn't been for a trolley car, Earle Leonard Nelson might have lived up to his aunt's pious expectations.

While playing catch with a playmate one day, Earle raced after a runaway ball and was snared by the cowcatcher of a passing trolley car. The trolley dragged him fifty feet, his head bouncing on the cobblestones, before the car could be braked.

Aunt Lillian and Earle's cousin Rachel stayed at his bedside for five days as little Earle fought death. He recovered slowly, battered and broken as he was. His bones mended, but the doctors continued to worry about the terrible blow to his skull.

Six weeks later, Mrs. Fabian reported that Earle was 'all mended and all well. The accident hasn't changed him a bit.'

But had Aunt Lillian had the psychic gift to see into Earle's mind, her blood would have run cold. For the little boy's brain had been grotesquely altered, distorted into some unrecognizable blob of horror.

At first, Earle lapsed into sullen moods of brooding silence. He would take his bible to his room and read it, underscoring passages.

Then he began pulling his cousin's pigtails so viciously that the little girl screamed in pain. At such times, a twisted smile would dart across Earle's mouth.

His aunt scolded him for this, and Earle, playing upon the naïve ignorance of his guardian, would drop to his knees and plead for forgiveness, groveling and sniveling. He would then run off to his room and babble over his Bible for hours.

Nothing Mrs. Fabian attempted altered the dark course Earle followed. She began to find him peeping at his cousin Rachel through a keyhole while the blossoming girl was undressing for bed.

Even as a child Earle's hands had been big, almost outsized, and extremely powerful. In celebration of his twenty-first birthday in 1918, Earle Nelson used those massive hands to drag a neighbour girl to her basement, where he tore away her dress and tried to rape her.

Her screams were heard by her father, who raced to the basement. It took two policemen to hold Nelson after he was arrested.

Authorities no longer agreed with Mrs. Fabian that Earle was merely an odd young man whose peculiar manners and attitudes were the result of a tragic accident. He was dangerous, a powerful bully and a threat to the safety of those around him.

The rape charge was upheld, and Nelson was convinced and sent to the state penal farm for two years. Within a week Nelson escaped, only to be recaptured immediately.

Six months later, he broke out again, and police tracked him to Mrs. Fabian's home. They found him standing in the rain, leering at his cousin Rachel as he watched her undress for bed through a bedroom window.

The penal farm couldn't hold Nelson, so he was transferred

to the state penitentiary. But the penitentiary couldn't hold him either. He escaped on December 4, 1918.

After that, Earle Leonard Nelson disappeared and didn't resurface for nine years. Police files later revealed that Nelson married a young schoolteacher on August 12, 1919, using the alias Roger Wilson.

The young couple's marital life was anything but blissful. Nelson constantly raged at his wife over the smallest if imagined slights. He accused her of flirting with every male on the street, from salesmen to streetcar conductors.

Like a preaching prophet of old, he screamed in full public view that his wife was a woman of sinful ways, a whore.

The girl finally had a nervous breakdown. But she found no peace in the hospital. Nelson visited her there and, with vulgar expressions pouring from his mouth, tore the sheets from her bed and threw himself on her.

Doctors and nurses ran to Mrs. Nelson's room after hearing her screams. Nelson raved at the doctor for interrupting his carnal pleasures. Then he accused the doctor of having intercourse with his wife. Indignant, Earle left the hospital. His wife, luckily for her, did not see him again for seven years.

The next six years in the life of Earle Nelson remain a blank, a curtain of obscurity that has never been lifted.

Nelson stepped from this maw on February 20, 1926, appearing on the doorstep of a boarding house in San Francisco.

The landlady, Mrs. Clara Newman, watched the young man in rather drab clothes approach her front door.

'Are you Mrs. Clara Newman?' the young man asked. Mrs. Newman looked him over, noticing that he was neat, clean, and of medium build and had piercing blue eyes.

'Are you the lady who has advertised a room for rent?'

'I have three rooms vacant at the moment,' Mrs. Newman said.

Something red-hot entered Earle Nelson's mind and caused a glow in his eyes as he watched the attractive Mrs. Newman lead him up the stairs to the room. He ravaged her body with his eyes—the neatly turned ankle, the swaying buttocks beneath her dress.

On the third floor, Mrs. Newman suddenly felt the young

man's arm around her throat. He yanked the struggling woman to him and grabbed the pearl necklace around her neck, twisting it into her soft flesh until she hung limp and dead from his arm.

As the pain in his head reached a white-hot pitch, Nelson gave himself up to necrophilia and ravaged the dead woman again and again.

The murdered woman's nephew, Richard Newman, found her and rattled off his story to the police later that evening.

Richard had passed both Nelson and his Aunt Clara on the stairs as the landlady took her prospective boarder to his room. His description was limited because he had only glanced at Nelson: a man standing five-foot-six with dark complexion and blue eyes. That was all.

But the San Francisco officers knew something more about Nelson. He was a maniacal sex pervert with a taste for murder. From the looks of Mrs. Newman's ravished body, he had enjoyed himself and would want more of the same.

Nelson moved South and on March 2, 1926, struck again. Mrs. Laura Beale, strangled and raped, was found dead and naked in one of the rooms of her boarding house. Again, witnesses described a short, dark-complexioned man with strange blue eyes.

On June 10 Mrs. Lillian St. Mary was found ravished and stuffed beneath a bed in her rooming house. Sixteen days later, Nelson's insatiable appetite for sexual fulfillment through death was appeased with the murder of a Santa Barbara landlady, Mrs. George Russell.

On August 16 Nelson raped and strangled an Oakland landlady, Mrs. Mary Nesbit. Then, for several months he held back. Police thought that his sexual perversion had subsided.

But it had taken Nelson time to work his way up to Portland, Oregon, where he attacked Mrs. Beta Withers on October 19. The following day Nelson killed Mrs. Mabel Fluke. Both victims were boarding-house landladies and both were strangled and ravished after being murdered.

Police intensified their search, but that didn't stop Nelson from killing and then raping Mrs. Virginia Grant, also a Portland landlady.

Nelson's ninth victim was in San Francisco, Mrs. William Edmonds. He then raced back to Portland and murdered and raped Mrs. Blanche Myers.

Ten victims and still no clues. The state of California was panicking, and the heat was so intense that Nelson decided to leave the West Coast. He ambled across the Plains States, and before the year was out, he murdered and violated two more landladies, Mrs. John Bernard of Council Bluffs, Iowa, on December 23, and Mrs. Germania Harpin of Kansas City, Missouri, on December 28.

With this last stop, Nelson added one more gruesome and perverted act to his ghoulish list: he strangled and ravished Mrs. Harpin's eight-month-old daughter.

Nelson's bloody trail can be charted by the bodies he left from coast to coast. He struck in the East on April 27, 1927, in Philadelphia, where he strangled Mary McConnell.

The berserk killer moved to Buffalo, New York, where he killed and raped Jennie Randolph. Then he swung back to Detroit and murdered Minnie May and Mrs. M. C. Atorthy on June 1.

While the entire nation was throwing dragnets out for the blue-eyed killer, Nelson moved to Chicago, where he murdered Mrs. Mary Sietsome on June 3. She was his last victim in the United States, and like all his other victims except the Harpin baby, she was a landlady.

Earle Nelson realized he could not forever elude the armies of police looking for him. He headed for Canada, and on June 8 he rented a third-story room from a Winnipeg landlady, Mrs. August Hill.

Mrs. Hill was impressed with her new and devout lodger. He even appeared at her door-step carrying a Bible.

That night, sixteen-year-old Lola Cowan disappeared. Lola was widely known and loved in Winnipeg. The lovely girl sold artificial flowers made by her crippled sister to support their family.

On June 9, 1927, police began combing the city for the girl. The following evening, a Winnipeg man returned home to find his children at play.

'Where is your mother, children?' William Patterson asked.

The children broke into sobs when they informed him that she had been gone all day. In a quick check of the neighbourhood, Patterson could find out nothing.

A devoutly religious man, Patterson went to his bedroom and knelt at his bed in prayer for his wife's safe return. After finishing, he glanced down and saw his wife's hand protruding from beneath the bed. He peered under and gasped in shock.

Emily Patterson lay naked beneath the bed, dead. She had been strangled and then raped after death.

George Smith, Winnipeg's chief of detectives, told his men: 'I think that we must operate on the assumption that the madman who has been killing all those landladies in the States has crossed over into Canada. Mrs. Patterson had been strangled by a man with extremely powerful hands and then, after death, she had been sexually molested. It is the same pattern.'

Someone pointed out that Mrs. Patterson was not a landlady, and Smith countered that the killer had changed his *modus operandi*. He not only had killed and ravished the Patterson woman but this time had done something he had not done before—he had stolen things: a complete set of Mr. Patterson's clothes, $70 in currency, Mrs. Patterson's wedding ring, and a Bible.

He had also done another strange thing—he had left behind his old clothes.

'Then we do have some clues,' a lieutenant put in.

'The clothes he left behind were probably stolen from a clothesline somewhere,' Smith said.

Smith kept his men working around the clock for the next few days, and issued bulletins all over Canada that the sex fiend had struck in Manitoba and was probably trying to escape from Winnipeg.

On a routine check of boarding houses detectives interviewed a Mrs. Hill, who denied taking in any suspicious borders recently.

'You're certain that no new lodgers have come to your house lately?' one asked her.

'None since Mr. Wilson last Wednesday.'

Mrs. Hill described Mr. Wilson as 'rather on the short side, dark, with blue eyes.'

The detectives immediately realized that this matched the killer's description and raced to Wilson's room.

There, a thick and sickening smell greeted them. Mrs. Hill apologized for the odor and opened a window.

'Good God, man' an officer cried out to his partner. 'Look here!'

Under the bed, they discovered the body of a naked girl. Her body was mutilated almost to the point of obliteration. It was the flower girl, Lola Cowan.

Mrs. Hill's husband, August, comforted his hysterical wife and then turned to the officers saying, 'To think that that fiend lay sleeping in that room for three nights with that poor dead girl under his bed!'

The dragnet that went out for 'Roger Wilson' was the most desperate and intense in Canadian history.

But Earle Leonard Nelson was now an expert at escape. He showed up in Regina, 200 miles west, the next day and rented a room. This time, he went after a fellow boarder, an attractive girl who worked at the telephone company.

Her screams, as he tore at her, brought an alert landlady, and Nelson fled, police on his trail within minutes.

In Winnipeg Smith got the report and told his men, 'my hunch is that he's trying to get back to the States. Things are becoming much hotter in Canada than he had anticipated. If he's heading for the border, he'll have to cross prairie country. That should make him easy to spot.'

Smith was right, and for the first time police began closing in on the most murderous strangler on the American continent.

Two constables, Grey and Sewell, on the alert for the strangler, were patrolling twelve miles north of the international border, outside the small farming community of Killarney.

There they saw a man walking leisurely down the roadway. He wore a plaid shirt and corduroy pants.

Pulling up alongside of him, the officers asked him who he was.

'My name is Wilson. I'm a stock hand and I work on a ranch near here.'

'We're looking for a man who is responsible for the deaths of twenty women,' Constable Grey blurted. He watched for some telltale sign from the stranger in the road.

A loud laugh greeted him as Nelson coolly said, 'I only do my lady-killing on Saturday nights.'

'I think you'd better ride back to Killarney with us,' Grey said, 'so we can check on your story.'

Nelson was nonchalant. 'That's fair enough. I guess you fellows have to play it safe when there's a killer on the loose.'

Constables Grey and Sewell locked Nelson in the small local jail. They handcuffed him to the bars of his cell and took away his shoes. Then they called Chief Smith in Winnipeg.

Sewell thought they had the wrong man and told Smith so as he and Grey stood in the telephone office. 'He sure looks like he might be the killer but he says that his name is Roger Wilson and he works on a ranch near here. Besides that, he is just too calm to be guilty of anything.'

Smith exploded. 'That must be the strangler!' he shouted wildly at Sewell. 'He used the name Roger Wilson here in Winnipeg and once before in San Francisco. It may be a coincidence but I am coming down there to question the man. Is Constable Grey with him now?'

'No, sir. He's here with me in the telephone office.'

'What! Don't let that man out of your sight! I want one of you with him at all times! And don't be taken in by his calmness and innocent appearance. Remember, twenty women are now dead because they made the same mistake.'

It was only fifteen minutes since the constables had locked up Nelson, but when they rushed back to the jail, he was gone. He had picked the locks from the handcuffs and the jail doors.

A 500-man posse was quickly formed, and all the women of Killarney were locked safely behind doors. Chief Smith sent detectives to the area by plane, and he led fifty men to the isolated village on the next train.

While the frantic search for Nelson went on, he was sleeping like a baby in William Allen's barn, only one block from the jail.

Nelson rose in the morning and calmly walked to the train station. He lounged in the waiting room until the morning express came into view.

With the air of a man confident of escape, Nelson walked slowly to the train. Just as he was about to board it, dozens of men rushed down the steps of the car, Chief Smith pointing out their target.

With his hands bent behind his back, the powerful little man was led away.

Nelson faced trial in Winnipeg for the murder of Mrs. Patterson. All through the damning testimony, the brutal killer displayed not the slightest bit of emotion. His blue eyes gazed in a stare at some inner vision and a smile played subtly about his lips.

His aunt and wife came to visit him in Winnipeg, but he only stared blankly at them, saying nothing.

A verdict of guilty was brought in on November 14, 1927, and he was condemned to death.

Earle Leonard Nelson mounted thirteen steps to the gallows on January 12, 1928. He stood on the gallows, and just before the hangman lowered the black hood over his sensitive face, he broke his strange silence.

His voice was high-pitched, the words tumbling and joining rapidly: 'I am innocent. I stand innocent before God and man. I forgive those who have wronged me and ask forgiveness of those I have injured. God have mercy!'

The hood went down, the trap snapped open, and Earle Nelson swung into space.

J.R.N

# 1927

# ALBERT SNYDER
## A 'Perfect Crime'

A chilly-looking blond with frosty eyes and one of those marble, you-bet-you-will chins, and an inert, scare-drunk fellow that you couldn't miss among any hundred men as a dead set-up for a blond, or the shell game, or maybe a gold brick.

Mrs. Ruth Snyder and Henry Judd Gray are on trial in the huge weatherbeaten old courthouse of Queens County in Long Island City, just across the river from the roar of New York, for what might be called, for want of a better name, The Dumbbell Murder. It was so dumb.

They are charged with the slaughter four weeks ago of Albert Snyder, art editor of the magazine *Motor Boating*, the blond's husband and father of her nine-year-old daughter, under circumstances that for sheer stupidity and brutality seldom have been equalled in the history of crime.

It was stupid beyond imagination, and so brutal that the thought of it probably makes many a peaceful, home-loving Long Islander of the Albert Snyder-type shiver in his pajamas as he prepares for bed.

They killed Snyder as he slumbered, so they both admitted in confessions—Mrs. Snyder has since repudiated hers—first whacking him on the head with a sash weight, then giving him a few whiffs of chloroform, and finally tightening a strand of picture wire around his throat so he wouldn't revive.

This matter disposed of, they went into an adjoining room and had a few drinks of very bad whiskey used by some Long Islanders and talked things over. They thought they had committed 'the perfect crime,' whatever that may be. It was probably the most imperfect crime on record. It was cruel, atrocious, and unspeakably dumb.

They were red-hot lovers then, these two, but they are strangers now.

Mrs. Snyder, the woman who has been called a Jezebel, a lineal descendant of the Borgia outfit, and a lot of other names, came in for the morning session of court stepping along briskly in her patent-leather pumps, with little short steps.

She is not bad-looking. I have seen much worse. She is thirty-three and looks just about that, though you cannot tell much about blonds. She has a good figure, slim and trim, with narrow shoulders. She is of medium height, and I thought she carried her clothes off rather smartly. She wore a black dress and a black silk coat with a collar of black fur. Some of the girl reporters said it was dyed ermine; others pronounced it rabbit.

They made derogatory remarks about her hat. It was a tight-fitting thing called, I believe, a beret. Wisps of her straw-colored hair straggled out from under it. Mrs. Snyder wears her hair bobbed, the back of the bobbing rather ragged. She is of the Scandinavian type. Her parents are Norwegian and Swedish.

Her eyes are blue-green and as chilly-looking as an ice cream cone. If all that Henry Judd Gray says of her actions the night of the murder is true, her veins carry ice water. Gray says he dropped the sash weight after slugging the sleeping Snyder with it once, and that Mrs. Snyder picked it up and finished the job.

Gray, a spindly fellow in physical build, entered the courtroom with quick, jerky little steps behind an officer, and sat down between his attorneys, Samuel L. Miller and William L. Milliard. His back was to Mrs. Snyder, who sat about ten feet away. Her eyes were on a level with the back of his narrow head.

Gray was neatly dressed in a dark suit, with a white starched collar and subdued tie. He has always been a bit on the dressy side, it is said. He wears big, horn-rimmed spectacles, and his eyes have a startled expression. You couldn't find a meeker, milder-looking fellow in seven states, this man who is charged with one of the most horrible crimes in history.

He occasionally conferred with his attorneys as the examination of the talesmen was going forward, but not often. He sat in one position almost the entire day, half slumped down in his chair, a melancholy-looking figure for a fellow who once thought of 'the perfect crime.'

Mrs. Snyder and Gray have been 'hollering copper' on each other lately, as the boys say. That is, they have been telling. Gray's defense goes back to old Mr. Adam, that the woman beguiled him while Mrs. Snyder says he is a 'jackal,' and a lot of other things besides that, and claims that he is hiding behind her skirts.

Some say Mrs. Ruth Snyder 'wept silently' in court yesterday. It may be so. I could detect no sparkle of tears against the white marble mask, but it is conceivable that even the very gods were weeping silently as a gruff voice slowly recited the blond woman's own story of the murder of her husband by herself and Henry Judd Gray.

Let no one infer she is altogether without tenderness of heart, for when they were jotting down the confession that was read in the courtroom in Long Island City, Peter M. Daly, an assistant district attorney, asked her:

'*Mrs. Snyder, why did you kill your husband?*'

He wanted to know.

'Don't put it that way,' she said, according to his testimony yesterday. 'It sounds so cruel.'

'Well, that is what you did, isn't it?' he asked in some surprise.

'Yes,' he claims she answered, 'but I don't like that term.'

A not astonishing distaste, you must admit.

'Well, why did you kill him?' persisted the curious Daly.

'To get rid of him,' she answered simply, according to Daly's testimony; and indeed that seems to have been her main idea throughout, if all the evidence the state has so far developed is true.

She afterwards repudiated the confession that was presented yesterday, with her attorneys trying to bring out from the state's witnesses that she was sick and confused when she told her bloody yarn five weeks ago.

The woman, in her incongruous widow's weeds, sat listening intently to the reading of her original confession to the jury, possibly the most horrible tale that ever fell from human lips, the tale of a crime unutterably brutal and cold-blooded and unspeakably dumb.

Her mouth opened occasionally as if framing words, and once she said, not quite distinctly, an unconscious utterance, which may have been a denial of some utterance by the lawyer or perhaps an assurance to her soul that she was not alive and awake.

Right back to old Father Adam, the original and perhaps the loudest 'squawker' among mankind against women, went Henry Judd Gray in telling how and why he lent his hand to the butchery of Albert Snyder.

She—she—she—she—she—she—she—she. That was the burden of the bloody song of the little corset salesman as read out in the packed courtroom in Long Island City yesterday.

She—she—she—she—she—she. 'Twas an echo from across the ages and an old familiar echo, at that. It was the same old 'Squawk' of Brother Man whenever and wherever he is in a jam, that was first framed in the words:

'She gave me of the tree, and I did eat.'

It has been put in various forms since then, as Henry Judd Gray, for one notable instance close at hand, put it in the form of eleven long, typewritten pages that were read yesterday, but in any form and in any language it remains a 'squawk.'

'She played me pretty hard.' . . . 'She said, "You're going to do it, aren't you?"' . . . 'She kissed me.' . . . She did this. . . . She did that. . . . Always she—she—she—she—she ran the confession of Henry Judd.

And 'she'—the woman accused—how did she take this most gruesome squawk?

Well, on the whole, better than you might expect.

You must remember it was the first time she had ever heard the confession of the man who once called her 'Momsie.' She probably had an inkling of it, but not its exact terms.

For a few minutes her greenish-blue eyes roared with such fury that I would not have been surprised to see her leap up, grab the window sash weight that lay among the exhibits on the district attorney's table, and perform the same offices on the shrinking Gray that he says she performed on her sleeping husband.

She 'belabored him,' Gray's confession reads, and I half-expected her to belabor Gray.

Her thin lips curled to a distinct snarl at some passages in the statement. I thought of a wildcat and a female cat, at that, on a leash. Once or twice she smiled, but it was a smile of insensate rage, not amusement. She once emitted a push of breath in a loud 'phew,' as you have perhaps done yourself over some tall tale.

The marble mask was contorted by her emotions for a time; she often shook her head in silent denial of the astounding charges of Gray, then finally she settled back calmly, watchful, attentive, and with an expression of unutterable contempt as the story of she—she—she—she ran along.

Contempt for Henry Judd, no doubt. True, she herself squawked on Henry Judd, at about the same time Henry Judd was squawking on her, but it is a woman's inalienable right to squawk.

As for Henry Judd, I still doubt he will last it out. He reminds me of a slowly collapsing lump of tallow. He sat huddled up to his baggy clothes, his eyes on the floor, his chin in hand, while the confession was being read. He seems to be folding up inch by inch every day.

He acts as if he is only semiconscious. If he was a fighter and came back to his corner in his present condition, they would give him smelling salts.

The man is a wreck, a strange contrast to the alert blond at the table behind him.

The room was packed with women yesterday, well-dressed richly befurred women from Park Avenue and from Broadway, and others not so well-dressed from Long Island City, and the small towns farther down the island. There were giggling young schoolgirls and staid-looking matrons, and, my friends, what do you think? Their sympathy is for Henry Judd Gray!

I made a point of listening to their opinions as they packed the hallways and jammed the elevators of the old courthouse yesterday and canvassed some of them personally, and they are all sorry for Gray. Perhaps it is his forlorn-looking aspect as he sits inert, numb, never raising his head, a sad spectacle of a man who admits he took part in one of the most atrocious murders in history.

There is no sympathy for Mrs. Snyder among the women and very little among the men. They all say something drastic ought to be done to her.

If you are asking a medium-boiled reporter of murder trials, I couldn't condemn a woman to death no matter what she had done, and I say this with all due consideration of the future hazards to long-suffering man from sash weights that any lesser verdict than murder in the first degree in the Snyder-Gray case may produce.

It is all very well for the rest of us to say what *ought* to be done to the blond throwback to the jungle cat that they call Mrs. Ruth Brown Snyder, but when you get in the jury room and start thinking about going home to tell the neighbors that you have voted to burn a woman—even a blond woman—I imagine the situation has a different aspect. The most astonishing verdict that could be rendered in this case, of course, would be first degree for the woman and something else for the man. I doubt that result. I am inclined to think that the verdict, whatever it may be, will run against both alike—death or life imprisonment.

Henry Judd Gray said he expects to go to the chair, and adds that he is not afraid of death, an enviable frame of mind, indeed. He says that since he told his story to the world from the witness stand, he has found tranquility, though his tale may also have condemned his blond partner in blood. But perhaps that's the very reason Henry Judd finds tranquility.

He sat in his cell in the county jail in Long Island yesterday, and read from one of the Epistles of John.

'Marvel not, my brethren, if the world hate you. We know that we have passed death unto life, because we love the brethren. He that loveth not his brother abideth in death. Whosoever hateth his brother is a murderer: and ye know that no murderer hath eternal life abiding in him.'

A thought for the second Sunday after Pentecost.

In another cell, the blond woman was very mad at everybody because she couldn't get a marcel for her bobbed locks, one hair of which was once stronger with Henry Judd Gray than the Atlantic cable.

The jury deliberated ninety-eight minutes before condemning Mrs. Snyder and Gray to die in the electric chair. Before his execution, Gray received a letter of forgiveness from his wife, who had shunned him after his arrest. He then announced: 'I am ready to go. I have nothing to fear.' Mrs. Snyder, saying God had forgiven her, died with a prayer on her lips.

D.R.

# 1928
# The Riddle of Birdhurst Rise

Birdhurst Rise, South Croydon, is one of the most respectable roads in a solidly respectable district. The houses, very late Victorian or early Edwardian, have a foursquare red brick or rendered ugliness that made them appropriate homes, in the earlier years of the century, for those pillars of the middle class who felt quite certain of their own good place in a properly ordered society. The purple weed of poison, which flourishes in the close air of bourgeois comfort, found a good forcing-ground in Birdhurst Rise.

In 1928 Mrs. Violet Sidney, a widow in her late sixties, lived at Number 29 with her unmarried daughter Vera; a little further down the road lived another, Grace, with her husband Edmund Duff, and three children; and only a minute's walk away, in the adjacent South Hill Park Road, lived her son Thomas, with his wife and children. To some people this very near association might seem emotionally stifling, but, as all the neighbours agreed, the Sidneys were really a remarkably devoted family. Grace's husband had spent much of his life in the Colonial Service before his retirement, and Grace was in and out of her mother's house almost every day. Thomas also was a frequent visitor, and came almost every Sunday with his wife and children, to lunch. It was in this happy family that there occurred three deaths by poison, deaths which offer a mystery as fascinating as the famous case of Charles Bravo and a mystery which like the Bravo case is still unsolved.

On 26th April, 1928, Edmund Duff returned from a short fishing holiday in Hampshire. He told his wife that he felt as if he had a chill, a remark to which she did not pay much attention, as he was a mild hypochondriac. However, Dr. Elwell, a friend of the family, came round to see him. Duff complained of a dry throat and a slight headache. His temperature was just over 99. He had the symptoms of influenza, and the doctor advised aspirin, quinine, and bed. Before going to bed, however, Duff ate supper, which was prepared by the maid. He had chicken, potatoes, bread and cheese, and a bottle of Bass. This was brought, as always, in a stoppered bottle standing in a pewter mug, and Duff removed the stopper himself. Later it was found that another bottle was missing and Mrs. Duff said afterwards that she thought he had snaffled it from the larder. Duff was the only person in the house who drank beer.

After his meal Duff seemed rather worse, and on the following morning he complained to the doctor, who called again, that he had been beastly sick. Later that day Mrs. Duff ordered a bottle of whisky, which was delivered just after one o'clock. Duff had two or three whiskies, with soda. Still he continued to vomit, and had severe back and stomach cramps, and in the evening Mrs. Duff telephoned to the doctor. He found Duff in a state of collapse, and administered digitalis and strychnine. Vainly, however. On the evening of 27th April, in the presence of his deeply distressed wife, Edmund Duff died.

Both Dr. Elwell, and his partner Dr. Binning were puzzled. Duff was a healthy man of fifty-nine, and it seemed likely to them that he had died from some sort of food poisoning. They advised a post mortem. By a fortunate chance for the murderer, this was conducted by a genial, slapdash Irishman named Dr. Robert Brönte. At the inquest Dr. Brönte gave evidence that there was no sign of poisoning. The coroner asked if he was perfectly satisfied? Absolutely, Brönte said. Poisoning could be excluded. A verdict of death from natural causes was returned.

Had Dr. Brönte's examination been more careful, it is likely that the two other deaths would not have occurred.

The Duffs had been married for seventeen years, in which they had had their full share of misfortune. Two of their children had died, one in 1919, and the other in 1924. They had been unlucky, also, when Mrs. Duff came into a legacy of £5,000, for they invested the money and lost it all. Since then they had been living on Duff's pension of £400 a year, with the addition of some work he did for a firm of paper manufacturers in the City, for which he was paid £3 10s. 0d. a week. The pension ceased at his death, so that Grace Duff was left with no money at all, other than two insurance policies, which were worth £1,500 together.

She used this money to buy the house in Birdhurst Rise, and her family gave her an income of about £400 a year. Most of this money was provided by her mother who, alone in the family, had rather disliked Duff. Financially, Grace Duff had not lost anything by her husband's death, but the actual change in her situation, as she said afterwards, was from that of a happy married woman with no financial responsibilities, to a miserable widow dependent on family charity.

The next death occurred nearly ten months later. The household at Number 29 consisted of Mrs. Sidney, Vera, and a daily woman named Mrs. Noakes. There was also a very old gardener, deaf and nearly blind, who worked for Mrs. Sidney and occasionally for Grace Duff. Vera Sidney was a strong and rather athletic woman, a good golf player, who drove and looked after her own car. She was usually very healthy, but for some weeks had been making entries in her diary, saying that she was feeling extremely tired, and occasionally sick. In early February she had a heavy cold, and said that she felt rheumaticky.

On the night of Monday, 11th February, Vera Sidney had some soup for supper. It was prepared by Mrs. Noakes, from carrots, onions, turnips and soup powder. Vera was usually the only person in the household who took soup, but this evening Mrs. Noakes had some, and gave a little to the cat. They were all violently sick.

On Tuesday, Grace Duff went round twice to her mother's house, and found her sister in bed. She was very poorly, and said she had been sick all night. On Wednesday morning, however, when Mrs. Duff telephoned and asked 'How is the invalid?' she was told that Vera had had a hot bath and had gone out to look after the car, which needed some attention.

On Wednesday there was soup again for lunch, and veal to follow it. Mrs. Noakes had thrown away the rest of the other soup, and had cleaned the saucepan. Now she had made some more, from the same ingredients and in the same way. Wise in her generation, she did not drink any herself to-day, nor did she give it to the cat.

When the soup came on the table, Vera said: 'Here is the wretched soup that made me ill on Monday.'

'Oh nonsense, Vera,' said her mother. 'That can't have done you any harm.'

Vera drank a plateful of the thick brown stuff. Her aunt, Mrs. Greenwell, who had come to lunch, had about six mouthfuls, and then felt she could not take any more. Mrs. Sidney had none at all. Then they ate the veal.

The results were drastic. Both Mrs. Greenwell and Vera were extremely sick, and had diarrhoea. Mrs. Greenwell was ill for six days, and then recovered. Vera was not so lucky.

Grace Duff went round on Wednesday afternoon, and found her dreadfully sick. 'I think it is the veal,' Mrs. Noakes said. Mrs. Sidney gave Vera castor oil, but she continued to vomit. Mrs. Duff thought it was gastric flu, and did not realize that her sister was seriously ill. She went home.

When she went round again on Thursday morning, it was to find that the mother had been up all night, and that Vera was extremely ill. Dr. Elwell and Dr. Binning had both seen the patient, and had diagnosed gastric influenza. Later, Mrs. Duff went round to see her brother Thomas who, rather oddly, had been told nothing about the illness. He said that he had been indoors a week himself with influenza, and they agreed that there was a lot of gastric flu about.

Vera Sidney was in suffering all that day, and died at about midnight. Afterwards, her mother asked whether there would have to be an inquest. 'No,' Dr. Binning said. 'There is no question of that.' The doctors' verdict was that she had died of gastric influenza. She was buried in the family grave at Queen's Road Cemetery, Thornton Heath.

After Vera's death Mrs. Noakes wanted to leave, but was persuaded to stay on for a little while so that Mrs. Sidney should not have to make an immediate change. The old lady grieved very deeply for her daughter. She had a weak heart and high blood pressure, and her frequent fits of giddiness alarmed her children. So, too, did her obvious depression. 'I don't know how I can go on living,' she said to both of them, but she never spoke of suicide, which she believed to be morally wrong. Dr. Binning saw her and prescribed a metatone tonic with strychnine in it, which she took intermittently.

On 4th March, rather less than three weeks after his sister's death, Thomas Sidney called on his mother, as he had been doing almost every day. This time they discussed Vera's will. She had left £2,000 to Grace Duff, £1,000 to Thomas Sidney, and had left to her mother a life interest on £2,000 expressing the wish that in the event of Mrs. Sidney's death, this sum should be equally divided between the two children. The rest of her estate (which amounted in all to some £5,500) was divided between her nephews and nieces.

On the following day Grace Duff came in, as she too did almost every day. Mrs. Sidney asked her to get some butter, and to put in an application at a registry office for another maid. After her daughter had left, just before lunch, Mrs. Sidney took her medicine. Mrs. Noakes, going in to lay the lunch, saw her mistress making a wry face as she put down the wineglass on the sideboard.

'My last dose of medicine tasted so nasty,' she said.

'Did you shake it up?'

'No, I don't think I have been doing so, Kate.'

The dose was practically the last in the bottle, and they agreed that that was the reason for the nasty taste. Mrs. Sidney then had lunch, but immediately after it she felt ill. When her daughter came back at one o'clock she said, 'I have had some poison.'

Grace Duff smelt the medicine. 'It doesn't smell very nice,' she said. She mixed some salt and water and took it in to her mother, to make her sick. Then she rang up the doctor.

When Dr. Binning arrived, he found Mrs. Sidney sitting in a chair in the dining-room, her face ash grey, her whole appearance that of a stricken woman. She told him that she had been poisoned, and that the medicine had a nasty taste. He looked at the bottle, which had just enough liquid in it to cover the bottom, with a sediment that looked like sago grains. Shortly afterwards they got the sick woman up to bed, and at about two o'clock Thomas Sidney came round. When told what had happened he said: 'Where is the medicine bottle? That must be looked after.' He found the bottle on the dining-room table, bit did not uncork or smell it.

Mrs. Sidney died at 7.15 that evening, in the presence of her son and daughter, Dr. Binning and Dr. Elwell, and a specialist they had called in. Again the doctors found that there was no need for a post mortem. It must be remembered that Dr. Binning and Dr. Elwell knew the family well, and knew how devoted the members of it were to each other; they knew also that the publicity involved in an inquest would be repugnant to them; and perhaps they remembered that in the case of Duff, when an inquest had been held, death had been found due to natural causes. Mrs. Sidney was laid beside her daughter and son-in-law.

But not for long. On 22nd March, the bodies of mother and daughter were exhumed. Sir Bernard Spilsbury conducted the post mortems. The Home Office analyst, Dr. Ryffel, extracted 1.48 grains of arsenious oxide from Vera Sidney's organs, the remains of a much larger dose. In the case of Mrs. Sidney 2.38 grains of arsenic were removed, and another grain was traceable. Her medicine bottle was examined. One grain of arsenious oxide was present in the quarter-teaspoonful of liquid left in the bottle.

Two months later, as the police pushed further back into the case, Duff's body was exhumed, and examined by Spilsbury. Dr. Brönte was found to have left the major part of the intestines unexamined, and it appeared that the parts previously analysed were the lung and trachea. Whether this was due to a mistake by Brönte or by the analyst was never finally established. Duff had been dead more than a year, but arsenic was discovered in almost every tissue tested.

Spilsbury was able to decide some very important points. He was able to say that in Duff's case the fatal dose had been taken within twenty-four hours of death. In the case of

Vera Sidney he said that the symptoms were consistent with a small dose of arsenic having been administered on Monday evening, and a fatal dose at lunch on Wednesday. In the case of Mrs. Sidney, both he and the analyst agreed that the dose of medicine before the last must have produced obvious symptoms of poison, unless the arsenic had been put into the bottle after that penultimate dose had been taken—that is, probably on the day of Mrs. Sidney's death.

Mrs Sidney's estate, which amounted to some £11,000, was divided equally between her children.

The inquests on all three victims were prolonged, exhaustive, and indecisive. The two chief witnesses were, naturally, Grace Duff and Thomas Sidney. Dressed each day in black, Mrs. Duff gave her evidence with composure, leaving court when the proceedings became most painful. Thomas Sidney, a tall, spare, grey-suited figure who gave his occupation as that of society entertainer, was inclined to argue with the Coroner, and on certain points was shown to have been inaccurate. He had loosely said, in relation to his sister's death, that he 'had had a week indoors with influenza', when in fact he had gone out for a two-hour walk on at least one day of that week. But at the time he answered these questions, as he pointed out, he had had no idea that death by poisoning was involved. The prolonged questioning upset him, and at one point he burst out:

> '*I should not mind being charged with the murder of my mother and sister. I should sleep quite soundly at nights, because I should know quite well what would be the result. I should have the experience of going into a jail, and it would be very useful to me in my lectures afterwards.*'

Arsenious oxide was plentiful available. Thomas Sidney kept a tin of weedkiller for the garden, and a cardboard box containing rat poison, and produced them himself for Inspector Hedges. Lane, the old gardener, had a tin of liquid weedkiller which had been lying about in Mrs. Duff's garden, and which she had asked him to take away in case the children should play with it. There was a gallon tin of liquid weedkiller in the Duff's cellar. Opportunity was not lacking. The back door of the Sidney house was often left ajar, with a mat against it. The beer at the Duffs was kept in the larder, adjacent to the back door, and that door also was often open.

The jury brought in an open verdict, of murder against some person or persons unknown; but they added in the case of Mrs. Sidney that suicide could not be excluded. The addition seems a strange one, in view of the fact that Mrs. Sidney had a strong moral disapproval of suicide, and said at once she had been poisoned by the medicine. In September, 1929, the police announced that they had given up work on the case; and the triple poisonings at South Croydon remain unexplained to this day.

An armchair detective would be rash to jump in with an explanation of what may always remain officially a series of unsolved crimes. The most one can do is to outline certain points which, taken together, dispose completely of a theory suggested at the time, that the murderer was a maniac striking at random. It is possible to show that the three murderers were very deliberately planned and cunningly executed. A table of ways and means will help to show this.

| MEANS OF VICTIM | METHOD | ADMINISTERING POISON |
|---|---|---|
| Edmund Duff | Arsenious oxide | Bottled beer (or, just possibly whisky) |
| Vera Sidney | Arsenious oxide | Soup |
| Mrs. Sidney | Arsenious oxide | Medicine |

In every case the poison was administered in a liquid, so that the murderer was somebody who knew that liquid arsenic has very little taste, and would not be noticed in beer or soup. But there are other points of similarity: in each case, the victim was feeling unwell before the poison was given. (Spilsbury decisively disposed of the idea that arsenic could have been administered to any of the victims over a long period of time.) Edmund Duff came home from Hampshire with a mild attack flu. Vera Sidney had been unwell for several days. Mrs. Sidney suffered From fits of giddiness, and said that she did not know how she could go on living.

The unknown murderer acted upon this already-prepared ground so that the doctors, although puzzled by the deaths, were able reasonably to attribute them to natural causes. In the first case, that of Duff, they insisted upon a post mortem: but when, through the mistake of Dr. Brönte or the analyst, this proved negative, they hesitated to ask for the post mortems in the other cases. The murderer, then, was somebody able to choose exactly the right time for the administration of poison.

There is one more deduction to be made, and it is an important one. The murderer was scrupulously careful in each case to aim the poison at only one person; partly, no doubt, to avoid the suspicion aroused by multiple deaths occurring simultaneously. In the Duff household only Edmund Duff drank beer or whisky; in the Sidney household only Vera Sidney took soup; and, naturally, only Mrs. Sidney drank the medicine. It is true that, in what one may call the trial run for Vera Sidney on Monday night, when she was given arsenic only in sufficient quantity to make her sick, Mrs. Noakes also took soup, but she gave evidence that this was unusual. But at Wednesday lunchtime, when Vera Sidney took the fatal dose, her aunt Mrs. Greenwell was also present, and drank enough soup to make her ill. In view of the murderer's scrupulous care to avoid involving any person other than the intended victim, the deduction to be made is this: *the murderer was somebody who did not know that Mrs. Greenwell was coming to lunch.*

There remain, on any count, two unsolved mysteries. How did the poison get into Duff's bottle of beer, which as the maid testified was properly stoppered, and had its paper cover untouched? And how did it get into the paper packets which Mrs. Noakes used for preparing the soup? In fifty years' time when it may be possible to speculate freely, criminal historians will no doubt offer answers to these questions; at present the file of the Croydon poisonings must carry the label, *Unsolved.*

J.S.

# 1928

# CHUNG YI MAIO
## Death of the Jade Bride

---

Wai Sheung Siu, delicate little dark-eyed lady, quaintly pretty as a Chinese doll, was the daughter of a fabulous father. Old Sheung Siu must have been the wealthiest man in Macao, that pocket Portuguese colony on the Canton River. Ruthless head of a powerful tong, his Macao estate had been turned into a fortress, garrisoned by more than fifty devoted and well-armed men. For here his treasures were housed, together with his wives, concubines, their twenty-one offsprings and, at times, his favourite child and sole heiress, Wai Sheung Siu. Old Sheung possessed the finest collection of jade in the world. Exhibited at Burlington House in London, it had staggered connoisseurs. In fact, I based a fiction story upon this exhibit.

And dainty little Wai Sheung, completing her education in Europe and the United States, was also (acting as her father's agent) getting rid of some of his treasures and depositing huge sum of money in various European and American banks. When old Sheung died, Wai Sheung inherited his vast fortune, and his jade.

Here, you will see, is a figure that might properly have stepped out of the chronicles of Dr. Fu Manchu, a girl Nayland Smith could have wanted to meet, but a character, like that of her father, I should have hesitated to offer as anything other than a creature of fantasy.

But the fortified palace of the Canton River didn't appeal to Wai Sheung. She divided her legacy between herself and her twenty-one brothers and sisters, and went back to Columbia University to continue her studies. It was during this post-graduate course that romance found her.

Fate took the form of Chung Yi Maio, at a dance at the International House. Whether or not Wai Sheung knew that Chung's father had cause to hate her own father, we shall never know. But she seems to have fallen in love with him at first sight. As their romance deepened, they had many dates, often dining in a favourite restaurant in New York's small but colourful Chinatown. Whether Chung returned her love must remain for ever in doubt, but as was brought out later, love must have struggled fiercely with family loyalty in his heart.

Chung Yi Maio was the son of prosperous Peking merchant who had left him a considerable heritage and then commited suicide. When he met Wai Sheung, Chung had broken away from unhappy family associations (which include ferocious tong warfare), studied law in several United States universities, and become a Christian.

And so, on May 12, 1928, the jade heiress became the jade bride.

Chung told chinese wedding guests that he and his wife were flying to Chicago, where he had friends, and then to San Francisco. He planned, he said, to sail from San Francisco to China.

Their itinerary followed schedule as far as Chicago only. Here they certainly bought plane tickets for San Francisco, but got up in the small hours of the night, motored to Indiana, and took an early morning plane for Montreal.

In Montreal they secured passage in a steamer to Glasgow, and on June 18, they registered at the Borrowdale Gates Hotel in Grange, beside Derwentwater, in the heart of the beautiful Cumberland Lake District.

This highly remarkable honeymoon tour seems to me to throw a new light upon the grim event to come. Their sudden change of plans in Chicago, the hurried voyage to Scotland surely suggest that their journey may have become a *flight!*

The gentle-mannered Chung Yi Maio and his petite Chinese bride brought an unfamiliar breath of the Orient into the little Cumberland village. Wai Sheung, in particular, always exquisitely dressed, wearing exotic but obviously valuable jewellery, became an object of intense interest.

'I have been looking forward to showing my husband your lovely Lake District,' Wai Sheung confided to the hotel manager. 'I came here before, you see, several times, when I stayed in England.'

After lunch on the following day, the 19th, the Maios, she carrying a gay beach umbrella and he a camera, went out arm in arm through the hotel garden. A police officer on vacation from

Southport was the last person ever to see them together—or the last of whom any record exists.

The connecting link in this mysterious story is a farm labourer working in a field beside Lake Derwentwater. He noticed a bright umbrella propped open on a beach. From the field all he could see of the woman under the umbrella was the hem of a dress and a pair of tiny feet.

He must have been a pathetically stupid oaf. Throughout all the afternoon the figure under the umbrella never stired, but he hadn't even a normal human impulse to go over and find out why. He downed tools and trudged off to the local pub.

Here it seems to have occured to him to mention the matter. The Southport police inspector on vacation was present and overheard him.

'Why,' he called out, 'it's the little Chinese girl! I was passing the wicket gate about half-past two and I saw the pair of them strolling down the lake.' Within half an hour, police from Grange and Keswick were on their way to the spot.

They found the open umbrella, and under it she lay—the little jade bride. Wearing her smart frock, she sat propped up against the bank, the once-pretty ivory face contorted in strangulation. Twine and two lengths of window-cord had been knotted around her slender neck until life was choked our of her body. . . . Which brings us to the most intriguing feature of this altogether extraordinary case—the unaccountable behaviour of Chung Yi Maio.

An intelligent and highly educated young man, already building up a profitable clientèle as an attorney, his proceedings on this fateful day of June 19 completely defy analysis. Remember, he was Chinese. The Chinese think calmly, even under stresses which might break one of another race, and they plan carefully.

At four o'clock he returned alone to the hotel and went up at once to his room. A chambermaid brought tea, but—

'Thank you,' Chung said. 'I'll wait for my wife. She went into Keswick, shopping. I came home as I have a severe cold.' (He had.)

But the afternoon passed. Night came. At 8.15 Chung inquired if his wife had returned. He inquired again at nine. In the meantime, the hotel manager had put through several calls to Keswick, but failed to get any news of Mrs. Maio.

The first news came in the person of Inspector Graham of the Keswick police. He found Chung Yi Maio in bed!

'I understand your wife has not returned?'

'No. It's very disturbing.'

'Why did you let her go to Keswick alone?'

'She wished it. She insisted that I return and go to bed as I am suffering from a severe chill.'

'Mr. Maio,' the inspector told him, 'I have a bad news for you. Your wife is dead.'

The autopsy indicated that Mrs. Maio had died at some time between two-thirty and 5 p.m. Strangulation must have been almost instantaneous. A granny knot and reef knots had been used to tie the strangling cord. There were no other marks of violence—and no sign had been found of a struggle at the spot where the body lay.

Mrs. Maio's platinum wrist-watch was still ticking on her wrist. But Chung declared that she had worn also a necklace and a diamond ring as well as a money-belt.

Police Superintendent Barson searched the Maios' hotel apartment. He found a case containing pearls, jewelled bangles, gold pieces, and some fine jade. Other items, notably a diamond solitaire and a wedding-ring, were tucked away in odd places.

Chung Yi Maio was arrested and charged with the murder.

The attorney he employed protested: 'You have no right to hold this man. You have no evidence to justify the charge.'

But Chung was kept in jail for four months and then put on trial before Mr. Justice Humphreys. Some facts presented to the jury were so bizarre and contradictory that, even now, I fail to see how they arrived at that verdict. These facts were:

1. Under Chinese law, all Wai Sheung possessed was her husband's only while she lived. With tears in his eyes, Chung Yi Maio pointed out that he could have had no possible object in murdering her, since upon her death her estate would go to her twenty-one brothers and sisters.

2. The knots on the cords used to strangle the victim were seaman's knots, which Chung had no knowledge of how to tie.

3. Chung's father had been nearly brought to ruin by the Siu Tong, of which his wife's father was formerly head. A vow

had been sworn that every member of the Siu family must be liquidated.

4. New York police authorities reported that late in May, 1928, Chung Yi Maio was summoned to a meeting of his late father's tong and assigned to execute Wai Sheung Siu. His friends put forward the theory that he planned to double-cross the tongs, which he had long since renounced, and fly with his bride to England; that the pair had been followed by hatchet-men from the American tongs.

5. Two Chinese had followed them on the dock at Glasgow; and two Chinese were in Keswick on the day of the murder, as several witnesses testified.

6. There was no evidence of a struggle at the fatal spot.

One thing in particular seems to have prejudiced the jury against him. Chung's leaving his bride of five weeks to wander alone in a strange country, and his remarkable behaviour during the hours that followed her disappearance.

He was found guilty and executed at Strangeways Prison, Manchester, December 12, 1928.

Do you agree with the jury's verdict?

S.R.

# 1930

# SIDNEY FOX

## Insurance and Arson

---

Sidney Fox, perhaps the most dastardly criminal in our annals, had, as it was proved beyond doubt at the trial at Lewes, strangled his mother in the Margate hotel bedroom before he set light to the room and gave the alarm. Either he hoped that the fire would not be extinguished till all the evidence of his handiwork had been obliterated, or at least, that the woman would be certified as having died from asphyxiation. The inquest passed off without any suspicions being aroused and Sidney Fox prepared to claim the insurance money from a short-term policy he had taken out on his mother's life. And here the luck that had hitherto been with him failed him utterly.

Insurance people are proverbially fair in their dealings, but there was something a little peculiar in a claim on an accident policy in which the insured had met with accidental death within an hour of the policy lapsing. The company patronised by Mr. Fox placed the matter in the hands of their solicitor, the famous Mr. Crocker who later spread the net that brought Harris and his firebugs to justice, and on Mr. Crocker's advice the claim was contested. And, following the lead of the insurance company, the police of Margate went, somewhat tardily perhaps, into action. An exhumation was ordered and Sir Bernard Spilsbury took charge of the affair. Under the distinguished doctor's expert examination, certain facts became quickly apparent. That Mrs. Fox had died of asphyxiation was definitely ruled out, as there were none of the customary signs in the air passages that are a feature of such cases. Neither was there any distinctive colouring in the blood to suggest the presence of carbon monoxide. Moreover, there were small but definite bruises on the tongue and at the base of the larynx which were, according to the medical evidence, conclusive. Sir Bernard stepped down from the witness-box leaving the jury firmly convinced that the unfortunate Mrs. Fox had died of strangulation and that she had ceased to breathe before the smoke from the fire reached her. Fox's previous record was one long recital of crime and vice. It was suspected that he had once before attempted murder. He was swindler, pervert, blackmailer, everything that is despicable, and his execution at Maidstone Prison on April 8th, 1929, rid the world of one of its foulest inhabitants. The timing of the murder of his mother within an hour of her policy lapsing is surely the stupidest of the many stupid acts that bring criminals to the gallows.

C.E.S.

# 1930
# PETER KÜRTEN
## The Sadist

---

*In the case of Obliger, I also sucked blood from the wound
of her temple, and from Scheer from the stab in the neck.
From the girl Schulte I only licked the blood from her
hands. It was the same with the swan in the Hofgarten.
I used to stroll at night through the Hofgarten very often,
and in the spring of 1930 I noticed a swan sleeping at the
edge of the lake. I cut its throat. The blood spurted up and
I drank from the stump and ejaculated.*

—*PETER KÜRTEN*

'From the medico-legal standpoint,' wrote Dr. Karl Berg—who
devoted an entire volume, *The Sadist*, to his subject—'I know
of no more interesting personality in criminology than (Peter)
Kürten.' One may well add that there are few studies of sex
criminals as interesting and informative as Dr. Berg's.

Kürten so captured Berg's interest and imagination by reason
of the criminal's unusual intelligence and psychological insight,
the variety of his offenses, and especially the variety of his
*modus operandi*, the latter contributing signally to Kürten's
success in eluding the police, since it is almost axiomatic in
such cases that nothing will deflect the criminal from his habitual
method of operation, even though he may understand very well
that such stereotyped behaviour will eventually lead to his
downfall. (The details have, in other words, symbolic value;
the crime is a ritual, and everything must be just so.)

Kürte, a resident of Düsseldorf, Germany, was variously a
strangler, a stabber, a hammer killer, a rapist, a vampire, an
arsonist, a thief, an informer, and a sadist who derived pleasure
not only from actual attacks on his victims, but from sadistic
fantasies and from the witnessing of accidents and catastrophes.
Following his arrest, which might never have come about save
for his emotional breakdown ('There arrives for every criminal
that moment beyond which he cannot go.')—Kürten admitted to

some 79 crimes, all of which his remarkable memory permitted him to describe in detail, though they had been committed over a period of more than thirty years. The first was an attempted strangulation in November of 1899, Kürten leaving the girl for dead, though police concluded that she must have survived since there was no record of a body's being found at that time. The last was in May of 1930—an attempted murder. He was executed in July of 1931, after being found guilty of nine murders and seven attempted murders. However, the number of his murders was at least thirteen, and the attempted murders also exceeded in number the total for which he was formally convicted.

Kürten's biography reveals that his childhood was unfortunate in many respects. His father was a drunkard who abused the members of his family, and who served a prison term for incest committed with one of Kürten's sisters. Several members of the family were or became alcoholics, and Kürten described several of his sisters as greatly 'oversexed' and himself as having been the victim of an abnormally powerful sex urge, which awakened in him prematurely. Two of his brothers served long prison sentences. The family was often in the direst poverty.

In discussing his childhood, Kürten recalled that when he was about nine years of age he drowned a boy, perhaps accidentally, while playing on a raft in the Rhine. Later he pushed into the river another boy, who was carried away by the tide and also drowned. Whether these incidents actually occurred or were false memories is not made clear.

Also at the age of nine, Kürten became the protégé of a dog-catcher who lived in the same house. Among other things, this dog-catcher taught him to torture animals by breaking off their tails and pricking them with pins, and to masturbate them—this last technic being described to the boy as a certain method for winning the undying affection of the animal.

When he was thirteen or fourteen, Kürten was fully awakened sexually. He had observed repeatedly, in the one-room apartment where the large family lived, the copulations of his mother and father, and he 'knew all about sexual matters.' His sadism had also been brought into consciousness, by his experiences with the dog-catcher.

About this time, Kürten strangled a squirrel he had captured and for the first time experience orgasm as the result of a sadistic act. He next attempted coitus with a girl, but unsuccessfully, and conceived the notion of copulating with animals. This plan he carried out, with goats and sheep available in neighbouring stables. But bestiality afforded no great satisfaction, and 'soon after that' he 'became aware of the pleasure of the sight of blood.' He then began to torture animals rather than have intercourse with them, stabbing pigs and sheep and experiencing orgasm. This behaviour he described as lasting over a period of several years, after which he 'only had connection with females.'

There followed imprisonments for theft, which he described as being motivated by economic necessity. He did not described sexual pleasure as resulting from his thefts, though this would not have been surprising considering the many facets of his perversion.

In prison, Kürten became thoroughly embittered against what he regarded as an unjust and oppressive society. He acquired a considerable knowledge of criminal techniques and of perverted and esoteric sexual practices, and became something of a father confessor to the homosexual prisoners—while taking a student's posture before the burglars and other professional criminals. Also, and importantly, in prison he developed the capacity to bring about orgasm by psychic masturbation, or entirely mental means—fantasying sadistic acts and other sexually stimulating situations. All his sexual experience while in prison was of this type—(manual) masturbation seeming to him to be both repugnant and pedestrian, and homosexual intercourse apparently holding no allure for him.

Kürten's sadistic attacks on women—and occasionally on men and children—began, as mentioned, in 1899. After that, he reported committing no further assaults until 1913, though he was guilty of three acts of arson in 1904. Undoubtedly he would have yielded to his sadistic impulses sooner, but from 1905 to 1913 he was in prison. In the year 1913, after his release, he strangled three women, made three assaults with an ax, and was guilty of one arson. But in the same year, his criminal adventures were once again interrupted, by another prison sentence, which lasted until 1921. In 1921, on his release, there was a single case of strangulation. After that, according to his confession, there were no more assaults until 1925, after which year his criminal activities mounted in intensity and frequency, reaching a crescendo in the year 1929 (23 attacks) and remaining at this high pitch until his breakdown in 1930 (10 attacks).

As mentioned, Kürten was exceptionally versatile in his sexual behavior and in the manner in which he committed his crimes. In the beginning, he employed an ax. Later, he used scissors—this confusing the police, since he used scissors open, stabbing with only one of the blades, thus leading them to think that a knife was the weapon employed. When the scissors broke off in the body of one of his victims, Kürten did not buy another pair of scissors, as another criminal would have done, but began to use a hammer—striking at the head, and usually first at temple, of his victim. One of these hammers also was broken, on a woman named Wander, and Kürten observed, with his customary grisly humor, that 'her head was harder than the hammer.' He also used, briefly, a knife, but he preferred the hammer and the scissors. These he could have in the house without throwing any suspicion on himself. The dagger, however, he kept hidden out of doors when he was not using it; and he was of course aware of how difficult it would be to explain were he to be searched and the dagger found in his possession.

The method of strangling, or throttling, was used twenty-four times. But in only one case did Kürten express any certainty that the throttling was the cause of death; and even that instance was regarded as dubious by the medical examiners. The murders were often committed by stabbing or the cutting of the throat while the victims were unconscious as a result of the throttling. On six occasions, Kürten began to throttle his victims while having coitus with them. In other occasions, he had the coitus first, and then proceeded to the strangulation. About nine of the women manages to fight free of his grip on their throat and so save their lives.

It is instructive—though not surprising to the student—to note that several of the woman Kürten attempted to throttle did not report him to the police and even to continued to see him on subsequent occasions. With his keen insight, Kürten observed that 'some victims made it rather easy for me to overpower them.' (And one thinks of those women who invariably 'have to go out' when a ripper or some other murderer is thought to be abroad.)

Although Kürten was greatly stimulated sexually by the act of throttling his victims, it was the sight of their blood that was crucial—and was most often required to bring on his orgasm. On occasion, he consumed the blood, as, for example, when he killed (after coitus) a girl he had met, stabbed at her throat, and then drank the blood while continuing to stab at her breast. In this case, he drank so much of the blood as to cause him to vomit. He also admitted drinking blood from the throat of one other victim and from a wound on the temple of another. In one more case, he licked the blood from the victim's hands; and he reported experiencing an ejaculation after decapitating a swan in a park and placing his mouth over the stump of the neck.

The considerable variation in the number of stab wounds on the bodies of the victims was particularly puzzling to the police and the criminologists. Sometimes there would be only a few such wounds; in other cases, there would be dozens. Kürten cleared up this problem; and his explanation of course sheds light on many other cases of multitude stab wounds of murder victims.

The explanation was very simple: He would continue to stab victims until he experienced orgasm. The number of his hammer blows was to be similarly explained. One might add that we see here an obvious parallel to the act of coitus: Sometimes, only a few thrusts of the penis will bring about ejaculation; on other occasions, dozens, or hundreds, may be required. When one reads in a newspaper of a killer striking again and again in his 'blind rage,' it is possible to suspect that it may have been another kind of frenzy that possessed him.

Occasionally, Kürten would have sexual intercourse with his victim while she was either dead or dying. However, one must agree with Dr. Berg that he was in no sense a necrophile. It was more likely to be the resistance of his victim than her passivity that stimulated him; and above all it was the blood that provided his climax. Thus, when he copulated with a dead or dying victim, it was only because he had not yet managed to experience his climax; and he would continue to mutilate the body, watching—and sometimes listening to—the spurting or the flow of the blood.

Kürten is not to be understood, either, as a torturer—or as the kind of sadist who derives pleasure from the conscious suffering of his victims. In his final address to the court, after his conviction, he disputed the contention of the chief prosecutor and denied that he had ever tortured anyone. There is no reason to doubt his statement. When using the hammer, he would first strike at the victim's temple, producing unconsciousness. When using the knife or the scissors, his usual procedure was to first throttle his victim into unconsciousness. He derived no pleasure from either the mental or the physical suffering of the victim, though he was sometimes stimulated, as mentioned, by the victim's resistance to his attempt to strangle her. But always the crucial and climactic act was the one producing the flow of blood, and there was no reason to inflict conscious suffering on the victim to obtain that stimulus.

Like probably most 'sex fiends,' Kürten did not at all look the part. He was a fashionable and immaculate dresser, and took great care to be well groomed. His face is pleasant and intelligent, and he was described by some who knew him as handsome.

Both Kürten's intelligence and his remarkable memory made a powerful impression on Dr. Berg, who interviewed him many times and came to know him quite well. Kürten's memory was so extraordinary that he could described in detail a room where he had committed a crime seventeen years earlier. He had been in the room on only one occasion, and then under circumstances one would expect to preclude any reportorial concern with the physical surroundings. But pictures of the room confirmed his description in every respect.

With great good humor and a delight in the gathering horror of his listeners, Kürten spent a number of days making his confession to the police. One crime after another was unfolded with a wealth of detail, so that it began to seem as if the confession were to be a kind of nightmarish Thousand Nights and a Night. Only when he dealt with events at the moment of his erotic climax or just before was Kürten's memory likely to fail. Thus, he sometimes did not recall blows struck or stab wounds inflicted at the height of his sexual frenzy.

Kürten's mind was many-faceted. He was exceptionally quick-thinking, was unusually well informed on a broad range of subject matter, and had a rare insight into both his own psychology and the psychology of his victims. On one occasion, when he had very nearly betrayed himself to a detective by returning to the scene of his crime—as he habitually did, through usually very cautiously—he quickly outwitted the man and diverted suspicion from himself. On another occasion, he swiftly turned the tables on a girl who was threatening to denounce him to the police. His co-workers had no inkling of his mental disturbance, and even his wife did not suspect him of being the famed 'Dusseldorf Murderer,' though on several occasions she became aware of his adulteries.

Though there were a few noteworthy exceptions, Kürten proceeded generally with great caution and cunning. The men he attacked were drunk. When he killed children, it was not because they were children, but because they offered such easy prey. If he encountered difficulty in overpowering a victim, he was never too lustful to beat a hasty retreat, either smoothing the matter over, or taking to flight.

For the legal interrogators, Kürten had one version of his motivation; for the medical examiners, another. Dr. Berg feels that it was with himself and the other medical men that Kürten was completely honest (though the reader of *The Sadist* is likely to have a reservation or two about accepting that).

In his dealings with the attorneys and with the police, Kürten insisted that he was driven to commit his crimes by a desire to strike back at the society that had sent him to prison and treated him brutally there. He derived great pleasure, he said, from the fears he aroused in the people by his crimes, and from their outrage. He would return to the scenes of the crimes in order to enjoy this outrage. He said nothing of sexual gratification.

(Kürten did not wish to be regarded as a lust-murderer. That he had raped some of his victims, he could not deny. Medical evidence—semen found in the vagina of one victim, in the anus of another, etc.—established that. But he sought to persuade the police and the prosecutors that his murders were primarily motivated by a desire to lash out at social authority.)

The 'medical version,' however, was quite different. Sexual satisfaction was always, Kürten said, his primary motive. In this regard, it was only due to the difficulty of obtaining victims that he did not kill more often.

Unlike many lust-murderers, who are satiated by a killing and experience no desire to commit another crime for some while afterwards, Kürten's appetites were never appeased, and his crimes knew no periodicity. Night after night he would roam the city streets, feeling immensely frustrated when he was unable to accomplish his objective. On one occasion, having the opportunity, he claimed three victims in two days. He could experience one orgasm after another in a very brief period of time.

(These 'medical version' confessions were made, many of them, after the trial and while he was awaiting execution. Much of what he disclosed about his sex desires and practices seems to have been with the understanding that the information would not be used at his trial. He did not wish to be treated sensationally as a sex criminal in the newspaper. But he had no objection to being written up as a scientific case study.)

Kürten described himself, Dr. Berg concurring, as a psychopath and a megalomaniac. To the end, he was unable to experience any sort of remorse for his crimes—or to say that he would not, if freed, at once commit others. He regretted any suffering endured by his victims; and any grief caused to their families; but in no way did he regret the crimes themselves. At his trial, and up to the time of his execution, he behaved calmly, intelligently, and with dignity. In the courtroom he admitted his offenses, but insisted upon 'keeping the record straight' as to particulars.

Berg, as others have before him in similar situations, often found it difficult to believe that the man with whom he so quietly and lucidly conversed could be a monster guilty of the most savage and degenerate crimes; and that the details so copiously provided referred not to fantasies but to actual events, and ones in which the narrator had been the main and villainous actor.

Arson also provided Kürten with sexual excitation and emission. However, by the time he was arrested—Kürten, breaking down, confessed to his wife and had her deliver him to the police so that she could claim the reward for the Düsseldorf Murderer—he had begun to desire stronger titillations in this regard. Previously he had set fire to haystacks, barns, forests, and a few dwelling places. But the idea had begun to ripen in him of setting fire to an orphanage, and committing similar crimes, which might have resulted in the deaths of large numbers of persons.

As the time of his execution approached, Kürten made a half-hearted attempt to obtain a pardon or commutation of his death sentence to life imprisonment. When this failed, he wrote letters of consolation to the families of thirteen of his victims and then went quietly and with characteristic composure to the block.

About his own execution, Kürten had expressed some curiosity. Would he, he inquired of Dr. Berg, after his head had been chopped off, still be able to hear, at least for a moment, the sound of his own blood gushing from the stump of his neck?

That would be, he remarked, the pleasure to end all pleasures.

R.E.M.

# 1931

# WILLIAM H. WALLACE
## Britain's Most Baffling Crime

Mr. Justice Wright lifted the black cap and fitted it on his head. 'The murder of this woman.' he declared, 'is unexampled in all the annals of crime! William Herbert Wallace, for having killed your wife, Julia, I condemn you to be hanged by the neck until you are dead.' On that rainy morning the judge of the Liverpool Assizes believed that the death sentence ended the case. But no jurist was ever more mistaken.

The monstrous killing of Julia, one winter's night in 1931, was unique because every circumstance that pointed to the prisoner's guilt could also be argued to prove his innocence. Famous authors have written about this crime. But in none of the writings can you find one mention of the secret hearing at which the prisoner's fate was really decided by what was truly a jury of his peers. Not even Mr. Justice Wright knew anything about that unprecedented process, which I tell here for the first time in print.

In appearance the soft-voiced insurance agent whom Mr. Justice Wright consigned to the gallows resembled that timid soul of caricature, Caspar Milquetoast. A lanky, bloodless fellow, William Herbert Wallace was taller than six feet; his hair was silvery. In neatly pressed suit and stand-up collar he peered at life quietly through gold-rimmed spectacles. Artistic and methodical, after eighteen years of married life he had remained patient with Julia's untidiness, rigid ideas and old-fashioned clothes. Whenever she got too much for him he fled to a chess club, where the dire history begins on the freezing evening of January 19, 1931.

There was to be a championship match in the warm, smoke-laden clubroom beyond the bar of the North John Street pub. But at 7 p.m., when the games began, the insurance agent had not arrived. A telephone call came for him and a barmaid answered. The caller said his name was 'Mr. R. M. Qualtrough.' Though his voice seemed far away, he was in a happy mood. It was his daughter's birthday and he intended taking out insurance in her favor. Would the agent call upon him next evening? Address: 25 Menlove Gardens, East. Fifteen minutes later, Wallace came in and was given the message. He then battled for two hours against a stubborn chess opponent, finishing as winner.

The next evening at 6:45 he set forth to find his unknown prospect. After a long ride on a tramcar he was seen by many persons wandering through the dimmish lanes of Menlove Gardens, North, South and West. Policemen, shopkeepers and others told him repeatedly that there was no such district as Menlove Gardens, East. Nor had they ever heard of any Mr. Qualtrough. Plainly he had been hoaxed. But why?

On the witness stand Wallace testified that alarm now entered his soul. Hurrying home, he arrived at 8:45, to find his front and back doors bolted. This is what he told some neighbors who came out to watch him. Try the back door again, they advised; and when he did, it yielded. A low light was burning in the kitchen, but no Julia was there. Upstairs he climbed. His wife was in neither bedroom; there was no answer to his gentle calls. Where else to look except in the front parlor, which they almost never used? On its threshold the husband struck a match and by its flicker saw his wife stretched on the floor.

With some heavy implement, never found, Julia had been pounded to death. More than a score of lethal blows had been rained on her head. She was lying neatly with her feet near a fireplace gas burner. A rolled-up mackintosh was tucked under her shoulders. The tail of the raincoat was partly burned; so was Julia's skirt, although the burner was not lit. But there was blood on it. Indeed, what object in the parlor had escaped the scarlet shower? Sofa cushions and hearthrug were darkened with damp stains; blood was on the walls, on the ceiling, on the chandelier.

Not even in such a shambles did the self-controlled insurance agent quail. Soft-voiced, he called in the neighbors, led them into the parlor. Then he led them out. They lit a fire in the kitchen range and sat and talked. When the police came the bereaved husband was in a rocking chair, stroking a pet black cat and looking them straight in the eye. Not all the questioning—days and nights of it—could break his calm; not even when they charged him with bludgeoning Julia to death.

In the view of most judges, circumstantial evidence is far better than fallible human memory, but only if the linked-up facts are overwhelming and complete. Were they so in this case? The public was convinced of it and already abhorred William Wallace as a monster. In theory it was Wallace who had made that telephone call, disguising his voice and leaving a bogus message for himself as an alibi. Quite by accident, telephone engineers were able to trace the call to a street-corner kiosk only four hundred yards from the prisoner's house, just at the time Wallace would have passed it when walking to the club. There had been trouble getting coin returns from that booth, and all calls were carefully recorded.

The rest of the crime, in the prosecutor's view, had been planned with the cunning of an expert chess player. Wallace was to be pictured by the jury as arriving home the next evening, going upstairs ostensibly to change but really to strip naked. Then he dons a mackintosh. He descends, enters the parlor and calls to his wife from the dark. He beats her to death, then carefully lays her out. Cold, he lights the gas burner, and Julia's skirt catches fire. He smothers the blaze with the mackintosh, turns off the burner, goes upstairs and bathes. At last, dressed and stainless, Wallace hastens out, making a great show of looking for a nonexistent man. After two hours he goes home to play-act some more. Where was the weapon? Thrown away on the journey to Menlove Gardens. A charwoman will swear there was, in the parlor, an iron rod fifteen inches long; and it is there no more.

The public antipathy to his client began to frighten Hector Monro, who had been appointed counselor for the defense. Wallace's life savings amounted to less than £400 and a proper defense would cost £1500 at least. No great trial lawyer, Monro wanted to call in a courtroom star who could give the accused man a fighting chance—but where was he to raise the money? Relatives could not help, nor would the officials of the insurance company. Monro decided to appeal to the trade union of insurance collectors, to which Wallace belonged. When he arrived in London, however, the union officers rebuffed him.

'But you're condemning a fellow worker without a hearing. Why not be fair to him?'

'How?' asked the president of the union. An answer, like a conjurer's rosebush, suddenly bloomed in the counselor's brain.

'Put him on trial yourselves!' pleaded Monro. 'Let me be prosecutor *and* defense attorney. You be the jury. I'll give you the whole case *against* him—and the case *for* him. Then you can decide.' So, after closing time, in the offices of the insurance company there was held a murder trial unique in the history of bloodshed. Some twenty members of the executive committee of the union sat as a jury. As convincingly as he knew how, Monro set forth the police theory.

'That,' he wound up, 'is the worst the King's attorney can bring against my client. Now what can be said for him? Remember that you are not called upon to decide who killed the woman. The jury has only one thing to decide: Is it certain, beyond a reasonable doubt, that the husband did it? True, that bogus telephone call was made near my client's house. But that is a point in his favor. If he was plotting murder, would he dare to use that phone, when some neighbor might notice him? More likely the murderer, keeping watch on the house, would use the booth to throw suspicion on the husband. Remember, the waitress will testify that the telephone voice was unfamiliar to her.

'Was Julia still alive when the husband left the house at 6:45? Fifteen minutes before, a milk boy had talked with Julia on her doorstep. So, if you believe him guilty, this man had only about ten minutes for the whole horrible job. Can anybody believe that a man could rain twenty-one blows on a woman's head, put out a fire, compose her body, bathe off bloodstains, dress himself and get out of the house, all in ten minutes? A surgeon professor will testify that those blows were dealt in a frenzy of ferocity. Can anyone imagine that timid man in a frenzy? For fifty-two years he has lived without a blemish on his reputation. And since the murder was discovered not one of his statements has been disproved.

'Most important of all—if he did it, can you tell me why? Hatred of his wife? He and his wife got on like Darby and Joan. Some other woman? No; not now, not ever. Robbery? Of what—£4 in the house? His wife's insurance? She had only a small policy. This man gains nothing by his wife's death, except loneliness. I can assure you that the prosecutor will not advance one sensible reason for my client to have murdered his wife.'

Wallace's twenty fellow workers heard the evidence fairly. In that quiet business office they put their heads together and brought in a verdict: Innocent! The whole unprecedented proceeding had to be cloaked in secrecy, for it could well have been held to be in flagrant contempt of British law. Not very long ago the editor of a London newspaper spent two months behind bars for discussing, in fictional form, a crime yet to be tried in court.

Convinced that there was not a rag of evidence to prove their associate guilty, the union members set out to raise money. Within a few days eminent counsel was engaged to conduct the defense. The trial lasted four days. Ten men and two women on the jury heard the prosecutor promise that although he could suggest no motive he would nevertheless prove the prisoner's guilt. Then came the parade of his witnesses. After that, for one full day the accused man himself stood impassive in the witness box, firm of voice as he denied everything. The jurors took but one hour to reach their unanimous verdict: guilty. And Mr. Justice Wright pronounced the death sentence.

What to do now? Never in British legal history had a Court of Criminal Appeal quashed a conviction for murder on the ground that the jury's verdict was unreasonable. But the union pushed the appeal on that ground alone. And one day three judges in scarlet robes listened to the arguments and decided there was a reasonable doubt. They unanimously set Wallace free.

Retiring to a tiny farm far from Liverpool, William Herbert Wallace installed in his lonely home a system of lights and burglar alarms. Guns were always at hand. He wrote that someone unknown was coming to finish him off, as Julia had been finished. After two years of terror he died a natural death. Was the fearful old fellow really a murderer? To this day you can have an argument on that in any pub in Liverpool. No one will ever know.

A.A.

# 1931

# A.A. ROUSE
## The Phoney Phoenix

---

The man who stood in the dock became one of those subjects for hilarious and impious jokes, on and off the music-hall stage, that are from time to time produced by British courts of justice. There was contradictory evidence by experts, a summing up by a Judge who obviously put considerable faith in the evidence offered, again by Sir Bernard Spilsbury, and after the trial more appeals to the Home Secretary and further bickering in those columns of the Press devoted to the outpourings of people with figurative axes to grind.

It was the trial before Mr. Justice Talbot during the 1931 Northampton Winter Assizes of Alfred Arthur Rouse, a man whose liking for alcohol in most forms was exceeded only by his fondness for philandering with young women foolish enough to listen to his practised tongue. A man who was described by the Judge who sentenced him to death as a 'most facile liar', and that when he was addressing the jury. It was also a trial in which a familiar barrister appeared in an unusual role. Mr. Norman Birkett, the eminent K.C., whose reputation at that time as a distinguished counsel for the defence was a very enviable one, appeared in the robes of counsel leading for the prosecution. The defence, on this occasion led by Mr. A. P. Marshall, included a figure to become redoubtable in English courts, Mr. Donald Finnemore, later Mr. Justice Finnemore, a popular and respected Judge. The trial of John Reginald Halliday Christie, over which he presided, is included later in this book.

Rouse, the doubtful hero of bawdy ballads, was a man who attempted in real life what novelists have for long tried to create—the perfect crime. The most ironical feature of a bizarre crime was that Rouse might have been successful in that attempt had he thought of one detail omitted from his carefully made calculations.

This man who was a past-master at telling tavern tales, whose glib tongue had smoothed his passage from many a rough situation, actually forgot to have a story ready to tell in case the unexpected happened. It seems incredible unless one accepts that Justice really does work best with a bandage around her head and covering her eyes. The man whose tongue and wits had always co-operated with perfect co-ordination was stumped for a convenient lie when he most needed it.

Rouse was born in Herne Hill, South London, ten years after Adelaide Bartlett and her grocer husband left the district to take up residence at the Cottage in Merton Abbey. His father might possibly have supplied Adelaide with stockings or her husband with socks. He was a hosier, and his son Arthur, despite the separation of his parents when he was six and the break-up of his home, grew up to be the kind of lad of whom a tradesman and his wife could be proud. He was good at schoolwork, could use his hands deftly, and was fond of music. He went regularly to church in his teens, and by the time he was leaving them he had a fairly good position with bright prospects. Before he was twenty-one he had found the girl of his choice, and was planning an autumn wedding. His date with his bride-to-be was postponed by the outbreak of the same war that found a patriotic response in the mind and heart of Norman Thorn. Rouse was married at the end of 1914. It was a Khaki wedding, and a few months later, in the spring of 1915, he went with his Territorial battalion to France. He caught what was known as a blighty wound in May, after being overseas for barely three months. A shell bursting at Givenchy struck him in the head and thigh.

He was brought back to England a stretcher case, and he was still convalescing when he had a letter from France which announced that he was the father of a French girl's child. In the next fifteen years he was to receive quite a few such letters from young women who found him attractive and hard to resist. But in those years Rouse changed from the young warrior in a hurry to join up. His wounds, which left him scarred physically and possibly mentally, became the seal of a new-found cynicism. In the age of the Bright Young Things and the Charleston and the regular broadcasts of the Savoy Orpheans, Arthur Rouse tried to live to the tempo of the times. But he tried to do it with no comfortable lining to his pocket. He went from job to job, and finally ended his search by accepting the fact that Fate had fashioned him to be a commercial traveller. He was a hard drinker, a fast traveller in his Morris car, and, as he might have described himself, a rare one with the women.

By 1930, a year when unemployment figures were depressing those who read them, many folks would have envied Arthur Rouse his place in the social scale. He was travelling for a firm that manufactured men's braces and sock suspenders, and with commission was clearing around £500 a year. He had his car and a house which he was buying through a building society.

But by that year life was becoming over-complicated for the man who had acted so injudiciously the part of Cupid's king-size gift to the other sex. Almost half his income disappeared on regular payments for the house and car and to his wife. With the other half he was paying out on at least two maintenance orders, sending money towards a child's upkeep in Paris, and paying for a child that was not his wife's, but lived in his home. His money was used up before he had it. His future prospects were in pawn. There were towns in England he had to avoid on his commercial journeys because of the demands likely to be made on him by women he had seduced with his fine words and pretensions to being a bachelor of means. Some eighty seduction cases were subsequently traced to him. His wife, unable to have children, had stood for his incredible infidelities, and had even agreed to become foster-mother to one of his illegitimate offspring. But in 1930 she had reached the end of wifely patience with a man who could not or would not change his lecherous ways. She told him she wanted a separation.

He was in a perturbed and brooding state of mind, worrying about lack of money and how to make more, when he read of a murder at Epsom around Derby time. A waitress named Agnes Kesson had been found strangled and lying in a ditch near the Downs. The police made exhaustive inquiries, but got nowhere. The murderer had got away with his crime. That fact intrigued and fascinated the man hard pressed to pay his debts. He thought about it for weeks, toyed with the idea of how he might beat the police. What one man could do, surely Arthur Rouse could improve on and better. Not merely a murder, but the complete obliteration of a personality. The personality of Alfred Arthur Rouse.

He lived with the idea for weeks, until he was convinced he saw how to work this adroit disappearance that would solve all his financial problems and simplify life so that he could hope to enjoy it again. He must find some unknown who had no relatives. He must kill this unknown and destroy his body so that it could not be recognized. But the crime must be so contrived that the unrecognizable corpse must be accepted as that of Arthur Rouse. Then he would be officially dead, and the police would not seek him. He could disappear at his leisure, adopt a completely new identity, and start a fresh life among strangers.

The man haunted by debts and pressed by daily circumstances into an ever-growing position of helplessness saw this fantastic possibility as promise of heaven on earth. But first he had to create his own miniature hades. He had to find the necessary unknown. He had to plan, and most carefully. Fire would best serve him. And he had the means of driving to a lonely place. But a fire is a very conspicuous and attractive spectacle on the public highway, in a city street, or even in the open countryside.

Except for one night in the year. November the 5th. Bonfire Night. Guy Fawkes' Night.

When he realized that he knew he had hit upon his perfect crime. He must find an unknown, promise him anything to ensure the man travelled with him in his car on the night of November the 5th. Out in the country it would be simple. A swift blow or a shot, a dousing with a spare can of petrol, a match, and all he would have to do would be to think up a new name. It was so perfect, as he outlined the crime to himself and went over the various details, that he was excited and thrilled. This would be the best lie he had ever told, and he wouldn't have to say a word to be believed. The authorities would do it all for him, say all that was to be said. It was so foolproof, he wanted to laugh.

The only joke he would be unable to share with bar-room cronies would be the truth about the phoney phoenix. Who would believe him, anyway? If he told them, they wouldn't fall for such a tall story. It was well-nigh past belief. Even for the man who had thought it up.

Yet forty-eight hours after Bonfire Night 1930 he sat in Hammersmith police-station and made a statement to a detective-sergeant. It wasn't the story he had lived with so long. But it was still incredible.

It read:

> *I picked the man up on the Great North Road. He asked me for a lift. He seemed a respectable man and said he was going to the Midlands. I gave him a lift. It was just this side of St. Albans. He got in, and I drove off, and after going some distance I lost my way. A policeman spoke to me about my lights. I did not know anything about the man, and I thought I saw his hand on my case, which was in the back of the car. I later became sleepy and could hardly keep awake. The engine started to spit, and I thought I was running out of petrol. I wanted to relieve myself, and said to the man, 'There is some petrol in the can. You can empty it into the tank while I'm gone,' and I lifted the bonnet and showed him where to put it in. He said, 'What about a smoke?' I said, 'I have given you all my cigarettes as it is.' I then went some distance along the road, and had just got my trousers down when I noticed a big flame from behind. I pulled my trousers up quickly and ran towards the car, which was in flames. I saw the man was inside, and I tried to open the door, but I could not as the car was then a mass of flames. I then began to tremble violently. I was all of a*

> *shake. I did not known what to do, and I ran as hard as I could along the road, where I saw the two men. I felt I was responsible for what had happened. I lost my head, and I didn't known what to do, and I really don't known what I have done since.*

Possibly the only sure piece of truth in that statement is that Rouse lost his head. The car certainly became a mass of flames, but it took a trial to determine that Rouse himself was responsible for the fire, not the vagrant he had picked up. And most likely the unknown was picked up in a bar, not on the public highway. What is reasonably certain is that Rouse was on his way to Leicester that night and picked up his victim somewhere in North London or on the outskirts. The object of the journey was to collect some commission due from the firm for whom he travelled. What is known for certain is that at two o'clock the next morning Rouse's car was blazing in a lane not far from the village of Hardingstone. He started to walk down the lane, the man who had to think of a fresh identity. He saw the lights of another car coming towards him, and without thinking jumped into a ditch beside the hedge. He peered at the field on the far side of the hedge. In the bright moonlight it looked rutted with plough lanes, so he did not risk walking across it and leaving footprints. Actually the moonlight was deceptive. The field was grassed over. He could have walked through the hedge and into the new life he had risked so much to find.

Instead he waited until the car had gone by, then straightened and stepped back on to the road, and came almost at once face to face with two young men named Bailey and Brown. His appearance from the earth at their feet, as it seemed, startled them. They had started home not long before from a dance, and now stood staring at the stranger etched in bright moonlight. They saw clearly every feature of his face and clothes, and Rouse knew it.

One of the pair said, 'Hallo, what's that blaze?'

'Looks like someone's having a late bonfire,' was his rejoinder before stepping past them and striding out. That lonely lane was quite a step from the main Leicester road. He didn't have to turn and look back to know that they were on their way to stare at the blazing car and that soon the police would be told, and then the meeting with the hatless man rising from the ditch would be remembered and his description given. His memory of that next ten minutes was refreshed during the trial in January 1931, when Mr. Norman Birkett questioned him about his strange behaviour after he found the car blazing.

'I got panicky,' was Rouse's feeble excuse. 'It was my car and I thought there was a man inside.'

'What were you panicky about?' Mr. Birkett pressed.

'I consider I had every reason to be panicky,' replied the flustered prisoner. 'I admit I was panicky.'

Of what?'

'The blaze.'

Mr. Birkett leaned forward. 'Do you mean that the mere blaze frightened you?'

'Yes, and I thought a man was inside.'

'Was that not all the more reason why you should try to help or get help?' was the next relentless question.

'Yes.'

'You went to get help?'

'Yes.'

'Why did you stop?'

Rouse switched to his first statement to the police. 'I lost my head.' Mr. Birkett still pressed him. 'But why did you lose your head? Do you mean you thought you would be blamed?'

He received no direct answer as Rouse fumbled with the words, repeating himself. 'I lost my head. I don't know why I lost my head, but I lost my wits. I will put it that way.'

The jury were not very impressed. They had heard evidence that Arthur Rouse had been actually things so many ways since he had walked from the fire. He had actually walked to a crossroads and secured a lift on a night lorry, and was set down in London. In a London hospital was a girl who was expecting her second baby. Arthur Rouse was the father. In a Welsh village was a nurse who had told her family she was married to him. She was expecting her first baby by him. She was also expecting him to arrive in Wales on November 6th. Because his plans had gone badly awry, he went to Wales.

He was there when his wife was taken to Northampton by the police. This news was in the newspapers on the 7th. He realized he had to bluff it out, and it was already late. He couldn't remain in hiding. He returned by coach to London, and made the statement to the sergeant at Hammersmith. He was taken to Angle Lane police-station, in Northampton. There he met Bailey and Brown in daylight. He looked identical with the man they had last seen in the light of the moon.

But by this time the police had a few more questions ready. For instance, a mallet had been found lying on a grass verge fourteen feet from the Holocaust. When asked about this by Inspector Lawrence, Rouse said readily, 'It's possible the man I left in the car may have used the mallet to undo the stopper of the can of petrol.'

But in cross-examination at the trial he said he had taken the stopper out of the petrol can, and had used the mallet's handle.

This was only one of very many discrepancies between his original and subsequent statements and the evidence he gave on the fourth day of his trial when he stepped into the witness-box. There, under fire from Mr. Birkett, he tried to recapture his nerve, and adopted a callous attitude towards the fire, the dead man, and even the trial he was undergoing. Some of his answers had a smart-aleck flavour, and he went to great lengths to provide a false verisimilitude to some of his flights of fancy.

For instance, there was a detail about the same mallet that had to be explained satisfactorily, and he attempted to do that. A human hair had been found on the mallet. His ingenious explanation started with his wife.

'My wife trained as a hairdresser,' he told the court. 'She never went into the business seriously at all, but two or three times she has occasionally—not every week—cut neighbours' hair or her friends' hair, including my own occasionally, and that is the only way I can account for the hair, because the rags I used for cleaning the car, which are given to me by her, are usually my old shirts and things of that description, and they were always used as being the most convenient rag handy for covering up the head and shoulders to prevent the hair from falling to one's clothes.'

It was quite a rigmarole, disjointed, and obviously thought out as uttered. But he suddenly became more matter-of-fact, and went on: 'As a matter of fact, it is practically the only thing that is used, and as I was handed the shirts as I wanted them, it is possible that on one occasion the shirt I had in the garage or in the car for cleaning contained, we will say, a few cut hairs. I might mention that I had knocked some dents out of the mudguard just a week or two previous, and I had used a cloth on the outside of the mudguard to prevent damaging the enamel. I particularly remember doing that, but what rag it was I do not remember.'

He could have saved himself the trouble and his listeners their wasted time. As Sir Bernard Spilsbury pointed out, the hair found on the mallet had not been cut. It still had its root. There could be little doubt that the mallet had been dropped after Rouse had knocked his victim unconscious with it.

The evidence offered by Colonel Cuthbert Buckle, a director of a firm of fire assessors and a witness for the Crown, was particularly damaging to the prisoner. He related how he had found the union nut in the carburettor lead a complete turn loose. He had loosened a similar union on a police car.

He said: 'I found a union like this on it, and gave it three-quarters of a turn. The petrol flowed quite quickly, and it filled an ordinary half-pint tumbler absolutely to the brim in one minute twenty seconds.'

One feature concerning the burned-out Morris Minor was never adequately cleared up. Rouse's insurance carried a £1000 indemnity for death occurring to either himself or a passenger in the car. If he had thought of collecting some time later, how would he have gone about it without revealing his true identity?

At one point he was asked if he were an engineer. With recovered cockiness he replied: 'I dare say I am. I'm not a doctor, nor a crime investigator, nor an amateur detective. I'm an engineer.'

So he could have fixed the car's engine. His stupid bravado and its effect was not lost on a jury that remained utterly unimpressed by his antics in the witness-box. Especially as a mechanical expert called by the defence had been more or less demolished when Mr. Birkett shrewdly asked him, 'What is the coefficient of the expansion of brass?'

The time came, on that last day of January, for Mr. Justice Talbot to sum up. His address was very much to the point, and after hearing it the jury knew where they stood. They were not much longer than half an hour bringing in their verdict of guilty.

As the Judge delivered the death sentence two women in court sobbed brokenly. Both had borne the prisoner's children, and they were thoroughly grief-stricken.

Rouse duly appealed against his sentence, and at the hearing Sir Patrick Hastings, who led Mr. Finnemore, put forward an ingenious argument. He said that in such a case, where the victim's identity had not been established by the investigating authorities, a motive should have been proved. He quoted a precedent of the claim, no less than a ruling made quite a few years before by Lord Chief Justice Cockburn. The appeal failed, and when he learned the news Rouse decided to make a full confession. It was published only after he had met the hangman. He describes his victim as a down-and-out he met in a public-house at Whetstone. 'The sort of man no one would miss.'

Possibly that confession is true in the main, although he was such an inveterate liar one may be pardoned for doubting anything he said. The stark fact remains that, as a killer, he was out of luck. If only he had said to Brown and Bailey: 'Quick, help me. There's been an accident to my car,' he might well have got away with murder. Edgar Wallace, for one, was of this opinion.

*The Law Journal*, which had entered the lists after the conviction of Thorne, commented somewhat aloofly after the trial at Northampton had closed, 'Few will have the courage to assert that the evidence was such as of itself to leave no reasonable doubt as to the guilt of the accused.'

By that assessment the Northampton jury that found Alfred Arthur Rouse guilty was composed of brave men. That was more than likely, but they were also shrewd citizens who refused to be bamboozled by a callous liar.

L.G.

# 1932

# BRUNO HAUPTMANN
## The Lindbergh Kidnapping Case

On a May day in 1927, Charles A. Lindbergh, an obscure young American of Scandinavian stock, completed the first New York-to-Paris transatlantic flight. He had sailed alone with no fanfare and now stood for a little moment out of eternity, a diffident figure, silhouetted, as no man before or since, against the skyline of the world. That world, in the disillusionment which followed the first great war, was craving a hero as parched earth craves the rain. Young Lindbergh gave back to mankind its lost self-respect, and it took him to its heart.

That is why every home in this country—every mansion, every shanty—felt that it, too, had been violated when, five years later, on the second morning of March 1932, America learned at breakfast of the monstrous horror which had visited the recluse Lindbergh household at Hopewell in New Jersey.

Twenty-month-old Charles A. Lindbergh, Jr., the hero's first-born, has been stolen from his crib by some thief who, in the early dark, had reached the nursery window by means of a homemade extension ladder.

On the window sill he had left a crude note signed with a device by which his coming demands for ransom might be identified.

On the ground they found the ladder which had apparently broken under his weight as he climbed down from the nursery. He had made that ladder with his own hands and it was to be the death of him.

The emotion flooding the country next day eventually fused all its disparate detective forces into concerted action, and enlisted countless ardent amateurs. All over America volunteers yearned to help, and of those haphazard fishermen, the one that got the real bite was a garrulous, old Mr. Fixit named John F. Condon, who was briefly famous in the headlines under his nickname, 'Jafsie.' 'Jafsie's' naïve offer to act as intermediary, inserted in the *Bronx Home News*, was the one to which the kidnaper responded because he, too, lived in the Bronx. Through Jafsie, on April second, that kidnapper, using as his credentials the baby's sleeping garment which Mrs. Lindbergh herself had made, kept a cruel tryst with the baby's father on the edge of a cemetery.

In the dark they came within earshot of each other, as Colonel Lindbergh was later able to testify.

In exchange for fifty thousand in cash, the kidnaper gave some fictitious information as to where the stolen baby would be found, collecting that ransom in the full knowledge that the baby lay dead in a hasty grave in a thicket five miles from the Lindbergh home. There the body was found by chance on a day in May. In September two years later the New York police arrested one Bruno Richard Hauptmann. This Hauptmann, a young German carpenter with a burglarious past, had sneaked into this country in 1923.

Like Adolf Hitler, with whom he had not a little in common, he was a recognizable neurotic by-product of the German surrender of 1918. More particularly he was a smoldering megalomaniac who, in his grandiose daydreams, nourished a consuming jealousy of the world's hero whom he especially resented on behalf of his own boyhood hero, Richthofen, the wartime German ace. It was for Richthofen he was to name his own son, born after he had killed Lindbergh's. And it was the life of Richthofen that he read in his cell as awaited trial.

To strike at Lindbergh and to do it singlehanded, just as Lindbergh had flown the Atlantic singlehanded, that had been the diseased ambition which nerved Hauptmann for his reckless undertaking and for the gleeful, contemptuous swindle by which, on the edge of a Bronx cemetery, he completed his triumph.

He owed his capture to the alertness of a filling-station attendant, when he was so careless as to pay for some gas with one of the Lindbergh ten-dollar bills. Indeed, it is probable that he never would have been caught at all if America's departure from the gold standard in 1933 had not called in all gold notes and thus made any left in circulation easier to spot. Once Hauptmann's hands had felt the ransom money, they never resumed, for so much as a single day, the humble service of his old trade. Instead, he happily divided his waking hours between travel, sport and Wall Street speculation.

Even so, the police found hidden in his garage fourteen thousand dollars in ransom bills, for his possession of which he could offer only an implausible explanation.

While a ten-dollar bill led to his arrest, it was the ladder which convicted him. From the inexorable testimony of Arthur Koehler, a forestry expert in the federal employ, the lay world learned for the first time that a piece of man-used wood can, by plane marks, saw marks, wood grain, annual rings, knot holes, and nail holes, be a witness as telltale as a fingerprint. By evidence which, unlike the dubious dicta of handwriting experts, the jurors could recognize with their own eyes, the state was able to prove beyond all doubt that part of the wood in the ladder—it had to be made in three parts so that he could carry it in his car—had been cut from the flooring in the attic of the house where Hauptmann lived.

Hauptmann was tried, not in New York for extortion, but in New Jersey for murder. To insure the public satisfaction by his conviction on a crime carrying the death penalty, the commonwealth was obliged to stretch a point. For, as the New Jersey laws stood at the time, it had to establish the fact that the baby was killed, whether intentionally or not, during the commission of the burglary, and although the district attorney blandly gave the bemused jurors their choice of believing either that the death blow was received in the nursery itself or afterwards when the ladder broke, there was no shred of evidence to show that it had not actually been killed much later and many miles away.

Indeed, only one person could really have told when that baby was killed, and that person was silenced forever by the State of New Jersey on April 3, 1936. The lone vulture remained secretive to the last.

Hauptmann's trial was the climax of the world's greatest manhunt and therefore the prevailing atmosphere in the old courthouse at Flemington, N.J., was not inappropriately that of a sporting event. There was, however, one unforgettable moment when all the hubbub ceased.

That was when Anne Morrow Lindbergh took the witness stand and identified the sleeping garment which her own hands has sewn for her small son. In that hushed moment the case, stripped to its essentials, was revealed for what it really was—evil incarnate standing accused by every American hearth.

A.W.

# 1933

# KENNETH NEU

## 'Look at those nerves!'

Affable, twenty-five-year-old Kenneth Neu was a heart's delight to women young and old, sporting wavy brown hair, piercing blue eyes, and chalk-white teeth. He had a talent of sorts for singing and dancing; his ambition was to be a nightclub entertainer, but though he warbled his way through many a honky-tonk, Mr. Neu's real talent was in murder.

Little is known of Kenneth Neu's early life, except that he drifted young into vagrancy and then upper-class trampdom during the early 1930s. Without any special training, Neu wholeheartedly believed himself blessed with a marvelous voice and dancing feet. (The voice was adequate; the feet could patter somewhat-less-than-dazzling, uneducated steps.)

Neu badgered almost all the nightclub owners in Manhattan to allow him to sing with their bands. The pay he politely requested was no more than a handout, a not-unusual ploy; the country was swamped with young men on the bum during the Depression and any job for any price meant survival. Neu's skimpy talent assured him limited engagements. By September 2, 1933, Neu found himself wandering through Times Square, broke and tired, too weak even to sing a song for quarters.

A middle-aged man named Lawrence Shead spotted him and invited him to his hotel room for a drink, telling Neu that he owned a string of theaters in Paterson, New Jersey, and that he might be able to advance his career. Neu spent the next twenty-four hours drinking with Shead, asking about the promised job. Shead put him off, plying Neu with imported liquor, and eventually making homosexual advances. Kenneth

Neu finally had enough and told Shead he was through with the game.

'I want you to feel good,' Shead told the would-be crooner, putting his arms about him. 'We're going to have some real fun.'

Neu exploded. He lashed out at his scabrous benefactor landing a blow to Shead's head that sent him to the floor. Shead got up, belching revenge. The two men fought wildly about the room. As Shead fell off balance, Neu grabbed an iron from a shelf and crashed it onto the older man's head. He then jumped upon Shead and strangled him, but he was choking a corpse.

He then went to the bathroom and took a shower. He put on one of Shead's best suits, stuffed the businessman's wallet into a pocket and left.

A week later Kenneth Neu was strolling the streets of New Orleans, singing in what nightclubs could endure his act. He met a waitress named Eunice Hotte and told her he would take her to New York: 'We'll have a big time in the big town.'

'Are you sure you'll have the money, Kenneth?'

'I'll have it,' beamed the enterprising Neu. He found it at the Yung Hotel some hours later, in the pockets of Sheffield Clark, Sr., head of a Nashville, Tennessee, hardware firm. After striking up a conversation with the elderly Clark in the lobby, Neu pawned his watch, bought a blackjack, and returned to the hotel. He went to Clark's room and demanded money. Clark refused and Neu blackjacked him to death. He took three hundred dollars of Clark's money and the parking stub of the merchant's car, and was soon driving northward with a deliriously happy Eunice Hotte at his side.

To avoid Clark's license plate's being detected, Neu replaced it with a crudely scrawled sign reading 'New Car in Transit.' This guaranteed a speedy arrest. New Jersey police pulled Neu over and he was soon in a station giving a dozen different stories for the sign. Detectives learned that a young man answering Neu's description was wanted for killing a prominent Patterson, New Jersey, businessman.

'Did you ever know a man named Lawrence Shead?' they asked Neu.

The boyish dancer grinned. 'Sure, I killed him. This is his suit I'm wearing now!'

Neu just as happily admitted killing Clark. He was extradited to Louisiana and placed on trial for the Clark murder. Though lengthy arguments ensued over Neu's sanity, he was convicted and judged mentally fit to be executed. Upon hearing the jury's verdict, Kenneth Neu bowed to the judge, turned to the jury and

cried out: 'Gentlemen, you have my best wishes.' With that he went into a wild dance and sang 'Sweet Rosie O'Grady' at the top of his lungs before being led away.

Neu's conduct while awaiting execution in Parish Prison in New Orleans was a virtuoso performance. He sang and danced all the time in his cell, giving out interviews to startled reporters as he flipped a coin and shouted: 'Look at those nerves, boys! Look at those nerves!'

On the morning of his execution, February 1, 1935, Neu treated guards to a song he had composed entitled 'I'm Fit as a Fiddle and Ready to Hang.' He gingerly tapped his way up the gallows stairs and did a clog dance upon the steel trap. As the hood was being lowered over his head, Kenneth Neu finished his last performance by crooning 'Love in Bloom.' The trap sprung open and Neu shot downward, his neck breaking almost instantly. From the guards and visitors present there was no applause, only silence for a bad actor.

J.R.N.

# 1934

# TONY MANCINI
## The Brighton Trunk Mystery

Tony Mancini had become so hopelessly entangled in lies and concealments that few would have given anything for his chances

when, in December 1934, he faced a judge and jury at Lewes Assizes, charged with the murder of Violet Sanders, known as Violette Kaye. Mancini's mean and shiftless life had been one of ups and downs, good luck and bad, mostly bad; no doubt he deserved nothing better. But at the crisis of his life he had the fortune to attract the interest and sympathy of the greatest criminal advocate of the day, Mr. Norman Birkett K.C. It was certainly not for the modest fee that was marked upon his brief that he accepted the defence in this difficult case, one of the toughest he ever handled. Rather, it must have been an obstinate feeling that although the Crown seemed to have an "open and shut" case against this little gutter rat, somehow the truth was in him when he said, quite simply: "I did not kill her. Strange as it is, I used to love her."

Mancini, aged twenty-six, was a convicted thief, a worthless young man existing in the sleazy half-world of dance hall, pool room and all-night café. One of the many false things about him was the name Mancini, which he appears to have assumed merely to impress a girl who had a romantic attachment for Italians. (His real name was Cecil Lois England; he was also known at various times as Hyman Gold and Jack Notyre.) In August 1933, having lately been released from prison, he got a job at a café not far from Leicester Square, and it was there that he met Violette Kaye, forty-two years of age, a former vaudeville dancer turned prostitute. When, a few weeks later, the café closed down, leaving Mancini without any immediate prospect of employment elsewhere, Miss Kaye suggested that he should set up house with her in Brighton, where she promised him at least a roof over his head, a sufficiency of food and drink, and a weekly sum as pocket money. It seems to have been a quite disinterested offer, made out of genuine affection; all she asked in return was that Mancini should make himself scarce when she was entertaining a client.

Accordingly, to Brighton they went, prostitute and souteneur, happy with an arrangement that suited them both very well. They were constantly on the move. Indeed, in six months they lived at twelve addresses. In March 1934 they moved to their thirteenth address, which consisted of two basement rooms at 44 Park Crescent, approached from the area by a flight of steep and badly worn steps. They furnished the rooms with a few odd pieces, not much more than a bed, a washstand, a table and one or two chairs. Here life went on as before, Violette Kaye picking up business as and where she could, Mancini keeping faithfully out of the way. But in May the pattern was broken. Mancini got himself a job at the Skylark Café, situated below the Front, near the foot of West street. Miss Kaye did not altogether approve of this. She rarely allowed a day to pass without visiting the café, being concerned to make sure that Mancini did not become too familiar with any of the women who frequented it. On Thursday 10th May she was in the Skylark, where, being the worse for drink, she took violent exception to some joking remark which Mancini made to one of the waitresses, and made a noisy and embarrassing scene. Eventually she was persuaded to leave, no doubt to Mancini's great relief. She appears to have gone straight home, for shortly afterwards she was seen at 44 Park Crescent by a man named Thomas Richard Kerslake, who had called with the melancholy news that one of her regular clients, a bookmaker, had been certified insane and had been removed to an asylum. Kerslake had a conversation with Miss Kaye at the area door; she seemed to him to be *distrait* and nervous. In the flat he heard men's voices. The next morning Mancini turned up as usual at the café. Something was said about Violette Kaye. "She's left," said Mancini. "Gone to Paris." That morning Miss Kaye's sister-in-law, who lived in London, received a telegram which read: GOING ABROAD GOOD JOB SAIL SUNDAY WILL WRITE—VI. But Vi never wrote.

On the following Monday, after his day's work at the Skylark was over, Mancini purchased second-hand a large black trunk, for which he paid seven and sixpence. Later that evening the landlord of the house in Park Crescent called on Mancini at the basement flat. "Vi has left me," Mancini told him. "She has gone to France and I can't afford to run this place myself." The next day he departed, taking with him all his belongings—including the newly acquired trunk, loaded on a hand-cart. All that was left with the landlord to remind him of his late tenants was a peculiar stain in one of the cupboards—which someone had vainly tried to wash away. Mancini had taken a room at 52 Kemp Street. He arrived with the trunk, which he placed in a convenient corner. For two months Mancini lived in that little room, and during all that time the trunk remained undisturbed in its corner. Comments were made about the trunk, particularly about the offensive smell which seemed to emanate from it. ("Do you keep rabbits?" one visitor inquired curiously.) Mancini casually evaded all such inquiries and they were not pursued.

How long Mancini would have been content to live with that shabby trunk in that shabby room is now beyond conjecture. Events were to make up his mind for him. On 14th June the body of a woman, minus the head and legs, was found in a trunk which had been deposited in the left-luggage office at Brighton Station ten days earlier. This gruesome discovery attracted immense notoriety as the "Brighton Trunk Murder". In view of what the police investigation was to uncover, it had later to be restyled the "Brighton Trunk Murder No. 2", and, as such, it has remained unsolved. The police had first to establish the identity of the victim. In this they did not succeed—have not done so to this day—but in the course of their inquiries hundreds of persons were questioned, among them Tony Mancini. He had no difficulty in convincing the police that he knew nothing of the crime. Nor did he. Nonetheless, he was so badly frightened that he resolved upon immediate flight. On 15th July, the day after his encounter with the police, he caught an early morning train to London. Later that day police officers called at the house in Kemp Street to put some further questions to Mancini. They found the trunk that he had left there.

They opened it. Inside was the decomposing body of Violette Kaye. Two days later, in the small hours of the morning, Mancini was picked up on the London–Maidstone road. "Yes, I'm the man," he said. "I didn't murder her, though. I wouldn't cut off her hand. She's been keeping me for months." At Mancini's trial before Mr. Justice Branson, Mr. Birkett put forward a defence based upon a single word—panic. "There is a feature of this case," he told the jury, "that has never been in dispute—the concealment of the body and the lies told to explain it. But concealment and lies, remember, are not murder. Consider the position in which this man found himself. When he went home that night from work and found the woman dead, his immediate reaction was one of sheer terror. 'I shall be blamed', he thought, 'and I cannot prove my innocence.' So he went out; he walked about; he turned over this dreadful situation in his mind; and when he returned he put the body in the cupboard and nailed the door upon its hideous secret. Members of the jury, once that is done all the rest follows. Once you have started on the road of lies, you are compelled to keep on telling lies. There is no going back." The point was driven home when Mancini, himself, went into the witness-box. Here is a key passage from his examination by Mr. Birkett:

Q: Did you live with Violette Kaye at Brighton?
A: I did, sir.
Q: Where did she get money?
A: She was a loose woman, and I knew it.
Q: Did she appear to be in fear?
A: Yes. That's why we're always on the move.
Q: Was she often intoxicated?
A: Often.
Q: How did you get on together?
A: Strange as it is, I used to love her.
Q: Had you any quarrels?
A: None.
Q: Does that cover the whole time you were together?
A: Every second she was alive.
Q: How did she behave when she came to the Skylark Café on Thursday 10th May?
A: She was staggering a little. She wasn't herself. She was affected by something. All the week she had been rather strange.
Q: What time did you get home that night?
A: About half-past seven.
Q: What did you do when you saw her lying on the bed?
A: At first glance I thought she was asleep. I caught hold of her shoulder and I said, "Wake up." Then I saw blood on the pillow and on the floor.
Q: When you found she was dead why didn't you fetch the police?
A: I? I fetch the police? Where the police are concerned, a man who's got convictions never gets a square deal.

The last answer has a genuine ring, surely. It uncovers in a few words a way of thinking which is entirely natural to a man bruised and buffeted by his perpetual conflict with authority, bitterly resented of the "unfairness" of life, for which everyone is to be blamed but himself. That, one feels, is how such a man, a man with a chip on his shoulder, would react. There was a stir in court. It was with the Moment of Truth. Earlier, in the handling of the Crown witnesses, Mr. Birkett had been at his most impressive. His cross-examination of Sir Bernard Spilsbury, the eminent pathologist, had been particularly effective. Indeed, Sir Bernard had been brought very near to agreeing that the depressed fracture of the skull, which was said to be the cause of death, might have been due to a fall down the area steps, admittedly very difficult to negotiate, particularly by a person under the influence of drink or drugs. Mr. Birkett gathered up all the points in a brilliant closing speech. He asked the jury not to dismiss from their minds the possibility that Violette Kaye might have fallen down the steps. But if it *were* murder, who was the killer? "Violette Kaye was a prostitute," said Mr. Birkett. "That man [pointing to Mancini in the dock] lived upon her earnings, and I have no word to say in extenuation, none. But you must consider the world in which such people live and the dangers to which they are exposed. Isn't it reasonably probable that in this woman's life—an unhappy, a dreadful, an unspeakable life—blackmail may have played a considerable part? Somewhere in his world are the people whom Kerslake heard speaking in the flat when he went there on 10th May. The finding of the body was proclaimed from the housetops. Those who were in the flat that day—they had a tale to tell. But not a word, never a word." He ended: "I asked you for, I appeal to you for, and I claim from you, a verdict of 'Not Guilty'." Mr. Birkett paused, and then, looking squarely at the jury, added two tremendous words of exhortation—"Stand firm!" The jury took nearly two and a half hours to decide upon their verdict—acquittal. "Not guilty, Mr Birkett," breathed Mancini. In a daze he went on repeating the words—"Not guilty, Mr. Birkett."

E.S.S.

Years later, in a 'confession' published in a popular Sunday newspaper, Tony Mancini admitted that he *had* killed Violette Kaye.

R.G.J

# 1935

# BUCK RUXTON

## The Dismembering Doctor

---

Buck Ruxton (formerly known as Bukhtyar Rustomji Ratanji Hakim), a Parsee doctor practising in Lancaster, was delighted to read in the *Daily Express* that unidentified human remains found in September 1935 in the ravine below the bridge of Gardenholme Linn on the main road from Moffat to Edinburgh were those of *a man and woman*. 'You see, Mrs. Oxley,' he remarked to the charwoman, 'it is a man and a woman; it is not our two.' He burst out laughing. By 'our two' the excitable Dr. Ruxton meant his wife, Isabella, and the nursemaid for his children, twenty-years-old Mary Jane Rogerson; nothing had been seen of either for several weeks past. Dr. Ruxton had, at various times, sought to explain their absence by saying: (*a*) that they had gone to Scotland for a holiday; (*b*) that they had gone to Blackpool; (*c*) that Mrs. Ruxton had gone to London; (*d*) that she had gone off with another man; (*e*) that Mary Rogerson was pregnant and that Mrs. Ruxton might have taken her away with the idea of procuring an illegal operation. But already rumour was suggesting that the ravine where the Gardenholme Linn ran into the river Annan had been their more likely destination.

Dr. Ruxton's satisfaction with the newspaper report was short-lived. It is true that preliminary examination had suggested that one of the mutilated bodies was that of a man. But this error was soon corrected. They were, indeed, 'our two'. These pitiable remains, the severed heads, mutilated so as to be unrecognizable, the sundered limbs, the torn bodies, skilfully dismembered, disjointed, parcelled up, thrown into a ravine a hundred miles way, provided mute and ghastly witness to what may happen when jealousy rages in a man's blood like fire, consuming him utterly.

Buck Ruxton—he had taken the name by deed poll—was a Bachelor of Medicine of the Universities of Bombay and London, and a Bachelor of Surgery of the University of Bombay. In 1927 he met Isabella Van Ess (*née* Kerr), who worked in an

Edinburgh restaurant. At the beginning of 1928 she left her husband, a Dutchman, and went to live with Dr. Ruxton as his wife. In 1930 the doctor set up in practice at 2 Dalton Square, Lancaster. There is no doubt he was deeply attached to Isabella—'My Belle', as he called her—and she to him. This did not prevent them from quarrelling bitterly and continually. 'We were the kind of people who could not live without each other,' Dr. Ruxton was to say at his trial, quoting the French phrase, 'Who loves most chastises most'. Buck Ruxton was a man with little control over his tongue, and none at all over his emotions, a man given to passionate outbursts of rage, during which he would look and act like a lunatic. He suffered agonies over what he supposed to be his wife's infidelities—these were entirely imaginary—and she had only to look at another man to bring upon herself, wild threats, and sometimes physical violence.

In September 1935 he was obsessed with the suspicion—again baseless—that Mrs. Ruxton was having an affair with a young man in the Town Clerk's Department of the Lancaster Corporation. This provided the disturbed background for all his actions at this time; he has to be regarded as a man made frantic by jealousy, whose emotional balance, always precarious, was now even more finely poised than ever. On Saturday, 14th September, Mrs. Ruxton drove her husband's car to Blackpool to meet her two sisters and to see the illuminations. At 11.30 p.m. she left Blackpool to drive back to Lancaster. Undoubtedly, she returned home, for the car was there the next morning. But no one ever saw Mrs. Ruxton alive again. At Ruxton's trial, leading counsel for the Crown, Mr. J. C. Jackson K.C., attempted a reconstruction of what had happened inside the doctor's house after Mrs. Ruxton's return:

'You will hear that Mrs. Ruxton had received before her death violent blows in the face and that she was strangled. The suggestion of the prosecution is that her death and that of the girl, Mary, took place . . . on the landing at the top of the staircase, outside the maid's bedroom. . . . I suggest that when she went up to bed a violent quarrel took place; that he strangled his wife, and that Mary Rogerson caught him in the act and so had to die also. Mary's skull was fractured; she had some blows on the top of her head which would render her unconscious, and then was killed by some other means, probably a knife, because of all the blood that was found down those stairs.'

All this was presumed to have happened in the early hours of Sunday, 16th September. Dr. Ruxton was occupied for some time thereafter cutting up and dismembering the two bodies and draining the blood vessels. He also had to find time to remove the numerous traces of his crime. At 4.30 p.m. on the Sunday he called at the house of Mrs. Mary Hampshire, a patient of his, and asked her if she would help him to prepare for the decorators, who were coming in the morning, by scrubbing down the stairs. Mrs. Hampshire went back with him to the house. She found that the carpets had been removed from the stairs and landing right up to the top floor. Straw was scattered about on the staircase; more straw was sticking out from under the doors of the two bedrooms occupied, respectively, by Dr. Ruxton and his wife. Both these doors were locked. Dr. Ruxton asked Mrs. Hampshire to clean the bath, which was a dirty yellow colour. Carpets—two from the landings and the stair carpet—one in particular badly stained with blood, were lying in the backyard, as well as a bloodstained shirt and some badly stained—and partly burned—towels. Dr. Ruxton told Mrs. Hampshire that she could have the carpets in the yard, and other stair carpets in the waiting-room, also a blue suit, copiously stained with blood, which he said he had been wearing when he had cut his hand with a tin-opener whilst opening a can of peaches for the children's breakfast. (Undoubtedly, Dr. Ruxton had a badly cut hand.) But at his trial the prosecution held that it was not the sort of injury that could have been made by a tin-opener. Mr. Jackson suggested either that the knife had slipped whilst the doctor was dismembering the bodies, or that he had deliberately cut his own hand to be able to account for the blood on the carpets and in other parts of the house.)

Later, Mrs. Hampshire tried to clean the most badly stained of the carpets by throwing twenty to thirty buckets of water over it; at the end of this operation the water running off the carpet still had the colour of blood. Late that Sunday night, or so it was charged against him, the doctor set out for Moffat with the parcelled remains of Mrs. Ruxton and the nursemaid in the back of his car. Having arrived at Gardenholme Linn, he threw the parcels over the bridge, and drove back to Lancaster.

Some parts of the remains had still to be disposed of, either at Moffat or elsewhere, and it was not until the following Thursday that Dr. Ruxton was able to rid himself of the last of his unpleasant parcels. Mrs. Oxley, the charwoman, at work in the kitchen, heard him go up and down the stairs and backwards and forwards to his car. When he drove off Mrs. Oxley discovered that the doors which had been locked were open again.

On 29th September that a Miss Susan Johnson, on holiday at Moffat, looked from the bridge at Gardenholme Linn and saw in the gully below a human arm. A little further downstream four bundles containing human remains were retrieved, together with two severed heads, a thigh bone, and two arms. The first bundle was wrapped in a blouse, the second in a pillow-slip, and the other two in pieces of a bed sheet. One of the two heads was wrapped in a pair of children's rompers. Further search in the Linn and along the river Annan resulted in the discovery within the next day or two of other remains. On 28th October a left foot, wrapped in a page torn from the *Daily Herald*, was discovered about nine miles south of Moffat on the main Edinburgh–Carlisle road. Finally, on 4th November, a right forearm and hand were found on the Edinburgh road, south of the bridge over the Linn.

The field of inquiry was drastically narrowed by the fact that among the various bundles, together with straw that had been used for packing, was part of the issue of the *Sunday Graphic* for 15th September. This turnd out to be the special 'slip' edition containing pictures of Morecambe Carnival which was sold only in Morecambe and Lancaster and surrounding districts; a copy of this edition had been delivered to Dr. Ruxton's house. The blouse was identified as one which had belonged to Mary Rogerson; her mother was able to recognize it by the patch under one arm. Similarly, the rompers were identified—through a peculiar knot in the elastic—as a pair belonging to one of Dr. Ruxton's children. The strips of sheeting also proved to be highly important. They were compared with a sheet taken from Mrs. Ruxton's bed, and were found to be identical with it; a fault in the selvedge (revealed under a microscope) was common to both, showing them to be the product not only of the same loom, but of the same warp whilst in the loom. The piecing together of the various remains, so as to make up (although not completely) two female bodies, was undertaken by Professor James Couper Brash, Professor of Anatomy in the University of Edinburgh. He was one of a brilliant team of professors in the Universities of Edinburgh and Glasgow whose work on this case—the reconstruction and examination of the bodies, and the systematic establishment of their identity, in spite of the care that had been taken to efface every recognizable peculiarity—has long been regarded as a classic achievement of forensic medicine.

The trial of Dr. Buck Ruxton for the murder of his wife was opened at Manchester Assizes before Mr. Justice (afterwards Lord Justice) Singleton on 2nd March 1936. It lasted eleven days. Two of those eleven days—or the greater part of them—were occupied with the examination and cross-examination of Dr. Ruxton. An early exchange between himself and Mr. Norman (afterwards Lord) Birkett K.C., the distinguished counsel who appeared in his defence, set the tone for much that was to follow:

> *Mr. Birkett:* It is suggested here by the Crown that on the morning of the Sunday after your wife had come back you killed her?
> *Dr. Ruxton:* That is an absolute and deliberate and fantastic story; you might as well say the sun was rising in the west and setting in the east.
> *Mr. Birkett:* It is suggested by the Crown that upon that morning you killed Mary Rogerson?
> *Dr. Ruxton:* That is absolutely bunkum, with a capital B, if I may say it. Why should I kill my poor Mary?

The high-pitched note is characteristic. Dr. Ruxton made the worst possible witness. He was voluble, discursive, and often hysterical, his evidence being repeatedly interspersed with paroxysms of weeping. One had the impression of a man at the edge of total collapse who was fighting for his life with increasing desperation—and mounting despair. The jury found Dr. Ruxton guilty; he was hanged at Strangeways Prison, Manchester, on 12th May.

E.S.S.

# 1935
# ROBERT JAMES
## The Reluctant Rattlesnakes

The case which I call in my own mind 'The Case of the Reluctant Rattlesnakes' began in early August of 1935. On the third, which was a Sunday, Mary Busch James took off her starched white smock for the last time in a beauty parlour and barber shop in down-town Los Angeles, owned and operated by her husband, Robert S. James, with whom she worked side by side.

Mary was a very pretty woman of twenty-seven, softly curved, with heavy honey-coloured hair and sunny blue eyes. Everybody liked her. Her husband was busy with a customer. Bob James was a slim, well-groomed fellows with a clever, sensitive face and a marvellous pair of hands. He could do anything with hair, and woman as well as men flocked to him. Mary drew Bob aside and said: 'I don't feel well, Daddy, and I think I had better go home.'

The Jameses had been married three months, and Mary was expecting a baby. Bob agreed at once. He wanted to go with her, but Mary wouldn't let him leave the shop. She told him with a smile that she'd be perfectly all right once she got off her feet. Bob James called a taxi and put his wife into it. The taxi drove off in the direction of suburban La Canada, where the Jameses lived, and, as far as the shop was concerned, that was the last seen of Mary Busch James—alive.

Bob James came in on Monday morning, but Mary was still a bit under the weather. She had said she'd be in later if she felt better. Mary didn't appear. Customers kept Bob James a bit later than usual, and he didn't leave the shop for home until seven-thirty. With him were two friends he had invited for dinner, Viola Lueck, an old pal of Mary's, and Viola's boy friend, Jim Pemberton.

The James house was pink stucco with gaily striped awnings, set well back behind shrubbery in the middle of a grove of pepper and bamboo and eucalyptus trees. It had a flower garden and a fish-pond. Mary loved her goldfish. Bob James and his guests arrived home at around eight-fifteen. To Bob's surprise there were no welcoming lights. The house was dark and Mary didn't come running to meet him. They went inside. Mary wasn't in the pretty living-room or in the orchid-tiled bathroom or in the bedroom or in the immaculate kitchen.

They went out under the pepper trees—and found her.

In the garden was the fish-pond, with goldfish darting about in the clear water, on which pink and white waterlilies floated. A bearded little cement gnome in the middle sat cross-legged contentedly smoking a pipe. The gnome was smiling down at Mary Busch James, dress in pyjamas of crimson silk, sprawling, face down, half in and half out of the pool, her head in the water.

Jim Pemberton rushed to the phone. His call brought radio cars zooming. A doctor arrived. Mary was dead.

At first glance what had happened seemed plain. Tears streaming down his face, Bob James cried: 'The baby . . . Mary got dizzy spells . . . She loved to watch the gold-fish . . .'

Apparently Mary had fallen forward into the water, perhaps striking her head on the stony rim of the pool as she went down. Alone, with no one to come to her assistance, she had drowned.

There was no head injury, but the dead woman's right leg was swollen and discoloured to the knee, and there was a gash a quarter of an inch long in the pad of her right big toe. The medical verdict was that she had been cut by a sharp instrument, or bitten by a powerful insect or a snake.

In the house the police found a note that appeared to be in Mary's writing. It was to her sister. It said, in part: 'Dear Sis, Just a line to let you know I am pretty sick. My leg is all swollen; something bit me while I was watering the flowers this morning. This is my old blue Monday, but Daddy will he home tonight, and he takes good care of me. Be sure and write me soon . . .'

Robert James was dazed, couldn't seem to get it through his head that his wife was dead. She had been so happy when he kissed her good-bye that morning. The only thing that troubled her was nausea, which in her condition was natural. He gave a straightforward account of his movements. He left the house at seven-thirty and was at the shop all day except for a ten-minute interval round noon. Viola Lueck, Jim Pemberton, and the shop personnel corroborated this.

Then one of the detectives made a discovery. He found a cluster of black widow spiders in a dark corner of the garage, that shouldn't have been there. The authorities went into a huddle. They were about to proclaim the death of Mary Busch James suspicious because of the spiders, the toe gash, and the swollen leg, when they were stopped cold.

A neighbour, a retired English Army officer named Dinsley, told the police that he had noticed a woman walking around the Jameses' garden that morning and that she was alone. As a result, the coroner's jury split on whether Mary Busch James had died by drowning, or whether her death was accident, suicide, or murder.

The bride of three months was consigned to her grave and there the case rested, for a while. Then James tried to collect insurance policies on Mary's life amounting to $21,400. Payment was refused and he entered suit. The police went on digging into the past of Robert S. James. They found plenty.

Mary was Bob's fifth wife. His real name was Lisenba. The first, second, and fourth marriages ended in divorce. The third wife, Winona Wallace James, had died, like Mary, from drowning, but in a bath-tub in a tourist cabin.

On their honeymoon James and Winona were driving in Colorado when the car went out of control and over an embankment. James managed to escape by jumping. Winona was in the car, alive, her only injury a temporary loss of memory. She and James went to a tourist cabin. On the following day Robert James and a delivery-boy who helped him carry in groceries found Winona dead.

The verdict was accidental drowning. James collected eighteen thousand dollars.

In 1933 he collected on policies on his mother's life. In 1934 Oneal Wright, a sailor nephew, was killed in a motorcar accident. James was the beneficiary to the tune of five thousand dollars.

In February of 1936 District Attorney Fitts ordered an all-out investigation. The house in which James was then living was wired, with the police on the receiving end. Women, women, and more women. They got James with a young girl on statutory grounds, and he received a sentence of from one to fifty years on three counts. The murder of Mary Busch James remained unsolved.

It was Charles H. Hope, a friend and drinking companion of James, who finally supplied the answers. Pulled in, Hope finally broke down and the whole frightful story came out.

James had paid Hope one hundred dollars to buy a pair of rattlesnakes for 'a friend'. The first pair James placed in his chicken-coop wouldn't even kill a chicken. The second, in a cage with a rabbit, died the following day, leaving the rabbit with a slightly sore leg. The third set was put to the use for which they had been obtained.

On August 4, Hope arrived at the James bungalow to find Mary, in a thin night-dress, gagged and blindfolded and strapped to a table. James opened the lid of the box containing the rattlesnakes and placed Mary's left foot in the box. Hope left the house. He came back that night and the two men did some drinking in the James garage. Robert James said that the snakes hadn't done the job; his wife was still alive. He watched the black spiders for a while. He was very restless. Presently he left the garage and went into the bungalow. At about four o'clock in the morning James came out and told Hope that his wife was dead.

The two men carried Mary to the fish-pond and pushed her head into the water.

'How did she die?' Hope asked.

James replied: 'She died in the bath-tub.'

Disappointed by both the rattlesnakes and the spiders, he apparently had recalled the manner of his third wife's death and decided to profit from it again.

Hope pleaded guilty, turned State's evidence, and received a life sentence.

James, after the Supreme Court of the U.S. ruled against him, was the last man to die by the rope in California. He was hanged in San Quentin.

H.R.

# 1936

# ALBERT FISH

## The Cannibal Killer

Horrific murders may be monstrous, but their perpetrators are not by definition monsters. They are human beings. Some of them are good-looking human beings. Some of them have charm.

It would surely be logical to suppose that a type of crime which a normal person rightly believes he could never, under any circumstances, even be tempted to commit would automatically lead him to consider a person who did commit it so grossly abnormal as to be incapable of responding to punishment or deserving of it. But the opposite is true. The more horrific a murder the greater the general desire to see its perpetrator punished as severely as, or more severely than, the law permits.

This is no doubt due, in part, to a terror of the unthinkable, but it is none the less perverse for that. A prime example is afforded by the notorious case of Albert Fish, which is excellently described by Dr Fredric Wertham in his book *The Show of Violence*. In 1928, Albert Fish, who was a mild-mannered man approaching 60 and the father of six children, called at the home of a Mr and Mrs Budd in New York on the pretext of offering their son a job. The Budds also had a daughter, Grace, who was aged 10. Fish said he would like to take Grace to a children's birthday party which his sister was giving, and the Budds, a little hesitantly, consented.

They never saw her again. But six years later they received an unsigned letter, which read in part: '. . . I came to your flat on the third of June, 1928, and under the pretense of taking your daughter Grace to a party at my sister's I took her up to Westchester County, Worthington, to an empty house up there, and I choked her to death. I cut her up and ate part of her flesh.'

This letter was eventually traced back to Fish, and provided an accurate account of what he had done. He subsequently elaborated in it six signed confessions and in statements to

Dr Wertham. He said he had cut off Grace's head before dismembering the body; he had taken part of the body home with him, had cooked them in various ways with carrots and onions and strips of bacon, and had eaten them over a period of nine days.

That was not all. There was, according to Dr Wertham, no known perversion that Fish had not indulged in. He had eaten his own excrement; he had put pieces of cotton, saturated with alcohol, up his rectum and set fire to them; he had, over a period of years, stuck needles into his body in the region of his genitals, and a series of x-ray photographs by Dr Wertham showed that twenty-nine of these needles—some eroded with rust—were still lodged in him. In pursuit of his sado-masochistic pleasures he had molested at least a hundred children. Nor had Grace Budd presented him with his first or only chance to practise cannibalism. Estimates, after his arrest, of other child murders he had committed ranged from five to fifteen. Finally, Fish was what is commonly called a 'religious maniac'. For the past ten years, he had been suffering from auditory hallucinations; voices had been urging him to new feasts of atonement.

Dr Wertham diagnosed Fish's condition as a 'paranoid psychosis', or, in other words, believed that Fish was legally insane—that he did not know that what he was doing was wrong. But there were psychiatrists to take the opposite view for the prosecution, and in the end the public got what they wanted, and Fish went to the electric chair. Subsequently, it came out that though a majority of the jury who condemned Fish to death believed that he was legally insane, they decided he ought to be executed anyhow!

G.P.

# 8
# MASS MURDERERS,
# AND MORE
## (1944–58)

# DOCTOR PETTIOT
## Sixty-Three Victims

With sixty-three victims, Dr. Pettiot of France can be reckoned the greatest mass murderer of his time. He planned a near-perfect scheme of murder for gain. He was a murderer of great audacity who, after his murders had been detected by the most stupid of blunders, slipped from the net, to expose himself finally by the sin of vanity.

Pettiot's great scheme of murder for profit, conceived in 1941 and carried on until 1944, was the culmination of a long criminal career in which, under the cloak of the magic word 'doctor' he escaped retribution time and again. Satisfied before the war by petty gain from abortions, thefts, drug trafficking, and occasional murders, Pettiot saw his great opportunity in the conditions of German-occupied France from which many were anxious to escape to avoid deportation to forced labour camps and worse. Such people would, Pettiot knew, disappear without remark, their relatives and friends thinking that they had been seized by the Gestapo and the Gestapo thinking that they had escaped abroad.

The discovery of Dr. Pettiot's 'murder factory' in the rue Leseur came about through his own carelessness. For several days in March 1944, that highly respectable street had been filled with evil-smelling black smoke, belching from the chimney of No. 21. On the 11th March, the occupier of No. 20 could stand the stench no longer and he telephoned the police and fire brigade.

While the firemen waited in the street, the police hammered at the door of No. 21. They could get no reply but on the door was a card directing enquiries to 66 rue Camartin which proved to be the residence of Dr. Marcel Pettiot. When the police telephoned, Pettiot said he would come straight over.

But the firemen could not wait. They told the police there was a risk of the house catching fire and setting the whole street aflame. It was too risky to wait for the owner who, anyhow, would hardly object to his house being saved.

The firemen battered down the door and went in. Two minutes later they came rushing out, shouting, 'This is no job for us. The place is full of corpses.'

Reaching the cellar, the police staggered back aghast. In the centre was a furnace belching black, acrid smoke and on the floor and against the walls were piled corpses in every stage of dismemberment. Some had been simply hacked to pieces, others split from neck to groin. Stray heads, limbs, trunks, and torsos littered the floor and from the stove stuck out a half-consumed body. In all, the pieces comprised twenty-seven bodies.

While the police were taking this in, a tall dark stranger entered the cellar, looked round and withdrew as discreetly as he came, sauntering out of the front door of the house. Accosted by a police sergeant, he said he was Dr. Pettiot, the owner of the house who had been sent for.

When the sergeant told him he must wait, Pettiot drew the man aside and whispered, 'You do not understand, you have discovered the execution chamber of the Resistance. The bodies in the cellar are those of Germans and collaborators.' Drawing himself up, and with flashing eyes, he declared, 'I am a patriot, you must let me slip away or the Gestapo will get me.'

To the dreaded word 'Gestapo' there could be only one reaction. The sergeant let Dr. Pettiot go. He disappeared without trace which was by no means difficult at a time only a few months before the Allied landings and the liberation of Paris.

The full story of Dr. Pettiot's crimes was revealed when the police traced his brother who lived at Auxerre, in the Department of Yonne. In his keeping were found the possessions of the sixty-three victims Pettiot had lured to the rue Leseur on the promise that he would get them out of occupied France. His agents told them they were to go to his house, carrying all their worldly goods and wealth.

Pettiot bought and altered No. 21 rue Leseur for the purpose of his scheme. From his consulting-room a passage, traversed by three doors, ran to a sound-proof, cell-like room, in the wall of which was a door, a false one.

When the client called, Pettiot explained that he would leave on his journey straight away, but first he must be inoculated against the diseases prevalent in the country of his destination.

With the sharp jab of the needle the formalities were complete and Pettiot led the man to his 'secret exit', where he would be picked up by one of his agents.

As the victim passed into the cell-like room, supposedly the ante-chamber to freedom, he saw the door in the opposite wall. Unable to find the handle he turned back to ask the good doctor but the door by which he had entered was shut and it, too, had no handle. By this time the drug with which Pettiot had injected him had begun to work, and the doctor was able to watch the man's death agonies through a magnifying glass set in the wall.

When he saw that life was extinct, Pettiot removed the body, dropping it into a pit in the courtyard, filled with quicklime. This was screened from prying eyes by a high wall he had had built.

Why Pettiot changed his plan of disposal and started burning bodies in 1944 is obscure. If he thought that incineration was a better means of disposal, he miscalculated for he forgot that dense clouds of smoke coming from his chimney would excite remark.

He changed his plan, probably, because with approaching liberation he saw the end of his 'murder factory' in sight. He could hardly abandon the house with the remains of sixty-three people slowly dissolving in the lime pit.

Paris was liberated before Pettiot was found. While the full horrors of the rue Leseur had been revealed in the French newspapers and Dr. Pettiot had been named as the wanted man, the suggestion that he had been an agent of the Gestapo could not be made until the Germans had gone.

When in September, Pettiot read a newspaper article accusing him of being, as well as a murderer, a traitor to France, he wrote to the newspaper *Resistance* denying that he had any connection with the Gestapo and claiming that the people he had killed had been collaborators and Germans only.

His letter was given to the Chief of the Parisian Resistance Movement who was asked to compare it with the handwriting of his men and particularly with those who had joined in the last few weeks.

Within fourteen days Pettiot was identified as 'Captain Henri Valery' who had joined the Resistance only six weeks before.

At his trial in March 1946, Pettiot made no attempt to deny that he had killed sixty-three people. He claimed that they were all enemies of France, and that he had only been doing his duty as a loyal Frenchman and as the leader of the Resistance Group *Grey Fox*. He had, he declared, smuggled many patriots to safety.

But Pettiot could not name any of the Germans or collaborators he had killed and none of those whom he had aided to escape came forward to speak on his behalf. Asked who else had belonged to Group *Grey Fox*, he could supply only names of famous resistance workers who were dead.

Another thing he failed to explain was his arrest, *and release*, by the Gestapo in 1942 and 1943. He had been suspected, he said, of helping saboteurs to escape from France and he accounted for his release by saying that the Gestapo found that they had insufficient evidence against him.

Suspecting the nature of his activities, the Gestapo had sent a spy to ask Pettiot to get him out of France. Pettiot, not knowing who he was, killed him like the others. But the Gestapo assumed that Pettiot *had* smuggled him abroad, a charge that the doctor could hardly deny.

On what terms Pettiot stood with the Germans has never been cleared up, but it is significant that his capture did not come until after they had gone. Certain aspects of his pre-war career suggest that Pettiot was under powerful protection.

When the trial jury returned with their verdict on the 4th April, the foreman's words were drowned by the pandemonium in court so that Pettiot had to beseech those near to tell him the result. When he was sentenced to death he screamed, 'I will be avenged.'

Just before dawn of the 25th May, Pettiot, asleep in his cell, was seized and bound and told that his appeal had failed and that his hour had come. 'Marcel Pettiot, now is the time for you to be brave,' the executioner shouted in his ear.

Led to the guillotine, Pettiot whispered to the executioner that he wished to relieve himself. When the executioner suggested that he would not have to wait long, Pettiot replied with a shrug, 'When one sets out on a voyage, one takes all one's luggage with one'. A few seconds later he was dead.

Marcel Pettiot, born in 1897, the son of a minor postal official, began his career as a criminal by robbing letter-boxes. When he was conscripted into the Army in 1916, he stole rugs from a casualty clearing station.

After the war he qualified as a doctor and built up an excellent practice at Villeneuve where he became first a town councillor and then the Mayor. While still a bachelor, he employed an unusually attractive housekeeper who, after becoming noticeably pregnant, suddenly disappeared and was never again seen alive.

In 1930 one of his patients, Madame Debauve, who kept a shop was robbed and killed. Local gossip accused Pettiot but it quietened down after his chief accuser, whom the doctor was treating for rheumatism, died suddenly. Pettiot certified his death to have been from natural causes. When enquiry was made in 1945 into these two deaths it was found that the police dossier on the former Mayor of Villeneuve had unaccountably disappeared.

While still Mayor, Pettiot was convicted of thefts from the municipal stores, and, on his release, he and his wife and son removed themselves to Paris, where we next hear of him being discharged for the theft of a book from a shop with the recommendation that he submit himself to psychiatric treatment.

But throughout these vicissitudes Pettiot retained his status as a doctor. With the start of the war, Pettiot turned to trafficking in drugs, and a woman who accused him of administering drugs to her daughter, on the excuse that he was curing her of addiction, mysteriously disappeared.

When Pettiot turned to mass murder in 1941 he had served a long apprenticeship in crime.

R.F.

# 1946

# NEVILLE HEATH
## The Cruel Bluff

He was a young man with a hard face, who had practised a cruel bluff. To fool the police into accepting his insanity as proved, he had brutally killed a second victim. His first had died in such conditions that he knew full well the manhunters searching for him must know they were hunting either a wanton sadist, capable of the extremes in cruelty, or a madman. His gamble was whether he would be adjudged insane. He was clever and unscrupulous in the manner in which he made his frenetic play for life. He preferred to roll loaded dice and deal cards from a cold deck. He was that kind of gambler. But his gamble against Scotland Yard and British Justice was an abortive effort. Perhaps he knew that when he first stepped into the dock on the morning of Tuesday, September 24th, 1946, in the sure knowledge that all Britain was agog to learn how his ordeal shaped. So far as the man himself was concerned it was virtually an ordeal of silence. From the moment of entering the box on the first day to the end of the trial he spoke only three words.

His name was Neville George Clevely Heath, a name to be remembered long after his death with abhorrence and a feeling of terror. He was a lustful, self-indulgent murderer without a single redeeming feature.

He was sane, but not normal. If he were, then the human race would be self-destroyed within a few depressive generations.

His life was a shabby catalogue of deception and crime, vicious, venal, and vindictive. He lived and died a man with no charity in his heart, no decency in his cesspool of a mind.

He was born in Guildford in 1917, left school at the age of seventeen, and in 1936 received a short-term commission in the R.A.F. It might be said that he and Frederick Field were pirate ships that passed in the night. Field deserted from the R.A.F. the year Heath entered and accepted his commission. His piratical ways were soon made manifest. Within a year

and a half he was court-martialled, and his Service crimes
were indicative of a thrusting personality. He stole a car, was
A.W.O.L., and escaped while under arrest. In September 1937
he was a civilian again, and two months later was on probation
after a not very edifying episode in which he posed as a Lord
Dudley, known to neither Burke not Debrett. Within eight
months he became acquainted for the first time with the interior
*décor* of the Old Bailey. This was the occasion when he was sent
to Borstal for three years. War came, Heath was released, and
the Army accepted him. For a time he was not sailing under
pirate colours, and he procured another commission. But in
less than two years the Army had found out its mistake. In
July 1941 it sent him back to Britain from the Middle East,
court-martialled and cashiered for the second time.

But he jumped his troopship in Durban, reached Johannes-
burg, fabulous city of get-rich-quicks, and undertook another
striking metamorphosis. Overnight he became a gallant captain
of the Argylls, with a Military Cross to boot. But when his frauds
were likely to be brought home to him he joined the South
African Air Force. In the name of Armstrong he procured
his third commission. Some sort of cycle was completed in his
adventurous and anti-social career when he was seconded to the
R.A.F. His luck wasn't good in the air. His aircraft was hit on
its first operation over enemy territory, and he had to bale out.
When the war was over he elected to go back to South Africa,
where he had left a wife. He arrived to find her faith in human
nature sufficiently shattered for her to be in the midst of divorce
proceedings. At the end of 1945 the S.A.A.F. fell in line with
line with the R.A.F. and British Army. Heath was thrown out.
He returned to England, and two months later was fined for
wearing a uniform and decorations to which he was not entitled.
That was in April 1946.

A couple of months later he booked a room in a hotel in
Notting Hill, an area of London that has witnessed some
notorious crimes of violence. He gave his own name, but
described himself as a lieutenant-colonel. He arrived with
his inamorata of the hour, who purported to be his wife
for the purposes of convenience. Within the next day or two
this lady disappeared, and afterwards she had good reason to
consider herself fortunate. Margery Gardner took the brunt of

any annoyance and frustration Heath felt at being faced with the prospect of nocturnal solitude. She kept a rendezvous with him at the Panama Club, in South Kensington, on the evening of 20th of June, four days after he had arrived at the Pembridge Court Hotel. She was an easy-going woman with an easy-come, easy-go philosophy, two years older than Heath. Born in Sheffield, she was separated from her husband, and liked to think she had an artistic temperament. Certainly she had taken drama lessons and had studied elocution. Her latest intention when she met Colonel Bill Armstrong of the South African Air Force was to paint.

It was Colonel Bill Armstrong she kept a date with at the Panama Club, and with whom she returned to the hotel in Pembridge Gardens. It was a night when Colonel Armstrong was flush. He had received payment for agreeing to fly a reporter to Denmark. It was a night, too, when he had drunk more alcohol than usual, and he had never acquired the reputation of a temperate man under any of hid other aliases, Graham, Blyth, or Denvers, or even under his legal name Neville George Clevely Heath. Margery Gardner knew him only as Bill Armstrong, and even on the night she became the colonel's lady had no true knowledge of his corkscrew career. They left the club after midnight, arrived at the hotel shortly before one o'clock, and entered without being observed or heard.

The next afternoon Superintendent Reginald Spooner, chief of F Division's C.I.D., was called to the hotel and entered the room that had been occupied by Heath. It was a shambles. Margery Gardner's mutilated body lay half covered with blood-soaked bedclothes. It was very obvious to eyes grown accustomed to the sordid secrets of human perversion in a big city that her death had occurred during a fierce orgy of uncontrollable eroticism, and that the partner responsible for her sad condition must have been a pervert with untamable instincts and bestial impulses.

That partner had vanished with his baggage. Photographs of the scene he left after carefully locking the door and leaving the blinds drawn are now safely stored in the Yard's Black Museum, together with a certain riding-crop.

Chief Superintendent Tom Barratt personally took charge after hearing Spooner's report. Chief Superintendent Fred Cherrill arrived and collected finger-prints. Detective-Inspector

Shelley Symes from Ladbroke Grove police-station put the local police to work. His heartfelt comment that Friday afternoon was, 'Nice plateful for the week-end!'

Within hours the Yard men knew who they were looking for. Neville Heath's photo appeared in the *Police Gazette,* and a nation-wide dragnet was cast. Before twenty-four hours had passed the view had been expressed at more that one conference that the killer of Margery Gardner must be a lunatic. But by this time the story of Neville Heath's past few months in London was beginning to take appalling shape. He had arrived in February, and within a few days had created a remarkable disturbance in a London hotel, when shouts for help brought the staff hurriedly to a room where Heath was discovered naked, bending over a naked woman who had been stunned. Her hands were tied. This disturbing couple were asked to leave, and they did so without delay. The woman proffered no charge against the room's occupant, whose name might have rung a bell with Margery Gardner. It was Colonel Bill Armstrong. From that occasion to the night of the 20th of June, Heath's peregrinations to and fro across London's western suburbs had resulted in legendary tales being told of this fair-haired man with bleak eyes who practised erotic excesses of a kind calculated at that time to get banned a book that carried in print even bare hints of what they comprised.

When the police were certain of the true character of the killer they sought, they knew they could not afford to fail. Such a man had only one chance of escaping what the law would consider just retribution. He might try to justify a plea of insanity. To do this he might run a brutal, calculated bluff by killing again, in similar circumstances.

That too was bruited at the police conferences while the hunt was up. At those conferences they had the sobering results of Dr. Keith Simpson's post-mortem examination of the woman who had been thrashed and tortured, and the results of analyses undertaken by Dr. Henry Holden, director of the Metropolitan Police Laboratory, who had proved that all the blood samples taken from the room were of the same group as the dead woman's. There had been no struggle, only fatal submission to a brutality that resulted in murder. No other explanation was conceivable or tenable.

Meanwhile, where was Heath, the most urgently wanted man in the British Isles?

He had journeyed to Brighton, and along the coast to Worthing, where he put up at a hotel and contacted the young woman who had been accommodating on the 16th. But when his name appeared in Sunday's newspapers, with the report that the police wished to interview him because they thought he could help in their investigation of the Notting Hill murder, Heath decided to lose himself. He told the lady who had once called herself Mrs. Heath that he was driving ot London. He told her on the 'phone. She did not see him again.

Instead of going to London, he continued along the coast the Bournemouth, where in another hotel he became Group Captain Rupert Brooke. He took stock of the situation. There was a letter from him in the post, and he was already running the first part of his bluff. The letter was to Tom Barratt at the Yard and was signed not with an alias, but his own name. It ran:

> *Sir,*
>
> *I feel it to be my duty to inform you of certain facts in connection with the death of Mrs. Gardner at Notting Hill Gate. I booked in at the hotel last Sunday, but not with Mrs. Gardner, whom I met for the first time during the week. I had drinks with her on Friday evening, and whilst I was with her she met an acquaintance with whom she was obliged to sleep. The reasons, as I understand them, were mainly financial. It was then that Mrs. Gardner asked if she could use my hotel room until two o'clock and intimated that if I returned after that I might spend the remainder of the night with her.*
>
> *I gave her my keys and told her to leave the hotel door open. It must have been almost three o'clock when I returned to the hotel and found her in the condition of which you are aware. I realized that I was in an invidious position, and rather than notify the police I packed my belongings and left. Since then I have been in several minds whether to come forward or not.*

The remainder of the letter purported to give a description of the unknown companion with Margery Gardner, explained that a notice in the personal column of a certain newspaper would find him ready to negotiate and be helpful, and informed Barratt that the instrument that had inflicted such horrible wounds on the dead woman was being forwarded. If he had said weapon instead of instrument it would have been more truthful, but the promise was a lie in any case. No riding-crop arrived by post.

For ten days Rupert Brooke, who bore no facial resemblance to a dead poet, remained at the hotel. On July 3rd he invited to tea and dinner a Miss Doreen Marshall, who was at that time staying alone at the Norfolk Hotel while recovering from influenza. She must have regretted the impulse that made her accept, for after sitting with Heath in the lounge of the Tollard Royal Hotel until midnight she decided to call it a day. Heath insisted on accompanying her back to the Norfolk. She did not reach her hotel. She had waited too long before leaving, and had become Heath's second victim, necessary for the completion of his cruel bluff.

Heath was not seen to return to his hotel, but at four-thirty in the morning the shoes outside his door were found to be covered with drying mud and damp sand. Two days passed, and then Miss Marshall's non-appearance at the hotel started comment and speculation, which became horrified certainty when on July 8th, the naked body of a young woman was found under her own clothes and some branches in Branksome Chine. Her death had resulted from a knife thrust, but her body was marked with terrible mutilations and bruises. Unlike Margery Gardner, there had been no submission by Doreen Marshall. The ex-Wren had fought desperately with her assailant. The end had been the same. The pattern of sadistic fury was identical with the handiwork of the Notting Hill killer.

But by July 8th Heath had been in custody for forty-eight hours. A sharp-eyed Bournemouth detective named Souter had recognized Group Captain Rupert Brooke as the Neville Heath described in the *Police Gazette*. A cloakroom ticket in his possession produced a suitcase deposited on June 23rd at Bournemouth railway station, and in this was the riding-crop he had omitted to send to Superintendent Barratt. In his hotel room the police found a blood-stained handkerchief, still knotted, and caught in the knot hairs from the head of Doreen Marshall. She had been gagged, like Margery Gardner, and obviously the knot had been tied in the nape of her neck after she had been punched unconscious.

It was all of a horrible piece.

He was invited to make a statement. He was in no position to refuse.

He started with a tale about Doreen Marshall being unofficially engaged to an American named Pat and receiving invitations to car rides from another, who was staying at the same hotel. He claimed they talked about general topics and that he persuaded her to remain with him until half past eleven.

The statement continued:

> *At about eleven-thirty, the weather was clear and we left the hotel and sat on a seat in the Undercliff overlooking the sea. From this stage onwards my times are vague, because I had no wrist-watch. We must have talked for at least an hour, probably longer, and then we walked down the slope to the Pavilion. Miss Marshall did not wish me to accompany her, but I insisted on doing so at least part of the way. I left her at the pier and watched her cross the road and enter the gardens. Before leaving her I asked her if she would come round the following day, but she said she would be busy for the next few days, but would telephone me on Sunday if she could manage it. I have not seen her to speak to since then, although I thought I saw her entering Bobby's on Thursday morning. After leaving Miss Marshall I walked along the sea-front in a westerly direction and up the path from Durley Chine and to the cliff-top, and so back to the hotel, whereupon I went to bed. It rained heavily before I reached the hotel.*

He had just completed this not very inspired piece of fiction when Spooner arrived from London. Spooner had already spent many late nights working in his shirt-sleeves to cover the thousands of statements and reports that had flowed into his office, but he when looked at Neville Heath he was taking in the features of a man whose story he knew thoroughly, from his schooldays clear through in his arrest for murder. That story was to be told in ten weeks' time to a crowded Old Bailey court, a most unusual procedure, but in this case to comply with the requests of the defence, and Spooner was the man who would tell it.

The trial, when it opened, achieved wide international notoriety. It was reported on the Continent and in the United States. Within the space of a short summer Neville Heath had earned a dark fame that internationally linked his name in criminal history with those of Jack the Ripper, Peter Kurten, Henry-Désiré Landru, and Hermann W.Mudgett—and in case this last is unfamiliar, it is the true name of the man who styled himself H. H. Holmes, the Chicago Bluebeard of the nineties, finally traced by the Pinkertons.

Some of the evidence was so nauseating that it was told only in part. It would have turned the strong stomach of Scotland's Jamie the First, who personally went hunting Sawney Beane and his cannibal tribe in the early fifteenth century. Possibly Heath was born out of his rightful century, but it wouldn't have provided much of a defence at the Old Bailey in September 1946 against the case presented by Mr. Anthony Hawke, senior Treasury counsel and son of the late Mr. Justice Hawke, who led for the Crown.

The defence offered by Mr.J.D. Casswell, K.C., was one to make headlines: partial insanity. In a crowned court rigid with attention he said, addressing the jury, 'I am going to invite you to say that as a result of the evidence you have heard and are due to hear on the part of the defence, the defence is that of partial insanity.'

Heath's bluff was soon to become apparent.

Mr. Casswell continued: 'This is an astonishing case. The probability is that Heath knows no more about what his state of mind is than any of us do about our own minds. It is something which is a natural part of his nature, and it is natural to him and would not appear extraordinary. You must decide whether Heath was insane, not now, not when he wrote the letter, not when he gave his statements to the police, but at the time when the terrible acts were committed.'

He put some questions to the jury.

'Why have the public taken such an interest in this case?' he asked them. 'Is it because two terrible and apparently motiveless crimes have been committed by the same man within the short space of a fortnight? Not a man who was unintelligent, but a man who had seen a good deal of the world, a man who had been three times commissioned. That is the sort of man you have to deal with, and yet you find within the short space of a fortnight these two astonishing and apparently motiveless crimes being committed by him. And the second one, as you will hear, where the injuries were far more terrible, was apparently, in my suggestion, due to a progressive mania. That second one was committed when the man must have known that the police were hunting for him throughout Britain. Yet he makes no effort at a disguise except a change of name.'

If there had been any cat in the bag, it was out when Heath's defending counsel spoke those words, and followed them with others to support the plea of partial insanity at the time of the crimes' commission, for the prosecution had linked the two murders, and Heath stood charged with both. In support Mr. Casswell called upon Dr. William Henry Duval Hubert, the well-known psychiatrist, who after answering a number of questions, stated, 'He is not an ordinary sexual pervert, but he is suffering from moral insanity, and at times he is quite unaware that what he is doing is wrong.'

At this point of glances of most people in the court turned from the man in the witness-box to the one in the dock. Heath remained perfectly still, apparently quite unmoved. Was that part of the bluff? He must have been holding his mental breath.

'In your view is he cerfitable as morally insane?' Mr. Casswell asked the psychiatrist.

'Yes. I think he appreciated what he was doing and appreciated the consequences, but did not appreciate that what he was doing was wrong.'

When Dr. Hugh A. Grierson, the senior medical officer at Brixton Prison, where Heath had been on remand, was called, he took an opposite view.

Mr. Hawke asked him, 'Do you take the view that he did not know it was wrong?'

'I do not take that view,' Dr. Grierson replied firmly.

Nor did Dr. Hubert Turner Young, senior medical officer at Wormwood Scrubs, in whose opinion Heath was a psychopathic personality and a sadist.

Heath, as expected, was not put in the witness-box. He had to play out the remainder of his bluff in silence. But the case was drawing to its close that third day, and it became obvious the verdict would be reached without continuing the trial another day. In strained silence Heath had to contain himself before he learned whether the terrible death he had brought to Doreen Marshall would serve the macabre purpose for which it was intended, and convince a jury of ten men and two women that when he cut and gouged her body he was partially insane. Counsel for the Crown and counsel for the defence took almost the same time over their last addresses to the jury, the former forty-seven minutes, the latter fifty. Mr. Justice Morris took twice as long, one hour and thirty-nine minutes, over his summing-up. He had a difficult and unusual case to put in its strictly legal perspective, and went thoroughly into the insanity issue, explaining firmly that legal insanity could not be permitted to become an easy or vague explanation of some conduct which was shocking because it was also startling. The law of insanity, he made clear beyond misunderstanding, was not to become a refuge for those who could not challenge a charge which was brought against them.

The attentive prisoner in the dock must have realized that this coldly uttered clarification of the issue was destroying his cruel bluff.

The learned Judge came to his peroration.

'It is for you to say whether this defence is made out,' he instructed the jury. 'If you believe this, your verdict will be one of guilty but insane. If you are of the opinion that it has not been made out, it will be your duty, whether you regard it or not as as unhappy one, to return a verdict of guilty.'

When he had finished none of the jury members was looking at the prisoner. The double-murderer, self-confessed, must have known that his gamble on reaching Broadmoor Lunatic Asylum had failed. The bluff was over, a bluff no longer. The jury retired shortly after half-past four. They were absent fifty-nine minutes. The slim, hard-eyed, stiff-faced figure in pin-striped flannel suit and wearing an R.A.F. tie was brought back to the dock. He stood at attention facing Mr. Justice Morris. The traditional termination of an historic and memorable trial was enacted.

The clerk turned to the foreman of the jury, inquired, 'Are you agreed upon your verdict?'

'We are, my lord,' the foreman replied gravely.

'Do you find the prisoner guilty or not guilty?'

'Guilty.'

'You find him guilty of murder?'

'Yes.'

No mention of insanity for Heath's straining ears.

'And that is the verdict of you all?'

'That is.'

The foreman sat down, and there was a stir in court as the clerk turned to the stiffly erect prisoner, and addressed him in level tones.

'Prisoner at the bar, you stand convicted of murder. Have you anything to say why the court should not give judgment according to the law?'

There was a pause. Heath's face was seen to twitch. He spoke his third word at his trial, the other two being his plea of 'Not guilty.'

He said, 'Nothing.'

His thoughts might have been miles away, as far as a hotel room in Notting Hill or even a clump of rhododendrons in Branksome Chine where the soft loam was trampled by thrashing feet.

Mr. Justice Morris adjusted the black cap. When he spoke his voice was so low that it was not easily heard by people straining for each word.

'Neville George Clevely Heath, you have been found guilty of a terrible crime. The sentence of the court upon you is that you be taken from this place to a lawful prison and thence to a place of execution and you should there be hanged by the neck until you are dead.'

The Judge's voice became softer, a quiet droning sound in that place where the formula for legalized death is an impressive cliché

His last words rang a little. 'May the Lord have mercy upon your soul.'

The trial was over, and the result within a very few minutes was spinning across continents. He was to die, but his memory would be darkly cherished by students of criminology. He was unique, evil beyond credence. But not, as he had hoped to prove, beyond sanity. He was now of the company of Greenacre and Neill Cream, a killer

with whom Patrick Mahon and Norman Thorne, Henry
Wainwright and Frederick Field, might feel outclassed in
pointless butchery.

He did not appeal to the Court of Criminal Appeal, which was
founded a bare ten years before he was born. But he did try a
desperate last attempt to sell his cold bluff with members of the
special medical board appointed by the Home Secretary to hear
final pleas of criminal insanity.

Their report was unanimous opinion that he was sane.

He met Albert Pierrepoint by appointment on the morning of
October the 26th, 1946.

L.G.

# 1946

# LEY AND SMITH
## The Chalk-Pit Murder

Thomas John Ley formerly Minister of Justice in New South
Wales, Australia, died from a meningeal haemorrhage in
Broadmoor Criminal Lunatic Asylum (now Broadmoor Institution) on 25th July 1947, four months after he and a man
named Smith had been jointly convicted of the notorious
'Chalk-pit Murder', that nightmare essay in *Grand Guignol*.
The processes by which it was to be revealed in all its
strangeness and horror began on the afternoon of Saturday,
30th November 1946, when Walter Tom Coombs, returning
to his home at Woldingham, Surrey, came upon the dead
body of a man lying across a newly dug trench at the top
of an old chalk-pit a little way off the road. Two pieces of
rope were twined loosely around the body and there were
deep grooves in the neck. It was concluded from a post-
mortem examination that the man had been slowly strangled,
having first received a severe blow on the head—sufficient to
cause unconsciousness—and another in the stomach. This was
later somewhat elaborated to suggest that the man had been

hanged, but hanged without a 'drop', or, at any rate, that death had been caused by a rope which had been 'pulled upwards'. In the dead man's pocket was a card which quickly led to the identification of the body as that of John McMain Mudie, a barman at the Reigate Hill Hotel, Reigate, Surrey, who had been missing since the previous Thursday, 28th November.

Mudie, was a decent, unoffending, kindly person, of whom everyone spoke well. Events were to show how cruelly he had been sacrified to the insane illusions of a man whose portly dignity and consequential air, helped to conceal the fact that he was a hopeless paranoic. Thomas John Ley enters the story at a very early stage in the police investigation. He was born at Bath, Somerset, in 1880, but was taken by his parents to Australia whilst still a boy. After leaving school he went to work as a butcher's boy, but by diligent study so far improved himself that he was eventually able to qualify as a solicitor. In 1917 he was elected to the Legislative Assembly of New South Wales and in due course became Minister of Public Instruction, them Minister of Labour, and finally, from 1922 to 1925, Minister of Justice. In the latter year, he was elected to the Australian House of Representatives, but lost his seat in 1928.

He had combined his busy public life with a career as company promoter. Some of his enterprises in this line had been distinctly dubious, and when the police started to make inconvenient inquiries, Ley thought it prudent to return to the land of his birth. He came to London in 1929, and was followed some months later by Mrs. Brook, a widow, who afterwards became his mistress. Maggie Evelyn Byron Brook was the unwitting, and unlikely, cause of Mudie's death. At the time of the murder she was sixty-six years of age and of homely appearance, hardly the sort of woman, it might have been thought, to drive a man to desperate deeds. But by 1946, despite the fact that it had been twelve years since he and Maggie Brook had been lovers, Ley was in the grip of a possessive jealousy that had long since passed the limit of what is possible to a sanely constituted mind. He was presently inhabiting a world of pure fantasy in which the unfortunate Mrs. Brook had only to exchange a casual word with a man for Ley to be convinced that his ageing *inamorata* had taken to herself a new lover. Mudie comes upon the scene in June 1945. He was at that time a lodger in the house at Wimbledon where Mrs. Brook had a flat, and one day, in a luckless moment for him, the landlady introduced him to Mrs. Brook as he was passing through the hall. They exchanged a few polite words. Mrs. Brook never saw or spoke to him again. Out of this trivial incident, magnified and distorted by the workings of a diseased mind, grew a monstrous conspiracy which took eighteen months to mature.

On 14th December, a fortnight after the discovery of Mudie's body, a curious trio presented themselves at New Scotland Yard—an ex-boxer named John William Buckingham, now engaged in the hire-car business; his son (also John William); and a Mrs. Lilian Florence Bruce, a cook-housekeeper from Putney. They had a remarkable story to tell. Mr. Buckingham, the father, described how in the early autumn of 1946, the hall porter at the Royal Hotel, Woburn Place, Bloomsbury, had advised him to get in Touch with Ley, who, it appeared, was looking for a car driver who could keep his mouth shut. Buckingham had telephoned Ley, and had met him at the Royal Hotel next evening, by appointment. Ley had not been alone. With him had been a certain Lawrence John Smith, the foreman of the workmen engaged upon converting Ley's home at 5 Beaufort Gardens, Kensington, into flats. At this and later meetings Buckingham had been given to understand that, as a solicitor, Ley was interested in protecting two women, mother and daughter, who were being blackmailed by the barman at the Reigate Hill Hotel. What Ley had wanted was to decoy Mudie to the house in Beaufort Gardens, to confront him with the proof of his blackmailing activities, and extract from him a promise to leave the country. Various ways of getting Mudie to the house had been discussed. Finally, it had been agreed that, posing as a woman of means, Mrs. Bruce, the cook-housekeeper, a friend of Buckingham *père*, should visit the Reigate Hill Hotel once or twice, and, having thus scraped an acquaintance with Mudie, invite him to be barman at a cocktail party she was supposed to be giving at Beaufort Gardens on 28th November.

All had turned out as planned. Mudie had agreed to act as barman at the party, since, by a not so curious chance, the date chosen for it happened to be his half-day off. Mrs. Bruce, accompanied by the younger Buckingham, had called for Mudie and had driven him up to London, arriving at Ley's house at about 7 p.m. Smith and Buckingham *père* had been lying in wait just inside the basement door. Buckingham had thrown a blanket over Mudie's head, and Smith had tied his ankles and wound a rope round his body. In this helpless condition, he had been 'jumped along' the passage and into a room which Ley used as an office. There Mudie was placed in a swivel-chair in front of a desk and gagged with a piece of rag. Buckingham had then left, first receiving from Ley, who all this while had been standing on the stairs, an envelope containing two hundred one-pound notes, as his and his son's and Mrs. Bruce's share in the kidnapping. Buckingham did not see Smith again until the following Tuesday, 3rd December. Smith had then told him: 'The old man was very pleased with the way things went off. Mudie has signed a confession and was given five hundred pounds and got out of the country.'

Ley was interviewed at Scotland Yard. There, in the presence of his solicitor, he made a long statement which amounted to a denial of everything that had been said both by Buckingham and by Smith. He had never mentioned Mudie to Smith; there had been no plot, no kidnapping. The statement ended: 'So far as my knowledge goes, Jack Mudie has never been at 5 Beaufort Gardens, and I have never seen him there.' On 28th December, Ley, Smith, and Buckingham were arrested and jointly charged with murder. But later Buckingham was released, and at the trial of Ley and Smith, which took place at the Old Bailey before the Lord Chief Justice, Lord Goddard, he was called as a Crown witness. The pair made an odd contrast in the dock; Ley, portly and prosperous-looking, suave, well-dressed; Smith, the working man, thirty years Ley's junior, and in appearance and demeanour the very opposite of his companion. Evidence was given which strongly suggested that on the day before the kidnapping Smith had visited the chalk-pit at Woldingham. From this the jury were invited to draw the conclusion that he had been on a reconnaissance, and had selected the chalk-pit—conveniently remote from Kensington—as a suitable place at which to 'dump' the body of the unfortunate Mudie. A verdict of 'Guilty' was returned against both prisoners, and 8th May was fixed as the date for their execution. But on 5th May, the Home Office announced that following a medical inquiry into Ley's mental condition he had been found to be insane, and had been removed to Broadmoor. That being so, it was inevitable that Smith should be reprieved also; in his case the death sentence was commuted to one of life imprisonment.

E.S.S.

# 1947
# Death of the Black Dahlia

Beth Short was known as the Black Dahlia. Why? Perhaps because of the lovely hair that fell over her shoulders. Perhaps because of her love for the black dresses she wore so well. Or perhaps because a fortune-teller might have picked out a card that said: 'The colour for you is—black!'

Her story has always fascinated me—not because I was so intimately connected with it from the time the city editor of the Los Angeles *Herald Express* called and said: 'This one is for you,' not only because I saw her tortured and mutilated body—but because of the strange and mysterious character of the Black Dahlia herself.

It was an anonymous telephone call that sent Los Angeles police to a vacant lot near the corner of Crenshaw and Santa Barbara Boulevards, where two officers found the nude body of a young girl, cut in two at the waist, and bound with rope. A beautiful girl, with black hair and grey-green eyes.

There was nothing, not even a scrap of clothing, to provide a clue to her identity, let alone the identity of her murderer. The Los Angeles *Examiner* arranged for her finger-prints to be sent by sound photo to the F.B.I. in Washington. If she had ever worked in a defence plant, or been in trouble with the law, her prints would be on file. The report came back quickly. The murdered girl was Elizabeth Short, last known address Santa Barbara, California. Born July 29, 1924, in Hyde Park, Massachusetts.

The call went out for information on Elizabeth Short, twenty-two, dark hair, eyes green, five foot three. The hunt for the Black Dahlia slayer had begun.

It was a Long Beach druggist who introduced Beth Short's nickname into the case. 'She'd come into our drugstore frequently,' he said. 'She'd usually wear a black two-piece beach costume which left her midriff bare, or she'd wear black lacy things. Her hair was jet-black. She was popular with the men who came in here, and they got to calling her the Black Dahlia.'

Police questioned everyone who had been in her company, or even remembered seeing her, but the results were baffling. Many people had known Beth Short—but nobody knew very much about her.

The crime itself was an unusually hideous one. Beth Short had been tortured before death put an end to her agony. The torturer had then severed the body at the waist, bound it with ropes, and transported it to where it had been found.

It was learned that Beth Short—penniless and homeless—recently had spent a month at the home of a girl friend in San Diego, and that from there she left to meet a former bandsman in the Air Force who was known only as 'Red'.

In two days' time, Red was in police custody. He readily admitted that he knew Beth Short and sometimes called her the Black Dahlia, but without further evidence he was exonerated as a suspect.

Several people had seen and talked with Beth in the days before her death. All told the same story—that the girl was a lost soul, obviously sick in heart and mind, wandering about town aimlessly, and scared of something she refused to talk about.

Something of Beth's life was told in letters that police found tucked away in her luggage located at a bus station in Los Angeles. These were love letters, neatly tied in ribbon, and revealing a story of men, heart-break, more men, and more heart-break.

A sense of guilt which plagued Beth's unfaithful heart revealed itself in letters which she wrote but never mailed. Desperation was their keynote. They revealed her as a beautiful, passionate girl, desperate for love and for protection.

In the days after the discovery of the Black Dahlia's tortured and mutilated body, tips poured in.

A girl who worked as a dancer in Hollywood night spots said she saw Beth Short sitting alone in the 'Gay Way' bar on South Main Street six days before she was murdered. Another girl acquaintance repeated that she saw her that same night, sitting in the lobby of an apartment hotel embracing a young man 'dressed like a petrol-station attendant'. The head bar-tender at a Hollywood Boulevard bar said he saw her five days before she died in the company of two girls of 'dubious reputation', looking 'seedy, as if she had slept in her clothes'.

Four days before the Black Dahlia's death, a South Main Street bar-tender had seen her and an unidentified blonde girl in an argument with two sailors. The next morning, another tip revealed, she took a room with an unidentified man in an East Washington Boulevard hotel. That evening she was seen alone again by the same dancer who had seen her before, and in the same bar, the 'Gay Way'.

The day before the murder, a bus-driver saw the Black Dahlia board his bus in the Santa Barbara bus terminal and alight at the Los Angeles terminal. On the same day, late in the afternoon, she was in a café in San Diego with a man dressed in a green suit.

There the trail ended. Nobody seemed to know where the Black Dahlia was between that afternoon and the next morning—January 15, 1947—when her dismembered body was found in the vacant lot.

The police recalled that Beth Short had failed to pick up her bags at the bus station during the last five days of her life. Had she been prevented from doing so? Had she been held prisoner during those days, free to move around only as long as she was under guard or the surveillance of others?

Investigation of this angle was hardly under way when an anonymous letter seemed to crack the case wide open. Soaked in petrol and addressed with lettering clipped from newspaper, it was found to contain a note reading: 'Here is Dahlia's belongings. Letter to follow.'

In the envelope police found a black address-book known to have been carried by the murdered girl, a newspaper clipping telling of the marriage of a former sweetheart, Beth Short's birth certificate, and a baggage claim check for the suitcases the police already had found and examined. There was no doubt that these things had been taken out of the Black Dahlia's purse.

The following day another letter came. It read: 'Here it is. Turning in Wed., Jan. 29, 10 a.m. Have had my fun at police—Black Dahlia Avenger.'

Authorities knew that the Avenger might be a prankster. On the other hand, it is not unusual for the psychotic killer to taunt the police with such notes and eventually give himself up; and in this case vengeance might well have been the motive, because it was known that the Black Dahlia lived in constant fear.

It was obvious that the Avenger had access to Beth's purse, so if he was not the actual killer, he was someone who could throw some much-needed light on the case. Would he give himself up Wednesday as he had promised?

On Tuesday night a man giving his name as Voorhees gave himself up because he couldn't 'stand it any longer' and signed a one-line confession. In twenty-four hours his 'confession' was discredited as the fantasy of a mentally sick man. He could never have known Beth Short. His was not the first 'confession' nor the last, all the work of cranks.

As for the Avenger, apart from a last note saying: 'Have changed my mind', that was the last anybody ever heard about him. All other leads have proved equally fruitless.

Who killed Beth Short, the Black Dahlia? The police are still working to find out. They will never give up. I don't know, either, but I have made some interesting deductions.

Everybody knows that the body of Elizabeth Short was cut in two at the waist—but what everybody does *not* know is that the job was done with precision and every evidence of professional skill.

Elizabeth Short was only five feet three inches in height, and weighed no more than 105 pounds. Why did the killer bisect the body? For more convenience in transporting it?

If the killer was a man, he would have had little difficulty in carrying the body. But suppose he were an under-sized man—a cripple—or a woman?

It seems likely that the mad killer must have been a doctor, a trained nurse, an undertaker or an undertaker's assistant.

Of the four, I would bet on one of the last two. Here are my reasons. A doctor's office or even a private hospital is not a

handy place to mutilate a girl and then cut her body in half.
Patients, nurses, anybody can drop in. On the other hand, an
undertaking parlour offers privacy.

I believe that someone working in an undertaking parlour
tortured and killed the Black Dahlia.

C.R.

# 1947

# JAMES CAMB
## Murder Overboard

James Camb, steward in the Union Castle liner *Durban Castle,*
was convicted of the murder of twenty-six-years-old Eileen
(Gay) Gibson, whose body he pushed through the porthole
of Cabin 126, so that it was lost for ever in the trackless
ocean. At the time of her death Miss Gibson, having already
had some stage and radio experience, was hopefully looking
forward to fresh engagements on the strength of the success
she had had in repertory in South Africa. She was now on her
way home to England as a first-class passenger in the *Durban
Castle*, which had sailed from Cape Town on 10th October
1947. At 12.40 a.m. on 18th October, Miss Gibson retired to
her cabin, having spent the evening dining and dancing with
some shipboard acquaintances. At two minutes to three, the
bell rang in the first-class pantry on A deck; the indicator
showed that someone was ringing in Miss Gibson's cabin on B
deck. Frederick Steer, night watchman, went to the cabin. Two
lights were showing outside the door, indicating that both the
steward and the stewardess had been rung for. Steer knocked
and made to enter the cabin. The light was on. He opened the
door a few inches. It was then shut in his face. As it closed,
Steer had a quick glimpse of a man wearing a sleeveless singlet
and a pair of blue trousers, a man he recognized as one of his
shipmates. He returned to the pantry and reported to James
Murray, the head night watchman, that James Camb, a steward

on the promenade deck, was in Miss Gibson's cabin. Together, they went along to the cabin, but although they waited outside the door for four or five minutes, they heard no sound. It was time now for Murray to make his routine report to the bridge. To the Second Officer of the Watch he described what Steer had seen, but being reluctant to make trouble for one of the stewards, he allowed the officer to infer that the man in Cabin 126 was a passenger. The officer dismissed him, remarking that the morals of the passengers were their own affair.

Miss Gibson was missed at breakfast-time and, after fruitless attempts to find her, the captain gave the order to reverse course. It was a hopeless search, and after an hour the captain set the liner on her course again. Steer now informed the captain that it was Camb he had seen in Miss Gibson's cabin. Camb promptly denied that he had stirred from his own quarters after he had gone to bed at 12.45. Later in the day he was examined by the ship's surgeon, who found that on the steward's right wrist were marks which appeared to be consistent with scratches made by fingernails. An examination of the bed in Cabin 126 revealed bloodstained saliva stains on the sheets.

When the *Durban Castle* arrived at Cowes Roads on the night of 24th–25th October, Camb was taken to police headquarters in Southampton, where it was pointed out to him that to persist in his denial that he had been in Cabin 126 when Steer had knocked at the door would only make it the more difficult to accept any reasonable explanation of Miss Gibson's disappearance that he might later have to offer. Said Camb: 'You mean that Miss Gibson might have died from a cause other than being murdered? She might have had a heart attack or something?' The Crown suggested that this was the genesis of the defence Camb was afterwards to develop at his trial, which took place at Winchester Assizes before Mr. Justice Hilbery the following March. In the witness-box, Camb told how he had gone to Miss Gibson's cabin at about 11 p.m. on 17th October to ask her if she required a supper tray. There, half jokingly, he said, 'I have a good mind to bring a drink down and join you.' To which Miss Gibson replied, 'Please yourself; it's up to you.' At about 2 a.m., he went along to Cabin 126, where he found Miss Gibson lying on the bed wearing a yellow quilted dressing-gown. He sat on the edge of the bed talking to her for ten or fifteen minutes. Then he climbed on to the bed and lay down beside the girl, who undid her dressing gown; he saw that she had nothing on underneath it. Whilst he was making love to her she suddenly heaved, as if she were gasping for breath. Her body stiffened for a fraction of a second and then went completely limp. 'I was rather stunned for a moment,' said Camb. 'First of all I listened and felt for heart-beats. I could not find any, and I attempted, by massaging the stomach towards the heart, to bring back circulation. . . . I should say I was twenty or twenty-five minutes trying to revive her.' He was standing by the bed applying what he knew of artificial respiration when Steer tried to enter the cabin; he closed the door upon him. He did not think he had been recognized, yet a feeling of 'complete panic' overcame him. For about fifteen minutes longer he continued in his fruitless attempts to revive Miss Gibson; at length he was forced to conclude that the girl was dead. He went on: 'I confess now it sounds very foolish, but I hoped to give the impression that she had fallen overboard, and deny all knowledge of having been to that cabin, in the hope that the Captain's further inquiries would not be too severe. I lifted her up and pushed her through the porthole.' In cross-examination by Mr. G. D. Roberts K.C., who led for the Crown, Camb was asked:

> Q: What would you expect a passenger to do who, in the night, objected to the advances of a member of the crew?
> A: Shout.
> Q: Not much good shouting. Is not ringing the bells a much better thing for a passenger to do?
> A: They both amount to the same thing.
> Q: That is what she did, is it not?
> A: She didn't touch the bell.
> Q: Who did then?
> A: I don't know.
> Q: Are you suggesting the bells went off on their own accord?
> A: I cannot suggest how the bells were rung.
> Q: Did you have to work quickly to silence her before the bell was answered?
> A: I didn't have to silence her at all.

> Q: I suggest that is what you did, and got those
> scratches on your right wrist?
> A: No.

The medical evidence was clearly of vital importance. Some of the best-known pathologists in the country were called. All agreed that the usual features of strangulation were present—the bloodstained saliva marks on the sheet, the scratches on Camb's wrist, suggesting that the girl had tried to tear the murderer's hands from her throat. Two eminent medical men who were called for the defence considered, however, that the signs were equally consistent with death from natural causes. Camb was found guilty and was sentenced to death—but he did not hang. He was condemned whilst Parliament was preoccupied with the 'no hanging' clause which the House of Lords took out. The Home Secretary had publicly stated that there would be no executions whilst the matter was still at issue between the two Houses. Thus was James Camb's life preserved. He was released from prison in September 1959.

E.S.S.

## 1948

# RAYMOND FERNANDEZ
## Slaying the Lonely Heart

The legions opposed to capital punishment rarely shun any condemned prisoner, yet two murderous creatures utterly failed to rouse one cry of protest over their executions. So vile and cold-blooded were their slayings that no one signed a petition, waved a placard or moaned an epitaph for Raymond Fernandez and Martha Beck before they visited Sing Sing Prison's electric chair during America's struggling post-World War II era.

In less than two years, Fernandez and Beck traveled a path strewn with more than a dozen grisly killings. Oddly enough, though, murder was not this strange couple's aim, but only the side-effect of a cheap con game gone amuck.

It began simply enough with Fernandez operating a Lonely Hearts racket. The Hawaiian-born Spanish American was tall and thin, but heavy of jowl and thick of eyebrow. He covered a nearly bald pate with a trim, black wig. Most of the elderly females who fell for this gigolo's line thought of him as a Latin-lover type, although newsmen later dubbed him 'a rather seedy Charles Boyer.'

Fernandez concentrated on females in their late fifties and early sixties, answering their lonely hearts ads, sweeping them off their feet with lavish attention. He already had two wives and uncounted children before embarking on his career as a devout bigamist.

One advertisement Fernandez answered was from a lonely woman living in Pensacola, Florida. He was happy to learn the woman was young, but was shocked when meeting her. Mrs. Martha Beck, a registered nurse and a matron of a home for crippled children, was obese, weighing well over two hundred pounds. Oddly, Fernandez fell in love with the roly-poly Martha and admitted his con game. She astounded him by her enthusiastic approval of his livelihood. She, too, wanted to participate.

The couple embarked upon a sinister system of swindling the lovelorn. Fernandez would join a lonely hearts club, enamour a fading female with his dubious charms and then introduce the gullible lady to Martha, who pretended to be Raymond's sister. In many instances, the pair moved into the homes of ladies who married Fernandez.

Such was the case with Mrs. Delphine Dowling, an attractive twenty-eight-year-old widow living in Grand Rapids, Michigan. After accepting Raymond's marriage proposal, Mrs. Dowling allowed him and Martha to move into her home. The cautious widow, however, delayed the walk to the altar until she was 'sure of Raymond's affections.'

This blocked the couple's chances of obtaining Mrs. Dowling's money, and Martha could not bear for Raymond to make love to the woman. As had been the case many times before with reluctant ladies, Raymond and Martha brought about their own solution. Mrs. Dowling and her two-year-old daughter, Rainelle, disappeared in January, 1949.

When police, asked to investigate by suspicious neighbors, arrived at the Dowling home, Fernandez and Martha shrugged their shoulders. No, they did not know where Mrs. Dowling had gone, but the officers 'could search the house if you like.' The police did search, and found, not cleverly concealed at all, a wet patch of cement the size of a grave. Digging down four feet, police found the bodies of Mrs. Dowling and her little girl.

The 'Lonely Hearts Killers' broke down immediately upon questioning. Mrs. Dowling became too suspicious so they gave her an overdose of sleeping pills, they said. The woman, however, struggled against the drug and Fernandez shot her in the head.

They tried to placate Rainelle by buying her a dog, but when the child continued to cry for her mother, Mrs. Beck threw her into a washtub and held her down until she drowned. The killers even boasted there were other victims—seventeen, perhaps more.

Fernandez discussed his murders quite freely with Michigan police, removing his cheap wig and wiping away the beads of sweat that gathered on his glistening pate with a perfume-scented handkerchief thoughtfully provided by Mrs. Beck, who chuckled through the lengthy interrogations. 'I'm no average killer,' grinned Fernandez. He had been suave and sophisticated in his homicides, he told police. It was business, after all, a way of earning a living.

The lean figure in the lockup complained that Mrs. Dowling's demise netted him only five hundred dollars but he had made as much as six thousands dollars in swindling and killing other lonely heart victims. There was Mrs. Jane Thompson, a widow Fernandez married and took to Spain on a honeymoon. He had returned alone, sadly informing Mrs. Thompson's relatives that she had perished in a horrible train wreck, a railway accident never recorded in any book of disasters. The con man was consoled by Mrs. Thompson's mother, a Mrs. Wilson. He moved into the elderly woman's home and she disappeared a short while later.

Carefree with his conscience, Fernandez recalled a Mrs. Myrtle Young. Oh, yes, he had promised to marry her, taking the woman (and her savings) to Chicago in August 1948. 'Poor woman,' laughed the con man, 'she croaked of over-exertion.'

He went on to explain in descriptions both vivid and obscene—as was the conduct of both Fernandez and Mrs. Beck throughout their three-week trial—how he drove Mrs. Young to death by compelling her to partake of nonstop sex.

In the tragic instance of Mrs. Janet Fay, a sixty-six-year-old widow living in a Manhattan apartment, murder was nothing more than a jealous whim of Martha Beck. She and Fernandez had *already* obtained every penny of Mrs. Fay's savings. As they were preparing to desert the widow, Mrs. Fay cried out for her beloved Fernandez. Martha grabbed a hammer and crushed the woman's head. With a smile forcing her chubby cheeks wide, Martha Beck told the police: 'I turned to Raymond and said, "Look what I've done," and then he strangled her with a scarf.'

Mrs. Fay's remains were packed into a trunk and driven to a small house some miles from New York City where the killers neatly wrapped it in brown butcher paper, then buried it beneath four feet of concrete. Fernandez generously gave the Michigan police the address of the New York cottage, one, he stated, they had cunningly rented just for the purpose of housing the grisly remains of their victims.

Michigan authorities reckoned that since their state had no capital punishment, the murderers might be free on parole in a decade. However, Mrs. Janet Fay was from New York, and that state still punished first-degree murder with execution. Fernandez and Martha were turned over to New York authorities.

Removed to Long Island jail cells, Martha and Raymond shrugged indifference to their fate. So avid was their taste for murder mysteries that warders were kept busy buying pocket-edition thrillers for them. Their trial commenced in July 1949 before Judge Fredinand Pecora. Both pleaded not guilty by reason of insanity.

On one occasion, as Mrs. Beck was being led to the witness stand, her face coated with rouge, her mouth thick with bright red lipstick, she broke away, waddled quickly to Fernandez, and held him in a bearlike embrace, kissing him passionately on the mouth, then the cheeks, the forehead, the neck. As she was pulled away by several guards, leaving Fernandez proudly bearing a lipstick-covered face, Martha screamed to the court: 'I love him! I do love him, and I always will!'

Such theatrics aside, the odd couple was found sane. A jury took little time convicting them of the first-degree murder of the widow Fay. Judge Pecora sentenced them to death on August 22, 1949. Their strange residence in Sing Sing's Death House, prolonged by laborious appeals, remains an unsavory legend in that prison.

Mrs. Beck and Fernandez were placed in cells that allowed them to see each other through an open door that stood between the men's and women's wings of Death Row. They waved at each other and blew kisses. Fernandez regaled his fellow condemned prisoners with his sexual feats, so much that they sarcastically took to calling him the 'Mail-Order Romeo.' They shouted at him to shut up, but he all the more readily prattled on about his bedroom exploits, his warped logic being that since all thoughts of sex were abandoned by fear in those facing executions, his bragging about sexual conquests therefore proved him unafraid, manly, someone to be respected.

Yet his Death House neighbours found a way to jangle Fernandez' nerves. Any caustic remark about his lover Martha would provoke him to screaming rage. A prisoner once called to him, after returning from the exercise yard: 'Hey, Fernandez, that blimp of yours gave me a big greeting today. She wiggled at me!' Raymond Fernandez exploded, shaking the bars in a fury, screaming deaths threats.

Before they were brought back to court for one of their many appeals, Martha began the love-hate correspondence that marked their Sing Sing imprisonment, writing:

> *Martha's not getting on the stand again if we have a new trial. I don't want a new trial if we have to cut each other's throats. Nor do I want one if it means you will refuse to look at me, smile, or speak when possible. I can take everything except a cold shoulder from you . . .*
>
> *I am glad you waved this a.m. Thanks darling, from the bottom of my heart. Ray—please, Ray—accept these flowers and my love.*
>
> *Your own Birdbrain*
> *P.S.: If you don't return the flowers. I'll know you added my initials to the bow knot, joining our love together with a tie so tight that nothing can break it.*

The next missive promised, as usual, eternal love, one in which Mrs. Beck waxed thickly about the birds she could see flying free beyond the cell window:

> *If I have to get to the chair to prove my love—I'll go. . . .*
> *Maybe I can train them [the birds], darling, to fly to you*
> *with a message of love, for I never want you to forget I love*
> *you. To me you will always be the man I love.*

Thirty X's, standing for kisses, were marked at the bottom of the page, with the flirtatious footnote:

> *If only I could deliver them in person!*

Weeks later, Martha had learned that Fernandez was talking freely about their evil adventures and her weird fetishes, laughing about such quirks with other prisoners in his wing. She dashed off the following vitriol to him:

> *You are a double-crossing, two-timing skunk. I learn*
> *now that you have been doing quite a bit of talking to*
> *everyone. It's nice to learn what a terrible murderous*
> *person I am, while you are such a misunderstood, white-*
> *haired boy, caught in the clutches of a female vampire. It*
> *was also nice to know that all the love letters you wrote*
> *'from your heart' were written with a hand shaking with*
> *laughter at me for being such a gullible fool as to believe*
> *them.*
> *Don't waste your time or energy trying to hide from*
> *view in church from now on, for I won't even look your*
> *way—the halo over your righteous head might blind me.*
> *May God have mercy on your soul.*
>
> M. F. Beck

Keeping pace with Martha's furious correspondence, the couple's lawyers filed appeal after appeal, all being denied, including that of the Supreme Court on January 2, 1951. The date for their execution was set for March 8, 1951. Two others,

Richard Powers and John King, both twenty-two, were slated to die at 11:00 P.M. on that date. The young killers, who had murdered a man in an armed robbery, taunted Fernandez to the end, studding their bravado with lines such as 'Don't forget, Ray, old boy, we got a date for Thursday, March eighth, at eleven o'clock. And don't forget to bring Martha!'

At this, Fernandez would grit his teeth and yell: 'You dirty punks, I'll still be around when you're both dead!' The lonely hearts killer was making reference to a Sing Sing rule that when more than one inmate is executed on the same day, the weaker goes to the chair first; he was, in his own estimation, the only one who 'wasn't yellow.'

On the appointed day, Powers and King did go first, weeping and shaking, being supported by guards into the 'little green room.'

The thirty-five-year-old Fernandez could not muster any appetite and sent his last meal to other prisoners. He did smoke a Havana cigar and handed over a note, his last official words, to warders for subsequent publication. It read:

> *People want to know whether I still love Martha. But of course I do. I want to shout it out. I love Martha. What do the public know about love?*

Martha Beck, age thirty, told her female guards that she was sick and tired of people thinking of her as a fat woman. She would show them. She ordered a simple last meal of fried chicken, fried potatoes and a salad—two helpings each. For the waiting newsmen, Mrs. Beck had written a final message:

> *My story is a love story. But only those tortured by love can know what I mean. I am not unfeeling, stupid or moronic. I am a woman who had a great love and always will have it. Imprisonment in the 'Death House' has only strengthened my feeling for Raymond.*

Fernandez was not, as he had boasted, the last to go to the electric chair that night. He followed Powers and King into the execution room, led wobbly legged and sagging by struggling guards. Mrs. Martha Beck was the last to go, thought by the authorities to be the strongest of all the condemned killers. There was a noticeable smile on her lips as she plopped down into the chair.

J.R.N

# 1949

# J.G. HAIGH
## The Acid-Bath Killer

Haigh was born in 1909, at Stamford in Lincolnshire. His father was an electrical engineer. Both parents belonged to that religious sect which calls itself 'The Peculiar People'—the Plymouth Brethren—and discipline in the home was strict and sanctimonious. He was an only child. He disliked games, loved music and drawing, became a choir-boy and won a divinity prize. At the grammar school he was also known as a ready and resourceful liar with a taste for practical jokes of the kind which inflict pain on the victim. After he left school he worked for a time in a second-hand car showroom, then as an electrician in a cinema, then as a salesman. When he was twenty-five, he was arrested on charges of obtaining money under false pretences by means of a hire-purchase swindle. He was sentenced to fifteen months' imprisonment. When he came out of prison he worked briefly for a firm of cleaners before being sacked for dishonesty. He then went south and set up, under a false name, as a solicitor. He was quite a skilful forger and by selling non-existent shares managed to defraud his 'clients' of over thirty thousand pounds before he was arrested again. This time, he was sentenced to four years' penal servitude.

He was thirty-one when he came out of Dartmoor. It was 1940; but for a man of his ingenuity it was not difficult to secure exemption from National Service on the grounds that he was in a reserved occupation. He then took to stealing from evacuated houses. In 1941 he was caught and sentenced to twenty-one months' hard labour. As a convict on licence, he also had to serve the balance of his previous sentence. He spent his time in prison studying law and doing some curious experiments with mice; he found that they could be dissolved in sulphuric acid. He was released in the autumn of 1943, and went to work for an engineering firm in Crawley. The following year he started a sideline business of his own. He rented a basement in Kensington and fitted it up as a workshop for repairing the pin-tables and automatic machines used in some amusement arcades. They were owned by a man named McSwann. Of the six persons whom Haigh is known for certain to have murdered, McSwann was the first.

In his statements to the police and the psychiatrists who examined him, Haigh always insisted that it was only the desire to drink human blood which made him murder, and that the desire always became overwhelming following a recurring nightmare about a forest of trees dripping with blood. He also claimed, as if for good measure, that he frequently drank his own urine. However, if we omit those embellishments and consider only the verifiable facts, a more convincing picture emerges.

Haigh needed money badly. McSwann had plenty. When he told Haigh that he was 'dodging the call-up,' Haigh saw that the situation had possibilities. He ordered some carboys of sulphuric acid and a forty-gallon tank. When McSwann next came to the workshop, Haigh hit him on the head with a cosh, dissolved the body in the acid and poured the solution down the drain.

His next move was to go to McSwann's elderly parents, tell them that their son had gone north into hiding from the army authorities and that he, Haigh, had agreed to look after the amusement arcades in their owner's absence. The explanation was accepted. He now proceeded, using a forged power of attorney, to gain possession of all the dead man's property and assets. When the old McSwanns heard that he had sold some of the pin-tables and began to ask questions, he took them separately, and on the pretext of having arranged a meeting with their son, to the basement workshop, killed them and dissolved their bodies in acid. Having supplied himself with a further power of attorney, he then took possession of their property also. By murdering the McSwann family, he made more than ten thousand pounds.

His subsequent murders—of the two Hendersons and Mrs.

Durand-Deacon— followed the same pattern. All were done for profit. After his arrest, and when he had had time to realise that his vampire motivation needed support, he confessed to a further three murders. In those cases, he claimed, there had been no coincidental profit; the victims had been killed only for their blood. He did not know their names. The police could find no evidence at all that they had ever existed. The inevitable conclusion was that Haigh had invented them. The nightmare was described convincingly enough, and Haigh may very well have been troubled by such dreams; but the blood-drinking episodes that they were said to have engendered seemed to belong to a clinical picture sketched, too hastily, by Bram Stoker.

In Haigh's account of the murder of Mrs. Durand-Deacon, he described how, after he had shot her, he collected a glass of her blood and drank it. He went on to describe his preparations for disposing of the body. Then, he corrected himself. Before pumping the acid into the tank, he had gone out to a nearby restaurant for a cup of tea. It was perhaps necessary to mention this. He was known in the restaurant and someone might have remembered seeing him there at that time. He wanted to appear completely truthful. But he destroyed his effect. Tea? On top of a nice glass of fresh blood? The defence plea of insanity never really had very much chance of succeeding.

E.A.

# 1952

# GASTON DOMINICI

## The Dirty Old Man Murders

Old Gaston Dominici was a peeping Tom. Not obsessed like David Berkowitz. But an occasional, almost accidental one. That
at least is the inference I draw from the triple murder of the Drummonds in Upper Provence on 5 August 1952.

The question originally posed by his miniature massacre was: who did it? That question, though, has long since been decided. Gaston did. As a jury found proved after a twelve day trial. The question still unanswered in many minds is: Why? What accursed combination of intent and circumstances led to an illiterate but hitherto harmless rustic slaughtering – at the age of seventy-six – three people who were strangers to him? People whom he had never before seen, whose names he did not know.

I think that, too, may now be explained with confidence. Having the advantage of time for thought and distance for perspective, one may venture to reconstruct the crimes from inception to completion.

Sir Jack Drummond was an English biochemist of international standing. During the second World War he played a major part in controlling the nation's diet as Lord Woolton's right hand man at the Ministry of Food. Afterwards he was director of scientific research at Boots. In the early fifties, overwork and exhaustion laid him low. Recovering, he set off in his station wagon for a recuperative holiday abroad. With him went his wife and their ten-year-old daughter Elizabeth. They drove south across France to Villefranche on the Côte d'Azur, camping *en route* and on excursions inland. The place they picked to camp about midnight on 4 August was a hundred yards from Gaston Dominici's farm. Nearly all the Dominici family lived at or near the farm: sons, daughters, daughters-in-law, sons-in-law, grandchildren of Gaston and his wife (a toothless, withered faggot nicknamed 'the Sardine'). They were landowning peasants, comfortable financially –

like the kulaks, rather than the moujiks of czarist Russia –
but quintessential peasants all the same. Depending on, and
obeying, the paterfamilias.

As the head of a suburban family nightly 'locks up' his
house, so old Gaston Dominici nightly 'locked up' his farm.
With a gun slung on his shoulder – more from habit than
for use – he patrolled the borders, alert for trespassers or
poachers. Notionally a duty, this also was a pleasure. The
sole chance to behave as he felt inclined. He need not do
anything strenuous or useful. He could do as the poet advises
– stand and stare. At the mulberry tree which he had pruned
that morning. At the unforthcoming soil which he had tilled that
afternoon. At the suddenly illuminated landscape as head-lamps
hurried by towards Grenoble or Marseilles. Old Gaston enjoyed
these solitary perambulations. Going along at a countryman's
unfatiguing saunter, he would often stay out for an hour or even
two. Always something to interest one who kept his eyes open.

That August night brought something exceptionally interesting, and the eyes of old Gaston opened wide. Some sort of a
vehicle – too long for a car, too much window for a van – lay in
a woody recess just off the main road. People, several people,
moving to and fro; it was fine and not pitch dark, Gaston could
see them clearly. Who were they? What did they want? Rather
suspicious, very curious, Gaston stood and stared.

There were three of them. A man – one certainly was a
man. And a woman – yes, another certainly was a woman; old
Gaston appreciatively traced the rounded curves. And the third,
skipping and jumping, was a child, a little girl. They were taking
things from the vehicle and putting them on the ground. Sheets?
Mattresses? A folding bed? Reminded old Gaston of his army
bivouacking on summer manoeuvres nearly fifty years ago. His
gaze firmly fixed on the gratuitous spectacle, he never moved an
inch, he never made a sound.

Their preparations finished, they started to undress. Under
the stars, in such an isolated spot, they might reasonably think
themselves secure from observation. The woman, though,
instinctively withdrew behind the wagon. Ironically, this took
her closer to old Gaston. As the female wear was cast aside,
concupiscence – long impotent or dormant – stirred his loins.
Forgetful of prudence, he stepped forth to get a better view.

He was spotted instantly. They jumped to conclusions, only partly justified. If a woman, however innocently, disrobes where men may see her, she must be ready for male stares. But Lady Drummond's innate modesty was shocked; Sir Jack's nerves, after illness, were hypersensitive. He construed it as a calculated insult to his wife. Gaston may not have understood the foreign words. He fully understood the foreigner's attitude. Was he to be reviled and threatened, almost in his own domain, by an alien unauthorized intruder? Gaston's indignation boiled up and overflowed. In rage and fright, he raised his gun, levelled it . . . and, hardly realizing what he did, he fired. And, without pausing, fired again, Sir Jack fell dead.

The rest was not, as superficially appears, the result of a savage running mindlessly amock. It was rather the result of reasserted peasant cunning. Murder had been done. Murder meant the guillotine. No one must live to tell the tale. And so Lady Drummond died – three bullets through her heart. And so Elizabeth, running desperately for life, was killed with the butt of a rifle in which no bullets remained.

When the police visited the Dominicis – after the bodies had been discovered by a wayfarer – nobody of course could tell them anything. 'Me? I was in bed all night,' old Gaston said, and the other members of the family rallied round. But some of them at least knew more than they at first would say, and later on at least some of these said some of it. Enough to put old Gaston behind bars, where he confessed and then retracted, time and time again, until the day he stepped into the dock. The death sentence was commuted into life imprisonment, and in 1960 he was set free on compassionate grounds. Old age.

Voyeurism – much associated with the old – is one of the milder sexual aberrations. It is not a crime, though it may give rise to one, or merge with one – most commonly, a trivial 'breach of the peace'. Here, diluted voyeurism gave rise to murder. None would have died on the Marseilles-Grenoble road that night if Sir Jack Drummond had been undressing alone.

E.L.

# 1953

## REG CHRISTIE

## The Monster of Rillington Place

Christie committed eight murders between 1940 and 1953, and was hanged in July 1953. He differed in only one respect from other 'shy killers': there was an authoritarian character structure. As a special reserve constable at the beginning of the war, he became notorious for his officiousness; he enjoyed reporting people for minor blackout offences. The first four victims were killed between 1940 and 1950, always when his wife was away on visits to relatives in Sheffield. In 1952, he murdered his wife, and buried her under the floorboards. Three more sex crimes followed in quick succession in the following months. The method was to persuade the woman to inhale gas, on the pretext of curing asthma or catarrh with Friar's Balsam, then to rape her while unconscious. The murder – by strangulation – was apparently an afterthought, to protect himself.

The interesting feature of the case is his moral collapse. The first two victims were carefully buried in the tiny back garden, and no suspicion fell on Christie. The third victim was Mrs. Beryl Evans, a woman who lived with her husband in the flat upstairs. Christie persuaded her husband that he was a skilled abortionist. The abortion was to take place when the husband – Timothy Evans – was at work. It seems unlikely that Christie intended to kill her – his chances of getting away with it were too small. But the sight of her nakedness was too much for him; he battered her unconscious, strangled her, then raped her. He later murdered the fourteen-month-old daughter, Geraldine. When Evans came home from work, Christie seems to have succeeded in frightening him so much that he ended by confessing to the murder of his wife. (Evan's I.Q. was exceptionally low, but it is still a mystery how he came to confess to Christie's crime.) Evans was hanged in 1950. Many years later, as a result of a public inquiry, he was finally exonerated.

Beryl Evans was murdered in 1949; Mrs. Christie in December 1952. After disposing of her body, Christie seems to have lost all caution, as if determined to have any orgy before he was caught. In early January, a prostitute named Rita Nelson entered 10 Rillington Place; she was anaesthetized, strangled and raped, and her body was pushed into the corner of a deep closet in the kitchen. About ten days later, Christie strangled and raped another prostitute, Kathleen Maloney. He left the body in the chair all night and went to bed; the next morning, it was wrapped in a blanket and pushed into the closet. During the next few months, the squalid little flat was allowed to become filthy and untidy. Christie had no job, and made no attempt to get one. And in the case of his final victim, he abandoned all attempt to cover his tracks. In early March, he met a girl named Hectorina Mclennan and her lover, a lorry driver called Baker. They spent three nights at his flat, sleeping in chairs or on the floor. On the fourth day, Christie approached Hectorina Mclennan outside the labour exchange, while Baker was signing on, and asked her back to the house. She told Baker where she was going; and went back with Christie. He strangled her, raped her, and put her in the cupboard. Baker called later to asked if Christie knew where she was; Christie said he didn't, and they drank a cup of tea in the kitchen; later, Christie went out with him and helped him search for her.

A week later, he sub-let the flat to another couple, collected £7 13s. for rent in advance, and wandered off, leaving the bodies in the cupboard that was now disguised by a layer of wallpaper. The owner of the house, finding the flat sub-let, told the new tenants to leave, and looked into the cupboard. In spite of the hue and cry that followed, Christie made no attempt to escape from London, even registering at a Rowton House under his own name; he walked around becoming increasingly dirty and unshaven, until he was recognized by a policeman on Putney Bridge. What happened to him in those last weeks of freedom? It is tempting to suppose that he ceased to be responsible for his actions. Yet he continued to plan and calculate; even when on the run, he met a pregnant girl in a café, and told her he was a medical man who could perform an operation . . .

What is clear is that, beyond a certain point, Christie found himself lost in a kind of maze. His early murders – of Ruth Fuerst and Muriel Eady – were carefully planned; the women were invited back to the house when his wife was on holiday, murdered, then buried in the back garden; no suspicion fell on Christie. In his confession, Christie described his feeling as he looked at the body of Muriel Eady, after raping and strangling her: '. . . once again I experienced that quiet, peaceful thrill. I had no regrets.' It was as deliberate as a fox stealing a chicken. The murder of Beryl Evans was less calculated; but in the aftermath, Christie showed his usual skill and calculation. At the Evans trial, he was a cool and competent witness, and a barrister wrote; 'Christie bore the stamp of respectability and truthfulness.' But the murders of 1953 were neither calculated nor competent. If Christie had buried his victims in the back garden, and continued to work at his job (with British Road Services), his chances of escaping detection would have been high. None of the three women was likely to be missed. His only problem was to prevent his wife's sister from becoming suspicious; but she lived in Sheffield, and Christie had already explained that Ethel's rheumatism was so bad that she was unable to write letters. But the time for calculation was past; Christie was on the same down hill slope as Sade, driven by an obsession that turned his life into a desert. His will to destruction was also a will to self-destruction. He was no longer in control; now the 'worm' possessed him; hence the curiously aimless, head-in-sand, magical behaviour of those last months of freedom.

C.W.

# 1954

# DOCTOR SAM SHEPPARD
## The 'Mysterious Stranger'

Dr. Sam Sheppard, the convicted murderer of his wife, set out to achieve one of the most difficult feats open to a killer. Having killed his wife Marilyn, on the night of the 4th July, 1954, he created a 'mysterious stranger', a burglar who had slain his wife and knocked him unconscious. He tried to make his story fit the facts. But he couldn't.

Some of Sheppard's blunders were unavoidable: few murderers would have avoided them but as a doctor, he should have realized that the removal of his wife's watch from her wrist after the blood had congealed would show that it had been taken off some time after death. This suggested either that the 'mysterious stranger' had returned to remove the watch, which was unlikely, or that its removal had been part of a plan to fake a burglary.

The Sheppard case is one of the most celebrated of recent American murder trials. In a country in which the homicide rate averages 12,000 a year, a murder case must be of outstanding interest to warrant national newspaper coverage. The Sheppard case did more than that for it rated almost daily mention in the British Press. To some degree it was a 'problem' case: whether or not Sheppard was rightly convicted is still hotly debated, and many veteran criminologists think that on the evidence he should have been acquitted. The jury's verdict was a compromise decision: they found him guilty of murder in the second degree when, to all appearances, he was either guilty of murder in the first degree, carrying the death penalty, or not guilty at all.

Sheppard, aged thirty, made an income of $12,000 a year from his partnership in the family practice and ownership of a hundred-bed osteopathic hospital at Bayview, about ten miles from Cleveland, Ohio.

He was a fine surgeon, tall, good-looking, and popular. He had married his boyhood sweetheart, and they lived with their small son in an old frame house, the garden of which ran down to a private beach on Lake Erie. Sam had expensive personal tastes: he spent his money on British sports cars but he was mean to his wife, begrudging her the household gadgets which are the glory of the American housewife.

The exact relationship between Sam and Marilyn is difficult to define. At the trial he swore that he loved her deeply but testimony was given that he had talked of divorce and it was undisputed that for fifteen months he had been carrying on an affair with his laboratory assistant, Susan Hayes. Motive did not have to be proved to convict him of the murder of his wife; and no adequate reason was advanced as to why he might have killed her when divorce, even for a doctor, carries no social stigma in

America. The early hours of a summer morning are not a usual time for blind rages and sudden blows.

There was no hint of motive in anything that immediately preceded the murder. The Sheppards spent the evening of the 3rd July with friends, Don and Nancy Aherne, who came to dinner and stayed to watch TV. Sheppard, after a long day's work, lay on a couch and dozed off, the guests being let out at 12.30 a.m. by Marilyn. When they left Sam was fast asleep wearing trousers, a T-shirt, and a corduroy jacket. The Ahernes did not hear Marilyn lock the front door and it is probable that it was seldom locked at night.

At 6.10 a.m Sheppard telephoned another friend, Major Houk, saying, ' My God, Spen, get over here right away. I think they've killed Marilyn.' When Mr. and Mrs. Houk got to the house they found Sam Sheppard in a chair, with his face bruised, naked from the waist up and with his trousers dripping wet. In the bedroom Marilyn lay on her back on the bed, having been given, it was later discovered, twenty-seven smashing blows on the head. She was quite cold and had been dead for some time.

Sam's brothers were called and he was rushed to the family hospital, it being said that he was injured seriously. The prosecution at the trial claimed that his injuries were faked and were no more than superficial. When he was finally made available for questioning he said that he had been sleeping in the living-room. He was awakened by hearing Marilyn moaning. He went upstairs and saw a vague form. He was knocked out by a blow. When he recovered consciousness he found his wife dead. He heard a noise downstairs and chased a shadowy figure out of the house and down to the beach where he was again knocked out. The attacker was a big bushy-haired man. Recovering consciousness he found himself lying on the beach with the waves washing over him. He went back to the house and again passed out. When he awakened he telephoned the first friend he thought of.

Such was Dr. Sheppard's story. The police considered it a pack of lies.

No 'mysterious stranger', far less a bushy-haired burglar, had been seen in the district. The supposed burglar had taken nothing except the doctor's T-shirt, yet he had ransacked drawers, ignored money, and had discarded Marilyn's wrist-watch which he must have come back to steal from the body. Having murdered Mrs. Sheppard he had been content merely to knock out the only probable witness against him. Why had he not used the same weapon to kill the husband?

There were no finger prints on Dr. Sheppard's desk, not even his own, and the surface looked as though it had been carefully dusted. The drawers had been opened. To open them it was necessary to pull back the desk chair, and it had been replaced correctly. This feat required considerable local knowledge for one of the castors came off if the chair was moved. How did the burglar know this?

No murder weapon was found, yet there was an indication of its nature. In his investigation the Coroner, Dr. Samuel Gerber, one of the America's foremost homicide experts, found a clue. Turning over the pillow on the bed he noticed faint blood-stains, suggesting that the murder weapon had been temporarily laid there. The marks indicated that it had been a claw-like weapon, perhaps a surgical instrument. Faint stains found on the stairs, and recognized only after chemical tests as human blood, suggested that the killer had carried the still dripping weapon from the house.

The loss of Sheppard's T-shirt was difficult to account for. According to him the bushy-haired stranger had taken it because his own shirt was blood-stained, but it was equally possible that the doctor had destroyed it himself for that reason. There was another odd fact: when Sheppard went to sleep he was wearing a corduroy jacket, yet when the Houks arrived just after 6 a.m. the corduroy jacket was lying on the couch neatly folded.

According to Sheppard, he had been knocked unconscious the second time on the beach by the lake. He was awakened by the waves lapping over him. The lake was very rough that night and it is a medical fact that a person lying unconscious face down in water drowns and is not revived.

On the bank by the lake was found a bag, which lad been taken from Dr. Sheppard's desk, containing his wrist-watch and signet ring. The watch had stopped at 4.15 a.m. and the fact that it was stained with blood, while the inside of the bag was clean, indicated that it had been placed there after the blood had dried.

The time the watch had stopped was nearly two hours before his telephone call of alarm.

Unconvincing as was Dr. Sheppard's story, it might have been difficult to disprove to the satisfaction of a jury, had it not been for the evidence that he had been having an affair with Susan Hayes. His guilty passion gave a reason why Sam and Marilyn might have quarrelled, a quarrel in the early hours of the morning resulting in his attack on her, or why he might have wanted to eliminate her.

As Susan Hayes had left the hospital some time before and had gone to live in California, the police might never have got on to her existence in relation to Sheppard if they had not found a list of Californian telephone numbers in his wallet which they traced to her. Sheppard, they learned, had visited California early in 1954 and had stayed with Susan at the house of some friends. His meanness was his undoing. If he had taken her to an hotel, their stay together might never have come to light. Questioned by the police, Susan Hayes admitted the affair but the defence claimed, that as Sheppard could have her whenever he wanted, there was no need for him to murder his wife to get her.

The jury at the trial, which lasted from the 16th October to the 17th December were asked to return one of four possible verdicts, or find Sheppard not guilty of any crime. They could find him guilty of murder in the first degree, carrying the death penalty, or first degree murder with a recommendation to mercy, carrying a sentence of life imprisonment; alternatively they could find him guilty of second degree murder, also carrying a life sentence but with better chances of parole, or guilty of manslaughter for which the sentence ranged from one to twenty years' imprisonment.

After a deliberation of 102 hours, the jury of seven men and five women found him guilty of second degree murder and he was sentenced to life imprisonment. It was a surprise ending to a case which has given rise to great controversy, and the verdict shows the fallacy of the 'degree' system, which was so rightly turned down in the recommendations of the British Royal Commission on Capital Punishment.

In most American Courts, the jury are directed by the Judge only on points of law. The vast difference in the time of deliberation from British jurors reflects both the difficulty in deciding upon the 'degree' of murder on which to convict and the absence of any direction on the evidence.

The case against Sheppard consisted chiefly of a set of suspicious circumstances growing out of a flimsy attempt to fake the story of a bushy-haired burglar to hide the real killer's guilt. As a doctor Sheppard should have been able to make his story more convincing. While his murder of his wife was in no sense a 'medical murder', he failed to use the trained mind of a doctor to disguise his crime. The police, through long and painful experience, have learned that when a wife is killed, the murderer is usually the husband and seldom a 'mysterious stranger'.

R.F

# 1957

# ED GEIN
## Horror Heaped upon Horror

'Searchers after horror haunt strange, far places,' wrote H. P. Lovecraft in the opening of his story, 'The Picture in the House.' 'For them are the catacombs of Ptolemais, and the carven mausolea of the nightmare countries. They climb to the moonlit towers of ruined Rhine castles, and falter down black cobwebbed steps beneath the scattered stones of forgotten cities in Asia. The haunted wood and the desolate mountain are their shrines, and they linger around the sinister monoliths on uninhabited islands. But the true epicure in the terrible, to whom a new thrill of unutterable ghastliness is the chief end and justification of existence, esteems most of all the ancient, lonely farmhouses of backwoods New England; for there the dark elements of strength, solitude, grotesqueness and ignorance combine to form the perfection of the hideous.'

Lovecraft's tale then goes on to describe a visit to one of these 'silent, sleepy, staring houses in the backwoods' inhabited by a weird eccentric whose speech and dress suggest origins in a bygone day. An increasingly horrible series of hints culminates in the revelation that the inhabitant of the house has preserved an unnatural existence for several centuries, sustaining life and vigor through the practice of cannibalism.

Of course it's 'only a story.'

Or—is it?

On the evening of November 16, 1957, visitors entered an ancient, lonely farmhouse—not in backwoods New England but in rural Wisconsin. Hanging in an adjacent shed was the nude, butchered body of a woman. She had been suspended by the heels and decapitated, then disemboweled like a steer. In the kitchen next to the shed, fire flickered in an old-fashioned pot-bellied stove. A pan set on top of it contained a human heart.

The visitors—Sheriff Art Schley and Captain Lloyd Schoephoester—were joined by other officers. There was no electricity in the darkened house and they conducted their inspection with oil lamps, lanterns, and flashlights.

The place was a shambles, in every sense of the word. The kitchen, shed, and bedroom were littered with old papers, books, magazines, tin cans, tools, utensils, musical instruments, wrapping paper, cartons, containers, and a miscellany of junk. Another bedroom and living room beyond had been nailed off; these and five rooms upstairs were dusty and deserted.

But amidst the accumulated debris of years in the three tenanted rooms, the searchers found:

two shin bones;

a pair of human lips;

four human noses;

bracelets of human skin;

four chairs, their woven cane seats replaced by strips of human skin;

a quart can, converted into a tom-tom by skin stretched over both top and bottom;

a bowl made from the inverted half of a human skull;

a purse with a handle made of skin;

four 'death masks'—the well-preserved skin from the faces of women— mounted at eye-level on the walls;

five more such 'masks' in plastic bags, stowed in a closet;

ten female human heads, the tops of which had been sawed off above the eyebrows;

a pair of leggings, fashioned from skin from human legs;
a vest made from the skin stripped from a woman's torso.

The bodies of 15 different women had been mutilated to provide these trophies. The number of hearts and other organs which had been cooked on the stove or stored in the refrigerator will never be known. Apocryphal tales of how the owner of the house brought gifts of 'fresh liver' to certain friends and neighbors have never been publicly substantiated, nor is there any way of definitely establishing his own anthropophagism.

But H. P. Lovecraft's 'true epicure of the terrible' could find his new thrill of unutterable ghastliness in the real, revealed horrors of the Gein case.

Edward Gein, the gray-haired, soft-voiced little man who may or may not have been a cannibal and a necrophile, was—by his own admission—ghoul, a murderer, and a transvestite. Due process of law has also adjudged him to be criminally insane.

Yet for decades he roamed free and unhindered, a well-known figure in a little community of 700 people. Now small towns everywhere are notoriously hotbeds of gossip, conjecture, and rumor, and Gein himself joked about his 'collection of shrunken heads' and laughingly admitted that he'd been responsible for the disappearance of many women in the area. He was known to be a recluse and never entertained visitors; children believed his house to be 'haunted.' But somehow the gossip never developed beyond the point of idle, frivolous speculation, and nobody took Ed Gein seriously. The man who robbed fresh graves, who murdered, decapitated, and eviscerated women when the moon was full, who capered about his lonely farmhouse be-decked in corpse-hair, the castor-oil-treated human skin masks made from the faces of his victims, a vest of female breasts and puttees of skin stripped from women's legs—this man was just plain old Eddie Gein, a fellow one hired to do errands and odd jobs. To his friends and neighbors he was only a handyman, and a *most* dependable and trustworthy babysitter.

'Good old Ed, kind of a loner and maybe a little bit odd with that sense of humour of his, but just the guy to call in to sit with the kiddies when me and the old lady want to go to the show. . . .'

Yes, good old Ed, slipping off his mask of human skin, stowing the warm, fresh entrails in the refrigerator, and coming over to spend the evening with the youngsters; he *always* brought them bubble gum . . .

A pity Grace Metalious wasn't aware of our graying, shy little small-town handyman when she wrote *Peyton Place!* But, of course, nobody would have believed her. New England or Wisconsin are hardly the proper settings for such characters; we might accept them in Transylvania, but Pennsylvania—néver!

And yet, he lived. And women died.

As near as can be determined, on the basis of investigation and his own somewhat disordered recollections, Gein led a 'normal' childhood as the son of a widowed mother. He and his brother, Henry, assisted her in the operation of their 160-acre farm.

Mrs. Gein was a devout, religious woman with a protective attitude toward her boys and a definite conviction of sin. She discouraged them from marrying and kept them busy with farm work; Ed was already a middle-aged man when his mother suffered her first stroke in 1944. Shortly thereafter, brother Henry died, trapped while fighting a forest fire. Mrs. Gein had a second stroke from which she never recovered; she went to her grave in 1945 and Ed was left alone.

It was then that he sealed off the upstairs, the parlor, and his mother's bedroom and set up his own quarters in the remaining bedroom, kitchen and shed of the big farmhouse. He stopped working the farm, too; a government soil-conservation program offered him a subsidy, which he augmented by his work as a handyman in the area.

In the spare time he studied anatomy. First from books, and then—

Then he enlisted the aid of an old friend named Gus. Gus was kind of a loner, too, and quite definitely odd—he went to the asylum a few years later. But he was Ed Gein's trusted buddy, and when Ed asked for assistance in opening a grave to secure a corpse for 'medical experiments,' Gus lent a hand, with a shovel in it.

That first cadaver came from a grave less than a dozen feet away from the last resting place of Gein's mother.

Gein dissected it. Wisconsin farm folk are handy at dressing-out beef, pork, and venison.

What Ed Gein didn't reveal to Gus was his own growing desire to become a woman himself; it was for this reason he'd studied anatomy, brooded about the possibilities of an 'operation' which would result in a change of sex, desired to dissect a female corpse and familiarize himself with its anatomical structure.

Nor did he tell Gus about the peculiar thrill he experienced when he donned the grisly accouterment of human skin stripped from the cadaver. At least, there's no evidence he did.

He burned the flesh bit by bit in the stove, buried the bones. And with Gus's assistance, repeated his ghoulish depredations. Sometimes he merely opened the graves and took certain parts of the bodies—perhaps just the heads and some strips of skin. Then he carefully covered up traces of his work. His collection of trophies grew, and so did the range of his experimentation and obsession.

Then Gus was taken away, and Gein turned to murder.

The first victim, in 1954, was Mary Hogan, a buxom 51-year-old divorcée who operated a tavern at Pine Grove, six miles from home. She was alone when he came to her one cold winter's evening; he shot her in the head with his 32-caliber revolver, placed her body in his pickup truck, and took her to the shed where he'd butchered pigs, dressed-out deer.

There may have been other victims in the years that followed. But nothing definite is known about Gein's murderous activities until that day in November, 1957, when he shot and killed Mrs. Bernice Worden in her hardware store on Plainfield's Main Street. He used a .22 rifle from a display rack in the store itself, inserting his own bullet which he carried with him in his pocket. Locking the store on that Saturday morning, he'd taken the body home in the store truck. Gein also removed the cash register, which contained $41 in cash—not with the intention of committing robbery, he later explained in righteous indignation, but merely because he wished to study the mechanism. He wanted to see how a cash register worked, and fully intended to return it later.

Mrs. Worden's son, Frank, often assisted her in the store, but on this particular Saturday morning he'd gone deer-hunting. On his return in late afternoon he discovered the establishment closed, his mother missing, the cash register gone. There was blood on the floor. Frank Worden served as a deputy sheriff in the area and knew what to do. He immediately alerted his superior officer, reported the circumstances, and began to check for clues. He established that the store had been closed since early that morning, but noted a record of the two sales transactions made before closing. One of them was for a half gallon of antifreeze.

Worden remembered that Ed Gein, the previous evening at closing time, had stopped by the store and said he'd be back the next morning for antifreeze. He'd also asked Worden if he intended to go hunting the next day. Worden further recalled that Gein had been in and out of the store quite frequently during the previous week.

Since the cash register was missing, it appeared as if Gein had planned a robbery after determining a time when the coast would be clear.

Worden conveyed his suspicions to the sheriff, who sent officers to the farm, seven miles outside Plainfield. The house was dark and the handyman absent; acting on a hunch, they drove to a store in West Plainfield where Gein usually purchased groceries. He was there—had been visiting casually with the proprietor and his wife. In fact, he'd just eaten dinner with them.

The officers spoke of Mrs. Worden's disappearance. The 51-year-old, 140-pound little handyman joked about it in his usual offhand fashion; he was just leaving for home in his truck and was quite surprised that anyone wanted to question him. 'I didn't have anything to do with it,' he told them. 'I just heard about it while I was eating supper.' It seems someone had come in with the news.

Meanwhile, back at the farmhouse, the sheriff and the captain had driven up, entered the shed, and made their gruesome discovery.

Gein was taken into custody, and he talked.

Unfortunately for the 'searchers after horror,' his talk shed little illumination on the dark corners of his mind. He appeared to have only a dim recollection of his activities; he was 'in a daze' much of the time during the murders. He did recall that he'd visited about 40 graves through the years, though he insisted he hadn't opened all of them, and denied he'd committed more than two murders. He named only nine women whose bodies he'd molested, but revealed he selected them after careful inspections of the death notices in the local newspapers.

There was a lie-detector test, a murder charge, an arraignment, a series of examinations at the Central State Hospital for the Criminally Insane. He remains there to this day.

The case created a sensation in the Midwest. Thousands of 'epicures of the terrible'—and their snotty-nosed brats—made the devout pilgrimage to Plainfield, driving bumper-to-bumper on wintry Sunday afternoons as they gawked at the 'murder farm'. Until one night the residence of the 'mad butcher' went up in smoke.

I was not among the epicures. At that time I resided less than 50 miles away, but had no automobile to add to the bumper crop; nor did I subscribe to a daily newspaper. Inevitably, however, I heard the mumbled mixture of gossip and rumor concerning the 'fiend' and his activities. Curiously enough, there was no mention of his relationship with his mother, nor of his transvestism; the accent was entirely on proven murder and presumed cannibalism.

What interested me was this notion that a ghoulish killer with perverted appetites could flourish almost openly in a small rural community where everybody prides himself on knowing everyone else's business.

The concept proved so intriguing that I immediately set about planning a novel dealing with such a character. In order to provide him with a supply of potential victims, I decided to make him a motel operator. Then came the ticklish question of what made him tick—the matter of motivation. The Oedipus motif seemed to offer a valid answer, and the transvestite theme appeared to be a logical extension. The novel which evolved was called *Psycho*.

Both the book and a subsequent motion picture version called forth comments which are the common lot of the writer in the mystery-suspense genre.

'Where do you get those perfectly *dreadful* ideas for your stories?'

I can only shrug and point to the map—not just a map of Wisconsin, but *any* map. For men like Edward Gein can be found anywhere in the world—quiet little men leading quiet little lives, smiling their quiet little smiles and dreaming their quiet little dreams.

Lovecraft's 'searchers after horror' do not need to haunt

strange, far places or descend into catacombs or ransack mausolea. They have only to realise that the true descent into dread, the journey into realms of nightmare, is all too easy—once one understands where terror dwells.

The real chamber of horrors is the gray, twisted, pulsating, blood-flecked interior of the human mind.

R.B.


# 1958

# CHARLES STARKWEATHER
## 'A Little World All Our Own'

There was always something a little odd about Charlie Starkweather. Not his all-American love of comic books, hot rods, and hunting; he did strange things.

Once when he was driving a garbage truck in Lincoln, Neb., Charlie sat behind the wheel and shouted obscenities at passersby.

(From his confession: 'The more I looked at people the more I hated them because I knowed they wasn't any place for me with the kind of people I knowed. I used to wonder why they was here anyhow? A bunch of goddamned sons of bitches looking for somebody to make fun of . . . some poor fellow who ain't done nothin' but feed chickens.')

Still no one suspected little Charlie would become one of the bloodiest mass murderers of all time.

Starkweather, nineteen, was infatuated with the James Dean image and wore his red hair long (by 1950s standards). Small, stocky, and pigeon-toed, he wore a cheap pair of cowboy boots several sizes too large, the toes of which he stuffed with crumpled newspapers.

His small stature kept him from dating girls his own age. So he selected diminutive Caril Ann Fugate for his sweetheart.

Caril Ann was only fourteen but well developed. She had a sexy, hip-swinging way about her. And she was a rebel, like

Charlie. She delighted in telling her stepfather, Marion Bartlett, to go to hell.

Little Red, as Starkweather was called by his friends, and Caril Ann made a mumbling, awkward pair of lovebirds. Charlie was on the shy side.

Yet it was this withdrawn boy who would blithely slaughter eleven people and terrify the Plains States area in the late, wintry days of January, 1958.

A lone victim of Starkweather's wrath was gas station attendant Robert Colvert. Little Red drove into Colvert's station on December 1, 1957 and robbed him at gunpoint. He then drove the 21-year-old Colvert to the open plains beyond Lincoln and killed him, shooting him several times in the head.

The mass slaughter began in Caril Ann's living room two months later. Charlie was waiting for her to come home from school. He had brought along his slide-action .22-calibre hunting rifle, the one possession he was seldom without.

Mrs Bartlett was annoyed. She didn't like Charlie, and his fondling of the rifle made her uneasy. Suddenly she started shouting angrily at him.

As Little Red remembered later: 'They said they were tired of me hanging around. I told Mrs Bartlett off and she got so mad that she slapped me. When I hit her back, her husband started to come at me, so I had to let both of them have it with my rifle.'

Caril Ann arrived just as the argument began. She watched the berserk bantam saunter into her little sister's room and choke two-year-old Betty Jean to death by pushing his rifle down her throat.

Then she switched on one of her favourite TV programs while Charlie made sandwiches in the kitchen.

Charlie hid Bartlett's body under rags and newspapers in the chicken coop behind the house. He dragged Mrs Bartlett's corpse to an abandoned outhouse a few yards away and covered it with newspapers.

Next he dumped the baby's body into a cardboard box and joined Caril Ann to watch television.

(From his confession: 'Don't know why it was but being alone with her [Caril] was like owning a little world all our own . . . lying there with our arms around each other and not talking much, just kind of tightening up and listening to the wind blow or looking at the same star and moving our hands over each other's face . . . I forgot about my bow-legs when we was havin' excitement. When I'd hold her in my arms and do the things we done together, I didn't think about bein' a red-headed peckerwood then . . . We knowed that the world had give us to each other. We was goin' to make it leave us alone . . . if we'd a been let alone we wouldn't hurt nobody . . .')

Caril Ann worried that relatives might show up. So Charlie wrote on a piece of paper: 'Stay a Way. Every Body is Sick With the Flu.' They tacked the note to the front door.

It wasn't long before Mrs Bartlett's older daughter stopped to visit. She thought the note fishy and pounded on the door. Caril Ann refused to let her in.

Puzzled and angry, the sister told her husband the fourteen-year-old was acting strangely. He called the police.

When officers arrived, Caril Ann again refused to open up.

'Everybody in this house is sick with the flu,' she said. 'The doctor told me not to let anybody inside.'

'He didn't mean your relatives, did he?'

'I certainly wouldn't let my sister come in here with her baby.'

Caril Ann played her role faultlessly. Perhaps, as her lawyer argued later, she was protecting visitors from the killer who lurked behind the door.

The officers were persistent. 'Why would your brother-in-law call us over something like this?' one asked.

'Ask him. I don't know what goes on in his head. He doesn't like me, for one thing. And he always has to be worrying about something.'

Two days later, Caril Ann turned her grandmother away. The woman angrily went to Lincoln's assistant police chief, Eugene Masters.

'There's something fishy going on,' she asserted. 'Caril's voice just didn't sound right, like she was covering something up.'

Two officers accompanied the woman back to the Bartlett house. Ignoring the 'Flu' sign, they entered. The house was empty.

At first they thought the entire family may have gone to the doctor. Then the Bartlett son-in-law, followed by Starkweather's brother, found the bodies.

Police quickly learned that Caril Ann and Charlie had packed bags into Little Red's hot rod and roared off. They ordered their arrest on 'suspicion.'

'Suspicion' hardened to belief when a gas attendant in Bennet, sixteen miles away, reported Charlie and Caril had stopped for gas and to repair a flat.

Little Red bought a box each of .22 rifle cartridges and .410 shotgun shells.

On January 29 Charlie's car was reported to be parked next to August Meyer's farmhouse. Sheriff Merle Karnopp, with a large body of officers, crept up on the house at dawn.

'Charles Starkweather!' Karnopp roared through a bullhorn. 'Come out with your hands in the air!'

No response. At Karnopp's signal nine tear gas bombs were shot through the farmhouse windows. The deputies moved in, guns drawn.

An officers kicked open a door and almost vomited. 'Starkweather and the girl are gone,' he told Karnopp. 'They left the farmer with his head nearly torn off by a shotgun.'

A short time later a nearby farmer, Evert Broening, found the bodies of Robert Jensen, 17, and Carol King, 16, shot through their heads in an abandoned storm cellar near the Meyer place.

Police figured that Jensen was killed for his automobile. Carol, the coroner reported, had been stripped naked and viciously raped before being killed.

(From his confession: 'I began to wonder what kind of life I did live in this world, and even to this day, I'm wondering about it, but it don't matter how much I used to think about it. I don't believe I ever would have found a personal world or live in a worth-while world maybe, because I don't know life, or for what it was. They say this is a wonderful world to live in, but I don't believe I ever did really live in a wonderful world.')

Two hundred lawmen combed the plains around Lincoln, but they were too late for wealthy industrialist C. Lauer Ward. A relative got suspicious when the businessman failed to appear at work; he found a 1950 Ford in Ward's garage in place of Ward's '56 Packard.

Officers broke into the Ward home to find Ward sprawled in the foyer with a bullet in his head.

In a bedroom were the mutilated bodies of Clara Ward and her maid, Lillian Fenci. Both women had been tied and gagged, then stabbed repeatedly.

(From his confession: 'Nobody knowed better than to say nothin' to me when I was a-heavin' their goddamn garbage.')

By now 1,200 men, including 200 National Guardsmen, were looking for little Red and his girlfriend. Charlie had made the Big Time.

Luck let Charlie slip through massive dragnets into Wyoming. Outside the small town of Douglas, he came on a car parked along the highway.

Shoe salesman Merle Collison, Starkweather's last victim, had pulled over for a nap. Starkweather sent a bullet through the window.

Collison. frightened, got up.

'Come on outta that car, mister!' Starkweather shouted, gesturing wildly with his rifle.

As Collison stepped out of the car, Starkweather pumped nine bullets into him, killing him instantly and blowing him back into the car.

'We got us another car, honey!' Charlie shouted.

(From his confession: 'People will remember that last shot, I hope they'll read my story. They'll know why then. They'll know that the salesman just happened to be there. I didn't put him there and he didn't know I was coming. I had hated and been hated. I had my little world to keep alive as long as possible, and my gun. That was my answer.')

The killer leaned over Collison's body and tried to release the emergency brake, but it was stuck. Passing oil agent Joseph Sprinkle, pulled over to help what he though were motorists in trouble. Starkweather brandished his rifle.

'Help me release this brake or I'll kill you!' Starkweather yelled.

Sprinkle spotted Collison's body and knew what he could expect. When Charlie reached forward to help the oil man release the brake, he grabbed the rifle.

'You bastard!' Starkweather screamed. 'Gimme my rifle! Jump him Caril! Get my shotgun!'

The fourteen-year-old girl stared, petrified as she saw another car, a police squad, approaching fast, red warning light spinning.

As Deputy Sheriff William Rohmer drove up, Caril Ann ran toward him.

'Help! It's Starkweather!' she yelped.'He's going to kill me! He's crazy! Arrest him!'

Sprinkle tore the rifle out of Starkweather's hands and the killer darted for his car. Rohmer couldn't fire because Caril Ann was in the way.

The deputy threw the girl into his car and took after Charlie, radioing to police ahead. Another Sheriff's car took up the chase at 115 miles an hour. A shot blew out the rear window of Little Red's car.

Outside Douglas, Wyo., Starkweather suddenly braked and staggered out, holding his right ear. 'I'm hit!' he squealed. 'You lousy bastards shot me!'

While Sheriff Earl Heflin held a shotgun on the killer, Police Chief Robert Ainsley looked him over.

'You're a real tough guy, aren't you?' he asked in disgust. Charlie had a superficial cut from flying glass.

At first, Starkweather tried to protect Caril Ann: 'Don't take it out on the girl. She had no part in any of it.' He shouted that Caril had been his hostage.

Later when she cried innocence and branded him a killer in court he turned on her.

'She could have escaped at any time she wanted,' he said. 'I left her alone lots of times. Sometimes when I would go in and get hamburgers, she would be sitting in the car with all the guns. There would have been nothing to stop her from running away.

'One time she said that some hamburgers were lousy and we ought to go back and shoot all them people in the restaurant.

'After I shot her folks and killed her baby sister, Caril sat and watched television while I wrapped the bodies up in rags and newspapers.

'We just cooked up that hostage story between us.'

As Starkweather had no mercy for his playmate in death, the jury ignored her plea of innocence. Caril Ann Fugate was sentenced to life in prison, though she continued to sob her not guilty plea as they led her from the courtroom.

Starkweather went to his death in the Nebraska State Pentitentiary only a few miles from the shack he called his home. He entered the death room on June 24, 1959. Only hours before, the Lions Club in Beatrice, Nebraska had asked that he donated his eyes to their eye bank following his death.

'Hell no!' Little Red roared from his cell. 'No one ever did anything for me. Why in the hell should I do anything for anyone else?'

Starkweather sat down in the electric chair at exactly midnight, saying nothing. He wore a badly-fitted death mask that made the ritual all the more grotesque. Five jolts of electricity—2,200 volts in each charge—were sent into his body and at 12:03 a.m. prison doctor Paul Getscher dramatically announced to witnesses present: 'Charles Starkweather is dead!'

Outside the prison gates, thirty teenagers in blue jeans and bobby socks milled around. A young girl stepped forward and told a reporter: 'Some of us knew him. Some of us wanted to be with him at the end.'

J.R.N.

# 9
# THE SICK SIXTIES, AND BEYOND
## (1961–88)

# 1961

# JAMES HANRATTY

## The A6 Murder

In August 1961, Mr. Michael John Gregsten and Miss Valerie Storie were scientific workers on the staff of the Road Research Laboratory at Langley, near Slough in Buckinghamshire. Gregsten was a happily married man of thirty-four with two young children. Miss Storie was twenty-two and single. They were both members of the Laboratory staff motor club, and regularly took part in the club rallies.

Shortly before eight o'clock on the evening of Tuesday, August 22, they set out with maps and notebooks in Gregsten's car to survey the route of an eighty-mile rally which they were organising for the following Sunday. The car was a grey, four-door Morris Minor saloon.

Just after eight o'clock, they stopped briefly for a drink at the Old Station Inn, Taplow and then drove on along the route as far as Dorney Reach. There, they stopped just off the road by the edge of a cornfield. It was about 8.45 then and beginning to get dark. They had been there about twenty minutes, discussing the route and the timings and making their notes, when there was a tap on the window beside Gregsten.

What happened to the car and its occupants during the next ten hours was described by counsel at a hearing before the Ampthill Magistrates' Court in November. However, on that occasion Miss Storie's own evidence was heard *in camera*. This account is based on her evidence given at Bedfordshire Assizes in the following January.

She said that when Gregsten started to wind down the window, the man outside who had tapped on the glass thrust a gun inside. He said: 'This is a hold-up. I am a desperate man. I have been on the run for four months. You do as I tell you, you will be all right.'

He then demanded the ignition key. Gregsten handed it over. The gunman locked the driver's door and got into the back of the car.

He kept talking. He said that he had not eaten for two days and that he had been sleeping out for the past two nights. He flourished the gun and remarked that he had not had it very long. 'This is like a cowboy's gun,' he added. 'I feel like a cowboy.'

Miss Storie thought the remark about sleeping out peculiar, because it had rained heavily the previous night and, as far as she could see, the man's clothes appeared 'immaculate.'

The gunman now returned the ignition key and told Gregsten to drive farther off the road into the field. Gregsten did so. The gunman then demanded their money and valuables. In the darkness, Miss Storie was able to remove most of the money from her handbag before handing it over.

The gunman went on talking. He complained again that he was hungry. In desperation they told him to take the car and the money and go—anything, if he would just leave them. He asked if there was something to eat in the car. Told that there wasn't, the gunman seemed to forget about food. He said, 'there's no hurry,' and added that every policeman in England was looking for him. He would wait until morning, then tie them up and leave.

To the wretched victims the whole thing must have been as bewildering as it was terrifying. They had given the man money and other valuables, they had offered to let him take the car and leave them stranded in the middle of a cornfield, they had tried to appease him in every way. But he did not seem to know *what* he wanted. In her evidence Miss Storie referred again and again to his indecision. The suggestion made later (though not by Miss Storie) that his sole motive from the beginning had been that of rape is difficult to accept. The confused behaviour is typical of a certain type of psychopath. It is probable that at that point he did not know what he meant to do.

The three had been sitting in the car for about an hour when a door in a near-by house opened. By the light inside they could see someone putting away a bicycle. The gunman became alarmed. 'If that man comes over here,' he told them, 'don't say anything. If you say anything, I will shoot him and then I will shoot you.'

Nobody came over, and after a while the gunman began talking again about being hungry. He could not stand it any longer, he said. He would go and find something to eat. He told Gregsten to get out, that he would drive. Gregsten, he decided, would be placed in the boot of the car.

Miss Storie's account of the arguments she had had to use in order to dissuade the gunman from putting this last proposal into practice is frightening. The Moris Minor is a well-designed car, but it is small. The very thought of cramming a full grown man, alive, into the boot seems absurd. Yet, it was not until Miss Storie had declared desperately that there was a leak in the exhaust system and that the fumes from it would kill anyone placed in the boot, that the gunman could be persuaded to abandon the plan.

This grotesque discussion took place outside the car. It is interesting, not only for its high fantasy content, but because, *for the first time*, Miss Storie saw that the gunman had a folded handkerchief tied 'gangster fashion' over the lower part of his face. He had a Cockney accent she recalled. For 'things' and 'think,' he said 'fings' and 'fink.'

The gunman finally decided that he would return to the back seat and that Gregsten should drive, with the revolver at the back of his head to ensure that he followed the directions given.

The drive began. Directed by the gunman they went through Slough towards Stanmore. During this part of the drive, the gunman removed the handkerchief from his face, but warned Gregsten and Miss Storie to keep their eyes on the road ahead. Miss Storie said that she did not see his face clearly during the drive. He talked a lot, however. There was self-pity. He said that he had been in a remand home and that he had 'done the lot' and had never had a chance in life. There were friendly overtures. He returned their watches to them. Near London Airport, he told Gregsten to stop at a garage and gave him a pound note with which to buy petrol. There was a threepenny piece in the change. The gunman gave it to Miss Storie as a 'wedding present.' At Stanmore, he allowed Gregsten to stop and buy cigarettes from a vending machine. Miss Storie lighted cigarettes for Gregsten and herself, and handed one to the gunman behind them. As he took it, she noticed that he was wearing black gloves.

At Kingsbury the gunman directed them on to the A5 road to St Albans, and then on to the A6 road to Bedford. By then

Gregsten had been flashing the car's reversing light in an effort to attract attention of some passing motorist. He did succeed in making one driver slow down and point to the rear of the car. The gunman saw the signal and misunderstood it. He made Gregsten stop, and then checked that the rear lights were on. Miss Storie also said that Gregsten had managed to convey to her that he intended, if they saw a policeman, to turn the car up on to the pavement near him. However, during the drive, which covered forty-three miles, they saw no policeman.

The gunman, meanwhile, had forgotten his hunger and now said that he needed somewhere to have a sleep. He would tie Gregsten and Miss Storie up first. At Deadman's Hill, on the A6 road at Clophill, near Luton, he saw a lay-by and told Gregsten to turn into it. Gregsten did so. When the car came to a standstill, he was told to switch off the lights.

There was some rope in the car. The gunman tied Miss Storie's wrists, not very securely, to a door handle. Earlier in the evening there had been a duffel bag full of laundry in the back of the car. The gunman had made them move it to the front. Now, he told Gregsten to pass it into the back seat. It may have been that he had decided to use the bag as a pillow. We don't know. As Gregsten heaved the bag over, the gunman shot him twice in the back of the head.

Gregsten fell forward and Miss Storie began to scream. The gunman told her to stop. Miss Storie sad to him: 'You shot him, you bastard. Why did you do that?'

'He frightened me,' was the reply. 'He moved too quick. I got frightened.'

She could hear the blood pumping from the wounds in Gregsten's head. She pleaded with the gunman to get a doctor, or let her go for help. This produced more indecision. He replied: 'Be quiet, will you, I'm thinking.'

She went on pleading and he repeated the sentence. Then, he took a piece of the laundry in the duffel bag and put it over the dying man's face. As he did this, he said to Miss Storie: 'Turn round and face me. I know your hands are free.'

They were indeed free, and she had been trying to conceal the fact from him. Now, she turned and faced him.

He told her to kiss him. She refused.

At that moment, the headlights of a car passing on the road lit up the gunman's face.

'This,' Miss Storie said in her evidence, 'was the first opportunity of really seeing what he looked like. He had very large, pale blue, staring icy eyes. He seemed to have a pale face. I should imagine anyone should have, having just shot someone. He had jet brown hair, combed back with no parting. The light was only on his face for a few seconds as the vehicle went past, then we were in complete darkness again.'

Miss Storie admitted that her vision was poor without glasses; but, at that moment, she was wearing her glasses and could see well.

The gunman now forced her to kiss him. She noted that he was clean shaven.

He then ordered her to get into the back of the car with him. When she refused, he threatened to shoot her. 'I will count five. If you haven't got in, I will shoot.'

She got in. He threatened her again, made her take some clothing off, and then raped her. Her revulsion seemed to amuse him. 'You haven't had much sex, have you?' he said when it was over.

He now made her help him drag Gregsten's body out of the front seat, and show him how to start the car. He seemed about to drive off. She went to Gregsten's body, which was lying on the concrete of the lay-by a few yards away.

The gunman got out of the car and came over to her. He said: 'I think I had better hit you in the head or something to knock you out, or else you will go for help.'

Miss Storie promised that she would not do so and implored him to go. She gave him one of the pound notes she had previously hidden.

The Gunman started to walk away, then suddenly turned and began shooting. He fired four shots at her, then reloaded the gun and fired six more. Of the ten shots, five hit her. One bullet lodged in the spine and paralysed her legs.

When the gunman moved her with his foot, she feigned death. Finally, he drove away.

It would have been understandable if, after the nightmare hours she had already lived through, Miss Storie had lost all ability to think. Yet, wounded and paralysed though she was, she realised that if she died, there would be no witness to what had happened. She tried to write a description of the gunman by forming letters with small stones on the concrete—'blue eyes and brown hair.' She failed because there were not enough stones within her reach; she could not move to get more. She called for help, but none came. She lay there with the dead Gregsten for the remainder of the night. At 6.40 in the morning, a labourer on his way to work heard her call and went for help.

The hunt for the gunman began. Detective Superintendent Acott of Scotland Yard took charge of the investigation.

That same day, a man telephoned the police and reported that the missing car was abandoned in Avondale Crescent, Ilford, forty-two miles from the final scene of the crime. The informant gave a name and address which later proved to be false; but the car was where he had said it was, and the seats were still bloodstained.

The following day, a cleaner working in the bus garage at Rye Lane in South London found a loaded .38 Enfield revolver and five boxes of ammunition under the rear seat of a 36A bus. Tests soon established that this was the murder weapon.

Miss Storie was in Bedford General Hospital in a critical condition and several days elapsed before she was able to amplify the first brief statements she had made to the police. On August 29, however, Scotland Yard issued two portraits built up with her help on the Identi-kit system.

Identi-kit is an American device, now widely used in criminal investigation. It consists of hundreds of transparencies each embodying a different facial characteristic. By means of superimposition, a witness's description is gradually translated into a visual statement which can be photographed.

After publication of the pictures, a number of men answering the description were questioned by Scotland Yard. Some four weeks later, on September 24, an identification parade was held in a ward at Guy's Hospital, where Miss Storie was now recuperating after an operation to remove two of the bullets from a lung.

Among those in the parade was a man who bore a marked resemblance to one to the Identi-kit portraits, and who was about to be charged with causing 'grievous bodily harm' to another woman.

Miss Storie did not identify that man at the parade, though, in a discussion with a doctor and the police afterwards, she agreed that there might be a resemblance. During the parade, she had picked out another man known to be innocent.

On October 6, a man calling himself Jimmy Ryan telephoned Superintendent Acott at Scotland Yard.

The man's real name was James Hanratty. He was twenty-five years old and already well known to the police. At school he had been considered unteachable. At fifteen he could neither read nor write. In 1952, an episode of amnesia had ended in his being diagnosed, after psychiatric examination in an institution, as a mental detective. He had become a burglar. At nineteen he had received further psychiatric treatment. The following year, while in prison, he had made a suicide attempt. Prison psychiatrists had described him then as a potential psychopath. During the months preceding the murder, he had burgled a number of houses in the Stanmore-Harrow area.

In his telephone conversation with Superintendent Acott, Hanratty said that he had heard that the police suspected him. He went on: 'I want to talk to you and clear up this whole thing, but I cannot come in there. I am very worried and don't know. . . . I know I have left my fingerprints at different places, and done different things, and the police want me. But I want to tell you, Mr. Acott, that I did not do that A6 murder.'

The Superintendent tried to keep him talking, but Hanratty had had enough.

'I'm so upset I don't know I'm doing and what I'm saying,' he declared; 'I've got a very bad head and suffer from blackouts and lose my memory. Look I will have to go now and think it over.'

The Superintendent tried again to persuade him to come in and make a statement. Hanratty hesitated.

'I will phone you tonight between ten and twelve and tell you what I have decided,' he replied. 'I must go now. My head's bad and I've got to think.'

He pronounced the word 'think' as 'fink,' as do a great many other Londoners.

Hanratty, again using the name Ryan, next called a newspaper, explained his problem to an assistant news editor and asked for advice. He said that he had an alibi for the night of the murder, that he had in fact been in Liverpool at the time with business friends, but that he could not involve them. The inference was that the business on which they had been engaged had been criminal. The news editor advised him to go to the police.

Superintendent Acott received a second telephone call. It was as unproductive as the first. Hanratty ended it by saying: 'Now I must go, Mr. Acott. I want to talk to you but you will catch me. I am going, Mr. Acott.'

The following day he telephoned yet again, this time from Liverpool.

He said that the three friends who could prove his alibi for the night of the murder refused to help him. 'You can't blame them because they are fences. You know what I mean, they receive jewellery. . . . I don't know what to do. . . .'

The Superintendent said that he would have to have some corroboration from witnesses and asked for the names of the three men. Hanratty refused to give the names.

Five days later he was arrested in Blackpool. Again he refused to give the names of the three men. The Superintendent warned him of the seriousness of his position and told him that two empty cartridge cases had been found in a hotel room he had occupied on the night before the murder.*

Hanratty considered that this last fact completely cleared him, because, 'I told you I have never had any bullets and never fired a gun.' He appeared to feel that a simple denial on his part ought to be enough. As to the need for corroborative evidence of his whereabouts on the night of the murder, he said: 'I am a very good gambler, Mr. Acott. I have gambled all my life. I am going to gamble now. I am not going to name the three men. I can get out of this without them.'

He was mistaken.

On the morning after the murder two motorists in the Ilford area had noticed a grey Morris Minor being driven erratically and dangerously. One of the motorists had been sufficiently incensed to shout at the driver of the Morris; both had been close enough to see his face. At an identity parade both identified Hanratty. On the other hand, a passenger in one of the cars, who recalled that the driver of the Morris had had a 'horrible smile,' attended two identity parades and picked out a different man each time, neither of them Hanratty.

Miss Storie had by then been moved to the spinal injuries centre at Stoke Mandeville Hospital for further treatment. On October 14 yet another identification parade was held. There were thirteen men in the parade, Hanratty among them.

On this occasion, Miss Storie asked that each man be told to say the sentence, 'Be quiet will you, I'm thinking.' After fifteen or twenty minutes, she identified Hanratty.

The following day he was charged with the murder of Gregsten.

His trial began at Bedfordshire Assizes on January 22, and lasted twenty-two days.

James Hanratty may or may not have been a mental defective in the medical sense of the term; he may or may not have been a psychopath; he was, without a doubt, a deeply stupid man. If he was guilty—and most probably he was—he made the prosecution's task easier than it need have been. If he was innocent, he made his own counsel's task infinitely more difficult, and contributed handsomely to his own destruction.

His story about the three men in Liverpool, whose names he knew and who could if they chose give him an alibi, was a lie. But he went on telling it after his arrest. He told it to his solicitor, and he told it to his defending counsel. He told it after the Magistrates' Court hearing and his committal. It was not until early in February, after he had heard the prosecution's case at his trial, that he let his legal advisers know that he had been deceiving them. He said that on the night in question he had really stayed in a bed-and-breakfast house in Rhyl in North Wales.

In the witness box, he explained himself this way: 'I didn't tell Superintendent Acott, because at that point I did not know the name to the street, the number of the house, or even the name of the people in the house. At that stage I knew that I was only wanted for interviewing, not for the actual A6 murder charge, which I found out later, or the truth would have been told straight away. I know I made a terrible mistake by telling Superintendent Acott about these three men, but I have been advised that the truth only counts in this matter, and might I say here every word of that is the truth.'

His counsel then asked him: 'Will you explain to my Lord and the jury why it was that after telling Mr. Acott this story you persisted in it for so long?'

'Because, my Lord, I am a man with a prison record,' was the answer; 'and I know that in such a trial as this it is very vital for a man once to change his evidence in such a serious trial. But I know inside of me, somewhere in Rhyl this house does exist, and by telling the truth these people will come to my assistance.'

Thanks to prompt and energetic inquiries made by the defence team, a Rhyl landlady was found who thought she remembered him. She 'felt' that he had stayed at the house on or about the date in question. She could not be certain though, and could not produce her visitors' book for that time as it had been destroyed.

However, Hanratty did not *have* to prove an alibi. His defence was that they had the wrong man. The prosecution's case for having the right man rested on Miss Storie's identification of him at the parade on October 14, the identification of the two motorists, and on very little else. Prosecution efforts to connect him with the murder weapon, through the cartridge cases found in the hotel, were frustrated when the hotel manager, upon whose evidence the police had relied, proved to be a man with a long criminal record who admitted that he had lied in order to 'help' the police, and also confused Hanratty with another man.

With the annihilation of this witness the defence may well have felt that they were making headway. If so, they had reckoned without their client.

On the eighth day of the trial, the prosecution called upon a rather odd type of man to give evidence. He was twenty-four, and had, he readily admitted, a criminal record.

In November of the previous year he had been in Brixton Prison awaiting trial on a fraud charge. Hanratty had also been in the prison on remand at that time. The witness said that they had spoken to one another in the exercise yard on a number of occasions. Eventually, he said, Hanratty had told him that he (Hanratty) was the A6 killer, and had spoken of Miss Storie and how he had raped her. According to the ex-convict, Hanratty had also said that he was 'sort of choked' that Miss Storie was living, as she was the only witness against him.

The defence, of course, claimed that it was all a pack of lies. In his summing-up, the Judge advised the jury to approach this evidence 'with care.' It is possible to believe the ex-convict's story nevertheless. A man of Hanratty's mentality would be quite capable of telling a fellow prisoner that he was the 'A6 killer' simply in order to make himself seem important.

Certainly, the jury did not find Hanratty's an easy case to decide. They were out almost ten hours. After six hours of deliberation, they sent a letter to the Judge requesting additional guidance. Its content is significant.

'May we have a further statement from you regarding the definition of reasonable doubt. Would you confirm that we judge the case on reasonable doubt, or must we be certain sure of the prisoner's guilt to return a verdict?

'Will you please also comment on the summing-up quoted by defence counsel, with a special reference to circumstantial evidence on the previous case, and the bearing on this case with regard to identification and the cartridge cases found at the Vienna Hotel?

'Would you please comment on the point made that when there is circumstantial evidence which admits of more than one theory, then the theory in favour of the defence must invariably be adopted?'

The jury returned to court to hear the Judge's reply.

He reminded them that he had said that they must be 'sure' and went on: 'Well, if you have a reasonable doubt, not a mere fancy sort of doubt, if you have a reasonable doubt you cannot be sure.'

On the question of identification, he said: 'You have to be quite sure that the evidence of identification was such that you, and each of you, can feel sure that, as a result of that identification, it was the prisoner that has been identified.'

Hanratty was found guilty, and in April he was hanged.

There was, and is, no reasonable doubt that he was guilty. But when we are taking the irreversible step of executing a man, should there be *any* permissible kind of doubt, even the 'mere fancy' kind?

Well, doubtless there has to be. Otherwise, nobody would *ever* be executed.

E.A.

# 1962–4

# ALBERT DESALVO

## The Boston Strangler

Like Jack the Ripper with the whores of Whitechapel during the autumn of 1888, the Boston Strangler created an empire of suspense and fear. But over a longer period, a wider area, and with an entirely different sort of woman.

The Strangler's dominion lasted eighteen months – from June 1962 to January 1964. It covered not only Boston – Back Bay, Beacon Hill – but points on the periphery: Cambridge, Salem, Lynn. His prey were not prostitutes, either cheap or costly; varying in social or economic status, they were all what are called 'straight' girls by prostitutes themselves. Girls, perhaps, is a misnomer, for the Strangler took high toll of the elderly; his first five victims were, in order, aged fifty-five, fifty-seven, sixty-
eight, seventy-five, sixty-seven. Those that came later tended to be younger: twenty-three, twenty, even nineteen. One of the very last in line, however, was fifty-six. The grand total cannot be determined – least of all from his own subsequent account. Sex criminals are selective in their reminiscences. But it was certainly not less than a dozen.

Like Byrne, he murdered to get sex, either by 'normal' copulatory penetration, or by 'playing around' (his own informative expression), or by 'the insertion of a foreign body'. When he did these things, he sometimes knew that the woman was aware; sometimes that she was unconscious: sometimes that she was dead. Sometimes he simply did not know one way or another – and does not seem to have cared.

His campaign had a terrible simplicity, the separate engagements an artistic uniformity. A call at the entrance of a large apartment block. A quick inspection of the plates beside the buzzers. A marking down of one flat – otherwise at random – which happened to be labled with a woman's name. An assurance – gained by oblique enquiry – that the female occupant was there quite on her own. An entry obtained by plausible excuse; 'I'm from the landlord, come to inspect ceilings, windows, pipes. A tour ostensibly searching for leaks, cracks, draughts. A blow on the head or an arm round the neck when her back was turned. Stripping off – her always, himself occasionally. After sex, the body posed suggestively and lewdly, the breasts tilting upwards, the bare legs straddling wide.

The Strangler – Albert DeSalvo. How do we know *who* he was? Because in the end, still undetected, he owned up. But only after he has partially paid for a mistake – or, on a charitable view, an unwonted act of mercy.

In October 1964 DeSalvo committed a rape which was not combined with murder. The woman was able to give the police his full description. It corresponded with that of a man they had in the past had tabs on. A man who had worked with immunity a minor sexual con trick – persuading women to let him 'measure' them, bust and thigh, on the pretext that he was recruiting 'models'. This man, brought in, was identified by the woman who had been raped – and spared. Before the judge he behaved so strangely that he was committed, until further order, to a State mental hospital. While there, he confessed to being the Strangler – on condition that his confession would not be used against him. But the police could confirm that what he said was true from the multitude of details he supplied. Nature of injuries, colour of bras, décor, furniture. Details never disclosed to the press and public. Details which only the Strangler could have known.

The Strangler – what sort of an individual was DeSalvo? In his mid-thirties, medium height, athletically built, with hands which were too large and eyes which were too small. He was a casual labourer with a 'record' – but only of pretty crimes, mostly breaking and entering; never a charge, still less a conviction, for any sex offence. 'A good provider and family man', he was fond of his two small children; he complained, though, that his wife was 'cold' and often refused him intercourse – a serious matter because DeSalvo was plainly oversexed ('Five or six times a day don't mean much to me').

The Strangler – why did he do it? Many will say, no need to ask. But randy husbands and frigid wives are neither new nor rare, and extra-marital sex does not postulate rape and murder. DeSalvo had given, for what it is worth, a personal explanation. 'I'm driving to work and I'm building the image up then I get release right in my underwear but five minutes later I'm ready again and the image comes back and the pressure mounts in my head, you understand me?'

I for one understand him perfectly. He is pleading what psychiatrists call an irresistible impulse. What less fanciful folk call an impulse unresisted. Mrs. DeSalvo hit the nail upon the head, remonstrating with her tiresomely tumescent spouse. 'Al, you can learn by yourself to control yourself. It is just a matter of self-control.'

E.L

# 1964–5

# 'JACK THE STRIPPER'
## The Thames Nude Murders

The case of the Thames nude murderer – sometimes known as 'Jack the Stripper' – provides a striking example of the build-up of a sexual obsession into aimless destructiveness. The 'Stripper's' crimes produced one of the biggest manhunts in British criminal history, which ended – typically – with his suicide.

Between February 1964 and January 1965, the bodies of six women – mostly prostitutes – were found in areas not far from the Thames. The first of the bodies, that of a thirty-year-old prostitute named Hanna Tailford, was found in the water near Hammersmith Bridge. She was naked except for her stockings, and her panties had been stuffed into her mouth. Her jaw was bruised, but this could have resulted from a fall. On 18th April, the naked body of Irene Lockwood, a twenty-six-year-old prostitute, was found at Duke's Meadows, near Barnes Bridge, not far from the place where Hanna Tailford had been found. She had been strangled, and, like Hanna Tailford, she had been pregnant. A fifty-four-year-old Kensington caretaker, Kenneth Archibald, confessed to her murder, and he seemed to know a great deal about the girl; but at his trial, it was established that his confession was false, and he was acquitted. There was another reason for believing in his innocence; while he was still in custody, another naked girl was found in an alleyway at Osterley Park, Brentford. This was only three weeks after the discovery of Irene Lockwood's body. The dead girl – the only one among the victims who could be described as pretty – was identified as a twenty-two-year-old prostitute and striptease artist, Helen Barthelemy. There were a number of curious features in the case. A line around her waist showed that her panties had been removed after death, and there was no evidence of normal sexual assault. But four of her front teeth were missing. Oddly enough, the teeth had not been knocked out by a blow, but deliberately forced out; a piece of one of them was found lodged in her throat. Medical investigation also revealed the presence of male sperm in her throat. Here, then, was the cause of death; she had been choked by a penis, probably in the course of performing an act of fellatio. The missing teeth suggested that the killer had repeated the assault after death. It was established that she had disappeared some days before her body was found. Where, then, had her body been kept? Flakes of paint found on her skin suggested the answer, for it was the type of paint used in spraying cars. Clearly, the body had been kept somewhere near a car spraying plant, but in some place where it was not likely to be discovered by the workers.

The 'nude murders' became a public sensation, for it now seemed likely that they were the work of one man. Enormous numbers of police were deployed in the search for the spray-shop, and in an attempt to keep a closer watch on the areas in which the three victims had been picked up – around Notting Hill and Shepherds Bush. Perhaps for this reason, the killer decided to take no risks for several months.

The body of the fourth victim – Mary Fleming, aged thirty – found on 14th July, confirmed that the same man was probably responsible for all four murders. Her false teeth were missing; there was sperm in her throat; and her skin showed traces of the same spray paint. She had vanished three days earlier.

Her body was found, in a half-crouching position, near a garage in Acton, and the van was actually seen leaving the scene of the crime. A motorist driving past Berrymede Road, a cul-de-sac, at 5.30 in the morning, had to brake violently to avoid a van that shot out in front of him. He was so angry that he contacted the police to report the incident. It he had made a note of the van number, the nude case would have been solved. A squad car that arrived a few minutes later found the body of Mary Fleming in the forecourt of a garage in the cul-de-sac.

The near-miss probably alarmed the killer, for no more murders occurred that summer. Then, on 25th November, 1964 another naked body was found under some debris in a car park at Hornton Street, Kensington. She was identified as Margaret McGowan, twenty-one, a Scot. Under the name Frances Brown, she had been called as a witness in the trial of Stephen Ward, and Ludovic Kennedy described her (in his book on the trial) as a small, bird-like woman with a pale face and fringe. Margaret McGowan had disappeared more than a month before her body was found, and there were signs of decomposition. Again there were traces of paint, and a missing front tooth indicated that she had died in the same way as the previous victims.

The last of the stripper's victims was a prostitute named Bridie O'Hara, twenty-eight. She was found on 16th February, 1965, in some undergrowth on the Heron Trading Estate, in Acton. She had last been seen on 11th January in the Shepherds Bush Hotel. The body was partly mummified, which indicated that it had been kept in a cool place. As usual, teeth were missing, and sperm was found in the throat. Fingermarks on the back of her neck revealed that, like the other victims, she had died in a kneeling position, bent over the killer's lap.

Detective Chief Superintendent John du Rose was recalled from his holiday to take charge of the investigation in the Shepherds Bush area. The Heron Trading Estate provided the lead they had been waiting for. Investigation of a paint spray shop revealed that this was definitely the source of the paint found on the bodies – chemical analysis proved it. The proximity of a disused warehouse solved the question of where the bodies had lain before they were dumped. The powerful spray guns caused the paint to carry, with diminishing intensity, for several hundred yards. Analysis of paint on the bodies enabled experts to establish the spot where the women must have been concealed: it was underneath a transformer in the warehouse.

Yet even with this discovery, the case was far from solved. Thousands of men worked on the Heron Trading Estate. (Oddly enough, Christie had been employed there.) Mass questioning seemed to bring the police no closer to their suspect. Du Rose decided to throw an immense twenty-mile cordon around the area, to keep a careful check on all cars passing through at night. Drivers who were observed more than once were noted; if they were seen more than twice, they were interviewed. Du Rose conducted what he called 'a war of nerves' against the killer, dropping hints in the press or on television that indicated the police were getting closer. They knew he drove a van; they knew he might have right of access to the trading estate by night. The size of the victims – who were all short women – suggested that the killer was under middle height. As the months passed, and no further murders took place, du Rose assumed that he was winning the war of nerves. The killer had ceased to operate. He checked on all the men who had been jailed since mid-February, all men with prison records who had been hospitalized, all men who had died or committed suicide. In his book *Murder Was My Business,* du Rose claims that a list of twenty suspects had been reduced to three when one of the three committed suicide. He left a not saying that the could not bear the strain any longer. The man was a security guard who drove a van, and had access to the estate. At the time when the women were murdered, his rounds included the spray shop. He worked by night, from 10 p.m. to 6 a.m. He was unmarried.

This is clearly a case of the obsessive mentality – even more so than in the case of Christie. Christie's pecularity was his inability to have intercourse with a woman who was fully conscious; the Stripper was interested only in fellatio. (This was not revealed at the time of the case, and it is only hinted at in du Rose's book.) If he was the killer of Hanna Tailford and Irene Lockwood – as seems likely – then his obsession had still not reached a climax. Presumably he had been paying prostitutes to satisfy his need. The death of Hanna Tailford could have been – as du Rose says – accidental, at the height of his sexual satisfaction, guiding her head with his hand on her neck, the other probably gripping her hair, he may have lost control, and choked her with the glans of his penis – as if an apple had been jammed in her throat, as du Rose explained in an article written after his retirement. But accident is unlikely – otherwise, why should he have stuffed her panties into her mouth, presumably to make sure she was dead? When he killed Irene Lockwood, he knew in advance what he intended to do. He picked her up on the night of 7th April. The murder almost certainly took place in the back of his van. After this he stripped her, and threw her body in the river. One writer on the case has suggested that the victims were stripped to avoid identification; but this would clearly be pointless; why should the murderer care whether the women were identified, or how soon? The stripping was a part of his sexual need, the desire to feel himself totally dominant. His fantasy involved a naked woman, and it involved treating her mouth as a vagina – hence the removal of teeth. In the later murders, the bodies were kept in the warehouse for several weeks – not because he was waiting for a favourable moment to dispose of them (after all, the longer he waited, the more chance there was that they would be discovered in the warehouse) – but in order to repeat his perverse acts. The last corpse was kept longer than any of the others, and was dumped on the Trading Estate. This may have been partly out of fear of being stopped with the corpse in his van – although the police cordon had not been formed at that time. But it is more likely the same indifference that overtook Christie; murder had become a *habit*, and destructiveness involved an element of self-destruction.

C.W.

# 1965

# IAN BRADY
## The Moors Murders

---

The two accused were Ian Brady, twenty-seven at the time of his arrest in October 1965, and Myra Hindley, his mistress, twenty-three. Brady, an illegitimate child, was born in a slum district of Glasgow's Clydeside; his mother was at work, and he was brought up by a neighbour with three children of her own. At the age of eleven, he got a scholarship to Shawland Academy, a school where most of the students were from middle-class homes, and he seems to have developed his attitude of resentment from this period. He began committing thefts and burglaries, and from the age of thirteen to seventeen he was on probation for a series of such offences. He moved to Manchester with his mother in 1945, and was soon sent to correctional school for a year. He was of above average intelligence, introverted, bad-tempered, and with a well-developed sadistic streak. In 1959 he became a stock clerk in a chemical company in Manchester. A great deal of his wages went on cheap Spanish wine and pornographic literature. By the time Myra Hindley joined the firm as a typist in 1961, Brady's tendencies were well-developed; he was interested in obscene photographs – in taking them as well as buying them – and in torture; he felt that modern society was totally decadent and corrupt, and that in such a society any healthy-minded person would inevitably be an outcast and a criminal. Hitler was his ideal, and he owned a great many books about concentration camps and tortures.

When Myra Hindley became infatuated with him, Brady was not interested; perhaps he felt she looked too healthy. She was a perfectly normal girl with religious tendencies, who had been brought up in an affectionate family; she loved children and animals. But when he began to realise that she possessed masochistic tendencies, his interest grew. At the trial, no evidence was offered about the development of their relationship, but the police uncovered a great deal. She became his mistress, then joined him in posing for pornographic pictures taken with a camera with a timing device. Brady soon convinced her that religion was a sign of weak mindedness. In 1963, Brady moved into the house in which Myra lived with her grandmother. One month later, a sixteen-year-old girl named Pauline Reade vanished; she lived close to them. Although her body was not found until twenty years later when police took Myra back to the moors, it was clear much earlier that this was their first victim. Six months later, in November 1963, twelve-year-old John Kilbride vanished on a Saturday afternoon. He was last seen in a busy marketplace at Ashton-under-Lyne. That day, Myra Hindley hired a mini.

Six months later, Keith Bennett, aged twelve, disappeared on his way to see his grandmother. This was in the Longsight district, where Brady had lived for may years with his mother. And six months after this, on Boxing Day, 1964, a ten-year-old girl named Lesley Ann Downey left her home to go to a nearby fair, and vanished. By this time, Brady, Myra Hindley and the grandmother had moved to a house in Wardle Brook Avenue, Hattersley, closer to the moors where certain bodies were buried. . . .

In August 1964, Myra's sister Maureen had married a youth with a police record, sixteen-year-old David Smith. When Brady learned about the police record he suddenly became very interested in Smith, and was soon proposing that they should rob a bank. He invited Smith and Maureen to the house a great deal, gave them wine, and preached the doctrines of the Marquis de Sade – that society has made laws for the protection of the law-givers and the oppression of people stupid enough to accept them. Smith was soon writing in his diary such sentences as, 'Murder is a hobby and a supreme pleasure'; 'God is a superstition, a cancer which eats in the brain'; 'People are like maggots; small, blind and worthless'. The sentiments themselves are hardly more extreme than those held by Swift; but Brady was soon explaining to Smith that he had put them into practice – that he had killed 'three or four people' and buried their bodies on the moors. It was his first major mistake. On 5th October 1965, Brady told Smith to bring his own library of murder and pornography to Wardle Brook Avenue; he and Myra took two suitcases to Manchester Central Station. They intended to stage a murder to initiate Smith into the pleasures of crimes of violence. In a pub in Manchester, they picked up Edward Evans, aged seventeen, whom Brady later alleged to be a homosexual. Evans agreed to go home with him, and when Evans and Brady were comfortably installed in the living-room with a bottle of cheap wine, Myra hurried off to fetch David Smith, who lived nearby. Almost as soon as Smith arrived, there was a loud scream, and Smith rushed into the sitting-room to see Brady attacking Evans with a hatchet. Brady hit him fourteen times before he stopped moving. Then he poured two glasses of wine and offered one to Smith. The latter was afraid for his own life, and took a drink. Brady told him to feel the weight of the hatchet – no doubt with the intention of getting Smith's fingerprints on it. Then Smith helped him carry the body upstairs. Myra's grandmother, who had heard the scream, was told that Myra had dropped the tape recorder on her toe. Smith finally said: 'Well I'd better be getting along now', and to his surprise, Brady agreed. He rushed home to tell his wife the story. The following morning they hurried to the phone and the police closed in on the house in Wardle Brook Avenue, and discovered the body of Edward Evans wrapped in a blanket in a bedroom. Evans had kicked Brady on the ankle as he writhed on the floor; it was this that decided Brady not to bury him for another twenty-four hours.

The suitcases in Manchester Central Station were discovered through the cloakroom ticket; they proved to contain pornographic books and photographs, and two tapes. Some of the photographs showed Lesley Ann Downey, with a scarf around her eyes, posing naked for the camera; one of the tapes had her voice on it, begging her kidnappers to allow her to go home, and asking them not to hurt her.

The photographs led the police to an area of the moors between Lancashire and Yorkshire, where they finally uncovered two bodies that were identified as Lesley Ann Downey and John Kilbride. Both bodies were too far decomposed for the pathologist to determined how they had died, but the boy's trousers had been pulled down, suggesting that some form of sexual assault had occurred.

In May 1966, Brady and Myra Hindley were both sentenced to life imprisonment, and a few months later, a paragraph appeared in the newspapers stating that Myra Hindley had been moved into solitary confinement for her own safety.

It was not ascertained until much later that they had killed Pauline Reade and Keith Bennett and that there may have been other victims too. It will be noticed that the murders occurred roughly every six months – and in fact, Brady told David Smith as much. Lesley Downey was killed on 26th December 1964, and Edward Evans on 6th October 1965. Yet Brady told Smith he was 'not really ready for another one yet'. Was there another victim in June or July, 1965?

Although the Moors case has been the subject of several books (the best of which is by Emlyn Williams), it still presents many mysteries, the chief one of which concerns the relationship between Brady and Hindley. Was this another 'master and slave' relationship, like Leopold and Loeb? Was Brady also homosexual? Were the murders genuinely sadistic, or were they a sort of anarchistic gesture, like Ravachol's? The only thing that can be said is that there is no precedent for this type of murder – that is, for an intellectually unbalanced male to persuade a perfectly normal and affectionate girl to take part in child murder. The couple even spent Christmas Eve of 1964 sleeping out on John Kilbride's grave, and Brady took a photograph of Myra Hindley holding her dog and looking down at it. The couple will probably spend the remainder of their lives in prison; but it would be more to the point if a psychologist could get them to explain exactly why they committed the murders.

C.W.

# 1966

# RICHARD SPECK
## 'Born to Raise Hell'

Towards midnight on 13th July 1966, Speck entered a nurse's hostel at Jeffrey Manor, in Chicago's south side, and went upstairs. He knocked on the door of a Philippine nurse, Corazon Amurao, twenty-three, who was asleep. The nurse opened the door, and saw the rather goodlooking, pockmarked young man who wore his hair swept straight back, and who smelt of alcohol. He was holding a small black gun. When he saw her room was empty, he ordered the nurse down the hall to another bedroom, where three girls were sleeping, then made all four go to yet another room, where there were two more. He told them, speaking softly, that he did not intend to harm them, but that he needed enough money to get to New Orleans. He tied up and gagged six of them with strips cut off sheets, and collected the money of each. At 12.30, three more nurses rushed into the dormitory. Speck pointed the gun at them too, assured them that no harm would come to them, and tied them up. Then he began to take them out of the room, one by one. The girls probably assumed that his intention was rape; when Corazon Amurao suggested getting free and attacking the man, one of the nurses told her that they hadn't better start anything, in case they provoked him. Corazon Amurao decided to roll under the bed. She stayed there all night as the man came in and took the girls out one by one. At five o'clock, when the killer had not reappeared for a long time, she crept from under the bed, and looked outside. What she saw there sent her screaming to a balcony, where she attracted the attention of neighbours. When the police arrived, they found the eight nurses, all dead. They were scattered all over the house. Gloria Davy, twenty-two, was the only one who had been ravished; she was one of the nurses who came in late. She lay naked, face down, on the living-room couch; she had been strangled and savagely slashed. Mary Ann Jordan, twenty, was stabbed in the heart, neck and left eye. Susan Farris, twenty-one, had been mutilated before she was strangled. The other five had been strangled and stabbed. Six of them were still tied up. But the killer had lost count – he thought he had killed every girl in the dormitory, and he had left one alive to describe him.

Miss Amurao remembered one thing clearly about the killer – a tattoo 'Born to raise hell' on his upper left arm. Apart from this, the police had two clues: the knots were tied in a manner that suggested a seaman, and the girls' hands had been tied with the palms together, in the way that a policeman handcuffs suspects; this suggested an ex-convict. And he had mentioned wanting to get back to New Orleans several times. With these clues, it proved remarkably easy to identify the killer. Half a block from the hostel there was a seamen's employment bureau. There, the police discovered that a man had been asking about a ship to New Orleans. His application form had a photograph clipped to it; he was Richard F Speck, aged twenty-five. The surviving nurse identified the photograph as that of the killer, and the alarm went out for Speck. When he saw his photograph in the newspaper, he realised that his chances of escape were nil. He slashed both his wrist with a razor. On Sunday the 17th, four days after the murders, a doctor in Cook County

Hospital recognised the 'Born to raise hell' tattoo, and Speck wearily admitted his identity. It emerged that he had spent the day before the murders – Wednesday – drinking beer near the nurses' hostel, and trying to catch a glimpse of the nursing staff sunbathing from the park behind the hostel. He also took drugs – 'yellow jackets' and 'red birds' – sodium amytal and sodium seconal – and was last seen at eleven o'clock. He claimed he could remember nothing of the murders. When he left the hostel, in the early hours of the morning, he went into a bar, and seemed in a cheerful mood; he told a fellow customer that his knife had come from Vietnam and had killed several people, and he put one arm round the bartender's neck and pretended to cut his throat. He had been drunk all day, and spent a few hours with a prostitute, whom he paid thirty dollars. Later, he went off with another prostitute and paid her five dollars. Obviously, drink had the effect of awakening his sexual appetites. This prostitute went back to his room in a cheap hotel on Dearborn Street, and later told the manager that Speck had a gun. The manager notified the police, who called on him. Speck said the gun belonged to the prostitute. And when the police moved out, he also moved out quickly; the police were notified half an hour later that the man wanted for the murder of the nurses was Richard Speck, and they rushed back to the hotel; Speck had already gone. By Saturday night, Speck was broke again, and was in the Starr Hotel on West Madison Street. He asked a man in the next room for a drink, but the man told him to go to hell. At midnight, Speck knocked on the man's door and fell into the room with his wrists slashed.

Investigation of Speck's background revealed that he was born in Kirkwood, Illinois, on 6th December 1941. At twenty, he married a fifteen-year-old girl, Shirley Malone, and they had a daughter. The marriage was not a success and – for reasons that have not yet been made public – Speck had a passionate hatred for his wife; he told friends that he was going back to Texas to kill her if it was the last thing he did. Significantly, the only nurse who was sodomised, Gloria Davy, bore a close resemblance to his wife. While he was still living with his wife, Speck had been arrested in Dallas, Texas, for pressing the blade of a knife against the throat of a young woman who was parking the car. He was sentenced to eighteen months in jail, but was released a few months later. Authorities at Huntsville, Texas, wanted him as a parole violator, but he moved on before they could catch him. There seems to be some reason for believing that after his release from jail, Speck went on a murder rampage that culminated in the killing of the eight nurses. On 10th April 1966, a pretty divorcee, Mary Pierce vanished from the tavern in Monmouth, Illinois, where she worked. Her naked body was found three days later in the pigsty behind the tavern. Speck, who was in Monmouth staying with his brother and working as a carpenter, had asked the divorcee for a date and been refused. A week later, a sixty-five-year-old woman was raped and robbed; but by the time the police arrived to question him, Speck had left town. He took a job on an ore boat on the Great Lakes, but was dismissed on 2nd July, in Indiana Harbour. That day, in the nearby Indiana Dunes Park, three girls vanished, leaving their clothes behind them in a car.

These were the crimes of which Speck was suspected by the police; there had also been four attacks on women in Benton Harbour, near Indiana Harbour, in February 1966; the ages of the women ranged from seven to sixty, and all were strangled and stabbed, like the eight nurses.

The theory of the psychiatrist who examined Speck in prison, Dr. Marvin Ziporyn, is that Speck was in a trance-like state due to drugs on the night of the murder of the nurses, and that the sight of the girl who resembled his wife – whom he had sworn to kill – triggered some mechanism of violence. He believes that Speck may have wandered around Chicago after the murders completely oblivious of what he had done. If, in fact, Speck had committed any of the crimes mentioned above, this theory would cease to fit the facts. Speck was a neurotic, and had been since childhood; once, in a fit of frustration with his father, he had hit himself on the head with a hammer and caused an injury; later, he suffered more head injuries in a bar-room brawl. In compiling the *Encyclopedia of Murder*, I observed that many 'insane' killers had suffered head injuries – Earle Nelson (the 'gorilla murderer') and Lock Ah Tam, for example. But, above all, his personality was quiet and pleasant (I spoke to a man who knew him in Chicago, who described him as a 'charmer'), and his sexual desires were violent. This is always a dangerous combination – as can be seen in the case of Christie, and of so many murderers discussed in this book – Gein, Nelson, Kürten. A nurse who went out with him in Hancock, Michigan (where Speck had an emergency operation to remove his appendix) described him as very gentle, but with an enormous amount of hatred in him.

Speck was sentenced to death; but at the time of writing, he is still appealing against the sentence. A few months after his murders, on 12th November 1966, eighteen-year-old Robert Benjamin Smith walked into a beauty parlour in Mesa, Arizona – where he was a high school student – and forced five women and two little girls to lie face down on the floor; then he went around and shot them one by one in the back of the head. (He explained later, 'I wanted to be known'. When Speck heard of the crimes, he remarked: 'Boy, I'd like to get my hands on that guy. I'd kill him.' Psychologists found it hard to understand Smith's motives; he was an excellent student, and had no hostility towards his parents.

C.W.

# 1967

# ZODIAC
## The Sign of Death

It was just a few days before Christmas, 1968, and the roundish hills outside Vallejo, just north of San Francisco, were covered with a thin layer of white frost. Moonlight flooded the scene and gave the entire area a ghostlike whiteness. But this stark beauty went unnoticed by the young couple parked on lonely Lake Herman Road. David Faraday, seventeen, and Bettilou Jansen, sixteen, were on their first date. Nervous and excited over the possibilities of romance they had eyes only for each other.

Suddenly a lone figure approached the car. Crouching by the driver's window the now visible man pulled out a 22-caliber pistol and aimed it at young David's head. A shot rang out, and then another, and then another. Inside the car, blood spurted from David's head. Across the seat Bettilou screamed. After a moment's hesitation, she yanked the door open and began to run frantically. But she was not fast enough and five more bullets brought her to the ground. It was all over in minutes. An innocent young couple lay dead, the only clue to their murder the nine shell casings spread around the area.

Police investigating the murders leaned towards jealousy as the motive. Fellow students and friends of the couple were hauled in and interrogated. The police got nowhere because the Lake Herman Road killings were not isolated slayings. The motive was not personal jealousy. The Zodiac Killer was at work. He would be heard from again.

Interest in the double killing died as the investigation petered out. Over the spring and into the summer, the area around Vallejo returned to normal. Then, on July 4, Zodiac struck again. This time the victims were a twenty-two-year-old Vallejo waitress and a nineteen-year-old friend. That fateful night the two were parked alone in nearby Blue Rock Springs Park. Again the two were so deeply involved with each other that they missed the approach of the lone figure. For the first time there was a moment of warning, however short and useless. Turning a strong flashlight on the young man, the killer blinded and immobilized him for a brief moment before filling the interior of the car with bullets. This time Zodiac employed a powerful 9-millimeter handgun. Ten shots smashed through the car. Then the deadly figure turned and fled.

The waitress died a short time later but the young man miraculously survived the four bullet wounds and lived to give a sketchy description of his assailant. Blinded by the light, he remembered only that the man was fairly heavy and wore glasses.

A short time later, the Vallejo Police Department received an anonymous phone call. A man spoke very matter-of-factly. 'I just shot the two kids at the public park. With a 9-millimeter automatic. I also killed those two kids Christmas.' The caller hung up and the hunt was on.

The case gained even more notoriety when, on August 1, letters from the killer showed up simultaneously at the Vallejo newspaper and at both major San Francisco dailies.

Each message contained a handwritten note and one-third of a cryptogram. The cryptogram was a mysterious series of letters and signs that defied easy interpretation.

As a means of establishing his identity in the note, the killer gave several details of the killing not known to the public. He listed the brand of bullets used and described the positions of the bodies. He also described the clothing worn by one of the female victims.

The note had several misspellings (possibly deliberate, as the complexity of the Cryptogram certainly indicated the killer was a man of some intelligence) and closed with a warning. If the newspapers didn't publish the encoded message for all to see, the murderer would go on a killing spree. The note was signed with what would soon become known as his symbol, a circle divided by a cross.

The papers published the Cryptogram and the note along with a message to the killer asking for more proof of his identity. As publicity was undoubtedly part of the killer's motivation, he responded quickly. The *San Francisco Examiner* soon received a letter with still more details of the crimes. This time the killer gave himself a symbolic name as well as a symbolic signature. 'This is Zodiac speaking,' the letter began. Headlines were born.

The authorities expended a good deal of effort in attempts to crack the encoded message. In his last letter Zodiac had stated that when the police solved the Cryptogram they would be able to catch him. A variety of experts were called in and the message was even fed into a computer. Nothing worked.

Finally two amateurs in Salinas (a high school teacher and his wife who had never tried to break a code before) were piqued by what they read in the newspaper. They tackled the job on their own and succeeded. The message they decoded sent chills through their hearts. 'I like killing people because it is more fun than killing wild game in the forest because man is the moat dangerus anamal of all to kill something gives me the most thrilling expeerence.

'The best part of it ia thae when I die I will be reborn in paradice and all the I have killed will become my slaves. I will not give you my name because you will trs to sloi down or stop my collecting of slaves for my afterlife.'

The message gave no solid clue to Zodiac's identity but it did give some insight into his motives. Sexual inadequacy, said more than one psychiatrist after reading the decoded statement.

Despite intensive investigative efforts by police, nothing new in the case happened until Zodiac struck again. This time the victims were two college students picnicking north of the city. Now Zodiac approached in broad daylight. Hiding his face with a square hood reminiscent of a medieval executioner's mask, he pulled a gun on the terrified young people and tied them up with a rope. Once they were helpless, Zodiac pulled out a long, sharp knife and plunged it into the man's back. He struck five more times before turning on the young woman. While he was stabbing her in the back, she turned over convulsively. The mad killer then proceeded to stab her in the torso twenty-three more times, the wounds forming the outline of a bloody cross.

Afterwards Zodiac walked over to the couple's white sports car and wrote on it the dates of all the murders he had committed. Amazingly enough, the young man survived despite his severe injuries. Because of the hood, however, there was little new information that he could give police.

Thirteen days later Zodiac killed again, this time inside the city of San Francisco itself. A cab driver, a part-time student working on his Ph.D., was the new victim. Zodiac hailed the cab and shot the driver from a backseat near a playground in Presidio Heights. When he finished his grisly work, he tore a piece out of the man's now bloody shirt and fled on foot. This time, however, there was a witness. Unbeknownst to Zodiac, the crime and his flight had been observed.

A short time later, police circulated a description of a man twenty to twenty-five, with a reddish crew cut and thick glasses. Armed with the description, police finally began to hope for an arrest. Working backwards through all of the data in the Zodiac case, they attempted to pin down a suspect fitting the new profile. They were unsuccessful, although they did manage to come up with details of an earlier murder that they now attributed to Zodiac.

By this time the entire city and its suburbs were in a state of terror. The killer had struck randomly in different areas and at different kinds of people. Nobody felt safe. Women and men alike began looking over their shoulders. Public outcry for an arrest reached epic proportions.

A few days after the cab murder Zodiac heightened the sense of panic by writing a letter in which he stated that a school bus might be his next target. He just might shoot out the front tires, he said, and pop off the kiddies as they came bouncing out. Whatever Zodiac's intentions were, this last letter moved the city to a siege mentality. Police escorts were assigned to school buses and many parents either kept their children at home or took them to school in cars.

But Zodiac never struck at a school bus. In fact he never struck again. In the months that followed he sent a steady stream of letters to the newspapers, either taking credit for some new murder or twitting the police for failing to capture him. Each lead was checked out but either no evidence of a murder could be found or the guilt for it was indisputably attached to someone else. As the letters continued to arrive and as they began to embody little more than the Zodiac's perverted sense of humor, the newspapers began to bury them on the back pages.

In March of 1971 Zodiac wrote his last letter. Nothing has been heard from or about him since. Despite a massive police hunt that involved forces all across the Bay area, despite nationwide publicity and appeals for help, and despite an aroused citizenry armed with a description, very little is known about Zodiac. The police theorize that he is either in a hospital or dead. Others think he may be in jail, serving time for some relatively innocuous offense.

Still another possibility haunts the Bay area. The Zodiac may be neither dead, nor jailed, nor hospitalized. He may be walking the streets of San Francisco, his murderous urges under control for the moment. He may be the model of a normal citizen on the outside, but a walking time bomb inside, a killer in suspension waiting for some hidden impulse to drive him on to new mass murders.

J.P.

# 1969

# CHARLES MANSON

## Helter Skelter

The Manson case belongs in the category of horrific murders, but it also (up to the present) stands on its own.

At midnight on 9 August 1969 the home of Sharon Tate, the film actress, above the Hollywood hills, was invaded by four unwelcome young strangers. One of them, Linda Kasabian, was to deny any active part in the proceedings that followed and to testify against her confederates. The other three, Susan Atkins, 21, Patricia Krenkwinkel, also 21, and Charles Watson, 23, murdered the pregnant Sharon Tate and four of her friends with unbridled brutality and apparent enjoyment. On the following night, they were joined by Leslie Van Houten, 20, in the no less savage and (for them) thrilling annihilation of Leno LaBianca, owner of a chain of Los Angeles grocery stores, and his wife Rosemary. The four murderers and Linda Kasabian were members of a hippie colony or 'Family' whose 'father' was a 34-year-old prisoner on parole named Charles Manson. Manson believed himself to be Jesus Christ, or at any rate encouraged his children to believe that he was, and his word was their law. He had commanded them to kill.

Manson, Susan Atkins, Patricia Krenkwinkel and Leslie Van Houten stood trial together, while Watson, who succeeded in evading extradition from Texas for over a year, was tried separately after his return to California. Under Californian practice, there is one trial to establish the fact of guilt (or innocence), and in the case of a conviction for first degree murder a second trial to enable the jury to recommend whether the penalty should be death or life imprisonment. In this case, all five defendants were convicted of first degree murder, and all five of them were subsequently sentenced to death. However, well before they had had time to exhaust the means of appeal available to them, capital punishment was abolished in California, and their sentences were consequently reduced to life imprisonment. They were, all of them, entitled to apply for parole in 1978, and some of them have now been released and are at liberty. As far as one can tell, this is the one matter most people in California are chiefly concerned about.

Late in 1974 Vincent Bugliosi, the young deputy district attorney who led for the prosecution, published in collaboration with Curt Gentry a long and very detailed book about the murders entitled *Helter Skelter*. One may note that he entitles the epilogue 'A Shared Madness' and (for example) writes of Susan Atkins when he first met her, 'She was crazy. I had no doubt about it. Probably not legally insane, but crazy none the less.' Yet though Mr. Bugliosi holds that 'the primary duty of a lawyer in a public prosecution is not to convict, but to see that justice is done', he was avowedly determined not only to secure convictions, but to win a recommendation from the jury for death in each case.

One may consider the question of Manson's sanity in the light of what the prosecution alleged was his motive for ordering the killings. Aaron Stovitz, who was associated with Bugliosi, strongly recommended something simple enough for a jury to be relied on to understand: for instance, the possibility that Manson was hoping to raise the $625 needed to bail out Mary Brunner, mother of one of his several offspring, who had been arrested the night before the Tate murders for stealing a credit card. But Bugliosi preferred what he was convinced was the real motive: 'to instil fear into the pigs' and bring on 'Helter Skelter', or a war between blacks and whites which would end in the total extermination of the whites. Bugliosi realized that a jury would dismiss this motive as too fantastic for belief unless he could find what he calls 'the missing link'—the thing that Manson had personally to gain from Helter Skelter. He did, in fact, discover this when he learned of the 'bottomless pit' in the desert, where Manson intended to take refuge with his followers. For Manson was certain that the time would come when the black man would realize that he couldn't handle things without being told by the white man what to do, and he would be forced to ask Charlie for help. The Family, by then multiplied to 144,000 (as prophesied in the Book of Revelations), would emerge from the bottomless pit a pure white master race, and Charlie would rule the world. Thus the motive, as Bugliosi saw it, was clear: murder done out of lust for power and gain. 'In his sick, twisted, disordered mind, Charles Manson believed that he would be the ultimate beneficiary of the black-white war and the murders which triggered it.'

If that was, indeed, his motive—and Bugliosi had plenty of evidence to prove that it was—it must surely follow that Manson was a lunatic, except according to the strictest interpretation of the legal or M'Naghten test under which no one is held to be insane who knows that what he is doing the law considers wrong.

Even more importantly, it is certain that the federal penal authorities bear a large measure of responsibility for the fact that the murders took place at all. 'God, Vince,' a reporter said to Bugliosi outside the courtroom, 'did it ever occur to you that if Barrett had revoked Manson's parole in, say, April, 1969, Sharon and the others would probably still be alive today?' The real point was much stronger than that. For while Samuel Barrett, Manson's parole officer, was given plenty of cause to revoke Manson's parole before the murders, Manson himself had not wanted this parole when it was granted him in 1967. In fact, he pleaded with the authorities to let him stay in prison, saying that prison had become his home and that he did not think he could adjust to the outside world. His request was refused, despite the fact that the only chance of success in the free community that he had—and this was no more than a chance—was to be placed in the charge of some skilled and understanding person who could devote his whole time to him. As it was, he was dealt with like every other parolee: made answerable to a man who had 150 other people either on parole or probation to look after. And Manson made it clear in a talk with Bugliosi, which took place in June 1971, after the case was over, that he was glad be be back in prison, again calling it his 'home'.

Psychiatry, which has been called the science of prediction, should also acknowledge some blame. Manson was the illegitimate son of a 16-year-old girl. She lived with numerous men, and married one of them who gave Manson his name. In 1939, when he was 5, his mother was sentenced to five years for armed robbery, and Manson was cared for by an uncle and aunt who were deeply religious. What influence they had on him, if any, is not known; but his mother reclaimed him after she was paroled in 1942, and he went to share her drunken and promiscuous existence until she wearied of him. After a brief time in care at a school in Indiana from which he absconded, Manson's career of crime began. It took him through several states, landed him in various institutions, educational at the start but later punitive, and included burglary, armed robbery, fraud, forgery, sodomy and pimping, with a high proportion of federal as opposed to state offences, for which penalties are likely to be far more severe.

During his periods of liberty, he was twice married. He had a son by his first wife Rosalie. The son was born while he was once more in jail. Though he had beaten Rosalie at times, he called her 'the best wife a guy could want'. She subsequently went to live with another man, and divorced him. His second wife Leona was a known prostitute for whom he pimped. He had been granted probation in 1959 instead of a ten-year sentence, on Leona's plea that she was pregnant by him, which was a lie, and that they were deeply in love. In February of the next year, Manson introduced himself to one Jo Anne Samuels as the president of '3-Star Enterprises, Nite Club and TV Enterprises'. He persuaded this girl to invest all her savings in the company, which didn't exist, drugged and raped her room-mate, and got Jo Anne herself pregnant. On 23 June 1960 he was sent to serve out his ten-year sentence, the judge observing that 'if there ever was a man who demonstrated himself completely unfit for probation, he is it'. After spending a year in the Los Angeles County Jail, he arrived at the United States Penitentiary at McNeil Island, Washington, in July 1961.

It is understandable that Manson should have come to consider prison his 'home' and have dreaded leaving it, for he did comparatively well at the McNeil Island penitentiary, and found in it a security which he had learned did not exist for him in the outside world. He was, it is true, chronically unstable in his interests, and those interests were largely of an outré or trendy kind. For example, he studied scientology under the guidance of a fellow-convict, and, according to his own claim, ultimately attained the highest level of 'beta clear'. Again, in 1964, when the Beatles and Beatlemania came to the United States, Manson learned to play the steel guitar. The last report on him before his release was made in August 1966, and said that 'he has come to worship his guitar and music', but also said that he had 'no plans for release as he says he has nowhere to go'.

Since the age of 12 Manson had spent seventeen years in institutions, and his remaining three years in the free world during the same period had been constantly criminal. Two psychiatrists had seen him. The first of them, Dr. Block, met him when he was 17, and after treating him with individual psychotherapy over a period of three months plainly failed to recognize the extreme potential dangerousness in him. For in the belief that he 'needed to be trusted' he recommended his transfer from the National Training School for Boys in Washington, D.C., to the minimum security Natural Bridge Honor Camp, where in less than three months he was found guilty of an offence which got him sent to the Federal Reformatory at Petersburg, Virginia. He held a razor blade against another boy's throat while committing an act of sodomy on him.

The other pyschiatrist to see Manson was Dr. Edwin McNeil, who interviewed him on two occasions in response to a judge's request. The first was in 1955 when he appears merely to have listened to what Manson had to say for and about himself, and then to have made a routine sort of report which one would suppose might have come from anybody else: 'It is evident that he has an unstable personality and that his environmental influences throughout most of his life have not been good . . . In my opinion this boy is a poor risk for probation; on the other hand, he has spent nine years in institutions with apparently little benefit except to take him out of circulation. With the incentive of a wife and probably fatherhood, it is possible that he might be able to straighten himself out. I would, therefore, respectfully recommend to the court that probation be considered in this case under careful supervision.'

The second occasion on which Dr. McNeil saw Manson was before Leona made her plea, and this time his recommendation was against the probation order which the judge none the less made. But Dr. McNeil still did no more than interview Manson. He had as little success as Dr. Block had had in predicting the magnitude of the menace in him; nor did he suggest that the proper place for a man of his kind was not a prison, where he could merely be kept out of circulation for a few years, but a secure hospital where he could be retained indefinitely and to which he would probably have been perfectly willing to go.

The power that Manson exhibited after his release on parole—a power of which there had been no evidence in his previous criminal career—to attract and dominate a 'family' of both sexes is for the moment inexplicable, except in psychic terms. Bugliosi said of the other defendants, 'True, Watson, Atkins, Krenkwinkel, and Van Houten committed these murders because Charles Manson told them to, but they would never have committed these murders in a million years if they did not already have murder in their guts, in their system. Manson merely told them to do what they were already capable of doing.' Can one really believe so simple an explanation? Not, surely, when one considers that Robert Beausoleil, 22, Mary Brunner, 23, Steve Grogan, 17, and Bruce Davis, 26, who all belonged to the Manson Family, were proven murderers, and at least six others were known either to have done murder or been willing to do it. They were all drop-outs. They may all have been 'crazy', though 'not legally insane'. But did Manson really collect so many in so short a time with 'murder in their guts, in their system'?

I was present by chance on one day only of the Sharon Tate trial, which lasted more than six months. I had been warned that it would be an exceptionally dull day confined to legal arguments. The prosecution had just concluded its case, and it had at once appeared that there was a dispute between the defendants and their counsel. The three girls had wished to testify to their own guilt in order to exculpate Manson. Rather than permit them to do this the defence had decided to rest its case. The session had ended in an unresolved deadlock. It was presumed that Manson had ordered the girls to take the blame for him, and that they were determined to obey him.

Even if this was so, Manson must obviously have changed his mind by the next day, because as soon as the proceedings began in the half-empty courtroom (comparatively few people, including reporters, were interested in legal arguments as opposed to blood) he took everyone by surprise with an offer to testify himself. The judge accepted this offer—I suspect gratefully, for it got him out of a very tricky situation—with the proviso that Manson should testify in the first place in the jury's absence in order that the admissibility of his testimony might be tested, and under these circumstances he was allowed to make a statement rather than be questioned by his counsel.

Manson spoke for more than an hour. It was a rambling, disorganized, largely irrelevant, and, I suppose, essentially mad speech, but utterly compelling; and I know that I, and I imagine everyone else who heard it, came away with the conviction that there must be some extraordinary power in Manson. 'I never growed up to read and write too good', he said near the beginning, which was the simple truth, but I felt he was making grammatical errors of this sort purposely to win our sympathy. Later, he lambasted us: 'If I could, I would jerk this microphone off and beat your brains out with it, because that is what you deserve, that is what you deserve.' At one point, he pictured himself as a sort of Peter Pan playing with his children a make-believe game of pirates and Indians in the woods; at another he betrayed bitterness about being forced to accept his parole: 'It's all your fear. You look for something to project it on, and you pick on a little old scroungy nobody that eats out of a garbage can, and that nobody wants, that was kicked out of the penitentiary, and that has been dragged out of every hellhole you can think of, and you drag him into a courtroom.' But he also revealed a flash of humour after the judge had asked him to stick to the issues. 'Mr. Bugliosi is a hard-driving prosecutor, polished education, a master of words, semantics. He is a genius. He has got everything a lawyer would want to have except one thing—a case.'

Manson admitted that he might have implied that he was possibly Jesus Christ, but said that he himself hadn't yet decided what or who he was. 'You can do anything you want with me, but you cannot touch me, because I am only my love . . . If you put me in the penitentiary, that means nothing because you kicked me out of the last one. I didn't ask to get released. I liked it in there because I like myself.'

At the same time, though he took a while to get round to it, Manson denied his own guilt clearly and unequivocally. After saying that 'these children', by which he meant the three female defendants, would have to explain whatever they had done, he told us, 'I have killed no one and I have ordered no one to be killed.' That part of his speech at least was relevant, and would have been admissible had he chosen to repeat it in front of a jury.

But amazingly, he did not so choose. He made his denial before the court officials and the few spectators who could not in any way influence the verdict. And when the judge asked him whether he wished to testify in the presence of the jury, Manson replied, 'I have already relieved all the pressure I had.'

On his way back from the stand to his seat (there is no dock in a Californian court) I saw Manson speak hurriedly to the girls, and I guessed at the time that he was 'unprogramming' them, though I could not hear what he said. However, Bugliosi reports in his book: 'As Manson left the stand and passed the counsel table, I overheard him tell the three girls: "You don't have to testify now." The big question: what did he mean by "now"? I strongly suspected that Manson hadn't given up but was only biding his time.'

But though Bugliosi does not admit as much, his 'strong suspicion' was never fulfilled. And it is a question whether it was, in fact, Manson's idea originally that the girls should testify as they had planned, or whether he deliberately took the stand himself, without hope of doing himself any good thereby, to keep them off it.

It is not enough to call Manson insane, and leave it at that, though it might have been a lot fairer than what has been done to him. One wants to know the source of these strange powers, which evidently didn't exist before he was forced out of the federal penitentiary at McNeil Island. He was a little man—only five feet two. Boys murdered for him as well as girls, and though most of the girls claimed to be desperately in love with him, not all of them did. Leslie Van Housten, for instance, told the psychiatrist who examined her that 'Charles was short. That is something that always turned me off.'

According to Bugliosi, Manson alone among the killers 'merits special handling', though by 'special' he evidently means particularly tough. For a while he was transferred to a maximum security 'adjustment centre' at Folsom Prison. The Warden of San Quentin said before his transfer: 'It would be dangerous to put a guy like Manson into the main population, because in the eyes of other inmates he didn't commit first-class crimes. He wa convicted of killing a pregnant woman, and that sort of thing doesn't allow him to rank very high in the social structure. It's like being a child molester. Guys like that are going to do time hard wherever they are.'

At Folsom Prison Manson lost all the inmate privileges that would normally be allowed him; no psychiatrist or anyone else who might be interested in his case went near him. He has since then been re-transferred to San Quentin, and was there when his chief disciple 'Squeaky' Fromme made a completely bungled effort to assassinate President Ford in 1975. But he is still presumably doing his 'time hard'; and even assuming that that is the kind of 'special attention' which he merits, it is not the kind from which society can hope to derive any benefit.

G.P.

# 1970

# DALE NELSON
## A Regular Guy

Dale Nelson was a *regular* guy (sociable, jolly, hail-fellow-well-met) only at intervals – when he had gone on a spree. At other times he was introverted, taciturn, even surly; without enemies but equally without close friends among his widely scattered neighbours in West Creston. But always an *ordinary* guy without any exceptional characteristics or proclivities. No one ever thought of him as a potential man of mark. No one ever thought of him as a potential criminal either.

He was thirty-one, living with his wife and three young children in a wooden shack on a dirt road which meandered through an expanse of open bush. He made a precarious living as a freelance logger, employed, when jobs were going, by local companies. His family liabilities might have been better met through an occupation yielding steadier employment, but Nelson liked hard physical labour out of doors. Nor did the consequent financial uncertainties greatly mar the harmony of his domestic life. Admittedly, once or twice he had struck his wife in anger, coincidentally with one of the aforementioned sprees. But those were isolated, unrepresentative incidents. Speaking broadly, Nelson was a good father and a good husband.

On 4 September of that year Nelson had a spree. He made a day of it, from noon till almost midnight. In and out of hotels and bars and liquor stores. With buddies or alone. Vodka, brandy, beer, wine – enough to float a battleship; but Dale Nelson could carry it with the best. At the end, getting into his car, he felt fit enough to drive. And apparently he was. But he did not drive home. Although not far away.

He drove first to the house of Maureen McKay, a relative by marriage, separated from her husband, living alone with her four-year-old daughter. From there he drove two hundred yards to the house of Shirley Wasyk, another relative by marriage, living along with three daughters, (aged twelve, eight and seven) while her husband was away at a logging camp. From there he drove two miles further to the tiny farm of a man named Phipps, the last human dwelling before uninhabited wastes.

At Mrs. McKay's house, finding on reconnaissance that she had grown-up company, Nelson slunk away without even a knock or ring. At Mrs. Wasyk's, he battered her to death and strangled the seven-year-old daughter; the twelve-year-old and the eight-year-old escaped. Do you inhale the faint scent of a bitter family feud? If so, mistakenly. Nelson had no relatives out at the Phipps farm, had had virtually no dealings with the farmer or his woman or their children (aged from ten years to eighteen months). Nonetheless, with rifle, club or knife, he killed them all. Eight people murdered within an hour or so. And still the worst is to be told of his iniquities.

In addition to the murders named, he ripped open the seven-year-old Wasyk girl from chest to groin, thrust his mouth into her stomach and ate undigested food; then having made off with her body into the wastes, dismembered it, hiding somewhere the heart and genitals. He subjected the eight-year-old Wasyk girl to cunnilingus, and he abducted from the Phipps farm another eight-year-old girl, dead or dying, and (in the wastes) subjected her to buggery.

The Crown drew the inference – difficult to refute – that Nelson's real objective was possession of the young girls, and that murder of the rest was only incidental. The removal of obstacles to the gratification of his appetites. This inference gains extra credibility from an event which stands out as extraordinary even among so many extraordinary events. Nelson had not removed the seven-year-old's body on his first exit from the Wasyk house. He had run out precipitately on hearing the siren of police cars summoned by an unharmed but apprehensive Mrs. McKay. Later, though, when the police had temporarily dispersed to evacuate other homesteads and scour environs, with infinite audacity he crept back inside, snatched the child's body, and drove on to the Phipps farm with his mutilated prize. Thus, in due course, he was able to head into the wastes with *two* young girls at his disposal for renewed atrocity.

Accepting the Crown's hypothesis concerning his objective, the vital question still awaited answer. What had occasioned this obscene explosion? Nelson had undoubtedly consumed a lot of alcohol, but not so as to prevent him controlling a car at speed along the unsurfaced tracks which zig-zagged through West Creston. Drunkeness, in any event, was no defence to a murder charge or charges, unless it had made him incapable of forming the intent (when he might be convicted of manslaughter instead – followed, almost inevitably, by very long imprisonment). There was a hint, though no proof, of drugs, that he was 'smashed' on 'acid': 'Must have been the LSD' were almost the first words he spoke to his police captors, but he revoked them in a later statement (though past use by him of LSD was proved). It soon became apparent that the one defence promising succour was insanity.

This defence comprised four main constituents. 'Crazy' remarks uttered by Nelson during the aftermath: 'I had no reason to do anything. It seemed like it wasn't me.' 'Hallucinations' experience by Nelson in his cell: mosquitoes, a large dog, Japaneses girls on his bunk. (Holt, more than fifty years before, had complained of dogs and insects, but Japanese girls lay beyond the limits of his fancy.) A psychiatrist, of course: 'Schizo-affective psychosis. . . . A fluctuating condition. . . . Unable to appreciate that his actions in the Wasyk and Phipps homes were wrong.' (The Crown, of course, called psychiatrists in rebuttal.)

Much the most important constituent, however, much the strongest card that defence counsel had to play, was the nightmarish narrative; the entirely undisputed record of the facts. No, the jury couldn't imagine themselves doing anything like it. But, yes, Nelson did know what he was doing. And yes, Nelson did know that it was wrong. The M'Naghten Rules directed them to a proper verdict.

The sub-human Nelson, though, did not forfeit his life. Bad ideas as well as good ideas are borrowed, and the Canadian Criminal Code had recently been amended to place different types of murder in different compartments (as did our own Homicide Act of 1957). The West Creston murders were not now capital. The Code fixed Nelson's penalty. Imprisonment for life. Sane or insane, he could not have hoped for anything better. His trial only settled *where* he was to be confined.

E.L.

# 1971

# EDWARD PAISNEL
## The Beast of Jersey

Edward Paisnel was a remarkable man. He kept the country-dwellers on the Channel Island of Jersey under a reign of terror for *more than fifteen years*; he took youngsters from their beds in lonely but inhabited houses, and then subjected them to unspeakable obscenities; he wore on these nocturnal expeditions grotesque garb and a terrifying mask; he kept those accoutrements, when not required, in a secret room; he dabbled – if no more – in black magic and Satanism, collecting dubious books and chalices and relics; he maintained all the while the image of a respectable citizen – a self-employed contractor and jobbing gardener.

And, incidental to these things – he confirmed one strongly held belief and upset another. The former – that a full moon stimulates weird behaviour. The latter – that robbers (whether looking for cash or jewels or children) steer clear of a house where adults are at home.

The domiciliary raids began in 1957. Thereafter they recurred sporadically; sometimes in swift bursts, once after an uninterrupted break of three whole years. The total sum of Paisnel's crimes defies exact enumeration, but twenty – the moderate police estimate – will serve.

A Paisnel operation passed, usually, through six stages. First, patiently casing the joint until he was familiar with windows and doors and juxtaposition of the rooms. Second, entry and abduction, effected by threat or force or fraud ('Don't shout or I'll kill you'; 'My knife is sharp'; 'I have a gun'). Third, expertly blindfolding the abductee as reinsurance of the protection afforded by his mask. Fourth, leading or dragging the victim to a neighbouring field. Fifth, an act of rape – or sodomy – with a girl, an act of sodomy – or fellatio – with a boy. Sixth, at high risk, escorting his coerced sexual partner back to the house, back to the room, back even to bed. Solicitous, tender almost – but the jobbing gardener was always nice with children.

Two of Paisnel's most audacious enterprises demonstrate how the system worked in actual practice.

A boy – a boy of nine. Innocent, truthful, rather babyish for his age. Peacefully sleeping, barely a yard from his small brother. Wakened by a torch flashing into his eyes.

'Come on,' says a muffled voice. 'Come on.'

The boy peers unavailingly into the bright light. Is it Daddy? Surely no; Daddy and Mummy have kissed him goodnight, and gone into their bedroom. Anyway, Daddy wouldn't play a joke like this. At *this* time. Who then?

'Come on. Come on.'

The boy can glimpse the stranger now. A funny-looking person! *Terribly* funny. Puffy cheeks. Flabby lips. Dirty, straggly hair. Nasty-like. Afterwards the boy speaks of him as the Bogey Man.

'Come on.'

'Where? What for?'

'Sssh. Quiet, now. Or I'll cut your throat. See?'

The boy sees – sees a penknife in the stranger's hand. Ordered to get up, he does. Half dazed, half afraid. His small brother, in the other bed, sleeps on.

'Piggyback?' suggests the stranger, in a whisper.

Yes, the boy likes piggybacks. It works like the classical bait of sweets. Carrying him, the stranger tiptoes softly down the stairs.

There are french windows at the back. They go through, down the garden, across some waste ground. The boy is no longer dazed, but much more afraid.

'Drop them,' says the stranger.

'Drop what?' says the boy.

A rough hand feels inside the gap in his pyjamas. . . .

A girl – a girl of fourteen. Living with her widowed mother. In a cottage; modern, spruce, comfortable, but secluded. Stirring in her beauty sleep. Hearing a knock and noises in the hall below. Wondering if she is dreaming. Then a loud shout. Calling her by name.

'Stay in your room and lock the door.'

Her mother's voice. No dream. No doubt. No possible mistake. Her mother's vice – but in a tone she has never heard before. Stricken with terror. Quivering with alarm.

The girl leaps up. As she opens her bedroom door, the front door slams.

'Mother . . . Mother. . . .'

Only an empty soundlessness. As though the cottage also holds its breath. Wondering, the girl goes down the stairs.

'Mother . . . Mother. . . .'

But Mother is hastening to the nearest house for help.

From somewhere a rough hand reaches out of the darkness. A hard punch fells the girl. A rope is tied around her neck.

'Come on.'

As she resists and pulls away, automatically she tightens the rope until she nearly chokes.

'Come on.'

She has no option. Barefoot, led as by a halter, she advances with her captor into the open air.

'I've killed before, and I'm ready to kill again. Drop them. And lie down.'

The girl – who blames her? – chooses a fate marginally better than death. . . .

E.L.

# 1972

# GRAHAM YOUNG

## A Psychopathic Murderer

---

1972 was a vintage year for those who are fascinated by poisoners, by murderers whose minds are 'disturbed', by compulsive killing and by the whole disputed area of madness and the Law. It was the year in which Graham Frederick Young was sentenced at St. Albans Crown Court to life imprisonment for murdering Mr. Robert Egle, head storeman at Hadlands Laboratories, Mr. Frederick Biggs of Chipperfield, and of attempting to murder David John Price Tilson, and Jethro Batt, as well as administering poison to Ronald Hewitt and Diana Smart.

The case created a public uproar not only because this dangerous psychopath had been using his work mates as guinea pigs in poison experiments, but because the whole sordid and dreadful affair could have been avoided if anyone had paid the slightest attention to what Mr. Justice Melford Stevenson had said ten years earlier, in 1962, when Young had been charged with poisoning his father and sister. The Judge had sent Young to Broadmoor Criminal Lunatic Asylum with the most positive recommendation that he should not be released for 15 years without the Home Secretary's consent. Young in fact was released, in February 1971, nine years later, and within three months had started a mad poisoning spree with the dreadful results that ended in his second trial.

Apart from the fact that he was released far too soon the authorities—who acted of course on medical advice—might have been warned by the fact that Young, even as a boy of fourteen, was administering poison to relations, friends, and acquaintances as opportunity offered in a motiveless way. This was the real hallmark of the mad, compulsive killer. He was not actuated by hate, or greed, or sexual desire; in his abnormal and deranged mind he was a chemical genius and those privileged to aid him in his experiments with poison by becoming his victims were merely 'interesting' in so far as they provided him with more knowledge of various types of poison, details of lethal doses, and the time it took the 'subject' to die. This was what had made Mr. Justice Stevenson write his awful warning. 'Such people are always dangerous and are adept at concealing their mad compulsion which may never be wholly cured.'

However, Home Secretaries these days are nothing if not fashionable and Mr. Justice Eveleigh made no comment when he passed the sentence of life imprisonment. There was in fact no need for comment. The whole dreadful sequence of events had been fully reported in the Press and once again we were indebted to detailed and accurate reporting of the case and its bizarre history for the measures which at last the authorities felt impelled to take in order to prevent, if they could, a recurrence of this tragedy.

The story of Graham Frederick Young I find totally fascinating because it shows the madness of a man beginning to show itself in the child, and that insanity never alters basically while he grows up. Young was a compulsive and cunning poisoner as a boy. He remained a compulsive and cunning poisoner as a man.

In July 1962 Young was top chemistry pupil at John Kelly Secondary School, Willesden. His knowledge of poisons was phenomenal. His friends were chemists from whom by forged prescriptions he obtained poisons. He started in a simple way by putting antimony in a cream biscuit and giving it to his best school friend, John Williams. He laced his sister's tea with belladonna. He sprinkled his father's food with an antimony 'dressing.' He had a perfectly normal family life. His father and sister were good to him. He owed them no grudge. Fortunately an alert science master caught this brilliant pupil with an authorised poison and reported the matter which led to his arrest. Had it not been for this Frederick Young might well have a juvenile murderer. As it was his three victims, after being very ill, recovered.

When detectives searched Young's room they found the same kind of books that Ian Brady the Moor murderer had in his possession. There was the same dedication to Hitler, but whereas Brady worshipped the cult of de Sade, this fourteen-year-old boy had a whole library on poison—and on poisoners. They were his heroes. William Palmer, Pritchard,

George Chapman, right down to Mrs. Merryfield who was very properly hanged in 1953 at a time when the good, clean crack of the rope was still putting the fear of God into killers and forcing the robbers to leave their guns at home.

There was no doubt that Young was a very bright boy indeed. The chemists he consorted with thought of him as a prodigy and a 'chemical genius.' Perhaps he was, but it was genius horrible and lethally perverted.

Young had ten shillings a week pocket money and out of this slender income he managed to build up a formidable library on poison. He read every book he acquired avidly so that the mind of this schoolboy was filled with the idea of poison to the exclusion of all else. It was the only subject that really interested him. It was his life.

At his first trial this good-looking schoolboy with his curly chestnut hair admitted the charges and gave no explanation.

At this trial the Judge heard the evidence of Dr. Christopher Fysh, chief Medical Officer of the remand centre where Young had been placed. Dr. Fysh said that Young was suffering from 'A psychopathic disorder'. Asked by the Judge whether he was likely to repeat this kind of crime, Dr. Fysh, who seems to have been a practical as well as an experienced doctor, said; 'I think it is extremely likely.' Again this dreadful warning was apparently forgotten or overruled with the dreadful results that led to the second trial.

The life that Young led in Broadmoor may come as a surprise to readers who have been left behind in the great swing to liberalism in prison administration; 'Young's prolific reading made him well-informed. He had access to all daily and Sunday newspapers. He was able to borrow books—on poison of course, from Berkshire County Council's mobile library. He could out-talk most of the inmates and nurses on a variety of subjects and was especially brilliant on medical matters and poisons.

From 7 am daily he was free to do as he liked, although he spent most of his time reading in his room. However, as he grew up he did grow a Hitler-type moustache and brushed his hair across his forehead, even making himself a Swastika emblem. He watched television in the 'common room'—connoisseurs of phraseology will notice the University nomenclature—and radio in his room was allowed after he had become a parole patient for good behaviour. He kept and carefully tended a budgerigar. This bird seems to have suffered no ill effects and in the companionship between the boy and the bird we glimpse perhaps the only sight of sanity in the story of Graham Young. He grew deadly nightshade in the garden and extracted belladonna from it. He put sugar-soap in the patients' tea as a joke, which was not appreciated.

Not a bad life, really. No expense, no worry, some companionship, time for study and assured privacy. No freedom, but no worries.

Perhaps the weirdest escapade of this extraordinary boy was to devise a way of getting drunk without alcohol, which was forbidden. Young and his small circle used carbon monoxide taken from a gas automatic lighter. The flame was extinguished and the escaping gas was charged into the tea and milk. It was very intoxicating. Several drunken parties seem to have taken place in the common room. Obviously Young had a most ingenious mind.

Throughout his time at Broadmoor he made no special secret of the fact that he was fascinated by murder, preferably by poison but not exclusively. He was an admirer of Christie, the horror killer of Rillington Place and knew every detail of the crimes that Christie committed. He even knew how many layers of wallpaper Christie had used to cover his foul crimes . . .

Mr. Geoffrey Foster of Hadlands, Young's employer, described him as above average intelligence, but Mr. Foster would never have employed him had he known of Young's Broadmoor record. This was suppressed to enable him to be 'rehabilitated' in a good job and, as the authorities explained, to ensure that he would rejoin normal society. There was of course never any chance of Graham Young rejoining normal society. Putting aside all the lawyers' jargon and all their definitions of insanity, and setting aside the medical 'scientific' approaches, Young was as mad as a hatter, and he revealed his madness most in the extraordinary cunning he showed in conning the Broadmoor doctors that he was totally cured when in reality his insanity had grown with the years.

Dr. Edgar Unwin was responsible for Young under the medical superintendent Dr. Patrick McGrath. Young, who could have the most winning manner if he chose, seems to have fooled both these very experienced doctors, Dr. Unwin being a psychiatrist of repute, and Dr. McGrath an expert in his field of medicine.

Dr. Unwin in recommending Young to a Training centre at Slough before he got his job with Hadlands wrote: 'This man has suffered a deep-going personality disorder necessitating hospitalisation throughout his adolescence. . . . He has however made an extremely full recovery and is now entirely fit for discharge—his sole disability now being the need to catch up his lost time.'

It is easy to be wise after the event. Dr. Unwin made a mistake. It may well be that Young would have deceived any psychiatrist, such was his gift for making a good impression. When Hadlands had agreed to employ him the Slough Training Centre were equally enthusiastic about their trainee. No mention was made of Broadmoor by anyone. That was a thing of the past, A letter of thanks that Young wrote to Mr. Foster shows how tactful and pleasing Young could be:

> *Dear Mr. Foster,*
> *Thank you for your letter of the 26th instant offering me the job of assistant store keeper.*
> *I am pleased to accept your offer and will therefore report for work on Monday the 10th of May at 8.30 am.*
> *May I take this opportunity of expressing my gratitude to you for offering me this position notwithstanding my previous infirmity as communicated to you by the placing officer.*
> *I shall endeavour to justify your faith in me by performing my duties in an efficient and competent manner.*
> *Until Monday week, I am,*
> *Yours faithfully,*
> *Graham Young*

It is just right, flawless. The little hurdle of the 'previous infirmity' is lightly touched on as a thing of the past, all the more reason for gratitude and faithful service to justify his employer's faith in him. It is a polite letter but not servile, even friendly, and it is the letter of an educated and intelligent man who knew exactly what to say and how to express it.

The newspapers went to town on the story of Graham Young suggesting that there had been negligence or at least dire mistakes. I disagree. I think that everyone from the Home Secretary and his advisers to the Hadlands Director, the staff at the training centre, and the Broadmoor doctors, were taken for a ride by a psychopath of exceptional cunning and address, capable of ingratiating himself with the able, experienced and compassionate men who were deceived by cleverly contrived symptoms of sanity and a balanced, moderate approach which Graham Young could invoke at will. He was a consummate actor. He was insane only about murder. He was otherwise not only normal but extremely clever. His work at the training centre had been exemplary. Those in charge of him did not doubt for a moment that so able and industrious a young man would make good.

So the scene seemed to be set for success and there was confidence at Hadlands that the new man in the store was a very lucky find indeed. Young began working with Robert Egle, the chief store keeper, Mr. Biggs, and Mr. Hewitt.

Mr. Egle was the first to go. The doctors never thought for one moment he had been poisoned. He was cremated. Young had killed him with thallium, a little known drug which Young had studied for ten years. As other members of the staff either died or were terribly ill without reason suspicion grew until detectives were called in and searched Young's room. Experienced policemen as they were they had never seen anything like it. There was a whole library on poison and poisoners. There were some very odd drawings of two hands administering poison to a victim. There were Nazi relics and literature. A favourite decorative theme of the room was a skull and crossbones.

Even with all this Young was able to play cat and mouse with the doctors who were called in. He even got himself appointed firm representative at the funeral of Mr. Egle . . . It is of course common for murderers to obtain some sexual satisfaction from attending their victim's funeral but there is no evidence of sexuality in the record of this macabre man.

Eventually as sickness increased in Hadlands it became known as 'the Bovington bug.' It was dreaded. Everyone feared that they might catch it.

So we have the extraordinary picture of a happy and well-ordered firm of moderate size—there were about eighty employees—reduced to tension and suspicion because they felt themselves haunted by an unspecified disease that might strike anyone down at any moment.

Graham Young made the most discreet but painstaking enquiries as to the condition of those struck down with the 'Bovington bug'. He was genuinely absorbed in the reaction to the poisons which he had administered. Whether the victim lived or died seemed unimportant. When Mr. Briggs perished, Young who seems to have liked him said, 'Dear old Fred. I'm so sorry.'

Thallium is tasteless and odourless. Graham Young knew his poisons.

A Committee was appointed under the amiable chairmanship of Lord Butler, the Master of Trinity College, Cambridge, to look into the whole matter and to recommend what—if anything—should be done.

G.S.

# 1973

# DEAN CORLL

## Loved Kids

---

Dean Arnold Corll was born on Christmas Eve, 1939. The impending war seemed far away from Fort Wayne, Indiana, and the boy seemed healthy and normal. His parents, Arnold Corll, a factory mechanic, and his wife Mary, were both twenty-three.

'They fought and fussed before they got married,' said a relative, who didn't want to be named in view of what happened later, 'and they fought and fussed right up to the end.' Details are vague, but it seems that the marriage broke up round about the end of World War II, when their names vanish from the Fort Wayne phone book, the city directory and the court records.

Arnold Corll may have gone off to do some kind of farm work in the south. Mary must have remarried – though there's no record of a divorce – because she now became known as Mary West. She had custody of two boys from an earlier marriage, as well as of Dean and his younger brother Stanley, and a girl was born from this new alliance. After a few moves, in 1954 the family settled in Vidor, Texas.

Dean Corll was known as a pleasant, quiet boy. 'Dean was a good boy;' said the anonymous relative, 'But the good ones are so often used by the damnable ones.' He was brought up in the Methodist church, but apparently only attended at Christmas and Easter. 'I never saw him with a cigarette,' she added, 'And I never heard him curse. He was almost too good, tried to do favors for people, always tried to make the best of every situation.'

His teachers at Vidor High School found him punctual, neat, quiet and never a troublemaker, but his grades were unimpressive. 'High school was a struggle for him. He had to work, helping out his mother, and he had odd jobs here and there.' The only real interest we know of is music: Dean played the trombone in the school stage band, and other members recall him as 'a good musician.' The band leader couldn't remember him at all: 'He was there in the band, but when you've got a big band students just don't stand out in your mind unless they are outstanding musicians or unless they are discipline problems. Dean Corll was neither.'

His best friend in High School couldn't believe what they were saying about him later. 'Let me put it this way,' he said. 'If Dean Corll had knocked on my door last Wednesday night before this story broke, I would have invited him in for a beer. He liked girls just like the rest of us.' Together they went to drive-in movies, where they tried to make out with the local girls, and Dean is known to have dated at least two girls at this time.

The only other thing that people remember about Dean Corll is that he seemed to be slightly better off than some of the other kids. For one thing, he ran a car. Perhaps this was because he helped his mother out with her business, for she had not only opened a candy store but made pralines, which she sold to other stores and restaurants. 'Dean was a good outdoorsman,' said his friend. 'Sometimes we'd drive down near the Trinity River and pick up pecans. Dean made up the pralines with the pecans we picked up at the river.'

When Dean graduated, he joined the family business, but then there was a gap of two years when he returned to Indiana to look after his grandmother, who had recently lost her husband. 'He knew she'd be alone and would need someone to take her to church and places. He got a job up there and stayed with his grandmother for two years, but he always managed to send a little money to his mother down here.'

He came back to the family in 1962, and they went to live in the Heights area of Houston, Texas. Here they established the Corll Candy Company, with Mrs. West as President, Dean as Vice-President and brother Stanley as Secretary/Treasurer. The business seemed to flourish, and life went on smoothly for a couple of years. Again, nobody found anything bad to say about Dean, and there seem to be no clues as to how this mild, pleasant young man turned into one of the world's most sickening mass murderers.

Some have suggested that it began in the army. Dean was drafted in 1964, and was assigned to Fort Polk in Louisiana for basic training, moving on to Fort Benning, Georgia, to attend the Army's radio-repair school, after which he got a permanent assignment as a radio repairman at Ford Hood, Texas. He applied for a hardship discharge soon after arriving at Fort Hood, and returned to help his family with an honourable discharge soon afterwards. The army records are exemplary: 'Nothing derogatory. No time lost.'

It seems, however, that it was in this short spell in the army that Dean Corll became homosexual, overtly so anyway.

Soon, the Corll Candy Company moved to bigger premises at 55 West 22nd Avenue, directly opposite Helms Elementary School. Dean's mother, still President of the company, now had an apartment of her own. Dean became General Manager of the company as well as Vice President, and he now rented his own apartment just one block away from the business.

A neighbour recalled how she heard about the Corll factory: 'My son, David, would come home all excited, saying the man was giving away candy to the children. It was the talk of the neighbourhood.' But she had a strange feeling about this. 'I heard that the man was inviting the children to a back room where he kept a pool table. I could understand the free candy, maybe, but this sounded a little peculiar to me.'

She forbade her son from seeing the man with the candy. He was thirteen, and he vanished shortly afterwards. 'I'll never know whether he went back or not.'

At this time, Dean Corll, nearly six feet tall, weighed around 190 pounds with not much spare flesh. His brown hair was closely cropped, and he had friendly brown eyes. Still nothing very noticeable, nothing to account for what was to come.

He was visiting his separated father two or three times a week, keeping him posted on what was happening with the family, but whether this has anything to do with what happened next is unclear. What did happen was that the candy company was suddenly dissolved, Dean's mother and sister moved out to Colorado, and brother Stanley took a job as machine operator in Bellaire. Dean, no longer in the candy business, decided to train as an electrician with the Houston Power and Lighting Company, and he too moved house – in fact, he lived in a dozen different places over the next five years, one month a single room, next a town house, then a garden apartment or a bungalow. Something strange was happening.

In 1969, Dean became friendly with a fourteen-year-old boy called David Owen Brooks, whose father was a paving contractor in the Heights section of Houston. Brooks said that it was a homosexual alliance, with Dean paying him for anal intercourse. He may have been known to him earlier, from the free candy period. However it went, they shared a number of apartments. One day, said Brooks, he had returned without warning to Dean's apartment in Yorktown and discovered Dean naked, molesting two young boys who had been stripped and tied to a wooden board. Dean let the boys go free, and offered Brooks a car if he would keep quiet about what he had seen. Seemingly, the offer was accepted.

Or maybe the boys were later killed – at this point the story gets vague again. What is clear is that at some point David Brooks introduced another young man to Dean Corll. This was Elmer Wayne Henley, and he soon joined the weird menage; on another occasion when Brooks had returned to the apartment early, he had himself been knocked unconscious by Henley and then repeatedly raped by Corll. Still, they all managed to remain friends, and over the next couple of years they had quite a lot of fun, in their own way. . .

It ended in the early morning of August 8, 1973, and it was Henley who cracked. He called the police with a garbled story about how he had just killed a man, and a patrolman who went to the scene found three terrified teenagers – Henley, another boy, and a girl – whimpering outside the apartment. Henley, produced a .22 pistol which he had used, he said, to kill his friend Dean Corll, whose body lay face down in the hallway with six bullet-holes in it.

They had been invited there for a glue-sniffing party. Dean had been less than pleased to find a girl there, but the spree had gone ahead anyway, and they had all knocked themselves out inhaling paint fumes from a paper bag. When Henley came round, it was to find himself bound and handcuffed, with Dean ramming a gun into his stomach yelling 'I'll teach you a lesson.' It took all of Henley's charm to get out of this situation, but he managed to do it by promising Dean that he would help him to torture, kill and dispose of the other two. Henley's part of the deal was that he would rape the girl then kill her, while Dean did the same to the boy. Dean stripped the boy, still unconscious, and strapped him to the wooden board, but when Henley tried to rape the girl he – not surprisingly – couldn't make it, and again he pleaded with Dean to let her go. Dean ignored him, but Henley was able to grab the gun. 'Go on, kill me,' taunted Dean, and Henley did just that, pumping bullet after bullet into him, then releasing the semi-conscious teenagers.

It emerged that Henley had been procuring young boys for Dean Corll for some time, and he took detectives to a boathouse that Dean had rented in south-west Houston. The part that Dean used contained only a stripped-down car, but beneath the floor they found something wrapped up in plastic sheeting: a boy, with a rope cutting deep into his throat. There were sixteen more corpses buried in the boathouse – 'Wall-to-wall bodies,' remarked one detective – and that was by no means the end of it. At a piece of ground near the lake they found four more bodies, and another six on the beach at High Island. The final count was twenty-seven bodies, though Henley claimed that there were more that hadn't been found.

Henley was found guilty of six of the murders and sentenced to 594 years in jail, but in 1978 his conviction was overturned on a technicality. Brooks was convicted of one murder and sentenced to life. A full account of the Dean Corll case can be found in Jack Olsen's book *The Man with the Candy*; quotations from the book were printed on t-shirts and sold at the *Sex* boutique in London's Kings Road, the shop which was the springboard for The Sex Pistols and Sid Vicious.

R.G.J.

# 1977

# DAVID BERKOWITZ
## 'Son of Sam'

We put the letter on the table and read it again. In his opening paragraph he wrote:

> *Hello from the gutters of N.Y.C which are filled with dog manure, vomit, stale wine, urine, and blood. Hello from the sewers of N.Y.C which swallow up these delicacies when they are washed away by the sweeper trucks. Hello from the cracks in the sidewalks of N.Y.C. and from the ants that dwell in these cracks and feed on the dried blood of the dead that has settled into the cracks.*

'He's a pretty good writer,' somebody at the table said.

'Yes, he is,' I said.

The letter was from the person who called himself 'Son of Sam.' He prowled the night streets of New York neighborhoods and shot at young girls and sometimes their boyfriends too, and he had killed five and wounded four. He crept up on victims with a .44-caliber pistol. Most of the young women had shoulder-length brown hair.

One of the victims was Donna Lauria, who was a eighteen when the killer shot at her as she sat in a car with her girlfriend outside the Laurias' apartment house on Buhre Avenue in the Bronx. Donna Lauria was the only victim mentioned by the killer in his letter, which was sent to me at my newspaper in New York, the *Daily News*. So I took the letter up to the fourth-floor apartment of Donna Lauria's parents, and I sat over coffee and read the letter again and talked to the Laurias about it.

The killer had sent one communication before this one. He left a note to police after murdering a girl and boy as they sat in a parked car at a place only five blocks from where Donna Lauria had been killed. Both notes were hand-printed. In the sadness and tension of the Laurias' dining room, I read the letter again. After the first paragraph, it said:

> *J.B., I'm just dropping you a line to let you know that I appreciate your interest in those recent and horrendous .44 killings. I also want to tell you that I read your column daily and find it quite informative.*
>
> *Tell me, Jim, what will you have for July Twenty-Ninth? You can forget about me if you like because I don't care for publicity. However, you must not forget Donna Lauria and you cannot let the people forget her, either. She was a very sweet girl but Sam's a thirsty lad and he won't stop me killing until he gets his fill of blood.*
>
> *Mr. Breslin, sir, don't you think that because you haven't heard from [me] for a while that I went to sleep. No, rather, I am still here. Like a spirit roaming the night. Thirsty, hungry, seldom stopping to rest, anxious to please Sam. I love my work. Now, the void had been filled.*
>
> *Perhaps we shall meet face to face someday or perhaps I will be blown away by the cops with smoking .38s. Whatever, if I shall be fortunate enough to meet you I will tell you all about Sam if you like, and I will introduce you to him. His name is 'Sam the Terrible.'*
>
> *Not knowing what the future holds I shall say farewell, and I will see you at the next job. Or, should I say you will see my handiwork at the next job? Remember Ms. Lauria. Thank you.*

> *In their blood*
> *and*
> *From the gutter*
> *'Sam's Creation' .44*

*P.S.: J.B., please inform all the detectives working on the slayings to remain.*

*P.S.: J.B., please inform all the detectives working on the case that I wish them the best of luck. 'Keep Em digging, drive on, think positive, get off your butts, knock on coffins, etc.'*

*Upon my capture I promise to buy all the guys working on the case a new pair of shoes if I can get up the money.*

*'Son of Sam'*

Directly under the signature was a symbol the killer drew. It appeared to be an X-shaped mark with the biological symbols for male and female, and also a cross and the letter S.

When I finished reading the letter, Mike Lauria, the father, said to me, 'What do you think?'

'Want to see for yourself?'

He pushed the letter away from him: 'I don't want to see it.'

'Let me,' his wife, Rose, said.

'You don't want to see it,' the husband said.

'Yes, I do. I have a lot of the cards she used to get. Maybe the printing is the same.'

The husband shrugged. 'Go ahead then.'

We took out the first page that mentioned her daughter and gave Rose Lauria the rest. Her large, expressive brown eyes became cold as she looked at the printing. On the wall behind her was a picture of her daughter, a lovely brown-haired girl with the mother's features. The mother put the pages down and looked up. 'He's probably a very brilliant man, boy, whatever he is,' she said. 'His brain functions the opposite way.'

She looked up at the picture of her daughter. 'She was a dancer and a half. Every place you went, people used to praise her. Is it possible he saw her someplace and she didn't speak to him or something?'

Nobody knew. The .44 killer appeared to be saying that he

was controlled by Sam, who lived inside him and sent him onto the streets to find young people to shoot. He did this at close range: one young woman, walking home from college, held a textbook over her face, and he put the gun up to the book and killed her. The detectives, whose shoes he would buy, walked the streets at night and hoped for a match with the man with the .44. 'He's mine,' one of them, a friend of mine, said. 'The man is Jack the Ripper, and I'm making a personal appointment with him.'

The hope was that the killer would realize he was controlled by Sam, who not only forced him into acts of horror but would ultimately walk him to his death. I felt that the only way for the killer to leave this special torment was to give himself up to me, if he trusted me, or to the police, and receive both help and safety. If he wanted any further contact, all he had to do was call or write me at the *Daily News*. It's simple to get to me. The only people I don't answer are bill collectors. The time to do it was right then, however. We were too close to the July 29 that the killer mentioned in his letter. It was the first anniversary of the death of Donna Lauria.

'She was sitting in the car with her girlfriend Jody Valenti,' Rose Lauria was saying. Jody Valenti was wounded but recovered. 'Mike and I came walking up. We'd been to a wake. I went up to the car and I said, 'Tell me, Jody, what happened tonight?' 'Donna'll tell you when she gets upstairs.' Now my husband says to Donna, 'What are you doing here at 1.00 a.m., you got to work tomorrow.' I said to him, 'What is she doing that's wrong?'

'So we went upstairs. My husband says, 'I'm going to walk the dog.' He goes with the dog to the elevator, and I hear Jody's horn blowing downstairs. I called out in the hall to my husband. He says to me, 'Well, go look out the window and see.' I look out and here's Jody screaming that Donna's been shot.'

Rose Lauria, nervous now, got up from the table. 'You know the last month when he killed the two more around here? My husband and I were at a wedding. We were supposed to meet some people after it. We left the wedding, and I said to my husband, 'I don't want to meet anybody. Something's the matter. I want to go home.' And we just got inside at the same time the two got killed.'

'She was pacing around here like a cat,' Mike Lauria said.

He walked me downstairs to the street. He stood in an undershirt, with the sun glaring on his wide shoulders, and he pointed to the spot where his daughter had been shot.

'She was starting to get out of the car when she saw this guy on the curb. Right where we are. Donna said to Jody, 'Who's this guy now?' Then the guy did what he did. Jody, she can't get herself to come near my wife. Forget about it. I saw her a couple of weeks ago. She spoke to me from the car. Told me she got engaged. She couldn't even look at me. I told her. "All right, Jody, go ahead, I'll see you." I let her go home.'

He turned and walked back into his building. I took my letter from his daughter's killer and went back the street and out of his wounded life.

Everyone was waiting for the July 29 anniversary of the Lauria killing, but Son of Sam didn't strike until two days later, when he killed Stacy Moskowitz and wounded Robert Violante, both twenty, in a car in Brooklyn. It was the first time the killer had struck outside the Bronx and Queens, and terror gripped all New York City.

## NO ONE IS SAFE FROM SON OF SAM

the *New York Post* blared on August 1. But the killer had made a mistake. While stalking the Brooklyn victims, he had left his car in front of a fire hydrant, and the police ticketed it. They traced the licence number – 561 XBL – to David Berkowitz, 24, of Yonkers, a postal worker and former auxiliary policeman.

Suspicious about what a a Jew from Yonkers would be doing in a quiet Italian neighborhood in Brooklyn at that time of night, detectives went to his apartment on August 10. They found the car in front and, peering through the window, saw the butt of a submachine gun and a letter addressed to the police.

Berkowitz was arrested when he came out to start the car. 'I'm Son of Sam. O.K., you've got me,' he said. The letter in the car indicated that he had planned a machinegun raid that night on a Hampton's discotheque and that the authorities 'would be all summer counting the bodies.' In the car, police also found a loaded, .44-caliber Bulldog revolver, which turned out to be the weapon that had killed and wounded all those people.

Later, in taped interviews with a psychiatrist, Berkowitz said that 'howling and crying demons demanding blood' had ordered him to kill. 'I'm the Son of Sam, but it's not me,' he said. 'It's Sam who works through me. I'm David Berkowitz. That's all I want to be. They use my body.' In April, 1978, Brooklyn Supreme Court Justice Joseph Corso ruled that Berkowitz was competent to stand trial for the murder of Stacy Moskowitz.

Berkowitz pleaded guilty to six murders, and he was sentenced to 315 years in prison.

J.Br.

# 1978

# TED BUNDY

## 'I Feel Like a Vampire'

Carol DaRonch was an exceptionally attractive young woman, though a little naïve. She had just graduated from high school and was working as an operator for Mountain Bell in Utah when, one Friday evening in November 1974, she drove her Camaro into Murray to look for a birthday gift for her cousin. She was browsing in the Walden bookstore when she was approached by a pleasant young man in a sports jacket who said that he was Officer Roseland of the Police Department and that someone had tried to break into her car: what was its number, and would she accompany him to check over the vehicle?

It didn't occur to her to wonder how this officer had been able to locate her so easily – he was a good-looking, affable fellow, and she was trusting by nature – so off they went. The car had not been broken into, but Officer Roseland asked Carol if she would go with him to the Police Substation in the shopping mall to 'view a suspect'. Now she did smell a rat, and asked to see some identification, and a gold shield was quickly flashed in front of her. She went with him. The shield was counterfeit.

While the door of the Substation was in fact the rear door of a laundromat, and it was locked. Would she go along with him to the central Police Station? She thought it a little unlikely that the beat-up Volkswagen to which he took her was a police vehicle, but his manner was reassuring and cops worked undercover, didn't they?

He drove the car out of the parking lot in the direction of the Police Station, but Carol felt more and more uneasy, and when he told her to fasten her safety belt she refused. Suddenly 'Officer Roseland' was a maniac; he turned the car into a quiet side street, stopped, and slapped a handcuff on her wrist. She screamed, and suddenly there was a gun in his hand, pointing at her head. Even so, she managed to open the car door and make a lunge out of it, but he grabbed a crowbar and started beating her with it. Amazingly, she was able to fend off a violent blow that would have crushed her skull, and ran out into the road hobbling in one shoe, into the path of an oncoming car. It screeched to a halt, and she flung herself inside, and she was driven away to safety by a young married couple. The wife said later: 'I have never seen a human being that frightened in my life. She was trembling and crying and weak, as if she was going to faint.'

If she had known just what this young man was capable of she would have passed clean out, but nobody knew just then – although there were suspicions, and in fact Carol was shown a picture of one Ted Bundy that had been sent down from Seattle, but she failed to recognize him. Bundy was just one of many suspects for a series of crimes that had been going on in the Seattle area for several months. Young women had been vanishing. To be precise:

> In January a young girl called Sharon Clarke had had her head battered by an intruder with a metal rod. She recovered.
>
> Later the same month a student at the University of Washington, Lynda Ann Healy, disappeared from her room, leaving behind bloodstained sheets and a nightdress.
>
> On March 12 a student at Evergreen State College in Olympia, Washington, was on her way to a concert when she vanished.
>
> On April 17 another student, at Central Washington

*State in Ellensburg, Susan Rancourt, was on her way to see a movie. She too vanished.*

*On May 6 yet another student, studying this time at Oregon State University in Corvalis, was out for a walk at night, and failed to return. This was Roberta Kathleen Parks.*

*On June 1 a girl named Brenda Ball was seen leaving a pub near Seattle Airport with a man at two in the morning. She never came back.*

*On June 11 a student at the University of Washington named Georgeanne Hawkins was dropped by her boyfriend on the way back to her residence, and she too vanished.*

*On July 14 a pleasant young man with one arm in a sling was seen by various people trying to pick up girls at a picnic area by Lake Sammanish, Washington. One gave him the brush-off but he succeeded in persuading Janice Ott to help him get a sailboat on to the roof of his car, and people heard him introduce himself as 'Ted'. Janice Ott went off with him, and didn't come back. Later, a girl named Denise Naslund went to the lavatory by the lakeside, and didn't return.*

*On September 7 two hunters found some human bones on a hillside near Lake Sammanish, some of which were identified as the remains of Janice Ott and Denise Naslund, while a third girl remained unidentified.*

*On October 12 another hunter, this time in Clark County, Washington, discovered a skull with some hair and scalp still clinging to it, and this led to a police search which came up with the remains of two young women, one of whom was identified as Carol Valenzuela who had disappeared eight weeks earlier. The other remained unidentified.*

By now there was a full-scale panic in progress, and a million rumours in the air. The name 'Ted' and the arm in the sling caught some people's imaginations or memories: one woman in Ellensburg thought she recalled seeing a man with his arm in a sling on the night that Susan Rancourt went missing. Another said that a man with his arm in a sling had approached her in Seattle, but that she had given him the brush-off, upon which he freed his arm and drove away. There were other crimes and other suspects to confuse matters, and Ted Bundy was only one of two thousand names to be checked out, and by the time the police got around to him he had gone. To Utah.

*On October 2 a young woman named Nancy Wilcox disappeared.*

*On October 18 a girl called Melissa Smith, whose father was actually the Midvale Chief of Police, set out for a party but decided in the end not to go, and turned to walk home. She never made it.*

*On October 27 Melissa's body was discovered in the Wassatch Mountains to the east of Salt Lake City. She had been raped and strangled.*

*On October 31 Laura Aime was returning from a Halloween party in Orem, but vanished on the way.*

The attack on Carol DaRonch which opened this chilling catalogue took place on November 8, by which time this man had sexually abused and violently killed at least thirteen young women, and possibly quite a lot more besides. She had the closest of escapes, but this was a man who was not going to give up so easily, for later that same evening he was spotted trying to pick up a young French teacher. She refused, but later still a young student named Debbie Kent vanished on her way to an ice-rink. The horrendous list grew even longer:

*On November 27 Laura Aime's nude body was found in a canyon.*

*On January 12 there was a medical conference in the skiing village of Snowmass, Colorado. Caryn Campbell, engaged to one of the doctors, disappeared from her room in the evening.*

*On February 17 her naked body was found frozen in the ice, not far from the village. Like most of the victims, she had been brutally raped then battered to death.*

*On March 15 in Vail, Colorado, a young woman named Julie Cunningham went out to meet a friend, and vanished.*

*On April 15 another girl, Melanie Cooley, disappeared from Nederland, Colorado.*

*On April 25 her body was found – clothed this time, but her jeans had been pulled down and her head battered in with a rock.*

*On July 1 a girl named Shelley Robertson disappeared from Golden, Colorado. Her naked body was later found in a mine.*

*On July 4 an attendant at a gas-station in Bountiful, Colorado, vanished from her workplace. This was Nancy Baird.*

*On August 16 Ted Bundy was arrested.*

His Volkswagen, cruising the streets of Salt Lake City, had aroused suspicion and police had followed it. The driver tried to shake them off, which made them more suspicious still, and they finally pulled him up in an abandoned gas station. In the car they found an ice-pick, a ski mask, a crowbar and other such tools. At Bundy's apartment they found maps and literature relating to Colorado, and subsequent tests found that hairs discovered in the car matched those of Melissa Smith – who had vanished on October 27 of the previous year – and someone came forward to say that they remembered seeing Bundy at the skiing village of Snowmass at the time when Caryn Campbell disappeared. Back in Washington bits and pieces of Brenda Ball and Susan Rancourt turned up on Taylor Mountain.

No one could believe that Ted Bundy was this multiple sex-killer: he was handsome and intelligent, with an infectious sense of humour, and he was evidently a bright student, studying psychology in Seattle and law in Salt Lake City. But the evidence was good, and more was on the way. Carol DaRonch was brought back, and she was able to identify Bundy as the man who had tried to abduct her, while examination of his credit-card slips showed that he had been around at the times and the places of Caryn Campbell's and Julie Cunningham's disappearances. Bundy was charged with murder, and extradited to Colorado in January 1977.

From the start he was a popular prisoner, quickly gaining special privileges: he was permitted to eat health foods in jail, and was allowed to make his appearances in court without handcuffs. As a law student, he was also able to prepare his own defence, and began a long succession of delaying tactics, and it was while he was working in the law library in Aspen, Colorado, that he was able to make his first escape. He simply opened a window and jumped 30 feet to the ground below. He was caught eight days later, hiding out in disused buildings on Smuggler's Mountain, but the daring of the attempt added to his already considerable mystique.

Most of the evidence against Bundy was circumstantial, and some people began to think that what he was saying might even be true: that he was the victim of a string of coincidences, for he sure didn't look or act like any kind of maniac. Defending himself with considerable skill, Bundy brought into play a whole string of objections and delaying tactics – then, in December 1978, he escaped again. Somehow he had got hold of a hacksaw blade, and used it to cut a hole in the ceiling of his cell around the light fitting, then he just climbed through and walked free. This time he wasn't caught so easily.

He made it first to Chicago, then travelled south to Atlanta and Florida, living on stolen credit-cards and eventually taking a room in Tallahassee just two blocks from the students' dwellings for Florida State University.

*On January 15 a man was seen outside a sorority house holding a club. Shortly afterwards, a girl called Karen Chandler staggered out of one of the rooms, having been beaten about the head. Her friend Kathy Kleiner, still inside, had been beaten too and her jaw was broken. Elsewhere in the same building, Margaret Bowman was dead, strangled with her own tights, raped and bludgeoned, while Lisa Levy died of similar injuries on the way to the hospital.*

*Ninety minutes later, in another sorority house, a female student was awakened by bangs and cries from the next room. Cheryl Thomas was found whimpering and bloody, with her skull fractured, but she lived.*

*On February 8 Kimberley Leach, only twelve years old, left her classroom in Jacksonville to fetch something, and didn't return.*

*On April 7 the decomposing body of Kimberley Leach was found by a policeman in a disused shed near the Swanne River State Park. There were signs of 'homicidal violence to the neck region; and injuries to the pelvic area.*

It emerged that Ted Bundy had been living in Tallahassee under the name 'Chris Hagen', and there was a string of other crimes: more stolen credit cards, stolen cars, rent owing and so on. He was arrested again when a policeman noted that the car he was driving – another Volkswagen – was stolen, and it soon became clear that 'Chris Hagen' was in fact Ted Bundy, and that he had been around Tallahassee at the time of the sorority attacks and in Jacksonville in February. Worse was to come when police took an impression of Bundy's teeth, for they were found to match bite-marks that had been found on the buttocks of Lisa Levy's body in the sorority house.

This was the evidence that was finally to convict him, in a highly publicized trial in Miami. On being found guilty of a whole string of charges, Bundy said: 'I find it somewhat absurd to ask for mercy for something I did not do. The sentence is not a sentence of me. It's a sentence of someone who is not standing here today.' He was then sentenced to death, at which his mother said that his was not the end; there would be appeal after appeal – and there was, though time finally ran out for Bundy as this book went to press, with banner headlines around the world along the tasteful lines of 'BUNDY FRIES'. His final remarks were that his deeds had been caused by reading violent pornography when young.

Certainly, he had acquired a taste for this in Seattle, and had become a voyeur. Then he had developed a sudden violent impulse to follow a girl he saw on the street, and he had followed her until she got home. 'Sometimes I feel like a vampire,' he told detectives later. He also spoke of an 'entity', a malignant being inside him that gradually dominated him and drove him to rape. This sounds not unlike David Berkowitz and 'Sam', but whereas most killers of this type are socially inadequate types, Bundy is a puzzle. Beneath the surface charm and the articulate manner he was a loner, certainly, but it does not begin to explain why he did what he did.

R.G.J

# 1980

## MARK CHAPMAN
### The Slaying of a Superstar

Despite his desperate attempts for a decade to disassociate himself from The Beatles, John Winston Lennon, up to the time of his violent death at age forty at the hands of an unhinged fan, was umbilically linked with the singing foursome that became the world's most popular rock group. As the years ebb and flow that image will probably never change. It was no accident that Lennon arrived and departed the public eye inside of mass mania, even though this exceptionally talented man, called a musical genius by many, fought against just such a fate.

Lennon was born on October 9, 1940, into an unhappy Liverpool family. His father, an itinerant seaman, deserted him and his mother when John was three. Though his mother also deserted him, leaving him in the care of her sister, Lennon reserved a special hatred for his father. Years later, when the elder Lennon suddenly appeared at his son's door, the then super rock star took one look at him and, without a word, slammed the door in his face. He later said with a great deal of bitterness: 'I don't feel I owe him anything. He never helped me. I got there by myself.'

Such self-confidence sometimes ran to megalomania with John Lennon, even when he appeared to be joking. At one point when The Beatles were working their way to the zenith of worldwide public acclaim, Lennon remarked: 'We're more popular than Jesus now; I don't know which will go first—rock'n'roll or Christianity.' He was to regret the comment and considered it a moment when his pride jumped his wit. He made a public apology on August 12, 1966, in Chicago, saying he 'was sorry that he opened his mouth about Jesus Christ.'

Lennon had been shown the error of false pride by his fans, who undoubtedly prompted the apology; after his 'Jesus' remark thousands of fans gathered to publicly smash and burn Beatles albums. Had not the commercially minded Lennon made his retraction, he and his three partners might have seen their fabulous careers go up in smoke.

Those careers and the enormous success attending them proved Horace Greeley's belief that young men could make their fortunes by 'going west,' only in this instance it was traveling west from England to America, the land that lined the pockets of The Beatles with more gold than they could ever spend.

The idea for the group slowly took form when fifteen-year-old John Lennon met Paul McCartney in 1955 at a Liverpool party. This was at a time when rock'n'roll was an embryo, with singing stars such as Buddy Holly, Bill Haley, and Elvis Presley just beginning to emerge. McCartney and Lennon began to talk about music, and a year later Lennon formed his first band, The Quarrymen, which McCartney promptly joined. The name derived from Quarry Bank High School in Allerton, a suburb of Liverpool, which Lennon attended.

Lennon's autocratic ways soon alienated most members, who came and went, but McCartney stayed and George Harrison later joined the group, Ringo Starr being the last permanent member to join up. That John Lennon was always the recognized leader of the foursome was reflected in some of the names used for the group: Johnny and the Moondogs, and Long John and the Silver Beatles, the latter name used in 1959. Finally it came down to the Silver Beatles, and then just The Beatles.

In the beginning Lennon was thought of as a talented up-and-comer in England but a sarcastic type who would rather deliver a wry insult than a compliment. His first wife, Cynthia, with whom Lennon had a son, Julian, was to comment in her book *A Twist of Lennon:* 'I think he was the last stronghold of the Teddy Boys [British street thugs]—totally aggressive and anti-establishment.' Critic Stanley Reynolds, who knew Lennon and his group long before they cut their first album, later remarked: 'John Lennon was the hardest, toughest kid I ever met. He had an uncompromising attitude that would never give an inch. He was completely unbending and it shocked you meeting him because he was, after all, a young fellow and a civilian—so why was he at war? The truth was he was at war with the whole world.'

The group nevertheless caught on, and in February 1963 the first Beatles album, *Please Please Me*, began to climb the charts in England. A year later, on February 8, 1964, the group appeared for the first time on the Ed Sullivan TV show, and from that point onward The Beatles became a household word in America, whether the older generation wanted to hear it or not.

McCartney supplied the masterful tunes and Lennon the brilliant lyrics for the group. All the members supplied quips or puns by the score to a public eager for any word they cared to drop. Their songs, style, and personae became a vogue that lasted for six years and continues to linger like a stubborn ghost. Lennon led the way. If he changed his style of clothes, tens of thousands of fans changed from suits to casual wear. When he donned dark, grainy glasses—he was always myopic—identical glasses appeared on the faces of the faithful. He grew a thin droopy mustache. Thin droopy mustaches became the rage.

Meanwhile, Beatles albums came out with crescendo at the cash register—*A Hard Day's Night (1964), HELP! (1965), Sgt. Pepper's Lonely Hearts Club Band (1967), Yellow Submarine (1969), Let It Be (1970)*. Millions of dollars rolled in from their records and millions more from their films and personal appearances. The stage appearances toward the end of the groups's career became so hectic that the members were almost torn to pieces by uncontrollable, emotional fans.

John Lennon grew to hate the very throngs that raved about him and his group. He had to run police gauntlets through which fans grabbed, clutched, tore, and scratched for souvenirs, especially fanatical girls gone berserk to have a shred of clothing from their idols. Lennon would arrive home scratched and bruised, his necktie or scarf torn from his throat, his clothes in tatters, to collapse on a bed exhausted with the ordeal. 'Christ, Cyn,' he told his wife once, 'we'll have to get out of this death trap before they kill me. I had no idea it was going to be like this. It's like a bloody madhouse out there. We deserve every penny we get.'

Lennon's dissatisfaction with the fierce fans and the demands of albums and appearances began early; by 1966, the year he met artist Yoko Ono, he was thinking of quitting the group and striking out on his own to create a 'more classical' kind of music. Not until 1970 did Lennon and the rest of The Beatles break up, however, each going his own way with only Paul McCarney and The Wings having any kind of success similar to that enjoyed by the original group. Yoko Ono, of course, for whom Lennon left his first wife, was a great influence in his life. It was Yoko who persuaded Lennon to concentrate on his own creativity and discovery of self. He, like the other Beatles, spent the 1970s experimenting with self–analysis, drugs, and a search for gurus with all–knowing answers. Such self–indulgences might be expected of four young men who had, perhaps, too early in life been deluged with fame and riches.

It was also Yoko Ono who convinced Lennon to live in New York City, where the couple and their small child moved into the posh Dakota apartments. Oddly enough, he told a British interviewer three days before this death, he felt 'secure' by living in New York. 'It was Yoko Ono who sold me on New York,' Lennon said. 'I fell in love with New York.' Another irony was that the very vilolence that his own songs damned took his life. *Double Fantasy*, his last album, done with Yoko, plaintively asked how long society would tolerate its own destruction.

Toward the end Lennon had turned almost mystical, introspectively examining himself and the world about him. He was also fatalistic, believing that he would be destroyed by a nuclear holocaust long before reaching old age. He talked of this eventuality at great length with his son Julian.

Only hours before his end came, Lennon was interviewed by RKO Radio Network, telling interviewers: 'We're going to live, or we're going to die. If we're dead, we're going to have to deal with that; if we're alive we're going to have to deal with being alive. So worrying about whether Wall Street or the Apocalypse is going to come in the form of the great beast in not going to do us any good today.'

At 5 p.m. that night, December 8, 1980, Lennon and Yoko left the Dakota en route to a recording session. Several fans who habitually stood outside the swanky apartment complex pushed forward to get Lennon's autograph. One of the these was a cherubic young man with a copy of *The Catcher in the Rye* jutting from his jacket pocket. Lennon gave him his autograph and then climbed into a waiting limousine after his wife. The couple returned to the Dakota at 11 p.m. They got out of the limousine at curbside and began to walk toward the Dakota's courtyard.

The same young man with the cherubic face and thick mop of black hair who had gotten Lennon's autograph six hours earlier suddenly appeared, coming up from behind the couple and shouting: 'Mr. Lennon!'

Lennon turned about slowly to see the man suddenly drop into a military crouch, his legs spread apart as he aimed a .38 Charter Arms revolver at the singer-composer. Without another word he fired off five shots, which struck Lennon in the chest, back, and left arm. He took about six steps, crying out to Yoko: 'I'm shot.' He collapsed. His assailant calmly dropped the revolver as if he were throwing away a half-eaten hot dog, then sauntered to the side of the Dakota and sat down, pulling out the J. D. Salinger novel and reading it avidly.

Patrolman Jim Moran who was detailed to keep fans from getting too close to the Dakota—it was the home of many celebrities, including Lauren Bacall, Leonard Bernstein, and Gilda Radner—ran forward. He helped the wounded singer to his squad car, placing him in the back seat, then jumped behind the wheel, heading for a nearby hospital. 'Are you John Lennon?' Moran asked. Lennon was in acute pain and could not answer. He only nodded and groaned. By the time Lennon was taken into the emergency room at Roosevelt Hospital, he was dead from his multiple wounds.

The killer was quickly identified as a former mental patient named Mark David Chapman. The twenty-five-year-old murderer, who offered no resistance to police taking him from the scene of the killing, was a resident of Hawaii. In his pockets police found fourteen Beatles tapes, the Salinger novel, and $2,000. He offered no explanation for the murder.

The public reaction to the killing was one of national shock and sorrow. Hundreds of Lennon's fans gathered outside of the Dakota to sing and pray, offering condolences to Yoko. Mayor Edward Koch heard of the killing and immediately called for nationwide gun control of handguns. President-elect Ronald Reagan called the singer's death 'a great tragedy,' and President Jimmy Carter paid tribute to the genius and music of John

Lennon, saying: 'His spirit, the spirit of The Beatles—brash and earnest, ironic and idealistic all at once—became the spirit of a whole generation.'

Within twenty-four hours the hawks of commerce descended. Lennon's albums were being sold faster than stores could stock them. Hundreds outside the Dakota were wearing brand new T-shirts inscribed: 'John Lennon, 1940–1980, rest in peace.'

The killer had also advertised his love for The Beatles, police later learned. In the past Chapman had pinned buttons to his shirt that read 'John Lennon.' As his defense attorney later pointed out, however, he was not proudly advertising his support for Lennon as a loyal fan; he thought *he was* Lennon. Mark Chapman was decidedly a mental case. The twenty-five-year-old had tried to commit suicide in Hawaii in 1977 and once again in New York, only two weeks before he shot and killed the man he once thought to be a god on earth.

Chapman was born in Forth Worth, Texas, on May 10, 1955, the year John Lennon and Paul McCartney first met. He was raised in Atlanta and Decatur, Georgia, graduating from high school and going on to DeKalb Community College. He later worked for various charitable organizations such as the YMCA, aiding Vietnamese refugees at Fort Chaffee, Arkansas, in 1975 when he was twenty. By then he had already gone through his own rock band in high school, where he played guitar and emulated The Beatles. He had collected every record the group cut.

Slowly, authorities leaned how Chapman's obsession with the chief Beatle had led him to stalk John Lennon for several days until he killed him. Hours before he shot Lennon, Chapman was photographed as Lennon autographed an album for him.

As the facts emerged it was clear that Chapman's background was unnervingly similar to that of his victim. He, too, had come from a broken home; his parents divorced only two years before he murdered Lennon. He had struck out on his own as a 'wild and fantastic kid,' according to one YMCA coworker who labored alongside Chapman to rehabilitate Vietnamese refugees. Chapman had taken an oath never to touch drugs and was a 'born again' Christian. He was remembered as being a rabid Beatles fan, but became extremely upset whenever anyone mentioned Lennon's remark about being more important than

Jesus. 'Who in the hell are they to compare themselves to Jesus?' he would ask over and over at such times.

Chapman lived a nomadic life through the mid to late 1970s, working in Arkansas and Tennessee and traveling to Hawaii and Switzerland, studying various religions but seeming to get nowhere. In 1979 he met an attractive travel agent, Gloria H. Abe, a woman four years his senior and of Japanese descent (as was John Lennon's Yoko Ono). The couple wed in June, moving to Oahu, Hawaii, where Chapman worked in a print shop at the Castle Memorial Hospital near Kailua. He later got a job as a security guard in a Honolulu condominium.

It was while living in Hawaii that Chapman began to lose control of himself. He forbade his new wife to read newspapers or watch TV and insisted she break with all her old friends. Chapman at this time began calling the Church of Scientology, whispering: 'Bang, bang, you're dead!' He was working as a security guard in a building directly across from the church, whose members remembered him standing outside it and shouting abuse. 'He was a very very strange character,' said one parishioner.

A friend of those days watched Chapman deteriorate to the point where he became 'a jerk, a creep, just a negative person' who spent most of his time playing Beatles records or visiting art galleries to argue with spectators over the values of Salvador Dali and Norman Rockwell. Chapman was a kind and gentle person to other people who had never seen the vicious side of his character. He was later to tell police: 'I couldn't help myself. I've got a good side and a bad side. The bad side is very small, but sometimes it takes over the good side and I do bad things.' To one friend in Hawaii, Chapman was nothing more than an innocuous soul 'who ate a lot of peanuts.'

In the fall of 1980 the five-feet-eleven-inch Chapman left his wife. He removed his name tag from his security guard uniform and substituted the name 'John Lennon.' He abruptly quit his job on October 23, 1980, going to the employee logbook to sign out for the last time. He signed the name of 'John Lennon,' then scratched it out.

By then Chapman was definitely two people, according to psychiatrists, a complete schizoid personality that had lost itself to the image of Beatle John Lennon, so much so that he began to take on the singer's powerful identity. 'Chapman probably came to see himself as the real John Lennon,' reported Dr. Robert Marvit of Honolulu. 'He probably felt he could find his rightful place as John Lennon if he got rid of the imposter.'

To Chapman, Lennon's retreat from the public eye, his rebuttal of the brash and wild image of his former days, represented a cowardly withdrawal from an anti-establishment posture. John Lennon was a sell-out, a drop-out, a person who no longer fought the good fight (whatever that fight might have been). He took to calling Lennon 'a phony, a fake,' and, in these remarks, he apparently began to substitute himself for the aggressive, take-charge John Lennon that was no more.

Four days after quitting his job Chapman went to J&S Enterprises, a shop only one block distant from Honolulu's main police station, and purchased a .38 caliber snub-nosed Charter Arms pistol, known as an 'undercover special,' used by detectives. Chapman was granted permission to buy the weapon since he had no police record at the time.

Next, Chapman borrowed $2,500 from a credit union and flew to New York on Saturday, December 6, 1980. He stayed at the West Side YMCA that night and the next day, checked into an $82-a-night room in the Sheraton Centre Hotel. Then he began to keep his daily vigil for Lennon outside the Dakota, briefly talking to other Beatle fans who stood about for long periods in hopes of catching a glimpse of their idol.

On December 8 he approached amateur photographer Paul Goresh, who was hoping to catch a few candid shots of Lennon.

'Are you waiting for Lennon?' he asked Goresh.

'Yes,' replied the photographer.

'I'm Mark,' Chapman told Goresh, 'I'm from Hawaii.'

'Where did you get that accent?'

'I'm originally form Atlanta, Georgia.'

'Where are you staying in New York?'

At that Chapman bristled. 'Why do you want to know?'

Chapman walked away, then returned to say: 'Sorry. I'm staying at the Sheraton. I've spent the last three days trying to see Lennon. I want him to autograph his new album.'

Then Chapman's fallen idol appeared with Yoko Ono. He timidly approached the great entertainer and held out the album *Double Fantasy,* an ominously revealing title, given

Chapman's strange aberrations. The star wrote on the album the words: 'John Lennon, 1980,' and walked off with Yoko to a waiting limousine. Chapman then turned to Goresh and said in amazement: 'John Lennon signed my album. Nobody in Hawaii is going to believe me.' Goresh also had a Lennon album, but it had not been signed.

Goresh stayed for two more hours, then decided to leave. Chapman asked him: 'Why don't you wait until they come home? He should be back soon. Then you can get your album signed.'

'I can get it another day.'

'I'd wait,' Chapman said. 'You never know if you'll see him again.'

'What do you mean? I always see him.'

Chapman shrugged: 'It's possible he could go to Spain or somewhere tonight, and you'll never get your album signed.'

Goresh left. Mark Chapman stayed behind to wait. A few hours later John Lennon was dead.

While awaiting trial, Chapman was guarded day and night. It was thought that he would attempt to take his own life, but he remained a docile prisoner. At his initial hearing he pled not guilty. His lawyer, Jonathan Marks, announced that he would present an insanity defense.

Psychiatrists came forward to testify that Chapman certainly was insane, 'a chronic paranoid schizophrenic,' according to Dr. Daniel Schwartz, who had examined Chapman in his cell. Schwartz claimed that Chapman's own miserable life with all its shortcomings was so unacceptable to him that he 'killed himself psychologically' when he murdered John Lennon. Further, to survive the thought that Lennon, his god, was a 'phony,' Chapman was compelled to make an 'abrupt break' with the singer.

At a hearing on June 22, 1981, Chapman told a judge that he had spoken to God and that God had instructed him to confess to the murdering of John Lennon. As his shocked lawyer stood by, Chapman pleaded guilty to second-degree murder.

On July 24, 1981, Chapman was sentenced to serve twenty years to life in prison for the murder of the top Beatle. His only response was to stand up and read a passage from J.D. Salinger's novel *The Catcher in the Rye,* about confused adolescence. At the time, the killer was wearing a bulletproof vest under a blue pullover shirt.

'Thousands of little kids,' droned Chapman as he read the passage concerning the book's hero, Holden Caulfield, and how he envisioned having to save hordes of children playing dangerously close to a cliff, 'and nobody's around—nobody big, I mean—except me. And I'm standing on the edge of some crazy cliff. What I have to do, I have to catch everybody if they start to go over the cliff—I mean if they're running and they don't look where they're going I have to come out from somewhere and catch them. That's all I'd do all day. I'd just be the catcher in the rye.'

The passage had great significance to Chapman, his lawyer later stated. For the convicted killer it meant that the world is phony and 'children should be saved from adulthood.'

These were the last words Mark David Chapman would utter to the world. Reported lawyer Jonathan Marks: 'And he said he does not plan to talk anymore.' With that Chapman left the court for Sing Sing.

John Lennon, however, goes on talking and singing in his albums, which continue to earn more than $10 million each year. He left an estate to Yoko Ono and their son, Sean, along with his other son, Julian, valued at more than $235 million. He also left his family a promise that he would try to contact them, especially Yoko, from 'the other side.'

Said his son Julian recently: 'I'm convinced Dad will contact Yoko because their minds were in tune . . . he said that if anything happened to him, he'd send a sign back to us that he was okay. He said he'd make a feather float down the room.

'Ever since his death I've been waiting for that sign. Every time I'm alone in a room, I find myself staring around, looking for the feather.'

J.R.N.

# 1981

# PETER SUTCLIFFE
## The Yorkshire Ripper

---

The reign of terror by the man who became who became known as the Yorkshire Ripper began on 29 October 1975, with the murder of Wilma McCann, and ended on 2 January 1981, when Peter Sutcliffe was arrested in Sheffield with a prostitute who was almost certainly intended as his fourteenth murder victim.

The attacks on Yorkshire women began on 5 July 1975, when a woman named Anna Rogulskyj was struck on the head with a hammer. On 15 August Olive Smelt was knocked unconscious by a hammer blow from behind. The attacker slashed both women – Mrs. Smelt's buttocks were cut. Both recovered after brain surgery.

On 29 October Wilma McCann, a Scotswoman who had separated from her husband and taken to prostitution, left her four children to go on a pub crawl in Leeds. In the early hours of the following morning, she was struck on the head from behind with a ball-headed hammer, then dragged into a playing field. Here the killer pulled up her dress, and inflicted injuries on the stomach, chest and in the genital area with a knife and, possibly, other tools.

From then on, the murders followed in regular succession. The Ripper's next victim, Emily Jackson, was a housewife who had three children. Her husband was a roofing specialist who often worked in the evenings; his wife would drive him to the job and collect him a few hours later. What Sydney Jackson did not know was that during those hours his wife supplemented her income by soliciting from the van she drove. On the evening of 20 January 1976 she failed to return for him and he took a taxi home. The following morning, his wife's body was found in a narrow passageway in Leeds, the head battered unrecognizably, and with fifty stab wounds in her chest.

More than a year passed before the Ripper struck again. Irene Richardson was separated from her husband; her two children lived with foster parents. She was not a professional prostitute, but had 'fallen on hard times' and hung around street corners. The Ripper picked her up on the evening of 5 February 1977 and drove her to Roundhay Park, Leeds. Her body was found the following morning by a jogger; she was lying near the sports pavilion.

A Bradford prostitute, Tina Atkinson, picked up the Ripper on 23 April and took him to her flat in Oak Avenue. The following morning a male friend found the door unlocked. Tina Atkinson was dead in bed; a police surgeon said she had been battered unconscious and been the victim of a 'frenzied sexual attack' – although she had not been raped.

Sixteen-year-old Jayne MacDonald was an unusually pretty girl who spent the evening of 25 June 1977 dancing at the Hofbrauhaus in the centre of Leeds, and was not far from her home, near Roundhay Park, when the Ripper knocked her unconscious, dragged her behind a fence, and stabbed her again and again. Possibly he mistook her for a prostitute – she lived only six doors from Wilma McCann in the notorious Chapeltown area.

On 27 July Maureen Long was walking through central Bradford when the Ripper drew up in his car and propositioned her. Soon afterwards, he was dragging the unconscious woman away from the street lights. But something disturbed him, and he left her there and hurried away. She recovered after a brain operation, and was able to say that her assailant had been driving a white Ford Cortina. She said he had blond hair – a detail that was discovered to be inaccurate when Sutcliffe was arrested four years later.

The Ripper crossed the Pennines, and claimed his next victim in Manchester on 1 October. During the early morning he encountered a twenty-year-old Scots girl, Jean Jordan, and took her to the Southern Cemetry. There he killed her with exceptional violence, stripping her naked and mutilating the body. He clothes were scattered all around. She was the common-law wife of a chef, Alan Royle, who had picked her up on his way home from work five years earlier when she had just run away from her home in Motherwell. The couple had two children, but they had begun to drift apart not long before her death, and she spent her evenings away from home with 'friends'. She had, in fact, worked as a prostitute and taken clients back to her flat while her husband was at work. The body was not found until nine days later, when the medical examination revealed that the murderer had killed her with eleven blows to the head, and stabbed her twenty-four times. Eight days later, he had returned to the body and torn off all the clothing then stabbed and slashed her several times more, tearing open the abdomen and making a long wound from the left shoulder to the right knee.

In this case, the police at last found a clue. In Jean Jordan's handbag there was a new £5 note, which had been issued at Shipley, Yorkshire, only four days before the murder. It seemed probable that the killer had handed it to her. The police traced the batch of notes to the depot where Sutcliffe worked as a lorry-driver, and questioned him. Since there appeared to be no evidence to connect him with the murders, he was cleared.

By early 1978 the hunt for the Ripper had become one of the largest police operations ever mounted in northern England. George Oldfield, the assistant chief constable in charge of the case, gave colleagues the impression that his search for the Ripper had become a personal crusade. Police work on the case was exhaustive; the police were willing to pursue any lead, no matter how tenuous.

The Ripper decided to move to Huddersfield to find his next victim: he felt that police activity in Leeds was becoming too intensive. Helen and Rita Rytka were eighteen-year-old twins, and much of their lives had been spent in the care of the social services. In 1977 they decided that prostitution was an easier way of making a living than factory work, and they would wait to be picked up by cruising cars. On the evening of 31 January Helen was picked up by a car shortly after nine, and Rita soon after. When Rita was dropped off later, there was no sign of Helen. And when Helen had still not returned by the next morning, Rita began to fear the worst. Later that morning, a lorry-driver noticed a pair of black lace briefs near a timber yard close to the flat shared by the twins. The yard foreman hung them up on a nail 'for the lads to laugh at'. Two days later Rita Rytka went to the police and reported that her sister had disappeared. The police immediately suspected another Ripper killing, and searched the timber yard. Helen's body was found underneath an archway, screened by timber, and lying under a piece of corrugated asbestos. She was naked, and had been battered unconscious, then stabbed in the chest area. Medical evidence showed that on this occasion, the killer had had sexual intercourse with her – probably after knocking her unconscious but before stabbing her.

By this time the police suspected that the Ripper was responsible for another disappearance. Ten days before Helen Rytka was killed, Yvonne Pearson had set out to ply her trade around Bradford's city centre; she left her two small children at home with a baby sitter. She never returned. Two months later a man crossing a piece of waste ground noticed a human arm protruding from under an abandoned settee. The head had been battered so violently that the skull had shattered into twenty-one fragments. Stuffing from the settee had been rammed down her throat, presumably to stifle screams or groans. Lack of stab wounds left some doubt whether this was another Ripper victim. Sutcliffe later admitted that he had been disturbed when another car drew up alongside.

In Manchester, on 16 May, a forty-year-old prostitute named Vera Millward was expecting a regular client who failed to turn up; so, leaving her two children in the charge of her common-law Jamaican husband, she went off in search of another client. At 1.15 a.m. a man visiting the Royal Infirmary heard three screams and a cry for help, then silence. The next morning, Vera Millward's body was found lying near a flower bed – a favourite site for prostitutes. The blows to her skull had been so violent that it had virtually disintegrated. She had also been stabbed many times.

So far, all the victims but Jayne MacDonald had been prostitutes and it seemed probable that the Ripper had mistaken her for one. But the next victim, nineteen-year-old Josephine Whitaker, was clearly not a prostitute. She had spent the evening of 4 April 1979 watching television at her grandparents' home in Halifax, then walked home towards midnight. The Ripper had attacked her as she was crossing Savile Park, fracturing her skull from ear to ear. Then he stabbed her frenziedly with a rusty screwdriver which had been specially sharpened. He pulled up her clothes and stabbed her in the vagina several times. The police found traces of oil on the body, and inferred – correctly – that the killer worked in an engineering factory.

It seemed clear that the killer was now prepared to murder any woman when the urge was upon him. The next victim was a student at Bradford University, Barbara Leach, who had spent the evening of 1 September at the Mannville Arms, not far from the university. She left at about 1 a.m., and told her friends she wanted a breath of air before going to bed at her flat in Grove Terrace. Her body was found a day later against a dustbin in a back alley, close to the spot where she had been last seen. She had been covered with old carpets held down with bricks. She had been stabbed repeatedly with a pointed weapon - the same rusty screwdriver that had killed Josephine Whitaker.

By this time there had been a new development in the case. In 1978 and 1979 the police had received three letters signed 'Jack the Ripper' threatening more murders. Then on 26 June 1979 the police received a cassette – addressed in the same handwriting as the three letters – containing the voice of the Ripper. Speaking with a slow Geordie accent, obviously reading aloud, the voice taunted George Olffield for failing to catch him: 'You can't be much good, can you?' He promised to strike again, and warned that if the police got too close he would probably 'top' himself (commit suicide). The tape was treated seriously – although after Sutcliffe's arrest it became clear that both tape and letters were from a hoaxer – and the police wasted much time looking for the letter-writer in the Wearside area. In July George Oldfield became ill from overwork on the case, and suffered a heart attack.

On 20 August Marguerite Walls, a civil servant in the Department of Education at Pudsey, worked late until 10.45, and was making her way home to Farsley when she encountered the Ripper. He knocked her unconscious with a blow on the head, then dragged her into a garden and ripped off most of her clothes. He then knelt on her ribs – breaking three of them – and strangled her with a piece of rope (Sutcliffe later explained that he did not have his knife with him). Then he covered the body with grass cuttings.

The next two victims survived. In October 1979 Sutcliffe walked up behind Dr. Upadhya Bandara, from Singapore, who was returning home from a course in the Nuffield Centre in Leeds, and threw a rope round her neck. He hit her on the head and dragged her down the road, then changed his mind – he later claimed to have apologized – and left her. A few weeks later, on 5 November, he came close to being caught when he attacked sixteen-year-old Theresa Sykes near her home in Huddersfield. Her boyfriend heard her screams and ran to her aid. The Ripper had knocked her to the ground, but he ran away.

Possibly it was this close shave with capture that made Sutcliffe decide to lie low for a while. His final murder took place more than a year later. Twenty-year-old Jacqueline Hill, a Leeds University student, had attended a meeting of voluntary probation officers on 17 November 1980, and caught a bus back to her lodgings soon after 9 p.m. An hour later, her handbag was found near some waste ground by an Iraqi student, and he called the police. It was a windy and rainy night and they found nothing. Jacqueline Hill's body was found the next morning on the waste ground. She had been battered unconscious with a hammer, then undressed and stabbed repeatedly. One wound was in the eye – Sutcliffe later said she seemed to be looking at him reproachfully, so he drove the blade into her eye.

This was the Ripper's last attack. On 2 January 1981 a black prostitute named Olive Reivers had just finished with a client in the centre of Sheffield when a Rover car drove up, and a bearded man asked her how much she charged: she said it would be £10 for sex in the car, and climbed in the front. He seemed tense and asked if she would object if he talked for a while about his family problems. When he asked her to get in the back of the car, she said she would prefer to have sex in the front; this may have saved her life – Sutcliffe had stunned at least one of his victims as she climbed into the back of the car. He moved on top of her, but was unable to maintain an erection. He moved her off again, and at this point, a police car pulled up in front. Sutcliffe hastily told the woman to say she was his girlfriend. The police asked his name, and he told them it was Peter Williams. Sergeant Robert Ring and PC Robert Hydes were on patrol duty, and they were carrying out a standard check. Ring noted the number-plate then went off to check it with the computer; while he radioed, he told PC Hydes to get into the back of the Rover. Sutcliffe asked if he could get out to urinate and Hydes gave permission; Sutcliffe stood by an oil storage tank a few feet away, then got back into the car. Meanwhile, the sergeant had discovered that the number-plates did not belong to the Rover, and told Sutcliffe he would have to return to the police station. In the station, Sutcliffe again asked to go to the lavatory and was given permission. It was when the police made him empty his pocket and found a length of clothes-line that they began to suspect that they might have trapped Britain's most wanted man.

To begin with, Sutcliffe lied fluently about why he was carrying the rope and why he was in the car with a prostitute. It was the following day that Sergeant Ring learned about Sutcliffe's brief absence from the car to relieve himself, and went to look near the oil storage tank. In the leaves, he found a ball-headed hammer and a knife. Then he recalled Sutcliffe's trip to the lavatory at the police station. In the cistern he found a second knife. When Sutcliffe was told that he was in serious trouble, he suddenly admitted that he was the Ripper, and confessed to eleven murders. (It seems odd that he got the number wrong – he was later charged with thirteen – but it is possible that he genuinely lost count. He was originally suspected of fourteen murders, but the police later decided that the killing of another prostitute, Jean Harrison – whose body was found in Preston, Lancashire – was not one of the series. She had been raped and the semen was not of Sutcliffe's blood group.)

A card written by Sutcliffe and displayed in his lorry read: 'In this truck is a man whose latent genius, if unleashed, would rock the nation, whose dynamic energy would overpower those around him. Better let him sleep?'

The story that began to emerge was of a lonely and shy individual, brooding and introverted, who was morbidly fascinated by prostitutes and red-light areas. He was born on 2 June 1946, the eldest of five children and his mother's favourite. His school career was undistinguished and he left at fifteen. He drifted aimlessly from job to job, including one as a grave-digger in the Bingley cemetery, from which he was dismissed for bad timekeeping. (His later attempt at a defence of insanity rested on a claim that a voice had spoken to him from a cross in the cemetery telling him he had a God-given mission to kill prostitutes.)

In 1967, when he was twenty-one, he met a sixteen-year-old Czech girl, Sonia Szurma, in a pub, and they began going out together. It would be another seven years before they married. The relationship seems to have been stormy; at one point, she was going out with an ice-cream salesman, and Sutcliffe picked up a prostitute 'to get even'. He was unable to have intercourse, and the woman went off with £10 note and failed to return with his £5 change. When he saw her in a pub two weeks later and asked for the money, she jeered at him and left him with a sense of helpless fury and humiliation. This, he claimed, was the source of his hatred of prostitutes. In 1969 he made his first attack on a prostitute, hitting her on the head with a sock full of gravel. In October of that year, he was caught carrying a hammer and charged with being equipped for theft; he was fined £25. In 1971 he went for a drive with a friend, Trevor Birdsall, and left the car in the red-light area of Bradford. When he returned ten minutes later he said, 'Drive off quickly,' and admitted that he had hit a woman with a brick in the sock. Sutcliffe was again driving with Birdsall in 1975 on the evening that Olive Smelt was struck down with a hammer.

In 1972 Sonia Szurma went to London for a teacher's training course and had a nervous breakdown; she was diagnosed as schizophrenic. Two years later, she and Sutcliffe married, but the marriage was punctuated by violent rows – Sutcliffe said he became embarrassed in case the neighbours heard the shouts, implying that it was she who was shouting rather than he. He also told the prostitute Olive Reivers that he had been arguing with his wife 'about not being able to live with her,' which Olive Reivers took to mean that they were having sexual problems. Certainly, this combination of two introverted people can hardly have improved Sutcliffe's mental condition.

Sutcliffe's first murder – of Wilma McCann – took place in the year after he married Sonia. He admitted: 'I developed and played up a hatred for prostitutes . . .' Unlike the Düsseldorf sadist of the 1920s, Peter Kürten, Sutcliffe never admitted to having orgasm as he stabbed his victims; but anyone acquainted with the psychology of sexual criminals would take it for granted that this occurred, and that in most of the cases where the victim was not stabbed, or was left alive, he achieved orgasm at an earlier stage than usual. The parallels are remarkable. Kürten, like Sutcliffe, used a variety of weapons, including a hammer. On one occasion when a corpse remained undiscovered, Kürten also returned to inflict fresh indignities on it. Sutcliffe had returned to the body of Jean Jordan and attempted to cut off the head with a hacksaw.

It was when he pulled up Wilma McCann's clothes and stabbed her in the breast and abdomen that Sutcliffe realized that he had discovered a new sexual thrill. With the second victim, Emily Jackson, he pulled off her bra and briefs, then stabbed her repeatedly – he was, in effect, committing rape with a knife. Sutcliffe was caught in the basic trap of the sex criminal: the realization that he had found a way of inducing a far, more powerful sexual sexual satisfaction than he was able to obtain in normal intercourse, and that he was pushing himself into the position of a social outcast. He admitted sobbing in his his car after one of the murders, and being upset to discover that Jayne MacDonald had not been a prostitute (and later, that her father had died of a broken heart). But the compulsion to kill was becoming a fever, so that he no longer cared that the later victims were not prostitutes. He said, probably with sincerity, 'The devil drove me.'

Sutcliffe's trial began on 5 May 1981. He had pleaded not guilty to murder on grounds of diminished responsibility, and told the story of his 'mission' from God. But a warder had overheard him tell his wife that if he could convince the jury that he was mad, he would only spend ten years in a 'loony bin'. The Attorney-General, Sir Michael Havers, also pointed out that Sutcliffe had at first behaved perfectly normally, laughing at the idea he might be mentally abnormal, and had introduced the talk of 'voices' fairly late in his admission to the police. On 22 May Sutcliffe was found guilty of murder, and jailed for life, with recommendation that he should serve at least thirty years.

C.W.

# 1983

## DENNIS NILSEN
### Killing for Company

---

Come with me to Muswell Hill in north London. It doesn't take
long from the West End—no more than fifteen minutes on the
tube from Leicester Square to Highgate. The bus journey takes
longer, even outside the rush hours, but is much more pleasant,
skirting Regent's Park, creeping up Parliament Hill, weaving
through Highgate Village and climbing towards the woods and
the golf course, finally reaching the rarified air of the capital
where it's safe to breathe—but not always safe to live to live,
particularly during the early 1980s.

Between Highgate Village to the south and to the north,
Alexandra Palace and the site of the one-time Ally-Pally
Racecourse, is Cranley Gardens. This is London at its sober,
'Sunday Best'. In Victorian times, the upper middle-class
residents of Muswell Hill could be observed in their horse-
drawn carriages and sartorial finery. The area has always been
a bourgeois backbone; an upmarket postcode to have and a
snob-value telephone number. Cranley Gardens epitomizes the
life of lace curtains and labradors.

Let us move along Cranley Gardens about twelve houses
among the odd numbers. We are outside No. 23. It looks
respectable enough—a tall, white-and-black fronted residence
with a neatly-manicured hedge and a low, rather superfluous
fence. The front door is hidden within a glass-structured porch.
The windows are fragmented into small squares and there are
twelve panes of glass in the front downstairs window, and six in
the attic window on the third-floor. The attic is very important,
as are the drains.

The drainage is good. However, this was not the case early in
February 1983, and the residents were protesting strongly.

Number 23, Cranley Gardens, had been divided into flats,
which was rather unusual for this district. Most of the houses
were owner-occupied, and at the time, No. 23 was rather letting
the side down. It was also shabby, and blocked drains, with the

inevitable odour, were provoking trenchant complaints from neighbours.

Detective Chief Inspector Peter Jay walked into this situation on the evening of February 9. Why should a senior detective be concerning himself with a domestic drainage problem? Let us turn back the clock twenty-four hours to the arrival of Michael Cottran, the Dyna-rod man, who had been called out by the owner of the house. Tenants had been complaining of being unable to flush their toilets throughout the weekend. Quickly he diagnosed a 'main drainage problem'. The tenant living on the ground-floor directed Cottran to the manhole which led to the drainage network.

Armed with a high-powered flashlight and his specialist tools, he lowered himself into the system, swiftly locating the blockage. There was no way that he could miss the large slabs of white flesh. 'Don't say anything to anyone,' he told the tenant, then reported his findings to his supervisor, who said he would conduct his own inspection the following morning.

During that night, tenants heard footsteps descending and ascending the stairs. 'I thought someone must be having a party, but I didn't hear any music,' one tenant was to comment later.

When Cottran returned in the morning with his chief, they discovered that the drains apparently had been cleared. However, nothing had been done about the stench and the two men decided to carry out a more thorough inspection, which produced a find that was to send both men scurrying to the surface.

Now you will understand the reason for the presence of Detective Chief Inspector Jay, from Hornsey CID, the following evening. He was leaning against the wall in the hallway when a thirty-seven-year-old civil servant, Dennis Nilsen, returned home to his top-floor flat.

'Mr. Nilsen?'

'Yes.'

'I'm Detective Chief Inspector Jay.'

'Oh, yes.'

'Do you mind if we have a chat?'

'No, of course not.'

Nilsen led the way.

Inside the flat were bottles of drink—whisky and beer—

modern table and chairs, a plain settee, television set, hi-fi system and a room with a spectacular view.

The bathroom was old-fashioned, with an ill-fitting window and a brown-stained, very deep enamel tub.

The kitchen was a typical bachelor's nightmare, and the bedroom was not much better. Chairs and the hooks behind the door were employed as coat-hangers. There was a sleeping-bag on the floor in one corner, and the bed looked as if it hadn't been made for a week or more. Dirty clothes spilled out of the wardrobe.

Jay said something to the effect that he expected Nilsen was wondering why he was there.

'Not really,' Nilsen replied.

Jay then explained that human flesh and the bones of fingers had been recovered from the drains of the house. When Nilsen made no comment, the detective said straight out: 'Where's the rest of the body, Mr. Nilsen?'

Without hesitation or fencing, Nilsen answered: 'It's in there, in two plastic bags.' He was pointing towards the wardrobe and he was telling no lie.

Nilsen was informed that he was being arrested and taken to Hornsey Police Station, and Jay's recollection is that the prisoner was perfectly resigned to his fate.

During the car ride to the police station, Jay wanted to know how many victims there were: 'Are we talking about one body or two?'

'Oh, no, more than that; much more. There have been fifteen or sixteen altogether.' Once again, he was not lying.

Dennis Nilsen, a former policeman and a bespectacled Job Centre employee, was Britain's worst mass killer up to that time, but he couldn't tell a lie. Killing came naturally, but lying did not.

Let us leave Cranley Gardens for a while and travel westwards across north London to Melrose Avenue, just south of Cricklewood, and only three blocks from Chatsworth Road, which is noted for the number of Rolls Royces parked in driveways. Most of the houses in Melrose Avenue—a long, far-reaching road disappearing in a straight line beyond the range of the eye—were built in the 1890s. They are bay-fronted with knee-high walls and modest gardens at the back. Most properties are red-bricked, but some houses have been painted. Number 195 is a case in point. It looked very smart in February 1983, with its virgin white façade, let down slightly by a house next door with a 'For Sale' sign in the rather overgrown restricted frontage.

The interest in No. 195, Melrose Avenue, in February 1983, arose from Nilsen's admission to Jay that he had murdered 'between twelve and thirteen' men at that address, which had been his home before moving to Cranley Gardens. The death-toll at the Muswell Hill address had been three.

There has never been anything extra-special about No. 195, Melrose Avenue. Until the 1960s, it had always been the private residence of one family, handed down through the generations. It offered larger than average rooms and lofty ceilings, typical of its era. 'Built to last', was the epithet of the estate agents when it went on the market. By the time Nilsen came on the scene, in November 1975, it had already been converted into flats. The three rooms on the ground-floor were ideal for his purpose. He wanted somewhere big enough to share with his male companion (who was never his lover), a mongrel bitch called Bleep, and a tom cat, which had been abandoned and befriended by Nilsen. He had a passion for animals, especially strays. There was a gentleness about him which the majority of work-colleagues admired. 'Wouldn't hurt a fly,' was an often-used phrase to describe Nilsen. It was absolutely true; he would never swat a fly, but a human being was different!

Undoubtedly, Nilsen was happier in his Melrose Avenue flat than he had been anywhere else. There was a garden, of which he was in charge. He mowed the lawn, grew flowers and trimmed the hedge. At weekends, he would take Bleep for long walks.

When he watched television or listened to his hi-fi, the cat would sleep in his lap. On summer evenings, at dusk, he would sit in the garden, eating a barbecue supper and drinking lots of beer. This was the happiest period of his life. The home was always kept spotlessly clean, Nilsen and his male flat-mate sharing the chores. Nilsen was the expert cook: once it had been his trade, while serving as a professional soldier. He had joined the army even before he was sixteen, as a junior soldier, and by the time he was nineteen he had transferred to the Catering

Corps, making quite a name for himself, and also travelling the world to places like Aden, the Persian Gulf, Cyprus and West Germany.

But military service is not an ideal life for a loner. If you cannot mix easily, you quickly become a target, not always for physical abuse but certainly for derision. Nilsen was capable of looking after himself physically, but he went through his entire army career—some twelve years—as an outsider.

As an army cook he had enjoyed a liberal amount of freedom, and during those twelve years he had developed into a heavy drinker, although he never became violent while under the influence. Alcohol tended to make him more reflective: he would compose poetry, read books about country matters, and attend concerts. All his life he had only one girlfriend. They went together on long walks, sharing an interest in the countryside. On Saturday nights, they would dance, but Nilsen had no idea how to extend the relationship. His girlfriend was attractive and intelligent, and would sit beside him while he recited his favourite poetry, often his own. She desperately yearned for the relationship to become physical but Nilsen had no experience. Finally, she had to take the initiative, which was greatly embarrassing to him.

After much soul-searching and many sleepless nights, Nilsen confronted the fact that he was in love. This made him morose, instead of happy. His emotions were causing him to panic. He wanted his girlfriend to become his wife, and wished to be able to hold her and tell her this, but he was terrified of rejection, which was so familiar to him. However, rather than risk being turned down, he dropped her, breaking her heart. Had he proposed, she would undoubtedly have accepted with delight. Dennis Nilsen would have become a happily married man. Today, perhaps, a proud father. Sixteen strangers would, possibly, still be alive.

In 1972, Nilsen had left the army to join the police; but that lasted only eleven months. He liked being in uniform because it reminded him of military life, but he resented the discipline which had been lacking in the Catering Corps, and found the pettiness irritating.

Rejection was a prominent theme in his life, which began on November 23, 1945, in Fraserburgh, Scotland. His parents were continually feuding. His Norwegian father, Olav Nilsen, frequently went 'missing' on drinking sprees which lasted days, sometimes weeks. When he returned, despairingly hung-over, he would lash out at his wife, Betty, and the children.

The marriage lated seven miserable years, long enough to make an indelible impression on Dennis, although he was only four years old at the time of the divorce. When his mother remarried in 1954, becoming Mrs. Betty Scott, a family decision was made which, in essence, was Nilsen's induction into the rejection syndrome. It was decided that for the remainder of his boyhood, he should be raised by his grandparents. Even so, he was immensely happy with his grandfather, Andrew Whyte, who thoroughly spoilt him. Many years later, Nilsen was to write: 'I loved Grandad Whyte more than anybody. He was truly my guardian angel. Nothing was too much trouble for him. He worshipped me and I him. He was my *real* father. I thought he would always be there for me to turn to. It never occurred to me that I might ever have to face life without him. Then he died. Just like that! Without warning. My world fell apart. I was devastated. It seemed that everything I ever loved died or went away. I had pets and they died or got lost. I had no confidence in the future. I was afraid what each new day would bring.'

Because of Nilsen's intense love of his grandfather, he was allowed to see his body in the coffin. 'I wish I hadn't,' he wrote in prison. 'It made me lose all faith. I realized he was gone forever, that he wouldn't be waiting for me, that life ended at death. I was shattered. It seemed so unfair. I wondered what would happen to me. Life without my grandad wasn't life at all.'

A few days later, his two racing pigeons were shot dead. The message he learned was that nothing lasted; hope was futile; the future could not be trusted; optimism was a trick, and the world was a devilish deception. The nature of future events had already been defined.

Nilsen's mother and her second husband were living in Strichen, not too far from Fraserburgh, and he moved in with them, staying until the August of 1961, when he joined the army at the first opportunity. 'I had to get away,' he told an NCO. 'I didn't belong. I've never belonged anywhere, except with my grandfather.'

Most of his contemporaries in the army believed he must

have been an only child because he seemed to display all the characteristics, but in fact he had an older brother and a younger sister. On one occasion he was spanked by his mother and sent to bed without supper because he had undressed in front of his brother. Apparently, his mother believed it was sinful and immodest for people of the *same sex*—even brothers and sisters—to see each other's private flesh.

'Flesh was a problem in our family,' Nilsen wrote while on remand. 'There's no way of escaping one's own flesh, but life would have been a lot easier if I didn't have any. Flesh was a constant source of embarrassment for my mother. She taught me to be wary of human flesh, but I still believe it can be beautiful, as long as it is not abused. People can abuse their flesh in such a variety of combinations: by eating too much and over-indulging in so many different ways.' He revealed that he was warned that if he ever caught a glimpse of his sister's naked body, nobody would be able to save him from hell. His hatred of homosexuals seemed to be rooted in this puritanical upbringing.

The most critical event in Nilsen's life was the decision by his friend at No. 195, Melrose Avenue, to leave London for a job in antiques in Devon. They had been together for two years and for Nilsen this separation was intolerable. He had never committed a crime in his life, and continued to commute between Muswell Hill and the Job Centre in Leicester Square. However, he was staying out late at night more and more, drinking excessively in the West End and following in the footsteps of his father.

'There's no way of running from your genes and your past, because they are pulling and you are chasing,' he once said. In addition to everything else, Nilsen was a deep thinker, a 'barrack-room philosopher'. He had the intelligence to be a success at most things. Instead, he chose to succeed at becoming one of Britain's most horrendous failures, which gave him a perverse sense of fulfilment.

Nilsen embarked on the road to hell on a night towards the end of December, 1978, when he was drunk in the Cricklewood Arms pub, *Cricklewood Broadway*. He invited an Irishman back to his Melrose Avenue flat, where the drinking continued throughout the night until both were in a drunken stupor. At some point, Nilsen proposed that his new-found drinking partner should stay so that they could celebrate the New Year together. The proposition was rejected and this seems to have provided the motive for the first murder. While the Irishman slept, Nilsen strangled him with a necktie.

After the murder, he stripped the body and scrubbed it from head to toe in a ritual cleansing fetish, which was to be repeated after every killing. When the wash was complete, he dried the body and dressed it: flesh had not only to be clean but covered. His first problem was what to do with the body. He did not own a car, so he had no means of removing it from the house. He opted for a hiding place within his flat: under the floorboards in his bedroom. And that is where the body remained for eight months, bandaged in plastic sheets, until August 11, 1979. When interviewed by the police, he remarked how amazed he was to discover that the body had decomposed scarcely at all between December, 1978, and August, 1979.

As soon as it was dark on the night of August 11, he had dragged the body to the bottom of the garden, where he had built a huge bonfire, and deposited the corpse in the middle of it. He also added rubber to mask the smell of burning flesh. That victim was never identified.

Nilsen's second victim was a Canadian, Kenneth James Ockenden, aged twenty-three, who was on a touring holiday. They met by chance early in December, 1979, in the *Princess Louise* pub in High Holborn. Nilsen asked him where he would be staying the night and Ockenden replied that he had an aunt and uncle in Carshalton and that is where he intended going: he had already been to Lake District.

Nilsen said that he could sleep at his place and, because it was late, Ockenden accepted the offer. Ockenden was not a homosexual, and there was no sexual attraction between them.

On the way back, they spent £20 on alcohol. While Nilsen cooked ham, eggs and chips, Ockenden watched television and, at the same time, listened through earphones to rock music on the hi-fi system. Not once did he remove these headphones. He ate his meal while still listening to the music and wasn't interested in making conversation.

'All I wanted to do was talk,' Nilsen told detectives. 'I thought to myself: "What a bloody good guest he's turned out to be!" I was livid.' To Nilsen, this was another kind of rejection.

Ockenden was strangled with a section of flex, while he sat in a chair, his head full of music.

This time Nilsen was unable to manipulate the body into a groove under the floorboards because of rigor mortis, so he left it covered under the bed for several days, before cutting it up. Then the pieces of flesh and bone were assembled neatly under the floorboards, where his first victim had been kept.

Ockenden had been carrying a large amount of money on him: Nilsen set fire to this after tearing it up. Stealing was a crime and Nilsen was no thief. He prided himself on his honesty.

Victim Number Three was a sixteen-year-old butcher, Martyn Duffey, who died in a similar fashion to the others, while he was drunk. Nilsen was to tell the police: 'It just happened. When I sobered up in the morning, he was dead on the floor. I don't remember how, or why, it happened. By then, I couldn't stop it. I knew it would happen again, sometime, but I didn't have a say in it anymore. Someone else, or something else, was controlling me.'

And so it went on, each new killing very similar to the previous one; a catalogue of casual meetings, followed by equally casual murder and cover-up. Some of the bodies were left around the rooms for several days before being hidden. Chunks of human meat were stored in a brick tomb in the garden shed, which was sprayed every day by Nilsen with a strong-smelling air-freshener. When he burned another victim on a bonfire, he used the opportunity to dispose of other flesh. Much of the killing became a blur for him. Some of the details were precise, others were very vague. He began to kill with only a hazy recollection of what he was doing and the reasons for his actions. Before leaving Melrose Avenue in October, 1981, he destroyed on yet another bonfire all the remaining evidence of his murderous activities.

Nilsen's first victim at No. 23, Cranley Gardens, was boiled in a large, black pot after being hacked into scores of separate pieces. The parts of one man were locked in a tea-chest, while the rest was flushed down the toilet. The head of the final victim was cut off and boiled in the big, black pot. While it was boiling, Nilsen took Bleep for a brisk walk.

When Nilsen's trial began at the Old Bailey on October 24, 1983, he was charged with six murders and two attempted killings. The defence argued that the murder charges should be reduced to manslaughter on the grounds of diminished responsibility, but Nilsen was against being judged insane and, on that score, he won the day.

On Friday, November 4, 1983, Nilsen was found guilty of all the murder charges and was given a 'life' prison sentence. It is worth noting that the jury were not in unanimous agreement: it was a 10–2 majority verdict.

In prison, Nilsen became a prolific writer, describing himself as a 'creative psychopath' who degenerated into a 'destructive psychopath' when he was drunk. He also revealed that after bathing and drying the bodies, he would powder them and himself all over. 'I also wanted to look like a corpse,' he disclosed. 'It is hard to know why I did all these things. I derived no pleasure from killing people, not as far as I can recall. I enjoyed cleaning them afterwards, though, scrubbing off all the dirt of their grubby lives. I have always been a loner, but I wanted to love and to be loved.'

The shed at the bottom of the garden of No. 195, Melrose Avenue was just like any other outdoor storehouse. There were spades, a couple of digging forks, hedge-clippers and a non-motor lawn mower, plus the type of tools that come in handy for home repairs. A fusty smell dominated my nose. In one corner were a few bricks, probably remnants of the makeshift structure in which parts of bodies had been entombed. How could such horror have been enacted amid all this domestic suburban ordinariness? The taciturn nature of the area and its residents, the sheer respectability of the neighbourhood, only heightened the sense of outrage. The enormity of the crimes was further magnified by the urbane docility of the murderer; a civil servant and a former policeman.

I stood where the bonfires had burned. No smell now. Most of the ash had been scattered by the varying winds of the different seasons. Some of it remained, though, having become a prisoner of the clinging top soil.

Perhaps the neighbours had complained among themselves on those nights when the Guys on the bonfires had not been dummies. The acrid smell, a combination of flesh and rubber, must have filled the night air with an unwholesome miasma, carried for several hundred yards on a steady, prevailing west wind.

However, no one had knocked on Nilsen's door to complain. Tolerance, preserved by the stoical stiff upper lip, was a strong feature of Nilsen's milieu.

New wallpaper, paint and furniture have changed the look of a monument that forever will be a memorial to so many young men who died in their prime for no better reason than it suited Nilsen's whim.

There is a high turnover of residents in both Melrose Avenue and Cranley Gardens. Each new year and every fresh face helps to push Nilsen and his houses of horror further back into oblivion, but total extinction is impossible. He, and others like him, will always be there to haunt the present, just as much as he did the past. The saying that *you never really know what goes on behind closed doors* is probably more applicable to the Dennis Nilsen case than any other.

However, when you make a study of murder, you soon discover that as one door closes, another immediately opens.

M.P.

# SOURCES AND ACKNOWLEDGEMENTS

ANTHONY ABBOT on William H. Wallace, from *Great True Stories of Crime, Mystery and Detection* (London: Readers' Digest, 1965), reprinted by permission of Readers' Digest Inc. ALISTAIR KERSHAW on Joseph Vacher, from *Murder in France* (London: Constable, 1955), reprinted by permission of the publishers. ALEXANDER WOOLLCOTT on The Minister and the Choir Singer, The Elwell Case and Bruno Hauptmann, from *Long, Long Ago* (New York: Viking Press, 1943). BILL McGOWRAN on Jack the Ripper, from *World's Strangest Stories* (London: Associated Newspapers, 1955). CHARLES E. STILL on Roland B. Molineux, William Guldensuppe and Sidney Fox, from *Styles in Crime* (New York: Lippincott, 1938). C.J.S. THOMPSON on Henri Girard, from *Poison Mysteries Unsolved* (London: Hutchinson, 1937). CHARLES KINGSTON on Thomas Wainewright, from *Law-Breakers* (London: Bodley Head, 1930); on Doctor Castaing, Doctor Smethurst, Doctor Lamson and Doctor Neill Cream, from *Enemies of Society* (London: Stanley Paul, 1927). CRAIG RICE on The Death of the Black Dahlia, from *My Favourite True Mystery* (London: Heinemann, 1956), copyright © 1955 by Craig Rice, reprinted by permission of Scott Meredith, Inc. COLIN WILSON on John Williams, H.H. Holmes, Reg Christie, Jack the Stripper, Ian Brady and Richard Speck, from *A Casebook of Murder* (London: Leslie Frewin, 1969); on Peter Sutcliffe, from *Encyclopaedia of Modern Murder* (London: Arthur Barker, 1983); all reprinted by permission of the author and David Bolt Associates. DAMON RUNYON on Albert Snyder, from *Trials and Other Tribulations* (New York: Lippincott, 1946), coyright © King Features, Inc., reprinted by permission of King Features, Inc. ERIC AMBLER on J.G. Haigh and James Hanratty, from *The Ability to Kill* (London: Bodley Head, 1963), copyright © Eric Ambler 1963, reprinted by permission of the author. EDWARD H. SMITH on Doctor Buchanan and Doctor Waite, from *Famous*

*American Poison Mysteries* (London: Hurst and Blackett, n.d.). EDGAR LUSTGARTEN on Fritz Haarman, Gaston Dominici, Albert DeSalvo, Dale Nelson and Edward Paisnel, from *The Illustrated Story of Crime* (London: Weidenfeld and Nicolson, 1976), copyright © the Estate of Edgar Lustgarten 1976, reprinted by permission of the publishers. EDMUND PEARSON on John Bender and G.J. Smith, from *Murder at Smutty Nose* (New York: Doubleday, Page & Co., 1938); on Major Armstrong and The Green Bicycle Mystery, from *More Studies in Murder* (New York: Smith & Haas, 1936). ELLERY QUEEN on Hollywood's Most Baffling Murder, from *My Favourite True Mystery* (London: Heinemann, 1956), copyright © Ellery Queen 1956, reprinted by permission of Scott Meredith, Inc. E. SPENCER SHEW on Patrick Mahon, The Luard Case, Tony Mancini, Buck Ruxton, Ley and Smith, and James Camb, from *A Companion to Murder and A Second Companion to Murder* (London: Cassell, 1962 and 1963, reprinted by permission of the publisher. FREDERIC BOUTET on Burke and Hare and Lacenaire, from *International Criminals Past and Present* (London: Hutchinson, n.d.). F.E. SMITH (Lord Birkenhead) on Charles Peace, from *Famous Trials* (London: Hutchinson, n.d.). FRANCIS ILES (Anthony Berkeley Cox) on Doctor Crippen, from *Great Unsolved Crimes* (London: Hutchinson, n.d.). FREEMAN WILLS CROFTS on The Gorse Hall Mystery, from *Great Unsolved Crimes* (London: Hutchinson, n.d.). GRIERSON DICKSON on William Palmer, from *Murder by Numbers* (London: Hale, 1958) reprinted by permission of the publisher. GILES PLAYFAIR on Albert Fish and Charles Manson, from *Crime in our Century* (London: Sidgwick and Jackson, 1977), copyright © 1977 Giles Playfair, reprinted by permission of the author. JUDGE GERALD SPARROW on Graham Young, from *Crime for the Connoisseur* (London: Leslie Frewin, 1974), reprinted by permission of the publisher. H. GREENHOUGH SMITH on Armand Peltzer, from *Stronger Than Fiction* (New York: Howell, Soskin, 1947). H. MONTGOMERY HYDE on William Kirwan, from *Cases That Changed the Law* (London: Heinemann, 1951), reprinted by permission of the publisher. HELEN REILLY on Robert James, from *My Favourite True Mystery* (London: Heinemann, 1956), copyright © 1956 Helen Reilly, reprinted by permission of the publisher. H.R.F. KEATING on Franz Muller and Samuel Dougal, from *Great Crimes* (London: Marks and Spencer), copyright © H.R.F. Keating, reprinted by permission of the author. HENRY T.F. RHODES on Pierre Voirbo, from *In the Tracks of Crime* (London: Turnstile, 1952). JOHN BROPHY on William Corder, George Chapman, Harry Thaw, Leopold and Loeb and Donald Merrett, from *The Meaning of Murder* (London: Whiting and Wheaton, 1966), reprinted by permission of the author's Estate. JIMMY BRESLIN on David Berkowitz, from *The New York Daily News* 1977, copyright © 1977 by Chicago Tribune – New York News Syndicate. J.C. ELLIS on Carlyle Harris and Thomas Alloway, from *Blackmailers & Co.* (London: Selwyn & Blount, n.d.). JAMES PURVIS on The Axeman of New Orleans and Zodiac, from *Great Unsolved Mysteries* (New York: Grosset and Dunlap, 1978), copyright © 1978 James Purvis, reprinted by permission of the publisher. JAY ROBERT NASH on Johann Hoch, Earle Nelson, Kenneth Neu and Raymond Fernandez, from *Murder, America* (New York: Simon & Schuster, 1980); on Charles Starkweather, from *Bloodletters and Badmen* (New York: Evans, 1973); and on Mark Chapman, from *Murder Among the Mighty* (New York: Delacorte, 1983); copyright © 1973, 1980, 1983 Jay Robert Nash, reprinted by permission of the author. JULIAN SYMONS on The Riddle of Birhurst Rise, from *A Reasonable Doubt* (London: Cresset Press, 1960), copyright © 1960 Julian Symons, reprinted by permission of Curtis Brown Ltd, London. LESLIE CHARTERIS on Ted Durrant, from *My Favourite True Mystery* (London: Heinemann, 1956), copyright © 1956 Leslie Charteris, reprinted by permission of the author. LEONARD GRIBBLE on James Rush, A.A. Rouse and Neville Heath, from *Famous Judges and Their Trials* (London: John Long, 1957), copyright © The Estate of Leonard Gribble 1957, reprinted by permission of Lois Gribble. MICHAEL PRINCE on Dennis Nilsen, from *Murderous Places* (London: Blandford, 1989), copyright © 1989 Michael Prince, reprinted by permission of the publisher. OSCAR SCHINGALL on The Dot King Case, from *My Favourite True Mystery* (London: Heinemann, 1956), reprinted by permission of the publisher. ROBERT BLOCH on Ed Gein, from *I, Witness* (New York: New York Times Book Co., 1962), copyright © 1962

Robert Bloch, reprinted by permission of the author. R.E.L. MASTERS on Peter Kurten, from *Perverse Crimes in History* (New York: The Julian Press, 1963), copyright © 1963 R.E.L. Masters, reprinted by permission of the author. RUPERT FURNEAUX on Doctor Pritchard, Doctor Pettiot and Doctor Sam Sheppard, from *The Medical Murderer* (London: Elek, 1957). RICHARD GLYN JONES on John Lee, Dean Corll and Ted Bundy, and the Introduction, appear for the first time in this book, copyright © 1989 Richard Glyn Jones. S.J. PESKETT on Jean-Baptiste Troppmann, from *Grim, Gruesome and Grisly* (London: Leslie Frewin, 1974), copyright © 1974 S.J. Peskett, reprinted by permission of the publisher. SAX ROHMER on Chung Yi Maio, from *My Favourite True Mystery* (London: Heinemann, 1956), reprinted by permission of the publisher. WILLIAM LE QUEUX on Bela Kiss, from *Stronger Than Fiction*. WEBB MILLER on Landru, from *Great True Stories of Crime, Mystery and Detection* (London: Readers' Digest, 1965), reprinted by permission of Readers' Digest Inc.

While every effort has been made to trace authors, publishers and copyright holders, in some cases this has proved impossible, and the editor would be glad to hear from any such parties so that any omissions can be rectified in future editions of the book.